T0143088

Lecture Notes in Computer Science 13376

More information about this series at https://link.springer.com/bookseries/558

Osvaldo Gervasi · Beniamino Murgante ·
Eligius M. T. Hendrix · David Taniar ·
Bernady O. Apduhan (Eds.)

Computational Science and Its Applications – ICCSA 2022

22nd International Conference
Malaga, Spain, July 4–7, 2022
Proceedings, Part II

 Springer

Editors
Osvaldo Gervasi ⓘ
University of Perugia
Perugia, Italy

Beniamino Murgante ⓘ
University of Basilicata
Potenza, Potenza, Italy

Eligius M. T. Hendrix ⓘ
Universidad de Málaga
Malaga, Spain

David Taniar
Monash University
Clayton, VIC, Australia

Bernady O. Apduhan
Kyushu Sangyo University
Fukuoka, Japan

ISSN 0302-9743 ISSN 1611-3349 (electronic)
Lecture Notes in Computer Science
ISBN 978-3-031-10449-7 ISBN 978-3-031-10450-3 (eBook)
https://doi.org/10.1007/978-3-031-10450-3

This Springer imprint is published by the registered company Springer Nature Switzerland AG
The registered company address is: Gewerbestrasse 11, 6330 Cham, Switzerland

Preface

These two volumes (LNCS 13375–13376) consist of the peer-reviewed papers from the main tracks at the 22nd International Conference on Computational Science and Its Applications (ICCSA 2022), which took place during July 4–7, 2022. The peer-reviewed papers of the workshops are published in a separate set consisting of six volumes (LNCS 13377–13382).

This year, we again decided to organize a hybrid conference, with some of the delegates attending in person and others taking part online. Despite the enormous benefits achieved by the intensive vaccination campaigns in many countries, at the crucial moment of organizing the event, there was no certainty about the evolution of COVID-19. Fortunately, more and more researchers were able to attend the event in person, foreshadowing a slow but gradual exit from the pandemic and the limitations that have weighed so heavily on the lives of all citizens over the past three years.

ICCSA 2022 was another successful event in the International Conference on Computational Science and Its Applications (ICCSA) series. Last year, the conference was held as a hybrid event in Cagliari, Italy, and in 2020 it was organized as virtual event, whilst earlier editions took place in Saint Petersburg, Russia (2019), Melbourne, Australia (2018), Trieste, Italy (2017), Beijing, China (2016), Banff, Canada (2015), Guimaraes, Portugal (2014), Ho Chi Minh City, Vietnam (2013), Salvador, Brazil (2012), Santander, Spain (2011), Fukuoka, Japan (2010), Suwon, South Korea (2009), Perugia, Italy (2008), Kuala Lumpur, Malaysia (2007), Glasgow, UK (2006), Singapore (2005), Assisi, Italy (2004), Montreal, Canada (2003), and (as ICCS) Amsterdam, The Netherlands (2002) and San Francisco, USA (2001).

Computational science is the main pillar of most of the present research, and industrial and commercial applications, and plays a unique role in exploiting ICT innovative technologies. The ICCSA conference series provides a venue to researchers and industry practitioners to discuss new ideas, to share complex problems and their solutions, and to shape new trends in computational science.

Apart from the six main tracks, ICCSA 2022 also included 52 workshops on topics ranging from computational science technologies and application in many fields to specific areas of computational sciences, such as software engineering, security, machine learning and artificial intelligence, and blockchain technologies. For the main conference tracks we accepted 57 papers and 24 short papers out of 279 submissions (an acceptance rate of 29%). For the workshops we accepted 285 papers. We would like to express our appreciation to the workshops chairs and co-chairs for their hard work and dedication.

The success of the ICCSA conference series in general, and of ICCSA 2022 in particular, vitally depends on the support of many people: authors, presenters, partic-ipants, keynote speakers, workshop chairs, session chairs, organizing committee members, student volunteers, Program Committee members, advisory committee members, international liaison chairs, reviewers, and others in various roles. We take this opportunity to wholehartedly thank them all.

We also wish to thank our publisher, Springer, for their acceptance to publish the proceedings, for sponsoring some of the best papers awards, and for their kind assistance and cooperation during the editing process.

We cordially invite you to visit the ICCSA website https://iccsa.org where you can find all the relevant information about this interesting and exciting event.

July 2022   Osvaldo Gervasi
                                                                    Beniamino Murgante
                                                                    Bernady O. Apduhan

Welcome Message from Organizers

The ICCSA 2021 conference in the Mediterranean city of Cagliari provided us with inspiration to offer the ICCSA 2022 conference in the Mediterranean city of Málaga, Spain. The additional considerations due to the COVID-19 pandemic, which necessitated a hybrid conference, also stimulated the idea to use the School of Informatics of the University of Málaga. It has an open structure where we could take lunch and coffee outdoors and the lecture halls have open windows on two sides providing optimal conditions for meeting more safely.

The school is connected to the center of the old town via a metro system, for which we offered cards to the participants. This provided the opportunity to stay in lodgings in the old town close to the beach because, at the end of the day, that is the place to be to exchange ideas with your fellow scientists. The social program allowed us to enjoy the history of Malaga from its founding by the Phoenicians...

In order to provoke as much scientific interaction as possible we organized online sessions that could easily be followed by all participants from their own devices. We tried to ensure that participants from Asia could participate in morning sessions and those from the Americas in evening sessions. On-site sessions could be followed and debated on-site and discussed online using a chat system. To realize this, we relied on the developed technological infrastructure based on open source software, with the addition of streaming channels on YouTube. The implementation of the software infrastructure and the technical coordination of the volunteers were carried out by Damiano Perri and Marco Simonetti. Nine student volunteers from the universities of Málaga, Minho, Almeria, and Helsinki provided technical support and ensured smooth interaction during the conference.

A big thank you goes to all of the participants willing to exchange their ideas during their daytime. Participants of ICCSA 2022 came from 58 countries scattered over many time zones of the globe. Very interesting keynote talks were provided by well-known international scientists who provided us with more ideas to reflect upon, and we are grateful for their insights.

Eligius M. T. Hendrix

Organization

ICCSA 2022 was organized by the University of Malaga (Spain), the University of Perugia (Italy), the University of Cagliari (Italy), the University of Basilicata (Italy), Monash University (Australia), Kyushu Sangyo University (Japan), and the University of Minho, (Portugal).

Honorary General Chairs

Norio Shiratori	Chuo University, Japan
Kenneth C. J. Tan	Sardina Systems, UK

General Chairs

Osvaldo Gervasi	University of Perugia, Italy
Eligius Hendrix	University of Malaga, Italy
Bernady O. Apduhan	Kyushu Sangyo University, Japan

Program Committee Chairs

Beniamino Murgante	University of Basilicata, Italy
Inmaculada Garcia Fernandez	University of Malaga, Spain
Ana Maria A. C. Rocha	University of Minho, Portugal
David Taniar	Monash University, Australia

International Advisory Committee

Jemal Abawajy	Deakin University, Australia
Dharma P. Agarwal	University of Cincinnati, USA
Rajkumar Buyya	Melbourne University, Australia
Claudia Bauzer Medeiros	University of Campinas, Brazil
Manfred M. Fisher	Vienna University of Economics and Business, Austria
Marina L. Gavrilova	University of Calgary, Canada
Sumi Helal	University of Florida, USA, and University of Lancaster, UK
Yee Leung	Chinese University of Hong Kong, China

International Liaison Chairs

Ivan Blečić	University of Cagliari, Italy
Giuseppe Borruso	University of Trieste, Italy

Elise De Donker	Western Michigan University, USA
Maria Irene Falcão	University of Minho, Portugal
Robert C. H. Hsu	Chung Hua University, Taiwan
Tai-Hoon Kim	Beijing Jiaotong University, China
Vladimir Korkhov	St Petersburg University, Russia
Sanjay Misra	Østfold University College, Norway
Takashi Naka	Kyushu Sangyo University, Japan
Rafael D. C. Santos	National Institute for Space Research, Brazil
Maribel Yasmina Santos	University of Minho, Portugal
Elena Stankova	St Petersburg University, Russia

Workshop and Session Organizing Chairs

Beniamino Murgante	University of Basilicata, Italy
Chiara Garau	University of Cagliari, Italy
Sanjay Misra	Ostfold University College, Norway

Award Chair

Wenny Rahayu	La Trobe University, Australia

Publicity Committee Chairs

Elmer Dadios	De La Salle University, Philippines
Nataliia Kulabukhova	St Petersburg University, Russia
Daisuke Takahashi	Tsukuba University, Japan
Shangwang Wang	Beijing University of Posts and Telecommunications, China

Local Arrangement Chairs

Eligius Hendrix	University of Malaga, Spain
Inmaculada Garcia Fernandez	University of Malaga, Spain
Salvador Merino Cordoba	University of Malaga, Spain
Pablo Guerrero-García	University of Malaga, Spain

Technology Chairs

Damiano Perri	University of Florence, Italy
Marco Simonetti	University of Florence, Italy

Program Committee

Vera Afreixo	University of Aveiro, Portugal
Filipe Alvelos	University of Minho, Portugal

Hartmut Asche   Hasso-Plattner-Institut für Digital Engineering gGmbH,
                                       Germany
Ginevra Balletto   University of Cagliari, Italy
Michela Bertolotto   University College Dublin, Ireland
Sandro Bimonte   TSCF, INRAE, France
Rod Blais   University of Calgary, Canada
Ivan Blečić   University of Sassari, Italy
Giuseppe Borruso   University of Trieste, Italy
Ana Cristina Braga   University of Minho, Portugal
Massimo Cafaro   University of Salento, Italy
Yves Caniou   ENS Lyon, France
Ermanno Cardelli   University of Perugia, Italy
José A. Cardoso e Cunha   Universidade Nova de Lisboa, Portugal
Rui Cardoso   University of Beira Interior, Portugal
Leocadio G. Casado   University of Almeria, Spain
Carlo Cattani   University of Salerno, Italy
Mete Celik   Erciyes University, Turkey
Maria Cerreta   University of Naples Federico II, Italy
Hyunseung Choo   Sungkyunkwan University, South Korea
Rachel Chieng-Sing Lee   Sunway University, Malaysia
Min Young Chung   Sungkyunkwan University, South Korea
Florbela Maria da Cruz   Polytechnic Institute of Viana do Castelo, Portugal
  Domingues Correia
Gilberto Corso Pereira   Federal University of Bahia, Brazil
Alessandro Costantini   INFN, Italy
Carla Dal Sasso Freitas   Universidade Federal do Rio Grande do Sul, Brazil
Pradesh Debba   Council for Scientific and Industrial Research (CSIR),
                                       South Africa
Hendrik Decker   Instituto Tecnológico de Informática, Spain
Robertas Damaševičius   Kaunas University of Technology, Lithuania
Frank Devai   London South Bank University, UK
Rodolphe Devillers   Memorial University of Newfoundland, Canada
Joana Matos Dias   University of Coimbra, Portugal
Paolino Di Felice   University of L'Aquila, Italy
Prabu Dorairaj   NetApp, India/USA
M. Noelia Faginas Lago   University of Perugia, Italy
M. Irene Falcao   University of Minho, Portugal
Florbela P. Fernandes   Polytechnic Institute of Bragança, Portugal
Jose-Jesus Fernandez   National Centre for Biotechnology, Spain
Paula Odete Fernandes   Polytechnic Institute of Bragança, Portugal
Adelaide de Fátima Baptista   University of Aveiro, Portugal
  Valente Freitas
Manuel Carlos Figueiredo   University of Minho, Portugal
Maria Celia Furtado Rocha   Federal University of Bahia, Brazil
Chiara Garau   University of Cagliari, Italy
Paulino Jose Garcia Nieto   University of Oviedo, Spain

Raffaele Garrisi	Polizia di Stato, Italy
Jerome Gensel	LSR-IMAG, France
Maria Giaoutzi	National Technical University of Athens, Greece
Arminda Manuela Andrade Pereira Gonçalves	University of Minho, Portugal
Andrzej M. Goscinski	Deakin University, Australia
Sevin Gümgüm	Izmir University of Economics, Turkey
Alex Hagen-Zanker	University of Cambridge, UK
Shanmugasundaram Hariharan	B.S. Abdur Rahman Crescent Institute of Science and Technology, India
Eligius M. T. Hendrix	University of Malaga, Spain and Wageningen University, The Netherlands
Hisamoto Hiyoshi	Gunma University, Japan
Mustafa Inceoglu	Ege University, Turkey
Peter Jimack	University of Leeds, UK
Qun Jin	Waseda University, Japan
Yeliz Karaca	UMass Chan Medical School, USA
Farid Karimipour	Vienna University of Technology, Austria
Baris Kazar	Oracle Corp., USA
Maulana Adhinugraha Kiki	Telkom University, Indonesia
DongSeong Kim	University of Canterbury, New Zealand
Taihoon Kim	Hannam University, South Korea
Ivana Kolingerova	University of West Bohemia, Czech Republic
Nataliia Kulabukhova	St. Petersburg University, Russia
Vladimir Korkhov	St. Petersburg University, Russia
Rosa Lasaponara	National Research Council, Italy
Maurizio Lazzari	National Research Council, Italy
Cheng Siong Lee	Monash University, Australia
Sangyoun Lee	Yonsei University, South Korea
Jongchan Lee	Kunsan National University, South Korea
Chendong Li	University of Connecticut, USA
Gang Li	Deakin University, Australia
Fang (Cherry) Liu	Ames Laboratory, USA
Xin Liu	University of Calgary, Canada
Andrea Lombardi	University of Perugia, Italy
Savino Longo	University of Bari, Italy
Tinghuai Ma	Nanjing University of Information Science and Technology, China
Ernesto Marcheggiani	Katholieke Universiteit Leuven, Belgium
Antonino Marvuglia	Public Research Centre Henri Tudor, Luxembourg
Nicola Masini	National Research Council, Italy
Ilaria Matteucci	National Research Council, Italy
Nirvana Meratnia	University of Twente, The Netherlands
Fernando Miranda	University of Minho, Portugal
Giuseppe Modica	University of Reggio Calabria, Italy
Josè Luis Montaña	University of Cantabria, Spain

Maria Filipa Mourão	Instituto Politécnico de Viana do Castelo, Portugal
Louiza de Macedo Mourelle	State University of Rio de Janeiro, Brazil
Nadia Nedjah	State University of Rio de Janeiro, Brazil
Laszlo Neumann	University of Girona, Spain
Kok-Leong Ong	Deakin University, Australia
Belen Palop	Universidad de Valladolid, Spain
Marcin Paprzycki	Polish Academy of Sciences, Poland
Eric Pardede	La Trobe University, Australia
Kwangjin Park	Wonkwang University, South Korea
Ana Isabel Pereira	Polytechnic Institute of Bragança, Portugal
Massimiliano Petri	University of Pisa, Italy
Telmo Pinto	University of Coimbra, Portugal
Maurizio Pollino	Italian National Agency for New Technologies, Energy and Sustainable Economic Development, Italy
Alenka Poplin	University of Hamburg, Germany
Vidyasagar Potdar	Curtin University of Technology, Australia
David C. Prosperi	Florida Atlantic University, USA
Wenny Rahayu	La Trobe University, Australia
Jerzy Respondek	Silesian University of Technology, Poland
Humberto Rocha	INESC-Coimbra, Portugal
Jon Rokne	University of Calgary, Canada
Octavio Roncero	CSIC, Spain
Maytham Safar	Kuwait University, Kuwait
Chiara Saracino	A.O. Ospedale Niguarda Ca' Granda, Italy
Marco Paulo Seabra dos Reis	University of Coimbra, Portugal
Jie Shen	University of Michigan, USA
Qi Shi	Liverpool John Moores University, UK
Dale Shires	U.S. Army Research Laboratory, USA
Inês Soares	University of Coimbra, Portugal
Elena Stankova	St Petersburg University, Russia
Takuo Suganuma	Tohoku University, Japan
Eufemia Tarantino	Polytechnic Universiy of Bari, Italy
Sergio Tasso	University of Perugia, Italy
Ana Paula Teixeira	University of Trás-os-Montes and Alto Douro, Portugal
M. Filomena Teodoro	Portuguese Naval Academy and University of Lisbon, Portugal
Parimala Thulasiraman	University of Manitoba, Canada
Carmelo Torre	Polytechnic University of Bari, Italy
Javier Martinez Torres	Centro Universitario de la Defensa Zaragoza, Spain
Giuseppe A. Trunfio	University of Sassari, Italy
Pablo Vanegas	University of Cuenca, Equador
Marco Vizzari	University of Perugia, Italy
Varun Vohra	Merck Inc., USA
Koichi Wada	University of Tsukuba, Japan
Krzysztof Walkowiak	Wroclaw University of Technology, Poland

Zequn Wang	Intelligent Automation Inc, USA
Robert Weibel	University of Zurich, Switzerland
Frank Westad	Norwegian University of Science and Technology, Norway
Roland Wismüller	Universität Siegen, Germany
Mudasser Wyne	National University, USA
Chung-Huang Yang	National Kaohsiung Normal University, Taiwan
Xin-She Yang	National Physical Laboratory, UK
Salim Zabir	France Telecom Japan Co., Japan
Haifeng Zhao	University of California, Davis, USA
Fabiana Zollo	Ca' Foscari University of Venice, Italy
Albert Y. Zomaya	University of Sydney, Australia

Workshop Organizers

International Workshop on Advances in Artificial Intelligence Learning Technologies: Blended Learning, STEM, Computational Thinking and Coding (AAILT 2022)

Alfredo Milani	University of Perugia, Italy
Valentina Franzoni	University of Perugia, Italy
Osvaldo Gervasi	University of Perugia, Italy

International Workshop on Advancements in Applied Machine-Learning and Data Analytics (AAMDA 2022)

Alessandro Costantini	INFN, Italy
Davide Salomoni	INFN, Italy
Doina Cristina Duma	INFN, Italy
Daniele Cesini	INFN, Italy

International Workshop on Advances in Information Systems and Technologies for Emergency Management, Risk Assessment and Mitigation Based on the Resilience (ASTER 2022)

Maurizio Pollino	ENEA, Italy
Marco Vona	University of Basilicata, Italy
Sonia Giovinazzi	ENEA, Italy
Benedetto Manganelli	University of Basilicata, Italy
Beniamino Murgante	University of Basilicata, Italy

International Workshop on Advances in Web Based Learning (AWBL 2022)

Birol Ciloglugil   Ege University, Turkey
Mustafa Inceoglu   Ege University, Turkey

International Workshop on Blockchain and Distributed Ledgers: Technologies and Applications (BDLTA 2022)

Vladimir Korkhov   St Petersburg State University, Russia
Elena Stankova   St Petersburg State University, Russia
Nataliia Kulabukhova   St Petersburg State University, Russia

International Workshop on Bio and Neuro Inspired Computing and Applications (BIONCA 2022)

Nadia Nedjah   State University of Rio De Janeiro, Brazil
Luiza De Macedo Mourelle   State University of Rio De Janeiro, Brazil

International Workshop on Configurational Analysis For Cities (CA CITIES 2022)

Claudia Yamu   Oslo Metropolitan University, Norway
Valerio Cutini   Università di Pisa, Italy
Beniamino Murgante   University of Basilicata, Italy
Chiara Garau   Dicaar, University of Cagliari, Italy

International Workshop on Computational and Applied Mathematics (CAM 2022)

Maria Irene Falcão   University of Minho, Portugal
Fernando Miranda   University of Minho, Portugal

International Workshop on Computational and Applied Statistics (CAS 2022)

Ana Cristina Braga   University of Minho, Portugal

International Workshop on Computational Mathematics, Statistics and Information Management (CMSIM 2022)

Maria Filomena Teodoro   University of Lisbon and Portuguese Naval Academy, Portugal

International Workshop on Computational Optimization and Applications (COA 2022)

Ana Maria A. C. Rocha	University of Minho, Portugal
Humberto Rocha	University of Coimbra, Portugal

International Workshop on Computational Astrochemistry (CompAstro 2022)

Marzio Rosi	University of Perugia, Italy
Nadia Balucani	University of Perugia, Italy
Cecilia Ceccarelli	Université Grenoble Alpes, France
Stefano Falcinelli	University of Perugia, Italy

International Workshop on Computational Methods for Porous Geomaterials (CompPor 2022)

Vadim Lisitsa	Sobolev Institute of Mathematics, Russia
Evgeniy Romenski	Sobolev Institute of Mathematics, Russia

International Workshop on Computational Approaches for Smart, Conscious Cities (CASCC 2022)

Andreas Fricke	University of Potsdam, Germany
Juergen Doellner	University of Potsdam, Germany
Salvador Merino	University of Malaga, Spain
Jürgen Bund	Graphics Vision AI Association, Germany/Portugal
Markus Jobst	Federal Office of Metrology and Surveying, Austria
Francisco Guzman	University of Malaga, Spain

International Workshop on Computational Science and HPC (CSHPC 2022)

Elise De Doncker	Western Michigan University, USA
Fukuko Yuasa	High Energy Accelerator Research Organization (KEK), Japan
Hideo Matsufuru	High Energy Accelerator Research Organization (KEK), Japan

International Workshop on Cities, Technologies and Planning (CTP 2022)

Giuseppe Borruso	University of Trieste, Italy
Malgorzata Hanzl	Lodz University of Technology, Poland
Beniamino Murgante	University of Basilicata, Italy

Anastasia Stratigea   National Technical University of Athens, Grece
Ginevra Balletto   University of Cagliari, Italy
Ljiljana Zivkovic   Republic Geodetic Authority, Serbia

International Workshop on Digital Sustainability and Circular Economy (DiSCE 2022)

Giuseppe Borruso   University of Trieste, Italy
Stefano Epifani   Digital Sustainability Institute, Italy
Ginevra Balletto   University of Cagliari, Italy
Luigi Mundula   University of Cagliari, Italy
Alessandra Milesi   University of Cagliari, Italy
Mara Ladu   University of Cagliari, Italy
Stefano De Nicolai   University of Pavia, Italy
Tu Anh Trinh   University of Economics Ho Chi Minh City, Vietnam

International Workshop on Econometrics and Multidimensional Evaluation in Urban Environment (EMEUE 2022)

Carmelo Maria Torre   Polytechnic University of Bari, Italy
Maria Cerreta   University of Naples Federico II, Italy
Pierluigi Morano   Polytechnic University of Bari, Italy
Giuliano Poli   University of Naples Federico II, Italy
Marco Locurcio   Polytechnic University of Bari, Italy
Francesco Tajani   Sapienza University of Rome, Italy

International Workshop on Ethical AI Applications for a Human-Centered Cyber Society (EthicAI 2022)

Valentina Franzoni   University of Perugia, Italy
Alfredo Milani   University of Perugia, Italy

International Workshop on Future Computing System Technologies and Applications (FiSTA 2022)

Bernady Apduhan   Kyushu Sangyo University, Japan
Rafael Santos   INPE, Brazil

International Workshop on Geodesign in Decision Making: Meta Planning and Collaborative Design for Sustainable and Inclusive Development (GDM 2022)

Francesco Scorza   University of Basilicata, Italy
Michele Campagna   University of Cagliari, Italy
Ana Clara Mourão Moura   Federal University of Minas Gerais, Brazil

International Workshop on Geomatics in Agriculture and Forestry: New Advances and Perspectives (GeoForAgr 2022)

Maurizio Pollino	ENEA, Italy
Giuseppe Modica	University of Reggio Calabria, Italy
Marco Vizzari	University of Perugia, Italy

International Workshop on Geographical Analysis, Urban Modeling, Spatial Statistics (Geog-An-Mod 2022)

Giuseppe Borruso	University of Trieste, Italy
Beniamino Murgante	University of Basilicata, Italy
Harmut Asche	Hasso-Plattner-Institut für Digital Engineering gGmbH, Germany

International Workshop on Geomatics for Resource Monitoring and Management (GRMM 2022)

Alessandra Capolupo	Polytechnic of Bari, Italy
Eufemia Tarantino	Polytechnic of Bari, Italy
Enrico Borgogno Mondino	University of Turin, Italy

International Workshop on Information and Knowledge in the Internet of Things (IKIT 2022)

Teresa Guarda	State University of Santa Elena Peninsula, Ecuador
Filipe Portela	University of Minho, Portugal
Maria Fernanda Augusto	Bitrum Research Center, Spain

13th International Symposium on Software Quality (ISSQ 2022)

Sanjay Misra	Østfold University College, Norway

International Workshop on Machine Learning for Space and Earth Observation Data (MALSEOD 2022)

Rafael Santos	INPE, Brazil
Karine Reis Ferreira Gomes	INPE, Brazil

International Workshop on Building Multi-dimensional Models for Assessing Complex Environmental Systems (MES 2022)

Vanessa Assumma	Politecnico di Torino, Italy
Caterina Caprioli	Politecnico di Torino, Italy
Giulia Datola	Politecnico di Torino, Italy

| Federico Dell'Anna | Politecnico di Torino, Italy |
| Marta Dell'Ovo | Politecnico di Milano, Italy |

International Workshop on Models and Indicators for Assessing and Measuring the Urban Settlement Development in the View of ZERO Net Land Take by 2050 (MOVEto0 2022)

Lucia Saganeiti	University of L'Aquila, Italy
Lorena Fiorini	University of L'aquila, Italy
Angela Pilogallo	University of Basilicata, Italy
Alessandro Marucci	University of L'Aquila, Italy
Francesco Zullo	University of L'Aquila, Italy

International Workshop on Modelling Post-Covid Cities (MPCC 2022)

Beniamino Murgante	University of Basilicata, Italy
Ginevra Balletto	University of Cagliari, Italy
Giuseppe Borruso	University of Trieste, Italy
Marco Dettori	Università degli Studi di Sassari, Italy
Lucia Saganeiti	University of L'Aquila, Italy

International Workshop on Ecosystem Services: Nature's Contribution to People in Practice. Assessment Frameworks, Models, Mapping, and Implications (NC2P 2022)

Francesco Scorza	University of Basilicata, Italy
Sabrina Lai	University of Cagliari, Italy
Silvia Ronchi	University of Cagliari, Italy
Dani Broitman	Israel Institute of Technology, Israel
Ana Clara Mourão Moura	Federal University of Minas Gerais, Brazil
Corrado Zoppi	University of Cagliari, Italy

International Workshop on New Mobility Choices for Sustainable and Alternative Scenarios (NEWMOB 2022)

Tiziana Campisi	University of Enna Kore, Italy
Socrates Basbas	Aristotle University of Thessaloniki, Greece
Aleksandra Deluka T.	University of Rijeka, Croatia
Alexandros Nikitas	University of Huddersfield, UK
Ioannis Politis	Aristotle University of Thessaloniki, Greece
Georgios Georgiadis	Aristotle University of Thessaloniki, Greece
Irena Ištoka Otković	University of Osijek, Croatia
Sanja Surdonja	University of Rijeka, Croatia

International Workshop on Privacy in the Cloud/Edge/IoT World (PCEIoT 2022)

Michele Mastroianni	University of Campania Luigi Vanvitelli, Italy
Lelio Campanile	University of Campania Luigi Vanvitelli, Italy
Mauro Iacono	University of Campania Luigi Vanvitelli, Italy

International Workshop on Psycho-Social Analysis of Sustainable Mobility in the Pre- and Post-Pandemic Phase (PSYCHE 2022)

Tiziana Campisi	University of Enna Kore, Italy
Socrates Basbas	Aristotle University of Thessaloniki, Greece
Dilum Dissanayake	Newcastle University, UK
Nurten Akgün Tanbay	Bursa Technical University, Turkey
Elena Cocuzza	University of Catania, Italy
Nazam Ali	University of Management and Technology, Pakistan
Vincenza Torrisi	University of Catania, Italy

International Workshop on Processes, Methods and Tools Towards Resilient Cities and Cultural Heritage Prone to SOD and ROD Disasters (RES 2022)

Elena Cantatore	Polytechnic University of Bari, Italy
Alberico Sonnessa	Polytechnic University of Bari, Italy
Dario Esposito	Polytechnic University of Bari, Italy

International Workshop on Scientific Computing Infrastructure (SCI 2022)

Elena Stankova	St Petersburg University, Russia
Vladimir Korkhov	St Petersburg University, Russia

International Workshop on Socio-Economic and Environmental Models for Land Use Management (SEMLUM 2022)

Debora Anelli	Polytechnic University of Bari, Italy
Pierluigi Morano	Polytechnic University of Bari, Italy
Francesco Tajani	Sapienza University of Rome, Italy
Marco Locurcio	Polytechnic University of Bari, Italy
Paola Amoruso	LUM University, Italy

14th International Symposium on Software Engineering Processes and Applications (SEPA 2022)

Sanjay Misra	Østfold University College, Norway

International Workshop on Ports of the Future – Smartness and Sustainability (SmartPorts 2022)

Giuseppe Borruso   University of Trieste, Italy
Gianfranco Fancello   University of Cagliari, Italy
Ginevra Balletto   University of Cagliari, Italy
Patrizia Serra   University of Cagliari, Italy
Maria del Mar Munoz   University of Cadiz, Spain
  Leonisio
Marco Mazzarino   University of Venice, Italy
Marcello Tadini   Università del Piemonte Orientale, Italy

International Workshop on Smart Tourism (SmartTourism 2022)

Giuseppe Borruso   University of Trieste, Italy
Silvia Battino   University of Sassari, Italy
Ainhoa Amaro Garcia   Universidad de Alcalà and Universidad de Las Palmas,
                           Spain
Maria del Mar Munoz   University of Cadiz, Spain
  Leonisio
Carlo Donato   University of Sassari, Italy
Francesca Krasna   University of Trieste, Italy
Ginevra Balletto   University of Cagliari, Italy

International Workshop on Sustainability Performance Assessment: Models, Approaches and Applications Toward Interdisciplinary and Integrated Solutions (SPA 2022)

Francesco Scorza   University of Basilicata, Italy
Sabrina Lai   University of Cagliari, Italy
Jolanta Dvarioniene   Kaunas University of Technology, Lithuania
Iole Cerminara   University of Basilicata, Italy
Georgia Pozoukidou   Aristotle University of Thessaloniki, Greece
Valentin Grecu   Lucian Blaga University of Sibiu, Romania
Corrado Zoppi   University of Cagliari, Italy

International Workshop on Specifics of Smart Cities Development in Europe (SPEED 2022)

Chiara Garau   University of Cagliari, Italy
Katarína Vitálišová   Matej Bel University, Slovakia
Paolo Nesi   University of Florence, Italy
Anna Vanova   Matej Bel University, Slovakia
Kamila Borsekova   Matej Bel University, Slovakia
Paola Zamperlin   University of Pisa, Italy

Federico Cugurullo   Trinity College Dublin, Ireland
Gerardo Carpentieri   University of Naples Federico II, Italy

International Workshop on Smart and Sustainable Island Communities (SSIC 2022)

Chiara Garau   University of Cagliari, Italy
Anastasia Stratigea   National Technical University of Athens, Greece
Paola Zamperlin   University of Pisa, Italy
Francesco Scorza   University of Basilicata, Italy

International Workshop on Theoretical and Computational Chemistry and Its Applications (TCCMA 2022)

Noelia Faginas-Lago   University of Perugia, Italy
Andrea Lombardi   University of Perugia, Italy

International Workshop on Transport Infrastructures for Smart Cities (TISC 2022)

Francesca Maltinti   University of Cagliari, Italy
Mauro Coni   University of Cagliari, Italy
Francesco Pinna   University of Cagliari, Italy
Chiara Garau   University of Cagliari, Italy
Nicoletta Rassu   Univesity of Cagliari, Italy
James Rombi   University of Cagliari, Italy
Benedetto Barabino   University of Brescia, Italy

14th International Workshop on Tools and Techniques in Software Development Process (TTSDP 2022)

Sanjay Misra   Østfold University College, Norway

International Workshop on Urban Form Studies (UForm 2022)

Malgorzata Hanzl   Lodz University of Technology, Poland
Beniamino Murgante   University of Basilicata, Italy
Alessandro Camiz   Özyeğin University, Turkey
Tomasz Bradecki   Silesian University of Technology, Poland

International Workshop on Urban Regeneration: Innovative Tools and Evaluation Model (URITEM 2022)

Fabrizio Battisti   University of Florence, Italy
Laura Ricci   Sapienza University of Rome, Italy
Orazio Campo   Sapienza University of Rome, Italy

International Workshop on Urban Space Accessibility and Mobilities (USAM 2022)

Chiara Garau	University of Cagliari, Italy
Matteo Ignaccolo	University of Catania, Italy
Enrica Papa	University of Westminster, UK
Francesco Pinna	University of Cagliari, Italy
Silvia Rossetti	University of Parma, Italy
Wendy Tan	Wageningen University and Research, The Netherlands
Michela Tiboni	University of Brescia, Italy
Vincenza Torrisi	University of Catania, Italy

International Workshop on Virtual Reality and Augmented Reality and Applications (VRA 2022)

Osvaldo Gervasi	University of Perugia, Italy
Damiano Perri	University of Florence, Italy
Marco Simonetti	University of Florence, Italy
Sergio Tasso	University of Perugia, Italy

International Workshop on Advanced and Computational Methods for Earth Science Applications (WACM4ES 2022)

Luca Piroddi	University of Cagliari, Italy
Sebastiano Damico	University of Malta, Malta

International Workshop on Advanced Mathematics and Computing Methods in Complex Computational Systems (WAMCM 2022)

Yeliz Karaca	UMass Chan Medical School, USA
Dumitru Baleanu	Cankaya University, Turkey
Osvaldo Gervasi	University of Perugia, Italy
Yudong Zhang	University of Leicester, UK
Majaz Moonis	UMass Chan Medical School, USA

Additional Reviewers

Akshat Agrawal	Amity University, Haryana, India
Waseem Ahmad	National Institute of Technology Karnataka, India
Vladimir Alarcon	Universidad Diego Portales, Chile
Oylum Alatlı	Ege University, Turkey
Raffaele Albano	University of Basilicata, Italy
Abraham Alfa	FUT Minna, Nigeria
Diego Altafini	Università di Pisa, Italy
Filipe Alvelos	Universidade do Minho, Portugal

Marina Alexandra Pedro Andrade	ISCTE-IUL, Portugal
Debora Anelli	Polytechnic University of Bari, Italy
Gennaro Angiello	AlmavivA de Belgique, Belgium
Alfonso Annunziata	Università di Cagliari, Italy
Bernady Apduhan	Kyushu Sangyo University, Japan
Daniela Ascenzi	Università degli Studi di Trento, Italy
Burak Galip Aslan	Izmir Insitute of Technology, Turkey
Vanessa Assumma	Politecnico di Torino, Italy
Daniel Atzberger	Hasso-Plattner-Institute für Digital Engineering gGmbH, Germany
Dominique Aury	École Polytechnique Fédérale de Lausanne, Switzerland
Joseph Awotumde	University of Alcala, Spain
Birim Balci	Celal Bayar University, Turkey
Juliana Balera	INPE, Brazil
Ginevra Balletto	University of Cagliari, Italy
Benedetto Barabino	University of Brescia, Italy
Kaushik Barik	University of Alcala, Spain
Carlo Barletta	Politecnico di Bari, Italy
Socrates Basbas	Aristotle University of Thessaloniki, Greece
Rosaria Battarra	ISMed-CNR, Italy
Silvia Battino	University of Sassari, Italy
Chiara Bedan	University of Trieste, Italy
Ranjan Kumar Behera	National Institute of Technology Rourkela, India
Gulmira Bekmanova	L.N. Gumilyov Eurasian National University, Kazakhstan
Mario Bentivenga	University of Basilicata, Italy
Asrat Mulatu Beyene	Addis Ababa Science and Technology University, Ethiopia
Tiziana Binda	Politecnico di Torino, Italy
Giulio Biondi	University of Firenze, Italy
Alexander Bogdanov	St Petersburg University, Russia
Costanza Borghesi	University of Perugia, Italy
Giuseppe Borruso	University of Trieste, Italy
Marilisa Botte	University of Naples Federico II, Italy
Tomasz Bradecki	Silesian University of Technology, Poland
Ana Cristina Braga	University of Minho, Portugal
Luca Braidotti	University of Trieste, Italy
Bazon Brock	University of Wuppertal, Germany
Dani Broitman	Israel Institute of Technology, Israel
Maria Antonia Brovelli	Politecnico di Milano, Italy
Jorge Buele	Universidad Tecnológica Indoamérica, Ecuador
Isabel Cacao	University of Aveiro, Portugal
Federica Cadamuro Morgante	Politecnico di Milano, Italy

Rogerio Calazan	IEAPM, Brazil
Michele Campagna	University of Cagliari, Italy
Lelio Campanile	Università degli Studi della Campania Luigi Vanvitelli, Italy
Tiziana Campisi	University of Enna Kore, Italy
Antonino Canale	University of Enna Kore, Italy
Elena Cantatore	Polytechnic University of Bari, Italy
Patrizia Capizzi	Univerity of Palermo, Italy
Alessandra Capolupo	Polytechnic University of Bari, Italy
Giacomo Caporusso	Politecnico di Bari, Italy
Caterina Caprioli	Politecnico di Torino, Italy
Gerardo Carpentieri	University of Naples Federico II, Italy
Martina Carra	University of Brescia, Italy
Pedro Carrasqueira	INESC Coimbra, Portugal
Barbara Caselli	Università degli Studi di Parma, Italy
Cecilia Castro	University of Minho, Portugal
Giulio Cavana	Politecnico di Torino, Italy
Iole Cerminara	University of Basilicata, Italy
Maria Cerreta	University of Naples Federico II, Italy
Daniele Cesini	INFN, Italy
Jabed Chowdhury	La Trobe University, Australia
Birol Ciloglugil	Ege University, Turkey
Elena Cocuzza	Univesity of Catania, Italy
Emanuele Colica	University of Malta, Malta
Mauro Coni	University of Cagliari, Italy
Elisete Correia	Universidade de Trás-os-Montes e Alto Douro, Portugal
Florbela Correia	Polytechnic Institute of Viana do Castelo, Portugal
Paulo Cortez	University of Minho, Portugal
Lino Costa	Universidade do Minho, Portugal
Alessandro Costantini	INFN, Italy
Marilena Cozzolino	Università del Molise, Italy
Alfredo Cuzzocrea	University of Calabria, Italy
Sebastiano D'amico	University of Malta, Malta
Gianni D'Angelo	University of Salerno, Italy
Tijana Dabovic	University of Belgrade, Serbia
Hiroshi Daisaka	Hitotsubashi University, Japan
Giulia Datola	Politecnico di Torino, Italy
Regina De Almeida	University of Trás-os-Montes and Alto Douro, Portugal
Maria Stella De Biase	Università della Campania Luigi Vanvitelli, Italy
Elise De Doncker	Western Michigan University, USA
Itamir De Morais Barroca Filho	Federal University of Rio Grande do Norte, Brazil
Samuele De Petris	University of Turin, Italy
Alan De Sá	Marinha do Brasil, Brazil
Alexander Degtyarev	St Petersburg University, Russia

Federico Dell'Anna	Politecnico di Torino, Italy
Marta Dell'Ovo	Politecnico di Milano, Italy
Ahu Dereli Dursun	Istanbul Commerce University, Turkey
Giulia Desogus	University of Cagliari, Italy
Piero Di Bonito	Università degli Studi della Campania, Italia
Paolino Di Felice	University of L'Aquila, Italy
Felicia Di Liddo	Polytechnic University of Bari, Italy
Isabel Dimas	University of Coimbra, Portugal
Doina Cristina Duma	INFN, Italy
Aziz Dursun	Virginia Tech University, USA
Jaroslav Dvořák	Klaipėda University, Lithuania
Dario Esposito	Polytechnic University of Bari, Italy
M. Noelia Faginas-Lago	University of Perugia, Italy
Stefano Falcinelli	University of Perugia, Italy
Falcone Giacomo	University of Reggio Calabria, Italy
Maria Irene Falcão	University of Minho, Portugal
Stefano Federico	CNR-ISAC, Italy
Marcin Feltynowski	University of Lodz, Poland
António Fernandes	Instituto Politécnico de Bragança, Portugal
Florbela Fernandes	Instituto Politecnico de Bragança, Portugal
Paula Odete Fernandes	Instituto Politécnico de Bragança, Portugal
Luis Fernandez-Sanz	University of Alcala, Spain
Luís Ferrás	University of Minho, Portugal
Ângela Ferreira	Instituto Politécnico de Bragança, Portugal
Lorena Fiorini	University of L'Aquila, Italy
Hector Florez	Universidad Distrital Francisco Jose de Caldas, Colombia
Stefano Franco	LUISS Guido Carli, Italy
Valentina Franzoni	Perugia University, Italy
Adelaide Freitas	University of Aveiro, Portugal
Andreas Fricke	Hasso Plattner Institute, Germany
Junpei Fujimoto	KEK, Japan
Federica Gaglione	Università del Sannio, Italy
Andrea Gallo	Università degli Studi di Trieste, Italy
Luciano Galone	University of Malta, Malta
Adam Galuszka	Silesian University of Technology, Poland
Chiara Garau	University of Cagliari, Italy
Ernesto Garcia Para	Universidad del País Vasco, Spain
Aniket A. Gaurav	Østfold University College, Norway
Marina Gavrilova	University of Calgary, Canada
Osvaldo Gervasi	University of Perugia, Italy
Andrea Ghirardi	Università di Brescia, Italy
Andrea Gioia	Politecnico di Bari, Italy
Giacomo Giorgi	Università degli Studi di Perugia, Italy
Stanislav Glubokovskikh	Lawrence Berkeley National Laboratory, USA
A. Manuela Gonçalves	University of Minho, Portugal

Leocadio González Casado	University of Almería, Spain
Angela Gorgoglione	Universidad de la República Uruguay, Uruguay
Yusuke Gotoh	Okayama University, Japan
Daniele Granata	Università degli Studi della Campania, Italy
Christian Grévisse	University of Luxembourg, Luxembourg
Silvana Grillo	University of Cagliari, Italy
Teresa Guarda	State University of Santa Elena Peninsula, Ecuador
Carmen Guida	Università degli Studi di Napoli Federico II, Italy
Kemal Güven Gülen	Namık Kemal University, Turkey
Ipek Guler	Leuven Biostatistics and Statistical Bioinformatics Centre, Belgium
Sevin Gumgum	Izmir University of Economics, Turkey
Martina Halásková	VSB Technical University in Ostrava, Czech Republic
Peter Hegedus	University of Szeged, Hungary
Eligius M. T. Hendrix	Universidad de Málaga, Spain
Mauro Iacono	Università degli Studi della Campania, Italy
Oleg Iakushkin	St Petersburg University, Russia
Matteo Ignaccolo	University of Catania, Italy
Mustafa Inceoglu	Ege University, Turkey
Markus Jobst	Federal Office of Metrology and Surveying, Austria
Issaku Kanamori	RIKEN Center for Computational Science, Japan
Yeliz Karaca	UMass Chan Medical School, USA
Aarti Karande	Sardar Patel Institute of Technology, India
András Kicsi	University of Szeged, Hungary
Vladimir Korkhov	St Petersburg University, Russia
Nataliia Kulabukhova	St Petersburg University, Russia
Claudio Ladisa	Politecnico di Bari, Italy
Mara Ladu	University of Cagliari, Italy
Sabrina Lai	University of Cagliari, Italy
Mark Lajko	University of Szeged, Hungary
Giuseppe Francesco Cesare Lama	University of Napoli Federico II, Italy
Vincenzo Laporta	CNR, Italy
Margherita Lasorella	Politecnico di Bari, Italy
Francesca Leccis	Università di Cagliari, Italy
Federica Leone	University of Cagliari, Italy
Chien-sing Lee	Sunway University, Malaysia
Marco Locurcio	Polytechnic University of Bari, Italy
Francesco Loddo	Henge S.r.l., Italy
Andrea Lombardi	Università di Perugia, Italy
Isabel Lopes	Instituto Politécnico de Bragança, Portugal
Fernando Lopez Gayarre	University of Oviedo, Spain
Vanda Lourenço	Universidade Nova de Lisboa, Portugal
Jing Ma	Luleå University of Technology, Sweden
Helmuth Malonek	University of Aveiro, Portugal
Francesca Maltinti	University of Cagliari, Italy

Benedetto Manganelli	Università degli Studi della Basilicata, Italy
Krassimir Markov	Institute of Electric Engineering and Informatics, Bulgaria
Alessandro Marucci	University of L'Aquila, Italy
Alessandra Mascitelli	Italian Civil Protection Department and ISAC-CNR, Italy
Michele Mastroianni	University of Campania Luigi Vanvitelli, Italy
Hideo Matsufuru	High Energy Accelerator Research Organization (KEK), Japan
Chiara Mazzarella	University of Naples Federico II, Italy
Marco Mazzarino	University of Venice, Italy
Paolo Mengoni	University of Florence, Italy
Alfredo Milani	University of Perugia, Italy
Fernando Miranda	Universidade do Minho, Portugal
Augusto Montisci	Università degli Studi di Cagliari, Italy
Ricardo Moura	New University of Lisbon, Portugal
Ana Clara Mourao Moura	Federal University of Minas Gerais, Brazil
Maria Mourao	Polytechnic Institute of Viana do Castelo, Portugal
Eugenio Muccio	University of Naples Federico II, Italy
Beniamino Murgante	University of Basilicata, Italy
Giuseppe Musolino	University of Reggio Calabria, Italy
Stefano Naitza	Università di Cagliari, Italy
Naohito Nakasato	University of Aizu, Japan
Roberto Nardone	University of Reggio Calabria, Italy
Nadia Nedjah	State University of Rio de Janeiro, Brazil
Juraj Nemec	Masaryk University in Brno, Czech Republic
Keigo Nitadori	RIKEN R-CCS, Japan
Roseline Ogundokun	Kaunas University of Technology, Lithuania
Francisco Henrique De Oliveira	Santa Catarina State University, Brazil
Irene Oliveira	Univesidade Trás-os-Montes e Alto Douro, Portugal
Samson Oruma	Østfold University College, Norway
Antonio Pala	University of Cagliari, Italy
Simona Panaro	University of Porstmouth, UK
Dimos Pantazis	University of West Attica, Greece
Giovanni Paragliola	ICAR-CNR, Italy
Eric Pardede	La Trobe University, Australia
Marco Parriani	University of Perugia, Italy
Paola Perchinunno	Uniersity of Bari, Italy
Ana Pereira	Polytechnic Institute of Bragança, Portugal
Damiano Perri	University of Perugia, Italy
Marco Petrelli	Roma Tre University, Italy
Camilla Pezzica	University of Pisa, Italy
Angela Pilogallo	University of Basilicata, Italy
Francesco Pinna	University of Cagliari, Italy
Telmo Pinto	University of Coimbra, Portugal

Fernando Pirani	University of Perugia, Italy
Luca Piroddi	University of Cagliari, Italy
Bojana Pjanović	University of Belgrade, Serbia
Giuliano Poli	University of Naples Federico II, Italy
Maurizio Pollino	ENEA, Italy
Salvatore Praticò	University of Reggio Calabria, Italy
Zbigniew Przygodzki	University of Lodz, Poland
Carlotta Quagliolo	Politecnico di Torino, Italy
Raffaele Garrisi	Polizia Postale e delle Comunicazioni, Italy
Mariapia Raimondo	Università della Campania Luigi Vanvitelli, Italy
Deep Raj	IIIT Naya Raipur, India
Buna Ramos	Universidade Lusíada Norte, Portugal
Nicoletta Rassu	Univesity of Cagliari, Italy
Michela Ravanelli	Sapienza Università di Roma, Italy
Roberta Ravanelli	Sapienza Università di Roma, Italy
Pier Francesco Recchi	University of Naples Federico II, Italy
Stefania Regalbuto	University of Naples Federico II, Italy
Marco Reis	University of Coimbra, Portugal
Maria Reitano	University of Naples Federico II, Italy
Anatoly Resnyansky	Defence Science and Technology Group, Australia
Jerzy Respondek	Silesian University of Technology, Poland
Isabel Ribeiro	Instituto Politécnico Bragança, Portugal
Albert Rimola	Universitat Autònoma de Barcelona, Spain
Corrado Rindone	University of Reggio Calabria, Italy
Ana Maria A. C. Rocha	University of Minho, Portugal
Humberto Rocha	University of Coimbra, Portugal
Maria Clara Rocha	Instituto Politécnico de Coimbra, Portugal
James Rombi	University of Cagliari, Italy
Elisabetta Ronchieri	INFN, Italy
Marzio Rosi	University of Perugia, Italy
Silvia Rossetti	Università degli Studi di Parma, Italy
Marco Rossitti	Politecnico di Milano, Italy
Mária Rostašová	Universtiy of Žilina, Slovakia
Lucia Saganeiti	University of L'Aquila, Italy
Giovanni Salzillo	Università degli Studi della Campania, Italy
Valentina Santarsiero	University of Basilicata, Italy
Luigi Santopietro	University of Basilicata, Italy
Stefania Santoro	Politecnico di Bari, Italy
Rafael Santos	INPE, Brazil
Valentino Santucci	Università per Stranieri di Perugia, Italy
Mirko Saponaro	Polytechnic University of Bari, Italy
Filippo Sarvia	University of Turin, Italy
Andrea Scianna	ICAR-CNR, Italy
Francesco Scorza	University of Basilicata, Italy
Ester Scotto Di Perta	University of Naples Federico II, Italy
Ricardo Severino	University of Minho, Portugal

Jie Shen	University of Michigan, USA
Luneque Silva Junior	Universidade Federal do ABC, Brazil
Carina Silva	Instituto Politécnico de Lisboa, Portugal
Joao Carlos Silva	Polytechnic Institute of Cavado and Ave, Portugal
Ilya Silvestrov	Saudi Aramco, Saudi Arabia
Marco Simonetti	University of Florence, Italy
Maria Joana Soares	University of Minho, Portugal
Michel Soares	Federal University of Sergipe, Brazil
Alberico Sonnessa	Politecnico di Bari, Italy
Lisete Sousa	University of Lisbon, Portugal
Elena Stankova	St Petersburg University, Russia
Jan Stejskal	University of Pardubice, Czech Republic
Silvia Stranieri	University of Naples Federico II, Italy
Anastasia Stratigea	National Technical University of Athens, Greece
Yue Sun	European XFEL GmbH, Germany
Anthony Suppa	Politecnico di Torino, Italy
Kirill Sviatov	Ulyanovsk State Technical University, Russia
David Taniar	Monash University, Australia
Rodrigo Tapia-McClung	Centro de Investigación en Ciencias de Información Geoespacial, Mexico
Eufemia Tarantino	Politecnico di Bari, Italy
Sergio Tasso	University of Perugia, Italy
Vladimir Tcheverda	Institute of Petroleum Geology and Geophysics, SB RAS, Russia
Ana Paula Teixeira	Universidade de Trás-os-Montes e Alto Douro, Portugal
Tengku Adil Tengku Izhar	Universiti Teknologi MARA, Malaysia
Maria Filomena Teodoro	University of Lisbon and Portuguese Naval Academy, Portugal
Yiota Theodora	National Technical University of Athens, Greece
Graça Tomaz	Instituto Politécnico da Guarda, Portugal
Gokchan Tonbul	Atilim University, Turkey
Rosa Claudia Torcasio	CNR-ISAC, Italy
Carmelo Maria Torre	Polytechnic University of Bari, Italy
Vincenza Torrisi	University of Catania, Italy
Vincenzo Totaro	Politecnico di Bari, Italy
Pham Trung	HCMUT, Vietnam
Po-yu Tsai	National Chung Hsing University, Taiwan
Dimitrios Tsoukalas	Centre of Research and Technology Hellas, Greece
Toshihiro Uchibayashi	Kyushu University, Japan
Takahiro Ueda	Seikei University, Japan
Piero Ugliengo	Università degli Studi di Torino, Italy
Gianmarco Vanuzzo	University of Perugia, Italy
Clara Vaz	Instituto Politécnico de Bragança, Portugal
Laura Verde	University of Campania Luigi Vanvitelli, Italy
Katarína Vitálišová	Matej Bel University, Slovakia

Daniel Mark Vitiello	University of Cagliari, Italy
Marco Vizzari	University of Perugia, Italy
Alexander Vodyaho	St. Petersburg State Electrotechnical University "LETI", Russia
Agustinus Borgy Waluyo	Monash University, Australia
Chao Wang	USTC, China
Marcin Wozniak	Silesian University of Technology, Poland
Jitao Yang	Beijing Language and Culture University, China
Fenghui Yao	Tennessee State University, USA
Fukuko Yuasa	KEK, Japan
Paola Zamperlin	University of Pisa, Italy
Michal Žemlička	Charles University, Czech Republic
Nataly Zhukova	ITMO University, Russia
Alcinia Zita Sampaio	University of Lisbon, Portugal
Ljiljana Zivkovic	Republic Geodetic Authority, Serbia
Floriana Zucaro	University of Naples Federico II, Italy
Marco Zucca	Politecnico di Milano, Italy
Camila Zyngier	Ibmec, Belo Horizonte, Brazil

Sponsoring Organizations

ICCSA 2022 would not have been possible without tremendous support of many organizations and institutions, for which all organizers and participants of ICCSA 2022 express their sincere gratitude:

Springer International Publishing AG, Germany (https://www.springer.com)

Computers Open Access Journal (https://www.mdpi.com/journal/computers)

Computation Open Access Journal (https://www.mdpi.com/journal/computation)

University of Malaga, Spain (https://www.uma.es/)

University of Perugia, Italy
(https://www.unipg.it)

University of Basilicata, Italy
(http://www.unibas.it)

Monash University, Australia
(https://www.monash.edu/)

Kyushu Sangyo University, Japan
(https://www.kyusan-u.ac.jp/)

University of Minho, Portugal
(https://www.uminho.pt/)

Universidade do Minho
Escola de Engenharia

Contents – Part II

Contents – Part I

High Performance Computing and Networks

Geometric Modeling, Graphics and Visualization

Advanced and Emerging Applications

Random Forest Based Deep Hybrid Architecture for Histopathological Breast Cancer Images Classification

Fatima-Zahrae Nakach[1], Hasnae Zerouaoui[1], and Ali Idri[1,2(✉)]

[1] Modeling, Simulation and Data Analysis, Mohammed VI Polytechnic University, Benguerir, Marrakech-Rhamna, Morocco
[2] Software Project Management Research Team, ENSIAS, Mohammed V University, Rabat-Salé-Kénitra, Rabat, Morocco
ali.idri@um5.ac.ma

Abstract. Breast cancer is the most common cancer in women worldwide. While the early diagnosis and treatment can significantly reduce the mortality rate, it is a challenging task for pathologists to accurately estimate the cancerous cells and tissues. Therefore, machine learning techniques are playing a significant role in assisting pathologists and improving the diagnosis results. This paper proposes a hybrid architecture that combines: three of the most recent deep learning techniques for feature extraction (DenseNet_201, Inception_V3, and MobileNet_V2) and random forest to classify breast cancer histological images over the BreakHis dataset with its four magnification factors: 40X, 100X, 200X and 400X. The study evaluated and compared: (1) the developed random forest models with their base learners, (2) the designed random forest models with the same architecture but with a different number of trees, (3) the decision tree classifiers with the best random forest models and (4) the best random forest models of each feature extractor. The empirical evaluations used: four classification performance criteria (accuracy, sensitivity, precision and F1-score), 5-fold cross-validation, Scott Knott statistical test, and Borda Count voting method. The best random forest model achieved an accuracy mean value of 85.88%, and was constructed using 9 trees, 200X as a magnification factor, and Inception_V3 as a feature extractor. The experimental results demonstrated that combining random forest with deep learning models is effective for the automatic classification of malignant and benign tumors using histopathological images of breast cancer.

Keywords: Breast cancer · Hybrid · Random forest · Transfer learning

1 Introduction

Breast cancer (BC) became the most common cancer globally as of 2021, accounting for 12% of all new annual cancer cases worldwide, according to the World Health Organization [1]. When BC is detected and treated early, the chances of survival are very high [2]. Computer aided detection and machine learning (ML) based intelligent automated prediction systems could improve the cancer diagnosis capability and reduce

O. Gervasi et al. (Eds.): ICCSA 2022, LNCS 13376, pp. 3–18, 2022.
https://doi.org/10.1007/978-3-031-10450-3_1

the diagnosis errors [3]. Moreover, these systems can provide decision support for the doctors for an opportunity of early identification of BC [4]. Research indicates that most experienced physicians can diagnose cancer with 79% accuracy while 91% correct diagnosis is achieved using ML techniques [5].

Over the past few decades, ensemble learning has drawn the attention of computational intelligence and ML researchers [6]. This increasing interest owes to its effective role at solving a large variety of ML problems, including feature selection, pattern recognition, confidence estimation, incremental learning, surfacing in application areas such as computer vision, medical research, geosciences, and many more [7, 8]. Ensemble learning methods were originally developed to improve the prediction power and stability of the classification model by combining several learners together [9]. In fact, theoretical and empirical studies have demonstrated that an ensemble of classifiers is typically more accurate than a single classifier [10]. However, improvement over the single best classifier or even on the average of the individual accuracies is not always guaranteed [11]. This improvement of performances relies on the concept of diversity [12], that is one of the three pillars of ensemble learning [8] (the other pillars are: generating ensemble members and combining them). The practical trade-off between diversity and accuracy of the ensemble learning is still an open question in ML [13] and many methods have been proposed to generate accurate and diverse sets of models [14]. The widely-used ensemble classification methods include bagging, boosting and stacking [15].

Deep learning (DL) is a new branch in the field of ML that can replace the manual feature extraction and selection with automatic learning of representative features [16]. Convolutional neural network (CNN) is one of the most effective DL models, which has also achieved a considerable performance in computer vision tasks and is also useful in transfer learning [17]. It is widely accepted that only the extracted features in the last convolutional layer are most suitable as the input vector of the classifier in most researches and applications of CNN models [18].

Since DL has the automatic feature extraction ability and ensemble learning can improve the accuracy and generalization performance of classifiers. This paper proposes a hybrid architecture that combines pre-trained DL techniques for feature extraction and random forest (RF) for binary classification of BC histological images over the BreakHis dataset at different magnification factors (MFs): 40X, 100X, 200X, and 400X. The main objective is to develop, evaluate and compare the hybrid RF models that are designed using: (1) three of the most recent DL techniques for feature extraction: DenseNet_201, MobileNet_V2, and Inception_V3 and (2) different number of trees (3, 5, 7 and 9).

Breiman [19] developed the concept of bagging in 1994 to improve classification by combining predictions of randomly generated training sets, the results proved that most of the improvement is obtained with unstable base models using only 10 bootstrap replicates, for that reason, the present study varies the number of trees between 3 and 9. The ML classifier that is frequently used to construct homogeneous ensembles is decision tree (DT) as reported in the systematic literature review [21], thus RF was used for classification. The three DL techniques (DenseNet_201, MobileNet_V2, and Inception_V3) were selected based on their performances as feature extractors (FE) for binary classification of breast pathological images over the BreakHis and FNAC datasets [20]. All the empirical evaluations used: four classification performance criteria (accuracy, sensitivity, precision and F1-score), 5-fold cross-validation, Scott Knott (SK) statistical test to select the best cluster of the outperforming models, and Borda Count voting system to rank the best performing ones. The present study discusses four research questions (RQs):

- **(RQ1): Do hybrid RF models perform better than their trees?**
- **(RQ2): What is the best number of trees of the outperforming hybrid RF model for each FE?**
- **(RQ3): Do hybrid RF models perform better than the DT classifiers?**
- **(RQ4): What is the best hybrid RF model for each MF and over all the MFs?**

The main contributions of this paper are the following:

1. Designing three DT models using different DL techniques as FEs: DenseNet_201, Inception_V3, and MobileNet_V2.
2. Designing twelve hybrid RF models (4 models with a different number of trees for each DL architecture).
3. Evaluating the twelve hybrid RF models over the BreakHis dataset, considering the four MFs (40X, 100X, 200X and 400X) as four datasets.
4. Comparing the performances of the twelve hybrid RF models using SK clustering test and Borda Count voting method.
5. Comparing the performances of the twelve hybrid RF models with their base learners (trees) using SK clustering test and Borda Count voting method.
6. Comparing the performances of the best hybrid RF model for each classifier and FE with the DT classifier using SK clustering test and Borda Count voting method.

The remaining sections of this paper are provided as follows. Section 2 presents an overview of the three DL techniques used as FEs and the DT classifier; it also defines transfer learning, bagging in general and RF in particular. Section 3 describes the related work. Section 4 presents the materials and methods followed throughout this research. Section 5 presents and discusses the empirical results. Section 6 outlines the conclusion and future work.

2   Background

The present study uses three pre-trained DL techniques: DenseNet_201, Inception_V3 and MobileNet_V2 as FEs with RF as a classifier to design the hybrid architectures. They have been implemented using transfer learning for feature extraction and the homogeneous ensemble learning method: bagging for classification. This section gives a summary of the different methods and techniques used.

2.1   Transfer Learning

Transfer learning is a ML technique that transfer the knowledge of a model from a related source task to a second related task. Transfer learning only works in DL if the model features learned from the first task are general [22]. This method optimizes its modeling by allowing rapid progress and improved performance. Compared with training from scratch, using a pre-trained convolutional neural network on a target dataset can significantly improve performance, while compensating for the lack of sufficient training data in the target task [23]. Transfer learning is widely used in computer vision, the models for image classification that result from a transfer learning approach based on pre-trained CNNs are usually composed of two parts: The convolutional base, which performs feature extraction, and the classifier, which classifies the input image based on the features extracted by the convolutional base. The typical way of conducting transfer learning with deep neural networks is usually expressed through the use of pre-trained models with 2 different methods:

- **Fine Tuning pre-trained models**: The idea of this method is to slightly adjust the parameters of a pre-trained model to allow knowledge transfer from the source task to the target task. Commonly used fine-tuning strategies include fine-tuning all the pre-trained parameters and fine-tuning few layers. The second strategy is made by unfreezing a few of the top layers of a frozen model base and jointly train both the newly added classifier layers and the last layers of the base model, in order to make it more relevant for the new specific task [24].
- **Pre-trained models as feature extractors**: This method uses the representations learned by a previous network to extract meaningful features from new samples. The main idea is to keep the convolutional base of the pre-trained model in its original form and then use its outputs to feed the classifier. This approach is much faster and give better results if the initial model was trained on a large benchmark dataset to solve a problem similar to the one in this research [25].

2.2 DL Techniques for Feature Extraction

Transfer learning with CNNs, well-trained on non-medical ImageNet dataset, has shown promising results for medical image analysis in recent years [26]. This study used the following pre-trained models for feature extraction:

- **DenseNet_201** is a convolutional neural network with 201 layers that connects each layer to every other layer in a feed-forward fashion. DenseNets have several compelling advantages: they alleviate the vanishing-gradient problem, strengthen feature propagation, encourage feature reuse, and substantially reduce the number of parameters [27].
- **MobileNet_V2** is based on an inverted residual structure where the residual connections are between the bottleneck layers. The intermediate expansion layer uses lightweight depth wise convolutions to filter features as a source of non-linearity. As a whole, the architecture of MobileNetV2 contains the initial fully convolution layer with 32 filters, followed by 19 residual bottleneck layers [28].
- **Inception_V3** is the third version in a series of DL convolutional architectures. It is a CNN with 42 layers with a default input size fixed to 299×299 [29]. It has a block of parallel convolutional layer with a filter size of (3×3), followed by three inception modules with 288 filters each, 5 instances of the factorized inception modules with

768 filters, and two inception modules with 1280 filters. The outputs are concatenated and sent to a SoftMax output layer.

2.3 Decision Tree (DT)

DT is a flowchart-like tree structure that classifies instances by sorting them based on feature values, where each node in a DT represents a feature in an instance to be classified, and each branch represents a decision rule, and each leaf node represents the outcome. the topmost node is known as the root node and it is the feature that best divides the training data [30].

2.4 Bagging

Bagging or "Bootstrap aggregating" is a homogenous ensemble method that improves the accuracy by decreasing the variance and reducing the overfitting [31]. This method generates sample subsets (bootstrap) by randomly sampling from the training dataset with or without replacement, in the first case many of the original examples of the training dataset may be repeated while others may be left out. The base learners are then trained on the generated subsets and their predictions are combined to get an aggregated prediction. The aggregation averages over the base learners' results when predicting a numerical outcome and does a majority vote when predicting a class. The training is performed in a parallel manner and the accuracy increases if perturbing the learning set causes major changes in the predictor built [19, 32].

2.5 Random Forest

RF classifier is a bagging ensemble that produces multiple DTs that will be used to classify a new instance by the majority vote [33]. Each DT node uses a subset of attributes randomly selected from the whole original set of attributes, and each tree uses a different bootstrap sample data. RF classifier has been attracting increasing attention due to its excellent classification accuracy and high efficiency; It is a computationally efficient technique that can operate quickly over large datasets [34].

3 Related Work

Motivated by the success of DL in computer vision, various studies employed pre-trained DL models for binary classification of BC histopathological images using hybrid architectures (the feature and classification tasks are done with different models). For instance, Zerouaoui et Idri [20] developed and evaluated twenty-eight hybrid architectures combining seven recent DL techniques for feature extraction (DenseNet 201, Inception V3, Inception ReseNet V2, MobileNet V2, ResNet 50, VGG16, and VGG19), and four classifiers (MLP, SVM, DT, and KNN) for a binary classification of breast pathological images over the BreakHis and FNAC datasets. The hybrid architecture using the MLP classifier and DenseNet 201 for feature extraction was the top performing architecture with higher accuracy values reaching 92.61%, 92%, 93.93%, and 91.73% over the four MF values of the BreakHis dataset: 40X, 100X, 200X, and 400X, respectively.

Kassani et al. [35] proposed ensemble model adapts three pre-trained CNNs: VGG19, MobileNet_V2, and DenseNet_201 to extract features and feed them into a multi-layer perceptron classifier. The proposed ensemble outperformed the single CNNs and the candidate ML classifiers, namely, DT, RF, XGBoost, AdaBoost and bagging.

Saxena et al. [36] investigated ten different pre-trained CNNs (AlexNet_43, VGG_16 and VGG_19; GoogLeNet, ResNet18, ResNet_50, ResNet_101, Inception_V3, Inception_ResNet_V2 and SqueezeNet) for extracting the features from BC histopathology images from the BreakHis dataset. For classification, they examined different classifiers which are: SVM, KNN, DT, RF, and boosting. They selected SVM with linear kernel for the classification since it performed better than the other classifiers. However, the selection of the classifier was only performed with ResNet_50 on MF 40X. The best performing models used SVM as classifier and as FE: ResNet50 for MF 40X, ResNet101 for MF 100X, ResNet50 for MF 200X, and AlexNet for MF 400X with an accuracy of 87.71%, 88.92%, 90.12% and 85.16% respectively.

4   Materials and Methods

This section presents the data preparation process, the experimental process followed to carry out all the empirical evaluations, the threats of validity and the abbreviations.

4.1 Data Preparation

The data preparation process followed for the BreakHis dataset in the current study is similar to the one that has been followed in [37]; thereafter we summarize the different steps of this process. The present study used intensity normalization to ensure that each input parameter (pixel, in this case) has a similar data distribution and to remove highlighted regions and shadows [38]. The input images were normalized to the standard normal distribution using min-max. Furthermore, before feeding input images into the proposed models, Contrast Limited Adaptive Histogram Equalization (CLAHE) is a necessary step to improve the contrast in images [39]. For the BreakHis dataset, 70% of the histological images represent the malignant class. To overcome this limitation, data augmentation [40] was used to resample the BreakHis dataset after the pre-processing step to increase the amount of data by adding slightly modified copies of already existing data or newly created synthetic data from existing data. After using data augmentation for the original BreakHis dataset, a new balanced dataset was obtained where the total number of benign samples was increased by 2 times to obtain the same number of malignant images.

4.2 Experimental Process

In this experiment, the models are evaluated using k-folds cross validation with k = 5. The empirical evaluations use RF, three DL techniques as FE: DenseNet_201, Inception_V3 and MobileNet_V2, and the BreakHis dataset which contains images with various MFs including 40X, 100X, 200X, and 400X. Moreover, the SK test [41] based on accuracy was used to cluster the models in order to identify the best SK clusters (i.e. containing the best models that are statistically indifferent in terms of accuracy). Thereafter, Borda Count [42] was used to rank the models belonging to each best SK cluster using accuracy, recall, precision and F1-score. Figure 1 shows the methodology followed to carry out all the empirical evaluations.

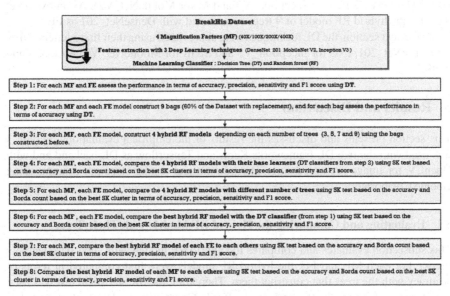

Fig. 1. Experimental process.

4.3 Threats of Validity

This paper used the k-fold cross validation as an internal threat with k = 5, The choice of k is usually 5 or 10, as these values have been shown empirically to yield test error rate estimates that suffer neither from excessively high bias nor from very high variance [43]. Transfer learning was also used to extract the features of the images with the most powerful DL techniques. For the external validity, this paper used the BreakHis dataset which contains histological images with four different MFs. Each MF can be considered as a dataset, which was helpful to compare the performance of the different models and FE for each MF. However, it would be interesting to study if the robustness of the models holds with different BC image datasets. For the reliability of the classifier performances obtained, this paper focused on four classification metrics (accuracy, recall, precision and F1-Score) to construct validity. The main reasons behind the choice of these performance criteria are: (1) most of the studies used them to measure the classification performance, and (2) the type of the data is balanced. Moreover, the conclusion was drawn by using the SK test and Borda count voting system with equal weights using these four performance criteria.

4.4 Abbreviation

In order to assist the reader and shorten the names of the models, this paper uses the following naming rules. The abbreviation of the hybrid RF models is RF, plus the abbreviation of the feature extractor, followed by the number of trees. The name of the FE technique used with the RF model is abbreviated using the first letter of the DL model (D for DenseNet_201, I for Inception_V3 and M for MobileNet_V2). As an example: RFD9 is the hybrid RF model of 9 trees constructed with DenseNet_201 as FE.

In the next section, the DL techniques were abbreviated using their first 3 letters (DEN for DenseNet_201, INC for Inception_V3 and MOB for MobileNet_V2) for tables and figures.

5 Results and Discussion

This section presents and discusses the results of the empirical evaluations. Python 3 was used with the two DL frameworks Keras and Tensorflow as DL backend and with OpenCV for image pre-processing. The training and testing steps are running using Google Colaboratory.

5.1 Evaluating and Comparing the Hybrid RF Models with Their Trees

This subsection evaluates and compares the hybrid RF models with their base learners (trees). For each MF and FE, the hybrid RF models were first compared in terms of accuracy with the trees that construct them. Thereafter, the SK statistical test was used to determine the best cluster, and finally Borda Count was used to rank the models belonging to the best SK cluster. Figures 2 shows the difference in % between the accuracy value of hybrid RF models and the mean accuracy value of their trees over the 4 different MFs. The number 3, 5, 7 or 9 refers to the number of trees that construct each RF model.

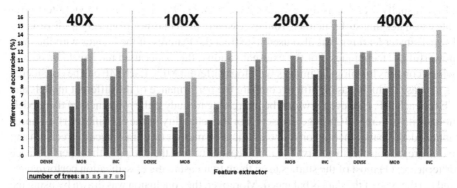

Fig. 2. Difference between the accuracy of the hybrid RF models and their trees over each MF and FE.

For each MF and FE, the observations of the results are as follow:

- The accuracy of the hybrid RF models is always better than the mean accuracy of their trees.
- The difference of accuracies increases with the number of trees that construct them (15.80% for the highest difference value with a RF of 9 trees, Inception_V3 and MF 200X and 3.31% for the lowest one with a RF of 3 trees, MobileNet_V2 and 100X).

Thereafter, the SK statistical test was used to determine the best cluster, it was found that for the majority of MFs and FEs two clusters were obtained; the best cluster contains the hybrid RF models while the other cluster contains all the trees. However, there are two exceptions for MF 100X and the hybrid RF model constructed using three trees:

- When using DenseNet_201 as FE, two clusters were obtained, the best one contains the hybrid RF model and one of its trees, while the other cluster contains the two other trees. Which means that statistically the hybrid RF model and one of its trees show the same predictive capabilities in terms of accuracy.
- When using MobileNet_V2 as FE, only one cluster was obtained, which means that statistically the hybrid RF model and its trees show the same predictive capabilities.

In order to identify which model is the best for MobileNet_V2 and DenseNet_201 as FE with MF 100X, the models of the best SK cluster of each MF and FE were ranked by using the Borda Count voting system based on accuracy, sensitivity, F1-score and precision. The results of the Borda Count voting method show that the hybrid RF models are always ranked first.

To conclude, hybrid RF models outperform their trees and the difference of accuracies between them and their trees is relatively important.

5.2   Evaluating and Comparing the Impact of the Number of Trees on the Hybrid RF Models Performances Over Each FE and MF

This subsection evaluates and compares the hybrid RF models implemented with the same FE but with a different number of trees (3, 5, 7 or 9) for each MF, in order to identify the number of trees that gives the best performance. The performances of the hybrid RF models were evaluated using four criteria: accuracy, precision, recall and F1-score. For each FE and each MF, the hybrid RF models were first compared in terms of accuracy.

Figure 3 shows the comparison of the mean accuracy values of the hybrid RF model using the four number of trees, the 3 DL techniques for FE over each MF value: 40X, 100X, 200X and 400X. It can be seen that:

- The best accuracy values were obtained when using the DenseNet_201 as FE for the MF 100X, and with Inception_V3 for the MF 40X, 200X and 400X. The worst accuracy values were obtained when using MobileNet_V2 for MF 40X, 200X and 400X, and when using Inception_V3 for MF 100X.
- The best accuracy values when using the DenseNet_201 as FE with the MF 100X reached 82.57% with a hybrid RF model of 9 trees, and with Inception V2 as FE the values were 84.31%, 85.88% and 82.35% with a hybrid RF model of 9 trees for the MF 100X, 200X and 400X respectively.

- The worst accuracy values when using the MobileNet_V2 were: 76.79%, 77.49% and 72.15% with a hybrid RF model of 3 trees for the MF 40X, 200X and 400X respectively. For MF 100X, the worst accuracy values when using the Inception_V3 was: 76.60%.

Thereafter, the SK statistical test was used to determine the best cluster, and finally Borda Count was used to rank the hybrid RF models belonging to the best SK cluster. It was found that the ranks are ascending: the hybrid RF models with more trees perform better than the others; but there are two exceptions. The hybrid RF model of 9 trees is outperformed by the hybrid RF model of 7 trees when using DenseNet_201 and MobileNet_V2 for MF 200X and MF 400X respectively.

In summary, (1) the hybrid RF models of 9 trees were generally ranked first, and (2) the hybrid RF models of 3 trees are always ranked last.

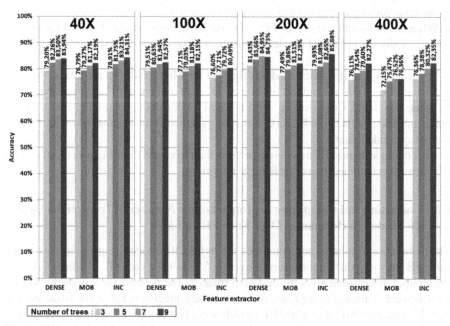

Fig. 3. Mean accuracy values of the hybrid RF models using different number of trees over each MF and FE.

5.3 Evaluating and Comparing the Best Hybrid RF Models and DT Classifiers

This subsection evaluates and compares the first ranked hybrid RF model found in RQ2 with the DT classifier over each MF and FE. Table 1 summarizes the testing accuracy values of the best hybrid RF model for each FE and the DT classifier designed using the same FE. Two different clusters were obtained for the results of SK test for the hybrid RF model and DT classifier over each FE and MF, where the first cluster was always represented by the hybrid RF model and the second one with the DT classifier. Therefore, the hybrid RF model outperforms the DT classifier for each MF and FE.

Table 1. Mean accuracy values of the best hybrid RF model and the DT classifier over each MF and FE.

FE MF	Hybrid RF accuracy (%)			DT accuracy (%)		
	DEN	**MOB**	**INC**	**DEN**	**MOB**	**INC**
40X	83.94	82.19	**84.31**	79.34	75.26	74.31
100X	**82.57**	80.49	82.15	76.39	76.39	74.31
200X	84.95	82.29	**85.88**	74.12	74.41	74.12
400X	82.27	76.52	**82.35**	73.20	70.04	72.55

5.4 Comparing the Best Hybrid RF Models of Each FE for Each MF and Over all the MFs

This subsection evaluates and compares the best hybrid RF models of the three FE for each MF and over all the MFs. Figure 4 shows the results of the SK test of the best hybrid RF models for each FE over each MF. It is observable that one cluster was obtained for MF 40X, 100X and 200X and two clusters for MF 400X.

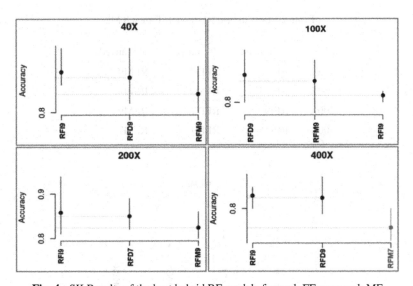

Fig. 4. SK Results of the best hybrid RF models for each FE over each MF

The hybrid RF models of the best SK cluster of each MF were ranked by using the Borda Count voting system based on accuracy, sensitivity, F1-score and precision. After using the Borda Count method it was found that:

- For MF 40X, the best hybrid RF model is constructed using Inception_V3 as FE with 9 trees. The second ranked hybrid RF model is constructed using DenseNet_201 as FE with 9 trees. The third one has 9 trees and was constructed with MobileNet_V2 as FE.

- For MF 100X, the best hybrid RF model is constructed using DenseNet_201 as FE with 9 trees. The second ranked hybrid RF model is constructed using MobileNet_V2 as FE with 9 trees. The third one has 9 trees and was constructed with Inception_V3 as FE.
- For MF 200X, the best hybrid RF model is constructed using Inception_V3 as FE with 9 trees. The second ranked hybrid RF model is constructed using DenseNet_201 as FE with 7 trees. The third one has 9 trees and was constructed with MobileNet_V2 as FE.
- For MF 400X, the best hybrid RF model is constructed using Inception_V3 as FE with 9 trees. The second ranked RF hybrid RF model is constructed using DenseNet_201 as FE with 9 trees. The third one has 7 trees and was constructed with MobileNet_V2 as FE.

Table 2 summarizes the three best hybrid RF models for each MF. It was found that the best ranked hybrid RF models always have 9 trees. For the feature extraction techniques: Inception_V3 was ranked first the most, DenseNet_201 was ranked second the most and MobileNet_V2 was ranked third the most.

Table 2. Best hybrid RF models for each MF

MF	1st ranked	2nd ranked	3rd ranked
40X	RFI9	RFD9	RFM9
100X	RFD9	RFM9	RFI9
200X	RFI9	RFD7	RFM9
400X	RFI9	RFD9	RFM7

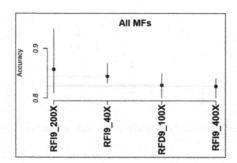

Fig. 5. SK Results of the best hybrid RF models of each MF

Figure 5 shows the results of SK test for the best hybrid RF models over the four MFs. Only one cluster was obtained that contains all the models, which means that the best hybrid RF models for each MF are statistically indifferent in terms of accuracy. In order to identify which hybrid RF model is the best over all the MFs, the hybrid RF models of the best SK cluster were ranked by using the Borda Count voting system based on accuracy, sensitivity, F1-score and precision. Table 3 presents the ranking results of the best hybrid RF models using the Borda count voting method based on accuracy, precision, recall, and F1-score. It was found that the best hybrid RF model over all the MFs uses MF 200X, the second-best model uses MF 40X, and the third-best model uses MF 100X.

Table 3. Best hybrid RF models over all the MFs

Model	MF	Accuracy (%)	Precision (%)	Sensitivity (%)	F1-score (%)	Rank
RFI9	200X	85.88	85.48	87.03	86.24	1
RFI9	40X	84.31	84.07	86.35	85.13	2
RFD9	100X	82.57	81.54	83.47	82.47	3
RFI9	400X	82.35	82.07	83.62	82.78	4

To sum up, the best hybrid architecture regardless of the MF is designed using the hybrid RF model with 9 trees as a classifier and Inception_V3 as FE, the second-best one is constructed using the hybrid RF model with 9 trees as a classifier and Inception_V3 as FE, the third best one is constructed using the hybrid RF model with 9 trees as a classifier and DenseNet_201 as FE. The fourth ranked one is designed using the hybrid RF model with 9 trees as classifier and Inception_V3 as FE.

6   Conclusion and Future Work

This paper presented and discussed the results of an empirical comparative study of forty-eight (48 = 4 MF × 3 DL techniques × 4 number of trees) hybrid RF models for BC histopathological image classification. This study used hybrid RF models for classification with different number of trees (3, 5, 7 and 9) and three DL techniques as FEs (DenseNet_201, Inception_V3 and MobileNet_V2). All the empirical evaluations used four performance criteria (accuracy, precision, recall and F1-score), SK statistical test, and Borda Count to assess and rank these models over the BreakHis dataset with its four MF (40X, 100X, 200X and 400X). The results showed that the hybrid RF models with the highest number of trees consistently perform well over all the MFs in terms of their accuracy, precision, recall and F1-score, and they also outperform the trees that construct them and the DT classifiers. As a result, this paper suggests that RF could be considered for the task of BC histological imaging classification with Inception_V3 as FE. Ongoing work focuses on implementing hybrid bagging ensembles using other classifiers as base learners to possibly improve the accuracy and comparing them with the hybrid RF models.

Acknowledgement. This work was conducted under the research project "Machine Learning based Breast Cancer Diagnosis and Treatment", 2020–2023. The authors would like to thank the Moroccan Ministry of Higher Education and Scientific Research, Digital Development Agency (ADD), CNRST, and UM6P for their support.

References

1. Breast Cancer Facts and Statistics. https://www.breastcancer.org/facts-statistics. Accessed 08 Apr 2022
2. Ginsburg, O., et al.: Breast cancer early detection: A phased approach to implementation. Cancer **126**, 2379–2393 (2020). https://doi.org/10.1002/cncr.32887
3. Yassin, N.I.R., Omran, S., El Houby, E.M.F., Allam, H.: Machine learning techniques for breast cancer computer aided diagnosis using different image modalities: a systematic review. Comput. Methods Programs Biomed. **156**, 25–45 (2018). https://doi.org/10.1016/j.cmpb.2017.12.012
4. Abdar, M., et al.: A new nested ensemble technique for automated diagnosis of breast cancer. Pattern Recogn. Lett. **132**, 123–131 (2020). https://doi.org/10.1016/j.patrec.2018.11.004
5. Hamed, G., Marey, M.A.E.-R., Amin, S.E.-S., Tolba, M.F.: Deep learning in breast cancer detection and classification. In: Hassanien, A.-E., Azar, A.T., Gaber, T., Oliva, D., Tolba, F.M. (eds.) AICV 2020. AISC, vol. 1153, pp. 322–333. Springer, Cham (2020). https://doi.org/10.1007/978-3-030-44289-7_30
6. Ho, T.K.: Multiple classifier combination: lessons and next steps. In: Bunke, H., Kandel, A. (eds.) Hybrid Methods in Pattern Recognition, pp. 171–198. WORLD SCIENTIFIC (2002). https://doi.org/10.1142/9789812778147_0007
7. Kuncheva, L.I.: Combining Pattern Classifiers, p. 382 (2014)
8. Polikar, R.: Ensemble learning. In: Zhang, C., Ma, Y. (eds.) Ensemble Machine Learning, pp. 1–34. Springer, Boston (2012). https://doi.org/10.1007/978-1-4419-9326-7_1
9. Sagi, O., Rokach, L.: Ensemble learning: a survey. WIREs Data Min. Knowl. Discov. **8**, e1249 (2018). https://doi.org/10.1002/widm.1249
10. Opitz, D., Maclin, R.: Popular ensemble methods: an empirical study. JAIR **11**, 169–198 (1999). https://doi.org/10.1613/jair.614
11. Oza, N.C., Tumer, K.: Classifier ensembles: select real-world applications. Inf. Fus. **9**, 4–20 (2008). https://doi.org/10.1016/j.inffus.2007.07.002
12. Kuncheva, L.I.: Measures of Diversity in Classifier Ensembles and Their Relationship with the Ensemble Accuracy, p. 27 (2003)
13. Brown, G., Kuncheva, L.I.: "Good" and "Bad" diversity in majority vote ensembles. In: El Gayar, N., Kittler, J., Roli, F. (eds.) MCS 2010. LNCS, vol. 5997, pp. 124–133. Springer, Heidelberg (2010). https://doi.org/10.1007/978-3-642-12127-2_13
14. El Ouassif, B., Idri, A., Hosni, M.: Investigating accuracy and diversity in heterogeneous ensembles for breast cancer classification. In: Gervasi, O., et al. (eds.) ICCSA 2021. LNCS, vol. 12950, pp. 263–281. Springer, Cham (2021). https://doi.org/10.1007/978-3-030-86960-1_19
15. Wang, G., Hao, J., Ma, J., Jiang, H.: A comparative assessment of ensemble learning for credit scoring. Expert Syst. Appl. **38**, 223–230 (2011). https://doi.org/10.1016/j.eswa.2010.06.048
16. LeCun, Y., Bengio, Y., Hinton, G.: Deep learning. Nature **521**, 436–444 (2015). https://doi.org/10.1038/nature14539
17. del Rio, F., Messina, P., Dominguez, V., Parra, D.: Do Better ImageNet Models Transfer Better... for Image Recommendation? arXiv:1807.09870 [cs] (2018)
18. Xu, G., Liu, M., Jiang, Z., Söffker, D., Shen, W.: Bearing fault diagnosis method based on deep convolutional neural network and random forest ensemble learning. Sensors **19**, 1088 (2019). https://doi.org/10.3390/s19051088
19. Breiman, L.: Bagging predictors. Mach Learn. **24**, 123–140 (1996). https://doi.org/10.1007/BF00058655
20. Zerouaoui, H., Idri, A.: Deep hybrid architectures for binary classification of medical breast cancer images. Biomed. Signal Process. Control **71**, 103226 (2022). https://doi.org/10.1016/j.bspc.2021.103226

21. Hosni, M., Abnane, I., Idri, A., Carrillo de Gea, J.M., Fernández Alemán, J.L.: Reviewing ensemble classification methods in breast cancer. Comput. Methods Prog. Biomed. **177**, 89–112 (2019). https://doi.org/10.1016/j.cmpb.2019.05.019
22. Guo, Y., Shi, H., Kumar, A., Grauman, K., Rosing, T., Feris, R.: SpotTune: Transfer Learning Through Adaptive Fine-Tuning, p. 10 (2018)
23. Pan, S.J., Yang, Q.: A survey on transfer learning. IEEE Trans. Knowl. Data Eng. **22**, 1345–1359 (2010). https://doi.org/10.1109/TKDE.2009.191
24. Alshalali, T., Josyula, D.: Fine-tuning of pre-trained deep learning models with extreme learning machine. In: 2018 International Conference on Computational Science and Computational Intelligence (CSCI), pp. 469–473. IEEE, Las Vegas, NV, USA (2018). https://doi.org/10.1109/CSCI46756.2018.00096
25. Ahmed, A., Yu, K., Xu, W., Gong, Y., Xing, E.: Training hierarchical feed-forward visual recognition models using transfer learning from pseudo-tasks. In: Forsyth, D., Torr, P., Zisserman, A. (eds.) ECCV 2008. LNCS, vol. 5304, pp. 69–82. Springer, Heidelberg (2008). https://doi.org/10.1007/978-3-540-88690-7_6
26. Morid, M.A., Borjali, A., Del Fiol, G.: A scoping review of transfer learning research on medical image analysis using ImageNet. Comput. Biol. Med. **128**, 104115 (2021). https://doi.org/10.1016/j.compbiomed.2020.104115
27. Wang, S.-H., Zhang, Y.-D.: DenseNet-201-based deep neural network with composite learning factor and precomputation for multiple sclerosis classification. ACM Trans. Multimedia Comput. Commun. Appl. **16**, 1–19 (2020). https://doi.org/10.1145/3341095
28. Sandler, M., Howard, A., Zhu, M., Zhmoginov, A., Chen, L.-C.: MobileNetV2: inverted residuals and linear bottlenecks. In: 2018 IEEE/CVF Conference on Computer Vision and Pattern Recognition, pp. 4510–4520. IEEE, Salt Lake City, UT (2018). https://doi.org/10.1109/CVPR.2018.00474
29. Inception V3 Deep Convolutional Architecture For Classifying Acute. https://www.intel.com/content/www/us/en/develop/articles/inception-v3-deep-convolutional-architecture-for-classifying-acute-myeloidlymphoblastic.html. Accessed 3 June 2021
30. Iqbal, M., Yan, Z.: Supervised machine learning approaches: a survey. Int. J. Soft Comput. **5**, 946–952 (2015). https://doi.org/10.21917/ijsc.2015.0133
31. Liang, G., Zhu, X., Zhang, C.: An Empirical Study of Bagging Predictors for Different Learning Algorithms, p. 2 (2011)
32. Bühlmann, P., Yu, B.: Analyzing bagging. Ann. Statist. **30** (2002). https://doi.org/10.1214/aos/1031689014
33. Adele Cutler, D., Cutler, R., Stevens, J.R.: Random forests. In: Zhang, C., Ma, Y. (eds.) Ensemble Machine Learning, pp. 157–175. Springer, Boston (2012). https://doi.org/10.1007/978-1-4419-9326-7_5
34. Oshiro, T.M., Perez, P.S., Baranauskas, J.A.: How many trees in a random forest? In: Perner, P. (ed.) MLDM 2012. LNCS (LNAI), vol. 7376, pp. 154–168. Springer, Heidelberg (2012). https://doi.org/10.1007/978-3-642-31537-4_13
35. Kassani, S.H., Kassani, P.H., Wesolowski, M.J., Schneider, K.A., Deters, R.: Classification of Histopathological Biopsy Images Using Ensemble of Deep Learning Networks. arXiv:1909.11870 [cs, eess] (2019)
36. Saxena, S., Shukla, S., Gyanchandani, M.: Pre-trained convolutional neural networks as feature extractors for diagnosis of breast cancer using histopathology. Int. J. Imaging Syst. Technol. **30**, 577–591 (2020). https://doi.org/10.1002/ima.22399
37. Zerouaoui, H., Idri, A., Nakach, F.Z., Hadri, R.E.: Breast fine needle cytological classification using deep hybrid architectures. In: Gervasi, O., et al. (eds.) ICCSA 2021. LNCS, vol. 12950, pp. 186–202. Springer, Cham (2021). https://doi.org/10.1007/978-3-030-86960-1_14
38. Nikhil, B.: Image Data Pre-Processing for Neural Networks. https://becominghuman.ai/image-data-pre-processing-for-neural-networks-498289068258. Accessed 12 May 2021

39. Yussof, W.: Performing Contrast Limited Adaptive Histogram Equalization Technique on Combined Color Models for Underwater Image Enhancement (2013)
40. Shorten, C., Khoshgoftaar, T.M.: A survey on image data augmentation for deep learning. J. Big Data **6**(1), 1–48 (2019). https://doi.org/10.1186/s40537-019-0197-0
41. ScottKnott: a package for performing the Scott-Knott clustering algorithm in R. https://www.scielo.br/scielo.php?script=sci_arttext&pid=S2179-84512014000100002. Accessed 20 May 2021
42. Borda Count | Mathematics for the Liberal Arts. https://courses.lumenlearning.com/waymakermath4libarts/chapter/borda-count/. Accessed 21 May 2021
43. Hastie, T., Tibshirani, R., Friedman, J.: Ensemble learning. In: Hastie, T., Tibshirani, R., Friedman, J. (eds.) The Elements of Statistical Learning. SSS, pp. 605–624. Springer, New York (2009). https://doi.org/10.1007/978-0-387-84858-7_16

Visualization and Processing of Structural Monitoring Data Using Space-Time Cubes

Luigi Barazzetti[1]📧, Mattia Previtali[1(📧)]📧, and Fabio Roncoroni[2]

[1] Department of Architecture, Built Environment and Construction Engineering, Politecnico di Milano, Piazza Leonardo da Vinci 32, Milan, Italy
{luigi.barazzetti,mattia.previtali}@polimi.it
[2] Polo territoriale di Lecco, via Previati 1/c, Lecco, Italy
fabio.roncoroni@polimi.it

Abstract. This paper aims to analyze space-time cubes for visualizing and processing multi-temporal spatial monitoring data. The proposed case study is the Cathedral of Milan (Duomo di Milano), which has a set of monitoring time series spanning more than half a century. Differential vertical movements are periodically measured for the cathedral columns, constituting a continuous spatio-temporal dataset for structural health monitoring. More specifically, the space time pattern mining toolbox in ArcGIS Pro was used to (i) create a space-time cube and (ii) perform advanced analysis using the monitoring dataset, including time-series clustering and forecasting operations.

Keywords: GIS · Monitoring · Space time cube · Time series

1 Introduction

Visualization and processing of multiple time-series associated with different georeferenced entities is a complex task requiring spatio-temporal algorithms and representation techniques. The dataset considered in this paper is a time-series collection of relative elevation values $Z_{t,i}$ measured by high precision geometric leveling. The considered points are monitoring benchmarks mounted on 59 pillars (index $i = 1, ..., 59$) of the Cathedral of Milan (Duomo di Milano), the Gothic masterpiece symbol of the city [1,2]. The spatial location (X_i, Y_i) of the columns is known and constant over time. In contrast, the elevation value $Z_{t,i}$ is the monitored parameter and represents the movement caused by subsidence.

Structural monitoring in the Cathedral of Milan using high precision geometric leveling started during the '60s, when the extraction of water from the ground in the city produced a rapid drop of the water table, resulting in differential vertical movements of the pillars and structural instability [3,4].

This paper does not describe other monitoring systems installed in the Cathedral, including both static and dynamic methods. The reader is referred to [5–7]

O. Gervasi et al. (Eds.): ICCSA 2022, LNCS 13376, pp. 19–31, 2022.
https://doi.org/10.1007/978-3-031-10450-3_2

for some examples. This paper aims to use space-time cubes to visualize and process time-series of vertical differential measurements, which are periodically calculated from elevation values derived by geometric leveling operations (Fig. 1). Least squares adjustment is used to obtain elevations with a precision of about ±0.1 mm, which is sufficient to track the movements over time.

Fig. 1. View of the pillars along the nave, the picture was acquired close to the central entrance of the cathedral.

Analysis and interpretation of monitoring time-series require efficient methods to provide facilitated access and visualization and support for data analytics, mainly when multiple spatio-temporal sequences are simultaneously used. Indeed, plotting in a single graph the data acquired for the different 59 locations (i.e., the columns of the Cathedral) provides a confusing representation and loses the spatial relationship between the columns.

The displacement of a column must be analyzed using an approach that considers the spatial position and the relationships with other columns. The monument comprises several interconnected structural elements (foundations, pillars, arches, vaults, tie-rods, etc.) with mutual interaction. The opportunity to simultaneously visualize monitoring data considering both spatial and temporal aspects is attractive and opens new possibilities to understand better structural behavior.

The idea is to use methods able to combine time series available as triplets $(X_i, Y_i, Z_{t,i})$ acquired overtime using an advanced representation with fixed spatial locations. In contrast, the third dimension corresponds to the variable's values at different times, which are adjusted elevation and their variations.

As mentioned, the problem faced in this paper is to exploit a space-time cube (STC) featuring both spatial and temporal structures. Space-time cubes became more popular in the last decade and emerged in connection with Big Data analysis and applications like weblogs, sensor networks, and cloud computing. In particular, the concept of space-time cube (also named hyper-cubes) was introduced in Business Intelligence to implement Data Dashboard and Data Warehouse concepts. The term "cube" is used in Business Intelligence to address a multidimensional data set. In database engineering and computer science, an OLAP (Online Analytical Processing) cube refers to a multidimensional array of data [8] that can be processed online [9]. In addition, Data-Cube structures gained significant attention recently for satellite imagery management and spatial data analytic domain. Examples of application domain for space-time cube are, among other, analysis of spatio-temporal pattern for COVID-19 spread [10], distribution of extreme weather events [11], modelling crime patterns in urban areas [12], road traffic and crash analysis [13]. A review of temporal data visualization based on space-time cubes (including different operations such as extracting sub-parts, flattening across space or time, and transforming the cube's geometry) is described in [14,15].

The work described in this paper was carried out with ArcGIS Pro v.2.9, which allows the creation and analysis of space-time cubes. The cube has rows, columns, and time steps, which correspond to X, Y, and Z coordinates, as shown in Fig. 2.

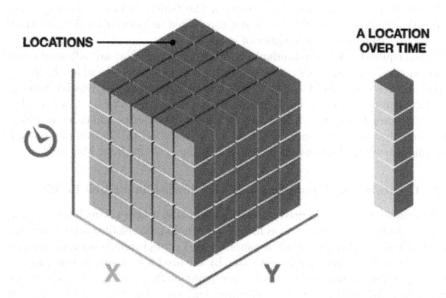

Fig. 2. Structure of the space-time cube, figure retrieved form https://pro.arcgis.com/.

The cube is saved using the Network Common Data Format (NetCDF), which is "a set of software libraries and self-describing, machine-independent data formats that support the creation, access, and sharing of array-oriented scientific data. The climate and forecast (CF) metadata conventions are designed to promote the processing and sharing of netCDF files", as described in www.ogc.org/standards/netcdf.

2   Creation of the Space-Time Cube

2.1   Data Description

The dataset used in this paper is a geometric leveling time-series collection acquired in the Cathedral of Milan. The installation of a geometric leveling monitoring network began in 1961 to track differential vertical movements induced by subsidence caused by water extraction from the ground.

The actual configuration of the leveling network still preserves continuity with original measurements. Benchmarks are installed on 59 pillars along the nave, the transept, and the apse. The frequency of data acquisition is based on two measurement campaigns in a year, in May and November. Readings are carried out with a high-precision level, and network geometry follows a rigid scheme with multiple closed loops with self-intersections. After completing a closed circuit, the misclosure (which should be theoretically zero) is compared to the tolerance c, which is estimated as $c = \pm 0.1\sqrt{n}$ mm, where n is the number of benchmarks in a closed loop. As the distance between the benchmarks is relatively short and rather constant, the distance is not considered in calculating the tolerance, which only depends on the number of points.

The acquired data (a redundant set of height differences) are adjusted using least squares, obtaining elevation values and their precision, which is in the order of ± 0.1 mm. The data set in this paper is based on the relative vertical displacements measured between May 1970 and November 2020, i.e., a period of about 50 years. Data are also available for a more extended period (back to 1965). However, the configuration used today is still based on the 1969 configuration. For this reason, the dataset presented in this paper starts from May 1970.

2.2   Creation and Visualization of the Space-Time Cube in 3D

Monitoring data are structured into tables reporting variations in elevation computed considering column n. 39 as fixed. The benchmark installed on this column is the historical reference for all measurements (i.e., its height is assumed as constant over time). This choice is motivated by the need for the monitoring project. It is impossible to find a stable reference point in the area because subsidence affects the cathedral and the surrounding buildings. For this reason, pillar 39 was chosen as a reference to capture differential vertical movements, i.e., those movements that could impact the stability of the cathedral.

The spatial location of the columns is known and stored in a point feature layer, allowing the creation of a spatio-temporal dataset. The reference system for planar coordinates is UTM-WGS84 32N, thus data are available as $East = X$ and $North = Y$ using metric units in meters. Vertical movements are instead reported in millimeters and can be estimated as $\Delta z_{t,i} = H_{t,i} - H_{1970,i}$, where H_i is the adjusted elevation using least squares, and index i refers to the pillar number. After importing the data in ArcGIS Pro, the reference system was changed to WGS1984 Web Mercator (Auxiliary Sphere).

The creation of the space-time cube was carried out using version 2.9. As mentioned, the point feature layer was used to define the spatial location of pillars with benchmarks. An one-to-many relationship was created to relate the point feature to a table with the measured variations $\Delta z_{t,i}$ and the corresponding date. The chosen time-step interval is six months and covers May 1970–November 2020.

The STC was generated without aggregation so that the different elements include the adjusted coordinates (Fig. 3). Color variation (from white to purple) along Z depends on the magnitude of differential movements. The interface provides facilitated access to specific data. For instance, selecting an element of the STC provides information about the pillar number and the measured variation at a particular time.

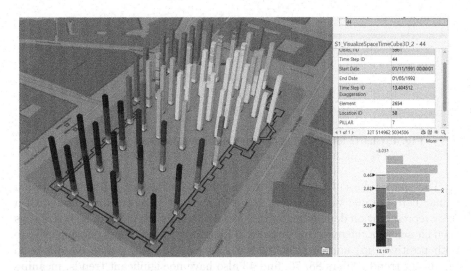

Fig. 3. The space-time cube encapsulating monitoring measurements. (Color figure online)

The space-time cube also has an associated attribute table, which can be used for queries. For instance, the user can visualize (in 3D) those time steps for all pillars with relative movements larger than a specif threshold or limit the query to just a subset of columns. Such options are useful when used together with other layers, which can be exploited to classify the pillars with additional information. For instance, columns can be grouped depending on their specific location inside the cathedral (i.e., nave, transept, apse, ...).

The time series collection can also be visualized using graphs. Figure 4 shows a chart created using data from pillars 74-75-84-85, i.e., the pillars of the tiburium, under the main spire (Guglia Maggiore) of the Duomo. Charts are not static representations, but they can be interactively inspected in ArcGIS Pro, and eventually exported. Query definition also applies to charts.

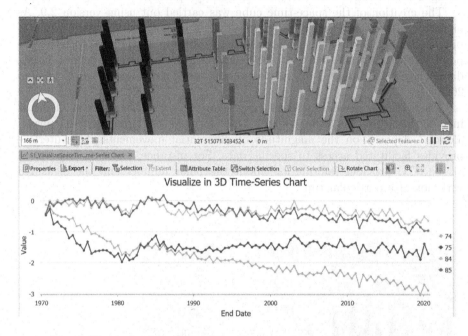

Fig. 4. Charts for the pillars of the tiburium generated using the STC.

The space-time cube can also be visualized in 2D, i.e., with a traditional planar cartographic visualization. Figure 5 shows the space-time cube with a color representation depending on the detected trends. As pillar n. 39 has always been chosen as a reference to compute differential displacements, movements are both positive (up) and negative (down). As can be seen, points 39 shows no significant trend. Pillars 88, 75, and 43 also have no significant trends, meaning that their movements tend to become constant over time. Instead, pillars of the apse and the nave have a positive trend, notwithstanding the magnitude cannot be quantified using such representation. Finally, a significant part of the transept shows a negative trend, indicating that the movements are the opposite if compared to the nave and facade. Additional results can be obtained using the created space-time cube. The next sections will illustrate some other operations that can be carried out to understand the differential movements better.

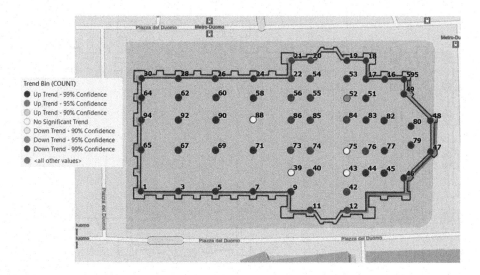

Fig. 5. Visualization of the trend related to different vertical movements (up or down) using pillar 39 as a fixed reference.

3   Time Series Clustering

Time-series clustering is the task of creating time-series groups depending on similarity parameters. Different options are available in ArcGIS Pro and Fig. 6 shows the results using two different methods: clustering based on the $\Delta z_{t,i}$ values and clustering based on correlation. The method based on the values compares $\Delta z_{t,i}$ magnitude, whereas clustering based on correlation determines if the time-series are correlated across time. Processing was done selecting 4 classes.

The two results can be interpreted as follows. In the case of clustering based on the value, a cluster is created for the pillars in the southern part of the transept (green). This area is historically the one characterized by maximum lowering. A second cluster (light green) is created around this area, which is surrounded by the pillars clustered in yellow mainly located on the apse, the northern part of the transept, and half of the nave. The last cluster (dark green) is mainly concentrated in the second half of the nave towards the facade.

Such a result can be compared with a visualization based on the interpolated surface of differential movements in the period 1970–2020 (Fig. 7). An interpolation based on rational basis splines was carried out to obtain a continuous representation from punctual data. Then, the grid model was represented with a similar color map used for the classification. The number of classes chosen is higher to better perceive the variations, so that colours of Figs. 6 and 7 do not match. However, they depict a similar trend in the value, indicating that the area with maximum negative displacement is the transept, whereas the largest positive values are in the area of the facade, especially in the North-West corner.

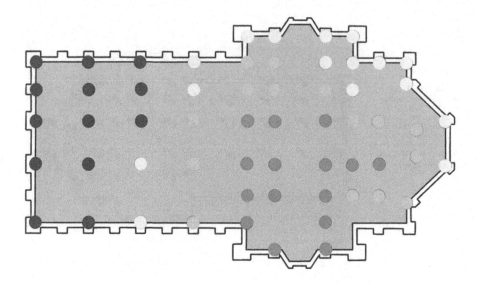

Fig. 6. Clustering based on $\Delta z_{t,i}$ values. (Color figure online)

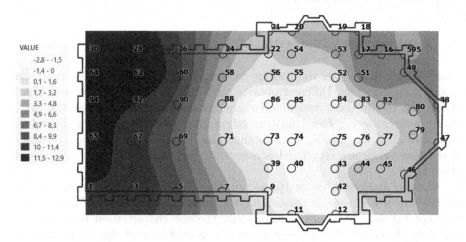

Fig. 7. Interpolated displacement map generated using rational basis functions. (Color figure online)

Figure 8 shows clustering results based on the correlation. The number of chosen classes is still 4. In this case, the achieved result shows groups of columns tending to increase (or decrease) in a similar way.

Column 39 forms a class because it is the only column with constant zero value. A second class (orange) is composed of columns mainly located in the southern part of the transept, including the 4 main columns of the tiburium that are located in the middle of the transept. The third class (rose) is made up of columns mainly located around those pillars in the second class. The last class (red) includes columns of the nave and the apse.

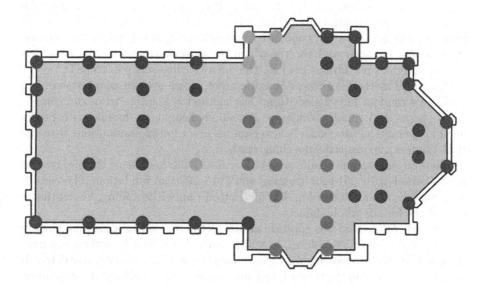

Fig. 8. Clustering results based on correlation. (Color figure online)

4   Time Series Forecast

Forecasting future values is one of the methods to find discontinuities in time series. A basic detection method could be based on forecasting the value at $t+1$ given the previously measured values at time $1, ..., t$. If the measured value at epoch $t+1$ is significantly larger than the forecast value (considering the precision of measurements, which is ± 0.1 mm in this case, and the forecast quality), the considered column could deserve more attention. In this way, a threshold could be set to identify anomalous variations.

Different options are available to perform time series forecasting using the space-time cube created in Arcgis Pro. The first option is based on curve fitting methods, which are used to interpolate the data using a specific function and then estimate future values. ArcGIS Pro offers different models: linear, parabolic, exponential, and S-shaped (using a Gompertz curve). All estimation methods can also be simultaneously run on the STC. An automatic selection of the best result is carried out using the validation root mean square error (RMSE), which is calculated on selected final time steps previously excluded during the fitting phase. The computed model is then evaluated at those time steps. The RMSE is equal to the square root of the average squared difference between the forecasted and original values of the excluded time step.

However, such methods were not used in this work because most of the time series do not follow those models, as it can be verified with a simple plotting and visual check of the time series.

The second method available in ArcGIS Pro is based on forecasting using the Holt-Winters exponential smoothing method. This algorithm decomposes the time series at each location cube into seasonal and trend components, assuming the seasonal behavior and the trend can be separated. Also in this case, this assumption does not always hold for the different time-series in the STC.

The third method is a forest-based forecast, which uses an adaptation of Leo Breiman's random forest algorithm. The method is suitable to model complicated shapes and trends, which are instead challenging to handle with predefined mathematical functions. It also requires fewer initial assumptions than the Holt-Winters exponential smoothing method.

Figure 9 shows some results achieved with such method, using the observation in the period 1970–2014 for training and 2015–2020 as validation. The considered columns are n. 40 (top) and n. 55 (bottom) notwithstanding, forecasting is carried out for the whole dataset.

No outlier detection was applied because all the time series come from already adjusted data (elevation values), in which methods to identify outliers are integrated. The used forecasting algorithm builds the model by values after detrending, i.e., values within the time window are linearly detrended, and the dependent variable is represented by its detrended value.

The statistics on the training dataset provided an average RMS of 0.05 mm and a standard deviation of ±0.01 mm. The RMS on the validation dataset gave an average of 0.27 mm and a standard deviation of ±0.015 mm. This last value is not significantly different from the evaluation precision achieved after Least Squares adjustment.

The forecasted value considers two additional time steps, i.e., the measurements for May and November 2021. Therefore, forecasting was carried out for the year 2021.

Statistics are also available for individual time series. In the case of column n. 40, the validation RMS is ±0.09 mm, whereas column n. 55 shows a larger validation RMS of ±0.21 mm. The method is also able to estimate a level of confidence for the forecasted value, which is illustrated at 90% in Fig. 9. As can be seen, the confidence level is different for the two time-series here proposed because the second one has a more irregular behavior.

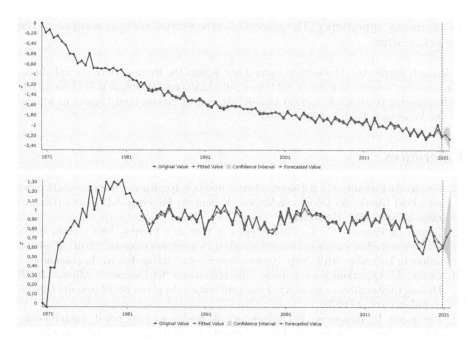

Fig. 9. Results after time-series forecasting for columns n. 40 (top) and n. 55 (bottom).

5   Conclusions

Efficient storage and visualization are essential in structural monitoring applications. The proposed work started from an important consideration: the monitoring system of vertical movements of the Cathedral of Milan is particularly
suitable for a GIS-based representation. Displacements of vertical movements
are measured using a set of benchmarks installed on the columns; therefore,
a space-time cube is an attractive opportunity to combine X, Y cartographic
coordinates and vertical variations measured over time.

After creating the STC, additional processing using all the time series was
carried out. Clustering algorithms allowed the creation of groups of columns with
similar movements, using both the values of the measured displacements and the
correlation between time series. Forecasting is helpful to predict future values
and verify if newly measured displacements are similar to forecasted values, i.e.,
establishing an alternative method to detect anomalous values. Therefore, such
a method is considered an integration of the traditional work carried out in the
Duomo.

Future work will consider the use of interpolated data in other specific locations. Interpolated maps of displacements (such as the one in Fig. 7) provide
information about the whole Cathedral. As the STC also supports multidimensional raster datasets, creating a STC not limited to the measured values seems

an interesting opportunity. The aim will be the extension of the analysis to the whole Cathedral.

Acknowledgments. The work is carried our within the framework of the collaboration between Veneranda Fabrica del Duomo di Milano and Politecnico di Milano. The authours want to thank Francesco Canali, director of Cantieri del Duomo di Milano for the Veneranda Fabbrica del Duomo.

References

1. Ferrari da Passano, C.: Il Duomo rinato: Storia e tecnica del restauro statico dei piloni del tiburio del Duomo di Milano. Veneranda Fabbrica del Duomo (Diakronia), Milan (1988). (in Italian)
2. Ferrari da Passano, C.: La Gran Guglia, il Duomo e l'acqua. Una piccola storia sulle vicissitudini e i misteri lungo i secoli ed i loro strani rapporti (2019). Puslihed online in Dicember 2019. http://www.risorsa-acqua.it/tag/ferrari-da-passano/
3. Croce, A.: Questioni geotecniche sulle fondazioni del Duomo di Milano. In: Il Duomo rinato: Storia e tecnica del restauro statico dei piloni del tiburio del Duomo di Milano, vol. 2 (1970)
4. Barazzetti, L., Roncoroni, F.: Relazione sulle misure eseguite per il controllo delle deformazioni del Duomo di Milano. Semestral report for the Veneranda Fabrica del Duomo di Milano, 39 p. (2020)
5. Alba, M., Roncoroni, F., Barazzetti, L., Giussani, A., Scaioni, M.: Monitoring of the main spire of the Duomo di Milano. In: Joint International Symposium on Deformation Monitoring, Hong Kong, China, 2–4 November 2011, 6 p. (2011)
6. Cigada, A., Dell'Acqua, L., Castiglione, B., Scaccabarozzi, M., Vanali, M., Zappa, E.: Structural health monitoring of an historical building: the main spire of the Duomo Di Milano. Int. J. Archit. Herit. **11**(4), 501–518 (2016)
7. Barazzetti, L., Canali, F., Della Torre, S., Previtali, M., Roncoroni, F.: Monitoring the Cathedral of Milan: An Archive with More Than 50 Years of Measurements. Lecture Notes in Computer Sciences, 16 p. (2021). in press
8. Gray, J., Bosworth, A., Layman, A., Pirahesh, H.: Data cube: a relational aggregation operator generalizing group-by, cross-tab, and sub-totals. In: Proceedings of the International Conference on Data Engineering (ICDE), pp. 152–159 (1996)
9. Dubler, C., Wilcox, C.: Just what are cubes anyway? A painless introduction to OLAP technology (2002). https://docs.microsoft.com/. Accessed Feb 2022
10. Mo, C., et al.: An analysis of spatiotemporal pattern for COIVD-19 in China based on space-time cube. J. Med. Virol. **92**(9), 1587–1595 (2020)
11. Allen, M.J., Allen, T.R., Davis, C., McLeod, G.: Exploring spatial patterns of Virginia Tornadoes using kernel density and space-time cube analysis (1960–2019). ISPRS Int. J. Geo Inf. **10**(5), 310 (2021)
12. Hashim, H., Wan Mohd, W.M.N., Sadek, E.S.S.M., Dimyati, K.M.: Modeling urban crime patterns using spatial space time and regression analysis. In: International Archives of the Photogrammetry, Remote Sensing Spatial Information Sciences (2019)
13. Wu, P., Meng, X., Song, L.: Identification and spatiotemporal evolution analysis of high-risk crash spots in urban roads at the microzone-level: using the space-time cube method. J. Transp. Saf. Secur. 1–21 (2021). https://doi.org/10.1080/19439962.2021.1938323

14. Bach, B., Dragicevic, P., Archambault, D., Hurter, C., Carpendale, S.: A descriptive framework for temporal data visualizations based on generalized space-time cubes. In: Computer Graphics Forum, vol. 36, no. 6, pp. 36–61 (2017)
15. Bach, B., Dragicevic, P., Archambault, D., Hurter, C., Carpendale, S.: A review of temporal data visualizations based on space-time cube operations. In: Eurographics Conference on Visualization (EuroVis 2014), pp. 23–41 (2014)

Modeling the Management and Efficiency of the Speculative Capital Market

George Abuselidze[1]([✉]) [ID], Olena Kireitseva[2] [ID], Oksana Sydorenko[3] [ID],
Viktor Gryschko[4] [ID], and Mariia Hunchenko[4] [ID]

[1] Batumi Shota Rustaveli State University, Ninoshvili, 35, 6010 Batumi, Georgia
george.abuselidze@bsu.edu.ge
[2] National University of Life and Environmental Sciences of Ukraine, Heroiv Oborony, 11,
Kiev 03041, Ukraine
[3] National University of Kyiv-Mohyla Academy, Skovorody, 2, Kyiv 04070, Ukraine
[4] National University «Yuri Kondratyuk Poltava Polytechnic», Pershotravnevyi Avenue, 24,
Poltava 36011, Ukraine

Abstract. The paper proves that as a result of the experience accumulation in using rigidly deterministic models, real opportunities have been created for the successful application of a more advanced methodology promoting modeling economic processes to consider stochastic and uncertainty: carrying out multivariate calculations and model experiments with a variation of the model design and its initial data; studying stability and reliability of the obtained solutions, identifying the zone of uncertainty, including reserves in the model: the use of techniques increasing the adaptability of the economic decisions in probable and unforeseen situations. The study outlines the general classification of economic and mathematical models including more than ten main features with the development of economic and mathematical research. The process of integration of different types models into more complex model constructions is carried out. It has also been proven that the formulated mathematical problem of the economic analysis can be solved by one of the most developed mathematical methods. It is emphasized that economic cybernetics makes it possible to analyze economic phenomena and processes as very complex systems from the point of view of the laws and mechanisms of control and the movement of information in them. It has been proven that many economic processes are studied by using econometric models, including ARMA models (mixed process of auto regression and moving average), GARCH (regressive models with conditional heteroscedastic errors), ECM (deviation correction models) and VAR (vector auto regression models). Accordingly, one of the important achievements is the ability to illustrate, using the constructed model, medium-term periodic fluctuations in technological changes and resource utilization due to external shocks associated with the development of technologies.

Keywords: Capital market · Speculative operations · Securities · Investment instruments · Speculator

O. Gervasi et al. (Eds.): ICCSA 2022, LNCS 13376, pp. 32–44, 2022.
https://doi.org/10.1007/978-3-031-10450-3_3

1 Introduction

Ensuring the stable development of the national market of speculative capital SOE is a prerequisite for the successful development of the real sector of the economy, since it provides the economy with a certain mobility, contributing to the overflow of financial resources from one industry to another and the technological modernization of the domestic economy. Currently, the capital coming from the export of agricultural and metallurgical products is not enough to reinvest in the modernization of the national economy. The development of high-tech and infrastructure industries in SOE, taking into account global demand trends, will allow the rapid accumulation of the capital within the country, and then it will be possible to invest in further transformation of the national economy.

The acceleration of the integration of the domestic economy into the world of economy increases the likelihood of external threats to the financial security of the country, because at the beginning of the economic crisis, capital outflows from regional financial markets abroad leading to the devaluation of the national currency, intensification of inflationary processes and the destabilization of the economic system [1, 2]. Taking this into account, research and disclosure of the economic essence, trends and contradictions in the development of the national market of speculative capital, the features of the mechanisms of its systemic regulation in the context of achieving the financial security of the country becomes relevant in the context of financial globalization. In addition, it is important to develop a modern financial theory of the systemic regulation of the capital market with the actualization of financial and competition policies.

The purpose of the article is to study the theoretical and methodological foundations of management and efficiency of the speculative capital market.

The theoretical foundations and practice of the securities market functioning, as well as the mechanisms for transforming the savings of business entities into investments through the securities market occupy a rather important place in the scientific research of foreign scientists: Pazarbasioglu & Ötker; C. A. Rodriguez; W. F. Bello et al.; Kletzer & Spiegel; A. Slobodianyk et al., and among others [3–7]. Modern features of the development of the securities market are considered in the works of the following scientists G. Abuselidze; J. Hull; I. Blank; J. Davis; T. Norfield; K. Singh; A. Steiner et al.; Xiao & Aydemir; J. D. Curto et al.; Zhang & Yue; Miao & LU; K. H. Liow; among others [8–20]. The research of both foreign and domestic scientists, are devoted to the problems of the stock market functioning and the study of the speculative movement of the investment capital E. Lesmana et al.; T. Choudhry et al.; Arnade & Hoffman; Floros & Vougas; W.F. Bello et al.; Slobodianyk & Abuselidze; Jylhä & Suominen; J. Rasmus; K. Peterson; D. Leblang [21–34]. Paying tribute to the scientific achievements of domestic and foreign scientists in the study of the development and functioning of the speculative capital market, it should be noted that the methodological foundations of the management and efficiency of the speculative capital market remain controversial and require further research.

2 Methodological Foundations

The theoretical and methodological basis are the principles of scientific knowledge, scientific achievements, reflected in the publications of domestic and foreign scientists in the field of economics, assessment and analysis of the management of the securities market, as well as forecasting heterogeneous financial time series.

The work applies the methods of logical, statistical, comparative analysis. In addition to general theoretical research methods, in the work, in order to build economic and mathematical models, methods for assessing forecast calculations, scenario modeling, factorial and graphical analysis were applied.

Classification of models for studying the economic processes and substantive problems, the models of the national economy as a whole and its individual subsystems and industries, regions, complexes of models of production, consumption, formation and distribution of income, labor resources, pricing, financial ties are distinguished.

In studies, at the national level, structural or structural-functional models are more often applied, since the interconnections of subsystems are of great importance for planning and management. Functional models are widely applied in economic regulation.

We can distinguish descriptive and normative models. Descriptive models explain observed facts or provide a probabilistic forecast. Normative models answer to the question: how should it be? An example of a normative model is the model of optimal planning, formalizing in one way or another the goals of economic development, opportunities and means of achieving them.

The descriptive approach is used to establish statistical patterns of economic processes, to study the possible development ways of any processes that do not change under conditions or proceed without external influences. Examples of descriptive models are production functions and customer demand functions based on the processing of statistical data. By the nature of the reflection of cause-and-effect relationships, there are rigidly determined models and models that take into account randomness and uncertainty. As a result of the accumulation of experience in using rigidly deterministic models, real opportunities have been created for the successful application of a more advanced methodology for modeling economic processes that take into account stochastics and uncertainty: carrying out multivariate calculations and model experiments with a variation of the model design and its initial data; studying the stability and reliability of the solutions obtained, identifying the zone of uncertainty, including reserves in the model: the use of techniques that increase the adaptability of economic decisions to probable and unforeseen situations. Models are spreading, they directly reflect the stochastics and uncertainty of economic processes and apply the appropriate mathematical apparatus: probability theory and mathematical statistics, game theory and statistical decisions, queuing theory, theory of random processes.

According to the ways of reflecting the time factor, economic and mathematical models are divided into: statistical and dynamic. In statistical models, all dependencies refer to one point in time. Dynamic models characterize the change in economic processes over time.

3   Results and Discussion

The general classification of economic and mathematical models includes more than ten main features. With the development of economic and mathematical research, the problem of classifying the applied models becomes more complicated. Along with the emergence of new types of models (especially mixed types) and new signs of their classification, the process of integrating models of different types into more complex model constructions is under way.

Economic and mathematical methods are applied in the field of mathematics, mathematical statistics and mathematical logic. The computer solution of economic and mathematical problems is implemented by using computational mathematics and the theory of algorithms.

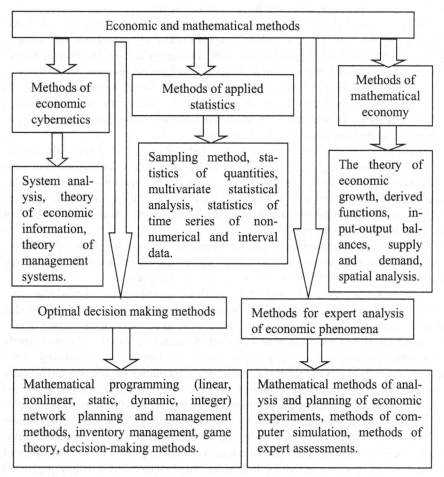

Fig. 1. Economic and mathematical methods in the study of management processes and the efficiency of the speculative capital market. Source: researched by the author based on summarizing research

Mathematical methods applied in the analysis can be systematized according to various criteria. The most appropriate is the classification of economic and mathematical methods by the content of the methods, that is, by belonging to a certain section of modern mathematics. Figure 1 shows the classification of economic-mathematical methods in accordance with the most frequently used sections of modern mathematics.

The formulated mathematical problem of economic analysis can be solved by one of the most developed mathematical methods. Therefore, the classification is largely arbitrary. For example, the problem of inventory management can be solved by mathematical programming methods and using queuing theory. A wide variety of methods can be applied in network planning and management. Operations research is sometimes defined so broadly that it encompasses all economic and mathematical methods.

The methods of elementary mathematics are applied in conventional traditional economic calculations when justifying resource requirements, accounting for production costs, justifying plans, projects, and balance sheet calculations.

The selection of classical methods of mathematical analysis in Fig. 1 is due to the fact that they are used not only within the framework of other methods, for example, methods of mathematical statistics and mathematical programming, but also separately. Thus, factor analysis of changes in many economic indicators can be carried out by using differentiation and other methods developed on the basis of differentiation.

Methods of mathematical statistics and probability theory are widely applied in economic analysis. These methods are applied in cases where the change in the analyzed indicators can be represented as a random process.

Statistical methods as the main means of studying massive, repetitive phenomena play an important role in predicting the behavior of economic indicators. When the relationship between the considered characteristics is not deterministic, but stochastic, then statistical and probabilistic methods are practically the only research tool. The most widely used mathematical and statistical methods in economic analysis are methods of multiple and pair correlation analysis.

To study one-dimensional statistical populations, a variational series, distribution laws, and a sampling method are applied. To study multivariate statistical populations, correlations, regression, variance and factor analysis are applied.

Econometric methods are based on the synthesis of three areas of knowledge: economics, mathematics and statistics. The basis of econometrics is an economic model, which is understood as a schematic representation of an economic phenomenon or process using scientific abstraction, reflecting their characteristic features. The most widely used method of analysis is "input-output". These are matrix (balance) models, built according to a checkerboard scheme and allowing representing the relationship between costs and production results in the most compact form. Convenience of calculations and clarity of economic interpretation are the main features of matrix models. This is important when creating systems for computer data processing. Mathematical programming is an important branch of modern applied mathematics. Methods of mathematical (primarily linear) programming are the main means of solving problems of optimization of production and economic activities. In essence, these methods are a means of planned calculations. Their value for the economic analysis of the fulfillment of the plans is that they allow to assess the intensity of planned targets, determine the limit of equipment groups, types of raw materials, and obtain estimates of the scarcity of the produced resources.

Heuristic methods (solution) are non-formalized methods for solving analytical problems associated with a survey and expert assessments of specialists, express their opinion on the basis of intuition, experience, with mathematical processing of various opinions to find the correct solution.

It is obvious that all existing models can be conditionally divided into two classes - material models, that is, objectively existing ones, and abstract models, existing in human consciousness. One of the subclasses of abstract models are mathematical models.

The application of mathematical methods significantly expands the possibilities of economic analysis, making it possible to formulate new statements of economic problems, and improving the quality of management decisions.

Mathematical models of the economy, reflecting with the help of mathematical relationships the basic properties of economic processes and phenomena, are an effective tool for studying complex economic problems. In modern scientific and technical activities, mathematical models are the most important form of modeling, and in economic research and the practice of planning and management, they are the dominant form.

Capital market participants apply to supply and demand information while making the decision on buying and selling. Ordinary people buy more goods for lower prices and less when prices rise. In the financial market, players are not inferior to them in practicality. Each price is an instant agreement on value that is reached by all market participants, each price reflects the actions or lack thereof - of all market participants. Thus, the chart can provide a look at the psychological state of the capital market participants. Chart analysis - analysis of the behavior of market participants.

Chart analysts study the behavior of the market, trying to identify the current price patterns. According to the axiom about "repeating history in the market", their goal is to find a winning option when repeating these models. It can take a trader from several months to several years of practical and theoretical work to study the "qualitative" identification of patterns on charts.

Assuming that history repeats in the market, therefore, it is necessary to develop a system capable of "remembering" past market situations and their corresponding consequences (that is, their continuation) in order to further compare with difficult situations in the market. The simplest solution to this problem would be a database in which you can record market situations encoded in a certain way. To make a forecast, it will be necessary to view all the records, which must be a huge number to achieve the forecast of the required accuracy. This idea is not constructive due to the complexity of data access, complexity of the criteria for comparing information.

The ability to "memorize" is inherent in systems implementing neural network principles of data processing. It is known that the forecast of a system based on artificial neural networks (ANN) can be trained in sufficiently large amounts of information, in which the system can detect dependencies, it cannot be detected when using other information processing methods.

The ANN idea has been developing for about half a century. Today, a large theoretical base has been accumulated in this area. In practice, predict systems based on neural network technologies are being introduced at an increasing pace (mainly in the USA).

The human brain neuron network is a highly efficient complex system with parallel information processing. It is able to organize (tune) neurons in such a way as to realize the perception of an image, its recognition many times faster than these tasks will be solved by the most modern computers. So, recognition of a familiar face takes place in the human brain in 100–120 ms, while a computer takes minutes or even hours for this.

Today, as it was 40 years ago, there is no doubt that the human brain works in a fundamentally different and more efficient way than any computer created by man. It is the fact stimulating and guiding the work of scientists on the creation and research of artificial neural networks for a number of years. The first experiments to reveal the secrets of the anatomical organization of the brain can be attributed to the research of Santiago Ramon y Cajal (1911) [35]. Using the method of staining neurons with silver salts, developed earlier by Camillo Golgi (silver selectively penetrates neurons, but does not impregnate other brain cells), Cajal saw that the brain has a cellular architecture. Cajal described neurons as polarized cells receiving signals from highly branched processes, called dendrites, and sendng information through unbranched processes called axons. The axon contacts the dendrites of other neurons through special structures - synapses affecting the strength of the impulse.

Golgi staining revealed a huge variety of neurons in terms of body shape, branching of dendritic parts, and axon length. Cajal found differences between cells with short axons interacting with neighboring neurons and cells with long axons projecting into other parts of the brain. Despite the differences in structure, all neurons conduct information in the same way. Connections between neurons are mediated by chemical transmitters - neurotransmitters - released from the endings of neuronal processes in synapses. We can assume that when passing through the synapse, the strength of the impulse changes by a certain number of times, which we will call the synapse weight. The impulses arriving at the neuron simultaneously via several dendrites are summed up. If the total impulse exceeds a certain threshold, the neuron is excited, forming its own impulse and transmiting it further along the axon. It is important to note that the weights of synapses can change over time, which means that the behavior of the corresponding neuron also changes. At the beginning of the century, neurophysiologists became aware of the extremely important role of synapses in the learning process. Indeed, brain signals passing through them can be amplified or attenuated in different ways. Noteworthy is the following fact, the brain of a newborn and an adult contains approximately the same number of neurons but only in an adult does it differ in the ordering of interneuronal synaptic connections. Perhaps, brain studying is the process of changing the architecture of the neural network, accompanied by the tuning of synapses.

Econometric methods of analysis are widely applied among researchers. Many economic processes are studied applying econometric models, including ARMA models (mixed process autoregression and moving average), GARCH (regression models with conditional heteroscedastic errors), ECM (deviation correction models) and VAR (vector autoregression models) [9, 14, 17–22, 36–48].

The model of the mixed process of autoregression and moving average order (p, q) is described by the following equation:

$$x_i = a_{i-1} + \cdots + a_p x_{i-p} + E_i - b_i E_{i-1} - \cdots - b_q E_{i-q} \tag{1}$$

where, xi is the value of the time series, iε1: n, n is the number of values of the series, E_i are independent, equally distributed random variables with an expectation equal to 0, αk, where kε1: p, bl, where l ε1: q are the coefficients of the model.

As a rule, research of ARMA models consists of several stages. At the first stage, the information is analyzed for stationarity. For this, visual analysis, analysis of the regression graph and its residuals, analysis of the graph of autocorrelation and partial autocorrelation functions, and Dickey-Fuller tests for unit roots are applied. If necessary, the output is modified to meet the requirements of the stationary process.

The next step is to evaluate the model. Modern computer packages include various methods for estimating ARMA (p, q) models: linear or nonlinear least squares method, maximum likelihood method. In particular, the estimates of the model coefficients must be significant, and the regression residuals e must be indistinguishable from the implementation of the white noise process (i.e., a process with constant mathematical expectation and variance and covariance function does not depend on a particular moment in time). To assess the significance of the coefficients, the Box-Pierce and Lewing-Box tests are applied. If the regression errors do not meet the necessary requirements, the model is modified and reevaluated.

If several models turned out to be adequate, then the choice between models of different orders is carried out according to two criteria: Akaike and Schwarz. Both criteria include 2 terms. The first term directly depends on the indexes of the order of the model p and q, and the second includes the sum of the squares of the residuals. The principle of model selection is to minimize the sum of the squares of the residuals and the order of the model. Therefore, in the best model, the values of the Akaike and Schwarz criteria are lower.

In a situation where for a regression model of the form:

$$x_i = \beta_l + \beta_2 z_{i2} + \ldots + \beta_k z_{ik} + u_i \tag{2}$$

where ui, are independent identically distributed centered random variables, it is assumed that the variance of errors at time it is equal to the conditional variance

$$\sigma_i^2 = V(u_1|u_{i-1}, u_{i-2}, \ldots, u_{i-p}) = E^2\left(u_i^2|u_{i-1}, u_{i-2}, \ldots, u_{i-p}\right) \tag{3}$$

and the conditional mathematical expectation E(ui | ui$-$1, ui$-$2,..., ui$-$n) is equal to zero, speaks of a model with conditional Heteroscedasticity [3, 20]. Such models are convenient for describing economic processes in which the amplitude of fluctuations of the indicator relative to its average tends to form temporary clusters - alternating periods of significant and minor deviations.

Various methods can be applied to simulate ui errors. In particular, they can be described as an autoregressive process, or as an ARMA (p, q) process. In the latter case, the model is called a generalized autoregressive model with conditional heteroscedasticity GARCH (p, q).

It can be shown that despite the fact that the conditional variance of errors in such models depends on time, the unconditional variance does not depend on time. Therefore, standard econometric procedures can be applied to evaluate the model.

When studying economic processes, a researcher often has several processes at his disposal, which, on the one hand, are non-stationary, and on the other hand, are related to each other for economic reasons. If it turns out that the indicated processes of the first order of integration (that is, their first differences are stationary), and some linear combination of these processes is stationary, then a stable long-term relationship between the quantities under study can be expected. In other words, if, for example, in the period t_i-1 consumption exceeded income, then in the period t_i consumption will decrease, and vice versa. That is the tendency to return (in the long term) to some kind of sustainable development.

Similar patterns can be described using the vidhlin correction model, which in a situation for two rows is set as follows:

$$\Delta x_i = c_1 + c_2 \Delta z_i + c_3 (x_{i-1} - \beta_0 - \beta_1 z_{i-1}) + E_i \qquad (4)$$

de x_i i z_i, $i \in 1: n$ is a pair of studied indicators, E_i, $i \in 1: n$ are independent identically distributed random variables, and the expression in brackets is a deviation correction mechanism.

For the successful application of such models, several conditions must be met. In particular, all coefficients c_k, k are $1: 3$ must be significant, coefficient c_3 must be negative, and there must be no autocorrelation in the residuals.

A separate problem when using ESM models is finding the coefficient β_l, $l \in 1: 2$. One of the most common methods for solving it is the construction of a regression x_i on z_i. From a theoretical point of view, estimates of the coefficients of such regression and estimates of their significance obtained using the least squares method do not make sense, since the processes x_i on z_i are nonstationary. However, the obtained linear combination, as the tests show, can satisfy the stationarity requirements.

In 1980, Christopher Sims proposed a new method for modeling economic equations, in which the traditional division into endo and exogenous variables did not occur [7, 30, 48]. In addition, there were no prior constraints on the variables. Instead, the economic model appeared directly in the analysis process. The proposed method of analysis is called the method of constructing vector autoregression models.

The construction of the model begins with setting a single vector of endo and exogenous variables x_i, $i \in 1: n$. The model itself is described by us as follows:

$$X_i = \sum_{k-1}^{t} A_k X_{i-k} + \varepsilon_i \qquad (5)$$

de A_k, $k \in 1 : l$ is a matrix of coefficients of the corresponding size, ε_i, $i \in 1 : n$ is a vector of grants.

Suppose that the series X_i is stationary, and the following requirements are met for the error vector:

- $E\varepsilon_I = 0$;
- $\mathrm{corr}(\varepsilon_{i_1}; \varepsilon_{i_2}) = 0$, $i_1 \neq i_2$, then there is no autocorrelation of errors;
- The components of the vector ε_I at each fixed time instant t_i can generally correlate, that is, ε corr $(\varepsilon_{kt1}; \varepsilon_{kt2}) \neq 0$, $t_1 = i_2$, $k \neq \varepsilon$.

Since, in the above assumptions, the autocorrelation formula of the residuals, the least squares method allows us to obtain consistent estimates. However, given that the correlation matrix is not diagonal, it makes sense to use multiple estimates of the least squares method.

The choice of the lag order l apply the general-to-specific principle using the likelihood method. First, the regressions with the number of lags l and l - 1 are sequentially estimated, then for each of the obtained regressions the natural logarithm of the likelihood function is calculated. The difference between the calculated values follows the distribution law x2, if the model coefficients with lag l are insignificant. Accordingly, based on the obtained value of the statistics, it is possible to draw a conclusion about the significance of the corresponding coefficients and exclude/leave them in the model.

As a result of using the above described models and their modifications, the researchers managed to obtain a number of practical results. In particular, Torben Andersen, Tim Bollerslev, Francis Diebold and Clara Vega, having studied the dynamics of exchange rates, found that unexpected macroeconomic events cause abrupt changes in the conditional average of the studied indicators [6, 27, 30]. At the same time, the market reaction is asymmetric: negative news causes stronger changes than positive news. In addition, the researchers obtained a number of interesting facts about macroeconomic news which are significant for exchange rates, influencing "controversial" factors, how the indicators of the currency market are related to the indicators of the stock market. Many of the obtained results are also confirmed by the works of Martin Evans and Richard Lyon, Peter Veronesi and Pierre-Luigi Balduzzi, G. Abuselidze, J. Davis, T. Norfield, Slobodianyk and Abuselidze [8, 11, 12, 27].

In another work, Ted Jaditz, using econometric tools, explores seasonal fluctuations in the variance of various macroeconomic indicators [10]. In the course of his research, Jadits comes to the conclusion that a significant part of macroeconomic indicators are subject to significant seasonal fluctuations, which must be taken into account both when predicting their dynamics and when trying to control them. Another important conclusion of the researcher is the assumption that for a successful analysis of economic indicators it is necessary to decompose them into a trend, a periodic component and seasonal deviations.

When studying the periodic components in the dynamics of certain macroeconomic indicators, researchers are most often interested in how periodic seasonal fluctuations and business cycles are related [28]. In particular, in their work [3, 4, 25] Diego Comin and Mark Gertler, using econometric methods, evaluated a model allowing to take into account the influence of short- and medium-term fluctuations in output at the stage of business cycles. The constructed model incorporated the influence of such variables as technological progress, resource utilization, investment in research and development, labor costs, and others. One of the important achievements is the ability to illustrate, using the constructed model, medium-term periodic fluctuations in technological changes and resource utilization due to external shocks associated with the development of technologies.

4   Conclusions

In studies, structural or structural-functional models are often applied, since the interconnections of subsystems are of great importance for planning and management. Functional models are widely applied in economic regulation.

The general classification of economic and mathematical models includes more than ten main features. With the development of economic and mathematical research, the problem of classifying the applied models becomes more complicated. Along with the emergence of new types of models (especially mixed types) and new signs of their classification, the process of integrating models of different types into more complex model constructions is under way.

Economic cybernetics allows you to analyze economic phenomena and processes as very complex systems from the point of view of the laws and mechanisms of control and the movement of information in them. Methods of cybernetic modeling and systems analysis are most widely used in economic analysis. The mathematical theory of optimal processes is used to control technical and economic processes and resources.

Having studied the dynamics of exchange rates, we found that unexpected macroeconomic events cause abrupt changes in the conditional average of the studied indicators. At the same time, the market reaction is asymmetric: negative news causes stronger changes than positive news.

Accordingly, we have reviewed the main existing methods of analysis and forecasting of indicators of the futures contracts market. The features of these indicators that we have indicated determine the fact that the main attention is paid to the methods of identifying the periodic components of their dynamics. The revealed advantages and disadvantages of the existing methods were taken into account when developing a modification of the spectral analysis method.

References

1. Abuselidze, G.: European integration of georgia and financial-economic condition: achievements and challenges. Euro. J. Sustain. Develop. **8**(1), 53–68 (2019). https://doi.org/10.14207/ejsd.2019.v8n1p53
2. Abuselidze, G., Mamaladze, L.: The impact of the COVID-19 outbreak on the socio-economic issues of the black sea region countries. In: Gervasi, O., et al. (eds.) ICCSA 2020. LNCS, vol. 12253, pp. 453–467. Springer, Cham (2020). https://doi.org/10.1007/978-3-030-58814-4_32
3. Pazarbasioglu, C., Ötker, I.: Exchange market pressures and speculative capital flows in selected European countries. IMF Work. Papers **94**(21), 1–72 (1994). https://doi.org/10.5089/9781451921571.001
4. Rodriguez, C.A.: Managed float: an evaluation of alternative rules in the presence of speculative capital flows. Am. Econ. Rev. **71**(1), 256–260 (1981)
5. Kletzer, K., Spiegel, M.M.: Speculative capital inflows and exchange rate targeting in the Pacific Basin: theory and evidence. Managing Capital Flows and Exchange Rates: Perspectives from the Pacific Basin. Cambridge University Press (UK) for Federal Reserve Bank of San Francisco (1998)
6. Abuselidze, G., Slobodianyk, A.: Investment of the financial instruments and their influence on the exchange stock market development. In: Econ. Sci. Rur. Develop. Conf. Proc. **52**, 203–221 (2019)
7. Copeland, T., Koller, T., Murrin, J.: Measuring and Managing the Value of Companies. Wiley, New Jersey, USA (2001)
8. Abuselidze, G.: Georgia's capital market: functioning problems and development directions in association with European Union. J. Appl. Econ. Sci. **13**(7), 1929–1938 (2018)
9. Hull, J.: Options, Futures and Other Derivatives. University of Toronto, Prentice Hall, Englewood Cliffs. New Jersey. USA (2016)

10. Blank, I.A.: Enterprise asset and capital management (2003)
11. Davis, J.: Speculative capital in the global age. Race Class. **44**(3), 1–22 (2003). https://doi.org/10.1177/0306396803044003022
12. Norfield, T.: Derivatives and capitalist markets: the speculative heart of capital. Hist. Mater. **20**(1), 103–132 (2012). https://doi.org/10.1163/156920612x634735
13. Singh, K.: Emerging markets consider capital controls to regulate speculative capital flows. VOX Research-based policy analysis and commentary from leading economists, vol. 5, (2010)
14. Steiner, A., Steinkamp, S., Westermann, F.: Exit strategies, capital flight and speculative attacks: Europe's version of the trilemma. Eur. J. Polit. Econ. **59**, 83–96 (2019). https://doi.org/10.1016/j.ejpoleco.2019.02.003
15. Slobodianyk, A., Abuselidze, G., Tarasovych, L.: The mechanism of integration of the Ukrainian stock market in the world stock market. E3S Web Conf. **157**, 04034 (2020). https://doi.org/10.1051/e3sconf/202015704034
16. Liow, K.H.: Dynamic relationship between stock and property markets. Appl. Finan. Econ. **16**(5), 371–376 (2006). https://doi.org/10.1080/09603100500390885
17. Xiao, L., Aydemir, A.: Volatility modelling and forecasting in finance. In: Forecasting volatility in the financial markets, pp. 1–45. Butterworth-Heinemann (2007). https://doi.org/10.1016/B978-075066942-9.50003-0
18. Curto, J.D., Pinto, J.C., Tavares, G.N.: Modeling stock markets' volatility using GARCH models with Normal, Student's t and stable Paretian distributions. Stat. Pap. **50**(2), 311 (2009). https://doi.org/10.1007/s00362-007-0080-5
19. Zhang, B., Yue, L.: Do the exchange rates matter for chinese stock market: evidence from ARDL-ECM estimation. J. Finan. **7**, 26–35 (2002)
20. Miao, S. S., Lu, Q.: Transmission effects of international rice price on domestic market: Based on ECM model. Finance Trade Res. **1**, 27–34 (2012)
21. Lesmana, E., Susanti, D., Napitupulu, H., Hidayat, Y.: Estimating the value-at-risk for some stocks at the capital market in Indonesia based on ARMA-FIGARCH models. J. Phys: Conf. Ser. **909**, 012040 (2017). https://doi.org/10.1088/1742-6596/909/1/012040
22. Choudhry, T., Hasan, M., Zhang, Y.: Forecasting the daily dynamic hedge ratios in emerging European stock futures markets: evidence from GARCH models. Int. J. Bank. Account. Financ. **10**(1), 67–100 (2019). https://doi.org/10.1504/IJBAAF.2019.099316
23. Arnade, C., Hoffman, L.: The impact of price variability on cash/futures market relationships: implications for market efficiency and price discovery. J. Agric. Appl. Econ. **47**(4), 539–559 (2015). https://doi.org/10.1017/aae.2015.24
24. Floros, C., Vougas, D.V.: Hedge ratios in Greek stock index futures market. Appl Finan Econ. **14**(15), 1125–1136 (2004). https://doi.org/10.1080/09603100412331297702
25. Bello, W.F., Bullard, N., Malhotra, K., Malhotra, A.: Global Finance: New Thinking on Regulating Speculative Capital Markets. Zed Books (2000)
26. Abuselidze, G., Beridze, L.: The role of alternative investments in the development of capital markets: in terms of the transformation of Georgia with the EU. In: Proceedings of the 4th International Conference on European Integration (ICEI), pp. 29–41 (2018)
27. Slobodianyk, A., Abuselidze, G.: Influence of speculative operations on the investment capital: an empirical analysis of capital markets. E3S Web Conf. **234**, 00084 (2021). https://doi.org/10.1051/e3sconf/202123400084
28. Jylhä, P., Suominen, M.: Speculative capital and currency carry trades. J. Financ. Econ. **99**(1), 60–75 (2011). https://doi.org/10.1016/j.jfineco.2010.07.006
29. Rasmus, J.: Speculative capital, financial crisis and emerging epic recession. Critique. **37**(1), 31–49 (2009). https://doi.org/10.1080/03017600802598179
30. Peterson, K.: Speculative Markets: Drug circuits and Derivative Life in Nigeria. Duke University Press (2014). https://doi.org/10.1215/9780822376477

31. Leblang, D.: Political uncertainty and speculative attacks. Coping with globalization: Cross-national patterns in domestic governance and policy performance (2002)
32. Abuselidze, G., Slobodianyk, A.: Value Assessment of Shares of Corporate Issuers by Applying the Methods of Fundamental Analysis in the Stock Exchange Market. In: Bogoviz, A.V. (eds.) The Challenge of Sustainability in Agricultural Systems. LNNS, vol. 206, pp. 25–39. Springer, Cham (2021). https://doi.org/10.1007/978-3-030-72110-7
33. Vasylieva, D., Kudyk, T., Lisovska, V., Abuselidze, G., Hryvkivska, O.: Ensuring the issuance of investment-attractive corporate bonds. E3S Web Conf. **295**, 01008 (2021). https://doi.org/10.1051/e3sconf/202129501008
34. Slobodianyk, A., Abuselidze, G., Buriak, R., Muzychenko, A., Momot, O., Romanova, L.: Stock trading indices: a mechanism for attracting speculative capital. In: Beskopylny, A., Shamtsyan, M. (eds.) XIV International Scientific Conference "INTERAGROMASH 2021." LNNS, vol. 246, pp. 897–905. Springer, Cham (2022). https://doi.org/10.1007/978-3-030-81619-3_100
35. Ramón y Cajal, S.: Histología del sistema nervioso del hombre y de los vertebrados. Madrid, Ministerio de Sanidad y Consumo, CSIC (1911)
36. Wurtz, D., Chalabi, Y., Luksan, L.: Parameter estimation of ARMA models with GARCH/APARCH errors an R and S plus software implementation. J. Stat. Softw. **55**(2), 28–33 (2006)
37. Karanasos, M.: Prediction in ARMA models with GARCH in mean effects. J. Time Ser. Anal. **22**(5), 555–576 (2001). https://doi.org/10.1111/1467-9892.00241
38. Ghahramani, M., Thavaneswaran, A.: Financial applications of ARMA models with GARCH errors. J. Risk Finan. **7**(5), 525–543 (2006). https://doi.org/10.1108/15265940610712678
39. Boubacar Maïnassara, Y., Saussereau, B.: Diagnostic checking in multivariate ARMA models with dependent errors using normalized residual autocorrelations. J. Am. Stat. Assoc. **113**(524), 1813–1827 (2018). https://doi.org/10.1080/01621459.2017.1380030
40. Sun, H., Yan, D., Zhao, N., Zhou, J.: Empirical investigation on modeling solar radiation series with ARMA–GARCH models. Energy Convers. Manage. **92**, 385–395 (2015). https://doi.org/10.1016/j.enconman.2014.12.072
41. Wang, Y., Wu, C.: Forecasting energy market volatility using GARCH models: can multivariate models beat univariate models? Energy Econ. **34**(6), 2167–2181 (2012). https://doi.org/10.1016/j.eneco.2012.03.010
42. Paolella, M.S.: Linear Models and Time-Series Analysis: Regression, ANOVA, ARMA and GARCH. Wiley (2018). https://doi.org/10.1002/9781119432036
43. Thornton, M.A., Chambers, M.J.: The exact discretisation of CARMA models with applications in finance. J. Empir. Financ. **38**, 739–761 (2016). https://doi.org/10.1016/j.jempfin.2016.03.006
44. Nwogugu, M.: Further critique of GARCH/ARMA/VAR/EVT Stochastic-Volatility models and related approaches. Appl. Math. Comput. **182**(2), 1735–1748 (2006). https://doi.org/10.1016/j.amc.2006.01.080
45. LeSage, J.P.: A comparison of the forecasting ability of ECM and VAR models. Rev. Econ. Stat. **70**(4), 664–671 (1990). https://doi.org/10.2307/2109607
46. OECD Composite Leading Indicators: Turning Points of Reference Series and Component Series (2014)
47. The international banking market report: Statistical Annex (2021). https://www.bis.org/statistics/index.htm?m=1037
48. The world federation of exchanges 2017 full year market highlights. https://www.world-exchanges.org/home/index.php/news/world-exchange-news/the-world-federation-of-exchanges-publishes-2017-full-year-market-highlights

The Influence of Changes in Oil Prices at the Inflation Levels: A Correlation-Regression Analysis

George Abuselidze[(✉)] [iD]

Batumi Shota Rustaveli State University, Ninoshvili, 35, 6010 Batumi, Georgia
george.abuselidze@bsu.edu.ge

Abstract. In the age of the global pandemic and during the war in Eastern Europe, inflation is increasing daily, affecting not only the socio-economic situation of developed but also developing and small open economy countries. Among the factors causing inflation are often indicated rising prices for petroleum products. Therefore, the aim of the paper is to make a correlation-regression analysis of the impact of changes in oil prices at the level of inflation. The majority of the empirical data covers the years 2000 to 2021. Quantitative data was analyzed in line with the objectives, resulting in the identification of particular issue tendencies. The paper examines the methodology of world prices for oil products and current factors. The characteristics of price formation in the global market and the indicators of the relationship between oil prices and the level of inflation are studied. The analysis of the impact of the dynamics of oil prices on inflation is established. The applicable conclusion was produced based on the examination of the information acquired through the characteristic and quantitative research methodologies.

Keywords: Inflation · Price · Oil market · Oil price shocks · SOE

1 Introduction

Over the last century, the significance of oil as an energy resource for the world economy has greatly increased. It originally had a fuel-energy function; later its role became much more important when mass-production and the use of automobiles were launched. Since then, oil has become a raw material of strategic significance and also plays a crucial role in the economic and political life of countries. The price of several products or services depends on the oil price, as it is involved in the production process of all fields. Despite technological advances, the transport sector is incredible without oil products, and it remains a major fuel-energy resource. Oil possession allows countries to determine the economic or political climate of the world. There has been a trend of frequent price changes in the oil market in recent years, it has increased dramatically and decreased at various intervals. Price manipulation has led to numerous crises all around the world.

OPEC still has a significant impact on the volume of oil supplies and price levels. However, its influence has been weakening recently and it is anticipated that this influence

© The Author(s), under exclusive license to Springer Nature Switzerland AG 2022
O. Gervasi et al. (Eds.): ICCSA 2022, LNCS 13376, pp. 45–57, 2022.
https://doi.org/10.1007/978-3-031-10450-3_4

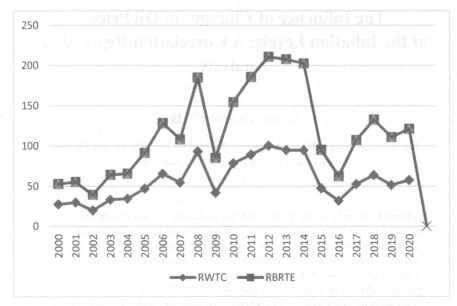

Fig. 1. Oil prices in 2000–2021. Source: Compiled by the author based on the [1, 2].

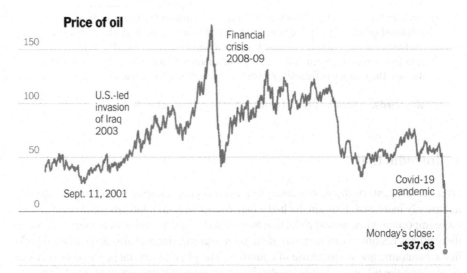

Fig. 2. Oil price change and global crises. Source: Compiled by the author based on the [3–7].

tends to disappear in the future. The fact is that today oil is a strategic resource and it has a great impact on the economies of both exporter and importer countries.

The aim of the research is to build an econometric model through selected factors and correlation-regression analysis of the obtained data. Based on the objectives of the research, we formulated H_0 and its anti-H_1 hypotheses:

H_0: The change in the price of oil on the world market affects the inflation rate of the oil - importing country;
H_1: The change in the price of oil on the world market does not affect the inflation rate of the importing country.

2 Methodology for Studying World Prices for Oil Products

Oil is one of the most important commodities whose price changes have a special impact on the world economy and macroeconomic factors such as inflation, GDP, recession, interest rates, exchange rates, among others. Consequently, the study of its price and price changes in general is still a topic of discussion for many economists and energy researchers. Numerous methods are used to predict accurately the prices of petroleum products and the events affecting the cost of crude oil. Econometric methods are especially popular among them, as well as recently widely used computational methods such as ANN and fuzzy expert systems, which are actively applied to financial markets as they are more flexible and accurate than other traditional methods. However, so far there is no agreement on which method is the most reliable.

Methodologies for studying the prices of petroleum products in the world literature are mainly divided into two categories: quantitative and qualitative methods. The quantitative method is divided into groups: econometric models including time, financial and structural models; non-standard models such as artificial neural networks (ANN) and Support Vector Machines (SVM). The qualitative method also includes various models, namely: Delphi method, Belief Networks, Fuzzy Logic, and Expert Systems, Web Text Mining method (WTM).

Quantitative methods are based on the past data and mathematical models and the main task are to predict short-term and medium-term prices.

One of the methods of studying prices is different variants of GARCH belonging to the econometric method. Morana (2001) applied a semi-parametric method to determine the price of a barrel which was based on the calculation of GARCH oil price fluctuations [8]. As a result, it was identified that this approach can be applied to determine forward prices as well as to calculate the price self-regulation interval. Moosa and Al-Loughani (1994) applied the GARCH-M model to prove that the future price is neither fair nor effective in the determination of the spot price [9]. Sadorsky (1999) using vector regression proved that changes in oil prices affect economic activity, but current changes in the economy have little effect on oil prices [10]. Sadorsky (2006) applied several one-sided and varied statistical models such as GARCH, TGARCH, AR, BIGARCH to calculate the daily change in profits from oil futures capital [11]. Postali and Picchetti (2006) applied the simple geometric Brownian method and asserted that their model was quite reliable for studying oil prices [8–13].

Peters (1994) opposes the application of similar models [14]. Most financial markets have fraudulent peaks, the Hens model, which is based on the normal assumption, excludes the aforementioned fraud. Moreover, the results of the Peters study suggest long-term memory. Dees et al. (2007) proposed a world oil market model to predict oil supply-demand and real prices to analyze the risks of each [15]. The model simulates, in particular, the determination of oil demand using behavioral equations, where demand is related to domestic government economic activity and real oil prices.

Adrangi *et al.* (2001) [16] investigated that oil prices are quite non-linear, while the results of a study by Panas and Nini (2000) point to the chaos of oil prices [17]. Gori *et al.* (2007) studied changes in the ratio of oil prices to consumption over the past decade and considered three possible scenarios for oil prices: parabolic, linear, and chaotic behaviors that predicted changes in oil prices and consumption [18]. Rehrl and Friedrich (2006) applied the LOPEX model to create a long-term scenario for the future delivery of world oil through 2010 [19]. However, the explanation of the facts is limited to idealized assumptions only.

ANN is inspired by the human brain biological system allowing it to study and analyze prices in the oil market. It is also widely used in business, science, or industry. Kaboudan (2001) presented a short-term monthly forecast of oil prices and proved that genetic programming (GP) gives more accurate results than the theory of randomness when ANN proved the discrepancy [20]. The following variables were studied: Monthly World Oil Production, Organization for Economic Co-operation and Development Consumption, World Crude Oil Shares, Monthly Change in Prominent US Securities, and Delayed FOB Crude Oil Price in US Imports. All variables except lagging prices did not prove to be useful. He also used GP and ANN to predict the cost of purchasing refineries at the price of petroleum products. Wang et al. (2004) applied the WTM and econometric method with intelligent forecasting techniques [21]. Based on the results, we can affirm the given model bearing the name TEI@I can predict better than the ANN and ARIMA models.

Fernandez (2007) predicted crude oil and natural gas prices using ANN, SVM, and ARIMA models and applied daily prices for 1995–2005 [22]. The results revealed that in the short run the ARIMA model is more reliable than the ANN and SVM, while in the long run, conversely, the ANN and SVM data are more accurate. Therefore, the length of the period is an important element of accurate price forecasting when applying this or that model.

As we can see the list of scientists applying different methods to study the prices of petroleum products is wide and it is clear that there is a substantial difference between the methods and models and different factors affect the accuracy of their price forecasting. However, as already mentioned, econometric methods are most often applied to predict oil price volatility. The second place is occupied by financial methods, followed by structural and non-standard models, and the last place is taken by qualitative methods.

3 Results and Discussion

Current developments in the world economy are closely interlinked and the market for strategic goods such as petroleum products has the potential to have a significant impact on the economies of countries [23–27]. A large share of public budget revenues is generated by revenues from oil exports because it is the most important source of tax revenue accumulation for importing countries and has a special fiscal effect [28, 29]. However, the relationship between oil prices and inflation levels is a topical issue for the study of world economists.

A study by Pederson (2011) in 46 countries confirmed the limited impact of oil price changes on core inflation [30]. However, 2010 study by S. Clerides entitled "Fuel

Retail Response to Oil Price Shocks in EU Countries" changes in oil prices directly affect the price of gasoline, although this will take some time [24]. In the long run, a single unit change in the price of oil in the international market will change the price of gasoline in the local market by the same amount. However, in the short term, gasoline prices for most EU countries account for only half of the change in international oil prices. It takes about 3 months for a full transfer of oil price change to gasoline prices in Europe. Price transfer is asymmetric. When oil prices rise, it is followed by a directly proportional increase in the price of gasoline, but the same does not happen in case of oil prices fall [24]. It is interesting that Georgia, unlike EU countries, is not characterized by the asymmetric transfer of prices. Both rising and falling Brent Crude Oil prices are symmetrically reflected in local gasoline prices.

For example, we can summarize how, on other equal terms, the increase in international oil prices by 10 US cents per liter is reflected (US $ 16 per barrel) in the overall inflation rate in Georgia and Europe (see Fig. 3).

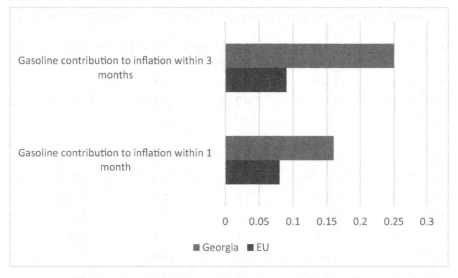

Fig. 3. Impact of oil prices on inflation rates in Georgia and Europe

If the price of "black gold" in the world market decreases, the economy of the exporting country begins to lose (decrease) the most important revenues from the sale of oil products. Accordingly, the issue of devaluation of the local currency is on the agenda. Mikhailov *et al.* (2019), Mukhtarov *et al.* (2019) [31, 32] applied modern mathematical models such as the VAR, the Granger method, the Dickey-Fuller test to determine the impact of oil prices on the Russian economy, and revealed that a 1% increase in GDP leads to local 1.47% strengthening of the currency, this fact is explained by the growth of the country's economy in general. And a 1% increase in oil prices leads to a strengthening of the ruble by 1.66%. Accordingly, we can affirm that the Russian economy depends on world oil prices. An increase of 1% in exports will also strengthen the ruble, as a foreign currency will flow in, which will ultimately increase supply in the interbank market.

To determine the impact of the oil price change on the inflation rate of importing countries, we conducted a correlation-regression analysis. Correlation-regression analysis shows the effect of the independent variable (in our case world oil prices) on the dependent variable (in our case the country's inflation and the price of gasoline in Georgia) and measures its magnitude. We took several countries as research objects: 1) South Korea, which is the largest importer of oil in the world. It ranks fourth in oil consumption and imports. For the analysis we took the world oil prices and the inflation rate in South Korea in 1990–2019; 2) China, which ranks first in terms of oil imports and consumption. For the analysis we took the world oil prices and the inflation rate in China in 1990–2019 [33–37]; 3) The US, which in addition to extracting oil, is also its importer. The US ranks second in the world in oil consumption and imports. For the analysis, we took the world oil prices and the inflation rate in the USA in 1990–2020 and 4) Georgia, which belongs to the importing country and is significantly dependent on the oil price (see Table 1).

Table 1. Impact of the oil price change on the inflation rate of importing countries

Years	World oil prices	Inflation rate in China	Inflation rate in the US	Inflation rate in Korea	Inflation rate in Georgia
1990	22.26	3.05	5.4	8.57	–
1991	18.62	3.55	4.2	9.33	–
1992	18.44	6.35	3	6.21	–
1993	16.33	14.61	3	4.8	–
1994	15.53	24.25	2.6	6.26	–
1995	16.86	16.79	2.8	4.48	162.71
1996	20.29	8.31	2.9	4.92	39.35
1997	18.86	2.78	2.3	4.43	7.08
1998	12.28	−0.77	1.6	7.51	3.56
1999	17.44	−1.4	2.2	0.81	19.19
2000	27.6	0.34	3.4	2.25	4.06
2001	23.12	0.71	2.8	4.06	4.64
2002	24.36	−0.73	1.6	2.76	5.58
2003	28.1	1.12	2.3	3.51	0.83
2004	36.05	3.82	2.7	3.59	5.65
2005	50.59	1.77	3.4	2.75	8.24
2006	61	1.64	3.2	2.24	9.16
2007	69.04	4.81	2.9	2.53	9.24
2008	94.1	5.92	3.8	4.67	9.99
2009	60.86	−0.72	−0.4	2.75	1.72

(*continued*)

Table 1. (*continued*)

Years	World oil prices	Inflation rate in China	Inflation rate in the US	Inflation rate in Korea	Inflation rate in Georgia
2010	77.38	3.17	1.6	2.93	7.11
2011	107.46	5.55	3.2	4.02	8.54
2012	109.45	2.62	2.1	2.87	−0.94
2013	105.87	2.62	1.5	1.3	−0.51
2014	96.29	1.92	1.6	1.27	3.06
2015	49.49	1.43	0.1	0.7	4
2016	40.76	2	1.3	0.97	2.13
2017	52.51	1.59	2.1	1.94	6.03
2018	69.78	2.07	2.4	1.47	2.61
2019	64.04	2.89	1.8	0.38	4.85
2020	49.99	2.39	1.25	0.54	5.22
2021	70.68	0.85	7.00	2.19	9.27
2022	117.25	2.08	8.5	1.65	12.8

Correlation-regression analysis of Chinese data gave us the following result: the coefficient of determination R^2 represents the part of the scatter explained by regression in the total scatter of the resulting variable and it is equal to 0.012. The closer this value gets to 0, the smaller the relationship between the dependent and independent variables is. There is no linear relationship between the variables and the selected model is unsuitable.

Statistical significance F (Significance F) is the probability that the null hypothesis (H_0) in our regression model cannot be rejected. Significance F = 0.25 - in our model, the null hypothesis is rejected or the H_1 hypothesis is true.

We provide a model with the obtained results:

$$Y = 5.86 - 0.037x$$

where Y is the inflation rate in Korea;

X - Change in world oil prices.

As we can see, there is an inverse relationship between the variables. An increase of one unit in oil prices reduces the inflation rate in China by 0.0037 points.

Correlation-regression analysis of US data gave the following results:

The coefficient of determination R^2 is equal to 0.008, ie the change in oil prices does not affect US inflation.

Significance F = 0.27 - The null hypothesis is rejected.

According to the data, we have the following model:

$$Y = 2.79 - 0.007x$$

The model shows that an increase in oil prices by one unit reduces the inflation rate in the US by 0.007 units.

The correlation-regression analysis of the South Korean data gave us the following result:

The coefficient of determination R^2 is equal to 0.19. That means that there is not any relationship between the variables i.e., the change in the dependent variable is entirely determined by random factors that are not included in the model. Significance $F = 0.009$ - Like other countries, we rejected the null hypothesis for Korea.

According to the results, the model is insignificant and the change in world oil prices has almost no effect on the inflation level of the importing country. Based on the data, we created a model: $Y = 70.376 - 6.459x$ which shows that rising oil prices are reducing South Korea's inflation rate.

Indeed, Georgia is not even in the top ten in terms of oil consumption and import in the world, but it is still interesting whether oil prices have an impact on the inflation rate of our country. Table 1 shows the dynamics of changes in oil prices in 1995–2020 and the level of inflation in Georgia by years.

Correlation-regression analysis of these data gave the same results: Oil prices have almost no effect on the country's inflation rate ($R^2 = 0.054$), we reject the null hypothesis (Significance $F = 0.13$) and we have an inverse relationship between these two indicators ($Y = 56.7 - 0.29x$).

As discussed above, the gasoline prices in the country are directly proportional to the price of world oil. For the analysis, we took the dynamics of world oil prices and gasoline prices in Georgia by months from 2013 to 2020 (see Table 2).

Table 2. Price of World Oil and gasoline prices in Georgia [38, 39]

Year/Month	Gasoline price in Georgia	Oil price in the world market	Year/Month	Gasoline price in Georgia	Oil price in the world market
2020/12	2.21	49.34	2016/12	1.79	58.93
2020/11	2.17	46.16	2016/11	1.69	54.24
2020/10	2.2	36.4	2016/10	1.66	51.36
2020/9	2.3	40.94	2016/9	1.59	52.92
2020/8	1.98	53.42	2016/8	1.59	49.17
2020/7	1.85	41.16	2016/7	1.58	45.8
2020/6	1.82	40.33	2016/6	1.55	53.11
2020/5	1.93	36.66	2016/5	1.53	54.16
2020/4	2.17	19.46	2016/4	1.47	50.83
2020/3	2.39	21.01	2016/3	1.47	42.63
2020/2	2.44	45.83	2016/2	1.49	37.7
2020/1	2.49	52.95	2016/1	1.53	37.59

(*continued*)

Table 2. (*continued*)

Year/Month	Gasoline price in Georgia	Oil price in the world market	Year/Month	Gasoline price in Georgia	Oil price in the world market
2019/12	2.52	42.95	2015/12	1.67	41.48
2019/11	2.53	56.83	2015/11	1.82	46.48
2019/10	2.53	55.75	2015/10	1.85	51.9
2019/9	2.54	55.8	2015/9	1.89	50.19
2019/8	2.52	56.86	2015/8	1.94	54.66
2019/7	2.51	60.45	2015/7	1.99	52.3
2019/6	2.43	60.46	2015/6	1.99	66.01
2019/5	2.37	55.32	2015/5	1.89	67.17
2019/4	2.29	66.27	2015/4	1.76	66.79
2019/3	2.24	62.67	2015/3	1.68	53.41
2019/2	2.27	59.96	2015/2	1.64	56.13
2019/1	2.31	56.59	2015/1	1.71	54.66
2018/12	2.36	47.86	2014/12	1.9	60.09
2018/11	2.38	53.53	2014/11	2.01	74.22
2018/10	2.41	68.38	2014/10	2.05	89.88
2018/9	2.39	76.84	2014/9	2.11	101.46
2018/8	2.37	73.29	2014/8	2.12	106.9
2018/7	2.37	72.27	2014/7	2.13	109.17
2018/6	2.31	77.93	2014/6	2.1	117.07
2018/5	2.23	70.59	2014/5	2.07	114.32
2018/4	2.15	72.48	2014/4	2.03	111.41
2018/3	2.17	68.9	2014/3	2.02	113.87
2018/2	2.21	65.58	2014/2	2.02	115.72
2018/1	2.25	69.26	2014/1	2.02	110.36
2017/12	2.27	64.89	2013/12	2.02	111.9
2017/11	2.18	61.65	2013/11	1.99	105.33
2017/10	2.12	58.40	2013/10	1.99	109.29
2017/9	2.05	55.44	2013/9	2.01	115.74
2017/8	2	50.96	2013/8	2	121.97
2017/7	1.97	54.28	2013/7	1.96	119.1
2017/6	2.05	49.77	2013/6	1.95	109.5
2017/5	2.05	52.28	2013/5	1.97	104.57

(*continued*)

Table 2. (*continued*)

Year/Month	Gasoline price in Georgia	Oil price in the world market	Year/Month	Gasoline price in Georgia	Oil price in the world market
2017/4	2.05	53.42	2013/4	2.05	106.45
2017/3	2.1	54.35	2013/3	2.1	110.66
2017/2	2.15	51.71	2013/2	2.06	105.03
2017/1	1.97	57.62	2013/1	2.03	112.11

In this case, the dependent variable is the gasoline price in Georgia, and the independent variable is the same - oil price in the world market.

We will have the following hypotheses:

H_0: The change in the oil price in the world market affects the gasoline price in Georgia;
H_1: The change in the oil price in the world market does not affect the gasoline price in Georgia;

Correlation-regression analysis gave us radically different results from the study discussed above. The coefficient of determination R^2 is equal to 0.004, i.e. the oil price in Georgia is influenced by factors that are not considered in our model. The null hypothesis presented by us has not been confirmed - Significance F = 0.5.

$Y = 2 + 0.0007x$ - The model shows that an increase in oil prices by 0.0007 units increases gasoline price in Georgia.

4 Conclusions

Inflation is an important economic indicator, as high inflation or deflation can damage a country's long-term economic growth potential [40]. Therefore, the goal of economic policy is to keep inflation at a level where long-term real economic growth is maximal (i.e., corresponds to its potential level).

Based on the results of the study, we rejected the H_0 hypothesis and confirmed the H_1 hypothesis that the change in oil prices on the world market does not affect the inflation rate of the oil-importing country and it does not affect the gasoline price in Georgia. However, in reality, this is not the case. The result of the correlation-regression analysis can be easily explained: depending on the variable - inflation is affected by many factors that are not considered in our model. For example, the economic and political situation in the country. The change in world oil prices indeed affects the inflation rate of the importing country, but its impact is very small and therefore was not revealed during the regression analysis in the model. As for the second model - we took the market price of gasoline in Georgia, which includes the costs of oil transportation, taxes, and several other factors that determine the fuel price in Georgia. Against the background of existing factors, the impact of changes in world oil prices on gasoline prices in Georgia has been greatly reduced in the model. Moreover, the reflection of oil prices on the gasoline price in the country takes some time, and this factor must be taken into account.

When oil prices rise in the world (sectorial inflation - rising prices in one sector increases prices in another sector) and as a result, fuel prices rise in Georgia and eventually the consumer price index, tightening monetary policy at such times will certainly not affect international oil prices, and it will only restrict the local economy, thereby causing slowing down the economy and rising unemployment. Consequently, central banks usually should not have to respond to these types of supply shocks (except when an increase in the consumer price index leads to an increase in inflation expectations in the country, which is necessary to tighten monetary policy), instead, the Ministry of Finance should respond through fiscal policy. In terms of productivity, in the current situation, we assume that orthodox and heterodox monetary methods should cohabit. At this time monetary and fiscal methods are converging and the gap between them is narrowing, which is the beginning of a new global economic paradigm in the history of world finance.

References

1. U.S. Energy Information Administration: Petroleum & Other Liquids. Data. Spot Prices (2021). https://www.eia.gov/dnav/pet/pet_pri_spt_s1_m.htm
2. Choi, S., Furceri, D., Loungani, P., Mishra, S., Poplawski-Ribeiro, M.: Oil prices and inflation dynamics: evidence from advanced and developing economies. J. Int. Money Financ. **82**, 71–96 (2018). https://doi.org/10.1016/j.jimonfin.2017.12.004
3. Abuselidze, G., Mamaladze, L.: The impact of the COVID-19 outbreak on the socio-economic issues of the black sea region countries. In: Gervasi, O., et al. (eds.) ICCSA 2020. LNCS, vol. 12253, pp. 453–467. Springer, Cham (2020). https://doi.org/10.1007/978-3-030-58814-4_32
4. Tsai, C.L.: How do U.S. stock returns respond differently to oil price shocks pre-crisis, within the financial crisis, and post-crisis? Energy Econ. **50**, 47–62 (2015). https://doi.org/10.1016/j.eneco.2015.04.012
5. Bhar, R., Malliaris, A.G.: Oil prices and the impact of the financial crisis of 2007–2009. Energy Econ. **33**(6), 1049–1054 (2011). https://doi.org/10.1016/j.eneco.2011.01.016
6. Berend, I.T.: A Restructured Economy: From the Oil Crisis to the Financial Crisis, 1973–2009. Oxford Handbooks Online. (2012). https://doi.org/10.1093/oxfordhb/9780199560981.013.0020
7. Lei, C., Yong, Z.: The properties and cointegration of oil spot and futures prices during financial crisis. Energy Procedia. **5**, 353–359 (2011). https://doi.org/10.1016/j.egypro.2011.03.060
8. Morana, C.: A semiparametric approach to short-term oil price forecasting. Energy Econ. **23**(3), 325–338 (2001). https://doi.org/10.1016/S0140-9883(00)00075-X
9. Moosa, I.A., Al-Loughani, N.E.: Unbiasedness and time varying risk premia in the crude oil futures market. Energy Econ. **16**(2), 99–105 (1994). https://doi.org/10.1016/0140-9883(94)90003-5
10. Sadorsky, P.: Oil price shocks and stock market activity. Energy Econ. **21**(5), 449–469 (1999). https://doi.org/10.1016/S0140-9883(99)00020-1
11. Sadorsky, P.: Modeling and forecasting petroleum futures volatility. Energy Econ. **28**(4), 467–488 (2006). https://doi.org/10.1016/j.eneco.2006.04.005
12. Postali, F.A., Picchetti, P.: Geometric Brownian motion and structural breaks in oil prices: a quantitative analysis. Energy Econ. **28**(4), 506–522 (2006). https://doi.org/10.1016/j.eneco.2006.02.011

13. Moshiri, S.: Asymmetric effects of oil price shocks in oil-exporting countries: the role of institutions. OPEC Energy Rev. **39**(2), 222–246 (2015). https://doi.org/10.1111/opec.12050
14. Peters, E.E.: Fractal Market Analysis: Applying Chaos Theory to Investment and Economics. Wiley (1994)
15. Dees, S., Karadeloglou, P., Kaufmann, R.K., Sanchez, M.: Modelling the world oil market: assessment of a quarterly econometric model. Energy Policy **35**(1), 178–191 (2007). https://doi.org/10.1016/j.enpol.2005.10.017
16. Adrangi, B., Chatrath, A., Dhanda, K.K., Raffiee, K.: Chaos in oil prices? Evidence from futures markets. Energy Econ. **23**(4), 405–425 (2001). https://doi.org/10.1016/S0140-9883(00)00079-7
17. Panas, E., Ninni, V.: Are oil markets chaotic? A non-linear dynamic analysis. Energy Econ. **22**(5), 549–568 (2000). https://doi.org/10.1016/S0140-9883(00)00049-9
18. Gori, F., Ludovisi, D., Cerritelli, P.F.: Forecast of oil price and consumption in the short term under three scenarios: parabolic, linear and chaotic behaviour. Energy **32**(7), 1291–1296 (2007). https://doi.org/10.1016/j.energy.2006.07.005
19. Rehrl, T., Friedrich, R.: Modelling long-term oil price and extraction with a Hubbert approach: the LOPEX model. Energy Policy **34**(15), 2413–2428 (2006). https://doi.org/10.1016/j.enpol.2005.03.021
20. Kaboudan, M.A.: Compumetric forecasting of crude oil prices. In: Proceedings of the 2001 Congress on Evolutionary Computation, pp. 283–287 (2001)
21. Wang, S., Yu, L., Lai, K.K.: A novel hybrid AI system framework for crude oil price forecasting. In: Shi, Y., Xu, W., Chen, Z. (eds.) CASDMKM 2004. LNCS (LNAI), vol. 3327, pp. 233–242. Springer, Heidelberg (2005). https://doi.org/10.1007/978-3-540-30537-8_26
22. Fernandez, V.: Forecasting commodity prices by classification methods: the cases of crude oil and natural gas spot prices (2007). http://citeseerx.ist.psu.edu/viewdoc/download?doi=10.1.1.87.2375&rep=rep1&type=pdf
23. Abuselidze, G., Slobodianyk, A.: Social responsibility of business and government in the conditions of the COVID-19 pandemic. E3S Web Conf. **210**, 15016 (2020). https://doi.org/10.1051/e3sconf/202021015016
24. Clerides, S.: Retail fuel price response to oil price shocks in EU countries. Cyprus Econ. Policy Rev. **4**(1), 25–45 (2010)
25. Charfeddine, L., Barkat, K.: Short-and long-run asymmetric effect of oil prices and oil and gas revenues on the real GDP and economic diversification in oil-dependent economy. Energy Econ. **86**, 104680 (2020). https://doi.org/10.1016/j.eneco.2020.104680
26. Adeosun, O.A., Tabash, M.I., Anagreh, S.: Oil price and economic performance: additional evidence from advanced economies. Resour. Policy **77**, 102666 (2022). https://doi.org/10.1016/j.resourpol.2022.102666
27. Talha, M., Sohail, M., Tariq, R., Ahmad, M.T.: Impact of oil prices, energy consumption and economic growth on the inflation rate in Malaysia. Cuadernos de Economia. **44**(124), 26–32 (2021). https://doi.org/10.32826/cude.v1i124.501
28. Bala, U., Chin, L.: Asymmetric impacts of oil price on inflation: an empirical study of African OPEC member countries. Energies **11**(11), 3017 (2018). https://doi.org/10.3390/en11113017
29. Abuselidze, G.: Competitiveness analysis of the georgian transport and logistics system in the black sea region: challenges and perspectives. In: Gervasi, O., Murgante, et al. (eds.) ICCSA 2021. LNCS, vol. 12952, pp. 133–148. Springer, Cham (2021). https://doi.org/10.1007/978-3-030-86973-1_10
30. Pedersen, M.: Propagation of shocks to food and energy prices: an international comparison. Central Bank of Chile, Santiago (2011)
31. Mikhailov, A.Yu., Burakov, D.B., Didenko, V.Yu.: Relationship between oil price and macroeconomic indicators in Russia. Finan. Theory Pract. **23**(2), 105–116 (2019). (In Russian) https://doi.org/10.26794/2587-5671-2019-23-2-105-116

32. Mukhtarov, S., Mammadov, J., Ahmadov, F.: The impact of oil prices on inflation: the case of Azerbaijan. Int. J. Energy Econ. Policy **9**(4), 97–102 (2019). https://doi.org/10.32479/ijeep.7712

33. Zaouali, S.: Impact of higher oil prices on the Chinese economy. OPEC Rev. **31**(3), 191–214 (2007). https://doi.org/10.1111/j.1468-0076.2007.00183.x

34. Jiang, M., Kong, D.: The impact of international crude oil prices on energy stock prices: evidence from China. Energy Res. Lett. **2**(4) (2021). https://doi.org/10.46557/001c.28133

35. Statista: Retrieved from Average annual Brent crude oil price from 1976 to 2021 (2021). https://www.statista.com/statistics/262860/uk-brent-crude-oil-price-changes-since-1976/

36. The World Bank. Retrieved from Inflation (2020). https://www.worldbank.org/en/home

37. National Statistics Office of Georgia: Retrieved from Consumer Price Index (2021). https://www.geostat.ge/ka/modules/categories/26/samomkhmareblo-fasebis-indeksi-inflatsia

38. Macrotendrs: Retrieved from Crude Oil Prices - 70 Year Historical Chart (2020). https://www.macrotrends.net/1369/crude-oil-price-history-chart

39. Gulf: Retrieved from Fuel Prices (2021). https://gulf.ge/ge/fuel_prices

40. Abuselidze, G.: Modern challenges of monetary policy strategies: inflation and devaluation influence on economic development of the country. Acad. Strateg. Manag. J. **18**(4), 1–10 (2019)

Cognitive Impairment and Dementia Data Modelling

Dessislava Petrova-Antonova[1](✉) (iD), Todor Kunchev[2], Ilina Manova[3] (iD), and Ivaylo Spasov[3]

[1] Sofia University, GATE Institute, FMI, Sofia, Bulgaria
`d.petrova@fmi.uni-sofia.bg`
[2] University Hospital "Sofiamed", Sofia, Bulgaria
[3] Rila Solutions, Sofia, Bulgaria
`{ilinam,ispasov}@rila.bg`

Abstract. Recently, a lot of data with variety factors and indicators of cognitive diseases is available for clinical research. Although the transformation of information to particular data model is straight-forward, a lot of challenges arise if data from different repositories is integrated. Since each data source keeps entities with different names and relationships at different levels of granularity, the information can be partially lost or not properly presented. It is therefore important to have a common data model that provides a unified description of different factors and indicators related to cognitive diseases. This paper proposes a hierarchical data model of patients with cognitive disorders, which keeps the semantics of the data in a human-readable format and accelerates the interoperability of clinical datasets. It defines data entities, their attributes and relationships related to diagnosis and treatment. The data model covers four main aspects of the patient's profile, including personal profile, anamnestic profile, related to social status, everyday habits, and head trauma history, clinical profile, describing medical investigations and assessments, comorbidities and the most likely diagnose, and treatment profile with prescribed medications. It provides a native vocabulary, improving data availability, saving efforts, accelerating clinical data interoperability, and standardizing data to minimize risk of rework and misunderstandings. The data model enables the application of machine learning algorithms by helping scientists to understand the semantics of information through a holistic view of patient. It is intended to be used by researchers in the field of Biostatistics, Bioinformatics, Neuroscience, etc. supporting them in content mapping and data integration from different datasets.

Keywords: Cognitive impairment · Dementia · Data model · Interoperability of clinical data

1 Introduction

Cognitive diseases are disorders of brain function that primarily affect cognitive abilities. While they can be the result of many medical conditions like a single or repeated head injuries, infections, toxicity, substance abuse, benign and malign brain tumors, many

O. Gervasi et al. (Eds.): ICCSA 2022, LNCS 13376, pp. 58–71, 2022.
https://doi.org/10.1007/978-3-031-10450-3_5

genetic diseases, etc., the majority of cognitive disorders are caused by neurodegenerative diseases, vascular damage to the brain and the various combinations between them. Cognitive disorders and especially dementia – a condition severe enough to compromise social and/or occupational functioning [1] – have a tremendous social significance to all the parties involved in their diagnosis and treatment. Patients undergo an ever-progressing cognitive decline and gradually lose independence, which puts a heavy burden on their caregivers – family members, hired professionals or the personnel of specialized institutions. Cognitive disorders also present a huge public and financial burden as the number of cases increases with every decade. Finally, they also pose several still unanswered moral and ethical issues.

The tendency for increased life expectancy led to an increased dementia morbidity as each decade of human life exponentially increases the chance of developing cognitive decline, something true for all types of dementia, but especially for the degenerative types. It is considered that about 5.5% of people over 65 have dementia and that the number of global cases is expected to double in every 20 years reaching the overwhelming number of 115 million until 2040 [2]. In the European Union, more than 160 million people are over 60, about 6.2% of Europeans have some form of dementia (or almost 10 million people) and European cases are expected to rise to 14 million until 2030 and almost 19 million until 2050 [3]. This data highlights the need for both global and national plans to combat this increase in dementia morbidity both clinically by an increased quality of dementia diagnosis and treatment and scientifically by increased dementia research. On a clinical level, diagnosis should be as accurate and as early as possible, pharmacological treatment should be prescribed as early as possible, the required infrastructure for cognitive rehabilitation should be present, vascular risk factors should be strictly controlled for the prophylaxis of vascular dementia, cases should be gradually followed-up and clinical guidelines should be updated as needed. This would result to early and adequate diagnosis of mild cognitive impairment with high risk of transforming to dementia, slowing down and prevention of late-stage cases of dementia where possible, significant decrease in morbidity and the subsequent medical and social burdens, reduction in medication and hospitalization needs and improvement of patients' and caregivers' quality of life [4].

Digitalization of medical data, particularly in cognitive diseases, could not only ease clinical management of those diseases by creating registries of patients, enabling strict follow-up, and creating a robust schedule of cognitive rehabilitation, but to also hugely amplify the ability to conduct large scale research by applying Big Data and Artificial Intelligence (AI) technologies. To this end, many digital repositories have been created around the world with the aim to enhance research on cognitive diseases [5], storing variety factors and indicators of the patient history and current state. Although the transformation of information to a particular data model is straightforward, a lot of challenges arise when data from different sources need to be integrated. Since each data source keeps entities with different names and relationships at different levels of granularity, a part of information can be lost or not properly presented during that transformation. Thus, interoperable data repositories are needed to enable data exchange and sharing in a standardized manner [6]. In such context, a great effort has been made on the development of ontologies in the biomedical domain as a whole and particularly in the dementia domain. The Mental Functioning Ontology is an upper-level ontology, which represents the aspects of mental functioning, including mental processes and qualities, while the Mental Disease Ontology describes and categorize mental disorders [7]. An ontological model representing the relationships between people with dementia and the entities they interact with is proposed by Pennington [8]. The risk factors that can cause dementia are modelled in In-MINDD ontology [9], while the focal-onset dementias are modelled by the SOLOMON ontology [10]. In addition, disease specific ontologies have been developed such as Alzheimer's disease ontology [11], Neurocognitive Integrated Ontology modelling Mild Cognitive Impairment related to as Alzheimer's disease [12] and Parkinson's disease ontology [13]. In addition, data models tailored to different data repositories exist such as the multidimensional data model for a Dementia Care Mapping data warehouse [14].

To the best of our knowledge, there is no comprehensive data model covering variety domains of cognitive diseases related to personal characteristics, anamnestic profile, clinical history, and treatment. Focusing on a single domain or part of them leads to loss of information for the characterization of cognitive diseases. Therefore, a common data model that integrates the information of multiple domains would be of great support to clinicians and researchers involved in the early detection, precise diagnosis, and treatment of the cognitive diseases. In order to avoid incorrect data transformations and loss of information and to enable data integration from variety of sources, the paper proposes a common hierarchical data model, which keeps the semantics of the data in a human readable format and accelerates interoperability of clinical datasets. The data model can be used by researchers as a standalone data model for clinical data as well as a middleware for mapping between different data models. It enables application of Machine Learning (ML) and Artificial Intelligence (AI) algorithms by helping data scientists to understand the semantics of information through a holistic view of patient.

The rest of the paper is organized as follows. Section 2 describes the approach followed for elaboration of the data model. Section 3 presents the developed data model. Section 4 gives conclusions and directions for future work.

2   Data Modeling Approach

This section describes the process followed for development of the patient's data model. It includes the following iteration step, shown in Fig. 1:

- Step 1: Definition of requirements to the data model.
- Step 2: Building of data model based on literature review and expertise of clinicians.
- Step 3: Formalization of data model using Unified Modelling Language (UML) [15], YAML Ain't Markup Language [16] notations and corresponding software tools.
- Step 4: Validation of data model.

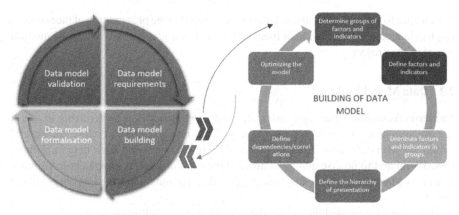

Fig. 1. Process of elaboration of the data model.

2.1 Data Model Requirements

This section presents the requirements that have been identified with the highest priority for creating the data model (Table 1).

Table 1. Data model requirements.

ID	Example	Type
DR1	The model should present the functional specification for the patient record reflecting the described structure in horizontal and vertical plan as well as the correlations and interactions between the included properties	Domain
DR2	The model should be oriented towards presenting data at the Patient level	Domain
DR3	The model should allow application for modelling all kind of cognitive disorders in unified way	Domain
DR4	The model should integrate information through biomedical abstractions, using proper medical terminology	Domain
DR5	The model should integrate diverse medical data at different levels of granularity	Domain
DR6	The model should have a temporal/historical dimension (analyzing patients' data over time)	Domain
DR7	The model should set correlations that discover a relationship between the patient's status, historical data, and disease progression	Domain
DR8	The model aligned with the external knowledge sources, such as ADNI database	Domain
TR1	The chosen format of presentation of the model must be known/popular and understandable to the medical expert and technical staff to be successfully validated	Technical
TR2	The model must provide a complete and non-contradictory structure to be used in the selection of the proper database and its creation	Technical

The full list of requirements includes others related to the presentation of the model in English language and inclusion of medical terms reviewed and approved by the medical expert in the project.

2.2 Data Model Building

The basic factors and indicators associated with cognitive diseases occurring in senior age are systematically analyzed based on in depth review of the literature and several interviews with clinicians. The data model is designed to provide basic data for follow-up work related to precise diagnosis and prognosis of disease development in patients, as well as generalized conclusions about dependencies and relations in the course of the disease.

The approach for building of the data model includes following steps:

1. Determining groups of factors and indicators, which are relevant to risk assessment, diagnosis of the disease and its development.
2. Defining factors and indicators and their description.
3. Distributing the factors and indicators in their corresponding groups.
4. Defining the hierarchy of presentation, where appropriate.
5. Defining dependencies/correlations between groups and/or factors and indicators, where they exist.
6. Optimizing the model.

Steps (1) and (2) are completed by conducting interviews with practicing neurologists and neuropsychologists in two neurological clinics in Sofia. The lead medical researcher in the project, using his personal expertise, defined the groups (3) and the distribution of the factors and indicators in them. The output of steps (4) and (5) are based on the performed functional analysis. Simultaneously, the team researched existing public databases related to studies of patients with proven Alzheimer's disease. Using the findings of the performed gap analysis, the data model is supplemented and optimized (6).

During the building of the data model, three main difficulties are encountered. First, there is a lack of previous centralized digital records of patients in Bulgaria, who are diagnosed with cognitive degenerative diseases in the senior age. Next, the access to existing relevant public digital databases is limited. Last, but not least the terminology is ambiguous, which complicates the performed gap analysis.

The presented data model claims to be innovative based on completeness and complexity of description (at existing levels, correlations, and relations) of the captured data.

2.3 Data Model Formalization

The main entities of the data model are specified using Unified Modelling Language (UML), while the whole model is implemented with "YAML Ain't Markup Language" (YAML). UML is a standardized modelling language, which uses mainly graphical notations to create and exchange meaningful models. It is independent form the development process and support extensibility of the models through extension of the core concepts. YAML is a data serialization language designed to be friendly and useful to people working with data. It is portable between programming languages as well as expressive and extensible, supporting serialization of native data structure. Since YAML is human readable, the validation of the data models created using it can be easily validated of the non-technical experts such as the case of the current data model.

2.4 Data Model Validation

Clinical expert in the field of cognitive diseases performed the evaluation and curation of the data model by checking the definition of data entities and their attributes as well as the consistency of the relationships. He was selected based on his clinical experience in leading neurological departments dealing with neurodegenerative states in Sofia, Bulgaria, and his research work on cognitive dysfunction in various neurological diseases. In addition, a mapping between the proposed data model and types of study data provided by Alzheimer's Disease Neuroimaging Initiative (ADNI) is performed [17]. The results shows that the data model covers all main data types – clinical, genetic, image and biospecimen.

3 Results

The data model defines data entities and their attributes and relationships needed to create a patient's profile. It is developed with the purpose of unifying and structuring the information relevant to four main domains of the profile – personal data, medical history data, objective clinical investigations and treatment prescribed. The model gives insights about the early life, midlife and old life risk and protective factors for dementia. Figure 2 presents a UML diagram of the main entities of the data model.

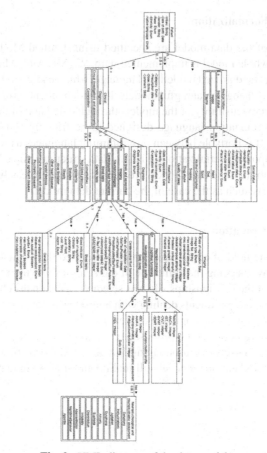

Fig. 2. UML diagram of the data model.

3.1 Personal Profile

The Personal profile includes the patient's personal data. The personal data is modelled as a Patient entity, including attributes such as date of birth, gender, race, ethnicity, and native language. Figure 3 shows the personal profile defined in.yaml format. The rest factors and indicators included in the data model are defined in a similar manner.

Age related cognitive decline is influenced by midlife and old age risk factors [18]. For example, older women are more likely to develop cognitive impairments than men of the same age. Differences in the development of dementia decreases between blacks and whites and increased between Hispanics and whites [19].

```
1    version: 1.0
2    patient:
3      description: 'Information of a patient'
4      type: object
5      properties:
6        initials:
7          description: 'Initials of a patient'
8          type: string
9        birthDate:
10          description: 'Birthdate of a patient'
11          type: date
12        gender:
13          description: 'Gender of a patient'
14          type: property
15          items:
16   >        oneof: …
20            type: string
21        race:
22          description: 'Race of a patient'
23          type: property
24          items:
25   >        oneof: …
30            type: string
31        ethnicity:
32          description: 'Ethnicity of a patient'
33          type: property
34          items:
35   >        oneof: …
39            type: string
40        nativeLanguage:
41          desciption: 'Native language of a patient'
42          type: property
43          items:
44   >        oneof: …
48            type: string
```

Fig. 3. Patient entity presented in .yaml format.

3.2 Anamnestic Profile

The medical history data, presented in the Anamnestic profile, is related to the patient's social status, everyday habits, and the presence of any head traumas, modelled as separate entities.

Social Status. The Social status entity is defined with attributes – years of education, marital state, coexistence (living alone, with a caregiver or in a specialized institution), employment, financial state, and computer literacy. The dementia risk is reduced by higher childhood education levels and lifelong learning [19, 20]. Recent studies shows that cognitive stimulation is more important in early life [17]. A reason for this could be that the people of intensive cognitive function seek out cognitively stimulating activities and education [21]. Similarly, there is relation between cognitive function and employment. People having jobs with a cognitive demand tend to show less cognitive decline before, and sometimes after retirement [22]. The social contact might be considered as a factor that reduces the risk for development of dementia, since it enhances the cognitive function. The marital state contributes to social engagement since the married people usually have more interpersonal contact. People who are living alone or widowed people are at a higher risk of dementia [23].

Habits. The Habits entity has attributes such as smoking, alcohol consumption, physical activity and sport, diet, drug abuse, duration, and quality of sleep. There is a strong evidence that the smoking increases the risk for developing dementia and its stopping reduces this risk, even in old age [24]. Similarly, the excessive alcohol consumption leads to brain changes and increased dementia risk [25]. Drinking more than 21 units (10 ml or 8 g of pure alcohol) per week is associated with a higher risk than drinking less than 14 units [26]. Drinking more than 14 units might be related to right sided hippocampal atrophy on MRI [27]. Regarding the diet, the recent studies are more focused on the nutrition rather than on dietary ingredients. According to WHO guidelines, a Mediterranean diet reduces the risk of cognitive decline or dementia [28]. The sleep disturbance has been linked with Aβ deposition, low grade inflammation, reduced glymphatic clearance pathways activation, increased Tau, cardiovascular disease, and hypoxia [18]. It could be part of natural history of the dementia syndrome and considered as a risk factor. There is evidence that the higher physical activity reduces the risk of dementia, but the interpretation depends on other factors such as age, gender, social class, comorbidity and cultural differences. Inactivity might be a prerequisite or consequence of dementia. According to WHO, the physical activity has a small effect on normal cognition, but more significant one on mild cognitive impairment [28].

Head Trauma. The Head Trauma entity is described with the date of the event, its severity, and the availability of head imaging at the time of the event – computed tomography (CT) or magnetic resonance imaging (MRI). The severe head trauma, caused by incidents, military exposures, recreational sports, firearms, and others is associated with widespread hyperphosphorylated tau pathology and increased dementia risk [29, 30].

3.3 Clinical Profile

The Clinical profile is described with data about medical investigations and assessments, comorbidities, and their severity and ultimately, as well as the most likely diagnose. It covers 6 aspects of diagnostics: Imaging, Neuropsychological and neuropsychiatric assessment, Cerebrospinal fluid biomarkers, Blood tests, Genetic data, and Comorbidities.

Imaging. CT and MRI scans are used for registration of the presence and severity of both neurodegenerative disease and vascular disease. MRI data might be assessed by several scales and scores as follows: global cortical atrophy scale (GCA), medial temporal lobe atrophy score (MTA) and posterior atrophy score of parietal atrophy (PCA, Koedam score) for neurodegeneration and the Fazekas scale for white matter lesions for vascular damage.

Neuropsychological and Neuropsychiatric Assessment. Neuropsychological and neuropsychiatric assessment is based on different tests for evaluation of cognitive domains (Table 2, rows 1–5) and neuropsychiatric state (Table 2, rows 6–10).

Table 2. Neuropsychological and neuropsychiatric assessment.

No	Cognitive domain/neuropsychiatric state	Test
1	General cognition	Mini-Mental State Examination (MMSE) and Montreal Cognitive Assessment (MoCA)
2	Verbal fluency	Isaac's Set Test (IST)
3	Verbal episodic memory	California Verbal Learning Test (CVLT)
4	Visuospatial memory	Brief Visuospatial Memory Test – Revised (BVMT-R)
5	Information processing and executive functioning	Symbol Digit Modalities Test (SDMT)
6	Presence and severity of depression	Beck's Depression Inventory (BDI)
7	Presence and severity of anxiety	Hamilton Anxiety Rating Scale (HAM-A)
8	Presence and severity of fatigue	Fatigue Severity Scale (FSS)
9	Presence and severity of neuropsychiatric and behavioural changes	Neuropsychiatric Inventory (NPI) questionnaire
10	Possibility for independent daily functioning	Lawton Instrumental Activities of Daily Living (IADL) scale

Cerebrospinal Fluid Biomarkers. Cerebrospinal fluid biomarkers are used to measure total tau protein (T-tau), phosphorylated tau protein (P-tau), beta-amyloid peptide 1–42 (Aβ42), P-Tau/T-tau ratio and Aβ42/Aβ40 ratio. Their interpretation is closely related to Personal profile of the patient, for example age and gender. Amyloid and tau indicate increased risk for development of cognitive impairment in older adults [18]. People with cognitive impairment and negative amyloid results is unlikely to be diagnosed with Alzheimer's disease in the next few years.

Blood Tests. Blood tests include levels of vitamin B12, B9, thyroid stimulating hormone, cholesterol, hemoglobin, glucose, creatinine, sedimentation rate, etc. Observational studies show that folate and B vitamins, Vitamin C, D, E, and selenium are potential protective factors against cognitive decline [31]. Apolipoprotein E is a protein responsible for transportation of the fats and cholesterol in the blood. At the same time, the APOE gene supports the production of the apolipoprotein E.

Comorbidities. Comorbidities are related to presence of arterial hypertension, dyslipidemia, diabetes, obesity, atrial fibrillation, carotid stenosis, autoimmune diseases and autoimmune vasculitis, psychiatric diseases, or other comorbid diseases. They may accelerate the progression of dementia [32]. For example, cognitive decline may be exacerbated in older people with type 2 diabetes [33]. Increased risk of a late life dementia correlates with persistent midlife hypertension [18]. In addition, the presence of cognitive disorder could affect and complicate the clinical care of other comorbid conditions [34].

Dementia Disease. The most likely dementia disease of the patient is described with one of the following diseases: Alzheimer's disease, vascular dementia, mixed dementia, Lewy body dementia, frontotemporal dementia, Parkinson's dementia, Parkinson's plus syndromes.

3.4 Treatment Profile

The Treatment profile is related to medications prescribed to the patient. The medications are divided in groups – medications for degenerative cognitive disorders, medications for cerebrovascular disease, antiplatelet and anticoagulant drugs, neuroleptic drugs, antidepressant drugs, medications for sleeping. Each medication is described with the date of prescription and the daily dosage in milligrams.

The neuroleptic drugs are sometimes used to treat the behavioral complications in presence of dementia. At the same time, they may worsen already poor cognitive function [35]. Regardless of sleep duration, people taking hypnotics are at greater risk of dementia than those who did not. For example, benzodiazepines are associated with falls and possibly dementia [36]. Antidepressants are widely used medication for treatment of anxiety and depression. Recent studies shows that the antidepressant therapy significantly increases the risk of dementia [37]. Along with the antidepressant, the urological and antiparkinsonian drugs with definite anticholinergic activity are associated with future development of dementia, with associations persisting up to 20 years after exposure [38]. In contrast, the antiplatelet drugs, which have a good tolerance in stroke prevention, may decrease the risk of vascular dementia [39].

4   Conclusions and Future Work

Cognitive can be the result of many medical conditions like a single or repeated head injuries, infections, toxicity, substance abuse, benign and malign brain tumors. Most of them are caused by neurodegenerative diseases, vascular damage to the brain and the various combinations between them. The medical investigations and assessments related to diagnosis and treatment of cognitive disorders are characterized by great variety, including medical imaging, neuropsychological and neuropsychiatric assessment, cerebrospinal fluid biomarkers, blood tests etc. The diversity of factors and indicators of cognitive diseases naturally implies the development of comprehensive data model describing history and status of patients with cognitive decline such as that proposed in this study. The main contribution and benefits can be summarized as follows:

- A common, actionable, and shareable data model is elaborated, allowing researchers in the field of Biostatistics, Bioinformatics, Neuroscience, etc. to conduct research efficiently using available datasets for patients with cognitive disorders.

- The data model delivers a native vocabulary, which improves data availability, saves efforts, and standardize data to minimize risk of rework and misunderstandings.
- The data model enables application of Machine Learning (ML) and Artificial Intelligence (AI) algorithms by helping data scientists to understand the semantics of information through a holistic view of patient.
- The data model accelerates interoperability of clinical datasets and support content mapping by classifying and semantically annotating the data.

The future work includes development of ontology of cognitive diseases on top of proposed data model. The ontology will be base for implementation of a graph database that integrates data from different sources for advanced data analytics. A dedicated Extract Transform Load (ETL) procedure and a corresponding tool are planned to be developed to import ADNI study data. Thus, the proposed data model will be validated based on actual health records.

Acknowledgements. This research work has been supported by GATE project, funded by the Horizon 2020 WIDESPREAD-2018-2020 TEAMING Phase 2 programme under grant agreement no. 857155, by Operational Programme Science and Education for Smart Growth under Grant Agreement no. BG05M2OP001-1.003-0002-C01 and by the Bulgarian National Science fund under project no. KP-06-N32/5.

References

1. Hugo, J., Ganguli, M.: Dementia and cognitive impairment: epidemiology, diagnosis, and treatment. Clin Geriatr Med. **30**(3), 421–42 (2014). https://doi.org/10.1016/j.cger.2014. 04.001. (Epub 2014 Jun 12. PMID: 25037289; PMCID: PMC4104432)
2. Prince, M., Bryce, R., Albanese, E., Wimo, A., Ribeiro, W., Ferri, C.P.: The global prevalence of dementia: a systematic review and metaanalysis. Alzheimer's Dementia **9**(1), 63-75.e2 (2013)
3. Alzheimer Europe. Dementia in Europe Yearbook 2019 (2019). https://www.alzheimer-eur ope.org/Publications/Dementia-in-Europe-Yearbooks. Accessed 21 Jan 2022
4. Bulgarian Society of Dementia, National consensus on dementia diagnosis, treatment and care (2015). http://www.dementia-bulgaria.com/index.php/en/events-en/nat-cons-15-en. Accessed 13 Feb 2022
5. Ashish, N., Bhatt, P., Toga, A.W.: Global data sharing in Alzheimer disease research. Alzheimer Dis. Assoc. Disord. **30**(2), 160–168 (2016)
6. Burgun, A., Bodenreider, O.: Accessing and integrating data and knowledge for biomedical research. Yearbook of medical informatics, pp. 91–101 (2008)
7. Hastings, J., Ceusters, W., Jensen, M., Mulligan, K., Smith, B.: Representing mental functioning: ontologies for mental health and disease. In: Towards an Ontology of Mental Functioning Workshop, Proceedings of the Third International Conference on Biomedical Ontology, pp. 1–5 (2012)
8. Pennington, D.R.: Keys to their own voices: social tags for a dementia ontology as a human right. Social Tagging for Linked Data Across Environments, p. 19. Facet Publishing (2018)
9. Roantree, M., O'Donoghue, J., O'Kelly, N., et al.: Mapping longitudinal studies to risk factors in an ontology for dementia. Health Inf. J. **22**(2), 414–426 (2016)

10. Skarzynski, M., Craig, A., Taswell, C.: SOLOMON: an ontology for Sensory-Onset, Language-Onset and Motor-Onset dementias. In: 2015 IEEE International Conference on Bioinformatics and Biomedicine (BIBM), pp. 969–972 (2015)
11. Malhotra, A., Younesi, E., Gündel, M., Müller, B., Heneka, M.T., Hofmann-Apitius, M.: ADO: a disease ontology representing the domain knowledge specific to Alzheimer's disease. Alzheimer's & dementia. J. Alzheimer's Assoc. **10**(2), 238–246 (2014)
12. Gomez-Valades, A., Martinez-Tomas, R., Rincon, M.: Integrative base ontology for the research analysis of alzheimer's disease-related mild cognitive impairment. Front. Neuroinform. **15**, 561691 (2021)
13. Younesi, E., et al.: PDON: Parkinson's disease ontology for representation and modeling of the Parkinson's disease knowledge domain. Theor. Biol. Med. Model. **12**, 20 (2015)
14. Khalid, S., Small, N., Neagu, D., Surr, C.: A Study proposing a data model for a dementia care mapping (DCM) data warehouse for potential secondary uses of dementia care data. Int. J. Healthcare Inf. Syst. Inf. **14**(1), 61–79 (2019)
15. Object Management Group, OMG Unified Modeling Language, Specification (2017). https://www.omg.org/spec/UML/2.5.1/PDF
16. Ben-Kiki, O., Evans, C., döt Net, I.: YAML Ain't Markup Language, 3rd edn (2009). https://yaml.org/spec/1.2/spec.html#id2763754. Accessed 25 Jan 2022
17. The Alzheimer's Disease Neuroimaging Initiative: General Procedure Manual. http://adni.loni.usc.edu/wp-content/uploads/2010/09/ADNI_GeneralProceduresManual.pdf. Accessed 02 Mar 2022
18. Livingston, G., Sommerlad, A., Orgeta, V., et al.: Dementia prevention, intervention, and care. Lancet **390**, 2673–2734 (2017)
19. Chen, C., Zissimopoulos, J.M.: Racial and ethnic differences in trends in dementia prevalence and risk factors in the United States. Alzheimer's & dementia (New York, N.Y.), vol. 4, pp. 510–520 (2018)
20. Norton, S., Matthews, F.E., Barnes, D.E., Yaffe, K., Brayne, C.: Potential for primary prevention of Alzheimer's disease: an analysis of population-based data. Lancet Neurol. **13**, 788–794 (2014)
21. Kajitani, S., Sakata, K., McKenzie, C.: Occupation, retirement and cognitive functioning. Ageing Soc. **37**, 1568–1596 (2017)
22. Xue, B., et al.: Effect of retirement on cognitive function: the Whitehall II cohort study. Eur. J. Epidemiol. **33**(10), 989–1001 (2017). https://doi.org/10.1007/s10654-017-0347-7
23. Sommerlad, A., Ruegger, J., Singh-Manoux, A., Lewis, G., Livingston, G.: Marriage and risk of dementia: systematic review and meta-analysis of observational studies. J. Neurol. Neurosurg. Psychiatry **89**, 231–238 (2018)
24. Chang, C.C., Zhao, Y., Lee, C.W., Ganguli, M.: Smoking, death, and Alzheimer disease: a case of competing risks. Alzheimer Dis. Assoc. Disord. **26**, 300–306 (2012)
25. Schwarzinger, M., Pollock, B.G., Hasan, O.S.M., et al.: Contribution of alcohol use disorders to the burden of dementia in France 2008–13: a nationwide retrospective cohort study. Lancet Public Health **3**, e124–e132 (2018)
26. Sabia, S., Fayosse, A., Dumurgier, J., et al.: Alcohol consumption and risk of dementia: 23 year follow-up of Whitehall II cohort study. BMJ **362**, k2927 (2018)
27. Topiwala, A., Allan, C.L., Valkanova, V., et al.: Moderate alcohol consumption as risk factor for adverse brain outcomes and cognitive decline: longitudinal cohort study. BMJ **357**, j2353 (2017)
28. WHO: Risk reduction of cognitive decline and dementia: WHO guidelines. Geneva: World Health Organization (2019)
29. Fann, J.R., Ribe, A.R., Pedersen, H.S., et al.: Long-term risk of dementia among people with traumatic brain injury in Denmark: a population-based observational cohort study. Lancet Psychiatry **5**, 424–431 (2018)

30. Barnes, D.E., Byers, A.L., Gardner, R.C., Seal, K.H., Boscardin, W.J., Yaffe, K.: Association of mild traumatic brain injury with and without loss of consciousness with dementia in US military veterans. JAMA Neurol. **75**, 1055–1061 (2018)

31. Hersi, M., Irvine, B., Gupta, P., Gomes, J., Birkett, N., Krewski, D.: Risk factors associated with the onset and progression of Alzheimer's disease: a systematic review of the evidence. Neurotoxicology **61**, 143–187 (2017). https://doi.org/10.1016/j.neuro.2017.03.006. (Epub (2017))

32. Savva, G.M., Stephan, B.C.: Alzheimer's Society Vascular Dementia Systematic Review Group: Epidemiological studies of the effect of stroke on incident dementia: a systematic review. Stroke **41**, e41–e46 (2010)

33. Whitmer, R.A., Karter, A.J., Yaffe, K., Quesenberry, C.P., Selby, J.V.: Hypoglycemic episodes and risk of dementia in older patients with type 2 diabetes mellitus. JAMA **301**, 1565–1572 (2009)

34. Keenan, T.D., Goldacre, R., Goldacre, M.J.: Associations between age-related macular degeneration, Alzheimer disease, and dementia: record linkage study of hospital admissions. JAMA Ophthalmol. **132**, 63–68 (2014)

35. McShane, R., Keene, J., Gedling, K., Fairburn, C., Jacoby, R., Hope, T.: Do neuroleptic drugs hasten cognitive decline in dementia? Prospective study with necropsy follow up. BMJ: British Med. J. **314**(7076), 266–270 (1997)

36. Ohara, T., Honda, T., Hata, J., et al.: Association between daily sleep duration and risk of dementia and mortality in a Japanese community. J. Am. Geriatr. Soc. **66**, 1911–1918 (2018)

37. Wang, Y.C., et al.: Increased risk of dementia in patients with antidepressants: a meta-analysis of observational studies. Behav. Neurol. **10**, 5315098 (2018)

38. Richardson, K., Fox, C., Maidment, I., Steel, N., Loke, Y.K., Arthur, A., et al.: Anticholinergic drugs and risk of dementia: case-control study. BMJ **361**, k1315 (2018)

39. Chabriat, H., Bousser, M.G.: Vascular dementia: potential of antiplatelet agents in prevention. Eur. Neurol. **55**(2), 61–9 (2006). https://doi.org/10.1159/000091981. (Epub, Mar 10. PMID: 16534208 (2006))

Application of Multi-criteria Analysis to Evaluate the Potential for the Occurrence of Cavities in Serra do Gandarela and Presentation in 3D Geological Modeling Software

Jonas de Oliveira Laranjeira[1,2](✉) ⑩, Diogo Sepe Aleixo[3],
Andréia Bicalho Henriques[4] ⑩, and Pedro Benedito Casagrande[4] ⑩

[1] Universidade Federal de Minas Gerais (UFMG), Escola de Engenharia Curso de
Pós-Graduação em Engenharia Metalúrgica, Materiais e de Minas, Av. Antônio Carlos 6627,
Belo Horizonte, Brazil
jonas.olaranjeira@gmail.com
[2] LB Mineração e Servicos, Rua Júpiter 69, Belo Horizonte, Brazil
[3] Universidade Federal de Minas Gerais (UFMG), LB Mineração e Servicos, Rua Júpiter 69,
Belo Horizonte, Brazil
[4] Universidade Federal de Minas Gerais (UFMG), Escola de Engenharia, Av. Antônio Carlos
6627, Belo Horizonte, Brazil
{abicalho,pcasagrande}@demin.ufmg.br

Abstract. The study of cavities and their areas of influence for purposes of environmental intervention has gained increasing relevance in Brazilian legislation. Serra do Gandarela is a geomorphological site, located in the State of Minas Gerais, which concentrates a large amount of speleological features, in addition to mineral resources. This article seeks to present multi-criteria analysis techniques in a GIS environment to measure the potential for the occurrence of cavities in the region in order to arrive at a map of the speleological potential of the site. The result will then be superimposed on a geological model developed for the region, in order to be able to observe transversal profiles in order to correlate the results considering the imputed geological and geomorphological factors. The importance of the analysis carried out is to expose the areas with the highest concentration of factors favorable to the development of cavities in regions close to mining activities, with the objective of guiding mining activities in a less harmful way to the environment. The suggestion of presentation in 3D platform is made to allow a more dynamic observation in addition to highlighting topographic and slope factors.

Keywords: Speleological potential · Serra do Gandarela · Geoprocessing · Geological modeling

O. Gervasi et al. (Eds.): ICCSA 2022, LNCS 13376, pp. 72–83, 2022.
https://doi.org/10.1007/978-3-031-10450-3_6

1   Introduction

Serra do Gandarela, located in the northeast portion of the Quadrilátero Ferrífero, in the State of Minas Gerais, is a geological site with one of the greatest geodiversities in the region (Passos 2015) [1]. Works such as that of Santos (2017) [2] approach the region as having a rich and unique association between biotic and abiotic aspects, including ferruginous formations of the Quadrilátero Ferrífero that are economically viable for mining. The map in Fig. 1 illustrates a digital elevation model of the Quadrilátero Ferrífero region with the nomenclature of the mountain ranges present at the site (Casagrande *et al.* 2019) [3].

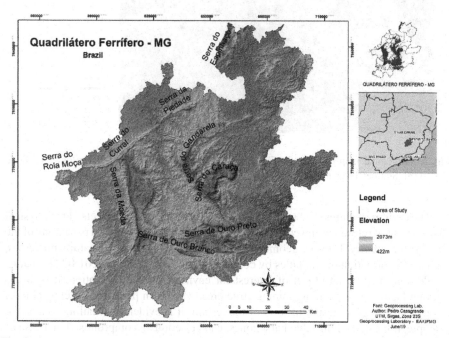

Fig. 1. Location Map of the Mountains Present in the Iron Quadrangle, contemplating the Serra do Gandarela. Source: Casagrande *et al.* (2019) [3]

Among the great geodiversities present in Serra do Gandarela, the most relevant for this research are the natural underground cavities. These are present mainly in the canga covers and in the lithologies of the Itabira Group, especially the Iron rocks of the Cauê Formation and mainly the Dolomitic Limestone rocks of the Gandarela Formation (Alkmin and Marshak 1998) [4]. Due to the great local geodiversity, the Gandarela National Park was created by Federal Decree, on October 13, 2014, with the aim of preserving the natural aspects of the region. Figure 2 illustrates the location of the National Park in relation to the geomorphological limits of Serra do Gandarela, also contemplating the lithologies of interest, simplified from the geological map prepared by Endo (2019) [5].

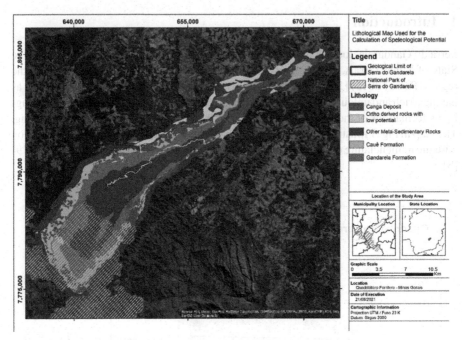

Fig. 2. Geological map of Serra do Gandarela considering the simplified lithologies of Endo (2019) [5]. Source: The authors

The cavities, features of abundant occurrence in the place, are aspects of the physical environment of relevance and environmental fragility, being considered patrimony of the union in the country. They are geomorphological features subjected to natural processes, such as the formation of sinkholes by collapse or subsidence (Souza 2018) [1]. That is, in addition to being an object of interest for environmental preservation, it is also a relevant factor when planning mining structures, which can present geotechnical risks through processes of destabilization of the terrain. It is evident that tailings dams, for example, if located on unstable karst zones, can be seriously compromised in a case of land subsidence, which can even be a trigger for their total or partial rupture.

In this way, the locations of some selected present mining structures were surveyed that can be confronted in the future with the potential for the occurrence of cavities to be calculated by multicriteria analysis. For this analysis, the area of the park was also considered. Figure 3 shows the location of the mining structures present and the area of the National Park.

Finally, the result obtained will be demonstrated on the Leapfrog Geo® 3D platform in order to be able to observe profiles containing geology, topography and speleological potential information integrated in a single interactive visualization platform.

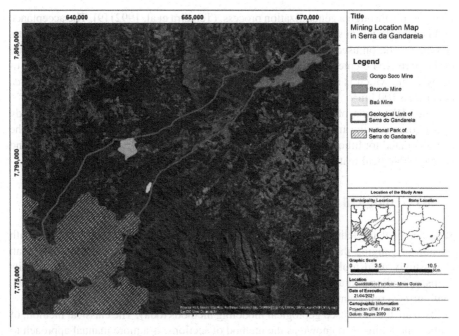

Fig. 3. Map representing the mining areas and the Gandarela National Park, which are present in Serra do Gandarela. Source: The authors

2   Multicriteria Analysis

When using an analysis based on data from Geographic Information Systems, one should always choose the best method according to the objectives of spatial analysis, discussing applications, restrictions and potentialities (Moura 2012) [6, 7]. The use of geoprocessing resources to carry out a spatial analysis requires the adoption of methodologies that follow a script based on discussions about the reasons for the proposed investigation. In other words, it is the choice of variables to be transformed into information plans and the choice of spatial analysis models that promote the combination of these variables that will provide the assertiveness of the proposed analysis. According to Moura (2004) [8], this choice of variables mentioned must be supported by bibliographic reviews, to approach a problem and reach a final solution, through successive approximations.

Moura (2012) [6, 7] also argues that, once it is necessary to perform numerical operations, it is of great interest to also perform the conversion of vector data into matrix data. In this matrix data, usually represented by a raster, each shape, other than a vector (where coordinates of the tie points are given), will be represented by a pixel of a certain resolution (pixel size). Thus, the entire extension of the studied space will receive a value, which can be density, existence or non-existence of information, represented in binary or classificatory format.

The author continues the discussion about the nature of the use of the raster format by saying that, by working with a surface that uses a discretized digital geometry, all morphological elements (points, lines and polygons) will be represented by sets of pixels, after passing through a generalization process. (Teixeira et al. 1992) [9]. The acceptance of this generalization will depend on the objectives necessary in the use of spatial data, and the resolution used must respond to the expectations of positioning and dimension of the portrayed elements. In the present case study, the pixels used will have a size of 20 by 20 m, which is adequate for the mapped scale, with a map representing an area larger than 100 km^2.

The elaboration of the map of the local speleological potential of a given study area is done by the multicriteria analysis from matrix data, taking into account the factors related to: lithology, geological structures, hydrography, slope, hypsometry and geomorphological features.

3 3D Geological Modeling

3D geological modeling is a technique widely applied in the mineral industry, with the aim of gauging the contents and volumes of mineral bodies. In addition, it is an increasingly used tool for understanding all the three-dimensional complexity of its forms, providing a more effective visualization, with the association of realistic images, configuring a representation in virtual reality - VR (Buchi 2018) [9].

Two are the most used geological modeling methods today. The classical method, of explicit modeling, also known as the method of sections, is a more manual approach to the construction of solids. The method used in this work was a more modern and more automated one, known as implicit modeling, performed in the Leapfrog Geo ® *software*. Three-dimensional models in implicit modeling can be generated from subsurface information such as soundings or also from geological maps, quickly and accurately.

The objective of presenting the results visualized on this platform is to introduce a pioneering and efficient program to generate 3D geological models widely used in mining (Buchi 2018) [10] in other related applications, as in the case presented in the environmental analysis.

4 Methodology

The work consisted in the elaboration of bibliographic reviews of the geological and geomorphological aspects of the area, in addition to seeking to reach an understanding of the relevant factors for the formation of cavities. Satellite images, geological maps and geodiversity maps were also analyzed and classified to delimit the study areas such as mining structures, the location of the cavities, the location of Serra do Gandarela and the homonymous National Park. The flowchart in Fig. 4 presents the methodological steps followed for the elaboration of the multi-criteria spatial analysis and its presentation in the geological model as a result.

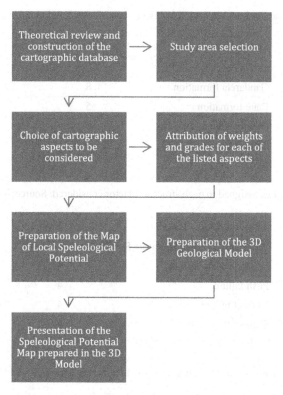

Fig. 4. Flowchart of methodological procedures. Source: The authors

Considering the available bibliographies and the methodology present in the Brazilian legislation, for the elaboration of the map of potential occurrence of cavities, factors were considered: Lithological, geological-structural, hydrographic and topographic. Considering each of these factors, a representative score for the potential for the occurrence of cavities was then listed. To achieve the result, the raster format was considered as input for each of the features, where each pixel had an extension of 20 m × 20 m and carried a numerical value referring to the assigned grade.

The tables numbered 1 to 4, presented below, show the value assigned to each of the features. In it, all factors of interest were considered, the topography being considered according to what was suggested by Embrapa (1999) [11], which considers slope classes according to what is presented in Table 4. The topography used was in accordance with the surveys performed by the Shuttle Radar Topography Mission (SRTM).

The highest scores given to each of these factors were according to the knowledge acquired by the author as well as data driven processes in the region. In lithological factors, for example, it is known that most of the cavities in the region are in canga formation, receiving a grade of 9, followed by the carbonates of the Gandarela Formation, which received a grade of 8. The other lithologies have a considerably lower potential, also getting lower grades. The same applies to the other structural, hydrographic and relief features (Tables 1, 2, and 3).

Table 1. Grades assigned to each lithological factor considered. Source: The authors.

Lithological type [Fat Lit]	Note
Canga cover	9
Gandarela formation	8
Cauê formation	5
Other sedimentary rocks	3
Orthoderived rocks	1

Table 2. Grades assigned to each structural factor considered. Source: The authors.

Structural factors [Fat Est]	Note
Axial Trace of the Gandarela Syncline	5
Indiscriminate failure	4
Push failure	4
Normal failure	4
Contacts	4

Table 3. Notes attributed to the hydrographic factors considered. Source: The authors.

Hydrographic factors [Fat Hid]	Note
Presence of drains	6
Absence of drains	1

Table 4. Notes attributed to topographic factors considered. Source: The authors.

Topographic factors [Fat Top]	Note
Slope 0 to 3%	1
Slope 3 to 8%	2
Declivity 8 to 20%	3
Declivity 20 to 45%	5
Declivity 45 to 75%	7
Slope >75%	9

The final potential map was then prepared, from the sum of all pixels present, according to the following formula, reaching the following result, shown in Fig. 5.

$$POT = \frac{[(1,5)Fat\ Lit + (1)Fat\ Est + (1)Fat\ Hid + (2)Fat\ Top]}{5,5}$$

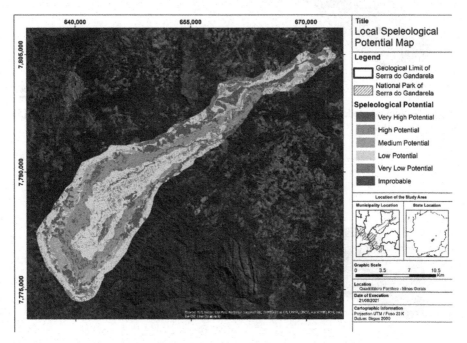

Fig. 5. Speleological potential map generated considering the listed factors Source: The authors

The weights 1.5 and 2 assigned to lithological and hydrographic factors respectively were considered according to the author's experience in addition to observations made by primary field data as well as secondary data. Both observations demonstrate that lithological and topographic factors have a greater influence than the others considered. Other simulations were also carried out with small variations, such as assigning weight 2 to both mentioned notes, but the formula presented was the one that presented the greatest adherence for the present case.

The next step was the preparation of the Geological Model of the area from the geological map used, prepared by Endo (2019) [5]. For this purpose, the "deposit" interpolator was used in the Leapfrog Geo Software, following the stratigraphic column suggested by the author with the layers following an average slope for the values found in the region, equal to 50/290. The geological model created is shown in Fig. 6, shown below.

The final step was to transform the ditch into pixels of the final potential map into a point cloud where each point represents a value that was imported into the geological model. The result obtained is presented below in plan and profile visualization, in Figs. 7 and 8, presented below.

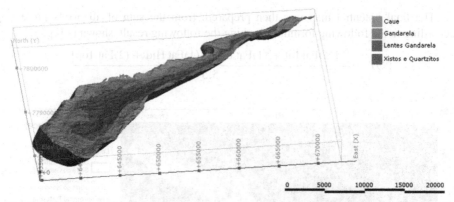

Fig. 6. Geological model elaborated considering the simplified lithologies of Endo (2019) [5] Source: The authors

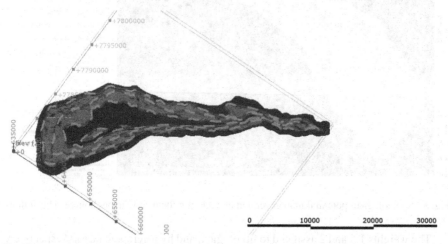

Fig. 7. Potential map represented as a cloud of points in geological modeling software. Source: The authors

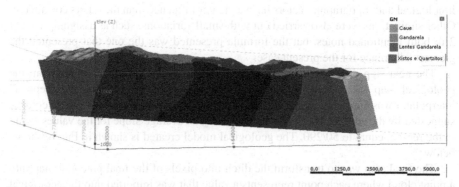

Fig. 8. Geological profile generated in the geological modeling software indicating the lithologies, the calculated slopes and the cloud of potential points. Source: The authors

5 Results Obtained

The results obtained revealed, when confronted with the cavities already mapped in the region, showed the following relationship, presented in Table 5, which indicates a good correlation of the potential map with reality. For this correlation, the database of the National Center for Research and Conservation of Cavities (CECAV/ICMBIO) was used, which is the official portal of the Brazilian government that provides the record of existing cavities in the country.

Table 5. Correlation of the speleological potential with the total area of occurrence of each potential, the number of cavities and the number of hectares for the occurrence of each cavity. Source: The authors.

Potential	Area (ha)	Number of cavities	Hectares/Cavities	% total of cavities
Very high	3923.7	229	17.1	47.80793319
High	7282.1	100	72.8	20.87682672
Medium	3882.5	81	47.9	16.91022965
Short	10452.3	59	117.2	12.31732777
Very Short	4430.7	10	443.1	2.087682672
Unlikely	885	0	–	0
Total	30856.3	479	–	100

We see in the table above that the potential is faithful since the number of hectares existing for each cavity increases when the potential increases, only in the average potential an exception occurs, with the number decreasing contrary to what was expected. Anyway, when comparing with the statistical data provided by the country's public data portal, provided by CECAV/ICMBIO, an excellent correlation is found with the results obtained, especially for high and very high potentials. Table 6 below presents the mentioned correlation:

Table 6. Correlation of the % of cavities found in the study according to the speleological potential according to what is available in public data from the Brazilian government. Source: The authors.

Potential	Total % of cavities by potential - study result	% total cavities by potential - Brazilian government
Very Tall and Tall	68.68475992	64
Medium	16.91022965	28
Low and a lot Short	14.40501044	8
Unlikely	0	0
	100	100

6 Conclusion

The present study presented as a result a map of the speleological potential of the Serra do Gandarela region. For its development, a bibliographic review was first carried out, which included geological aspects of the area, cavity legislation in Brazil, the history of mining rights in the study region, methods and tools applied in Geographic Information Systems (mainly multi-criteria analysis) and 3D Geological Modeling.

Using multicriteria analysis methods, it was possible to determine the speleological potential of the Serra do Gandarela region, a region rich in geodiversity and mineral requirements. For this, the geological map of the Quadrilátero Ferrífero prepared by Endo, in 2019, was used as a basis for the lithological, structural and hydrographic factors. For the topographic factors, the Shuttle Radar Topography Mission (SRTM) database was considered. Grades from 1 to 9 were then assigned to each of these factors, referring to each pixel, and then added up, according to the formula presented in Sect. 4 of this article, which was the one that presented the most consistent results.

After the elaboration of the speleological potential map, a table was extracted from the geoprocessing software, correlating the density of cavities per area for each potential. It was then evident that, in general, the areas presented as having greater speleological potential had, in fact, a greater number of existing cavities. The only exception was the medium potential, which presented more cavities per hectare than the high potential, still with an occurrence density below the very high potential. When comparing the data made available by the official portal of the government of the country, presented in Table 5, a good correlation of the occurrence of cavities by potential was found, which shows that the scores used as well as the weights assigned to each factor in the present formula in item 4 – methodology.

Parallel to the elaboration of the speleological potential map presented, a geological model of the area was made. For this, the same lithological and structural bases were considered, in order to represent the geology of the area and allowing the realization of cross-sections that are able to demonstrate the lithological, structural and topographic variations.

The potential map was then exported as a cloud of points so that each point refers to each pixel and loads the final grade assigned to its database. The exported point cloud was then superimposed on the mentioned geological model and the results analyzed in profile. Such analysis made it possible to observe the potential variation according to topographic and lithological factors, as well as predicted.

The study presented here aims to show the methodology for a speleological potential analysis as well as its results in the region selected as a target. In addition, it is also interesting to present the possibility of using geological modeling tools for environmental studies, since they allow a dynamic visualization in addition to being good for the administration of geographic databases.

References

1. Passos, R.M.: The Serra do Gandarela, a demarcation with marked cards. Mineral Technology Center. University Research Institute of Rio de Janeiro. Rio de Janeiro (2015)

2. Santos, D.J.: The geodiversity of the Serra do Gandarela National Park: Analysis of the potential for didactic use, with emphasis on the speleological heritage. Masters dissertation. Federal University of Minas Gerais, Institute of Geosciences (2017)
3. Casagrande, P.B.: Geology and geoprocessing applied to territorial planning. Minas Gerais, UFMG (2019)
4. Alkmin, F.F., Marshak, S.: Transamazonian Orogeny in the Southern São Francisco Craton Region, Minas Gerais, Brazil: evidence for Paleoproterozoic collision and collapse in the Quadrilátero Ferrífero. Precambrian Research, pp. 29–58 (1998)
5. Endo, I., et al.: Geological map of the Iron Quadrangle, Minas Gerais Brazil. Scale 1:50,000. Ouro Preto, Department of Geology, School of Mines – UFOP – Center for Advanced Studies of the Quadrilátero Ferríferfo (2019). www.qfe2050.ufop.br
6. Moura, A.C.M.: The choice of interpolators and visualization resources in the structuring of databases for the production of spatial information supported by geoprocessing. Geoprocessing Laboratory at the UFMG School of Architecture. Belo Horizonte, 21 p. (2012). http://www.arq.ufmg.br
7. Machado, S.A.: High spatial resolution sensors. Paper presented to the discipline of Advanced Systems and Sensors for Earth Observation. Graduate Program in Remote Sensing. National Institute for Space Research, São José dos Campos (SP) (2002)
8. Moura, A., Ana Clara, M.: Geoprocessing applied to the characterization and urban planning of Ouro Preto – MG. In: Jorge, X.-D.-S., Ricardo, Z. (eds.) Geoprocessing and Environmental Analysis – Applications, p. 227. Bertrand Brazil, Rio de Janeiro (2004)
9. Amandio, T., Antonio, C., Edmar, M.: Introduction to geographic information systems. In: Claro, R. (ed.) 80 p (1992)
10. Buchi, A.: Geological mapping using the BGS digital workflow and implicit modeling. Master's Thesis, Graduate Program in Geology, UFMG, Belo Horizonte (2018)
11. EMBRAPA Brazilian system of soil classification. EMBRAPA Information Production, Brasília (1999)

Acoustic Wavefields Simulation by the Ray Method with Approximation of a Broadband Signal Propagation

Dmitry Neklyudov[(✉)] [iD] and Maxim Protasov [iD]

Institute of Petroleum Geology and Geophysics SB RAS, prosp. acad. Koptuga 3,
Novosibirsk 630090, Russia
`neklyudovda@ipgg.sbras.ru`

Abstract. The paper presents a method for calculating frequency-dependent rays, which allows effective approximation of a broadband signal propagation. We provide comparative analysis of this method with the standard ray method and the finite-difference method. The developed algorithm is promising for modelling and inverse problems. We performed the numerical examples for the realistic Sigsbee model.

Keywords: Ray method · Broadband signal · Green function

1 Introduction

Asymptotic methods play an important role in solving direct and inverse problems in seismic. The ray method occupies a special place among them [1–3]. Based on it, key procedures for processing seismic data and constructing seismic images, such as Kirchoff depth migration, are implemented [4–6]. The ray method is used to calculate the travel times of seismic waves. However, it is also used to calculate wave fields in models with a moderate complexity. An important limitation of the ray method is the fact that it is based on a high-frequency approximation of signal propagation processes. It does not consider that the real seismic signals are broadband and have a limited spectrum [7, 8]. A high-frequency approximation often leads to "unphysical" behavior of the rays and the corresponding travel times calculated along the ray trajectories in models with sharp interfaces between regions with different values of physical parameters. The limited spectrum signals propagate within some volume surrounding the ray (the so-called Fresnel zone or in 3D "Fresnel volume"). Dominant frequency of the signal determines the width of this volume. The signal "feels" variations in the parameters of the medium within this volume and changes the direction of its propagation accordingly, [9, 10].

Several approaches can take the band limited waves nature into account with varying degrees of efficiency and weaken the influence of the high-frequency approximation used in the ray method [11–18]. The papers [19–21] consider the so-called "exact" frequency-dependent rays. They show such rays provide an efficient calculation of the

O. Gervasi et al. (Eds.): ICCSA 2022, LNCS 13376, pp. 84–96, 2022.
https://doi.org/10.1007/978-3-031-10450-3_7

travel times under salt bodies. However, "exact" frequency-dependent rays are computationally expensive, since the procedure requires knowledge of acoustic wavefield for a given frequency. Another approach proposed in [12] and considered in [22] is a simplified but highly effective method for approximating the propagation of broadband seismic signals in complex environments. The author (A. Lomax) calls it "the wavelength-smoothing technique". The method is based on the use of the Huygens's principle and the frequency-dependent velocity function. The key point of Lomax method is the fact that velocity used for ray tracing is determined by smoothing actual velocity along the normal to the ray at the current point over an aperture proportional to the wavelength (i.e. along some pre-defined portion of the wave front). Below we will call the rays constructed by this method as "Lomax rays". In the limiting case when the wavelength becomes infinite small, Lomax rays reduces to the standard rays described by classical ray theory. In this paper, we prove that Lomax rays might be quite promising in some seismic exploration applications. Particularly, we demonstrate the use of Lomax rays to calculate travel times and acoustic wave fields in complex environments and compare these results with results provided by much more computationally expensive finite-difference method for two-way acoustic wave equation.

2 Lomax Ray Calculation

In this section, we briefly present the algorithm for Lomax rays calculation and emphasize what exactly is their difference from standard rays. For a clearer presentation, we will focus on the two-dimensional case. All the above arguments work for the three-dimensional case. The key point in the Lomax method is velocity smoothing along the current position of the front (more precisely, in the normal direction to the ray). For the given frequency υ (we consider it as a certain parameter for now) the average velocity has the expression,

$$v_{sm}(\vec{x}_p, \nu) = \frac{\sum_{j=-N}^{N} w_j \cdot v(\vec{x}_j)}{\sum_{j=-N}^{N} w_j} \tag{1}$$

where w_j are the values of the smoothing function (we will mention this later), $v(\vec{x}_j)$ is the values of the velocities taken at certain points $\vec{x}_j$ along the front. These points are located symmetrically regarding the central point $\vec{x}_p = (x_p, z_p)$. The maximum distance from the central point (averaging aperture) is determined by the parameter θ, which is specified in wavelengths, $\theta \sim \lambda$, where $\lambda = \frac{v(\vec{x}_p)}{\upsilon}$, (for example $\theta = 1.5$). As a smoothing function, we use the Gaussian function (other options are possible): $w(x) = \exp\left\{-4\ln2\left(\frac{x}{2}\right)^2\right\}$.

Let a Lomax is constructed at some point $\vec{x}_p = (x_p, z_p)$. At this point a unit tangent vector $\vec{s} = (s_x, s_z)$ is given. The unit normal to the ray is $\vec{n} = (s_z, -s_x)$. In the normal direction $\vec{n}$, at a distance l from a central point on the ray, we define edge points $\vec{x}_1$ and $\vec{x}_2$ symmetrically (Fig. 2). At each of the three points, we calculate smoothed velocities using the expression (1): $\bar{v}_p = v_{sm}(\vec{x}_p, \nu)$, $\bar{v}_1 = v_{sm}(\vec{x}_1, \nu)$, $\bar{v}_2 = v_{sm}(\vec{x}_2, \nu)$. We use the same direction of smoothing along the normal $\vec{n}$ for the edge points $\vec{x}_1, \vec{x}_2$. Let us define the time step along the ray as dt. During this time, the central point $\vec{x}_p$ moves to the point $\vec{x}_p + d\vec{x}_p, d\vec{x}_p = (dx_p, dz_p)$ along the vector $\vec{s}$:

$$dx_p = \bar{v}_p dt \cdot s_x, dz_p = \bar{v}_p dt \cdot s_z \qquad (2)$$

The edge points move respectively at the distance $\bar{v}_1 dt, \bar{v}_2 dt$ (Fig. 2). Assuming that the front remains locally flat, from simple geometric considerations, one can get an expression for the correction to the tangent vector to the ray $d\vec{s}$ and find the tangent vector at the next point on the ray (Fig. 2):

$$ds_x = -\frac{d\bar{v}_p}{x_1 - x_2}dt \cdot s_z, ds_x = -\frac{d\bar{v}_p}{z_1 - z_2}dt \cdot s_x, d\bar{v}_p = \bar{v}_1 - \bar{v}_2 \qquad (3)$$

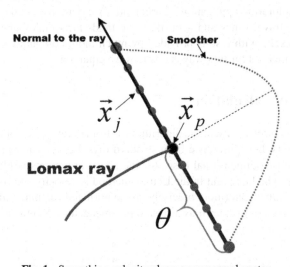

Fig. 1. Smoothing velocity along a ray normal vector.

Thus, there is a step-by-step movement along the ray. Note that the "Lomax" ray tracing is performed in a certain volume of the medium. Simultaneous movement of three points determines a next position of the front. The parameter l (the width of the flat front) turns out to be a very important parameter. We propose to determine it adaptively at each time step along the ray, dt, depending on the wavelength: $l = q \cdot \lambda$, where $q \sim 0.25 - 0.5$.

In the limit case, $l \to 0$, $dt \to 0$ one obtain a system of ordinary differential equation of Lomax ray:

$$\frac{d\vec{s}}{dt} = -(\nabla \bar{v}_p \cdot \vec{n})\vec{n}, \quad \frac{d\vec{x}}{dt} = \bar{v}_p \vec{s} \tag{4}$$

Equations (4) become equivalent to the equations of standard ray tracing when the averaged velocity $\bar{v}_p$ is replaced by the local velocity $v(\vec{x})$.

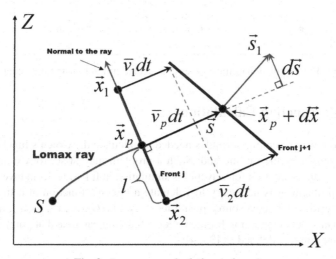

Fig. 2. Lomax ray calculation (scheme).

When constructing rays, we determine the traveltimes at the points of the medium through which each ray passes. Below, we need to determine the traveltimes on some regular grid. With Lomax rays, considering the specifics of their construction, it is possible to propose a natural algorithm for interpolating traveltimes given at irregularly spaced points on a ray to a regular grid. When constructing a Lomax ray, at each point of the ray, a certain volume of the medium is considered, which is determined by the wavelength at the current point. Let us calculate the ray. Moving along the ray, i.e. increasing traveltime by a constant increment dt, consider the position at time T_j. When constructing the ray up to the moment of time $T_{j+1} = T_j + dt$, the flat wavefront has passed through the area of the medium, concentrated inside the trapezoid. The bases of the trapezoid are two segments: the position of the front at the moment T_j and the position of the front at the moment T_{j+1} (Fig. 3). The points of a regular grid may be located inside this trapezoid. When such points are found, then the traveltimes are interpolated in these points according to the principle shown schematically in Fig. 3.

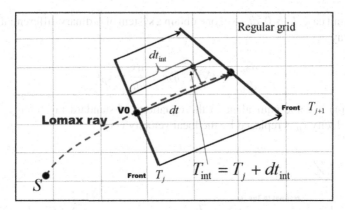

Fig. 3. Interpolation of traveltimes to a regular grid in Lomax ray tracing.

3   Green's Function Calculation

In this section, we present the formulas needed to calculate the Green's functions in the frequency domain by the ray method. Such a problem may arise, for example, when asymptotic methods are used for wavefields simulation in full-waveform inversion [23]. For such a problem, it is necessary to calculate a Green's function at a frequency ω on a regular grid with a fixed source position (x_S, z_S), i.e. $G(x, z, x_S, z_S; \omega)$. In the two-dimensional case, the expression for the Green's function calculated at point R with the source in the point S is defined as [3, 24]:

$$G(R; S) = S(\omega)A(S, R)\exp\{i\omega\tau(S, R)\}, \tag{5}$$

where $\tau(S, R)$ is traveltime along a ray between the points S and R, the multiplier $S(\omega) = \sqrt{\frac{1}{-i\omega}}$, $A(S, R)$ is an amplitude factor provided by the ray method:

$$A(S, R) = \sqrt{\frac{v(R)}{8\pi v(S) \cdot J(S, R)}}, \tag{6}$$

$v(S)$ is a value of velocity in corresponding point of velocity model, $J(S, R)$ is geometrical spreading along a ray:

$$J \sim \frac{\delta L}{\delta\theta_S}, \tag{7}$$

where δL is a width of a ray tube in point R, $\delta\theta_S$ is an opening angle increment in the initial point of the ray tube (see Fig. 4).

Having several rays calculated for a source position within the whole computational domain, it is possible to evaluate approximately the Green's function using the formulas (5–7), [3]. Since we use the approximate expression for geometrical spreading (7), ray coverage (or ray density) within the target area should be sufficient. As an alternative, one may use much more computationally expensive dynamic ray tracing [2, 3].

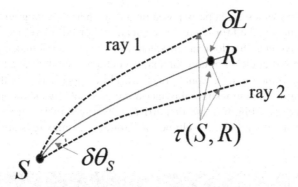

Fig. 4. Geometrical spreading calculation

4 Numerical Experiments

4.1 Lomax Ray Tracing Through a Salt Intrusion

Significant problems arise when the ray method calculates traveltimes below salt bodies. Salt bodies might have a very complex shape. Seismic wave velocities in salt are much higher than in sedimentary rocks surrounding a salt intrusion. Usually, it is very problematic to construct reliable rays passing through the salt body and calculate the corresponding traveltimes at those points of the medium that are located under the intrusion. As it is shown in [16, 21], frequency-dependent rays can help to solve this problem. Below we demonstrate that Lomax rays can penetrate through salt bodies successfully. Figure 5 shows a fragment of the well-known Sigsbee velocity model [25] with a salt body of complex shape (shown in yellow). Seismic wave velocity in salt is 4500 m/s meanwhile in surrounding area it doesn't exceed 3500 m/s. Point source is located near the surface, $Zs = 20$ m. Our task is to pass the rays through the salt intrusion and calculate the corresponding traveltimes in receivers located on the horizontal line in the depth below salt ($Zr = 4100$ m). For standard raytracing we used a code taken from well-known Seismic Unix freeware package [26]. Lomax rays are calculated using the code we developed. Figure 5a shows standard rays (black). As one can see, their behavior is irregular. At sharp, non-planar boundaries of the salt, the standard rays scatter. In the receiver line, where the first arrival traveltimes are calculated, "holes" are formed (i.e. intervals where the rays do not arrive at all). It is an obvious contradiction with the real physical process of wave propagation. Note that the rays are traced densely. Increment of the emerging angle from the source is very small (in this case, 0.02°). Maximum emerging angle is equal to 30° in this case. So totally 3000 rays were constructed (for illustrative purpose we plot each tenth ray in the figure). But it does not help to get the traveltimes on the entire line of receivers in depth. Figure 5b shows the Lomax rays calculated for a frequency of 5 Hz (shown in red). The parameter θ (smoothing aperture of local velocities) equals to 0.5 wavelength in each point of a ray. As one can see, Lomax rays' behavior is much more "physical" than the behavior of standard rays. Lomax rays pass through the salt body and arrive to receivers quite regularly. In Fig. 6 we compare first arrival traveltimes. Figure 6a demonstrates the traveltimes obtained by the Lomax rays which are superimposed on the synthetic seismogram calculated by the finite-difference method for scalar wave-equation. For full wavefiled simulation we used a Ricker wavelet with a dominant frequency of 15 Hz. The Lomax rays traveltimes are marked with red circles. For comparison, we demonstrate the traveltimes provided by standard rays (blue circles). Lomax rays' traveltimes perfectly fits the first arrival in the seismogram. To demonstrate this fact more precisely, we show the first arrival traveltimes separately (Fig. 6b): the first arrival traveltimes picked from the synthetic seismogram are shown in blue; traveltimes according to Lomax rays are shown as red

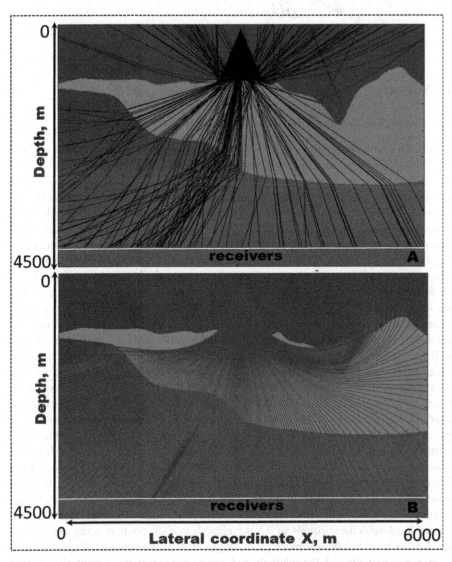

Fig. 5. Ray tracing in Sigsbee model. (a) Standard rays; (b) Lomax rays for frequency 5 Hz.

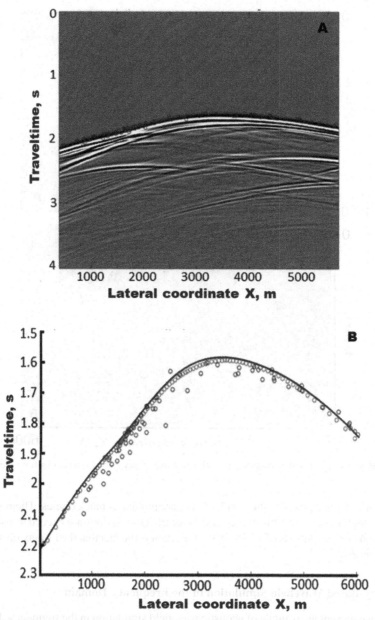

Fig. 6. (a) First arrival traveltimes along the Lomax rays (red circles) are superimposed on the synthetic common-shot gather; (b) comparison of first arrivals traveltimes: (blue) traveltimes computed by the finite difference method; (red circles) travel times along the Lomax rays calculated for frequency 5 Hz; (black) traveltimes along the standard rays. (Color figure online)

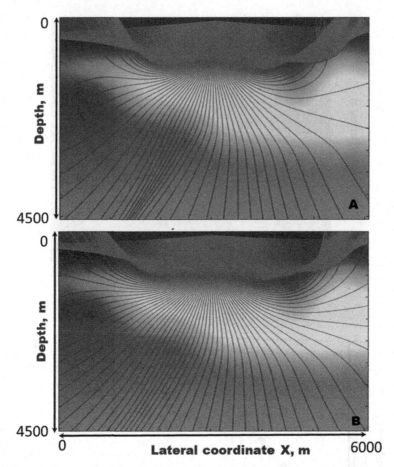

Fig. 7. Rays in the smoothed Segsbee model: (a) standard rays; (b) Lomax rays for a frequency of 10 Hz.

circles; traveltimes given by the standard rays are plotted as black circles. The residuals between the Lomax rays' traveltimes and exact traveltimes does not exceed 4 ms which can be considered quite satisfactory. Also important is the fact that the Lomax rays arrive at each receiver.

4.2 Ray-Based Wavefield Simulation in the Frequency Domain

Below, we present an example of acoustic wavefield simulation in the frequency domain using Lomax rays and compare results with the results provided by the standard finite difference method for acoustic wave equation. To simplify the comparison of results, in this example, we use a smoothed version of the Sigsbee velocity model (its fragment that was used in the previous example). Figure 7 shows a fragment of the smoothed Sigsbee model and the ray fields superimposed on it: Fig. 7a shows standard rays; Fig. 7b shows the Lomax ray constructed for a frequency 10 Hz. The parameter θ is equal to 0.5 wavelength in each point of a ray. Further, in Fig. 8 (left column) we show the traveltimes calculated using the ray method in each point of the model after interpolation on a regular grid in comparison with the first arrival traveltimes got by the finite difference method. As one can see, the traveltimes calculated using standard rays have "holes" at the edges of the computational domain (i.e. there are no rays passed through these areas) (marked by the black ovals in Fig. 8b). Thus, although the velocity model is smooth, the standard ray method cannot provide reliable traveltimes. The traveltimes provided by the Lomax rays practically coincide with the first arrival "finite difference" traveltimes (residuals do not exceed 5 ms). In Fig. 8 (right column) we show the wavefields in the frequency domain for a fixed frequency 10 Hz (real part) which correspond to traveltime in the left column. As one can see, the wavefield constructed using the Lomax rays corresponds much better to the wave field calculated by the finite difference method than the result got using the standard rays. In Fig. 9, we compare the vertical and horizontal sections

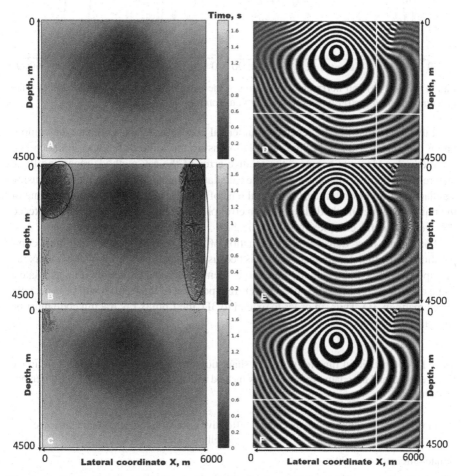

Fig. 8. (Left column) First arrival traveltimes distribution: (a) finite difference simulation; (b) standard ray method; (c) Lomax rays for a frequency of 10 Hz. (Right column) Corresponding wavefields for a fixed frequency 10 Hz: (d) FD simulation, (e) standard rays, (f) Lomax rays.

of the wavefields from Fig. 8d, 8f (corresponding locations are marked by the white lines) for the finite difference solution (shown in blue) and for the Lomax rays (red). Very satisfactory match is obvious. Thus, we show numerically that Lomax rays can effectively calculate wave-fields in fairly complex media.

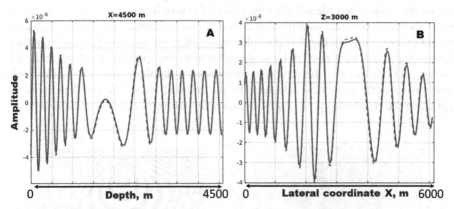

Fig. 9. Vertical (a) and horizontal (b) section of the wavefields from Fig. 8d, 8f: (blue) finite difference method, (red) Lomax rays. (Color figure online)

Table 1 summarizes the results of numerical experiments. We compare the computation time needed for wavefields simulation using the finite difference approach and ray methods. Also, we compare the relative error of the ray methods regarding finite difference modeling. One can see that the calculation time of the ray method, both using standard rays and Lomax rays, is several tens of times less than the calculation time of the finite difference method. The solution error provided by Lomax rays does not exceed 4% even for such a complex model as Sigsbee.

For a given rays' density, the construction of Lomax rays requires much more computational time than for standard rays. It is because at each time step along the Lomax ray multiple accesses to the velocity model (i.e. memory access) are required to calculate a value of the averaged velocity along the current position of the front. It will be especially problematic in 3D. Thus, in order to extend to 3D, the Lomax ray tracing code must be carefully optimized.

Table 1. Computational time for wavefield simulation for 1 source on 1 processor core in the Sigsbee model and the relative error of the ray method with respect to the result of finite difference modeling.

Method	Computational time	Relative error with respect to finite-difference modelling result
Finite-difference	~80 s	–
Standard rays	~2 s	7.5%
Lomax rays	~5 s	3.6%

5   Conclusion

In the paper, we consider "Lomax method" for calculating frequency-dependent rays. This method allows a simple and efficient approximation of a broadband signal propagation. We perform a comparative analysis of the Lomax method, the standard ray method and the finite difference method for calculating travel times and acoustic wavefields in complex media The relative error of wavefield calculated using Lomax rays regarding the finite difference solution is a percentage even for such a complex model as Sigsbee, while the computation time is more than an order of magnitude less in a two-dimensional case. Such results show the promise of using Lomax rays to calculate acoustic wavefields for solving inverse seismic problems in a three-dimensional environment.

Acknowledgments. The reported study was funded by RFBR and GACR, project number 20-55-26003.

References

1. Babich, V.M., Buldyrev, V.S.: Asymptotic Methods in Short-Wavelength Diffraction Theory. Alpha Science (2009)
2. Cerveny, V., Molotkov, I.A., Psencik, I.: Ray Theory in Seismology. Charles University Press, Prague (1977)
3. Cerveny, V.: Seismic Ray Theory. Cambridge University Press, Cambridge (2001)
4. Schneider, W.: Integral formulation for migration in two and three dimensions. Geophysics **43**, 49–76 (1978)
5. Bleistein, N.: On the imaging of reflectors in the earth. Geophysics **52**, 931–942 (1987)
6. Audebert, F., Nichols, D., Rekdal, T., Biondi, B., Lumley, D., Urdaneta, H.: Imaging complex geologic structure with single-arrival Kirchhoff prestack depth migration. Geophysics **62**, 1533–1543 (1997)
7. Kravtsov, Y., Orlov, Y.: Geometrical Optics of Inhomogeneous Media. Springer, Heidelberg (1990)
8. Ben-Menahem, A., Beydoun, W.B.: Range of validity of seismic ray and beam methods in general inhomogeneous media – I. General theory. Geophys. J. Int. **82**, 207–234 (1985)
9. Marquering, H., Dahlen, F.A., Nolet, G.: Three-dimensional sensitivity kernels for finite-frequency traveltimes: the banana-doughnut paradox. Geophys. J. Int. **137**, 805–815 (1999)
10. Dahlen, F.A., Hung, S.-H., Nolet, G.: Fréchet kernels for finite-frequency traveltimes—I. Theory. Geophys. J. Int. **141**, 157–174 (2000)
11. Cerveny, V., Soares, J.E.P.: Fresnel volume ray tracing. Geophysics **57**, 902–915 (1992)
12. Lomax, A.: The wavelength-smoothing method for approximating broad-band wave propagation through complicated velocity structures. Geophys. J. Int. **117**, 313–334 (1994)
13. Vasco, D.W., Peterson, J.E., Majer, E.L.: Beyond ray tomography: wavepaths and Fresnel volumes. Geophysics **60**, 1790–1804 (1995)
14. Bube, K.P., Washbourne, J.K.: Wave tracing: ray tracing for the propagation of band-limited signals: part 1 – theory. Geophysics **73**, VE377-VE384 (2008)
15. Protasov, M.I., Yarman, C.E., Nichols, D., Osypov, K., Cheng X.: Frequency-dependent ray-tracing through rugose interfaces. In: Proceedings of 2011 81st SEG Annual Meeting, pp. 2992–2996. SEG (2011)
16. Yarman, C.E., Cheng, X., Osypov, K., Nichols, D., Protasov, M.: Band-limited ray tracing. Geophys. Prosp. **61**, 1194–1205 (2013)

17. Vasco, D.W., Nihei, K.: Broad-band trajectory mechanics. Geophys. J. Int. **216**, 745–759 (2019)
18. Vasco, D.W., Nihei, K.T.: A trajectory mechanics approach for the study of wave propagation in an anisotropic elastic medium. Geophys. J. Int. **219**, 1885–1899 (2019)
19. Foreman, T.L.: An exact ray theoretical formulation of the Helmholtz equation. J. Acoust. Soc. Am. **86**, 234–246 (1989)
20. Protasov, M., Gadylshin, K.: Exact frequency dependent rays on the basis of Helmholtz solver, In: Proceedings of 2015 83rd SEG Annual Meeting, pp. 3739–3743. SEG (2015)
21. Protasov, M., Gadylshin, K.: Computational method for exact frequency-dependent rays on the basis of the solution of the Helmholtz equation. Geophys. J. Int. **210**, 525–533 (2017)
22. Chen, J., Zelt, C.A.: Comparison of full wavefield synthetics with frequency-dependent travel-times calculated using wavelength-dependent velocity smoothing. J. Environ. Eng. Geophys. **22**, 133–141 (2017)
23. Virieux, J., Operto, S.: An overview of full-waveform inversion in exploration geophysics. Geophysics **78**, WCC1–WCC26 (2009)
24. Operto, M.S., Xu, S., Lambare, G.: Can we quantitatively image complex structures with rays. Geophysics **65**, 1223–1238 (2000)
25. Paffenholz J., Stefani, J., McLain, B., Bishop, K.: SIGSBEE_2A synthetic subsalt dataset - image quality as function of migration algorithm and velocity model error. In: Proceedings of 2002 64th EAGE Conference and Exhibition, cp-5–00108, EAGE (2002)
26. Cohen, J.K., Stockwell, Jr. J.W.: CWP/SU: Seismic Un*x Release No.39: an open source software package for seismic research and processing, Center for Wave Phenomena, Colorado School of Mines (2005)

Urban and Regional Planning

An Approach Based on Linked Open Data and Augmented Reality for Cultural Heritage Content-Based Information Retrieval

Antonio M. Rinaldi[✉], Cristiano Russo, and Cristian Tommasino

Department of Electrical Engineering and Information Technologies,
University of Napoli Federico II, 80125 Via Claudio, 21, Napoli, Italy
{antoniomaria.rinaldi,cristiano.russo,cristian.tommasino}@unina.it

Abstract. Nowadays, many technologies are changing our way of life, including those related to extended reality. One of the most interesting is Augmented Reality (AR). Today, even if this technology seems to be discovered yet, it is widely applied in several contexts, including the fruition and conservation of cultural heritage. Such spread is mainly offered by the new and more powerful mobile devices, allowing museums and art exhibitions to use AR to offer new experiences to visitors. In this paper, we present an augmented reality mobile system based on content-based image analysis techniques and Linked Open Data to improve the user knowledge about cultural heritage. We use different image analysis techniques, and we present several experimental results to show the performance of our system.

1 Introduction

Cultural heritage (CH) often fails to be a successful attraction because it cannot fully capture people's interests. Moreover, the enjoyment of an archaeological site cannot be improved due to legal or environmental regulations, and it is often hard to recognize relevant details in a cultural landscape or understand their meanings.

A new way of enhancing cultural sites is to provide information to users quickly and intuitively. In this context, information has a strategic value to understanding the world around a user, and new technologies provide the ability to interact with places or objects in real-time [28,29]. Furthermore, cultural heritage goes towards decay, so future generations may not be able to access many artistic works or places.

Digital cultural heritage is a set of methodology and tools that use digital technologies for understanding and preserving cultural, or natural heritage [1]. The digitisation of cultural heritage allows the fruition of artwork from literature to paintings for current and future generations.

O. Gervasi et al. (Eds.): ICCSA 2022, LNCS 13376, pp. 99–112, 2022.
https://doi.org/10.1007/978-3-031-10450-3_8

Augmented reality (AR) represents a technique that has changed the way of enjoying art in recent years. In this context, the advancement of information technologies has made it possible to define new ways to represent and integrate natural and digital information [15]. Augmented reality allows information to be superimposed around the user without blinding him in his physical environment. Mixed reality overlays information on the real world and includes the ability to understand and use the environment around the user to show or hide some of the digital content. Indeed, virtual reality allows users to be completely immersed in a computer-generated environment while the real world is hidden when the device is in use. Additionally, there are new classifications of the reality-virtuality continuum, such as extended reality, in which the real world and virtual world objects are presented within a single display. Thus, extended reality includes all the previously mentioned categories [48].

Most applications that extensively use multimedia objects, such as digital libraries, sensor networks, bioinformatics and e-business applications, require effective and efficient data management systems. Due to their complex and heterogeneous nature, managing, storing and retrieving multimedia objects are more demanding than traditional data management, which can be easily stored in commercial (primarily relational) database management systems [18].

A solution to the problem of retrieving multimedia objects is to associate the objects with a specific description [24,32]. This description allows us to make a retrieval by similarity. How this description occurs depends on the type of object. An image description can be done in two ways: through metadata or visual descriptors, [18]. Content-Based Image Retrieval (CBIR) is the application of computer vision to image recovery. Its goal is to limit the use of textual descriptions and develop techniques for retrieving images based on automatically extracted multimedia characteristics from a user-requested image or user-specified image features. Moreover, novel data structure as knowledge graphs [35] could combine different data to improve their informative layers [25].

In the realm of the semantic web, [3], linked data is a way of publishing structured data that allows data to be linked together. The publication of linked data is based on open web technologies and standards such as HTTP, RDF (Resource Description Framework) and URI. The purpose of this data structuring is to allow computers to read and interpret the information on the web directly. The links also make extracting data from various sources through semantic queries. When linked data links publicly accessible data, it is referred to as linked open data (LOD) [50].

In this work, CBIR techniques are used via mobile devices that retrieve information in real-time through interaction with Linked Open Data. This information is superimposed on the scene under observation and shown to the user.

The paper is organised as follows: in Sect. 2 we provide a review of the literature related to CBIR and augmented reality for cultural heritage; Sect. 3 introduces the used approach along with the general architecture of the system; in Sect. 4 a use case of the proposed system is described and discussed; in Sect. 5

we present and discuss the experimental strategy and results; lastly, Sect. 6 is devoted to conclusions and future research.

2 Related Works

The application of technology to cultural heritage is a topic that has been widely discussed. The UNESCO 1970 convention stated that the presentation work should keep pace with the progress of "communication, audiovisual techniques, automatic data processing and other appropriate technologies, as well as cultural and recreational trends" [44].

In this context, AR is considered a feasible technology for the heritage sector because it is now possible to develop applications for consumer-level mobile technology [30].

Furthermore, thanks to the AR technologies, new values can be added to CH sites [9]. Visitors can explore unfamiliar surroundings enjoyably and thrillingly [12]. Consequently, this is one of the most significant benefits from a supply perspective because many tourists are looking out for exceptional and unforgettable on-trip experiences [49]. Besides enjoyment, investigators argue that the interaction between visitors and AR systems contributes to a richer CH experience [14], demonstrating an experience co-creation, i.e. user and provider jointly produce a valued outcome [26,47].

Augmented reality has been one of the technologies that have spread most in the artistic field, and its application has been studied often and from different points of view. Diek and Jung, for example, have identified the economic, experiential, social, epistemic, cultural, historical and educational values of the greater reality in the context of cultural heritage [45].

On the other hand, content-based image retrieval has also found extensive application in the field of cultural heritage, for example, in [22] where the authors used it for e-documentation of monumental heritage and 3D reconstruction. The widespread diffusion dictated the choice to bring this type of application to mobile systems that this device has had in recent years. Most people now own a smartphone, and therefore the costs to offer this type of experience to users are very limited.

Among the many examples of augmented reality applications on mobile systems for cultural heritage, we mention [42] where the authors propose a mobile application that uses augmented reality to provide users with information on natural monuments. For example, the authors in [17,43] have used CBIR to develop an application that acquires the images from a camera to exemplify the information retrieval process. They used this information to enrich the image shown to the user. In [16] the authors introduced applications that exploit SURF and the greater reality for the visualisation of information and 3D models of cultural heritage sites. In [4,10,27,37] there are other similar examples but with applications designed for mobile systems. Other descriptors are used in digital cultural heritage applications as in [46], where the authors use ORB, a similar algorithm that is faster in extracting and comparing features. The authors in [13] describe, together with an application that uses augmented reality and retrieval, the results of experiments conducted during some museum visits. These experiments aim to study how such a tool can transform visitors' learning experience.

An Italian example is the "Ducale" research project, which proposes ICT solutions for the Palazzo Ducale museum in Urbino. A mobile application that uses augmented reality and content-based image retrieval to enhance the museum visit experience is presented. In this project, the famous painting "Ideal City" becomes a case to exemplify a specific approach to digital mediation of cultural heritage [8].

In our work, we proposed a novel approach where the use of different descriptors is tested and used to have optimal performances in different real scene exposures using a mobile CBIR framework. Moreover, the retrieved images are integrated with Linked Open Data to retrieve textual data and give more information to users employing augmented reality.

3   The Proposed System

In this section, we detailed our system. Figure 1 shows the top-level architecture. An essential component of our system is the Multimedia Knowledge Base [31] that contains all indexed images with related external resource links, specifically with Linked Open Data (LOD). The use of visual information is an important improvement for the understanding of object meaning [40].

The system indexes the images using local features extracted with the Keypoint Detector, in our case are SIFT (Scale Invariant Feature Transform) [20], SURF (Oriented FAST and Rotated BRIEF) [2] and ORB (Oriented FAST and Rotated BRIEF) [38].

In particular, the modules that compose our architecture are:

- *Picture Loader*: it loads the pictures taken from a mobile phone;
- *keypoint Extractor*: it processes the pictures and applies a keypoint Detector to extract local descriptors;
- *keypoint Marker*: it compares the local features of input pictures with all indexed images and returns the best matching.
- *Augmenter Picture*: using a SPARQL query to retrieve the information from LOD;
- *Result Checker*: in case of wrong or missed matching, it helps the user add or select the correct matching.

In the following of this section, we detail the proposed framework with the used technologies and techniques. A keypoint Detector locates some features from an image and describes them. SIFT was proposed as invariant to rotation, affine transformations, intensity, and viewpoint change in matching features. SIFT is composed of four main steps. The first one applies the Difference of Gaussian (DoG) to estimate the scale-space extremes. The second one localities the key point removing the low contrast point. The third one assigns orientation

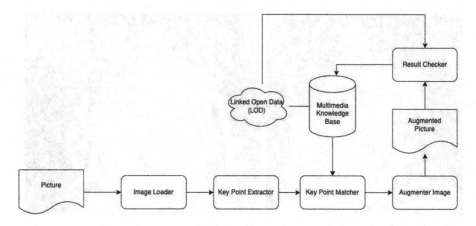

Fig. 1. System architecture

to key points using local image gradients. The last one generates a descriptor based on each keypoint image gradient magnitude and orientation.

SURF approximates the DoG with box filters. Instead of Gaussian averaging, the image uses a square to approximate the convolution because the square is faster with the integral image. SURF uses a BLOB detector based on the Hessian matrix to find the points of interest. The orientation assignment uses wavelet responses in horizontal and vertical directions by applying adequate Gaussian weights. For feature description, SURF uses wavelet responses. A neighbourhood around the key point is selected and divided into subregions, and then for each subregion, the wavelet responses are taken and represented to get the SURF feature descriptor. The sign of Laplacian which is already computed in the detection, is used for underlying interest points. The sign of the Laplacian distinguishes bright blobs on dark backgrounds from the reverse case.

ORB is a FAST keypoint detector based on a BRIEF descriptor with some modifications. Originally, to determine the key points, it used FAST. Then, it applies a Harris corner measure to find the top N points. Due to FAST does not compute the orientation and is a rotation variant, it computes the intensity weighted centroid of the patch with a located corner at the centre. The direction of the vector from this corner point to the centroid gives the orientation. Moments are computed to enhance the rotation invariance. In ORB, a rotation matrix is computed using the orientation of the patch, and then the BRIEF descriptors [5] are steered according to the orientation.

As shown in Fig. 3, the foremost step executed from the system is image acquisition, keypoint detection, image augmentation, visualisation of the result, and results checking. In this process user interacts with the system in only two cases, firstly to take a picture and lastly in case of wrong or missed matching.

In our framework, a user takes a picture using a mobile device that sends it to the server that extracts the keypoint and compares it with the indexed keypoint using the best matching techniques. Eventually, the server retrieves

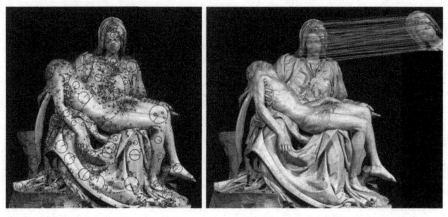

(a) Keypoint detection example   (b) Keyoint machining example

Fig. 2. An example on Pietà di Michelangelo

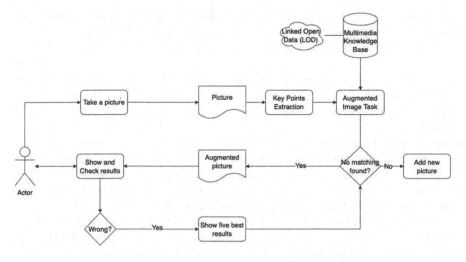

Fig. 3. Flow chart

the description from LOD, creates the augmented images, and sends it to the client (mobile device).

In detail, when a user sends an image to the server, it applies a keypoint detector that retrieves either keypoint and its description (Fig. 2). Then, the system matches the keypoint extracted from the input image and the indexed keypoint returning the LOD code id more similar to the input, namely, the one with the highest match rate. Moreover, it performs a SPARQL query to retrieve a title and description from a LOD source (i.e. DBpedia). Eventually, it creates augmented add this information to the images. We summarised such a process performed by the server in Fig. 4.

Moreover, we considered the case when our system fails, if the retrieved information is wrong or the system cannot find the match. Firstly, if the application retrieves a wrong result, the user can show the first five best results to select the correct result. If the system does not recognize anything or the proposed results are all wrong, the user can add new knowledge by adding a new picture together with the Wikipedia page link if it exists; otherwise, the picture is out to form our knowledge base.

Concerning the technologies used to develop our application, we used SOLR [41] as a retrieval system that, furthermore, indexes the local feature and the relations with the Linked Open Data. Apache Solr is an open-source search platform based on Apache Lucene that provides the methods for indexing and searching. Linked Open Data are the publisher's way of structured data that allows linking the data among them. LOD relies on standard web technologies like HTTP (Hypertext Transfer Protocol), RDF (Resource Description Framework) [6] and URI (Uniform Resource Identifier). In the retrieval process, we used the Brute Force Matcher to retrieve a code id of LOD used to perform a SPARQL [11] query to retrieve the information used then to augment the image.

In this work, we used LOD DBpedia [19], one of the most significant resources on the web. DBpedia is a Knowledge base built on several structured information found on Wikipedia. Namely, the last statistics report that the complete DBpedia data set features 38 million labels and abstracts in 125 different languages, 25.2 million links to images and 29.8 million links to external web pages; 80.9 million links to Wikipedia, and 41.2 million links to YAGO categories.

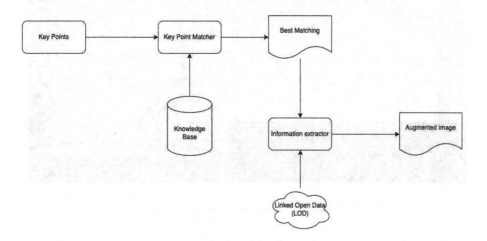

Fig. 4. Augmented image task detail

4 Use Case

In this section, we introduced a use case into the frame of the cultural heritage domain. This application has been developed to show the efficient use of the proposed framework implemented in a mobile application supported by augmented reality and the CBIR technique.

The goal, in this case, is to show the usefulness of our approach in a real scenario to support the user experience and his/her knowledge improvement. From an information retrieval point of view, the integration of LOD and CBIR is based on the mediation of the web as an important medium for publishing different kinds of cultural heritage contents, hence representing a valuable source of cultural heritage data.

We used as example the Pietà of Michelangelo Buonarotti housed in St. Peter's Basilica in Città del Vaticano. Figure 6a shows a picture taken by a user. The system processes the picture and extracts the key point with the respective descriptor, and performs matching with indexed images.

Figure 5 depicts the best matching. Then, the system queries DBpedia, retrieves the description, and overlaps it on the picture, as shown in Fig. 6b.

Fig. 5. Keypoint machining example

5 Experimental Results

This section introduces the experimental strategy and shows the results with related comments and discussion. Firstly, to choose the best keypoint Detector, we evaluated SIFT, SURF, and ORB, adding some "noises" to the images.

(a) Taken picture by user

(b) Picture with overlapped description

Fig. 6. Example

Specifically, we performed the following transformation: change of intensity and colour composition (I), noise (II), shearing (III), rotation (IV), fisheye distortion (V) and scaling (VI). In the case of rotation, we tried several angles, from 0 to 270, with step 45°, and in this work, we reported only the average results.

To evaluate the best keypoint detector we used the measure shown Eq. 1 as proposed by [23].

$$recall = \frac{\#\ correct\ matches}{\#\ correspondences} \tag{1}$$

Figure 7 summarised the result of such evaluation in terms of average matching rate. Therefore, SIFT is the best against I, II, IV and V transformations, and ORB is the best against III and VI transformations. The worst are ORB in I, II and IV transformations and SURF in V transformation.

However, accounting for the average results, SIFT is the best technique, so we choose it as a keypoint detector in our application.

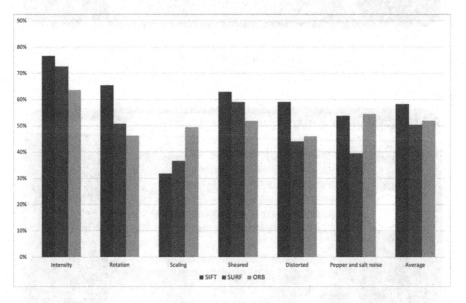

Fig. 7. Evaluation of SIFT, SURF, and ORB against intensity, scaling, rotation, sheared, fish-eye distortion, pepper and salt noise

6   Conclusion and Future Works

In this work, we proposed an application of augmented reality for the cultural heritage domain. Moreover, we developed a modular and easily extensible framework that uses local descriptors and Linked Open Data to provide a valuable and enjoyable experience for the user in the cultural heritage domain. The use of linked open data (LOD) and Semantic Web technologies, combined with the CBIR approach, has provided good results for the generation of SPARQL queries by the mobile interface.

In future work, we will improve our framework by adding new features integrating more one Linked Open Data [34] and robotic applications [21,39] to enhance the user experience. Moreover, to improve the accuracy of our system, we will extend our work using other feature descriptors, local or global, and other ones based on deep neural networks [36]. Moreover, we want to investigate the use of domain crawler [7] to improve the knowledge of our system if we do have not enough information from LOD and the use of novel knowledge structure to represent information [33].

References

1. Affleck, J., Kalay, Y., Kvan, T.: New Heritage: New Media and Cultural Heritage. Routledge, London (2007)
2. Bay, H., Tuytelaars, T., Van Gool, L.: SURF: speeded up robust features. In: Leonardis, A., Bischof, H., Pinz, A. (eds.) ECCV 2006. LNCS, vol. 3951, pp. 404–417. Springer, Heidelberg (2006). https://doi.org/10.1007/11744023_32
3. Berners-Lee, T., Hendler, J., Lassila, O.: The semantic web. Sci. Am. **284**(5), 34–43 (2001)
4. Bres, S., Tellez, B.: Localisation and augmented reality for mobile applications in culture heritage. Computer (Long. Beach. Calif), pp. 1–5. INSA, Lyon (2006)
5. Calonder, M., Lepetit, V., Strecha, C., Fua, P.: BRIEF: binary robust independent elementary features. In: Daniilidis, K., Maragos, P., Paragios, N. (eds.) ECCV 2010. LNCS, vol. 6314, pp. 778–792. Springer, Heidelberg (2010). https://doi.org/10.1007/978-3-642-15561-1_56
6. Candan, K.S., Liu, H., Suvarna, R.: Resource description framework: metadata and its applications. ACM SIGKDD Explor. Newsl. **3**(1), 6–19 (2001)
7. Capuano, A., Rinaldi, A.M., Russo, C.: An ontology-driven multimedia focused crawler based on linked open data and deep learning techniques. Multimed. Tools Appl. **79**(11), 7577–7598 (2020). https://doi.org/10.1007/s11042-019-08252-2
8. Clini, P., Frontoni, E., Quattrini, R., Pierdicca, R.: Augmented reality experience: from high-resolution acquisition to real time augmented contents. Adv. MultiMedia **2014** (2014). https://doi.org/10.1155/2014/597476
9. Cranmer, E., Jung, T.: Augmented reality (AR): business models in urban cultural heritage tourist destinations. In: APacCHRIE Conference, pp. 21–24 (2014)
10. Dastageeri, H., Storz, M., Koukofikis, A., Knauth, S., Coors, V.: Approach and evaluation of a mobile video-based and location-based augmented reality platform for information brokerage. In: ISPRS - International Archives of the Photogrammetry, Remote Sensing and Spatial Information Sciences, vol. XLII-4/W1, pp. 151–157, September 2016. https://doi.org/10.5194/isprs-archives-XLII-4-W1-151-2016
11. Valle, E.D., Ceri, S.: Querying the semantic web: SPARQL. In: Domingue, J., Fensel, D., Hendler, J.A. (eds.) Handbook of Semantic Web Technologies. Springer, Heidelberg (2011). https://doi.org/10.1007/978-3-540-92913-0_8
12. Fritz, F., Susperregui, A., Linaza, M.T.: Enhancing cultural tourism experiences with augmented reality technologies. In: The 6th International Symposium on Virtual Reality, Archaeology and Cultural Heritage VAST (2005)
13. Ghouaiel, N., Garbaya, S., Cieutat, J.M., Jessel, J.P.: Mobile augmented reality in museums: towards enhancing visitor's learning experience. Int. J. Virtual Reality **17**(1), 21–31 (2017)
14. Han, D., Leue, C., Jung, T.: A tourist experience model for augmented reality applications in the urban heritage context. In: APacCHRIE Conference, pp. 21–24 (2014)

15. Han, D.-I.D., Weber, J., Bastiaansen, M., Mitas, O., Lub, X.: Virtual and augmented reality technologies to enhance the visitor experience in cultural tourism. In: tom Dieck, M.C., Jung, T. (eds.) Augmented Reality and Virtual Reality. PI, pp. 113–128. Springer, Cham (2019). https://doi.org/10.1007/978-3-030-06246-0_9

16. Han, J.G., Park, K.W., Ban, K.J., Kim, E.K.: Cultural heritage sites visualization system based on outdoor augmented reality. AASRI Procedia **4**, 64–71 (2013). https://doi.org/10.1016/j.aasri.2013.10.011. https://www.sciencedirect.com/science/article/pii/S2212671613000127. 2013 AASRI Conference on Intelligent Systems and Control

17. Jing, C., Junwei, G., Yongtian, W.: Mobile augmented reality system for personal museum tour guide applications. In: IET International Communication Conference on Wireless Mobile and Computing (CCWMC 2011), pp. 262–265 (2011). https://doi.org/10.1049/cp.2011.0887

18. Candan, K.S., Sapino, M.L.: Data Management for Multimedia Retrieval. Cambridge University Press, Cambridge (2010)

19. Lehmann, J., et al.: DBpedia-a large-scale, multilingual knowledge base extracted from Wikipedia. Semant. Web **6**(2), 167–195 (2015)

20. Lowe, D.G.: Object recognition from local scale-invariant features. In: Proceedings of the Seventh IEEE International Conference on Computer Vision, vol. 2, pp. 1150–1157. IEEE (1999)

21. Madani, K., Rinaldi, A.M., Russo, C.: Combining linked open data and multimedia knowledge base for digital cultural heritage robotic applications. In: 2021 IEEE International Symposium on Multimedia (ISM), pp. 196–203. IEEE (2021)

22. Makantasis, K., Doulamis, A., Doulamis, N., Ioannides, M., Matsatsinis, N.: Content-based filtering for fast 3D reconstruction from unstructured web-based image data. In: Ioannides, M., Magnenat-Thalmann, N., Fink, E., Žarnić, R., Yen, A.-Y., Quak, E. (eds.) EuroMed 2014. LNCS, vol. 8740, pp. 91–101. Springer, Cham (2014). https://doi.org/10.1007/978-3-319-13695-0_9

23. Mikolajczyk, K., Schmid, C.: A performance evaluation of local descriptors. IEEE Trans. Pattern Anal. Mach. Intell. **27**(10), 1615–1630 (2005)

24. Moscato, V., Picariello, A., Rinaldi, A.M.: A recommendation strategy based on user behavior in digital ecosystems. In: Proceedings of the International Conference on Management of Emergent Digital EcoSystems, pp. 25–32 (2010)

25. Muscetti, M., Rinaldi, A.M., Russo, C., Tommasino, C.: Multimedia ontology population through semantic analysis and hierarchical deep features extraction techniques. Knowl. Inf. Syst. **64**, 1283–1303 (2022). https://doi.org/10.1007/s10115-022-01669-6

26. Neuhofer, B., Buhalis, D., Ladkin, A.: A typology of technology-enhanced tourism experiences. Int. J. Tour. Res. **16**(4), 340–350 (2014)

27. Olojede, A.: Investigating image processing algorithms for provision of information in rock art sites using mobile devices. Master's thesis, University of Cape Town (2016)

28. Purificato, E., Rinaldi, A.M.: Multimedia and geographic data integration for cultural heritage information retrieval. Multimed. Tools Appl. **77**(20), 27447–27469 (2018). https://doi.org/10.1007/s11042-018-5931-7

29. Purificato, E., Rinaldi, A.M.: A multimodal approach for cultural heritage information retrieval. In: Gervasi, O., et al. (eds.) ICCSA 2018. LNCS, vol. 10960, pp. 214–230. Springer, Cham (2018). https://doi.org/10.1007/978-3-319-95162-1_15

30. Rigby, J., Smith, S.P.: Augmented reality challenges for cultural heritage. Applied Informatics Research Group, University of Newcastle, Newcastle (2013)

31. Rinaldi, A.M., Russo, C.: A semantic-based model to represent multimedia big data. In: Proceedings of the 10th International Conference on Management of Digital EcoSystems, pp. 31–38. ACM (2018)
32. Rinaldi, A.M., Russo, C.: User-centered information retrieval using semantic multimedia big data. In: 2018 IEEE International Conference on Big Data (Big Data), pp. 2304–2313. IEEE (2018)
33. Rinaldi, A.M., Russo, C.: Using a multimedia semantic graph for web document visualization and summarization. Multimed. Tools Appl. **80**(3), 3885–3925 (2020). https://doi.org/10.1007/s11042-020-09761-1
34. Rinaldi, A.M., Russo, C., Madani, K.: A semantic matching strategy for very large knowledge bases integration. Int. J. Inf. Technol. Web Eng. (IJITWE) **15**(2), 1–29 (2020)
35. Rinaldi, A.M., Russo, C., Tommasino, C.: A semantic approach for document classification using deep neural networks and multimedia knowledge graph. Expert Syst. Appl. **169**, 114320 (2021)
36. Rinaldi, A.M., Russo, C., Tommasino, C.: A knowledge-driven multimedia retrieval system based on semantics and deep features. Future Internet **12**(11), 183 (2020)
37. Rodrigues, J.M.F., et al.: Mobile augmented reality framework - MIRAR. In: Antona, M., Stephanidis, C. (eds.) UAHCI 2018. LNCS, vol. 10908, pp. 102–121. Springer, Cham (2018). https://doi.org/10.1007/978-3-319-92052-8_9
38. Rublee, E., Rabaud, V., Konolige, K., Bradski, G.: ORB: an efficient alternative to SIFT or SURF. In: 2011 International Conference on Computer Vision, pp. 2564–2571. IEEE (2011)
39. Russo, C., Madani, K., Rinaldi, A.M.: An unsupervised approach for knowledge construction applied to personal robots. IEEE Trans. Cogn. Dev. Syst. **13**(1), 6–15 (2020)
40. Russo, C., Madani, K., Rinaldi, A.M.: Knowledge construction through semantic interpretation of visual information. In: Rojas, I., Joya, G., Catala, A. (eds.) IWANN 2019. LNCS, vol. 11507, pp. 246–257. Springer, Cham (2019). https://doi.org/10.1007/978-3-030-20518-8_21
41. Shahi, D.: Apache Solr: An Introduction. In: Apache solr, pp. 1–9. Springer, Berkeley (2015). https://doi.org/10.1007/978-1-4842-1070-3_1
42. Shin, C., Hong, S.H., Yoon, H.: Enriching natural monument with user-generated mobile augmented reality mashup. J. Multimed. Inf. Syst. **7**(1), 25–32 (2020)
43. Tam, D.C.C., Fiala, M.: A real time augmented reality system using GPU acceleration. In: 2012 Ninth Conference on Computer and Robot Vision, pp. 101–108 (2012). https://doi.org/10.1109/CRV.2012.21
44. Titchen, S.M., et al.: On the construction of outstanding universal value: UNESCO's world heritage convention (convention concerning the protection of the world cultural and natural heritage, 1972) and the identification and assessment of cultural places for inclusion in the world heritage list (1995)
45. tom Dieck, M.C., Jung, T.H.: Value of augmented reality at cultural heritage sites: a stakeholder approach. J. Destination Mark. Manag. **6**(2), 110–117 (2017). https://doi.org/10.1016/j.jdmm.2017.03.002. https://www.sciencedirect.com/science/article/pii/S2212571X16300774. Special edition on Digital Destinations
46. Ufkes, A., Fiala, M.: A markerless augmented reality system for mobile devices. In: 2013 International Conference on Computer and Robot Vision, pp. 226–233 (2013). https://doi.org/10.1109/CRV.2013.51
47. Vargo, S.L., Lusch, R.F.: From goods to service(s): divergences and convergences of logics. Ind. Mark. Manage. **37**(3), 254–259 (2008)

48. Vi, S., da Silva, T.S., Maurer, F.: User experience guidelines for designing HMD extended reality applications. In: Lamas, D., Loizides, F., Nacke, L., Petrie, H., Winckler, M., Zaphiris, P. (eds.) INTERACT 2019. LNCS, vol. 11749, pp. 319–341. Springer, Cham (2019). https://doi.org/10.1007/978-3-030-29390-1_18
49. Yovcheva, Z., Buhalis, D., Gatzidis, C.: Engineering augmented tourism experiences. In: Cantoni, L., Xiang, Z.P. (eds.) Information and Communication Technologies in Tourism 2013, pp. 24–35. Springer, Heidelberg (2013). https://doi.org/10.1007/978-3-642-36309-2_3
50. Yu, L.: Linked open data. In: Yu, L. (ed.) A Developer's Guide to the Semantic Web, pp. 409–466. Springer, Heidelberg (2011). https://doi.org/10.1007/978-3-642-15970-1_11

Effectively and Efficiently Supporting Visual Big Data Analytics over Big Sequential Data: An Innovative Data Science Approach

Alfredo Cuzzocrea[1,2]([✉]), Majid Abbasi Sisara[1,3], Carson K. Leung[4], Yan Wen[4], and Fan Jiang[5]

[1] iDEA Lab, University of Calabria, Rende, Italy
{alfredo.cuzzocrea,majid.abbasi}@unical.it
[2] LORIA, University of Lorraine, Nancy, France
[3] Department of Engineering, University of Trieste, Trieste, Italy
[4] Department of Computer Science, University of Manitoba, Winnipeg, MB, Canada
kleung@cs.umanitoba.ca
[5] Department of Computer Science, University of Northern British Columbia, Prince George, BC, Canada
Fang.Jiang@unbc.ca

Abstract. In the current era of big data, huge volumes of valuable data have been generated and collected at a rapid velocity from a wide variety of rich data sources. In recent years, the willingness of many government, researchers, and organizations are led by the initiates of open data to share their data and make them publicly accessible. Healthcare, disease, and epidemiological data, such as privacy-preserving statistics on patients who suffered from epidemic diseases such as Coronavirus disease 2019 (COVID-19), are examples of open big data. Analyzing these open big data can be for social good. For instance, people get a better understanding of the disease by analyzing and mining the disease statistics, which may inspire them to take part in preventing, detecting, controlling and combating the disease. Having a pictorial representation further enhances the understanding of the data and corresponding results for analysis and mining because a picture is worth a thousand words. Hence, in this paper, we present a visual data science solution for the visualization and visual analytics of big sequential data. The visualization and visual analytics of sequences of real-life COVID-19 epidemiological data illustrate the ideas. Through our solution, we enable users to visualize the COVID-19 epidemiological data over time. It also allows people to visually analyze the data and discover relationships among popular features associated with the COVID-19 cases. The effectiveness of our visual data science solution in enhancing user experience in the visualization and visual analytics of big sequential data are demonstrated by evaluation of these real-life sequential COVID-19 epidemiological data.

Keywords: Information visualization · Big data · Sequences · Data science · Visual data science · Data mining · Data analytics · Visual analytics · COVID-19

O. Gervasi et al. (Eds.): ICCSA 2022, LNCS 13376, pp. 113–125, 2022.
https://doi.org/10.1007/978-3-031-10450-3_9

1 Introduction

Big data is a phenomenon characterized by the ability to easily generate and collect large quantities of valuable data at rapid speeds from a wide variety of rich data sources. In recent years, the initiates of open data also led to the willingness of many government, researchers, and organizations to share their data and make them publicly accessible. Examples of open big data include biodiversity data [1], biomedical/healthcare data and disease reports (e.g., COVID-19 statistics) [2–5], census data [6], financial time series [7–11], music data [12], patent register [13, 14], social networks [15–17], transportation and urban data [18–22], weather data [23], and web data [24, 25].

There is valuable information embedded in those open big data [26–28] which also makes good use of data mining algorithms [29–34], data analytics methods [35–39, 56–58], visual analytics methods [40–43], and machine learning tools [2–44]. Hence, analyzing and mining these big data can be for social good. By analyzing and mining disease statistics, people can learn more about the disease, such as:

- An outbreak of SARS in 2003 was caused by a coronavirus (CoV) that was associated with SARS.
- Swine flu, which was caused by influenza A virus subtype H1N1 (A/H1N1) and led to a pandemic from 2009 to mid-2010.
- A MERS-CoV caused Middle East respiratory syndrome (MERS). During the period of 2012–2018, the disease was reported from the Middle East (e.g., Saudi Arabia), while in 2015, it was reported from South Korea.
- Zika virus disease, which was primarily transmitted by the bite of an infected mosquito. An outbreak was reported in Brazil during 2015–2016.
- SARS-CoV-2 caused coronavirus disease 2019 (COVID-19). In early 2020, this outbreak was reported to become a global pandemic, and it is still prevailing in 2021.

A better understanding of the disease may inspire people to take part in preventing, detecting, controlling and combating the disease.

We know well that "a picture is worth a thousand words". It is desirable to represent the discovered information and knowledge visually to make it easier to comprehend. This calls for an important branch of data science—visual data science, which makes good use of visualization and visual analytics techniques.

In IV 2020, we presented a big data visualization and visual analytics tool for visualizing and analyzing COVID-19 epidemiological data was presented by us [45]. By analyzing cumulative COVID-19 statistics, it visualizes the most common features (e.g., frequently used transmission methods, hospitalization status, clinical outcomes) associated with the majority of COVID-19 cases.

As COVID-19 has spanned more than a year, the cumulative statistics reveal numerical summary of some characteristics of COVID-19 cases for the entire period. However, temporal changes may be not revealed in these characteristics during this period. There is a need for a tool or solution to visualize and analyze COVID-19 epidemiological data on a temporal basis. This motivates our current work. As a non-trivial but logical extension to our big data visualization and visual analytics tool from IV 2020 work, a data science solution for visualization and visual analytics of temporal data—i.e., a COVID-19 sequence—in the current IV 2021 paper is designed and developed by us.

We designed and developed our data science solution in such a way that notably it visualizes and visually analyses not only COVID-19 data, but also other big sequences. For example, visualization and visual analytics of financial time series or stock prices helps financial analysts to get a better understanding of the trends (e.g., uptrends, down-trends) of a stock. Similarly, social scientists are helped by visualization and visual analytics of temporal employment data to get a better understanding of social and/or economic situations and impacts of any irregular events or shocks (e.g., COVID-19 pandemic).

Our major contribution to this paper is the design and development of a data science solution for visual analytics of big sequential data. Our solution visualizes temporal trends in the sequence. The findings (e.g., discovered information and knowledge) from the visual analytics on the temporal sequential data are also visualized by it. The tool reveals, for example, popular features associated with the data (e.g., popular transmission methods, hospitalization status, and clinical outcomes at certain times) and how these characteristics change over time. To illustrate our key ideas, we apply our solution to real- life COVID-19 sequences. Our solution applies to a real-life COVID-19 sequences for evaluating it.

The remainder of this paper follows the following format. The next section discusses background and related works. Our data science solution for visualization and visual analytics of big sequential data are described in Sect. 3. The results of the evaluation based on Canadian COVID-19 epidemiological data are presented in Sect. 4. Finally, conclusions are drawn in Sect. 5.

2   Background Analysis

As for application to visualization and visual analytics of COVID-19 data, they have developed many visualizers and dashboards since its declaration as a pandemic. In this regard, the following dashboards are noteworthy: (a) the COVID-19 dashboard created by the World Health Organization (WHO); (b) the COVID-19 dashboard developed by the Center for Systems Science and Engineering (CSSE) at Johns Hopkins University; and (c) the COVID-19 dashboard created by the European Center for Disease Prevention and Control (ECDC). They provide summary for global COVID-19 situations. Moreover, visualizers and dash- boards are provided by local governments (e.g., Government of Canada4) and media (e.g., TV5, 6, Wikipedia7) for local COVID-19 situations. A feature that these visualizers and dashboards all have in common is that they display the number of new/confirmed cases and deaths, as well as their cumulative totals. They serve the purpose of fast dissemination of these crucial numbers related to COVID-19 cases. However, we embed additional information and knowledge in the data and yet to be discovered.

To address this issue, we developed a big data visualization and visual analytics tool for identifying infrequent patterns in COVID-19 statistics. In terms of related works on visualizing frequent patterns, Jentner and Keim [46] surveyed several visualization techniques for frequent patterns. we can generalize these techniques into four categories:

- Frequent patterns are best represented visually through lattice representation [53]. With it, frequent patterns are represented as nodes in a lattice (aka concept hierarchy). Edges connect immediate supersets and subsets of a frequent pattern.
- Using pixels as the representation, a frequent k-itemset (a pattern consisting of k items) is represented by a pixel [47].
- Linear visualization, in which frequent patterns are represented linearly. For example, a frequent k-itemset in a polyline is represented by *FIsViz* [48] that connects k nodes in a 2-dimensional space. Rather than represent frequent patterns in an orthogonal diagram (i.e., a wiring-type diagram), *FpVAT* [42] represents them as frequent patterns.
- Tree visualization, in which frequent patterns are represented according to a tree hierarchy. For example, frequent patterns with a side-view of the pyramid are shown by *PyramidViz* [49], in which puts short patterns on the bottom of the pyramid and puts longer related patterns (e.g., extensions of short patterns) on the top. Likewise, *FpMapViz* [50], which shows frequent patterns by overlaying related patterns over shorter patterns, shows frequent patterns in the foreground and background.

Similar to the aforementioned tree visualization, our big data visualization and visual analytics tool [45] for visualizing frequent patterns from the cumulative COVID-19 statistics also follows a hierarchy so that patterns can be connected to their extensions. We can consider it as showing frequent patterns with a top-view. This scheme, however, instead of placing short patterns in the background and overlaying long related patterns in the foreground, places short patterns in the inner ring near the center and long related patterns in the outer ring (although they do not overlap or overlay with the inner ring). Immediate extensions of a pattern are put just outside (but touching) the sector representing the pattern. More specifically, we represent the frequent patterns and their related in a pie chart or a sunburst diagram (i.e., a doughnut chart).

To elaborate, when mining and analyzing a Canadian COVID-19 epidemiological dataset collected from Public Health Agency of Canada (PHAC) and Statistics Canada8 for the period from 2020 to May 29, 2021 (i.e., Week 21 of 2021), our big data visualization and visual analytics tool visualizes transmission methods of 1,368,422 COVID-19 cases in Canada. Figure 1 shows a frequent 1-itemset (i.e., a singleton pattern) {*domestic acquisition*}:82.35% and its patterns {*unstated transmission method*}:17.19% and {*international travel*}: 0.46%. These patterns reveal that 82.35% (as the white ring sector represent it) of these cases acquired the disease domestically via community exposures, 17.19% (as represented by the grey ring sector) were without any stated transmission methods, and the remaining 0.46% (as represented by the tiny light-blue ring sector) were exposed to the disease via international travel.

Expanding the frequent singleton pattern, we find a frequent 2-itemset (i.e., non-singleton pattern) {*domestic acquisition, non-hospitalized*}:52.41%. This reveals that, among those who domestically acquired the disease from community exposures, a large fraction (52.41%/82.35% $\approx$ 0.64) of them did not required hospitalization. This is shown in Fig. 2 that how our big data visualization and visual analytics tool represents this frequent 2-itemset by putting a green ring sector outside of (but touching) the white ring sector representing the domestic acquisition. In addition, the figure reveals that, while most of them did not require hospitalization, a significant proportion (25.83%/82.35% $\approx$

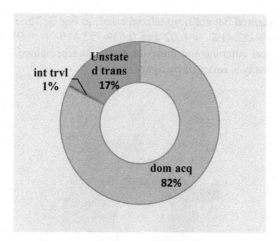

Fig. 1. Visualization of transmission methods.

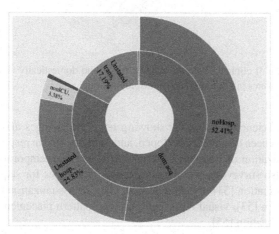

Fig. 2. Visualization of hospital status among those who domestically acquired COVID-19 via community exposures.

0.31) were not listed in hospitals (represented by the gray rings). Smaller fractions of them were admitted to the hospital. Specifically, it hospitalized $3.38\%/82.35\% \approx 0.04$ of them but did not require to admit to the intensive care unit (ICU), as the small yellow ring sector represents it; it admitted $0.73\%/82.35\% \approx 0.01$ of them to the ICU, as the tiny red ring sector represents it.

Among those who domestically acquired but not hospitalized, a significant number $(50.87\%/52.41\% \approx 0.97)$ of them recovered. In this direction, a frequent 3-itemset {*domestic acquisition, not hospitalized, recovered*}:50.87% indicates that, among those who domestically acquired but not hospitalized, a significant number $(50.87\%/52.41\% \approx 0.97)$ of them recovered. This pattern is represented by a golden ring sector, which was put outside of (but touching) the green ring sector representing the domestically acquired but not hospitalized cases, in Fig. 3. The remaining two tiny fractions (i.e., $0.91\%/52.41\% \approx 0.02$ and $0.63\%/52.41\% \approx 0.01$) belong to those without stated clinical outcome and those deceased, as represented by grey and black ring sectors respectively is revealed by figure.

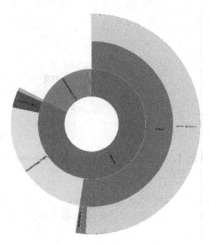

Fig. 3. Visualization of clinical outcomes among those who domestically acquired COVID-19 via community exposures but did not require hospitalization.

A visual data science solution for showing temporal changes and visualizing big sequential data has been designed, developed, and implemented in response to the observation that visualization of frequent patterns may not reveal temporal changes. Jenter and Keim [46] also surveyed several visualization techniques for sequential patterns. Individual representation [51] is included, flow diagram visualization [52], aggregated pattern visualization [53], visual representation with pattern placement strategies [54], and episode visualization [55].

3   An Innovative Data Science Approach for Supporting Visual Big Data Analytics Over Big Sequential Data Effectively and Efficiently

We develop a visual data science solution to explore and visualize temporal changes. It first collects and integrates data from a wide variety of rich data sources. Then the data is preprocessed and a temporal hierarchy to generalize the temporal data is built by it. A fine granularity of data can be collected depending on the application. Having the temporal hierarchy enables us to pick an appreciate level of data granularity. For instance, although it can collect dynamic streaming data at a rapid rate (e.g., per second, minute), may lead to more meaningful and interesting results may be led by analyzing data aggregated at a coarser level (e.g., hourly daily). COVID-19 statistics, for example, are usually updated every day. We observed that, analyzing the data on a yearly basis may miss some details, but analyzing them on a daily basis may lead to a huge solution space and may be sensitive to unnecessary fluctuation (e.g., delay in testing or reporting cases due to weekends). Consequently, they are appeared appropriate by analyzing them on a weekly basis.

In addition to choosing the appropriate level of temporal hierarchy, the next key step is to aggregate frequency counts at this level (for example, summing the frequencies over this period of time). The resulting frequent patterns help reveal frequently observed characteristics at a time instance. By repeating the mining procedure over all temporal points, then similarities and differences among frequent patterns discovered at these temporal points are compared and contrasted by us. Using COVID-19 data, we aggregate their daily counts of multiple features associated with the data on a weekly basis to obtain corresponding weekly counts. Then, we discover frequent patterns revealing characteristics (e.g., transmission method, hospital status, clinical outcome) of COVID-19 in a particular week (e.g., Week 8 of 2020).

In terms of visualization for sequential data, many related works focus on visualizing collections of individual sequences. Contrary to that, we focus here on visualizing patterns that occur in sequences. For example, instead of analyzing and visualizing the trend of each individual stock, our visual data science solution focuses on visualizing temporal changes in the composition of stocks. As another example, for sequences of COVID-19 data, our solution focuses on visualizing temporal changes in the composition of some features (e.g., raise or drop in the number of domestically infected cases among all transmission methods).

Pie charts and sunburst diagrams (i.e., doughnut charts) are tempting ways to visualize temporal changes over compositions of features. Given an outward sunburst diagram for a temporal point, one could repeat the mining and visualization process to generate multiple sunburst diagrams (with one diagram for each temporal point). While all information for analysis of temporal changes is captured by the stack of sunburst diagrams, it may be challenges to view and comprehend the details for each diagram, let alone discovering their temporal changes.

The visual data science solution represents and visualizes a feature's temporal composition by using stacked columns to make the composition easy to understand. We observe that, when visualizing the composition of a (categorical) feature, each record takes on a single value (including NULL) for the feature. Hence, for singleton patterns on a feature, the total number of records should be matched the sum of frequencies of each distinct value. If there are no singleton patterns on the k features, then the sum of the frequencies of the k features, since each one comes from a distinct domain, should be equal to the total number of records that exist. As a concreate example, with 2 transmission methods (i.e., domestic acquisition and international travel) and unstated transmission method (i.e., NULL) for the feature "*transmission method*", the sum of frequencies of these $2 + 1 = 3$ feature values should match the total number of records. With 3 hospital statuses (i.e., ICU, non- ICU hospitalized, not hospitalized) and NULL for an additional feature "*hospital status*", the sum of frequencies $(2 + 1) \times (3 + 1) = 12$ combinations of these two features should be matched the total number of records. As a result, the height of the stacked column indicates the frequency of all records at the particular time.

For easy comparison of compositions of features over n temporal points, our visual data science solution represents these n compositions with n stacked column arranged according to their temporal order. Absolute frequency at time t is given by The height of the entire stacked column. In some cases, the height of the entire stacked column or segments of it may reveal the uptrend or downtrend.

In addition, our solution provides users with an alternative representation, in which compositions are represented by 100% stack column. By doing so, we can easily observe the relative frequency (i.e., percentage composition) of different values of features. It is also possible to observe changes in relative frequency.

4 Experimental Assessment and Analysis

To evaluate our visual data science solution for visualizing and visually analyzing big sequential data, we applied it to the same real-life Canadian COVID-19 epidemiological dataset collected from Public Health Agency of Canada (PHAC) and Statistics Canada for the period from 2020 to May 29, 2021 (i.e., Week 21 of 2021) mentioned in Section II. Compositions of features associated with these 1,368,422 Canadian COVID-19 cases in stacked column or 100% stacked column charts are represented by our solution. The columns show the composition of features during the week.

For example, Fig. 4(a) shows sequences of stacked columns, in which each column represents the composition of two stated transmission methods. The number of cases for each week is clearly indicated by heights of each column. In each column, the (absolute) heights of the segments representing the domestically acquired cases, foreign-exposed cases, and cases without indication of the method of transmission are shown. In earlier weeks, observable numbers of cases were exposed via travel. In later/recent weeks, more cases whose transmission methods were unknown (and probably still under investigation). As the general pattern shows, the three waves of COVID-19 in Canada oscillate up and down (as well as peak and valley).

To clearly show the relative percentage of these three transmission methods (including NULL/unstated ones), our visual data science solution provides users with a representation in 100% stacked columns. See Fig. 4(b), the significant percentages of cases exposed via international travel—e.g., close to 50% of cases infected in Week 9 (i.e., March 01–07) of 2020 can be easily observed from which users. As a result of international travel restrictions, the numbers decreased from Week 14 (April 05–11) of 2020.

For user convenience, our visual data science solution also provides users with options to include or exclude NULL values. As an instance of excluding NULL values, the relative percentages of stated transmission methods of cases is shown by Fig.4(c).

Data Science solution reveals the frequencies of four "domestic acquisition", *-combinations of hospital status within the exposure group based on the most frequent transmission method (i.e., domestic acquisition). Figure 5(a) shows the frequencies of these hospital statuses—namely, not hospitalized, non-ICU hospitalization, ICU hospitalization, and unstated hospital status—by green, yellow, red and white segments of stacked columns. That majority of these domestically acquired cases were not hospitalized is revealed by the figure. As shown in Fig. 5(b) in Week 9 of 2020, almost 20%

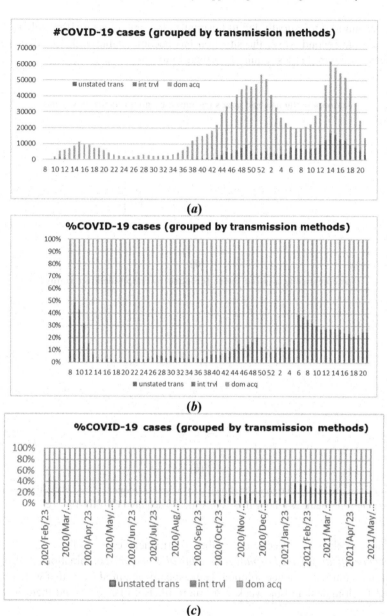

Fig. 4. Our visual data science solution showing (*a*) absolute frequency and (*b*) relative percentage of different transmission methods, as well as (*c*) relative percentage of stated transmission methods for Canadian COVID-19 cases from Week 8 of 2020 to Week 21 of 2021 (i.e., Feb. 23, 2020 to May 29, 2021).

of cases acquired domestically led to hospitalization, and close to 10% to ICU admission. Since the second wave, the situation has become stable with less than 10% of domestically acquired cases required hospitalization.

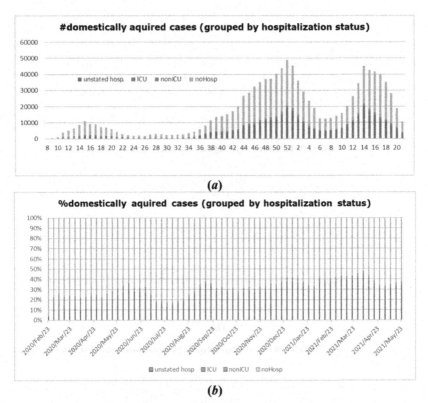

(a)

(b)

Fig. 5. Our visual data science solution showing (*a*) absolute frequency and (*b*) relative percentage of different hospital statuses among those domestically acquired COVID-19 cases.

Along this direction, the frequencies of the three ⟨*domestic acquisition*, *not hospitalized*, *clinical outcome*⟩-combinations also are visualized by our data science solution. Domestically acquired cases that were not hospitalized for longer than one week were more likely to be recovered than those that were.

5   Conclusions and Future Work

In this paper, we presented a visual data science solution for the visualization and visual analytics of big sequential data. The ideas through its applications to real-life COVID-19 epidemiological data are illustrated by us. In this approach, we represent feature values in stacked columns, which makes temporal comparisons easier. Although we evaluated and showed its practicality by using COVID-19 data, it can be applicable to visualization and visual analytics of other big sequential data. As ongoing and future work, visibility, interpretability and explainability of our visual data science solution in visualization and visual analytics of big sequential data are further enhanced by us.

References

1. Anderson-Grégoire, I.M., et al.: A big data science solution for analytics on moving objects. AINA **2**, 133–145 (2021)
2. Diallo, A.H., et al.: Proportional visualization of genotypes and phenotypes with rainbow boxes: methods and application to sickle cell disease. IV 2019, Part I, pp. 1–6 (2019)
3. Hamdi, S., et al.: Intra and inter relationships between biomedical signals: a VAR model analysis. IV 2019, Part I, pp. 411–416 (2019)
4. Pellecchia, M.T., et al.: Identifying correlations among biomedical data through information retrieval techniques. IV 2019, Part I, pp. 269–274 (2019)
5. Shang, S., et al.: Spatial data science of COVID-19 data. IEEE HPCC- SmartCity-DSS 2020, pp. 1370–1375 (2020)
6. Choy, C.M., et al.: Natural sciences meet social sciences: census data analytics for detecting home language shifts. IMCOM 2021, pp. 1–8 (2021)
7. Chanda, A.K., et al.: A new framework for mining weighted periodic patterns in time series databases. ESWA **79**, 207–224 (2017)
8. Jonker, D., et al.: Industry-driven visual analytics for understanding financial timeseries models. IV 2019, Part I, pp. 210–215 (2019)
9. Luong, N.N.T., et al.: A visual interactive analytics interface for complex event processing and machine learning processing of financial market data. IV 2020, pp. 189–194 (2020)
10. Morris, K.J., et al.: Token-based adaptive time-series prediction by ensembling linear and non-linear estimators: a machine learning approach for predictive analytics on big stock data. IEEE ICMLA 2018, pp. 1486–1491 (2018)
11. Prokofieva, M.: Visualization of financial data in teaching financial accounting, IV 2020, pp. 674–678 (2020)
12. Barkwell, K.E., et al.: Big data visualisation and visual analytics for music data mining. IV 2018, pp. 235–240 (2018)
13. Lee, W., et al.: Reducing noises for recall-oriented patent retrieval. IEEE BDCloud 2014, pp. 579–586 (2014)
14. Leung, C.K., et al.: Information technology-based patent retrieval model. Springer Handbook of Science and Technology Indicators, pp. 859–874 (2019)
15. Huang, M.L., et al.: Designing infographics/visual icons of social network by referencing to the design concept of ancient oracle bone characters. IV 2020, pp. 694–699 (2020)
16. Jiang, F., et al.: Finding popular friends in social networks. CGC 2012, pp. 501–508 (2012)
17. Singh, S.P., Leung, C.K.: A theoretical approach for discovery of friends from directed social graphs. IEEE/ACM ASONAM 2020, pp. 697–701 (2020)
18. Audu, A.-R.A., Cuzzocrea, A., Leung, C.K., MacLeod, K.A., Ohin, N.I., Pulgar-Vidal, N.C.: An intelligent predictive analytics system for transportation analytics on open data towards the development of a smart city. In: Barolli, L., Hussain, F.K., Ikeda, M. (eds.) CISIS 2019. AISC, vol. 993, pp. 224–236. Springer, Cham (2020). https://doi.org/10.1007/978-3-030-22354-0_21
19. Balbin, P.P.F., et al.: Predictive analytics on open big data for supporting smart transportation services. Procedia Comput. Sci. **176**, 3009–3018 (2020)
20. Leung, C.K., et al.: Effective classification of ground transportation modes for urban data mining in smart cities. DaWaK 2018, pp. 83–97 (2018)

21. Leung, C.K., et al.: Urban analytics of big transportation data for supporting smart cities. DaWaK 2019, pp. 24–33 (2019)
22. Shawket, I.M., El khateeb, S.: Redefining urban public space's characters after COVID-19: empirical study on Egyptian residential spaces. IV 2020, pp. 614–619 (2020)
23. Cox, T.S., et al.: An accurate model for hurricane trajectory prediction. IEEE COMPSAC 2018, vol. 2, pp. 534–539 (2018)
24. Leung, C.K., et al.: Explainable machine learning and mining of influential patterns from sparse web. IEEE/WIC/ACM WI-IAT 2020, pp. 829–836 (2020)
25. Singh, S.P., et al.: Analytics of similar-sounding names from the web with phonetic based clustering. IEEE/WIC/ACM WI-IAT 2020, pp. 580–585 (2020)
26. Dierckens, K.E., et al.: A data science and engineering solution for fast k-means clustering of big data. IEEE TrustCom-BigDataSE-ICESS 2017, pp. 925–932 (2017)
27. Leung, C.K., Jiang, F.: A data science solution for mining interesting patterns from uncertain big data. IEEE BDCloud 2014, pp. 235–242 (2014)
28. Muñoz-Lago, P., et al.: Visualising the structure of 18th century operas: a multidisciplinary data science approach. IV 2020, pp. 530–536 (2020)
29. Alam, M.T., et al.: Mining frequent patterns from hypergraph databases. PAKDD 2021, Part II, pp. 3–15 (2021)
30. Fariha, A., et al.: Mining frequent patterns from human interactions in meetings using directed acyclic graphs. PAKDD 2013, Part I, pp. 38–49 (2013)
31. Leung, C.K.: Big data analysis and mining. Encyclop. Inf. Sci. Technol. **4e**, 338–348 (2018)
32. Leung, C.K.: Uncertain frequent pattern mining. Frequent Pattern Mining, pp. 417–453 (2014)
33. Roy, K.K., et al.: Mining sequential patterns in uncertain databases using hierarchical index structure. PAKDD 2021, Part II, pp. 29–41 (2021)
34. von Richthofen, A., et al.: Urban mining: visualizing the availability of construction materials for re-use in future cities. IV 2017, pp. 306–311 (2017)
35. Casalino, G., et al.: Incremental and adaptive fuzzy clustering for virtual learning environments data analysis. IV 2020, pp. 382–387 (2020)
36. Huang, M.L., et al.: Stroke data analysis through a HVN visual mining platform. IV 2019, Part II, pp. 1–6 (2019)
37. Jiang, F., Leung, C.K.: A data analytic algorithm for managing, querying, and processing uncertain big data in cloud environments. Algorithms **8**(4), 1175–1194 (2015)
38. W. Lee, et al. (eds.): Big Data Analyses, Services, and Smart Data (2021)
39. Leung, C.K., Jiang, F.: Big data analytics of social networks for the discovery of "following" patterns. DaWaK 2015, pp. 123–135 (2015)
40. Afonso, A.P., et al.: RoseTrajVis: visual analytics of trajectories with rose diagrams. IV 2020, pp. 378–384 (2020)
41. Kaupp, L., et al.: An Industry 4.0-ready visual analytics model for context-aware diagnosis in smart manufacturing. IV 2020, pp. 350–359 (2020)
42. Leung, C.K., Carmichael, C.L.: FpVAT: A visual analytic tool for supporting frequent pattern mining. ACM SIGKDD Explor. **11**(2), 39–48 (2009)
43. Maçãs, C., et al.: VaBank: visual analytics for banking transactions. IV 2020, pp. 336–343 (2020)
44. Ahn, S., et al.: A fuzzy logic based machine learning tool for supporting big data business analytics in complex artificial intelligence environments. FUZZ-IEEE 2019, pp. 1259–1264 (2019)
45. Leung, C.K., et al.: Big data visualization and visual analytics of COVID-19 data. IV 2020, pp. 415–420 (2020)
46. Jentner, W., Keim, D.A.: Visualization and visual analytic techniques for patterns. High-Utility Pattern Mining, pp. 303–337 (2019)

47. Munzner, T., et al.: Visual mining of power sets with large alphabets. Tech. rep. TR-2005–25, UBC (2005). https://www.cs.ubc.ca/tr/2005/tr-2005-25
48. Leung, C.K., et al.: FIsViz: a frequent itemset visualizer. PAKDD 2008, pp. 644–652 (2008)
49. Leung, C.K., et al.: PyramidViz: visual analytics and big data visualization of frequent patterns. IEEE DASC-PICom-DataCom- CyberSciTech 2016, pp. 913–916 (2016)
50. Leung, C.K., et al.: FpMapViz: a space-filling visualization for frequent patterns. IEEE ICDM 2011 Workshops, pp. 804–811 (2011)
51. Cappers, B.C.M., van Wijk, J.J.: Exploring multivariate event sequences using rules, aggregations, and selections. IEEE TVCG **24**(1), 532–541 (2018)
52. Zhao, J., et al.: MatrixWave: visual comparison of event sequence data. ACM CHI 2015, pp. 259–268 (2015)
53. Chen, Y., et al.: Sequence synopsis: optimize visual summary of temporal event data. IEEE TVCG **24**(1), 45–55 (2018)
54. Stolper, C.D., et al.: Progressive visual analytics: user-driven visual exploration of in-progress analytics. IEEE TVCG **20**(12), 1653–1662 (2014)
55. Jentner, W., et al.: Feature alignment for the analysis of verbatim text transcripts. EuroVis 2017 Workshop on EuroVA, pp. 13– 18 (2017)
56. Cuzzocrea, A., et al.: Fragmenting very large XML data warehouses via K-means clustering algorithm. Int. J. Bus. Intell. Data Min. **4**(3/4), 301–328 (2009)
57. Ceci, M., Cuzzocrea, A., Malerba, D.: Effectively and efficiently supporting roll-up and drill-down OLAP operations over continuous dimensions via hierarchical clustering. J. Intell. Inf. Syst. **44**(3), 309–333 (2013). https://doi.org/10.1007/s10844-013-0268-1
58. Bellatreche, L., et al.: F&A: a methodology for effectively and efficiently designing parallel relational data warehouses on heterogenous database clusters. DaWak 2010, pp. 89–104 (2010)

Right Ownership as the Particularization of Territorial Formations in the Conditions of Decentralization Reform of Ukraine

Pavlo Ivanyuta[1] , Evgen Kartashov[2] , Nadiia Datsii[3] , Maksym Kovalskyi[4] ,
George Abuselidze[5(✉)] , and Olena Aleinikova[6]

[1] Vinnitsya Cooperative Institute, Akademiker Yangel, 59, Vinnytsia 21009, Ukraine
[2] University of Educational Management, Sichovykh Striltsiv, 52A, Kyiv, Ukraine
[3] Polissia National University, Staryi Boulevard, 7, Zhytomyr 10008, Ukraine
[4] Central-Western Interregional Department of the Ministry of Justice, Volodymyrska vul. 91,
Khmelnytskyi 29000, Ukraine
[5] Batumi Shota Rustaveli State University, Ninoshvili, 35, Batumi, Georgia
george.abuselidze@gmail.com
[6] Masaryk University (MUNI), Žerotínovo nám. 617/9, 601 77 Brno, Czech Republic

Abstract. On the modern stage the economic relationships in Ukraine, which constant by years, the characterized it stage of development of the state regulation, organically connect with right ownership into economics object, and beforehand, land. Here determined of through property relationships is legal regulation the state into transfer, accepted, appropriation by different of physical and juridical persons depend from fields of their activity. And existing innovation of this research to lie down in that, what objects of the right ownership, as forms of legal regulation of public relationships, clearly interconnected by territory borders, especially at the time reforming of local self-government and territorial organization of authority in Ukraine. And by this example is creation and open of transparent land market. The purpose of the article is to study the stages of development of state regulation of relations to ensure, provide and protect property rights by their types and forms, depending on the characteristics of territorial entities of Ukraine, which, of course, contain objects of different possessions. The article used methods of comparison and description, the method of decomposition, methods of observation and grouping. It should be concluded that the right of ownership in Ukraine is particularly subject to regulation by public authorities and local governments and is evidenced by the legal fact that establishes common relations in society and has a relationship with the territorial location of objects according to their purpose or benefits. And providing large sections of the population with property rights to objects such as property and land resources is directly related to the processes of zoning the territory of Ukraine.

Keywords: Territory · Territorial formations · Right ownership · Property ·
Thing · Land

O. Gervasi et al. (Eds.): ICCSA 2022, LNCS 13376, pp. 126–143, 2022.
https://doi.org/10.1007/978-3-031-10450-3_10

1 Introduction

Today, in the each district of Ukraine arise transformation of relationship system as well as general-national and local levels – this objective process, substantiated by necessity of decision sharp oppositions between achieving levels of development production volumes and system of society relations, that base objects and forms property. By basis decision of indicated oppositions is creation of legal conditions for existing of different ownerships forms that further to substantiated and formed of market aspects the economy.

By problem regard ownership, that already more years remain in Ukraine the non-decisional, are expansion of swindle and strippable off pertain ownership from parties firms, physicals persons and exclusion of the state from proper and from real guarantee of subjective properties rights. This are concerning availability and compliance existed norm-legal basis into Ukraine, and documental acceptation of the state regulation of public relationships regard transfer and granted as well as thing and non-thing property.

All this explain that territory of Ukraine by zoning is important nature-resources, labor, social, production, and also economic potential, that allow of farm entities to implemented its indirectly activity, to acquire and to get goods, guaranteed to conduct production process, has subject exchange, accumulation and, by individual condition, renewal. And process of state management, being from achievement independence of Ukraine, render until systemized crisis, led to worsening of economic situation in state, in result why happened inadequate and despondent attitude to most territorial formations, and characterized by the neglecting condition until properties, industrial, and also of agricultural complexes, cooperatives and other farm. In order to improvement this condition in field the state, and namely – by territorial management, should be implemented out of regulatory measures, that pertained to mutually-relationship in society and farm entities. Hereby is the ownership – as a basis for formation and stabilization of economic territorial systems.

Here necessary to noted and advantageous geographies condition of the territory of Ukraine on the earthly continent, which to characterize exit to sea relatively to transit movements in the direction of transport corridors Europe and Asia, that is, has the most branched infrastructure for all transportation [1, 2]. Hereby also substantiated a ownership, that concern out of all existing objects and complex, which are in territorial formations of the state, because in those condition they is ability to reproduction and receiving matter goods, being in economic and society relations.

Reliable providing of right ownership is task of each democratic state. In relation with this extraordinary interest casual the problems of warranting of right ownership of physical and juridical persons.

On modern stage of development World community observed considerable increase circle of right ownership: along with matter objects to appear out considerable quantity of non-things (bodiless) objects, which considered how rights that is value and monetary evaluation, but «ideally» property objects of a non-exist character.

The theoretical foundations of federalism, sovereignty of the federation and its constituent parts was considered and were studied by N. Koval, I. Sudak, Y. Bilyak, Y. Nehoda, A. Marchuk [3–5]. Researchers J. Holm-Hansen, S. Kropp, M. Marilyn, D. Sanders, C. Luck focused on the latest approaches to the problems of federalism [6–10]. The problems of Ukrainian decentralization were studied by N. Davydenko, A. Buriak,

I. Demyanenko, M. Buryak, I. Britchenko, M. Bezpartochnyi, M. Natalia, Z. Siryk, N. Popadynets, M. Pityulych, O. Chakii, I. Irtyshcheva, O. Panukhnyk, N. Lysyak. S. Kvitka, Y. Borodin, V. Yemelyanov, M. Moskalets, V. Zubchenko. A significant contribution to the study of federalism was also made by domestic researchers: A. Fenna, J. Erk, W. Swenden, etc. [11–15].

In modern scientific researches the situation of transformation economics of Ukraine – being from achievement independence in 1991, organically to connected with re-forming of relationship of right, particular ownership forms, that pertained out no only existing objects, but and features, which happened in each region.

Therefore basis task of this theme – determine position ownership in right relationship according territory formation in the state, and also substantiate it necessity improvement and reforming.

Learning of basis category right ownership on the territory of Ukraine give possibility maximally objectively to determine essential of process general privatization and prospective of their properties forms how thing and land plot – between differential parties of legal mutually-relationship.

2 Purpose of This Article

To lie down in research stage of development of the state regulation process regard given and protection of right ownerships by their kinds, forms and objects. Therefore it is right ownerships in Ukraine are clearly binding until her territory borders, based on what its state regulation impacted and lie down development – beginner from receiving of Ukraine independence and ending large-scale decentralization for formatting of Amalgamated of Territorial Communities, together with creation and opening of transparent land market.

This research of right ownerships into Ukraine depend from territorial formations direction for solve problems thus, in order to promotion law observance and given of equal conditions for physical and juridical persons, territory communes.

3 Materials and Methods

Legislate and norm-legal acts were use under the time of implementation of scientific researches, as: Laws of Ukraine, Codes of laws, Resolutions and etc.

For achievement of set purpose by writing of these article used methods of research: first performance it comparison of relations as well as right ownerships, dependency of arrangement objects ownership on the territorial formations during periods to begun from come independence of Ukraine, and next by method of description were researched directs of construction and functioning right ownership as base of regulation in territorial formations – on basis the experience gained in the state. And all this to connected, that right ownerships in Ukraine to depend by territorial formations of the state, as place of allocation the objects, by which to performance the economic relationships in society.

And on completion, implemented decomposition process method regard of provided rights ownership in field of economy and society relationship, and also monitoring methods regard changes in territorial formations conformably regulation and providing out right ownerships for society. And connection methods of decomposition and monitoring with others methods is in that, into territory of Ukraine took place such administration-territory reform, as formation of Amalgamation of Territorial Communities, where of enforcement and granted of right ownership are especial matter in the state regulation, particular – in improvement of opened and transparently land market.

To scientist-researches, which developed labors regard right ownership, should be noted Z. Romovska [22], that grounded the right ownership in cutter objects of thing and non-thing forms in process their granted and transfer of physical and juridical persons, K. Stashkiv [23] – regard leading of juristic process, connecting with possession of right ownership in district territorial formations, and T. Krysan [19] – regard granted and simultaneously protection of right ownership for physical persons.

But still is insufficient research of public relationship regard the right ownership, which are fact, fixed by concrete territorial border of the state, resulting in an happens ambiguous attitude no only through there persons, claimed on objects by place their allocation, and also and its state departments, who are authorized to regulate these questions, understand this only in total. Therefore authors of this article to ground research of public relationship regard the right ownership considering territorial formations, particular by stage their chances and recycling, where are objects of possession, for example land plots, for clearly concretization of juristically essence, quest od advantages, promotion perfection and improvement of the state regulation.

4 Results and Discussion

Go to market principles of economy in Ukraine has stronger non-equability of social-economic development the district and aggravation of territory opposition's within the state. This case to require an improvement of state regulation, what directed on over-coming the depressiveness of separation territorial formations, support of labor mobility population, creation conditions for functioning of new economy subjects. Exactly such conditions to lie down in assistance of regional economy system, realization of transfer pays, production of goods and services for society. All this possibility and needed to provide by setting realization right-relations regard objects ownership in connection territorial formations in the state.

It should be noted, that after decay USSR and today, the old economic complex, that to located on all territory district of Ukraine, in insufficiently measures, has provided of differentially development of society and communes, having historical, economical, nature and other particularities and also characterized out higher its potential. Therefore question as to ownership, conformably property things and lands, that related out to present economy complex and remained in separately territorial formations, stay sharp and are the most actual.

Ownership in most economic researches considered as natural matter properties and relations, that express a person's attitude toward things as your-self, and ownership seems as direct condition for consumption, because only appropriation of people of one or another thing are foreseen by process of its consumption. Therefore ownership considered as entity and object, as legal category, on basis which established by order of distributed the economic resources and as category, that determine law control of sure subjects of important goods and economically resources. Hence the ownership is substantiated no so much economic, how many political, legal factors and acts frequently to category no basic, but only superstructures.

But such determining of ownership is insufficient, how many need to consider right-relationship on level regions of Ukraine which to differed by diverse economic and industrial objects, natural riches, economic potential etc.

As a legal, category of right, ownership expresses conscious, willed actions, relationships pertain things. That is, ownership in a legal aspect is concept that embodies relations – as a form of a manifestation of real existing relationship regard property. This concept clearly confirmed evaluate thing by such areas, as: ensuring of agreement, creation of farms, share payments, privatization, revaluation of properties complexes etc. [25].

They concretely displaying their acquirement into law acts, norms and category of legal property, such as: Possession of land (fact); Use (consumption of object ownership); Disposal (determining of justify ownership – purchase, represent and so on).

After receiving of Ukraine independence in 1991, by arise possibility self and freely by state to manage of own territory, begun out the relationship in the field ownership. About this evidenced accepted by Verkhovna rada (parliament) of Ukraine Law «On ownership», which has a clear binding to territorial formations in the state, because the title of this law is following text «Ukrainian state is sovereign in regulating all property relationships», and is direction for ensuring the free economic self-determination citizens, as well as the use natural, economic, scientific-technical potentials to increase the life level of population.

At the same time, in 1996 by Verkhovna rada (parliament) of Ukraine accepted Constitution of Ukraine, where Art. 41 indicate that ownership an immutable (The constitution of Ukraine. 1996) [29]. It is worth noting that physicals are historically the first persons of ownership. And also in these year been accepted Law of Ukraine «On management of objects the state ownership», where by established requirement for physicals persons indicated on necessity of use objects – in depend from characteristics of property [19].

Substantiating it territorial bound of the state, that pertain relationship of right ownership, established by world community, need indicate a there principles: Right ownership guaranteed out, and their content and district established out legally; Ownership is obligatory its using must serve of society goods; Expropriation is permissible only for the general goods.

There are prevailed object of ownership is foremost condition (factors) production (land, their bowels, flora and fauna), which were organically connect in primarily society regard immediate subjects her appropriation – human.

But in the most-broadened kind *objects* of *right ownership*, which to envelop of territory units the state, are land plots, by clear territorial districting, differ in different price and reproductive characteristics, substantiating of separate objects of society and economy relationship in the state. And regulation of right-relationship in the state that pertained out land plots has perfected in 1998 by way of accepted Law of Ukraine «On land leasing», where lands of Ukraine as ownership forms by basis purpose appointed to split up:

- lands of agricultural appointed;
- lands for housing and public building;
- lands of nature-reserves and other nature-protectoral appointed;
- lands of health-improving appointed;
- recreational land;
- lands of historical-cultural appointed;
- lands of forest-economical appointed;
- lands of water fund;
- lands of industry, transport, connect, energy, military etc.

The obligatory mechanisms of regulation right ownership conformably property is documental per-fastening of right-relationship, as conclusion of agreement, particular on possession of land plot, which is most-broadening processes in the state [22].

Agreements on properties of land plot – legal document, that to certify the legal right on properties of land plot according by established dimension, and things, which arranging on these land, and also natural characteristics.

However, also to exist agreement purchase-sale of land plot – legal document, that to certify a trading relationship between seller and buyer as consent on possession, use, disposal of a land plot, that has its value and matter characteristics, example, place of arrangement. Also it should be noted agreement about land plot leasing – legal document, that evidenced trade relations between landlord and a landholder by according pay as consent on transference of land plot on established term, which has its value and is appropriate appointed depending from the field activity [20].

These above-mentioned documents to regulation legal norms that determine the concept, parties and content of agreement, as well as the order of its conclusion together with amendment and termination. Thus, the constitutional right of physical and juridical persons in the field of land relationship is exercised through the conclusion of agreements (Fig. 1).

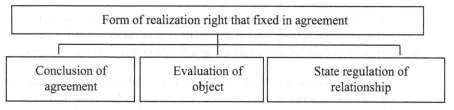

Fig. 1. Forms of realization right on land relationship

For example in the field of land relationship agreement considered three aspects (Fig. 2). Namely agreement of land relationship is an agreement of the parties, and right-relationship regard operations with land plot – this legal relation of property and receiver land share, and also seller and buyer.

Agreement of land relationship is also legal fact of realization buyer land plot other rights on use her and till and obligator of followed all laws and orders. As right institute at agreement on land operation – system of legal norms to purchase-sale of land plot. And

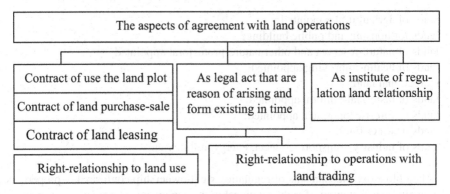

Fig. 2. The aspects of agreement with land operations

institute of agreement land operations is core of land relationship to other operations on objects possession, sale, purchase, leasing.

Especial form of agreement is a contract; him context, although defined by consent of parties, have to responded laws and other norm-legal acts.

From moment of conclusion agreement to ordinate right-relationship between seller and buyer arise right-relationship for use of land plot.

Depending from order of establishment rights and obligators is two kind of condition agreement: immediate, context which to determined parties at conclusion agreement; derivatives, the context which by established in laws, sub-laws and local norm-legal acts and which, as order, cannot be changed by agreement of the parties.

Conditions, are made by the parties at conclusion agreement (immediate), in turn, are divided into obligatory (necessity), without which agreement no must will concluded, and supplementary (facultative), no obligatory for existing agreement (Fig. 2).

Thus, agreements about operations with land plot – contract of parties, their mutual expression of will, that have purpose to establish between agree parties right-relationship (Fig. 3).

Under agreement the main obligators of the buyer land plot belong it primarily the appointed and application sphere. That is exploitation (cultivation) of buyer land plot accordingly by beforehand established appoint, and also improvement him – in depended from economic field.

The land plots territorially are found in different places, therefore farming realized on big square with movement of agricultural machines and mechanisms. And value of land plot to depend from there particularities, as:

– from the surroundings, including infrastructure;
– from permitted directions of use;
– from what is located on it;
– from natural condition;
– from the subsoil and composition of the surface sphere (not always);
– from political stability and fluctuation of demand;
– from condition of economics and level of development country, region;
– from condition of its own benefit characteristics.

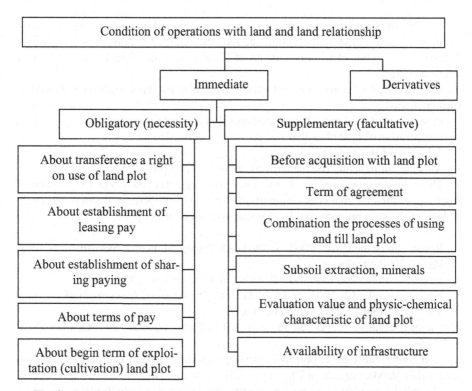

Fig. 3. Condition agreement of operations with land and land relationship classification

Thus, main complexes of right ownership on land that clear to display of territorial appliance properties and non-properties objects the state is: place of realization land operations; information provided of land market sharer about him condition; disclosed of subjects operation with land; determining price on land; establishment of form realization land operation (auctions, competition trading, right decision procedures and so on); preparation to realization land operation; execution of legal document; state (notarial) certificate about land operations; payment of customs duties; banking services of land operations; infrastructure of servicing land market; right ensuring of land operations; personnel provided of land market [17].

But in spite of on this, in the state still maintained old post-soviet relations of economic entities, which render uncertain as to right-relationship with questions of property, as well as violation of law ownership. Therefore, before the next stage of development of regulation right-relationship regarding the ownership, which started in 1999, it should be noted attributed to the President of Ukraine Leonid Kuchma Decrees «On pressing measures for acceleration reforming of agricultural sector the economic» and «On pressing measures for acceleration of property privatization in Ukraine», that also is straight relation to the state regulation of territorial formations.

And in further, this stage is based on the adoption of next norm-legal acts that regulate legal relationship on objects property with clear prescribing there are procedures, as buying, sale, exchange, representation, evaluation.

In 2001, the fundamental norm-legal act on regulation of land relationship has been developed and accepted by the Verkhovna rada of Ukraine the Land code of Ukraine. According Land code of Ukraine citizens of Ukraine to received property on land plot follow as [24]:

Acquisition of agreement on land operations, exchange, representation, others civil-legal contracts;

Free transfer from lands of state, communal and private properties;

Privatization of land plots that was previously granted to them in use;

Adoption of inheritance;

Allocate out in nature (on the terrain) of the land plot proper.

The main documents of legislative framework regulating the general provisions of processes evaluation, that concerning of all contracts is property evaluation, which no is share of the state property and legal restrictions on ownership are:

1. Resolution of the CMU, 2002, № 1531 «On Expert Monetary Assessment of Land Plots», 2002, October 11;
2. Law of Ukraine, 2004, № 1808-IV «On Land Evaluation», 2004 June 17;
3. National standard 1, 2003, № 1440 «General Principles of Assessment of Property and Main Rights», 2003 September 10;
4. National standard 2, 2004, № 1442 «The Real Estate valuate», 2004 October 28.

And conformably of all objects ownership generally it should be note drafted and accepted by Verkhovna rada of Ukraine the Civil code of Ukraine in 2003, where indication the full list of subjects ownership on property. Therefore was to this time has active Law of Ukraine «On property», where in Art. 11 signifying, that only citizen, or physical persons was recognized private owners – and this often led conflicts conformably of objects properties [28].

And since from acceptation of the Civil code of Ukraine served out the considerable broadening of subjects property, which led to radical economic and social changes in society, of quality changes in production managing as one on the functions of property (arising of management, marketing, employees of qualify managers), to development of new economic forms (individual, collective, mixed).

The each type of economic relations society is it prevailed object property. Only he characterized almost full:

Mutual-relationship human with nature;

Level productivity labor in society;

Particularity of appropriation means and results of production.

And in article 316 The Civil code of Ukraine is there understand of right ownership:

– right ownership is a right of person on thing (property), that they to realize accordingly by self-will, independently from will other entities;
– particular kind of right ownership is right of trust property, which to arise because of law or agreement.

A broadening of subjects properties it mean the democratization of management ownership, production, transformation of a significant part of society into immediate owners, which most-efficiency to realize its production activities [16].

Along with the state (what determined Law of Ukraine «On property»), and cooperatives (which early been subjects properties), now the owners became separate citizens, labor collectives, and also foreign states, international organizations, other legal entities.

Of course, so happened the great achievements in right-relationships with ownership but along with this stage of setting development of regulation on possession namely – period from 2004 is personified of negative phenomena, as self-appropriation and usurpation of objects property that is – raiding. And here there is a need to emphasize so problems regard right-relationships combine with appropriation and non-legal possession of objects property, such as:

- legal abuse of third entities, for example – advocates, which browsing official documents about financial condition of the economic, has falsified data about him debt;
- wishing of bank organizations by lending crediting of subjects economies forcedly to reason growth debt with purpose appropriation profit and value objects properties;
- non-legally decision of justices regard transaction of right ownership by other entities, which founded on imitation and falsification documents regard possession on objects properties;
- wishing of large oligarchic groups to appropriated of objects properties of other entities for own broadening its activities or receiving of additional goods.

And therefore here sharply staying question in regulation contradictions regarding right ownership no only on legal level, but and arise out necessity in reforming of state and department institutes – concerning discharge of they its function.

And only in 2018–2019 up for prevention of raiding on general-state level were introduction changes to Land code of Ukraine and adopted Laws of Ukraine «On State Registration of Corporeal Rights to Real Estate and Their Encumbrances» (to have accent as anti-raider law) and «About modification of some legislative acts of Ukraine concerning the decision of a question of collective ownership of the earth, improvement of rules of land use in massifs of lands of agricultural purpose, prevention of raiding and stimulation of irrigation in Ukraine», which to pertain a strongly of order registration business, real estate, lands plots, to disclosed information about objects ownership and their use, and also established clear requirements regard state power entities activity, for example, those authorized to conduct state registration of objects property. Here these norm-legal acts to justify a clear link to the territorial entities that the state has, therefore namely in their ensured registration of property right into real estate [27]. This also applies land plots, which within the limits established by the State land Cadaster are lease, use and disposal conformably their possession, purpose, and the prepared technical documentation [26].

Further after these it should be noted events of Ukraine, which was happen in 2014, that clear affected its territory, as, such as loos of Crimea and hostilities into Donbass. And therefore question to protection of right ownership on temporarily occupied territories stay very sharply. In ties with hereby are several aspects that attracting attention. One of them – compensation for property damaged by harm of war actions, that is fact destroyed, the second – property, illegally appropriate from citizens, who left him on occupied territory not on their will, the third – how to save property, that here remain, from misappropriation of unknown entities etc. [23].

And here receive compensation of harm by reasoned of war actions losses from state possibility only by availability of evidences its reasoning, reason-consequently connection and cost evaluation of losses.

Property located in ATO zone, can be sold. Ways of decision of this question are two: general powers of attorney of disposal property, which can be receive on occupied territory, how notaries have access notarial register of power of attorney, or register the contract in the territory controlled by Ukraine.

Here it should be noted, that accordingly to provisions of the Law of Ukraine «On providing rights and wills citizens and legal regime on temporarily occupied territory of Ukraine», guard and protection of right ownership on temporarily occupied territory realized accordingly to legislation of Ukraine. This Law protected preservation in righty aspect by properties right ownership on their real estate that arranged on temporarily occupied territory. For example, in the case conclusion transactions regard real estate with infringement legislation of Ukraine there is considered invalid from the moment of realization and does not created legal consequences.

Equally with there, exactly from 2014 until 2019, was happens a first stage of decentralization in Ukraine – the mentioned next stage of development regulation transaction as to ownership. Here the state policy of Ukraine in field local self-government to basis oneself for the interests residents of territorial communities and foreseen of decentralization their powers – that is transfer from entities of execute government to entities of local self-government a significant parts authorities, recourses and responsibilities. In base of this policy by lay provisions of the European Charter of local self-government and better world standards of society relationship in this field.

The legal sub-substantiation for core change of government power system and her territorial basis on all levels began to form in 2014.

In April 2014 the Government has approved a major approach document – the Concept of Reforming Local Self-Government and Territorial Structure of Power. Thereafter, the Action Plan was approved to implement the Concept, thus launching the reform.

By this time already formatter and to active the main package of new legislation, to improved priority initiatives. This refers to:

– Laws on amendments to the Budget and Tax Codes of Ukraine. Due to those amendments, local budgets increased by UAH 123.4 billion: from UAH 68.6 billion in 2014 up until UAH 275 billion in 2019;
– The Law "On Voluntary Amalgamation of Territorial Communities". It made possible to start forming a capable basic level of local self-government. By 2015–2019 in Ukraine 892 amalgamated territorial communities (the "ATCs") were already established. Those ATCs are composed of about 4500 former local councils (from nearly 12 thousand). International experts regard this rate of inter-municipality consolidation to be very high.

Also, the law introduced the institute of starosta (village headperson) in the ATCs who represent the interests of rural residents in the community council. Today, 800 starostas have been elected, more than 2,4 thousand individuals are acting starosta.

In 2018 Amalgamation of Territorial Communities by received in communally ownership nearly 1.5 million hectare lands of agricultural appointed by border of population points;

- The Law "On Cooperation of Territorial Communities". It established the mechanism of dealing with common problems faced by communities: waste management and recycling, development of joint infrastructure, etc. This mechanism to indicate of there are particularities: conclusion 530 cooperation agreements are already being implemented; 1188 communities already have taken of these acquirement;
- The Law "On Fundamental Principles of the State Regional Policy". The government support for regional development and the development of infrastructure in communities increased by 41.5 times over the period of reform: from UAH 0.5 billion in 2014 up until UAH 20.75 billion in 2019. By the setting of this support in districts and communes realized in 2015–2019 more 12 thousand projects;
- A package of laws pertaining to the enhancement of powers of local self-government entities and the optimization of administrative services provision. It allowed delegating powers to provide administrative services to local self-government bodies of respective level: individuals registration at the place of residence, issuance of national identity documents, state registration of physical and juridical persons, entrepreneurs, associations of citizens, civil registration, registration of proprietary rights, dealing with land issues, etc.

The new legislative framework significantly strengthened the motivation to intermunicipal consolidation in the country, created appropriate conditions and mechanisms in terms of legal framework for the establishment of capable territorial communities in villages, towns, and cities consolidating their efforts with the aim of resolving pressing problems. Also, the new model of financial support to local budgets has proved to be effective, which budgets obtained autonomy to certain extent and independence from the central budget.

And on Fig. 4 disclosed characteristic of territorial formations in Ukraine from 2014, together with achievement, what set a creation Amalgamation of Territorial Communities. Here is need to indication a role of right ownership in new-created Amalgamation of Territorial Communities over processes of purchase, exchange and transaction property and land, where by property relationship is population, starostas (village headperson) and economics, which there are stayed and leaded its activities, among them with settle of accordingly processes in just that one territorial formations of present years to realization administrative-territorial reform.

In 2019 President of Ukraine Volodymyr Zelensky has signed Law «On introduction changes to several legislate acts of Ukraine as to protection of right ownership» [30].

In Ministry of Justifying to self-duty indicated, that new law to promote a decreasing of quantities raiding usurpation of Real Estate and Corporeal Rights. The law to foreseen overcoming of main justifies gaps that create problems properties Real Estate and business.

So, the law to foreseen stopping of accrediting subjects activity; improvement obligatory of notarial witnessing od agreement about strangest out Corporeal Rights; improvement principle of one-timely till reasoning of notarial active and state registration rights; increasing responsibilities by infringement accordantly registering procedures.

And purpose these Law lie in decreasing of quantities raiding usurpation of Real Estate and Corporeal Rights, and also decrease of expense citizens and business, connected with protection ownership from unlawful encroachments.

And further President of Ukraine Volodymyr Zelensky has promised about opening of the transparently land market. Therefore by him affirmation, during the ban on the sale of agricultural land, about 5 million hectares of state land were illegally appropriated in Ukraine, and a shadow market for land turnover without taxes, official employment and social guarantees for people was formed inside the country.

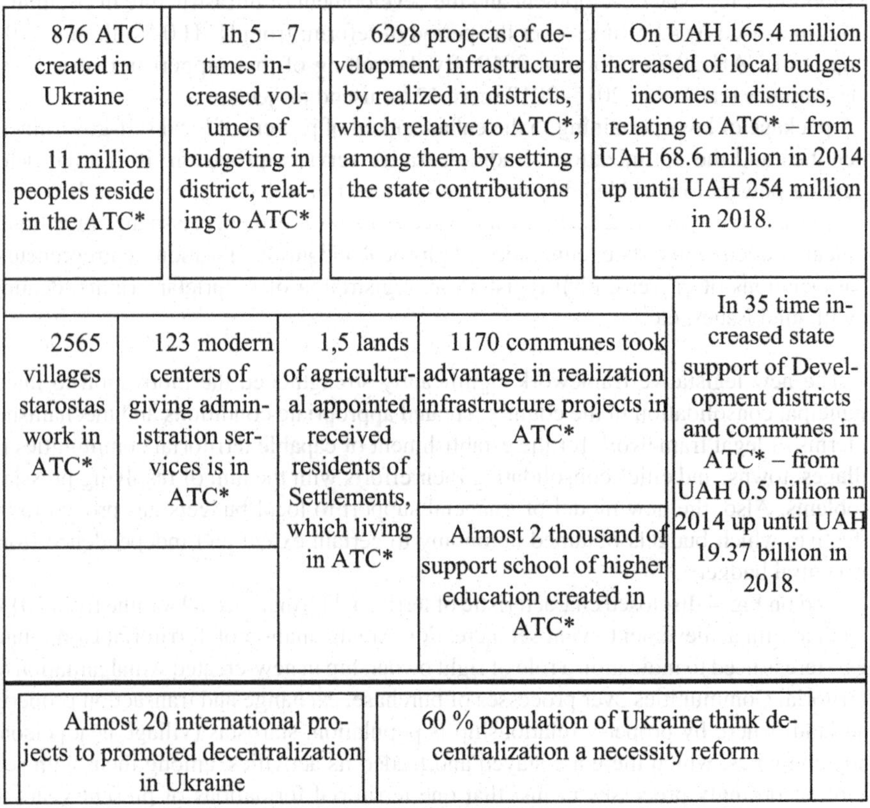

876 ATC created in Ukraine	In 5 – 7 times increased volumes of budgeting in district, relating to ATC*	6298 projects of development infrastructure by realized in districts, which relative to ATC*, among them by setting the state contributions	On UAH 165.4 million increased of local budgets incomes in districts, relating to ATC* – from UAH 68.6 million in 2014 up until UAH 254 million in 2018.
11 million peoples reside in the ATC*			

2565 villages starostas work in ATC*	123 modern centers of giving administration services is in ATC*	1,5 lands of agricultural appointed received residents of Settlements, which living in ATC*	1170 communes took advantage in realization infrastructure projects in ATC*	In 35 time increased state support of Development districts and communes in ATC* – from UAH 0.5 billion in 2014 up until UAH 19.37 billion in 2018.
			Almost 2 thousand of support school of higher education created in ATC*	

Almost 20 international projects to promoted decentralization in Ukraine	60 % population of Ukraine think decentralization a necessity reform

* ATC – Amalgamated of Territorial Communities

Fig. 4. Decentralization in Ukraine [18]

When in March 2020 were worked the first step in direction of opening land market – then Verkhovna rada has decreed law about improvement of lands current of agricultural appointed. And in May 2020 parliament has voted, and President of Ukraine Volodymyr

Zelensky has signed law about national infrastructure a geo-spatial dates, particular single geo-portal of open dates – information about all land, water, and forest recourses.

Equally with there, in July 2020 President of Ukraine Volodymyr Zelensky had signed a law on spatial planning of communities, because communities know best how to organize their lives: where to have a kindergarten, school, public roads or industrial facilities [21]. To fully complete decentralization, a decree was signed on the transfer of agricultural land from state to communal ownership. Accordingly statement President of Ukraine Volodymyr Zelensky knowingly, that «Local communities have received more than two million hectares of land, as well as the opportunity to allocate funds from land use to their development and well-being».

And in 2020–2021 was happens a second stage of decentralization in Ukraine [18]. Here Cabinet Ministers of Ukraine determined a support of decentralization reform in Ukraine one with priority task, that protection a development the local self-government and economic perfection of country whole. And base tasks discovered on Fig. 5 pertains of this stage decentralization. This period by became keying in question of formatting framework the local self-government: 2020, July 12 government had approved a new administrative-territorial order of basis level. Accordingly to ordinations of Cabinet Ministers of Ukraine, in Ukraine was formation 1469 Amalgamated of Territorial Communities, that to covering all territory of country.

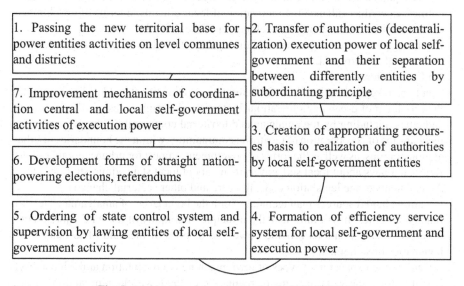

Fig. 5. Main tasks of decentralization in 2021–2022 [18].

15 July 2020 by Verkhovna rada of Ukraine accepted Resolution № 3809 «On appointed of the next local elections in 2020», that is – from 25 October 2020.

16 July 2020 by Verkhovna rada of Ukraine accepted changes to elections legislation.

17 July 2020 by Verkhovna rada of Ukraine accepted Resolution № 3650 «On creation and liquidation districts». Accordingly with this document, present in Ukraine 136 districts. Olds 490 districts parliament has liquated.

25 October 2020 has come local elections on new territorial framework of communes and regions.

All this create a solid foundation for next steps reform of local self-government, and also to promote of speeding-up reforms in field health guard, education, culture, social services, energy-efficiency and other sectors.

For continued reform necessity to be passed else row following important laws, as:

– "On Fundamental Principles of Administrative and Territorial Structure of Ukraine" (the draft Law has been prepared for consideration by the Verkhovna Rada (Parliament)). Subject to the effective Constitution, it determines the fundamental principles on which the administrative and territorial structure of Ukraine, types of settlements, the system of administrative-territorial entities, powers of the governmental authorities and local self-government bodies in terms of the administrative and territorial structure, procedure for the formation, liquidation, establishment and changing the boundaries of administrative-territorial entities and settlements, maintenance of the State Register of Administrative-Territorial Entities and Settlements of Ukraine should be based.
– "On Service in the Bodies of Local Self-Government" (it is currently being refined by the Verkhovna Rada (Parliament), subject to proposals of the President). It will ensure equal access to, and enhance the prestige of, service in local self-government entities, as well as enhance the motivation of local officials in terms of development of communities and individual development of the officials.
– Regarding government supervision of the legality of resolutions passed by the entities of local self-government.
– On Urban referendum;
– "On Urban Agglomerations". It will determine organizational and legal principles for the formation of urban agglomerations by territorial communities of villages, towns, and cities, including by the amalgamated territorial communities, the principles and mechanisms of co-operation of territorial communities within the boundaries of urban agglomerations, as well as the forms of government support for urban agglomerations.
– Renewal a laws about local self-government, about local state administrations etc.
– Amendments to the legislation on health care and other sectorial changes.
– Regarding land resources management within the boundaries of amalgamated territorial communities. It will introduce the principle of ubiquity of the ATC's jurisdiction in terms of land relations provide powers to dispose of the land plots outside the boundaries of settlements.
– Regarding the expansion of types of town planning documentation at the local level. It will remove the gaps in terms of regulation of the town planning and make any unauthorized use and allocation of land impossible.

In 2022 waiting out the introduction changes to Constitution of Ukraine regard decentralization, which are necessary for further promotion of the reform and its completion.

5 Conclusion

In this article by researched initiation and development of the right ownership such objects: property and land plots, because they required subject to the state regulation accordingly existing territorial formations, where are Amalgamated of Territorial Communities and residence there population. These above objects of ownership bind with natural and resource condition of territorial formations that is basis for leading of economic and public relationship in the state.

The state regulation of public relationship regard right ownership to property generalized conclusion agreements, that is most common juristically practice between granted and transparent thing and non-thing objects. Because field of public relationship regard right ownership clearly to monitoring a territorial affiliation thing and non-thing objects.

But in spite of on this, in the state still maintained old post-soviet relations of economic entities, which render uncertain as to right-relationship with questions of property, as well as violation of law ownership. And it all caused necessity of research stages of development public relationship regard of the right ownership in Ukraine, as acceptation of fundamental norm-legal acts with clearly prescribing there procedures, as purchase, sale, exchange, presentation, evaluation.

At the time researching stages of development of the right ownership in this article, together with chances, perfection and improvement existing and creation of new norm-legal acts, directed on democratization of management property, production, recycling much of society on direct economists and etc., grounded guide and mechanisms of these right relationship regard conditions transfer and granted objects, that happens out in Ukraine.

These research is consistent with that by consideration a stages of development of the right ownership in Ukraine, expanding the list of subjects property, recycling and addition norm-legal base, and also phenomena's, which happened into Ukraine among with large-scale decentralization by formation Amalgamated of Territorial Communities, together with creation and open of transparent land market to accord purpose of this scientific publication. And this to ground conflict resolution, which to happen in society regard procedures transfer and granted of objects property that fixed by territory borders, and on this basis – compliance with the law and granting equal condition of physical and juridical persons, territorial communes.

And creation of new society and economic relationship system on basis ownership on property and land plot, provided equally of right ownership on land physical and juridical persons, territorial communes and the state, and also warranting rights on land became key moment of development Amalgamated of Territorial Communities, which reorganized and to transformed being in 2014. But, in spite of, orientation of Ukraine on market relationship accordingly to Constitution of Ukraine, else need of radical changes the territorial formations in field of economies activity on property and land. And there exactly, with appearance Amalgamated of Territorial Communities in decentralization process, what being in 2014, the state stay on responsible stage of practical improvement land market relationship, that to pertain interests of each citizen of Ukraine. They should be efficiency in political, sociological, economics and ecological aspects. Here politics of liberalization of properties and land relationship the society, communes and economic complex obliged to base on un-permitting whenever un-substantial distractions or preconceiving regard transaction property and allocation lands shares, their separate, exchange or association, and obligatorily be sub-fastening of the effective legal leverage for protection entirety of property, rationally land massifs, and also un-permitting their of non-substantial splitting (parceling).

References

1. Abuselidze, G.: Competitiveness analysis of the georgian transport and logistics system in the black sea region: challenges and perspectives. In: Gervasi, O., et al. (eds.) ICCSA 2021. LNCS, vol. 12952, pp. 133–148. Springer, Cham (2021). https://doi.org/10.1007/978-3-030-86973-1_10
2. Datsii, O., Levchenko, N., Shyshkanova, G., Platonov, O., Abuselidze, G.: Creating a regulatory framework for the ESG-investment in the multimodal transportation development. Rural Sustain. Res. **46**(341), 39–52 (2021)
3. Koval, N.: Three faces of federalism in the foreign policy: Russian and German approaches to the "Ukraine Crisis". In: Decentralization, Regional Diversity, and Conflict, pp. 187–210. Palgrave Macmillan, Cham (2020)
4. Abuselidze, G., Sudak, I., Bilyak, Y., Nehoda, Y.: Political features of federalization of the most powerful countries in the world: experience for Ukraine. In: Proceedings of the 21 International Multidisciplinary Scientific GeoConference Surveying, Geology and Mining, Ecology and Management – SGEM 2021. SGEM, vol. 21, no. 5, pp. 797–804 (2021). https://doi.org/10.5593/sgem2021/5.1/s21.096
5. Marchuk, A.: Theoretical foundations of decentralization: its essence, forms and consequences. Moderní věda 37 (2018)
6. Holm-Hansen, J., Kropp, S.: The regional diversity of Ukraine: can federalization be achieved? In: The Accommodation of Regional and Ethno-Cultural Diversity in Ukraine, pp. 23–51. Palgrave Macmillan, Cham (2021)
7. Marlin, M.: Concepts of "decentralization" and "federalization" in Ukraine: political signifiers or distinct constitutionalist approaches for devolutionary federalism? Nationalism Ethnic Politics **22**(3), 278–299 (2016)
8. Sanders, D., Tuck, C.: The Ukraine conflict and the problems of war termination. J. Slavic Mil. Stud. **33**(1), 22–43 (2020)
9. Abuselidze, G.: The intergovernmental relations and their regulation in the context of decentralization of fiscal policy. In: E3S Web of Conferences, vol. 280, p. 02010 (2021). https://doi.org/10.1051/e3sconf/202128002010
10. Abuselidze, G.: Mechanism of transfer of financial resources to territorial units: a case study. In: European Proceedings of Social and Behavioural Sciences (EpSBS), vol. 82, pp. 192–200 (2020)
11. Davydenko, N., Buriak, A., Demyanenko, I., Buryak, M.: Assessment of the components of financial potential of the regions of Ukraine. J. Optim. Ind. Eng. **14**(1), 57–62 (2021). https://doi.org/10.22094/JOIE.2020.677816
12. Britchenko, I., Bezpartochnyi, M., Natalia, M.: Financial decentralization in Ukraine: prerequisites, problems, prospects. VUZF Rev. **4**(4), 25–44 (2019)
13. Siryk, Z., et al.: Decentralization of local self-government under the conditions of administrative-territorial reform in Ukraine. Accounting **7**(4), 781–790 (2021)
14. Dmytryshyn, M., Dmytryshyn, R., Yakubiv, V., Zagorodnyuk, A.: Peculiarities of Ukrainians' approval of decentralization reform. Adm. Sci. **11**(4), 104 (2021)
15. Kvitka, S., Borodin, Y., Yemelyanov, V., Moskalets, M., Zubchenko, V.: The subsidiarity principle and legal and economic aspects of the decentralization in Ukraine. Cuestiones Políticas **39**(68), 356–368 (2021)

16. Belgytsia, V., Antonova, L., Kozlova, L., Datsii, O., Datsii, N.: System of concepts communications of state institutions and society as the basis of national security and socio-economic stability. Financ. Credit Act. Probl. Theory Pract. **3**(38), 549–556 (2021). https://doi.org/10.18371/fcaptp.v3i38.237487

17. Datsii, O., Datsii, N., Zborovska, O., Aleinikova, O., Krasowska, O.: Marketing research of the state policy in the field of sanitation of the settlement territory. Financ. Credit Act. Probl. Theory Pract. **2**(37), 510–520 (2021). https://doi.org/10.18371/fcaptp.v2i37.230679

18. Decentralization Give Possibilities (2021). https://decentralization.gov.ua/about

19. Krysan, T.: Problems of the state-legal guarantying of right ownership for physical persons. Enterp. Econ. Right **1**, 38–41 (2012)

20. Oleshko, T., Kvashuk, D., Boiko, Y., Odarchenko, R., Krainov, V.: Analyzing digital image processing capabilities while growing crops. In: CEUR Workshop Proceedings, vol. 2654, pp. 240–250 (2020)

21. President of Ukraine Volodymyr Zelensky: The transparent land market is what we promised and what we are implementing, 24 May 2021. https://www.president.gov.ua/news/volodimir-zelenskij-prozorij-rinok-zemli-ce-te-sho-mi-obicya-68629

22. Romowska, Z.: Ukrainian Civilian Right. General Part: Academic Course: Textbook 2nd edn. Supplemented. Aleuta, KNT, Center of Educational Literature, Kyiv, 594 p. (2012)

23. Stashkiv, K.: In ATO zone the right ownership. Justify practice: ownership work. Ukrainian Jurist, 4 April 2015. http://jurist.ua/?article/869

24. The Land Code of Ukraine. Law 2768-III-VR/2001. The Verkhovna Rada of Ukraine, 25 October 2001. https://zakon.rada.gov.ua/laws/show/2768-14

25. The Law of Ukraine: on appraisal of property, property rights and professional appraisal activity in Ukraine. The Verkhovna Rada of Ukraine. Law 2658-III-VR/2001, 12 July 2001. https://rada.kiev.ua

26. The Law of Ukraine: On modification of some legislative acts of Ukraine concerning the decision of a question of collective ownership of the earth, improvement of rules of land use in massifs of lands of agricultural purpose, prevention of raiding and stimulation of irrigation in Ukraine. The Verkhovna Rada of Ukraine. Law 2498-VIII-VR/2018, 10 July 2018. https://zakon.rada.gov.ua/laws/show/2498-19#Text

27. The Law of Ukraine: On state registration of corporeal rights to real estate and their encumbrances. The Verkhovna Rada of Ukraine. Law 1952-IV-VR/2004, 1 July 2004. https://zakon.rada.gov.ua/laws/show/1952-15#Text

28. The Civil Code of Ukraine: The Verkhovna Rada of Ukraine. Law 435-IV-VR/2003, 16 January 2003. https://zakon.rada.gov.ua/laws/show/435-15

29. The Constitution of Ukraine: The Verkhovna Rada of Ukraine. Law 254к/96-VR/1996, 28 June 1996. https://zakon.rada.gov.ua/laws/show/254%D0%BA/96-%D0%B2%D1%80

30. Ukrinform: President has signed law about protection of law ownership (2019). https://www.ukrinform.ua/rubric-polytics/2802978-prezident-pidpisav-zakon-pro-zahist-prava-vlasnosti.html

A Virtual 3D City Model for Urban Planning and Decision-Making - The East Jerusalem Case

Andreas Fricke$^{(\boxtimes)}$ (ID), Jürgen Döllner, and Hartmut Asche

Hasso Plattner Institute, Digital Engineering Faculty, University of Potsdam,
Prof.-Dr.-Helmert-Str. 2-3, 14482 Potsdam, Germany
{andreas.fricke,juergen.doellner,hartmut.asche}@hpi.uni-potsdam.de

Abstract. This contribution presents an approach for generating and modelling spatially referenced, multi-dimensional urban models from remote sensing data for regions where no reliable reference data are available. The focus is on a modular service-oriented process chain covering the entire process from data acquisition to effective web-based visualization, addressing raw data, preprocessing, management, spatial analyses, visualisation and applications. The use case, investigated in the framework of a EU-funded multidisciplinary R+D project, is the cityspace of East Jerusalem (about 190 about 190 sqkm). Due to the controversial geopolitical situation, usable and high-resolution reference data of the complex, granular urban fabric is unavailable. Hence very high-resolution stereo aerial images (571 pcs. à 10 cm GSD) were acquired and photogrammetrically processed to build a high-resolution 3D reference point cloud. Corresponding semantic data from various sources and household surveys (3,500 pcs.) specially conducted were integrated into the data and managed within a unified, fully-referenced 3D database (open-source). The resulting virtual urban 3D model includes functionalities for geospatial exploration and analysis, allowing spatio-temporal applications, such as land use/management, social/technical infrastructure, or tourism for documentation, information, education as well as decision-making. It addresses both the local civil society and, through specific functions, urban planners and decision makers. Analysis and interaction functionalities are provided in a user-oriented and application-related framework, taking into account effective visualisation (cartographic and visual gestalt principles). The independent spatial reference of a multi-scale grid is used for spatial analyses and visualisation purposes. The generic construction of the dedicated virtual cityspace allows for the transferability of results.

Keywords: Service-oriented workflow · Lack of reference data · Virtual multi-dimensional model

© The Author(s), under exclusive license to Springer Nature Switzerland AG 2022
O. Gervasi et al. (Eds.): ICCSA 2022, LNCS 13376, pp. 144–159, 2022.
https://doi.org/10.1007/978-3-031-10450-3_11

1   Overview: Modelling

Abstraction and modelling serve as tools for understanding complex relationships. Models allow for complex systems to be made comprehensible and manageable. A model is an abstraction of reality under aspects relevant to problem solving. Thus, a model is - per se - always domain-specific [9]. A virtual city model designed for tourism purposes accordingly follows different principles or expectations than, for example, a model of the atmospheric circulation for meteorologists. As a rule, a model describes reality. By means of a model, it is possible - to a limited extent - to try out or simulate certain actions without directly manipulating objects within the real world. Regardless of their domain specificity, models are usually assigned to either data models or process models. Furthermore, modelling at its core involves abstraction and thus, to some extent, generalisation. Objects and entities of reality are consequently simplified in modelling. A model should describe or depict the real counterpart in terms of its objective characteristics and features so precisely and accurately that conclusions can be drawn about future events with a high degree of probability. Such a model can be seen as a kind of 'experimental sandbox'. Given a comprehensive synchronisation of the twin, which is mostly digital today, crown scenarios (e.g. accessibility of local transport), planning (e.g. housing construction) or simulations (e.g. flood modelling) may be transferred to reality with a high degree of probability. Figure 1 illustrates this relationship in a concise manner.

Fig. 1. Illustrated problem statement

1.1   Modelling: Virtual City Models

Virtual city models represent an application case where the spatial reference takes on an elementary and decisive factor [12]. Hence, at least two, usually three or more dimensions of a datum are already fixed by the spatial location.

The georeference of a datum therefore already represents a fixed characteristic of any city model, since the topology of space, i.e. the relationship between objects to each other, is decisive [13]. Consequently, a virtual multi-dimensional city model consists of geodata. Modern IT technologies, ubiquitous data availability, efficient management, processing and visualisation frameworks allow those models nowadays to be, by their appearance at least, deceptively close to reality. As already mentioned, this is the first stage of the fully synchronised replica of reality, the digital twin. An example of this is the current version of the simulation game Microsoft Flight Simulator, in which a large part of the real world has been reconstructed to scale as well as real weather events are synchronised at game time. Another example is the Google Earth system, which in the meantime has become a 'de facto standard' that can realistically represent spatial relationships and simple functionalities in almost every large metropolis in the world, in terms of appearance. The basis of virtual city models is usually municipal geodata, such as a digital elevation model, orthophotos, buildings of the real estate map, vegetation, street furniture, architectural models, development plans, domain-specific data, but also increasingly volunteered geographic information (e.g. OpenStreetMap), which is more and more available for urban areas and metropolises up-to-date, area-wide and in particularly high quality [3]. With the integration of these data stocks into a multi-dimensional city model, they can be used in a variety of ways and help, for example, to modernise urban planning and administrative processes and make them more transparent or allow applications, for example, in the areas of visualisation of traffic routing/flows, environmental analyses of noise and flood propagation, planning variants/scenarios in construction, energy and the economy. Furthermore, the presentation of e.g. geographic business locations or in city marketing for tourism purposes is an essential application [16]. The central task of the virtual (city) model, however, always includes communication and dissemination through the spatial representation, the 'spatial readability' and the ability of each person to efficiently and effectively derive connections and conclusions through orientation in space. As a result, a multi-dimensional (city) model can serve as a central information hub, analysis or information system, which above all makes it easier for decision-makers to visually link complex factual relationships to real structures and to share them in a universally easy-to-understand way [4].

1.2   Problem Statement and Application Domain

Typically, the essential factor 'data' is rarely considered in this type of model; most of the time, data is simply available. The case that a city model starts with data acquisition is hardly considered in the literature. Nevertheless, every city model is inevitably defined and characterised from the outset by its data. Within the framework of a research project funded by the European Union, the aim was to generate a model embedded in a web-based platform that allows both decision-makers and civil society to visualise spatial information and analysis results based on a virtual model of the urban Middle Eastern region of East Jerusalem.

Accordingly, the key research question is how to create spatially referenced, multi-dimensional virtual city models for spatial planning in urban areas that lack reliable spatial planning bases. The objective is therefore to construct 3D virtual city models for geospatial exploration, analysis, planning and decision-making, and to facilitate spatio-temporal applications for information, planning and participation of urban planning stakeholders (government and civil society). The application domain is the East Jerusalem region, the centre of the Jerusalem urban agglomeration. It is a complex cityscape (historical Oriental city with modern expansions), a complex situation of urban planning actors (Israeli municipality vs. Palestinian civil society), and a complex geopolitical status (UN two-state solution vs. Israeli annexation) [1,2]. As a result, there is a lack of reliable, up-to-date and high-resolution geodata for spatial planning applications [14].

2   Approach and Methodology

Given the lack of suitable reference data, the research question and the original objective, the creation of a virtual multi-dimensional city model, is expanded to include the transfer into a complex service-oriented process that is component-based or modularised. However, the objective of this process is to create a virtual multi-dimensional city model in the absence of suitable reference data, and to transform it into a complex service-oriented process that is component-based and modularised.

2.1   Related Work

Multi-dimensional virtual models are mainly available in large metropolitan regions or cities nowadays. This is primarily due to better data availability, both geometrically and semantically, compared to, for example, rural areas [13]. Open Data Portals or VGI, such as OpenStreetMap, also demonstrate their strengths in metropolitan areas [4]. Comparative work and processes for generating virtual city models - without adequate reference data - therefore usually disregard the aspect of data acquisition due to the initial situation described [5]. A comprehensive workflow, including data acquisition, is therefore as yet not available or usable, far less transferable [18]. Paradoxically, the 'de facto standard' for virtual city models, the CityGML standard, does present obstacles, because this conceptual model or exchange format only allows a standard-compliant transfer once a database is available. Acquisition is not part of this concept. Special methods and techniques for processing geodata, storing them and making them usable are partially available and used as sub-modules of the presented concept of a comprehensive workflow.

2.2   Service-Oriented Workflow

The comprehensive process presented in this paper 'from data to a feature-rich virtual city model' can be structurally divided into the essential segments 1)

(Raw)Data, 2) (Pre)Processing, 3) Management, 4) Analytics, 5) Visualisation, and 6) Applications. To a certain extent, this contribution represents a kind of bracket around already conducted own assessments and published results of research. An essential introduction to the service-based concept has already been given in [8]. Furthermore, in [6] it can be read how data acquisition was made in detail and how the necessary data stock was generated and managed. Finally, in [7] methods and techniques have been presented on how a virtual multi-dimensional city model can be created from acquired geometric geodata and semantic context. An overview of the workflow is shown in Fig. 2.

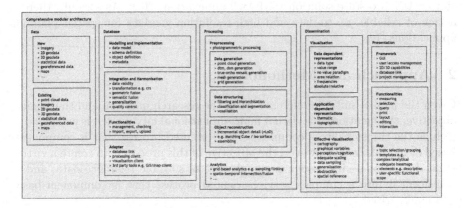

Fig. 2. Modularised overview of the service-oriented workflow

Data. An indispensable and important, base-relevant component of the workflow is geodata. Geospatial data, also known as geographic data or spatial data, refers to data and information explicitly or implicitly associated with a location in relation to Earth [9]. Common types of geographic data include vector files consisting of simple points, vertices and paths, raster files consisting of pixels and grid cells, geographic databases that typically store vectors and rasters (0D, 1D, 2D, 3D), and multi-temporal data that add a temporal component to the information (4D). Moreover, if further feature spaces are added by means of semantic enrichment, it can be referred to as multi-dimensional geodata. Such geographic data can be recorded and generated, for example, using telematics devices (GNSS or total stations), geographic aerial and satellite images, lidar or laser scanning, the Internet of Things, and VGI or geotagging. Authoritative or accessible geodata usually form the backbone of any application. In this case, it is about the most accurate representation possible of the geometric characteristics of an object and the semantics attached to it. In this context, it is referred to as geo-reference data. For a digital city model, geometric representations of the contained objects (including buildings) are crucial. Depending on the purpose of the model, further thematic data (demography, economy, traffic, official) and topological data (heights, environment, hydrography) are used for modelling [10].

Point clouds are particularly suitable for modelling the most accurate possible representation of reality. A point cloud or a point heap is a set of points of a vector space that has an unorganised spatial structure [5]. It is described by the points it contains, each of which is captured by its spatial coordinates. Point clouds with georeferencing contain points in an earth-related coordinate system. Additional attributes can be registered for the points, such as geometric normals, colour values, time of recording or measurement accuracy. As a result, the point cloud represents an ideal invariant reference data set. However, for the object formation (for example of a building) a multitude of digital processing techniques are necessary [5, 7].

Import. The integration of new data sources or the updating of existing data starts with the import. This must be carried out per data format or data source in order to comply with all technical limits. The import can be adjusted to the data collection system, as it does not change. However, the time of collection (for example, in a year) can change the data. The constancy of data collection by modern sensor systems usually makes it easy to fully automate the import process [15].

Cleaning. The first step is to check loaded data to remove errors and outliers. This step usually has to be done per data source and increases data quality from the beginning [15]. Secondly, in some cases the raw data needs to be adjusted by modelling accuracy (approximate and interpolate). Thirdly, it can be helpful to convert all data to the same coordinate projection to avoid later processing problems. Modern geoprocessing tools allow the on-the-fly integration of those subprocesses. The cleaning process can also be automated in most cases, but it does not replace a final check and quality approval; this remains mandatory [10].

Assessing. Each data source must be assessed in terms of its quality. This is because each source has a different accuracy and level of detail (for example, age or measurement accuracy of different recording systems). The same applies to official cadastral data [9]. Geospatial data can be generated or referenced using high-precision differential geodetic measurements, while other geospatial data is acquired using, comparatively simpler, handheld GNSS trackers to record a position (without reference station or post-processing of errors). The assessment process can also usually be automated for each individual data source, especially if reference data is available for verification. Metadata is suitable as documentation in this case [10].

Processing. Following processing, more information can be derived from the imported and cleaned data compared to the direct use of the raw data. For example, the diameter of tree crowns and the tree heights at the time of measurement can be calculated from laser scan or point cloud raw data, so that there is no need to resort to official cadastral data, which are updated less frequently. Aerial imagery can be used to determine the location and quality of objects for large areas without the need for small-scale measurements [18]. The disadvantage is that aerial photographs are sometimes not spatially resolved precisely enough to use the derived data directly, however. In this respect, data may sometimes need to be adapted for use in subsequent processing steps. Information about buildings, for example, can be very detailed and include protrusions and niches, for example. It may therefore be necessary or required, depending on the modelling purpose, to remove such details from the very beginning and procedurally recreate building models to make them more suitable for further processing steps [5]. Occasionally, the data must also be converted into another data format during processing. Nevertheless, data processing can usually be automated as well. This is especially true if the data source with its data semantics does not change and the structure of the data remains the same. If one of these points changes, the processing algorithms must be adapted.

Harmonisation. Various data sources have to be amalgamated in order to obtain an overall representation. Data of a city are versatile and consist for example of vector-based cadastral data derived from mobile maps and aerial imagery or volunteered geographic information. These different data have to be merged despite their temporal and spatial differences. For the fusion process, the results of the assessment are useful to select the best source as ground truth or reference for all other sources [13]. This selection must be made for each crucial element. The fusion of the data is the most difficult part of the whole process chain. Especially when different and many heterogeneous data sources are needed for further processing, the fusion process has to be adapted consistently. This is because the sources used usually do not provide updated data at the same time, or sometimes there is no data at all [17]. Therefore, the ground truth selection may also change. Information that is only tangentially linked to other data is easy to include in the description, whereas this is more complicated for data that is already an amalgamation of different data sources. This principle leads to a multi-stage fusion process. The more information is linked to other data, the more complex the fusion process is. For instance, as a result, information should separate the road infrastructure and street furniture, which may change their position and type more frequently, from the topographic description of a building. This makes it possible to update the road infrastructure layer without considering many dependencies. During the fusion it is also conceivable to make necessary spatial corrections if road infrastructure etc. are not completely necessary to the road layout. The fact that this correction can usually be made on-the-fly and is not kept in the data makes the undoing of a correction in an outdated road description dataset obsolete during the update process. Such fusion is essential when data sources need to be replaced. It could be the case that a data source (e.g. aerial imagery) may no longer be available, but a comprehensive cadastral survey becomes available and affordable.

Storing. The cleaned, processed and amalgamated data needs to be stored. For this purpose, simple and open description formats should be used. They are usually implemented in corresponding geographic information systems (GIS) or standards like OGC specified. In addition to geometry types (vector and raster), a distinction is also made in data types and forms of representation (discrete, continuous) [10]. Consequently, storing in the form of individual data sets merely creates a bundle of distributed databases arranged in a federated hierarchy. A crucial point is the linking of data. It is highly desirable to link as much information as possible directly across different database components. Therefore, domain-specific data formats should be avoided, as they are optimised for their specific use case and only contain the problem of implicitly representing certain features. Simple and open description formats that can be mapped to common geometric elements, with contextual information stored as attributes, should be preferred. The use of simple 3D features (Point, LineString and Polygon) for comprehensive modelling of, for example, a road environment, forms the basis for the versatile use of such a database [17]. The use of a simplified data model for objects enables detailed modelling of roads and buildings and their surroundings through relationships. With the help of mostly automated conversion, different and very specific output formats can be provided for domain-specific use, while simplified elements are translated into complex representations with the required spatial precision. Data storage is generally fully automatable. The data to be stored is known, as is the storage format. Once implemented, it can therefore be used again and again [10].

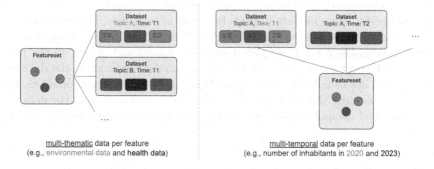

multi-thematic data per feature
(e.g., environmental data and health data)

multi-temporal data per feature
(e.g., number of inhabitants in 2020 and 2023)

Fig. 3. Object-oriented modelling to enable multi-thematic and multi-temporal processing

Versioning of data also plays an important role, especially when it comes to data describing flows. They can be used later to analyse progress and can be included in simulations to better assess the (temporary) impacts [10]. This is done either by storing different temporal versions of the same data layer as one consistent data set or by storing corresponding elements in multiple versions over time. They are further linked to related elements in different temporal versions. Object-oriented modelling then allows multi-thematic or multi-temporal processing of the features (objects) stored in the underlying databases, as shown in Fig. 3.

Referencing. Referencing is an important part of processing because there is no 'world format' for describing every piece of information. Meaningful references need to be made to meet the different requirements of stakeholders. An example could be the power infrastructure in the context of the building environment to assess the impact on the disturbance due to incidents. With regard to a Digital City Twin, other sensor data or Building Information Modelling (BIM) can also be linked without importing it into the database [3,4]. In this way, the actual data of the model can be accessed when needed and avoid dealing with complexity when it is not required. The linkage can be stored as additional attributes in a data set itself or as additional data layers in a specific description language. Based on the use case of the particular spatial data set, either only additional data is listed and linked in a catalogue service (CSW), or a federated database management system (FDBMS) is implemented, or a combination of both [10].

Export. The collected and processed data shall be exported in different data formats so that they can be used e.g. as 3D visualisation for decision making. It is important that each export based on the same data set does not export ambiguities [15]. Accordingly, each target format requires the implementation of its own exporter to avoid information and accuracy losses along the conversion chain that follows. Specific requirements for the target format should be implemented in the export and not in the prior data processing. Conversion between domain-specific, complex data formats is almost always lossy, introduces numerical challenges and leads to limited flexibility in incorporating future requirements. This makes a solid, simplified database model and design all the more important. Export can be fully automated, as can data storage, as the data and formats used are usually clearly defined. Besides the export functionalities, this section also includes the provision of interfaces to access data from the database in modules and components of the system. This includes database adapters and interfaces.

Analytics. However, the comprehensive, harmonised database in the form of a common database serves as an input for analyses. Furthermore, the challenges related to data harmonisation and fusion in some ways favour another approach [6]. In addition to the already existing spatial reference of each datum, another independent spatial reference such as a grid cell (for example, a square or hexagonal shape) allows the neutral calculation and processing of each datum for analysis purposes. Such spatial references can be hierarchically structured, thus also allowing an efficient implementation as well as application of spatial functionalities and queries (select, filter) or processing procedures (filter, intersect, compute). Furthermore, the choice of a grid as spatial reference allows a transfer of analysis results and calculations across, for instance, variable administrative units. It is therefore a generic approach.

Visualisation. Visualisation is the graphic representation of information, visual elements such as diagrams, graphs or maps. Visualisation is essential for analysing information and making data-related decisions. When it comes to spatial elements, it is also cartography, the art and science of graphically representing a geographical area [11]. This usually involves a flat surface, such as a map or diagram. Political, cultural or other non-geographical subdivisions may be superimposed on the representation of a geographical area. This is then referred to as a thematic map. With the increased emergence and availability of the third dimension or more, visualisation and cartography are conditionally reinventing themselves. The effective and efficient representation of multi-dimensional objects and relations is therefore also part of this complex. Interactive and dynamic visualisations compared to static variants can have advantages, but also many disadvantages. Similar to the visual representation of uncertainty, 3D visualisation raises the important question of whether it is useful. The answer is usually that it depends. In general, it turns out that people prefer to use 3D maps than their 2D counterparts. However, it also shows that people perform tasks less efficiently with 3D graphics than with simpler 2D visualisations. There is no scientific consensus on whether 3D visualisations are helpful to users, and due to the contextual nature of such a question, it is unlikely that there will be an answer in the foreseeable future. The current state of research suggests that 3D visualisations should be used with caution. In contexts where seconds matter (e.g. emergency management, disaster response), 3D visualisation tools could be a risky option. In contexts where the user's pleasure is paramount (e.g. a university campus map), on the other hand, they could be an excellent choice [11].

Applications. The applications of a digital city model are as versatile as they are limited. The availability of data and the degree of abstraction of the model usually limit many applications right from the start. Nevertheless, the spatial representation of a digital city model or twin touches on many areas, just like in reality. Energy supply, solar potential, traffic engineering, traffic flow analysis, civil engineering, municipal planning and analysis or tourism, to name just a few, show the versatility given appropriate data availability [3]. At the same time, in combination with the spatial and temporal dimension, an experience and analysis space can be created that makes planning or results tangible; for example, through augmented or virtual reality. Applications can be differentiated in terms of their taxonomy, such as semantics, the minimum level of detail, the level of spatial granularity, the spatio-semantic coherence, the nature of the output of the use case or the 'human-style' visualisation itself.

3 Implementation

Based on the described methodology, the construction of a georeferenced virtual city model from unstructured 3D point clouds is implemented. The realisation consists of the development and application of a component-based and modular comprehensive workflow from data acquisition to web-based dissemination of the content.

3.1 System Design

The system design is essentially based on open-source components. The system components are shown in Fig. 4 for an applied overview. For storage and management, a specially developed data model is implemented in a PostgreSQL, which, as described, is object-based. It allows, for example, to link and store changes in the state of an object (e.g. a building) over time. Individual modules and segments allow for targeted integration and harmonisation when importing data into or exporting data from the database. For the management of the database, a management system was developed that allows the administration and modification of the contained data via a graphical user interface. As the database is object-based, only vector data can be stored, which is why another module for raster data is an essential part of the system in supplement to the database. This is the software module 'GeoServer', which is open-source and provides additional management functionalities. Various self-developed data adapters or already existing standardised ones of the GeoServer form interfaces to further modules and third-party services or GIS and VIS systems. A large, still proprietary module (VC Map, VC Publisher) of the workflow represents the mapping and visualisation framework that makes the data available on a web-based platform. This system also serves to package the virtual representation of the East Jerusalem region. It allows for compilation and presentation in 3D using Cesium technology with extensibility through tools.

In addition to the dedicated component overview in Fig. 4, Fig. 5 illustrates an abstracted and genericised variant, which is, however, extended by the user types. Thus, in addition to the main modules 1) database, 2) mapping tools, 3) visualisation tools and 4) management tools, the respective user role is also shown. As an example, a tourism application is provided in the system, which only includes read rights and does not allow any changes to the data stock. The user role of the tourism operator, on the other hand, allows changes to the database via a graphical user interface after authentication. Furthermore, various standardised interfaces, such as WMTS or WFS, allow data integration into third-party tools and services for in-depth analyses, provided the corresponding user role and expert knowledge are available.

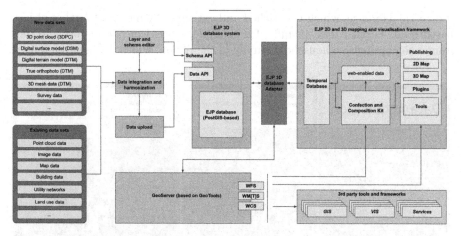

Refined system architecture - including the acquired software

Fig. 4. Overview of system components and their linkages

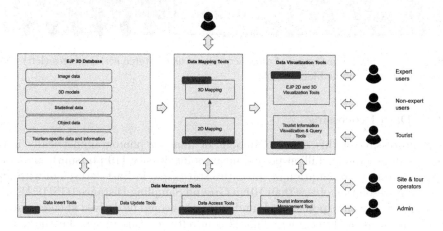

Fig. 5. Abstracted system overview including user types

3.2 Data Acquisition

For the region of East Jerusalem, there are no reference data available, neither for the whole area nor in a certain quality, in order to derive a digital model of the region. Consequently, valid and usable reference data must be acquired. As already described in [6,7], nadir stereo aerial images could be obtained during a flight campaign, which were processed photogrammetrically. An overview is shown in Fig. 6. This acquisition represents the geometric corpus respectively the geometric reference, which is enriched and extended by means of further object-based data. Further data include, for example, statistical parameters and data from a comprehensive household survey of the region, which was geo-referenced.

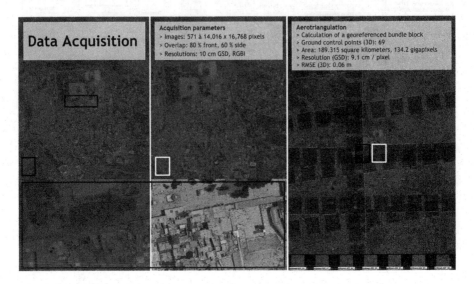

Fig. 6. Exemplary illustration of data acquisition using stereo aerial images (left) and calculation of a bundle block (right)

3.3 Data Processing

The processing of this massive amount of imagery photogrammetrically into point clouds (over 21 billion points, mean point density 119 pts/sqm), allows a very accurate representation of the entire status quo in East Jerusalem with an area-wide resolution of less than 10 cm Ground Sampling Distance (GSD). Using proprietary software, point clouds and 3D meshes could be derived and generated with unprecedented accuracy. This is a novelty for this region. Furthermore, due to the encapsulated and modularised process sections, the massive dataset could be analysed to detect, extract and reconstruct objects (such as buildings) geometrically. Details can be found in [7]. Semantics and thematic could then be assigned or linked to these objects in the database by means of harmonisation and integration modules as illustrated in Fig. 7.

Analyses on hierarchical grid reference allow versatile correlations and are very precisely available or referenceable due to the spatial resolution of the source data (10 cm GSD). The spatial 3D data visualisation and on-the-fly analysis is carried out using CesiumJS. The system components allow a transformation of necessary formats. CesiumJS is an open source JavaScript library for the creation of 3D globes and maps as well as interactive web applications with the sharing of dynamic geodata and is the 'de facto standard' in terms of performance, precision, visual quality and usability today. CesiumJS is based on open formats

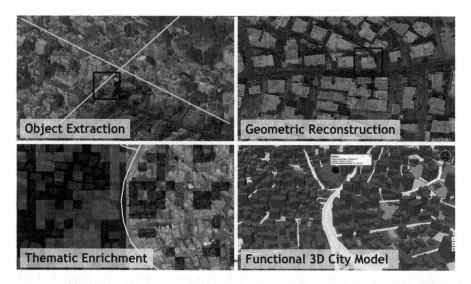

Fig. 7. Exemplary illustration of consecutive data processing, object reconstruction, semantic enrichment towards a feature-rich 3D city model

and designed for robust interoperability and scaling for large datasets. The final result is a 3D spatial virtual model of the East Jerusalem region that is usable and can add value through simple functionalities such as spatial selection or spatial queries.

4   Conclusion and Discussion

In summary, the comprehensive workflow presented can be applied to create a virtual city model in case of a lack of adequate or valid reference data. The encapsulated and independent modules allow the realisation of a feature-rich virtual city model of the East Jerusalem region. Another point to note is that this has generated the development and compilation of a comprehensive geodatabase, including up-to-date 3D geodata and thematic data of unprecedented breadth and depth. The choice of the grid for analysis purposes demonstrates independence and objectivity especially in regions where boundaries are changeable (administratively or by uncertainty). With hierarchical handling, it also allows efficient and effective processing of integrated and harmonised geodata in a common geodatabase. The interconnection of the modules in the overall system are appropriate as a documentation, information and dissemination platform for research, education and decision-making by civil society, municipal stakeholders and the general public. The sustainability and outlook of the contents of this contribution lie, among other things, in the maintenance and expansion of the existing database and the improvement and expansion of the dissemination tools. Furthermore, in the spirit of the VGI, the extension of crowd-sourcing tools to all user groups and sectors can be considered [13]. This includes providing specific access to the database and data processing functions for specific target groups. Moreover, this also includes the development of a mapping and visualisation system for the general public and the use of the collected data for the development of decision support functions and planning tools [3]. Hence, the field of the digital twin is clearly already touched upon, as it can act as a communication medium for versatile applications. It can be seen that a combination of 2D and 3D - regardless of the temporal dimensions - requires further research, given that added value can only arise in combination when it comes to effective forms of visualisation. The accuracy provided by the point cloud reference data is an excellent starting point. It can be assumed that in future developments point cloud processing will allow object-based representation forms to be derived on-the-fly, which can be used for monitoring or modelling purposes in the future [5,7]. Since the approach is detached from the spatial region, it is important to check whether it is transferable to other oriental cities (for example Cairo or Damascus) that are faced with similar data availability. However, due to the requirements and few limitations of the process, it can be assumed that this is possible and that adjustments may only be necessary within individual modules or segments.

Acknowledgements. The work discussed here is part of a larger R+D project on East Jerusalem with Palestinian, East Jerusalem, and NGO partners funded by the European Union. Part of this research work is supported by a PhD grant from the HPI Research School and the Chair of the Computer Graphics Systems department for Service-Oriented Systems Engineering at the Hasso Plattner Institute for Digital Engineering, University of Potsdam. The funding of both institutions is gratefully acknowledged.

References

1. Bittner, C.: OpenStreetMap in Israel and Palestine- 'game changer' or reproducer of contested cartographies? Polit. Geogr. **57**, 34–48 (2017)
2. Bittner, C., Glasze, G.: Who maps middle eastern geographies in the digital age? Inequalities in web 2.0 cartographies in Israel/palestine. In: Media and Mapping Practices in the Middle East and North Africa, p. 45 (2021)
3. Chamoso, P., González-Briones, A., De La Prieta, F., Venyagamoorthy, G.K., Corchado, J.M.: Smart city as a distributed platform: toward a system for citizen-oriented management. Comput. Commun. **152**, 323–332 (2020)
4. Chen, R.: The development of 3D city model and its applications in urban planning. In: 2011 19th International Conference on Geoinformatics, pp. 1–5. IEEE (2011)
5. Döllner, J.: Geospatial artificial intelligence: potentials of machine learning for 3D point clouds and geospatial digital twins. PFG-J. Photogramm. Remote Sens. Geoinf. Sci. **88**(1), 15–24 (2020)
6. Fricke, A., Asche, H.: Geospatial database for the generation of multidimensional virtual city models dedicated to urban analysis and decision-making. In: Misra, S., et al. (eds.) ICCSA 2019. LNCS, vol. 11621, pp. 711–726. Springer, Cham (2019). https://doi.org/10.1007/978-3-030-24302-9_52

7. Fricke, A., Asche, H.: Constructing geo-referenced virtual city models from point cloud primitives. In: Gervasi, O., et al. (eds.) ICCSA 2020. LNCS, vol. 12252, pp. 448–462. Springer, Cham (2020). https://doi.org/10.1007/978-3-030-58811-3_33

8. Fricke, A., Döllner, J., Asche, H.: Servicification – trend or paradigm shift in geospatial data processing? In: Gervasi, O., et al. (eds.) ICCSA 2018. LNCS, vol. 10962, pp. 339–350. Springer, Cham (2018). https://doi.org/10.1007/978-3-319-95168-3_23

9. Goodchild, M.F.: Geographical data modeling. Comput. Geosci. **18**(4), 401–408 (1992)

10. Haining, R.P.: The nature of georeferenced data. In: Fischer, M., Getis, A. (eds.) Handbook of Applied Spatial Analysis, pp. 197–217. Springer, Heidelberg (2010). https://doi.org/10.1007/978-3-642-03647-7_12

11. Kraak, M.J., Ormeling, F.: Cartography: Visualization of Geospatial Data. CRC Press, Boca Raton (2020)

12. Lehner, H., Dorffner, L.: Digital geoTwin Vienna: towards a digital twin city as geodata hub. PFG – J. Photogramm. Remote Sens. Geoinf. Sci. **88**(1), 63–75 (2020). https://doi.org/10.1007/s41064-020-00101-4

13. Lü, G., Batty, M., Strobl, J., Lin, H., Zhu, A.X., Chen, M.: Reflections and speculations on the progress in Geographic Information Systems (GIS): a geographic perspective. Int. J. Geogr. Inf. Sci. **33**(2), 346–367 (2019)

14. Maitland, C.: Maps, politics and data sharing: a Palestinian puzzle. In: Proceedings of the Sixth International Conference on Information and Communications Technologies and Development: Notes, vol. 2, pp. 76–79 (2013)

15. Nagy, G., Wagle, S.: Geographic data processing. ACM Comput. Surv. (CSUR) **11**(2), 139–181 (1979)

16. Prandi, F., Soave, M., Devigili, F., Andreolli, M., De Amicis, R.: Services oriented smart city platform based on 3D city model visualization. ISPRS Ann. Photogramm. Remote Sens. Spat. Inf. Sci. **2**(4), 59 (2014)

17. Uitermark, H.T., van Oosterom, P.J.M., Mars, N.J.I., Molenaar, M.: Ontology-based geographic data set integration. In: Böhlen, M.H., Jensen, C.S., Scholl, M.O. (eds.) STDBM 1999. LNCS, vol. 1678, pp. 60–78. Springer, Heidelberg (1999). https://doi.org/10.1007/3-540-48344-6_4

18. Vosselman, G., Dijkman, S., et al.: 3D building model reconstruction from point clouds and ground plans. Int. Arch. Photogramm. Remote Sens. Spat. Inf. Sci. **34**(3/W4), 37–44 (2001)

Economic Benefits of Noise Reduction from Road Transport in Mountain Areas

Federico Cavallaro[1], Alberto Fabio[2], and Silvio Nocera[2(✉)]

[1] Politecnico di Torino, Turin, Italy
[2] Università IUAV di Venezia, Venice, Italy
nocera@iuav.it

Abstract. Noise emissions are a relevant externality, which cause negative effects on affected population. Due to the topographic and physical characteristics of the geographical context, road transport in mountain areas is a main source of noise emissions. Adequate solutions have to be foreseen, able to reduce the impacts on affected population. First, this contribution describes alternative solutions to reduce the noise pressure along mountain roads. Then, it provides a method to evaluate their effectiveness based on a cost-effectiveness ratio and hedonic pricing. Two case studies located along a mountain road in South Tyrol (Italy) show the performances of different solutions in various contexts, suggesting the importance of evaluations that consider the territorial and settlement specificities. These results can be helpful for policy makers to define the most effective solutions to reduce transport externalities and to make mountain areas more liveable.

Keywords: Noise · Economic benefits · Transport externalities · Road transport · Mountain areas

1 Introduction

The impact of noise emissions at EU level is estimated at €1047B [1]. Together with global and local air pollution, accidents, congestion and habitat damage, noise is one of the main externalities generated by the transport sector [2]. Its effects on the affected population include physical and mental health problems, sleep disturbance hypertension, risk of stroke, diabetes and depression, agitation, stress, anxiety, and problems in children's cognitive development [3].

Some areas are more vulnerable than others under the same level of acoustic pressure. The mountain valleys are among them: here, sound can be amplified by topographic conditions, thermal inversion typical of cold months and nights, and the refraction of waves and wind, thus generating an amphitheatre effect that exacerbates the level of perceived sound and worsens the quality of life of the inhabitants [4]. Despite the temporary decrease in road and rail traffic volumes registered during the SARS-CoV-2 pandemic, traffic volumes along main roads are expected to increase, along with noise emissions, if adequate solutions are not implemented.

© The Author(s), under exclusive license to Springer Nature Switzerland AG 2022
O. Gervasi et al. (Eds.): ICCSA 2022, LNCS 13376, pp. 160–174, 2022.
https://doi.org/10.1007/978-3-031-10450-3_12

This paper discusses about the impacts of alternative solutions for reducing noise emissions along mountain roads, by evaluating the variation in market values of affected buildings and relating them with the construction and implementation costs. The rest of the paper is organised as follows: in Sect. 2, potential measures for the reduction of noise emissions are presented. Section 3 describes a method to evaluate them, based on a cost-effectiveness ratio and hedonic prices (HP). Section 4 tests the method in two selected case studies, showing the importance of tailored solutions according to the territorial context. Some conclusions end the contribution.

2 Measures to Reduce Noise Emissions from Road Transport

Measures to mitigate noise emissions from road traffic are numerous and can be distinguished according to their scope. Three groups of measures can be identified: at-source, propagation path, and at-receptor [5]. The selection of the correct intervention depends also on the specific geographical context: in rough terms, solutions can be divided into urban and rural ones, here including also marginal areas. A third classification depends on the nature of the measure, which can be either management or physical. A list of these measures, with their main characteristics in terms of costs and acoustic benefits, is presented in Table 1.

As for the management solutions, noise pollution depends on vehicular speed (the average speed is related to the noise pressure by a logarithmic relation: [6]) and traffic volumes on the road. Urban solutions aim mainly at limiting the vehicular circulation or the travel speed through traffic management solutions. At speeds below 50 km/h, a 10-km/h reduction may lead to a reduction of 2–3 dB L_{eq} [7]. This solution implies the construction of physical elements to moderate speed vehicles, like gateways, horizontal or vertical deflections. Their costs are normally not high and, according to the evaluation available in several Italian territorial price lists, are included between 1,000 € and 10,000 € for every element.

Another management solution to reduce noise pollution is traffic calming, which can be either total or limited to heavy traffic. In the former case, this solution is found to be more effective, with a reduction up to 7 dB [7]. In the latter case, the reduction can be estimated up to 3 dB. This solution has low costs, but it implies an alternative road for the traffic, such as a bypass or a ring road. In urban contexts, alternative roads can be easily identified and this measure can be introduced in areas that are particularly critic. In case the alternative road is not available (this is mostly valid in non-urban context), the costs for building a new infrastructure have to be considered. As an initial reference value, the guidelines of the Autonomous Province of Bolzano [8] suggest considering 1,500 €/m, but this value can increase up to 20,000 €/m in case of gallery or other main infrastructural works, such as bridges or viaducts.

Physical measures foresee other types of interventions to reduce noise impacts: installation of noise barriers, embankment, vegetation and realization of noise reducing asphalt pavement. Noise barriers are found to be more effective than vegetation, with an absorbing factor between 5 and 15 dB. They are effective only up to 100 m; if the distance is higher, the effect is negligible [5]. Unitary costs are equal to 1,000–1,500 €/m for a barrier that is up to 4 m high, with different values according to the typology and construction materials [8]. The average operational life of this solution is about 20 years [9]. The application of these solutions may lead to several issues. Especially in delicate contexts (such as the mountain ones), influences on landscape must be considered and solved with adequate solutions that minimize the visual impact. Transparent barriers may be suitable for this purpose, but attention has to be paid to the effects on birds. The continuity of the structure is another issue. Along secondary roads, it cannot be always guaranteed for their entire length, due to the existence of the access to the buildings and to local roads. Fragmented barriers have a lower effect.

Embankment is a more natural type of noise barrier, with a potential effect estimated at 5–10 dB of noise reduction. The cost of this solution is not easily definable, as it is highly dependent from the morphology of the terrain and the required ground works. The main issue related to this solution is the large area required, which is rarely available. The cost for tree planting and for maintaining the vegetation has also to be foreseen. Vegetation can be also used without embankment, but its benefits are lower than noise barriers [5]. Hence, the planting should be foreseen as a technical solution for noise abatement only if expected emissions are slightly above the maximum threshold.

The tyre-road contact is the main noise source for both passenger cars and for heavy vehicles, respectively at speeds over 35 and 60 km/h [10]. Traditional noise reducing pavement can lower noise emissions up to 2–4 dB for light traffic and 2 dB for heavy traffic, considering the different average speeds of the two classes of vehicles. The use of special types of asphalt on roads with speeds equal or higher than 90 km/h can increase these values up to 6–8 dB and 4–5 dB, respectively. Costs for this solution are 15 €/m² for the first type, and 30 for the second [8]. The application of these asphalts is recommended for extra-urban roads, with an average speed not below 50 km/h. Conversely, in urban contexts, this solution is less effective. The estimated duration of this material is up to 10 years [11]. However, performances can progressively decrease and reach values only 1–2 dB lower than traditional asphalt values in five years, due to the accumulation of the pollutants in the asphalt pores.

Table 1. Measures to reduce acoustic emissions, benefits and implementation costs

Type	Measure	Geographical scope	Acoustic benefits	Costs
Management	Speed calming (physical elements)	Urban (speed limit < 50 km/h)	2–3 dB	1,000–10,000 €/each
Management	Traffic calming	Urban	3–7 dB	n.a.
Physic	Noise Barrier	Urban/rural	5–15 dB	1,000–1,500 €/m
Physic	Embarkment	Rural	5–10 dB	n.a.
Physic	Vegetation	Urban/rural	n.d.	n.a.
Physic	Traditional noise reducing pavement	Urban/rural (speed limit > 50 km/h)	2–4 dB	15 €/m²
Physic	Special noise reducing pavement	Urban/rural (speed limit > 90 km/h)	6–8 dB	30 €/m²

Finally, noise abatement solutions may be also directly related to the source (i.e., the vehicles), including the reduction of noise from engine and other vehicle noises. In this sense, the diffusion of zero-emission vehicles (powered by electricity or hydrogen) or hybrid vehicles in the vehicular fleet may represent a valid support in the reduction of noise emissions. However, except for few public vehicles, this measure is mostly related to private citizens and firms; furthermore, it requires a long temporal horizon to be effective, due to the slow dynamics in the renewal of the vehicular fleet [12]. As such, policymakers can intervene only indirectly, by introducing subsidies or other incentives to encourage the shift towards these vehicles.

3 Methodology

To verify the impacts of selected measures in terms of noise reduction, HP is a possible solution [13]. HP calculates a variation in the market value of buildings as a consequence of the variation in noise emissions perceived by such buildings. The relationship is inverse: a decrease in perceived noise determines an increase in market values, and vice versa. This variation has to be compared to the installation/construction costs to realize the proposed interventions. To this aim, a cost-effectiveness ratio can be adopted, which is referred to a single year z, as in Formula (1):

$$CE_x^z = \frac{C_x^z}{B_x^z} \tag{1}$$

where CE is the cost-effectiveness ratio of a specific solution x, C are the implementation costs and B are the benefits, expressed as economic variation of market values after the introduction of x. Since each x has a different temporal horizon (for instance, the installation of a noise barrier is effective for a longer period than the pavement of a road with noise reducing pavement), it is appropriate to divide the implementation costs and the benefits by the years y of expected life, as in Formula (2) and (3), to obtain a yearly average value:

$$C_x^z = \frac{C_x}{y} \tag{2}$$

$$B_x^z = \frac{B_h + B_{com} + B_{ind} + B_{acc}}{y} \tag{3}$$

The comparison of CE from alternative solutions x allows determining the most effective solution in terms of noise reduction.

C_x can be calculated through parametric values given by territorial price lists, as provided by regional or provincial institutions, local Chambers of Commerce or equivalent institutions. The most complex aspect in Formula (1) is the calculation of B_x, which has to consider the different uses of involved buildings [14]. To this aim, we can distinguish among residential (h), commercial (com), industrial (ind) buildings, and accommodation and facilities (acc). They need to be analysed separately (Formulas 4–7), according to their average market prices (AP, expressed as €/m^2). These values have to be multiplied by the commercial area S of the buildings affected by noise (calculated as the sum of all surfaces of a building), by a noise sensitivity appreciation index (*NSAI*), defined as the percentage appreciation in prices per dB decrease in noise level, and by the reduction of noise *RNP* that is guaranteed by *x* for each building *i*. *NSAI* is theoretically different for each function: for instance, the variation in dB for residential buildings is expected to be more important than industrial areas, considering the type of activities performed. For the sake of simplicity, instead of considering the value of *RNP* for the single building, bands with a similar reduction of noise can be defined.

$$B_h = \sum_{i=1}^{n_h} AP_h \cdot S_h \cdot RNP_{i,x} \cdot NSAI_h \tag{4}$$

$$B_{com} = \sum_{i=1}^{n_{com}} AP_{com} \cdot S_{com} \cdot RNP_{i,x} \cdot NSAI_{com} \tag{5}$$

$$B_{ind} = \sum_{i=1}^{n_{ind}} AP_{ind} \cdot S_{ind} \cdot RNP_{i,x} \cdot NSAI_{ind} \tag{6}$$

$$B_{acc} = \sum_{i=1}^{n_{acc}} AP_{acc} \cdot S_{acc} \cdot RNP_{i,x} \cdot NSAI_{acc} \tag{7}$$

4   Impacts of Alternative Solutions on Noise Reduction: Two Case Studies from S.S.38 (Italy)

Strada Statale (S.S.) 38 dello Stelvio has been selected as location of two distinct case studies. This road is a typical mountain motorway, which connects Bolzano (South Tyrol) to Valtellina (Lombardy) through the Stelvio pass. Road traffic from S.S. 38 is one of the main sources of noise pressure in the area and object of specific monitoring by the Autonomous Province of Bolzano. The average traffic registered at the detection point of Laces in 2021 was equal to 11,642 vehicles/day, with the heavy component counting for roughly 6% of the total (687 veh/day) [15]. Before the SARS-CoV-2 pandemic, average values were higher, with more than 13.000 veh/day (Fig. 1). Traffic data are incomplete for years 2019 and 2020 (the detection point did not work properly between November 2019 and January 2020).

Impacts deriving from road traffic are represented by some noise maps elaborated by the Environmental Agency of the Province of Bolzano, according to the European standards with the L_{den} indicator, as foreseen by the Italian Legislative Decree 194/2005 [8]. These maps represent noise generated by road traffic, dividing their surroundings in areas of 5 dB intervals, comprised between 50 and 80 dB. Only major roads (i.e., roads with a yearly traffic volume higher than 3M vehicles) are mapped. This allows identifying those stretches of the provincial road where buildings are affected by a higher noise pressure. Values provided by these maps have then been assigned to the buildings located close to the motorway thanks to the software QGis. A unique noise exposition has assigned to each building included in the two study areas (the red rectangle in Fig. 2 and Fig. 3). If a building lies between two acoustic zones, the highest value has been considered. Recalling the methodology presented in the section above, geometric and typological information of buildings have also to be collected. The surfaces of the buildings are provided by the digital cadastral geometries, which are published on the

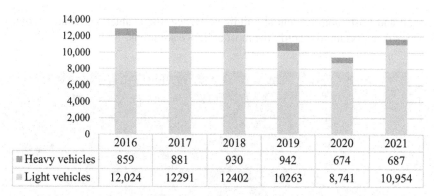

	2016	2017	2018	2019	2020	2021
▪ Heavy vehicles	859	881	930	942	674	687
▪ Light vehicles	12,024	12291	12402	10263	8,741	10,954

Fig. 1. Evolution of average daily traffic along S.S. 38, years 2016–2021 [15]

Geoportal of the Province of Bolzano [16]; whereas destination and number of floors of the buildings have been provided manually, with a visual analysis made through Google Street View. These values have been subsequently inserted in the attributes of the digital cadastral geometries.

If values registered along the road overcome the thresholds imposed by the Italian National Law (L. 447/95) and no compensation measures have been yet introduced, the impacts of alternative solutions can be evaluated in terms of effectiveness and acoustic benefits generated on the territory. Two stretches of S.S. 38 seem particularly interesting for the evaluation: they are located in the South Tyrolean municipalities of Laces and Castelbello-Ciardes. Practically, we limit our evaluation only on those areas with buildings, where the acoustic maps reveal a noise pressure higher than 55 dB. Indeed, under this value the national legislation for residential areas is respected and the adoption of such solutions does not provide significant marginal acoustic benefits to the exposed population. In both case studies, interventions under evaluation include a) the installation of noise barriers on the side(s) of the road where buildings are exposed to noise pressure (scenario 1); the pavement of the road surface with a noise reducing pavement (scenario 2); and the two measures adopted jointly (scenario 3). Theoretically, the number of alternative solutions to reduce noise pressure from road traffic is higher. For instance, the speed traffic moderation or the limitation of the circulation for heavy vehicles are possible alternatives, but it seems more appropriate in urban contexts or in areas where an alternative road network is available (see Sect. 2).

4.1 Laces

The portion of considered territory is an urbanized area located between the centre of Laces and the S.S.38. It includes 2- or 3-floor residential buildings, a petrol station with a mini-market discount, and a hotel with camping structure (Fig. 1). The accommodation facilities and the petrol station are at the same level of the road, and are directly accessible from it, while the residential zone is depressed and divided from the road by a river and some vegetation. Despite this, acoustic values registered in this area overcome the threshold value of 55 dB, with some peaks (up to 75 dB) in the band that is closer to the road and hosts non-residential buildings. Hence, the evaluation of the alternative measures is important to identify the most effective solutions.

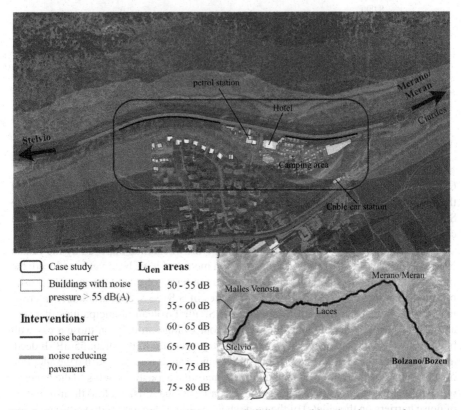

Fig. 2. Laces: noise pressure from road transport, buildings considered and proposed measures. Background map: [17]

Scenario 1 (NB_La) foresees the installation of two noise barriers. The first one is between the road and the bike lane along the Adige River, whereas the second is in substitution of the fence of the camping. These two barriers are interrupted to allow the access to the petrol station, hotel and camping. Total length of the two barriers is about 325 m. Assuming a parametric cost of 1,500 €/m [8], total construction costs are about 580,000 €. The effect of this solution is limited to 13 residential buildings and on the camping area. The range of noise reduction estimated in the second paragraph for this type of solution varies between 5 and 15 dB, according to the technical characteristics. To be cautionary, in the first band (the closest to the road, with an average noise pressure of 65 dB or more), we assume an intermediate reduction of 10 dB thanks also to the favourable conditions of the terrain and a reduction of 6 dB for the buildings subjected to a noise pressure of 60 dB, that are also situated further from the barrier. The benefits of this solution are expected to be valid at least for 20 years from the construction [9].

Scenario 2 (RA_La) proposes the substitution of the road pavement in simple asphalt, with a noise reducing pavement for a length of 860 m and a width of 8 m. The new road pavement is not limited to the place where buildings are located, but includes a broader part of the road, where the line is straight, and the travel speed of vehicles is higher. The total cost is about 100,000 € (assuming a unitary cost for the asphalt equal to 15 €/mq [8]). The impacts of this solution, which is expected to be operational 10 years [11] and requires two cycles of pavement for the period of 20 years under evaluation, involve all 24 buildings considered. With this solution, a potential noise reduction on light traffic from 2 to 4 dB, and 2 dB on heavy traffic may be obtained. As in scenario 1, we assume two different values for the buildings subjected to a noise pressure equal to 60 dB and 65 dB or more (respectively, green, light green and oranges colours in Fig. 2). Reduction is estimated at 2 and 3 dB, considering the reduced component of heavy traffic along the road and the speed limit of 90 km/h (the efficiency of noise reducing asphalt pavement increases with increasing speeds).

Scenario 3 (NB/RA_La) sums the costs and benefits deriving from the two scenarios previously described.

Table 2 and Table 3 present for each scenario the construction costs and the acoustic benefits, expressed as variation in the real estate according to Formulas 4–7. The market value of buildings is given as the average unitary values for residential, retail and accommodations in the municipality of Laces as derived from [18] and multiplied by the floor area of the buildings distinguished by destination. In other scenarios, we have assumed an appreciation index equal to 0.05%/dB for each function, according to [19]. This value has to be multiplied by the noise reduction described above.

Table 2. Laces: construction costs of acoustic measures in different scenarios

Scenario	Measure	Unitary cost*	Quantity	Total costs** €	Average costs €
Scenario 1: NB_La	Noise barrier	1,500 €/m	385 m	577,500	28,875
Scenario 2: RA_La	Noise reducing pavement	15 €/m^2	6,880 m^2	206,400***	10,320
Scenario 3: NB/RA_La	Noise barrier	1,500 €/m	385 m	577,500	39,195
	Noise reducing pavement	15 €/m^2	6,880 m^2	206,400***	

Note: *Source: [8]
**Referred to a period of 20 years for all measures
***Noise reducing pavement has to be renewed every 10 years

In absolute terms, scenario 3 presents highest values both in terms of yearly costs and benefits (with about 39,000 and 46,000 €/year, respectively); whereas the most economical solution is given by scenario 2 (10,320 and 18,750 €/year of costs and benefits). The installation of noise barriers only (Scenario 1) lies in the middle. Table 4 demonstrates that, despite the lower economic benefits, scenario 2 presents the most

Table 3. Laces: acoustic benefits in different scenarios

Scenario	Destination	Unitary value* €/m²	RNP	Surface m²	Benefits** €	Yearly benefits €
Scenario 1: NB_La	Residential	2,204	10 dB	724	79,718	3,986
		2,204	6 dB	4,975	328,884	16,444
	Commercial	1,557	6 dB	256	11,992	600
	Accommodation and facilities	1,693	10 dB	1,425	120,612	6,031
		1,693	6 dB	136	6,860	343
	Total			**7,516**	**548,066**	**27,403**
Scenario 2: RA_La	Residential	2,204	3 dB	724	23,915	1,196
		2,204	2 dB	6,706	147,803	7,390
	Commercial	1,557	3 dB	894	20,857	1,043
		1,557	2 dB	256	3,997	200
	Accommodation and facilities	1,693	3 dB	6,936	176,129	8,806
		1,693	2 dB	136	2,287	115
	Total			**15,652**	**374,988**	**18,749**
Scenario 3: NB/RA_La	Residential	2,204	13 dB	724	103,635	5,182
		2,204	8 dB	4,975	438,511	21,926
		2,204	2 dB	1,731	38,176	1,909
	Commercial	1,557	8 dB	256	15,989	799
		1,557	3 dB	894	20,857	1,043
	Accommodation and facilities	1,693	13 dB	1425	156,795	7,840
		1,693	8 dB	136	9,145	457
		1,693	3 dB	5,511	139,945	6,997
	Total			**15,652**	**923,053**	**46,153**

Notes: * Source: [18]

**Benefits are calculated for 20 years. NSAI is 0.05% for each destination and each scenario

Table 4. Laces: cost/effectiveness ratio of different scenarios

Scenario	Yearly costs of intervention €	Yearly acoustic benefits €	Cost-benefit ratio
Scenario 1: NB_La	28,875	27,403	1.05
Scenario 2: RA_La	10,320	18,750	0.55
Scenario 3: NB/RA_La	39,195	46,153	0.85

effective performance: economic benefits are nearly the double of the yearly construction costs, due to the fact that the benefits involve all buildings (differently from Scenario 1). The combined adoption of measures (Scenario 3) presents also a good cost-benefit ratio, which suggests the adoption of both technologies in case of higher initial pressure. The installation of noise barriers alone (scenario 1) seems not effective (cost-benefit ratio greater than 1).

As for the single destinations, some considerations can be useful. Residential buildings have a considerably appreciation, due to the high number of these buildings in the band that is the closest to the infrastructure. Accommodation facilities have a similar benefit in both scenarios 1 and 2: indeed, the camping benefits from the installation of noise barriers, whereas the noise adsorbing asphalt produces an increase of value also for the hotel. The joint adoption of the two solutions determines a high benefit on this type of destination (+305,885 €). In absolute terms, values of commercial buildings are negligible compared to other destinations. The petrol station and related commercial activities benefit somehow from the road pavement substitution. Conversely, the only building that registers a reduction of noise pressure originated by the noise barriers is a small activity situated next to the cable car station.

4.2 Ciardes

The second case study along the S.S. 38 is a small area near Ciardes, for which we investigate the same alternative measures and scenarios as in Laces. Here, the main destination of buildings is residential, with few manufacturing or rural activities (reported as "industrial" in Table 5 and Table 6). Differently from Laces, buildings are located on both sides of the road (mostly southward) and are depressed. The limit of the study area is given by the territorial context. At the western side, the boundary is coincident with the beginning of the urban area: here, the 50-km/h speed limit makes the noise reducing pavement ineffective; furthermore, in urban areas it is not possible to install noise barriers. At the eastern side, we consider the presence of a road tunnel as the natural boundary of our evaluations.

Scenario 1 (NB_Ci) foresees the installation of a noise barrier to protect 9 residential buildings on the southern side of the road. Other 16 buildings in the east area cannot be protected with a similar efficacy, because they have a direct access to the S.S. 38 through local roads. This prevents from the construction of a continuous barrier. The total length of the barrier is about 265 m, the construction cost is about 397,500 € and the expected effect on the buildings is a reduction of noise pressure by 10 dB. In this case, no differences in noise reductions are considered among buildings, because all of them are located in the proximity of the road and are all subjected to values of noise pressure between 65 and 75 dB. The considered operational lifetime of this infrastructure is 20 years.

In Scenario 2 (RA_Ci), the noise reducing pavement is extended for a length of 650 m and a width of 8 m, which means a construction cost equal to 78,000€. As in Lacies, this intervention has to be repeated two times in the 20 years, which is the temporal horizon of the analysis. The expected effect is the reduction of noise pressure by 2 dB. This value is lower than in the previous case study, due to the lower speed limit on this section of the road (70 km/h against 90 km/h in Laces).

Scenario 3 (NB/RA_Ci) is the sum of the measures adopted in NB_Ci and RA_Ci.

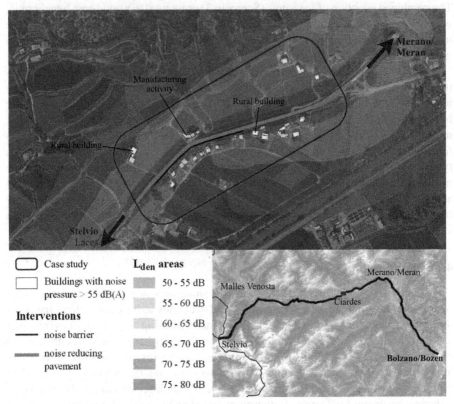

Fig. 3. Ciardes: noise pressure from road transport, buildings considered and proposed measures. Background map: [17]

Results deriving from the adoption of the different measures are quite clear: even though the installation of the noise barrier (scenario 1) is the solution that allows the highest benefits in absolute terms (see Table 6), the adoption of noise reducing pavement is the most effective solution. The cost-benefit ratio equal to 0.75 means that the introduction of this measure is convenient compared to the implementation costs. Differently from the previous case study, Scenario 3 has a cost-benefit ratio slightly greater than 1, which would suggest a cautionary approach in the adoption of joint measures as the technical solution to limit the noise pressure for the residential buildings that are close to the road (Table 7).

As for the single destinations, residential buildings are those that benefit the most (almost exclusively) from the introduction of the noise barrier and/or noise reducing pavement. In Scenario 2 and 3, no benefits for industrial buildings are visible because the surfaces, and hence their market values, are too limited to have an appreciable benefit for this destination.

Table 5. Ciardes: construction costs of acoustic measures in different scenarios

Scenario	Measure	Unitary cost*	Quantity	Total costs** €	Average costs €
Scenario 1: NB_Ci	Noise barrier	1,500 €/m	265 m	397,500	19,875
Scenario 2: RA_Ci	Noise reducing pavement	15 €/m^2	5,200 m^2	156,000***	7,800
Scenario 3: NB/RA_Ci	Noise barrier	1,500 €/m	265 m	397,500	27,675
	Noise reducing pavement	15 €/m^2	5,200 m^2	156,000***	

Note: * Source: [8]
**Total costs refer to a period of 20 years for all measures
***Noise reducing pavement has to be renewed every 10 years

Table 6. Ciardes: acoustic benefits in different scenarios

Scenario	Destination	Unit value* €/m^2	RNP	Surface m^2	Benefits** €	Yearly benefits €
Scenario 1: NB_Ci	Residential	1,596	10 dB	3,000	330,601	16,530
	Industrial	626	10 dB	–	–	–
	Total			**3,000**	**330,601**	**16,530**
Scenario 2: RA_Ci	Residential	1,596	2 dB	9,239	203,644	10,182
		561	2 dB	626	3,588	179
	Total			**9,865**	**207,232**	**10,362**
Scenario 3: NB/RA_Ci	Residential	1,596	12 dB	3,000	396,718	19,836
		1,596	2 dB	6,239	137,523	6,876
	Industrial	561	2 dB	626	3,588	179
	Total			**9,865**	**537,829**	**26,891**

Notes: * Source: [18] ** Benefits are calculated for 20 years. NSAI is 0.05% for each destination and each scenario

Table 7. Ciardes: cost/effectiveness ratio of different scenarios

Scenario	Yearly costs of intervention €	Yearly acoustic benefits €	Cost-benefit ratio
Scenario 1: NB_Ci	19,875	16,530	1.20
Scenario 2: RA_Ci	7,800	10,361	0.75
Scenario 3: NB/RA_Ci	27,675	26,891	1.02

5 Conclusions

Noise emissions are one of the most important transport externalities, as they affect population living close to the infrastructures, with direct impacts on their physical and mental status. This paper has presented and evaluated some technical solutions to reduce the perceived noise along mountain roads, which are known as critical areas characterized by high acoustic pressures. The evaluation is based on a cost-effectiveness ratio that compares the installation costs with the expected benefits of inhabitants, which in turn are calculated with the hedonic pricing method. Two case studies located along S.S. 38 in South Tyrol reveal the importance of tailored solutions, which need to be based on the morphological and settlement characteristics of the area.

This research derives from a change in the paradigm of development for mountain areas. In the past, the well-being of inhabitants of the valleys was often sacrificed in favour of the economic benefits deriving from tourists, with all related negative externalities (here including the noise and air pollution). However, in last years, this vision has been modified. This is not only due to an increased concern about environmental aspects, but also as a consequence of the tourist market, which seeks more and more genuine and less car-dependent products. Hence, the perspective of inhabitants and the added value that they can obtain regarding the market values of their properties can be used not only as indicator of the social benefit, but also as an indicator related to the tourist attractiveness of a region.

Other contributions revealed the importance of addressing the noise emissions from mountain roads, thus confirming the results of our evaluation: [20] measured noise emissions along an urban expressway in the mountainous city of Chongqing (China). A survey to local inhabitants revealed that acoustic environment was the priority environmental factor to be improved. [21] analysed the variation of traffic-related noise emissions from 1990 to 2016 in Bielsko-Biała, a mountainous city in Poland. Despite the improvement in the vehicle fleet, directing transit traffic to the city beltways, as well as the local use of noise barriers, the level of noise intensity increased at night-time, due to the increased road traffic. [22] made a literature review of noise abatement actions, finding that noise barriers are the most effective direct measure, whereas quieter pavements could have an important supporting role.

Some aspects need to be evaluated with a higher accuracy, starting from the adoption of a noise sensitivity appreciation index that is more tailored to the specificities of the context and continuing with the real reductions of noise guaranteed by alternative solutions. Moreover, costs based on parametric values may be helpful for a preliminary evaluation, but when coming to a more executive phase, analytical evaluations have to be provided. The analysis of future noise emissions should also consider the technological evolution: as recalled in Sect. 2, the increase in the number of electric vehicles, as well as the improvement of materials could contribute to the reduction of noise emissions. Finally, the two case studies presented in Sect. 4 have analysed the payback period of the interventions, without considering the issue of discounting. An analysis that includes also the discounted payback period may be helpful, paying particular attention to the choice of the rate that best represents the intervention from a social perspective. Issues related to discount rates and transport externalities may be a very delicate issue, as visible from the numerous criticalities raised during the evaluation of the impacts from greenhouse gas emissions [23].

Despite the need of deepening these methodological aspects, this paper has demonstrated that mountain sites with a limited number of buildings but crossed by important road infrastructures can obtain appreciable benefits in terms of noise reduction with the application of relatively economical measures. This aspect is fundamental in terms of policy and equity perspectives: indeed, targeted interventions may contribute to improving the quality of life for citizens living in such peripheral and rural contexts, and to avoiding negative consequences in terms of ageing, depopulation and significative tourism losses [24, 25].

References

1. van Essen, H., et al.: Handbook on the external costs of transport, version 2019-1.1. Publications Office of the European Union, Luxembourg (2020)
2. Nocera, S., Cavallaro, F.: Economic evaluation of future carbon impacts on the Italian highways. Procedia Soc. Behav. Sci. **54**, 1360–1369 (2012)
3. Potvin, S., Apparicio, P., Séguin, A.M.: The spatial distribution of noise barriers in Montreal: a barrier to achieve environmental equity. Transp. Res. Part D Transp. Environ. **72**, 83–97 (2019)
4. Heimann, D., de Franceschi, M., Emeis, S., Lercher, P., Seibert, P. (eds.): Living Near the Transit Route – Air Pollution, Noise and Health in the Alps. ALPNAP Brochure. Università degli Studi di Trento, Dipartimento di Ingegneria Civile e Ambientale, Trento (2007)
5. Sinha, K.C., Labi, S.: Transportation Decision Making: Principles of Project Evaluation and Programming. Wiley, Hoboken (2007)
6. Iannone, G., Guarnaccia, C., Quartieri, J.: Speed distribution influence in road traffic noise prediction. Environ. Eng. Manag. J. **3**(12), 493–501 (2013)
7. Ellebjerg, L.: Effectiveness and Benefits of Traffic Flow Measures on Noise Control. European Commision DG Research (2007)
8. Provincia Autonoma di Bolzano-Alto Adige: Linee guida per il risanamento acustico lungo le strade provinciali. http://www.provinz.bz.it/tourismus-mobilitaet/strassen/images/Linee_guida_risanamento_acustico_strade.pdf. Accessed 20 Mar 2022
9. EC, European Commission: Solar panels as integrated constructive elements in highway noise barriers. https://webgate.ec.europa.eu/life/publicWebsite/index.cfm?fuseaction=search.dspPage&n_proj_id=5115. Accessed 06 Oct 2021
10. Berge, T., Mioduszewski, P., Ejsmont, J., Świeczko-Żurek, B.: Reduction of road traffic noise by source measures—present and future strategies. Noise Control Eng. J. **65**(6), 549–559 (2017)
11. Bichajło, L., Kołodziej, K.: Porous asphalt pavement for traffic noise reduction and pavement dewatering – the pollution problem. In: VI International Conference of Science and Technology, INFRAEKO 2018 Modern Cities. Infrastructure and Environment, vol. 45, pp. 1–6 (2018). https://doi.org/10.1051/e3sconf/20184500114
12. Santos, G., Behrendt, H., Maconi, L., Shirvani, T., Teytelboym, A.: Externalities and economic policies in road transport. Res. Transp. Econ. **28**, 2–45 (2010)
13. Yao, Y.B., Dubé, J., Carrier, M., Des Rosiers, F.: Investigating the economic impact of noise barriers on single-family housing markets. Transp. Res. Part D Transp. Environ. **97**, 102945 (2021)

14. Cavallaro, F., Nocera, S.: Are transport policies and economic appraisal aligned in evaluating road externalities? Transp. Res. Part D Transp. Environ. **106**, 103266 (2022). https://doi.org/10.1016/j.trd.2022.103266
15. Istituto provinciale di statistica ASTAT - Provincia autonoma di Bolzano. https://qlikview.services.siag.it/QvAJAXZfc/opendoc_notool.htm?document=Traffico.qvw&host=QVS%40titan-a&anonymous=true&Select=LB555,00000012. Accessed 19 Mar 2022
16. Geocatalogo della Provincia di Bolzano. http://geocatalogo.retecivica.bz.it/geokatalog/#!. Accessed 19 Mar 2022
17. QGis QuickMapService – Google Maps Satellite
18. Borsino immobiliare.it. https://borsinoimmobiliare.it/quotazioni-immobiliari/trentino-alto-adige/bolzano-provincia/. Accessed 20 Mar 2022
19. de Schepper, E., Van Passel, S., Manca, J., Thewys, T.: Combining photovoltaics and sound barriers–a feasibility study. Renew. Energy **46**, 297–303 (2012)
20. Li, H., Xie, H.: Noise exposure of the residential areas close to urban expressways in a high-rise mountainous city. Environ. Plann. B Urban Anal. City Sci. **48**(6), 1414–1429 (2021)
21. Vaverková, M.D., Koda, E., Wdowska, M.: Comparison of changes of road noise level over a century quarter: a case study of acoustic environment in the mountainous city. J. Ecol. Eng. **22**(1), 139–150 (2021)
22. Tischmak, D.: Investigation into effective traffic noise abatement design solutions for mountain corridors. Report number: CDOT-2013-11 (2013)
23. Stern, N.: Stern review on the economics of climate change, UK Treasury (2006)
24. Cavallaro, F., Irranca Galati, O., Nocera, S.: Policy strategies for the mitigation of GHG emissions caused by the mass-tourism mobility in coastal areas. Transp. Res. Procedia **27**, 317–327 (2017)
25. Cavallaro, F., Ciari, F., Nocera, S., Prettenthaler, F., Scuttari, A.: The impacts of climate change on tourism mobility in mountain areas. J. Sustain. Tour. **25**(8), 1063–1083 (2017)

Short Papers

Short Papers

Uncertain Integration and Composition Approach of Data from Heterogeneous WoT Health Services

Soura Boulaares[1]([✉]), Salma Sassi[2], Djamal Benslimane[3], and Sami Faiz[4]

[1] National School for Computer Science, Manouba, Tunisia
`boulaaressoura@gmail.com`
[2] Faculty of law, Economic,and Management Sciences, Jendouba, Tunisia
[3] Claude Bernard Lyon 1 University, Lyon, France
`djamal.benslimane@univ-lyon1.fr`
[4] Higher Institute of Multimedia Arts, Manouba, Tunisia
`sami.faiz@insat.rnu.tn`

Abstract. In recent years, the usage of electronic health records (EHR), wearable devices, and health applications has expanded in popularity. Because of the abundance of data that has been accumulated and integrated, health self-management is becoming more practicable. Some of the difficulties that the current healthcare system is facing include smart homes and smart workplaces enabled by the internet of things. The Web of Things (WoT) is a subset of the Internet of Things that aims to connect everyday things to the Internet and manage interoperability. Furthermore, collaboration of health data with data from various devices at home and at work, as well as open data on the Internet, is critical for successful and accessible health self-management. Unfortunately, shared health data may be untrustworthy for a variety of reasons. Uncertainty can be caused by heterogeneity, incompleteness, unavailability, and data inconsistency. To address the problem of health data uncertainty, we provide a probabilistic approach for composing uncertain Health Connected Data and computing the probabilities to deliver the final degree of uncertainty. We also present a method for parsing typical WoT objects into a new programmatic form that mimics the uncertainty of health data. Using a health care use case, we show how our technique successfully integrates uncertain health data with home, work, and sport environment data for the WoT domain.

Keywords: Uncertain WoT · Uncertain IoT · REST · Data Uncertainty · Integration health data · Probability

1   Introduction

In today's modern information systems, individuals, networked devices, and businesses may create and publish vast amounts of data on the web via web APIs and public endpoints [15,19]. The data is then aggregated from multiple sources and used in mashups to provide value [19]. Data may come from disparate, inconsistent, or incomplete sources, disrupting the integration process [10]. The Web of Things (**WoT**) has revolutionized people's lives in recent years. Since 2020, the number of connected devices and apps has outnumbered the world's population, reaching more than 50 billion [8]. Furthermore, the emergence of the Internet of Things (**IoT**) has supported the creation of smart homes, smart work, and other smart technologies. Furthermore, in [5] medical care and health care systems are among the most enticing application areas for the **WoT**. As a result, the application of IoT technology in healthcare simplifies and improves people's lives [7]. Long-term and frequent treatment of chronic diseases by individuals and healthcare providers is necessary for successful and simple self-management.

Wearable gadgets, health apps, and EHR for healthcare monitoring have enabled more people to take charge of their own health. Many healthcare professionals have utilized EHR systems. Smart home, work, and health gadgets that are **WoT** enabled create a seamless environment for recording patient data and vital signs. The aforementioned devices, applications, and systems generate huge amounts of health data from the patient. The Collaborative health data, home and work environment data have the potential to support chronic disease patients with more effective and convenient self-management. However, the collaborative health data with home and work data and activity daily can provide a comprehensive overview and an increased understanding.

Unfortunately, all the data generated risk to become data silos and in heterogeneous format because most of the things used different network protocols. Interoperability plays an important role in smart healthcare, providing connectivity between different devices using different communication technologies. Hence, to resolve the above problems [9] uses **WoT** standards to bring up interoperability between things. The composition of this varied and unpredictable data is required by health data services. For a variety of reasons, the **WoT** services can be unpredictable. The results produced by various **WOT** health devices, for example, are not equivalent since they are positioned in distinct situations. The control of data uncertainty is required for reliable integration of health data with home and work resource environments, which is the goal of this research. Several types of uncertainty have been discovered in the evaluation of emerging **IoT** applications in healthcare, notably in **WoT**. Parameter uncertainty, structural uncertainty, methodological uncertainty, variability, heterogeneity, and decision uncertainty are all examples of uncertainty. Every day, an increasing number of devices join to the **WoT** connection. A smart healthcare network is made up of billions of devices and a massive quantity of data and information that can be analyzed. Can only succeed if it can give capabilities for dealing with heterogeneity and uncertainty. The aim of this work is to address the issue of Uncertain Health Data Composition in the context of **WoT**.

This paper is organized as follows: Sect. 2 covers the related works that dealt with the uncertainty of integration and composition. Section 3 describes our technique for coping with the unpredictable composition of **WoT** health data. Section 5 provides a use example that demonstrates the uncertain composition. Finally, we get to the conclusion of our paper.

1.1   Motivation Example

A patient utilizes **WoT** services and connected things to make decisions about his status at various times of the day and in various locations during his work and home activities. Figure 1 illustrates a Health Data example using a diabetic called Alex who works in a corporation "X". He utilizes **WoT** devices to self-monitor his health at home (**A**), at work (**B**), and when participating in sports (**C**). He measures the temperature (**T**) at home and at work using **WoT** equipment. Simultaneously, he has been utilizing **WoT** health device band services to track daily activities and lifestyle data. The patient intends to integrate his Blood Glucose (**BG**) with each scenario in order to obtain a monthly comprehensive view (home, work, sport). The data is transmitted to the doctor on a regular basis so that he may stay up to date on his patient's status.

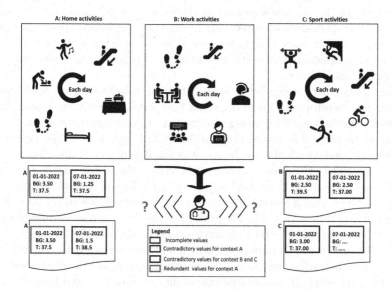

Fig. 1. Motivating example (Color figure online)

The values revealed in the three environments of home, work, and sport are all confusing. Using the data from context A for day 01-01-2022, we can observe that the **T** and **BG** numbers are redundant. In addition, the statistics for 07-01-2022 are incompatible. The contradictory values are colored blue and green, the redundant values are red, and the incomplete values are orange.

1.2   Challenges

When dealing with data uncertainty in **WoT** health service compositions, such as the one in the motivating example, the following challenges arise:

– How can the heterogeneity of values provided by different **WoT** devices, which are not equal because they exist in different contexts, be managed?
– How should the values supplied by the various **WoT** devices be handled if they're not equivalent since they are situated in separate places (home and workplace) and have varying measurement accuracies?
– How should data that represents the same device be handled in terms of redundancy, contradiction, and incompleteness?

2   State of the Art

The applicability of **WoT** in healthcare is critical for a variety of applications. Clinical therapy, remote monitoring, and situational awareness are the three phases of this criterion. The use of an autonomous medical data collection, integration, and composition technique eliminates the possibility of human error during the data integration and composition of Health Data. This will increase the accuracy of the diagnosis and lessen the possibility of human mistake in the gathering or transmission of potentially life-threatening information. There have been attempts to evaluate healthcare from many perspectives. We cover relevant efforts on two aspects in this section: handling heterogeneity in health data with and without uncertainty.

Many research on integrating health data to help healthcare professionals and patients monitor and make decisions have been undertaken. Kumar et al. described a method for integrating glucose data into the EHR to allow diabetic patients to monitor and assess their health [13]. Dexcom, a sensor technology that detects interstitial glucose levels, was employed to do this. The glucose readings are sent to the device vendor's IOS mobile phone app. Apple Healthkite receives the information. The data is then available for analysis within the HER. Authors in [6] created a mobile healthcare system that addressed connection and interoperability difficulties. The integration of the body sensors is accomplished through the use of the Restful web service. In [17], the e-health ontology is suggested to integrate and communicate health and fitness data from disparate IoT sources. The integration was accomplished by utilizing semantic web technologies to facilitate the integration and interoperability of data acquired from disparate IoT sources. The authors in [20] offered an approach for information fusion. To deal with data from disparate sources, a common format and information fusion paradigm for complimentary log aggregation and abstraction are required. They proposed an information fusion approach that reorganizes personal healthcare activity logs and visualizes them hierarchically in a harmonized fashion while delivering a comprehensible summary, as well as a sensor and activity model that classifies heterogeneous sensors. Other research works concentrated on integrating health data with semantics Health IoT ontology. Such as authors in

[18] they set out to characterize the semantic interoperability of medical items and data. They created an algorithm for analyzing the observed vital signs and providing appropriate therapy. The authors in [12], suggested a platform for integrating data from disparate source sources The integration of health data allows different stakeholders access to clinical decision-making and healthcare delivery. In [4], authors addressed variable composition of resources in the context of the social **IoT**. In [21], the authors proposed a portal-based home care platform for integrating various assistive devices and their associated online services. There are three layers to the integration: service, information, and device. The integration levels are intended to increase the adaptability of home health care systems. In [2], authors proposed a framework for aggregating health data and context The data collection intended to improve self-awareness, which led to targeted behavior modifications. A community initiative in [14] introduced JSON-LD to standardize Linked Data in JSON, and the syntax is completely compatible with regular JSON. The JSON -LD can be used to develop RESTful services as well as integrate the exposed data into the Semantic Web. These studies are more concerned with specific integration in healthcare. According to the following sections, to illustrate the uncertain integration of health data. Some approaches consider uncertainty in terms of fuzzy inputs and outcomes. In [1], authors provided a method for assessing decision-making units' performance under uncertainty (DMUs). It incorporates the Data Envelopment Analysis (DEA) approach for cross-efficiency. In [11] the authors suggested a model for a healthcare supply chain in an integrated healthcare system with unpredictable product complaints. Authors in [22] suggested a validation model for physical activity, offered in an IoT enabled customized healthcare setting for reducing irregular uncertainties and evaluating data dependability. In [16], the authors presented a dynamic paradigm for prioritizing surgical patients based on risks and uncertainty. Authors in [3], offered a probabilistic method to data synthesis in the context of the Linked Data web only. These publications are more concerned with specific integration in healthcare. According to the following sections, to illustrate the uncertain integration of health data. Unfortunately, these techniques generate a semantic interoperability difficulty because objects cannot interact with them. Furthermore, none of these techniques address the issue of integrating uncertainty in health data with IoT and, in particular, **WoT** devices.

3   Uncertain Composition of WoT Health Data

We discuss our approach to the unpredictable composition of health data with home and work contexts in this part. Furthermore, the fundamental rationale for integrating health in diverse situations (at home and at work) is to improve the thinking process. The collaborative health data is concerned with supporting chronic disease patients in better managing their symptoms. The management of data uncertainty is required for the trustworthy uncertain composition of data, which is the goal of this research. The health data services sources, API layer,

parser layer (JSON-LD to **JSON-LDpx(MUX,IND)**), uncertain composition
health data layer, and utility applications layer include our method. Figure 2
outlines the layered architecture for unpredictable health data composition with
home and work environments. To integrate uncertain health data, we begin
with the first layer, where we must combine health uncertain data from various
services. The API layer then simply requests data from services via APIs; for
WoT things, we serve data in JSON-LD serialization format (named as TD or
Thing description). JSON -LD format is used to showcase each service. In this
paper, we will focus on the parsing and composing of health data with **WoT**
devices.

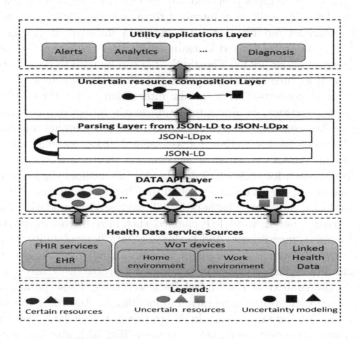

Fig. 2. Layered architecture of uncertain Health Data Composition

1. **The uncertain resource layer:** The first layer includes all of the healthcare domains that come after them. Allowing for a wider range of data and a
   wealth of information for a more comprehensive analyzing experience. These
   data are redundant, ambiguous, diverse, and large in scale, making integration, utilization, and composition problematic. The next phase (parsing) is
   to describe this uncertainty in such a way that data processing, integration,
   and composition become relevant tasks.
2. **Parsing layer:** We will describe the parsing algorithm (JSON-LD to **JSON-
   LDpx** procedure in this layer. This method finds JSON-LD file content that
   has been modified to probabilistic **JSON-LDpx** and then parses it into

JSON-LD format using the sendTo Parse class to determine whether the JSON-LD format is legitimate or not. If the grammatical syntax is correct, then continue with the process. The file is not parsed if it does not conform to the JSON-LD format. The following is the parsing algorithm:

Algorithm 1. Parsing JSON-LDpx

Require: JSON-LD files
Ensure: JSON-lDpx
  $JSON - LDpx \leftarrow 0$
  while $JSON - LD file not empty$ **do**
      if Same attribute and multiple values **then**
          $Attribute \leftarrow uncertain - Id$
          $Dist - IND \leftarrow (Uncertain - Id, v, p)$
          $\triangleright$ (value and probability)
          add.JSON-LDpx(Dist-IND)
      else if Same attribute and one value **then**
          $Attribute \leftarrow uncertain - Id$
          $Dist - MUX \leftarrow (uncertain - Id, v, p)$
          $\triangleright$ (value and probability)
          add.JSON-LDpx(Dist-MUX)
      else Error $\triangleright$ Empty file
      end if
  end while
  return JSON-LDpx

---

3. **Uncertain data Composition layer:** Smart home and work environment data are also considered health-related resources since they are tied to a person's health management. We propose an uncertain composition technique in this layer to combine health data services with **WoT** home and work services in the presence of data uncertainty. In order to accomplish efficient and effective health self-management, it is necessary to integrate and collaborate personal health management data with home and work contexts.

(a) The context of home and work are very important to enhance the reasoning process. Figure 2 describes the process of the uncertain health data composition with home and work environment. In the first step we request file **JSON-LDpx** from health service and **WOT** device service home and work. Then, we compute the probability in the uncertain sub-distribution IND and MUX. We propose a **WoT** probabilistic algebra (inspired from [3]) to compute the uncertainty of the final response degree. The computation of the sub-probability response **P** is as follow:

  – the uncertain sub-distribution (IND) with the OR operator:

$$\mathbf{OR} = \prod_{i=1}^{n} pi = p1 \wedge p2 ... \wedge p_n \tag{1}$$

– the uncertain sub-distribution (MUX) with the XOR operator:

$$\mathbf{XOR} = MAX(p1, ..., p_n) \tag{2}$$

Finally, we estimate the uncertainty of the final degree response by aggregating all the probabilities.

$$\mathbf{P} = \prod_{i=1}^{n} pi(IND) * pi(MUX) \tag{3}$$

4. **The utility applications layer** The doctor may use this layer to prescribe an acceptable therapy for the patient as well as to tell the patient about his condition and the necessary treatment.

4   Use Case of Uncertain Composition

To demonstrate the uncertain health data an example of motivation has been presented in Sect. 1. The motivation example has been presented focuses on the patient in different contexts at home, work, and when practices sport.

In each setting, the **WoT** devices offers distinct data values. The article's major goal was to answer the issue of data ambiguity and return the final degree of uncertainty in order to make an appropriate decision for health patients in each setting. This outcome will assist doctors in obtaining a relevant result among all the unclear options. The health data are modeled in **JSON-LDpx**. Table 1 describes the data values during one week provided by **WoT** device blood glucose (**BG**), **WoT** device temperature (**T**), and **WoT** device steps(S)in each context.

Table 1. The uncertain value of health data resources in each context

Time Context	Home Context	Work Context	Sport Context
01-10-2020	BG:3.5, T:37.5	BG:4.5, T:36.5	BG:1.00, S:300
02-10-2020	BG:2.5, T:33	BG:2.5, T:35.7	BG:0.99, S:200
03-10-2020	BG:1.5, T:40	BG:1.5, T:40	BG:2.25, S:1000
04-10-2020	BG:4.2, T:36.5	BG:3.5, T:36.5	BG:0.99, S:400
05-10-2020	BG:3.5, T:37	BG:3.5, T:37	BG:1.20, S:600
06-10-2020	BG:2.5, T:36	BG:2.5, T:40	BG:0.98, S:800
07-10-2020	BG:1.25, T:37.5	BG:1.5, T:38.5	BG:2.5, S:100

Figure 3 depicts the **BG** and **T** resources of Alex's residence. The representation of probabilistic data is passed to calculate the final degree in order to make an appropriate health patient choice. First, we compute IND's **BG** resource type. The **T** type of MUX is then computed. Finally, the final degree is computed. The probability response P(1) is computed as follows:

First, we use the OR operator to compute the probability in the unknown sub-distribution **BG** (IND) where we take only three possibilities:

$$\mathbf{OR(BG)} = \prod_{i=1}^{n} pi = p1 \wedge p2... \wedge p_7 = (0.1 * 0.2 * 0.3) = 0.006$$

Second, we compute The probability in the uncertain sub-distribution **T** (MUX) is calculated by the XOR operator:

$$\mathbf{XOR(T)} = MAX(p1,..,pi) = MAX(0.6, 0.2, 0.8, 0.5, 0.6, 0.2, 0.3) = 0.8$$

The final result: $\mathbf{P(Q1)} = (0.006 * 0.8) = 0.0020$

```
{  "@context": "http://schema/org",
   "@id": "http://hl7.org/fhir",
   "id":"http://iotschema.org/tempeture",
   "blood glucose": "@300",
   "tempeture":"@301",
   "dist":{
   "dist1":{ "iddist": "@300", "type":"IND",
   "val":[3.5,0.1,2.50,0.2,1.50,0.3,4.20,0.1,3.50,0.1,2.50,0.1,1.25,0.1]},
   "iddist": "@301", "type":"MUX",
   "val":[37.5,0.6,33,0.2,40,0.8,36.5,0.5,37,0.6,36,0.2,37.5,0.5]} } |
```

Fig. 3. JSON-LDpx(MUX, IND) data at home; BG and T

Figure 4 depicts the data values of Alex's **BG** and **T** resources. The representation of probabilistic values is passed to determine the final degree for making an appropriate health patient choice. First, we compute IND's **BG** resource type. The **T** type of MUX is then computed. The probability response P(2) is computed as follows: First, we use the OR operator to compute the probability in the uncertain sub-distribution **BG** (IND) where we take only three possibilities:

$$\mathbf{OR(BG\ )} = \prod_{i=1}^{n} pi = p1 \wedge p2... \wedge p_n = pi(0.3 * 0.1 * 0.1) = 0.003$$

The XOR operator is then used to compute **T** probability in the uncertain sub-distribution (MUX):

$$\mathbf{XOR(T)} = MAX(p1,..,pi) = MAX(0.6, 0.2, 0.8, 0.5, 0.6, 0.7, 0.6) = 0.8$$

The final result: $\mathbf{P(Q2)} = (0.03 * 0.8) = 0.0328$

```
{  "@context": "http://schema/org",
   "@id": "http://hl7.org/fhir",
   "id":"http://iotschema.org/tempeture",
   "blood glucose": "@200",
   "tempeture":"@201",
   "dist":{
   "dist1":{ "iddist": "@200", "type":"IND",
   "val":[4.50,0.3,2.50,0.1,1.50,0.1,3.20,0.17,3.50,0.16,2.50,0.15,1.50,0.02]},
   "iddist": "@201", "type":"MUX",
   "val":[36.5,0.6,35.7,0.2,40,0.8,36.5,0.5,37,0.6,36,0.2,40.5,0.5,38.5,0.6]} } |
```

Fig. 4. JSON-LDpx(MUX, IND) data at work; **BG** and **T**

Finally, the total degree of uncertainty for all resources is calculated using P(3) as follows:

$$\mathbf{P(Q3)} = (0.002 * 0.0328) = 0.0000656$$

According to the computation, the data values in each context differ. We have a better understanding of the patient's health in each situation, which helps us to improve our thinking and give the patient with suitable therapy. The ultimate outcomes in P1, P2, and P3 varies since the patient is in different conditions. Understanding health patients requires the calculating of probability. Furthermore, the unpredictability of health data from home, work, and sports **WoT** devices provides clinicians with a comprehensive perspective of patients' health for the most accurate analysis.

5   Conclusion

In this research, we provided an uncertain approach to compose health services that is incorporated in **WoT** standards. The capacity to integrate various categories of health services and **WoT** services has the ability to assist in self-management of health, particularly for those with chronic conditions. Contexts is an attempt to increase cognition in a variety of contexts while also providing appropriate therapy for the patient. We proposed a method for parsing conventional data into uncertain data in order to provide a probabilistic value to each data set. In addition, we provided an example of patient health in various contexts. Our method gives clinicians a visual overview of data uncertainty as well as a better user experience.

References

1. Alcaraz, J., Monge, J., Ramón, N.: Ranking ranges in cross-efficiency evaluations: a metaheuristic approach. J. Oper. Res. Soc. **73**(4), 1–15 (2020)
2. Bentley, F., et al.: Health mashups: presenting statistical patterns between wellbeing data and context in natural language to promote behavior change. ACM Trans. Comput. Hum. Interact. (TOCHI) **20**(5), 1–27 (2013)
3. Boulaares, S., Omri, A., Sassi, S., Benslimane, D.: A probabilistic approach: a model for the uncertain representation and navigation of uncertain web resources. In: 2018 14th International Conference on Signal-Image Technology and Internet-Based Systems (SITIS), pp. 24–31. IEEE (2018)
4. Boulaares, S., Sassi, S., Benslimane, D., Maamar, Z., Faiz, S.: Toward a configurable thing composition language for the SIoT. In: Abraham, A., et al. (eds.) ISDA 2021. LNNS, vol. 418, pp. 488–497. Springer, Cham (2022). https://doi.org/10.1007/978-3-030-96308-8_45
5. Cai, H., Da Xu, L., Xu, B., Xie, C., Qin, S., Jiang, L.: Iot-based configurable information service platform for product lifecycle management. IEEE Trans. Ind. Inf. **10**(2), 1558–1567 (2014)
6. Choi, J., et al.: The patient-centric mobile healthcare system enhancing sensor connectivity and data interoperability. In: 2015 International Conference on Recent Advances in Internet of Things (RIoT), pp. 1–6. IEEE (2015)

7. Daar, A.S., et al.: Grand challenges in chronic non-communicable diseases. Nature **450**(7169), 494–496 (2007)
8. Evans, D.: The internet of things: how the next evolution of the internet is changing everything. CISCO White Pap. **1**(2011), 1–11 (2011)
9. Guinard, D., Trifa, V.: Towards the web of things: web mashups for embedded devices. In: Workshop on Mashups, Enterprise Mashups and Lightweight Composition on the Web (MEM 2009), in Proceedings of WWW (International World Wide Web Conferences), Madrid, Spain, vol. 15, p. 8 (2009)
10. Halevy, A., Rajaraman, A., Ordille, J.: Data integration: the teenage years. In: Proceedings of the 32nd International Conference on Very Large Data Bases, pp. 9–16 (2006)
11. Imran, M., Kang, C., Ramzan, M.B.: Medicine supply chain model for an integrated healthcare system with uncertain product complaints. J. Manuf. Syst. **46**, 13–28 (2018)
12. Jayaratne, M., et al.: A data integration platform for patient-centered e-healthcare and clinical decision support. Future Gener. Comput. Syst. **92**, 996–1008 (2019)
13. Kumar, R.B., Goren, N.D., Stark, D.E., Wall, D.P., Longhurst, C.A.: Automated integration of continuous glucose monitor data in the electronic health record using consumer technology. J. Am. Med. Inf. Assoc. **23**(3), 532–537 (2016)
14. Lanthaler, M., Gütl, C.: On using JSON-LD to create evolvable restful services. In: Proceedings of the Third International Workshop on RESTful Design, pp. 25–32 (2012)
15. Larian, H., Larian, A., Sharifi, M., Movahednejad, H.: Towards web of things middleware: A systematic review. arXiv preprint arXiv:2201.08456 (2022)
16. Rahimi, S.A., Jamshidi, A., Ruiz, A., Aït-Kadi, D.: A new dynamic integrated framework for surgical patients' prioritization considering risks and uncertainties. Decis. Support Syst. **88**, 112–120 (2016)
17. Reda, R., Piccinini, F., Carbonaro, A.: Towards consistent data representation in the IoT healthcare landscape. In: Proceedings of the 2018 International Conference on Digital Health, pp. 5–10 (2018)
18. Rhayem, A., Mhiri, M.B.A., Gargouri, F.: HealthIoT ontology for data semantic representation and interpretation obtained from medical connected objects. In: 2017 IEEE/ACS 14th International Conference On Computer Systems and Applications (AICCSA), pp. 1470–1477. IEEE (2017)
19. Saeidnia, H.R., Ghorbi, A., Kozak, M., Abdoli, S.: Web-based application programming interface (Web APIs): vacancies in Iranian public library websites. Webology **19**(1), 133–141 (2022)
20. Seo, D., Yoo, B., Ko, H.: Information fusion of heterogeneous sensors for enriched personal healthcare activity logging. Int. J. Ad Hoc Ubiquitous Comput. **27**(4), 256–269 (2018)
21. Vuorimaa, P., Harmo, P., Hämäläinen, M., Itälä, T., Miettinen, R.: Active life home: a portal-based home care platform. In: Proceedings of the 5th International Conference on Pervasive Technologies Related to Assistive Environments, pp. 1–8 (2012)
22. Yang, P., et al.: Lifelogging data validation model for internet of things enabled personalized healthcare. IEEE Trans. Syst. Man Cybern. Syst. **48**(1), 50–64 (2016)

A Non Parametric Test for Decreasing Uncertainty Residual Life Distribution (*DURL*)

Hassina Benaoudia[1] and Amar Aissani[2(✉)] [ID]

[1] Department of Probability and Statistics, Faculty of Mathematics, University of
Science and Technology Houari Boumediene (USTHB), Bab Ezzouar, Algiers, Algeria

[2] Laboratory of Research in Intelligent Informatics, Mathematics and Applications
(RIIMA), Faculty of Computer Science, University of Science and Technology Houari
Boumediene (USTHB), Bab Ezzouar, Algiers, Algeria
aaissani@usthb.dz

Abstract. A new statistical test is presented to detect the monotonicity
of uncertainty (F is *DURL*) based on derivative criteria and the histogram
method. Some properties such as consistency and asymptotic normality
are discussed. Simulation by the Monte-Carlo method gives the critical
values of the statistics. We compare the power estimate with that of the
test based on the criteria of monotonicity of residual entropy. Finally, we
show on real survival data that the two tests lead to the same conclusions.

Keywords: Reliability · Information measures · Uncertainty ·
Lifetime distribution · Non Parametric Test · Decreasing Uncertainty
of Residual Lifetime (*DURL*)

1 Introduction

Uncertainty measures are useful in a variety of scientific activities, including Artificial Intelligence (Expert Systems) [19], Wireless and Sensor Networks [16]...
Measuring uncertainty can be provided by several methodologies: probability,
entropy, possibility, fuzzy sets, belief functions, etc. A random variable's differential entropy $H(f) = -E[log f(X)]$ can be thought of as a measure of its
information or uncertainty. However, if X represents the lifetime of a component (or system), this measure doesn't give any information about the remaining
lifetime of the system. A direct approach to measuring uncertainty in the residual
lifetime distribution has been provided in [11].

Let X be a nonnegative random variable representing the lifetime of a physical or biological component (or system) with cumulative distribution function
$F(x) = P(X < x)$ and density $f(x)$. As a result, the probability distribution
function for reliability (or survival) $\bar{F}(x) = P(X > x)$ i.e. the probability that
the component (or system) survives the time interval $(0, x)$. A distribution has
decreasing (increasing) uncertainty of residual life $DURL(IURL)$ if the function

O. Gervasi et al. (Eds.): ICCSA 2022, LNCS 13376, pp. 188–196, 2022.
https://doi.org/10.1007/978-3-031-10450-3_14

$H(f;t) = -E[\log f_t(X_t)]$ is decreasing (increasing) in t. Here $f_t(x)$ is the density of the random variable $X_t = X - t/X > 0$, the remaining lifetime of a system of age t and $H(f,t)$ is the dynamic residual entropy which measures the expected uncertainty contained in the conditional density of X_t about the predictability of the residual lifetime of the system.

Considerable attention has been given to testing the membership of a probability distribution to a non parametric class such as *IFR*(Increasing Failure Rate) or *DMRL* (Decreasing Mean Residual Life). The objective of this paper is to present a new statistic to test the membership to *DURL* class.

Section 2 describes classical non parametric reliability (aging) distributions. Section 3 focuses on the non parametric *DURL* (*IURL*) class and some of its properties, specifically the relationship with classical non-parametric reliability distributions. Section 4 introduces a new method for determining whether a probability distribution belongs to the *DURL* class. The test is based on derivative criteria and histogram method. The following properties of such a test are discussed: mean and variance of the statistic, consistency,asymptotic normality, critical values and power of the test. Finally, in Sect. 5, an illustrative example is given on real lifetime data in order to compare this test with that based on criteria of monotonicity of residual entropy [9].

2   Non Parametric Reliability Distributions

Usual probability distributions are "parametric" in the sense that they depend on some parameters. For example, the exponential distribution depends on only one parameter (mean or failure rate); the normal distribution depends on two parameters (mean and variance). However, we can show examples in which the chi-square test leads to accept two different distributions, Gamma and Raighley, which are both characterized by Increasing Failure Rate (*IFR*).

Indeed, in practice, an engineer is not always interested by the concrete parametric probability distribution itself, but simply in some "aging property" of the system. The more simplest example is given by Reliability or Survival analysis studies , in which practitioners are interested only in a stage of aging or rejuvenation; for example "Increasing(Decreasing) Failure Rate" i.e. *IFR*(*DFR*) [14]. So, we consider the class of all probability distributions with *IFR*(*DFR*)property. Because it contains a collection of probability distributions that share a common aging property, such a class is non-parametric rather than parametric.

Other stochastic models, such as queueing , insurance, medicine, or biological models, are also interested in the properties of such classes [15,17].

Now, in reliability, we are interested in the lifetime of the system. Let X be the system's failure time and denote its probability distribution function by $F(t) = P(X < t)$, $t \geq 0$, which is assumed to be absolutely continuous with density probability function $f(t)$.

The survival (or reliability) function, i.e. the probability of system survival over the period $(0,t)$, is represented by the function $\bar{F}(t) = 1 - F(t) = P(X > t)$. We are interested also about system's residual lifetime $X_t = X - t/X > t$ after it has survived until time t.

We denote by $F_t(x) = P(X_t < x/X > t) = \frac{P(t \leq X < t+x)}{P(X > t)}$, the probability distribution of the system's residual lifetime; by $\bar{F}_t(x) = P(X_t > x) = \frac{\bar{F}(t+x)}{\bar{F}(t)}$ the reliability of a system of age t. The function $\lambda_F(t) = \frac{f(t)}{\bar{F}(t)}$ represents the failure rate of the system at time t also called hazard or risk function. This is a local characteristic such as the density function and $\lambda_F(t)dt + o(dt)$ represents the probability of a failure during the interval of time $(t, t + dt)$ given no failure until time t.

We define now some usual non-parametric probability distributions [15,17]. In the following, by increasing (decreasing), we mean nondecreasing (nonincreasing).

Definition 1. *The survival function $\bar{F}$ has increasing (resp. decreasing) failure rate IFR (resp. DFR), if $\lambda_F(t)$ is increasing (resp. decreasing) in t on the interval $(0, t)$ [15, 17].*

This definition assumes that $F(.)$ is absolutely continuous. Otherwise, the definition remains valid by considering the relation between stochastic orderings and reliability theory. A non negative random variable X is $IFR(DFR)$ if and only if $X_t \geq_{st} (\leq_{st})X_{t'}$ for all $t \leq t'$. So, the stochastic order $\leq_{st}$ characterizes the $IFR(DFR)$ probability distribution.

Similarly, the order $\leq_{icx}$ (increasing convex order) characterizes another usual aging notion in Reliability i.e. $DMRL$ $(IMRL)$: Decreasing (Increasing) Mean Residual Life.

Definition 2. *The random variable X is DMRL(IMRL) if $X_t = \frac{\int_t^\infty \bar{F}(x)dx}{\bar{F}(t)}$ is decreasing (increasing) in $t \in [0, t]$ [15, 17].*

Definition 3. *A nonnegative random variable X is said to be IFRA (Increasing Failure Rate in Average) if the average of its cumulative failure rate over $(0, t)$*

$$\frac{\Lambda(t)}{t} = \frac{1}{t} \int_0^t \lambda(t) = \frac{-log\bar{F}(t)}{t} \tag{1}$$

is increasing in $t \geq 0$ [15, 17].

Remark 1. There is some relations between these non-parametric distributions (classification). If F is IFR then it is also $IFRA$ and $DMRL$ in the sense that the class $IFR \subset IFRA$ and $IFR \subset DMRL$, the inclusion is strict. But there is no relations between $IFRA$ and $DMRL$. The same relations are valid for the dual classes DFR, $DFRA$ and $IMRL$.

3   Decreasing Uncertainty of Residual Life ($DURL$) Class

Ebrahimi and Pellerey [10] present a similar notion of dynamical entropy to Shannon information measure [18], by considering the age of the system S at time $t, t > 0$. More precisely, the residual entropy expresses the uncertainty contained in the conditional density of the residual lifetime $X_t = X - t/X > t$ on the system's predictability of it's residual lifetime:

$$H(f;t) = - \int_t^\infty \frac{f(x)}{\overline{F}(t)} log \frac{f(x)}{\overline{F}(t)} dx \qquad (2)$$

$H(f;t)$ can be seen as a dynamic measure of uncertainty about S associated to its lifetime distribution. In other words, $H(f;t)$ measures the expected uncertainty contained in conditional density of the residual lifetime X_t of a system of age t i.e. given $X > t$. In this sense $H(f;t)$ measures the concentration of conditional probability distributions. Note finally that the dynamic entropy of a new system (of age 0) $H(f;0) = H(f)$ is the ordinary Shannon's entropy [10] and that the function $H(f;t)$ uniquely determines the reliability function $\overline{F}$ or equivalently the failure probability distribution F.

We can now define an uncertainty ordering. The non negative random variable X have less uncertainty than Y ($X \leq_{LU} Y$), if $H(f;t) \leq H(g;t), t \geq 0$. If X and Y are the lifetimes of two systems S and S', respectively, and if $X \leq_{LU} Y$, then the expected uncertainty contained in the conditional density of X_t about the predictability of the residual lifetime of the first system S is less than expected uncertainty contained in the conditional density of Y_t about the remaining lifetime of the second system S'. Intuitively speaking, the better system is the system that lives longer and there is less uncertainty about its residual lifetime.

Ebrahimi [11] defines two nonparametric classes of lifetime distributions based on the measure of uncertainty $H(f;t)$.

Definition 4. *A survival function $\overline{F}$ has decreasing (resp. increasing) uncertainty of residual lifetime DURL (resp. IURL), if $H(f;t)$ is decreasing (resp. increasing) in t [11].*

If a system has a survival probability distribution belonging to the class $DURL$, then as the system ages the conditional probability density function becomes more informative. So, if a system of age X has a $DURL$ distribution (resp. $IURL$), its residual lifetime can be predicted with more (resp. less) precision.

Remark 2. 1. If F is $IFR(DFR)$, then it is $DURL(IURL)$. So that, $IFR \subset DURL$ and $DFR \subset IURL$.
2. If F is $DMRL$, then it is $DURL$. So that, $DMRL \subset DURL$.
3. IF F $IURL$, then it is $IMRL$. So that, $IURL \subset IMRL$.

Example 1. The exponential distribution is the only continuous distribution which is both $DURL$ and $IURL$ [11]. In other words, the class EXP of all exponential distributions is the boundary between $DURL$ and $IURL$ classes.

Example 2. Let X be a random variable having Weibull distribution with survival function $\overline{F}(t) = 1 - e^{\lambda t^\alpha}, t > 0$. Then X is $DURL$ ($IURL$) for $\alpha > 1$ (resp. $0 < \alpha < 1$) [11].

The following two counter-examples show that $DURL$ property does not imply IFR, nor does it imply $DMRL$.

Example 3. Let

$$\bar{F}(t) = (1 - exp(-\lambda_1 t))(1 - exp(-\lambda_2 t)), t \geq 0. \tag{3}$$

be the reliability function of a system with two components in series with independent reliabilities that are exponentially distributed with parameters λ_1 and λ_2 respectively. Then one can verify that $\bar{F}$ is IFR, but not $DURL$ [12].

Example 4. A common structure of redundancy is k-out-of-n. Such a system functions if and only if at least k components function. Two important particular cases are series ($k = 1$) and paralell ($k = n$) structures. The $IURL$ class is not preserved for such a structure. A counter-example is given by a parallel system with two components having exponential distributions. Obviously, each component is $IURL$. The lifetime of the parallel system is strictly increasing. As a result, the system is $DURL$, rather than $IURL$ [1].

An original example is given by Ebrahimi an Kermani [12] showing that $DMRL$ doest not imply $DURL$. The authors gave also another example for a renewal process with inter-failure time distribution F which is $DMRL$ and for which the limiting distributions of the forward waiting time from a particular time t to the next failure and the length of the renewal interval that contains the point t are $DURL$.

We can point out an interesting mathematical property of $DURL$ non-parametric probability distribution:

Lemma 1. *A survival function $\bar{F}$ is DURL, if and only if $H(f; x) - H(f; y) \geq 0$ for all $y \geq x$* [11].

The statistical test of [9] is based on the above lemma, while the present test is based on the following:

Lemma 2. *If $L(f; t) = -H'(f; t) \geq 0$, then the corresponding survival function $\bar{F}$ is DURL(IURL). In other words, if we have negative (positive) local reduction of uncertainty, then $\bar{F}$ is DURL(IURL)* [11].

4   A Non Parametric Test for $DURL$

The main goal would be to test the hypothesis H_0: F is $DURL$ against the hypothesis H_1: F is not $DURL$. However, because $DURL$ is a non-parametric class of probability distributions, the statistical criteria under the null hypothesis H_0: $F \in EXP$ against H_1: $F \in DURL$ (and not exponential), where EXP is the class of all exponential probability distributions.

The alternative H_1 is based on uncertainty rather than aging.

4.1   Construction and Implementation of the Test

Under the hypothesis H_0, and according to Lemma 2, the function $H'(f;t) = 0$ and $\lambda_F(t) \neq 0$. As a result, the function $g(t) = H'(f;t) - 1 + \lambda_F(t) = 0$ under the assumption hypothesis H_0.

The test is built with the statistic $S(t) = E[g(t)] = \int_0^\infty g(t)f(t)dt$ which is estimated using an empirical probability density function and a histogram method based on a partition of the order statistics. According to the above-mentioned property, $g(t) = 0$ for H_0 and $g(t) < 0$ for H_1. The same logic applies to the empirical statistic $S_n(k)$: it is null under H_0 and negative under H_1. Small values of $S_n(k)$ favor H_1, whereas large values of $W_n(k) = -S_n(k)$ favor H_1.

So, at significance level α, we reject H_0 in favor of H_1 if $W_n(k) \geq C_{k,n}(\alpha)$, where $C_{k,n}(\alpha)$ is the critical point value determined by the $(1 - \alpha)$-quantile of the distribution of $W_n(k)$ under exponentiality.

4.2   Mean and Variance of the Test $W_n(k)$

We can calculate the mean $E(W_n(k))$ and the variance $Var(W_n(k))$ using tedious algebra. Thus, we can prove the convergence and the asymptotic normality of the statistic $W_n(k)$.

4.3   Consistency of the Test $W_n(k)$

We can prove the consistency of the test statistic $W_n(k)$ in the following sense

Theorem 1. *As* $n \to \infty, k \to \infty$, *and* $\frac{k}{n} \to 0$, *the statistic* $W_n(k)$ *converges to* S.

4.4   Normality of the Statistic $W_n(k)$

We can also prove the asymptotic normality of the statistic $W_n(k)$ as $n \to \infty$.

Theorem 2. *As* $n \to \infty$, *and* $k \to \infty$, *the normalized statistic* $kW_n(k)$ *converges to a standard normal distribution.*

Table 1. Critical values of $W_n(k)$

n	α			
	0.100	0.050	0.025	0.010
3	4.8006	5.5334	6.3069	7.0340
11	6.8219	7.5294	8.1805	8.7718
100	8.9363	9.5745	10.1214	10.7857

Table 2. Critical values of $-W_n(k)$

n	α			
	0.100	0.025	0.010	0.0001
3	2.3564	3.9297	5.3591	7.7634
10	−0.0337	1.2530	2.6525	4.1937
100	−3.4964	−2.5482	−1.6047	−0.4008

4.5 Critical Values of the Test $W_n(k)$.

Under the alternative hypothesis, the distribution of the statistic $W_n(k)$ is complicated. In this section, we determine critical values $C_{k,n}(\alpha)$ of the statistic $W_n(k)$ by means of Monte Carlo simulation. Simulations are provided for different confidence levels of $1 - \alpha$: $0.900, 0950, 0.975$ and 0.990 and different values of sample size n. We generated 5000 samples of exponential distribution with mean 1. We computed for each sample the corresponding values of the empirical statistic distribution $W_n(k)$ (for large spacings of the observations) and $-W_n(k)$ (for little spacings). A function in Matlab gives the critical values for each α and n. They are summarized in Table 1 and Table 2.

4.6 Power Estimates

We can obtain power estimates by using, again, Monte Carlo simulation. We have provided several experiments under Weibull $(1, \theta)$ and Gamma $(\theta, 1)$ alternatives.

Table 3 and Table 4, show simulated powers for different sample sizes n. Simulated results are based on 10000 iterations. We observe that the presented test performs relatively well when the parameter θ of the distributions reaches 20.

Table 3. Power Estimates for Weibull $(\theta, 1)$ of $W_n(k)$

θ	n		
	20	10	5
20	0.9990	0.9862	0.8921
10	0.9288	0.7831	0.5686
5	0.5568	0.3750	0.2591
3	0.2506	0.1784	0.1321
1	0.0555	0.0522	0.0526

5 Illustrative Example

As an illustration, and for comparison purposes, we consider the data set from the US National Cancer Institute, resulting from a study by Bryson and Siddiqui [5]

Table 4. Power estimates of $J_n(k)$ for Weibull $(\theta,1)$ (Ebrahimi [9])

θ	n		
	20	10	5
10	1.0	0.9570	0.9255
5	0.9869	0.8543	0.8476
3	0.9110	0.7468	0.7379
1	0.0510	0.0460	0.0430

Table 5. The ordered survival times (in days from diagnosis) (Bryson and Siddiqui [5]).

7	429	579	968	1877
47	440	581	1077	1886
58	445	650	1109	2045
74	455	702	1314	2056
177	468	715	1334	2260
232	495	779	1367	2429
273	497	881	1534	2509
285	532	900	1712	
317	571	930	1784	

which provides a real sample of residual life time of size $n = 43$. Table 5 contains the data.

We have computed the observed value of the statistic $W_n(k)$ on the basis of this sample, which gives the following estimation of the statistic $W_n(k) = 30.4629$. When comparing the result with the critical values of the histogram method given in Table 1, we see that the statistic exceeds all percentiles.

As a result, we can conclude that the above sample provide from a *DURL* distribution. That is, uncertainty about the residual lifetime of an individual from this population decreases over time. More simply, the uncertainty for the residual lifetime among patients tends to decrease for a long time and their remaining lifetimes can be predicted with more precision.

6   Conclusion

In this paper, we have presented a new statistical test for detecting monotonicity of uncertainty (F is *DURL*). This test is based on derivative criteria different from that of [9]. Some properties such as consistency, asymptotic normality, and power estimation have been discussed. Illustrations based on real survival data have been provided for comparison. A new test for decreasing uncertainty has been studied but based on the kernel estimation method, which leads to the same conclusions. We leave this question for a further paper.

Acknowledgement. The Ministry of Higher Education and Scientific Research $(DGRSDT)$ is funding the project, in part, through PRFU N° $C00L07UN16042022$ 0004.

We appreciate the fruitful discussions with Professor Mounir Mesbah when the second author visited the LPSM laboratory, University of Jussieu-Sorbonne in 2018.

References

1. Asadi, M., Ebrahimi, N.: Residual entropy and its characterizations in terms of hazard function and mean residual life function. Stat. Probab. Lett. **49**, 263–269 (2000)
2. Baratpour, S., Habibi Rad, N.: Testing goodness of fit exponential distribution based on cumulative residual entropy. Commun. Stat. Theory **41**, 1387–1396 (2012)
3. Baratpour, S., Habibi Rad, S.: Exponentiality test based on the progression type II censoring via cumulative entropy. Commun. Stat. Simul. Comput. **45**(7), 2625–2637 (2016)
4. Belzunce, F., Guillamon, A., Navarro, J., Ruiz., J.M.: Kernel estimation of residual entropy. Commun. Stat. Theory **30**(7), 1243–1255 (2001)
5. Bryson, M.C., Siddiqui, M.M.: Some criteria for aging. J. Am. Stat. Assoc. **64**, 1472–1484 (1969)
6. David., H.A.: Order Statistics, 3rd edn. Wiley, New York (2003)
7. DiCrescenzo, A., Longobardi, M.: Entropy-based measure of uncertainty in past lifetime. J. Appl. Probab. **39**, 434–440 (2002)
8. Ebrahimi, N., Soofi, E.S. Information functions for reliability. In: Soyer, R., Mazzuchi, T.A., Singpurwalla, N.D. (eds.) Mathematical Reliability: An Expository Perspective. International Series in Operations Research & Management Science, vol. 67. Springer, Boston (2004). https://doi.org/10.1007/978-1-4419-9021-1_7
9. Ebrahimi., N.: Testing whether lifetime distribution is decreasing uncertainty: J. Stat. Plan. Infer. **64**, 9–19 (1997)
10. Ebrahimi, N., Pellery, F.: New partial ordering of survival functions based on notion of uncertainty. J. Appl. Probab. **32**, 202–211 (1995)
11. Ebrahimi, N.: How to measure uncertainty about lifetime. Sankhya **58**, 48–57 (1996)
12. Ebrahimi, N., Kirmani, S.: Some results on ordering of survival functions through uncertainty. Stat. Prob Lett. **29**, 167–176 (1996)
13. Härdle, W.: Smoothing Techniques. Springer Verlag, Heidelberg (1991). https://doi.org/10.1007/978-1-4612-4432-5
14. Lai, C.D., Xie, M.: Stochastic Ageing and Dependance in Reliability. Springer Verlag, Heidelberg (2006). https://doi.org/10.1007/0-387-34232-X
15. Marshall, A.W., Olkin, I.: Inequalities: Theory of Majorization and Its Application. Academic Press, New York (1979)
16. Senouci, M.R., Mellouk, A., Oukhellou, L., Aissani, A.: Using the belief functions theory to deploy static wireless sensor networks. In: Denoeux, T., Masson, M.H. (eds.) Belief Functions: Theory and Applications. Advances in Intelligent and Soft Computing, vol. 164. Springer Verlag, Berlin (2012). https://doi.org/10.1007/978-3-642-29461-7_50
17. Shaked, M., Shantikumar, J.G.: Stochastic Orders and Their Applications. Academic Press, San Diego (1994)
18. Shannon, C.E.S.: A mathematical theory of communication. Bell System. Techn. J. **27**, 379–423 (1984)
19. Walley, P.: Measures of uncertainty in expert systems. Artif. Intell. **83**, 1–58 (1996)

Critical Points Properties of Ordinary Differential Equations as a Projection of Implicit Functions Using Spatio-temporal Taylor Expansion

Vaclav Skala$^{(\boxtimes)}$ (iD)

Faculty of Applied Sciences, Department of Computer Science and Engineering,
University of West Bohemia, 301 00 Pilsen, Czech Republic
skala@kiv.zcu.cz
http://www.vaclavskala.eu/

Abstract. This contribution describes a new approach to formulation of ODE and PDE critical points using implicit formulation as t-variant scalar function using the Taylor expansion. A general condition for the critical points is derived and specified for t invariant case. It is expected, that the given new formulae lead to more reliable detection of critical points especially for large 3D fluid flow data acquisition, which enable high $3D$ vector compression and their representation using radial basis functions (RBF).

In the case of vector field visualization, e.g. fluid flow, electromagnetic fields, etc., the critical points of ODE are critical for physical phenomena behavior.

Keywords: Critical points · Vector fields visualization · Numerical methods · Ordinary differential equations · Partial differential equations · Implicit functions · Radial basis functions

1 Introduction

Many physical and computational problems lead to formulations using ordinary differential equations (ODE) or partial differential equations (PDE) and different methods are used for their solution. Methods for solution of ODEs or PDEs are quite different from a solution of algebraic equations, as the solution requires specification of the initial conditions in the case of ODE, while in the case of PDE the boundary conditions have to be specified.

In the case of vector field visualization, e.g. fluid flow, electromagnetic fields, etc., the critical points of ODE are critical for physical phenomena behavior. The critical or null points are points in which the derivative $\dot{\mathbf{x}} = \mathbf{f}(\mathbf{x}(t))$ is *zero*, see Lebl [12], Smolik [16] and Skala [15]. Classification of such points helps in

Research supported by the University of West Bohemia - Institutional research support.

vector fields visualization Helman [7], Koch [11], Schuermann [13], Skala [15], Huang[8] and Smolik [16].

In the ODE case differential equations are usually given as:

$$\frac{d\mathbf{x}}{dt} = \mathbf{f}(\mathbf{x}(t), t) \tag{1}$$

or in a more general implicit ordinary differential form as:

$$F\left(\mathbf{x}, \frac{d\mathbf{x}}{dt}, \cdots, \frac{d^n \mathbf{x}}{dt^n}, t\right) = 0 \tag{2}$$

with initial conditions $\mathbf{x}_0 = [x_0(0), \ldots, x_n(0)]^T$. The implicit forms from the geometrical point of view was studied in Goldman [5,6] and Agoston [1]. In the majority of cases, the function f, resp. F are time independent, i.e. $\dot{\mathbf{x}} = \mathbf{f}(\mathbf{x}(t))$.

In the case of the partial differential equations (PDE), the differential equation is given in the implicit form as:

$$F\left(\mathbf{x}, u, \frac{\partial u}{\partial x_i}, \frac{\partial^2 u}{\partial x_i \partial x_j}, \frac{\partial^3 u}{\partial x_i \partial x_j \partial x_k}, \ldots, \frac{\partial u}{\partial t}, \frac{\partial^2 u}{\partial t^2}, \ldots, t\right) = 0 \tag{3}$$

where $\mathbf{x} = [x_1, \ldots, x_n]^{T1}$ are points fixed position in the domain, derivatives are in the domain axes direction, i.e. in the 3D case:

$$\frac{\partial u}{\partial x_1} \equiv \frac{\partial u}{\partial x} \qquad \frac{\partial u}{\partial x_2} \equiv \frac{\partial u}{\partial y} \qquad \frac{\partial u}{\partial x_3} \equiv \frac{\partial u}{\partial z} \tag{4}$$

Let us explore the ordinary differential equation case more in a detail. The following notation will be used:

- a - scalar value,
- $\mathbf{a}$ - vector,
- $\mathbf{A}$ - matrix,
- $\xi = (\mathbf{x}, t)$ spatio-temporal vector, i.e. $\mathbf{x} = [x_1, \ldots, x_n]^T$, $\xi = [x_1, \ldots, x_n, t]^T$
- $\eta = (\mathbf{x}_0, t_0)$

It should be noted, that $\mathbf{x}_i$ and t have different physical units, i.e. $[m]$ and $[s]$. In the following the ordinary differential equations (ODE) are explored.

2   Ordinary Differential Equations and Taylor Expansion

The ordinary differential equation (ODE) can be formulated as:

$$F(\mathbf{x}(t), t) = 0 \quad \text{or} \quad \dot{\mathbf{x}} = \mathbf{f}(\mathbf{x}(t), t) \quad \text{with} \quad \mathbf{x}_0 = \mathbf{x}(0) \tag{5}$$

where $\mathbf{x}_0 = [x_1(0), \ldots, x_n(0)]^T$ and n is the dimensionality of the ODE.

---

[1] It should be noted that in the case of the PDE the coordinatesx are as sumed to be time independent.

Now, the function $F(\mathbf{x}(t), t)$ has the following derivatives:

$$\frac{\partial F(\mathbf{x}(t), t)}{\partial \mathbf{x}} = F_{\mathbf{x}} = \mathbf{g}(\mathbf{x}, t) \qquad \frac{\partial F(\mathbf{x}(t), t)}{\partial t} = F_t = h(\mathbf{x}, t) \qquad (6)$$

$$\frac{\partial \mathbf{g}(\mathbf{x}(t), t)}{\partial t} = \mathbf{g}_t \qquad \frac{\partial^2 F(\mathbf{x}(t), t)}{\partial \mathbf{x}^2} = F_{\mathbf{xx}} = \mathbf{G}_x(\mathbf{x}, t) \qquad (7)$$

$$\frac{\partial^2 F(\mathbf{x}(t), t)}{\partial t^2} = F_{tt} = h_t(\mathbf{x}, t) \qquad \frac{\partial(h(\mathbf{x}(t), t)}{\partial \mathbf{x}} = \mathbf{h}_{\mathbf{x}} \qquad (8)$$

assuming, that $F_{\mathbf{x}t} = F_{t\mathbf{x}}$.

Let us explore the time dependency;

$$\frac{d}{dt}\left[\frac{\partial F(\mathbf{x}, t)}{\partial \mathbf{x}}\right] = \frac{d}{dt}[\mathbf{g}(\mathbf{x}, t)] = \frac{\partial \mathbf{g}(\mathbf{x}, t)}{\partial \mathbf{x}}\frac{d\mathbf{x}}{dt} + \frac{\partial \mathbf{g}(\mathbf{x}, t)}{\partial t}$$
$$= \mathbf{G}_{\mathbf{x}}\dot{\mathbf{x}} + \mathbf{g}_t \qquad (9)$$

$$\frac{d}{dt}\left[\frac{\partial F(\mathbf{x}, t)}{\partial t}\right] = \frac{d}{dt}[h(\mathbf{x}, t)] = \frac{\partial h(\mathbf{x}, t)}{\partial \mathbf{x}}\frac{d\mathbf{x}}{dt} + \frac{\partial h(\mathbf{x}, t)}{\partial t}$$
$$= \mathbf{h}_{\mathbf{x}}\dot{\mathbf{x}} + h_t \qquad (10)$$

Then the Taylor expansion in time for t-varying functions, see Bronson [3] and Skala [14], the following is obtained:

$$F(\xi) = F(\eta) + \frac{dF(\eta)}{dt}(t - t_0) + \frac{1}{2}\frac{d^2 F(\eta)}{dt^2}(t - t_0)^2 + \ldots \qquad (11)$$

As in the case of change of t, also $\mathbf{x}(t)$ is changed. Therefore, the first derivative in time is expressed as:

$$\frac{dF(\eta)}{dt} = \frac{\partial F(\mathbf{x}, t)}{\partial \mathbf{x}}\frac{d\mathbf{x}}{dt} + \frac{\partial F(\mathbf{x}, t)}{\partial t} \qquad (12)$$

and the second derivative as:

$$\frac{d^2 F(\eta)}{dt^2} = \frac{d}{dt}\left[\frac{dF(\eta)}{dt}\right] = \frac{d}{dt}\left[\frac{\partial F(\mathbf{x}, t)}{\partial \mathbf{x}}\frac{d\mathbf{x}}{dt} + \frac{\partial F(\mathbf{x}, t)}{\partial t}\right]$$
$$= \frac{d}{dt}[\mathbf{g}(\mathbf{x}, t)\frac{d\mathbf{x}}{dt} + h(\mathbf{x}, t)]$$
$$= \frac{\partial \mathbf{g}(\mathbf{x}, t)}{\partial \mathbf{x}}\frac{d\mathbf{x}}{dt} \bullet \frac{d\mathbf{x}}{dt} + \mathbf{g}(\mathbf{x}, t)\frac{d^2\mathbf{x}}{dt^2} + \frac{dh(\mathbf{x}, t)}{dt} \qquad (13)$$
$$= \mathbf{G}_{\mathbf{x}}(\mathbf{x}, t)\dot{\mathbf{x}}^2 + \mathbf{g}(\mathbf{x}, t)\ddot{\mathbf{x}} + \mathbf{h}_{\mathbf{x}}(\mathbf{x}, t)\dot{\mathbf{x}} + h_t(\mathbf{x}, t)$$
$$= F_{\mathbf{xx}}(\mathbf{x}, t)\dot{\mathbf{x}}^2 + F_{\mathbf{x}}(\mathbf{x}, t)\ddot{\mathbf{x}} + F_{\mathbf{x}t}(\mathbf{x}, t)\dot{\mathbf{x}} + F_{tt}(\mathbf{x}, t)$$

It should be noted, that $\mathbf{A}\mathbf{x}^2$ should be read as a quadratic form, i.e. $\mathbf{x}^T\mathbf{A}\mathbf{x}$.

Using the Taylor expansion for the function $F(\mathbf{x}(t), t)$:

$$F(\mathbf{x}(t), t) = F(\eta) + \frac{dF(\eta)}{dt}(t - t_0) + \frac{1}{2}\frac{d^2 F(\eta)}{dt^2}(t - t_0)^2 + R_n = 0 \qquad (14)$$

3   Critical points

It can be seen that the following identity for the critical points is valid by definition Lebl [12]:

$$F(\xi) = F(\mathbf{x}(t), t) = 0 \quad \forall t \geq 0 \quad , \text{ i.e. } \quad F(\xi) = F(\eta) = 0 \tag{15}$$

Using the Taylor expansion and the identities above, the following is obtained using linear and quadratic elements:

$$\frac{dF(\eta)}{dt}(t - t_0) + \frac{1}{2}\frac{d^2 F(\eta)}{dt^2}(t - t_0)^2 + R_n = 0 \tag{16}$$

Rewriting that the following is obtained:

$$\left(\frac{\partial F(\mathbf{x}, t)}{\partial \mathbf{x}}\frac{d\mathbf{x}}{dt} + \frac{\partial F(\mathbf{x}, t)}{\partial t}\right)(t - t_0)$$

$$+ \frac{1}{2}\left(\mathbf{G_x}(\mathbf{x}, t)\dot{\mathbf{x}}^2 + \mathbf{g}(\mathbf{x}, t)\ddot{\mathbf{x}} + \mathbf{h_x}(\mathbf{x}, t)\dot{\mathbf{x}} + h_t(\mathbf{x}, t)\right)(t - t_0)^2 + R_n = 0 \tag{17}$$

It should be noted, that $\mathbf{A}\mathbf{x}^2$ should be read as a quadratic form, i.e. $\mathbf{x}^T\mathbf{A}\mathbf{x}$. Then

$$(\mathbf{g}(\mathbf{x}, t)\dot{\mathbf{x}} + h(\mathbf{x}, t) + \mathbf{G_x}(\mathbf{x}, t)\dot{\mathbf{x}}^2)(t - t_0)$$

$$+ \frac{1}{2}(\mathbf{g}(\mathbf{x}, t)\ddot{\mathbf{x}} + \mathbf{h_x}(\mathbf{x}, t)\dot{\mathbf{x}} + h_t(\mathbf{x}, t))(t - t_0)^2 + R_n = 0 \tag{18}$$

In the case of 2D and 3D physical phenomena behavior, e.g. fluid flow Helman [7], electromagnetic field Drake [4] etc., there are critical points of the relevant ODE, which have to be analyzed Koch [11], Schuermann [13], Skala [15], Smolik [16,17,20].

The critical points are defined as $\dot{\mathbf{x}} = \mathbf{0}$. Using the linear and quadratic elements of the Taylor expansion the following equations for critical points is obtained:

$$h(\mathbf{x}, t) + \frac{1}{2}(\mathbf{g}(\mathbf{x}, t)\ddot{\mathbf{x}} + h_t(\mathbf{x}, t))(t - t_0) = 0 \tag{19}$$

In the case of t-invariant systems, i.e. $F(\mathbf{x}(t)) = 0$ and a pro $t \neq t_0$, the following is obtained:

$$\mathbf{g}(\mathbf{x}, t)\ddot{\mathbf{x}} = 0 \quad , \text{ i.e. } \quad \frac{\partial F(\mathbf{x})}{\partial \mathbf{x}}\ddot{\mathbf{x}} = 0 \tag{20}$$

It leads to a new condition:

$$F_\mathbf{x}(\mathbf{x}(t))\,\ddot{\mathbf{x}} = 0 \tag{21}$$

This is a significant result as it enables better and more reliable critical points detection needed for interpolation and approximation of large and complex 2D and 3D vector fields, e.g. Skala [15], Smolik [16,18,19].

Let us consider two simple ODE examples by Eq. 22 to demonstrate critical points and behaviour of the vector fields, see Fig. 1.

$$\begin{bmatrix} \dot{x} \\ \dot{y} \end{bmatrix} = \begin{bmatrix} xy - 4 \\ (x - 4)(y - x) \end{bmatrix} \qquad \begin{bmatrix} \dot{x} \\ \dot{y} \end{bmatrix} = \begin{bmatrix} 2x + y^2 - 1 \\ 6x - y^2 + 1 \end{bmatrix} \tag{22}$$

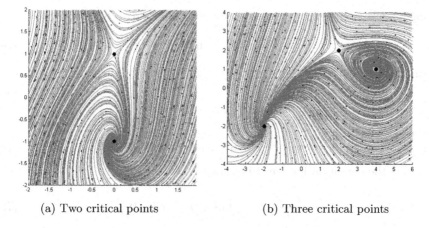

(a) Two critical points   (b) Three critical points

Fig. 1. Examples of vector fields in E^2 with two and three critical points

It can be seen, that critical points have a significant influence to the vector field behaviour. It should be noted, that if a vector field is given by an acquired discrete data, specific techniques are to be used for the critical points detection and the condition given by the Eq. 21 helps to robustness of this.

4 Example

Let us consider a differential equation $x\dot{y} + y = \sin(x)$ and its solution $y = \frac{1}{x}(c - \cos x)$ & $x \neq 0$.   In this case the implicit function

$$F(\mathbf{x}) = F(x, y) = (c - \cos x) - xy = 0 \qquad (23)$$

as $\mathbf{x} = [x, y]^T$. Then derivatives of the implicit function $F(\mathbf{x}) = 0$ are:

$$\frac{\partial F(\mathbf{x})}{\partial \mathbf{x}} = F_{\mathbf{x}} = [\sin x - y, -x] \qquad \frac{\partial F(\mathbf{x})}{\partial \mathbf{x}}\ddot{\mathbf{x}} = (\sin x - y)\ddot{x} - x\ddot{y} = 0 \qquad (24)$$

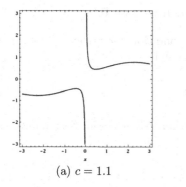

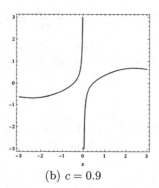

(a) $c = 1.1$ (b) $c = 0.9$

Fig. 2. Behaviour of the function $F(\mathbf{x}) = 0$ for different values c

Using a trick $x_1 = x$, $x_2 = y$, the differential equation can be rewritten as:

$$\dot{x}_1 = 1 \qquad \dot{x}_2 = (\sin x_1 - x_2)/x_1 \tag{25}$$

Verification

$$\begin{aligned}
\dot{x}_1 = 1 \quad \& \quad \ddot{x}_1 = 0 \qquad & x_1 \in R^1 \quad \& \quad x_1 \neq 0 \\
\dot{x}_2 = (\sin x_1 - x_2)/x_1 \qquad & x_2 \in R^1
\end{aligned} \tag{26}$$

Then

$$\ddot{x}_2 = [\dot{x}_1(x_2 - \sin \dot{x}_1 + x_1 \cos x_1) - x_1\dot{x}_2]/x_1^2 \tag{27}$$

Applying the condition for the t-invariant ODE

$$\frac{\partial F(\mathbf{x})}{\partial \mathbf{x}}\ddot{\mathbf{x}} = (\sin x - y)\ddot{x} - x\ddot{y} = 0 \tag{28}$$

$$\begin{aligned}
\frac{\partial F(\mathbf{x})}{\partial \mathbf{x}}\ddot{\mathbf{x}} &= \frac{x_1[\dot{x}_1(x_2 - \sin \dot{x}_1 + x_1 \cos x_1) - x_1\dot{x}_2]}{x_1^2} \\
&= \frac{\dot{x}_1(x_2 - \sin \dot{x}_1 + x_1 \cos x_1) - x_1\dot{x}_2}{x_1} \\
&= \frac{\dot{x}_1(x_2 - \sin \dot{x}_1)}{x_1} + \cos x_1 - \dot{x}_2 = 0
\end{aligned} \tag{29}$$

As $\dot{x}_1 = 1$, then

$$\begin{aligned}
\frac{\partial F(\mathbf{x})}{\partial \mathbf{x}}\ddot{\mathbf{x}} &= x_2 + \cos(1) - \sin(1) - \dot{x}_2 = 0 \\
\frac{\partial F(\mathbf{x})}{\partial \mathbf{x}}\ddot{\mathbf{x}} &= x_2 - (\sin(1) - \cos(1)) - \dot{x}_2 = 0
\end{aligned} \tag{30}$$

Using identity

$$\sin \alpha \pm \cos \beta = 2\sin(\frac{\alpha \pm \beta}{2})\cos(\frac{\alpha \mp \beta}{2}) \tag{31}$$

$$\frac{\partial F(\mathbf{x})}{\partial \mathbf{x}}\ddot{\mathbf{x}} = x_2 - 2\sin(1).\cos(0) - \dot{x}_2 = 0 \tag{32}$$

As $\dot{x}_2 = 0$ for any critical points, the new condition for critical points of t-invariant ordinary differential equation is obtained

$$\frac{\partial F(\mathbf{x})}{\partial \mathbf{x}}\ddot{\mathbf{x}} = 0 \tag{33}$$

It can be seen, that there is a formal connection to the Frenet-Serret formula, see Kabel [9], Kim [10] and WiKi [21].

5   Conclusion

This paper briefly describes a new condition for critical points of ordinary differential equations using the Taylor expansion, see Eq.21. This condition increases robustness of the critical points detection especially in the case of discrete acquired data.

A general form for t-varying differential equations is derived and specification for the t-invariant differential equations is presented. A simple example demonstrating the approach is given, too.

In future, the proposed approach is to be applied for more complex cases, when physical phenomena is described by the ordinary differential equations, e.g. Skala [15], Smolik [18], etc. using Taylor expansion for vector data Skala [14] without tensor representation, and in applications described by partial differential equations, e.g. Biancolini [2]

Acknowledgments. The author thanks to students and colleagues at the University of West Bohemia, Plzen and VSB-Technical University, Ostrava for their critical comments, discussions and especially to Michal Smolik for producing some images. Thanks belong also to the anonymous reviewers, as their comments and hints helped to improve this paper significantly.

References

1. Agoston, M.: Computer Graphics and Geometric Modelling: Implementation & Algorithms. Computer Graphics and Geometric Modeling, Springer, London (2005). https://doi.org/10.1007/b138805
2. Biancolini, M.: Fast Radial Basis Functions for Engineering Applications. Springer ,Cham (2018). https://doi.org/10.1007/978-3-319-75011-8
3. Bronson, R., Costa, G.B.: Matrix Methods: Applied Linear Algebra. Academic Press, Boston (2009)
4. Drake, K., Fuselier, E., Wright, G.: A partition of unity method for divergence-free or curl-free radial basis function approximation. SIAM J. Sci. Comput. **43**(3), A1950–A1974 (2021). https://doi.org/10.1137/20M1373505
5. Goldman, R.: Curvature formulas for implicit curves and surfaces. Comput. Aid. Geomet. Des. **22**(7 SPEC. ISS.), 632–658 (2005). https://doi.org/10.1016/j.cagd.2005.06.005
6. Goldman, R., Sederberg, T., Anderson, D.: Vector elimination: a technique for the implicitization, inversion, and intersection of planar parametric rational polynomial curves. Comput. Aid. Geomet. Des. **1**(4), 327–356 (1984). https://doi.org/10.1016/0167-8396(84)90020-7
7. Helman, J., Hesselink, L.: Representation and display of vector field topology in fluid flow data sets. Computer **22**(8), 27–36 (1989). https://doi.org/10.1109/2.35197
8. Huang, Z.B., Fu, G.T., Cao, L.j., Yu, M., Yang, W.B.: A parallel high-precision critical point detection and location for large-scale 3D flow field on the GPU. J. Supercomput. **78**(7), 9642–9667 (2022). https://doi.org/10.1007/s11227-021-04220-6
9. Kabel, A.: Maxwell-Lorentz equations in general Frenet-Serret coordinates. In: Proceedings of the 2003 Particle Accelerator Conference. vol. 4, pp. 2252–2254 (2003). https://doi.org/10.1109/PAC.2003.1289082

10. Kim, K.R., Kim, P.T., Koo, J.Y., Pierrynowski, M.R.: Frenet-Serret and the estimation of curvature and torsion. IEEE J. Select. Topics Signal Process. **7**(4), 646–654 (2013). https://doi.org/10.1109/JSTSP.2012.2232280
11. Koch, S., Kasten, J., Wiebel, A., Scheuermann, G., Hlawitschka, M.: 2D Vector field approximation using linear neighborhoods. Visual Comput. **32**(12), 1563–1578 (2015). https://doi.org/10.1007/s00371-015-1140-9
12. Lebl, J.: Notes on Diffy Qs: Differential Equations for Engineers. CreateSpace Independent Publishing Platform (2021)
13. Scheuermann, G., Kruger, H., Menzel, M., Rockwood, A.P.: Visualizing nonlinear vector field topology. IEEE Trans. Visual. Comput. Graph. **4**(2), 109–116 (1998). https://doi.org/10.1109/2945.694953
14. Skala, V.: Efficient Taylor expansion computation of multidimensional vector functions on GPU. Ann. Math. Informat. **54**, 83–95 (2021). https://doi.org/10.33039/ami.2021.03.004
15. Skala, V., Smolik, M.: A new approach to vector field interpolation, classification and robust critical points detection using radial basis functions. Adv. Intell. Syst. Comput. **765**, 109–115 (2019). https://doi.org/10.1007/978-3-319-91192-2_12
16. Smolik, M., Skala, V.: Classification of critical points using a second order derivative. Procedia Comput. Sci. **108**, 2373–2377 (2017). https://doi.org/10.1016/j.procs.2017.05.271
17. Smolik, M., Skala, V.: Spherical RBF vector field interpolation: experimental study. In: SAMI 2017 - IEEE 15th International Symposium on Applied Machine Intelligence and Informatics, Proceedings, pp. 431–434 (2017). https://doi.org/10.1109/SAMI.2017.7880347
18. Smolik, M., Skala, V.: Reconstruction of corrupted vector fields using radial basis functions. In: INFORMATICS 2019 - IEEE 15th International Scientific Conference on Informatics, Proceedings, pp. 377–382 (2019). https://doi.org/10.1109/Informatics47936.2019.9119297
19. Smolik, M., Skala, V.: Radial basis function and multi-level 2d vector field approximation. Math. Comput. Simul. **181**, 522–538 (2021). https://doi.org/10.1016/j.matcom.2020.10.009
20. Smolik, M., Skala, V., Majdisova, Z.: 3D vector field approximation and critical points reduction using radial basis functions. Int. J. Mech. **13**, 100–103 (2019)
21. WiKi: Frenet-Serret-formulas (2022). https://en.wikipedia.org/wiki/Frenet%E2%80%93Serret_formulas. Accessed 18 Jan 2022

Managing Non-functional Requirements in Agile Software Development

Ezeldin Sherif[(✉)], Waleed Helmy, and Galal Hassan Galal-Edeen

Information Systems Department, Faculty of Computers and AI,
Cairo University, Cairo, Egypt
ezeldinsherif@gmail.com, {w.helmy,galal}@fci-cu.edu.eg

Abstract. Agile software development is an iterative software development methodology that aims at maximizing productivity, effectiveness, and speed of delivery. There are a lot of benefits of Agile Software Development. However, there are still some challenges. For example, non-functional requirements are not treated as first-class artifacts during the development lifecycle, which causes many problems such as customer dissatisfaction and much rework which therefore affects time and cost. This paper explains different solutions that have handled non-functional requirements issues in Agile. The paper shows the strength and weakness of each solution, however, there is no single solution that handles all main activities of requirements engineering such as elicitation, analysis, validation and management in regards of non-functional requirements.

Keywords: Agile · Non-functional requirements · Scrum

1 Introduction

The term Agile implies agility, adaptability, and flexibility [1]. Agile software development entails breaking down a software project into smaller pieces. First, the development team works on the most important functions that are selected by the users. The team uses an iterative incremental development method for all selected functions and accordingly, makes each iteration's results into a running system. Agile software development (ASD) has become increasingly popular in the past decade due to its benefits such as an increase in team productivity, motivation and software quality. Due to changing market demands and the rapid speed of technological change, Agile is becoming an increasingly important [2]. Agile focuses more on working software, however less on non-functional requirements [3]. This causes increased cost or longer time-to-market in case of not properly dealing with non-functional requirements [4]. Therefore, this is our focus; as non-functional requirements must be treated as important as functional requirements in order to produce working quality software. The paper presents different solutions that manage non-functional requirements in ASD. This is how

O. Gervasi et al. (Eds.): ICCSA 2022, LNCS 13376, pp. 205–216, 2022.
https://doi.org/10.1007/978-3-031-10450-3_16

the paper is structured: Sect. 2 presents requirements engineering challenges in Agile, Sect. 3 presents solutions to handle those challenges and Sect. 4 provides the conclusion.

2   Requirements Engineering Challenges in Agile

There are many challenges in Agile requirements engineering, as shown in Table 1. The table shows 15 different research papers along with 16 challenges. The challenge labeled with "Yes" means that this challenge is mentioned in the given paper. The challenge that is labeled with "-" means that this challenge is not mentioned in the given paper. As noticed from Table 1, negligence of non-functional requirements and minimal documentation are two significant challenges in requirements engineering of Agile software development. Problems in neglecting non-functional requirements include too-minimal documentation of non-functional requirements, insufficient techniques to deal with non-functional requirements in Agile and focus on functionality [3,4]. According to Cao and Ramesh's empirical investigation, [6,7], Non-functional requirements (NFRs) are given less emphasis in the early stages of Agile since the client is more concerned with core operations. Non-functional requirements are frequently overlooked in Agile testing for a variety of reasons, including lack of awareness, experience, priority, culture, and time and expense constraints [20]. There are many different solutions that handled the negligence of non-functional requirements in Agile. Each solution handled the negligence in different perspective and each solution is described in section three.

Table 1. Challenges in agile requirements engineering

No	Challenge	[5]	[6]	[7]	[8]	[9]	[10]	[11]	[12]	[13]	[14]	[15]	[16]	[17]	[18]	[19]
1	**Neglect of NFR**	Yes	Yes	Yes	Yes	Yes	Yes	Yes	Yes	Yes	Yes	Yes	-	Yes	Yes	Yes
2	Minimal documentation	Yes	Yes	-	Yes	Yes	Yes	Yes	Yes	Yes	Yes	Yes	Yes	Yes	Yes	Yes
3	Inadequate/inappropriate architecture	Yes	-	Yes	-	Yes	-	-	-	Yes	Yes	Yes	Yes	Yes	Yes	Yes
4	Prioritization of NFR	Yes	-	-	-	-	-	-	Yes	-	-	Yes	-	-	Yes	Yes
5	NFR infeasibility	-	-	Yes	-	-	Yes	-	-	-	-	-	-	-	-	-
6	Teams interaction	-	-	Yes	-	-	-	-	-	-	-	-	Yes	-	-	-
7	Inadequate NFR verification	-	-	Yes	Yes	-	-	-	-	-	-	-	Yes	-	Yes	-
8	NFRs identification	-	-	Yes	-	-	Yes	-	-	-	-	Yes	-	-	-	-
9	Customer unavailability	-	-	-	Yes	Yes	-	-	Yes	Yes	Yes	Yes	Yes	Yes	Yes	Yes
10	Project budget and time estimation	-	-	-	-	Yes	Yes	-	Yes	Yes	Yes	Yes	Yes	Yes	Yes	Yes
11	Change of requirements	-	-	-	-	Yes	Yes	-	-	Yes	Yes	Yes	-	-	-	Yes
12	Problems related to prototyping	-	-	-	-	-	-	Yes	-	-	-	-	-	-	-	-
13	Not understanding the big picture	-	-	-	-	-	-	Yes	-	-	-	-	-	-	-	-
14	Lack of requirements traceability	-	-	-	-	-	-	-	Yes	-	-	-	-	-	-	-
15	Contractual limitations	-	-	-	-	-	-	-	Yes	Yes	Yes	-	-	-	-	Yes
16	Customer inability and agreement	-	-	-	-	-	-	-	-	Yes	Yes	Yes	-	-	-	-

3   Solutions to Handle the Challenges

This section presents related solutions that can handle non-functional requirements in Agile software development. As shown in Table 2, it consists of 7 different methods and methodologies to handle the non-functional issue(s) in Agile software development. As shown in Table 3, it consists of 10 different frameworks, tools, processes, and guidelines to handle the non-functional issue(s) in Agile software development. In each table, it shows the strength of each of the proposed solutions. The keyword "yes" means that the item does apply to that specific solution/research paper, and the keyword "no" means that the item doesn't apply to that specific solution/research paper. In general, requirements engineering phase consists of four main activities: requirements elicitation, analysis, validation and management. As showing in Tables 2 and 3, each solution tackles different perspectives of those activities, but there is no single solution that handles the four main activities of requirements engineering. There is a need for a solution that can handle those activities of requirements engineering in Agile along with functional requirements but without affecting the principles and values of Agile.

3.1   Methods/Methodologies to Handle Non-functional Requirements in Agile

This section explains 7 different methods and methodologies that handle non-functional requirements in Agile software development as it can be seen in Table 2.

Table 2. Different methods/methodologies to handle non-functional requirements in agile

Item/Paper	1	2	3	4	5	6	7
	NORMAP [21]	NERV [25]	MEDoV [27]	CEP [28]	Decision Tree [30]	ACRUM [33]	SENSoR [34]
Type of solution	Methodology	Methodology	Method	Methodology	Methodology	Method	Method
Inform client meaning of NFR	No	No	No	No	No	No	Yes
Handles functional requirements	Yes	Yes	No	Yes	No	Yes	No
Elicit NFR	No	Yes	Yes	Yes	No	No	Yes
Analyze NFR	No	Yes	Yes	No	No	Yes	Yes
Link NFR with functional requirements	Yes	Yes	No	No	No	Yes	No
Model NFR	Yes	No	Yes	No	No	No	No
Recommend NFR	No	No	No	No	No	No	No
Plan (prioritized) NFR	No	No	No	Yes	No	No	No
Schedule NFR	No	No	No	No	No	No	No
Predict NFR	No	No	No	No	Yes	No	No
Document NFR	Yes	Yes	Yes	Yes	No	Yes	Yes
Validate NFR	No	No	Yes	No	No	Yes	Yes

NORMAP. NORMAP is a simple framework for identifying, linking, and modeling non-functional requirements [21]. To support the goals, three areas of improvement were proposed. The first enhancement is the W^8 user story card model. It is basically an enhancement of the Agile index card (user story) technique in order to gather requirements in ASD. Each "W" in W^8 represents a question to be answered. It includes eight questions to capture functional and non-functional requirements. The first "W" is "who" is the actor, second "W" is "what" the user wants, the third "W" is "why" that captures business justification, fourth "W" is "within" estimated time frame, fifth "W" is "while it is nice to have" or in other words optional non-functional requirements, sixth "W" is "without ignoring" meaning required non-functional requirements, seventh "W" is "with a priority of" and last "W" is "which may impact" that captures a list of impacted requirements. The second enhancement is that NORMAP proposes an Agile requirements taxonomy, which divides requirements into functional (Agile Use Case) and non-functional (Agile Loose Case) categories. The third enhancement to link functional and non-functional requirements, "Before, after, override, and wrap" are examples of Aspect-Oriented "pointcut" operators used by NORMAP. The term "pointcut" refers to a point in time where an ACC is performed and linked to an AUC in order to avoid code tangling and crosscutting issues. In other words, it combines functional and non-functional requirements and links ACC to AUC. The NORMAP framework can be utilized semi-automatically or manually. NORMANUAL is the name of the manual framework, and NORMATIC is the name of the semi-automated framework. The proposed framework contains many steps, which increases the complexity of the framework. Therefore, it may contradict the principles and values of ASD. In addition, the framework was not validated in real-world Agile projects; however, it is validated using data-sets. The first dataset is a collection of unrelated requirements from several projects in a DePaul University software engineering course. The second dataset represents the European Union eProcurement Online System's requirements model. Also, the framework only focuses on identifying, modeling and linking non-functional requirements with functional requirements in Agile.

NERV. NERV is lightweight methodology to address NFRs in the early stages of Agile [25]. NERV handles NFRS elicitation, reasoning and validation in ASD. It is an improvement of NORMAP methodology. NERV uses Agile user story cards to capture functional requirements (including users, actions performed and reason for doing action), an NFRusCOM card for handling quality requirements information and capturing quality requirements' aspects, an NFR trigger card for eliciting quality requirements, and a non-functional requirements reasoning taxonomy for classifying quality requirements. It also employs NFR's quantification taxonomy to quantify the quality requirements' validation criteria, as well as the NERV Agility Index (NAI) to measure the degree of agility of each non-functional and functional need. It is validated using two case studies (datasets) and not real-world projects. Furthermore, NERV added six additional artifacts (NFR Elicitation Taxonomy, NFRusCOM Card, NFR Reasoning Taxonomy, NFR Quantification Taxonomy, NFR Trigger Card, and NAI), which may lead to Agile becoming a heavily documented methodology, which is contrary to the Agile Manifesto's objectives.

MEDoV. MEDoV consists of three phases. Phase one is setting project objectives with business goals by a deep understanding of customer values and expectations [27]. Phase one is carried out only once at the start of the project, however phases II and III are carried out again in each iteration. Eliciting and documenting requirements is part of phase two. Phase three performs requirements analysis, specification and validation. Much formal documentation is needed in order to specify requirements. There is the possibility of wasted efforts in understanding the KPI for each requirement.

CEP. CEP methodology is an extension of NERV and NORMAP [28]. The objective of this methodology is to develop an automated framework that captures, elicits and prioritizes non-functional requirements from requirements documents that contain images. The capture part was done using OCR, converting images into readable textual format. The elicitation part uses NFRL+, which elicits the non-functional requirements from digitized documents and images. The prioritization part is done by prioritizing the non-functional requirements by using weights. For example, the non-functional requirement of the weight of one has a higher priority than a non-functional requirement of five. The methodology is simple enough, but there are few details to explain how obtaining a solution is approached. For example, what if the document is written poorly or the requirements are not complete. In addition, the methodology was not validated in real-world Agile projects; however, it was validated using data-sets.

Decision Tree. This research uses the prediction model to extend the Capture Elicit Prioritize (CEP) methodology by using a simple decision tree to make predictions using historical non-functional requirements data [30]. By applying the decision tree, non-functional requirements that appeared three times or more are the ones that were predicted in the future iterations. This research only focuses on the prediction by using simple decision trees. The scope of the study is focused on prediction only. The proposed solution wasn't applied using real-life projects.

ACRUM. It's an Agile development method based on quality attributes [33]. There are three major activities in ACRUM along with Scrum activities: first activity is the AQUA (analysis of quality attributes), the second activity is the preparation of the correlation mapping table (Requirements Association Matrix) between requirements and its analysis, the third activity is failure or success of the quality attributes is verified through the Validation of Quality Attribute (VQA). It was validated using only two case studies.

SENoR. It is a method for eliciting NFRs, consisting of three steps: preparation, workshop and follow-up. The first step is preparation, which is the business case presentation [34]. According to ISO25010, the second step is a workshop, which consists of a series of short brainstorming sessions. Each session dedicated to one of the ISO25010's qualities sub-characteristic. The purpose of the second step is to elicit NFRs. The third step is follow-up which consists of analyzing non-functional requirements and introducing improvements, such as identifying contradictory or duplicated information. The output of this step is non-functional requirements and lessons learned. There are four roles in SENoR: moderator, presenter, recorder and experts. The Moderator is the person who leads the whole process. The presenter is the individual who explains the project's concept to the participants, the Recorder is the person who records the work of participants, and the Expert is the person who is an expert on specific content and defining its requirements. It only focuses on elicitation of the non-functional requirements.

3.2 Other Solutions to Handle Non-functional Requirements in Agile

This section explains 10 other solutions (frameworks, processes, tools and guidelines) that handle non-functional requirements Agile software development as it can be seen in Table 3.

Table 3. Other solutions to handle non-functional requirements in agile

Item/Paper	1	2	3	4	5	6	7	8	9	10
	NORMATIC [22]	NORPLAN [23]	NORVIEW [24]	CEPP [26]	NFRec Tool [29]	NFR recommendation System [31]	AgileRE [32]	Elicitation Guideline [35]	Framework for requirements elicitation [36]	Modeling NFR [37]
Type of solution	Tool	Metric	Framework	Study	Tool	Process	Tool	Guidelines	Framework	New artifacts
Inform client meaning of NFR	No	No	No	No	No	No	No	No	No	No
Handles functional requirements	Yes	Yes	Yes	Yes	Yes	No	Yes	Yes	Yes	Yes
Elicit NFR	No	No	No	Yes	Yes	No	No	Yes	Yes	No
Analyze NFR	No	No	No	No	No	No	No	No	No	No
Link NFR with functional requirements	No	No	No	No	Yes	No	Yes	Yes	No	Yes
Model NFR	Yes	No	No	No	No	No	No	No	No	Yes
Recommend NFR	No	No	No	No	Yes	Yes	No	No	No	No
Plan (prioritized) NFR	No	Yes	No	Yes	No	No	No	No	No	No
Schedule NFR	No	No	Yes	No	No	No	No	No	No	No
Predict NFR	No	No	No	Yes	No	No	No	No	No	No
Document NFR	Yes	Yes	Yes	Yes	Yes	No	Yes	Yes	Yes	No
Validate NFR	No	No	No	No	No	Yes	Yes	No	No	No

NORMATIC. NORMATIC is a Java-based visual modeling simulation tool that is part of the NORMAP framework [22]. It supports the three building blocks of the NORMAP framework, which includes identifying, linking and modeling non-functional requirements with functional requirements. The tool is designed to model functional and non-functional requirements in a visual environment that may be utilized in Agile methods like Scrum. The three NORMAP building components were used to create NORMATIC: Agile Use Case (AUC), Agile Loose Case (ALC), and Agile Choose Case (ACC). AUC includes requirement quality attributes; ALC identifies to address non-functional as a story, and ACC represents instances of a potential solution for identified ALC.

The proposed tool was validated using datasets, specifically two case studies only. The European Union Electronic Procurement System is the first dataset, and the PROMISE dataset is the second. So it wasn't used in real-world Agile projects to measure the tool's effectiveness, and the number of case studies is minimal. In addition, since this tool is part of the NORMAP framework, it has the same complexity as the framework, which may affect the concept of Agile software development by containing too many complicated steps. Also, NORMATIC is not web-enabled, and therefore it doesn't support the mobile computing environment, and today's trend is shifting toward web applications and mobile applications.

NORPLAN. NORPLAN is one of the components of the NORMAP framework [23]. NORPLAN's key components for calculating the plan include requirements quality metrics, risk-driven algorithms and project management metrics. NOR-PLAN's goal is to generate a potentially better requirements implementation sequence. This implementation sequence calculates technical and project management risks of all requirements (non-functional and functional), which will aid in planning which requirements will be implemented in future sprints/releases. In addition, riskiest-requirements-first and riskiest-requirements-last are the two priority techniques used by NORPLAN, instead of the normal business value prioritization scheme used in Agile software development methodologies.

First, NORPLAN was not implemented in real-world Agile software projects. Second, a high-business-value-first prioritization scheme should be considered as a first class artifact as it may cause conflict with client/customer business needs and therefore cause unnecessary issues such as losing a segment of the market. In other words, it disregards the Product Owner's requested priority of requirements. Third, since NORPLAN is part of NORMAP, it has a similar complexity with NORMAP which also contradicts the concept of Agile.

NORVIEW. NORVIEW is the last component of NORMAP framework [24]. The next step is to schedule and visualize the plan using different project management metrics after it has been developed in NORPLAN. This will aid Scrum teams in planning, scheduling and visualizing NFRs. NORVIEW is a tree-like direct visual representation of NORPLAN. NORVIEW is the last component of NORMAP and its purpose is to support planning and scheduling. This component could be a part of NORPLAN in order to reduce the number of components and therefore reduce complexity. In addition, same as for other components of NORMAP, it is not validated in the real-world Agile projects.

CEPP. This methodology gathers non-functional requirements metadata from documents and images [26]. It uses historical trending to predict non-functional requirements that could be overlooked in the early stages of ASD. Also, it prioritizes non-functional requirements using α β γ- framework where process α is used to subjectively prioritize needs in order to subjectively minimize the number of options. The objective is to provide effective techniques to predict and prioritize non-functional requirements. This methodology wasn't validated by either case studies or data sets.

NFRec Tool. The tool aids in the elicitation of non-functional needs by performing two tasks: project information structuring and non-functional requirement recommendation [29]. A developer can visualize suggestions of non-functional requirements for each user story in the current or future sprints, and therefore non-functional requirements will be considered early in the development. The tool should be analyzed and validated using different projects from distinct software development organizations.

NFR Recommendation System. It is a non-functional requirements recommendation system based on collaborative filtering to support Scrum practitioners [31]. It introduced one new role, Scrum Architect, and a new artifact called "semi-structured user story". This may affect the concept of agility and the Agile manifesto by getting close to traditional software development methodology. The dataset was insufficient to test recommendation systems in various domains.

AgileRe Tool. It is a tool that provides basic requirements management features such as persona creation, epic and user story management, role-based access for product owners, customer feedback, dashboard and reports [32]. This tool is accessible through the web browser interface. The tool covers many different features in regard to requirements; however, there is less focus on NFRs. In the tool, NFRs are included in the acceptance criteria.

Elicitation Guide. It contains elicitation guidelines for non-functional requirements in Agile methods, and it helps developers and users [35]. This guideline helps in two perspectives: the first is that developers interact with the customer or user for requirements elicitation. The second is that the team has to extract or elicit non-functional requirements from the requirements. More case studies are needed, especially in the software industry, and preferably a tool should be developed to help with the objectives of this solution.

Framework for Requirements Elicitation. Pre-elicitation, mid-elicitation, and post-elicitation are the three phases of the elicitation framework [36]. It combines mind mapping, Scrum, and the Joint Requirement Document (JRD). There is a lack of focus on non-functional requirements. The main parts of the proposed framework are:

- Phase I (pre-elicitation) is JRD to create an initial scope document.
- Phase II (mid-elicitation) is mind mapping that focuses on detailed requirements gathering.
- Phase III (post-elicitation): The requirements are sent to the Scrum process's product backlog as user stories.

Modeling NFR. It presents three building blocks for identifying, linking and modeling non-functional requirements with the functional requirement in order to improve software quality [37]. The first block is where functional requirements are modeled through AUC (Agile Use Cases). Second, non-functional requirements are modeled using ALC (Agile Loose Cases). The third is non-functional requirements; Potential solutions are modeling through ACC (Agile Choose Cases). Three new artifacts were introduced, which may compromise the principles of Agile. In addition, it was validated using datasets, and not real-life projects.

4 Conclusion

Agile software development is a one of the hot topics in the software engineering. It comes with its own challenges such as challenges in requirements engineering in Agile software development. There are many challenges within requirements engineering of Agile such as ignoring non-functional requirements and minimal documentation. In the past decade, there were many solutions that handled non-functional requirements in Agile in different ways. Each of those solutions had its own weakness and strength. However, there is no single solution that covers non-functional requirements elicitation, analysis, documentation, validation, recommendation, along with functional requirements. This can be a potential research point to reduce the issues of ignoring non-functional requirements in Agile software development.

References

1. Jarzębowicz, A., Weichbroth, P.: A systematic literature review on implementing non-functional requirements in agile software development: issues and facilitating practices. In: Przybyłek, A., Miler, J., Poth, A., Riel, A. (eds.) LASD 2021. LNBIP, vol. 408, pp. 91–110. Springer, Cham (2021). https://doi.org/10.1007/978-3-030-67084-9_6
2. Lu, H.-K., Lin, P.-C., Huang, P.-C., Yuan, A.: Deployment and evaluation of a continues integration process in agile development. J. Adv. Inf. Technol. 8(4), 204–209 (2017). https://doi.org/10.12720/jait.8.4.204-209
3. Jarzebowicz, A., Weichbroth, P.: A qualitative study on non-functional requirements in agile software development. IEEE Access 9, 40458–40475 (2021). https://doi.org/10.1109/ACCESS.2021.3064424
4. Behutiye, W., et al.: Management of quality requirements in agile and rapid software development: a systematic mapping study. Inf. Softw. Technol. 123, 106225 (2020). https://doi.org/10.1016/j.infsof.2019.106225
5. Schön, E.-M., Winter, D., Escalona, M.J., Thomaschewski, J.: Key challenges in agile requirements engineering. In: Baumeister, H., Lichter, H., Riebisch, M. (eds.) XP 2017. LNBIP, vol. 283, pp. 37–51. Springer, Cham (2017). https://doi.org/10.1007/978-3-319-57633-6_3
6. Behutiye, W., Karhapää, P., Costal, D., Oivo, M., Franch, X.: Non-functional requirements documentation in agile software development: Challenges and solution proposal. arXiv, pp. 515–522 (2017). https://doi.org/10.1007/978-3-319-69926-4

7. Alsaqaf, W., Daneva, M., Wieringa, R.: Agile quality requirements engineering challenges: first results from a case study. Int. Symp. Empir. Softw. Eng. Meas. **2017**, 454–459 (2017). https://doi.org/10.1109/ESEM.2017.61
8. Gaikwad, V., Joeg, P.: A case study in requirements engineering in context of agile. Int. J. Appl. Eng. Res. **12**(8), 1697–1702 (2017)
9. Elghariani, K., Kama, N.: Review on agile requirements engineering challenges. In: 2016 3rd International Conference on Computer Information Science ICCOINS 2016 - Proceedings, pp. 507–512 (2016). https://doi.org/10.1109/ICCOINS.2016. 7783267
10. Alam, S., Nazir, S., Asim, S., Amr, D.: Impact and challenges of requirement engineering in agile methodologies: a systematic review. Int. J. Adv. Comput. Sci. Appl. **8**(4), 411–420 (2017). https://doi.org/10.14569/ijacsa.2017.080455
11. Käpyaho, M., Kauppinen, M.: Agile requirements engineering with prototyping: a case study. In: 2015 IEEE International Requirements Engineering Conference RE 2015 - Proceedings, pp. 334–343 (2015). https://doi.org/10.1109/RE.2015.7320450
12. Inayat, I., Moraes, L., Daneva, M., Salim, S.S.: A reflection on agile requirements engineering: solutions brought and challenges posed. In: ACM International Conference Proceeding Series, 29 May 2015, vol. 25 (2015). https://doi.org/10.1145/ 2764979.2764985
13. Inayat, I., Salim, S.S., Marczak, S., Daneva, M., Shamshirband, S.: A systematic literature review on agile requirements engineering practices and challenges. Comput. Human Behav. **51**, 915–929 (2015). https://doi.org/10.1016/j.chb.2014. 10.046
14. Sunner, D., Bajaj, H.: Classification of functional and non-functional requirements in agile by cluster neuro-genetic approach. Int. J. Softw. Eng. Its Appl. **10**(10), 129–138 (2016). https://doi.org/10.14257/ijseia.2016.10.10.13
15. Saleh, M., Baharom, F., Farvin, S., Mohamed, P., Ahmad, M.: A systematic literature review of challenges and critical success factors in agile requirement engineering. In: International Conference on Information and Knowledge Management, pp. 248–254, July 2018
16. Batra, M., Bhatnagar, A: A research study on critical challenges in agile requirements engineering. Int. Res. J. Eng. Technol. **6**, 1214–1219 (2019)
17. Telesko, R.: Road to agile requirements engineering: Lessons learned from a web app project. Stud. Syst. Decis. Control **141**, 65–78 (2018). https://doi.org/10. 1007/978-3-319-74322-6_5
18. Ramesh, B., Cao, L., Baskerville, R.: Agile requirements engineering practices and challenges: an empirical study. Inf. Syst. J. **20**(5), 449–480 (2010). https://doi.org/ 10.1111/j.1365-2575.2007.00259.x
19. Saleh, M., Baharom, F., Mohamed, S.F.P.: Critical success factors and challenges in agile requirements engineering. Turkish J. Comput. Math. Educ. **12**(3), 1670–1682 (2021). https://doi.org/10.17762/turcomat.v12i3.989
20. Cruzes, D.S., Felderer, M., Oyetoyan, T.D., Gander, M., Pekaric, I.: How is security testing done in agile teams? A cross-case analysis of four software teams. Lect. Notes Informatics (LNI). In: Proceedings - Series of the Gesellschaft fur Informatik, vol. 292, pp. 133–134 (2019). https://doi.org/10.18420/se2019-40
21. Farid, W.M.: The Normap methodology: lightweight engineering of non-functional requirements for agile processes. In: Proceedings of the Asia-Pacific Conference on Software Engineering, APSEC, vol. 1, pp. 322–325 (2012). https://doi.org/10. 1109/APSEC.2012.23

22. Farid, W.M., Mitropoulos, F.J.: NORMATIC: a visual tool for modeling non-functional requirements in agile processes. In: Conference Proceedings on IEEE SOUTHEASTCON, no. 978 (2012). https://doi.org/10.1109/SECon.2012.6196989
23. Farid, W.M., Mitropoulos, F.J.: NORPLAN: non-functional requirements planning for agile processes. In: Conference Proceedings on IEEE SOUTHEASTCON (2013). https://doi.org/10.1109/SECON.2013.6567463
24. Farid, W.M., Mitropoulos, F.J.: Visualization and scheduling of non-functional requirements for agile processes. In: Conference Proceedings on IEEE SOUTH-EASTCON (2013). https://doi.org/10.1109/SECON.2013.6567413
25. Domah, D., Mitropoulos, F.J.: The NERV methodology: a lightweight process for addressing non-functional requirements in agile software development. In: Conference Proceedings on IEEE SOUTHEASTCON, vol. 2015-June (2015). https://doi.org/10.1109/SECON.2015.7133028
26. Maiti, R.R., Mitropoulos, F.J.: Capturing, eliciting, predicting and prioritizing (CEPP) non-functional requirements metadata during the early stages of agile software development. In: Conference Proceedings on IEEE SOUTHEASTCON, vol. 2015-June (2015). https://doi.org/10.1109/SECON.2015.7133007
27. Dragicevic, S., Celar, S., Novak, L.: Use of method for elicitation, documentation, and validation of software user requirements (MEDoV) in agile software development projects. In: Proceedings of the 6th International Conference on Computational Intelligence, Communication Systems and Networks, CICSyN 2014, pp. 65–70 (2014). https://doi.org/10.1109/CICSyN.2014.27
28. Maiti, R.R., Mitropoulos, F.J.: Capturing, eliciting, and prioritizing (CEP) NFRs in agile software engineering. In: Conference Proceedings on IEEE SOUTHEAST-CON (2017). https://doi.org/10.1109/SECON.2017.7925365
29. Ramos, F., et al.: Evaluating software developers' acceptance of a tool for supporting agile non-functional requirement elicitation. In: Proceedings of the International Conference on Software Engineering and Knowledge Engineering, SEKE, vol. 2019-July, August, pp. 26–31 (2019). https://doi.org/10.18293/SEKE2019-107
30. Maiti, R.R., Krasnov, A., Wilborne, D.M.: Agile software engineering & the future of non-functional requirements. J. Softw. Eng. Pract. **2**(1), 1–8 (2018)
31. Ramos, F., Costa, A., Perkusich, M., Almeida, H., Perkusich, A.: A non-functional requirements recommendation system for scrum-based projects. In: Proceedings of the International Conference on Software Engineering and Knowledge Engineering, SEKE, vol. 2018-July, pp. 149–154, July 2018. https://doi.org/10.18293/SEKE2018-107
32. Gaikwad, V., Joeg, P., Joshi, S.: AgileRE: agile requirements management tool. Adv. Intell. Syst. Comput. **661**, 236–249 (2018). https://doi.org/10.1007/978-3-319-67618-0_22
33. Jeon, S., Han, M., Lee, E., Lee, K.: Quality attribute driven agile development. In: Proceedings of the 18th International Conference on Evaluation and Assessment in Software Engineering, SERA 2011, pp. 203–210 (2011). https://doi.org/10.1109/SERA.2011.24
34. Kopczyńska, S., Nawrocki, J.: Using non-functional requirements templates for elicitation: a case study. In: 2014 IEEE 4th International Workshop on Requirement Patterns, RePa 2014 - Proceedings, pp. 47–54 (2014). https://doi.org/10.1109/RePa.2014.6894844
35. Younas, M., Jawawi, D.N.A., Ghani, I., Kazmi, R.: Non-functional requirements elicitation guideline for agile methods. J. Telecommun. Electron. Comput. Eng. **9**(3–4 Special Issue), pp. 137–142 (2017)

36. Saeeda, H., Dong, J., Wang, Y., Abid, M.A.: A proposed framework for improved software requirements elicitation process in SCRUM: implementation by a real-life Norway-based IT project. J. Softw. Evol. Process, **32** (2020). https://doi.org/10.1002/smr.2247
37. Farid, W.M., Mitropoulos, F.J.: Novel lightweight engineering artifacts for modeling non-functional requirements in agile processes. In: Conference Proceeding on IEEE SOUTHEASTCON (2012). https://doi.org/10.1109/SECon.2012.6196988

Non-linear Approximated Value Adjustments for Derivatives Under Multiple Risk Factors

Ivan Gallo[✉] [ID]

University of L'Aquila, 67100 L'Aquila, ABR, Italy
`ivan.gallo1@graduate.univaq.it`

Abstract. We develop a numerical method to approximate the adjusted value of a European contingent claim in a market model where the underlying's price is correlated with the stochastic default intensities of the two parties of the contract.

When the close-out value of the contract is chosen as a fraction of the adjusted value, the latter verifies a non linear, not explicitly solvable BSDE. In a Markovian setting, this adjusted value is a deterministic function of the state variable verifying a non-linear PDE.

We develop here a numerical method to approximate the PDE solution, as an alternative choice to the commonly used Monte Carlo simulations, which require large computational times, especially when the number of the state variables grows.

We construct the approximated solution by the simple method of lines and we show the method to be accurate and efficient in a simplified cases. We show numerical results in the case of both constant intensities and the situation where only one is diffusive.

Keywords: Value adjustments · Backward stochastic differential equation · Nonlinear valuation · Credit risk · Numerical method

1 Introduction

Before the financial crisis of $2007-08$, the value of a financial contract, such as an option, was determined by taking the conditional expectation of the discounted expected price, under a risk-neutral measure, without taking into account any credit risk (*default-free*). After the crisis, the need to introduce the effect of potential parties' defaults in the contract price became of great importance, and a theory of *Value Adjustments* was developed.

The first to be introduced was the CVA (*Credit Valuation Adjustments*), a positive quantity to be subtracted from the default-free price accounting for the possible losses due to the counterparty's default.

Over the years, the role of CVA increased considerably and became crucial when trading derivatives in the OTC markets, stimulating a lot of research in the field: for some examples, see [8, 10, 14].

© The Author(s), under exclusive license to Springer Nature Switzerland AG 2022
O. Gervasi et al. (Eds.): ICCSA 2022, LNCS 13376, pp. 217–227, 2022.
https://doi.org/10.1007/978-3-031-10450-3_17

When evaluating products with cashflows in both directions (such as forwards or swaps), in order to take into account default of either part, the need to consider further adjustments arose, such as DVA (*Debt Valuation Adjustments*), FVA (*Funding Valuation Adjustments*), LVA (*Liquidity Valuation Adjustments*), were introduced and we refer the reader to the papers by Brigo et al. [5–8] for a detailed discussion.

The adjusted value of a financial contract under a risk-neutral measure turn on the so-called "close-out value", which is a portion of a contractually agreed price to be paid as partial compensation when the default of one of the parties occurs. This adjusted value can be represented as the solution of a BSDE (backward stochastic differential equation).

If the close-out value is as a portion of the price of the defaultable contract itself, this BSDE equation becomes non-linear, hence not explicitly solvable.

The principal choice to a numerical approximation of the solution of this BSDE is Monte Carlo simulation techniques but usually have very long computational times. So this, we are looking for alternative methods.

Under the Markovian assumption of all market processes, it is possible, thanks to Feynman-Kac's formula, to express the derivative's value as a deterministic function of the state variables that satisfies a PDE with the final condition given by the product's payoff [9]. We can use an alternative numerical approach to solve the problem by discretizing this PDE.

More in detail, we consider the case of a European call option subject to liquidity, funding, and collateralization risks. We assume both parties to be defaultable with stochastic intensities chosen as CIR processes in order to ensure their positivity, being certainly a desirable feature.

Among computational papers about this topic, we also quote the recent [3,4]. Both follow the works by Piterbarg [19] and Burgard and Kiaer [9] that obtain PDE formulation by hedging arguments on suitable portfolios and the application of the Ito lemma for jump-diffusion processes. They apply finite elements methods and contraction methods to approximate the PDE solutions, but they are able to treat only deterministic intensities or, in the linear case, a single Gaussian intensity.

We used the simple method of lines to approximate the PDE with a system of ODEs, which can be solved by one-step methods, such as the Euler one. We implemented the method by Matlab software and we used Monte Carlo simulations as benchmark. In the more complex case, the presence of a 3-dimensional vector of processes makes the Monte Carlo simulations computationally prohibitive, while the method of the lines still provides a numerical solution in highly competitive times. The numerical results were extremely satisfactory as they matched the Monte Carlo method in accuracy with remarkably shorter computational times.

The paper is structured as follows. In the first section, we briefly describe the modeling of the problem, and we introduce the BSDE characterizing the adjusted contract's value. Next, we consider the specific case of a European call, and we obtain the associated non-linear PDE. The third section is dedicated to the method of the lines and its implementation in a simplified case.

2   Evaluation of European Claims Under the Intensity Approach

We consider a finite time interval $[0, T]$ and a complete probability space $(\Omega, \mathcal{F}, \mathbb{P})$, endowed with a filtration $\{\mathcal{F}_t\}_{t \in [0,T]}$ that represent the market generated by the processes S_t, r_t and other possible stochastic factors, where r_t is the risk-free interest rate process, determining the money market account and S_t representing the asset price (underlying). We assume to be in absence of arbitrage with $\mathbb{P}$ representing a risk-neutral measure selected by some criterion.

We consider exchanging some European claim between two financial parties $(1 = \text{Counterparty}, 2 = \text{Investor})$ with maturity T and payoff $\Phi(S_T)$, where Φ is a function as regular as needed.

We take the perspective of the investor with the objective to compute the contract value, that we denote by $\bar{V}_t$, taking into account all the cashflows (see [7] for more details).

Both parties might default, and we denote by τ_1, τ_2 the random variables representing their default times.

In general, those r.v.'s are not necessarily stopping times with respect to the filtration $\mathcal{F}_t$, generated by the market observables. To price the defaultable contract, we first need to extend $\mathcal{F}_t$, to $\mathcal{G}_t = \mathcal{F}_t \vee \mathcal{H}_t^1 \vee \mathcal{H}_t^2$, where $\mathcal{H}_t^i = \sigma(1_{\{\tau_i \leq s\}}, s \leq t)$, $i = 1, 2$, which is the smallest filtration making the random variables τ_i stopping times and then project the results back on $\mathcal{F}_t$. To do so, we assume that

- every $\mathcal{F}_t$-martingale remains a $\mathcal{G}_t$-martingale.;
- $\tau_i = \inf\{t \geq 0 | \int_0^t \lambda_u^i du > \xi_i\}$, where ξ_i are two independent standard exponential random variables, and λ^i for $i = 1, 2$ are two $\mathcal{F}_t$-predictable positive processes (see [7,17]);
- In this setting, $\lambda := \lambda^1 + \lambda^2$, is the default intensity of $\tau = min(\tau_1, \tau_2)$, and we set $\bar{\tau} = min(\tau, T)$.

Following Brigo et al. [7], we can write the $\mathcal{G}_t$-adapted value process of the defaultable derivative, $\bar{V}_t$, as the sum of the discounted default-free price and the adjustments due to default, funding, and collateralization risks which gets characterized as the solution of the following BSDE

$$\bar{V}_t = \mathbb{E}_t^{\mathcal{G}}\left[1_{\{\tau > T\}} e^{-\int_t^T r_s ds} \Phi(S_T) + \int_t^{\bar{\tau}} e^{-\int_t^u r_s ds} \pi_u du \right] - \mathbb{E}_t^{\mathcal{G}}\left[\int_t^{\bar{\tau}} e^{-\int_t^u r_s ds} (c_u - r_u) C_u du \right]$$

$$- \mathbb{E}_t^{\mathcal{G}}\left[\int_t^{\bar{\tau}} e^{-\int_t^u r_s ds} (\bar{f}_u - r_u)(\bar{V}_u - C_u) du \right] - \mathbb{E}_t^{\mathcal{G}}\left[\int_t^{\bar{\tau}} e^{-\int_t^u r_s ds} (r_u - \bar{h}_u) \bar{H}_u du \right]$$

$$+ \mathbb{E}_t^{\mathcal{G}}\left[e^{-\int_t^{\tau} r_s ds} 1_{\{t \leq \tau \leq T\}} \left(\epsilon_\tau - 1_{\{\tau_1 < \tau_2\}} LGD_1 (\epsilon_\tau - C_\tau)^+ + 1_{\{\tau_2 < \tau_1\}} LGD_2 (\epsilon_\tau - C_\tau)^- \right) \right].$$

$$\tag{1}$$

Some terms in the above are predefined by the contract's agreements, others depend on the price evolution. We summarize their meaning and measurability properties in Table 1.

Table 1. Summary of cashflows and their measurability properties

Symbol	Role	Assumption
$\Phi()$	Payoff at maturity	Lipschitz function of S_T
π	Contract dividends	$\mathcal{F}$-predictable
C	Collateral process	$\mathcal{F}$-predictable
$\bar{H}$	Hedging process	$\mathcal{G}$-predictable
ϵ	Close-out value	$\mathcal{F}$-predictable
c	Collateral rate	$\mathcal{F}$-predictable
$\bar{f}$	Funding rate	$\mathcal{G}$-predictable
$\bar{h}$	Hedging rate	$\mathcal{G}$-predictable
$LGD_i, i = 1, 2$	Loss Given Default	Constant

The close-out value ϵ_u is usually taken as portion of the default-free price or as the price of the defaultable claim: the first choice gives a solvable linear BSDE, while the second ($\epsilon_u = \bar{V}_u$) determines a non-linear BSDE, not explicitly solvable.

It is well-known that the default times are not market observables, so we have to translate in terms of $\mathcal{F}$ any risk-neutral evaluation, which would take place in the $\mathcal{G}$. That means that we must project on to the market filtration $\mathcal{F}_t$ the theoretical price represented by Eq. (1).

By the key lemma and its extensions (see [1,2,5,7,17]), if $\bar{V}_t$ is a $\mathcal{G}$-adapted process then there exists an $\mathcal{F}_t$-adapted process V_t such that $1_{\{t<\tau\}} V_t = 1_{\{t<\tau\}} \bar{V}_t$. We may therefore project Eq. (1) on $\mathcal{F}_t$, obtaining the following $\mathcal{F}$-BSDE:

$$
V_t = \mathbb{E}_t^{\mathcal{F}} \left[e^{-\int_t^T (r_s + \lambda_s) ds} \Phi(S_T) + \int_t^T e^{-\int_t^u (r_s + \lambda_s) ds} \Big(\pi_u - (c_u - r_u)C_u - (f_u - r_u)(V_u \right.
$$
$$
\left. - C_u) - (r_u - h_u)H_u + V_u \lambda_u - LGD_1 \lambda_u^1 (V_u - C_u)^+ + LGD_2 \lambda_u^2 (V_u - C_u)^- \Big) du \right],
$$
$$
\tag{2}
$$

where V_t, f_u, h_u and H_u are $\mathcal{F}$-adapted processes such that $1_{\{t<\tau\}} V_t = 1_{\{t<\tau\}} \bar{V}_t$, $1_{\{u<\tau\}} f_u = 1_{\{u<\tau\}} \bar{f}_u$, $1_{\{u<\tau\}} h = 1_{\{u<\tau\}} \bar{h}_u$, $1_{\{u<\tau\}} H_u = 1_{\{u<\tau\}} \bar{H}_u$.

If $\mathcal{F}_t$ is generated by a (possibly multidimensional) Brownian motion driving the market assets prices, by the martingale representation theorem, taking for granted the necessary integrability conditions, we can rewrite Eq. (2) as

$$
V_t = \Phi(S_T) + \int_t^T \Big(\pi_u + (f_u - c_u)C_u - f_u V_u - (r_u - h_u)H_u
$$
$$
- LGD_1 \lambda_u^1 (V_u - C_u)^+ + LGD_2 \lambda_u^2 (V_u - C_u)^- \Big) du - \int_t^T Z_u dW_u + \mathcal{M}_t
$$
$$
\tag{3}
$$

with W_t is a (vector) Brownian motion, Z_t, possibly square integrable, an $\mathcal{F}$-adapted (vector) process, and $\mathcal{M}_t$ is a martingale orthogonal to $\int_t^T Z_u \cdot dW_u$, possibly depending on further stochastic factors.

Missing a closed form solution for Eq. (3), one may try to construct an appropriate approximation procedure. In the literature, the most widespread method is Monte Carlo simulations (possibly coupled with deep learning-techniques as in [13]), which have very long computational times. It is then worth looking for alternative, less costly methods. This is possible when the underlying processes are diffusions, generating a Markovian vector.

3   Markovian BSDE and PDE for V_t

Under appropriate conditions, Eq. (3) has a unique adapted solution (V, Z) (see [7,18]) and in a Markovian setting, this is a deterministic function of the state variables. That is the case when $(S, \lambda^1, \lambda^2)$ are diffusion processes.

To analyze this case, we simplify the equation by assuming that

- the claim pays no dividends, hence $\pi = 0$;
- the rates r, f, c, h are deterministic bounded functions of time;
- the collateral process is a fraction of the process V_u, namely $C_u = \alpha_u V_u$, where $0 \le \alpha_u \le 1$ is a function of time;
- the process $H_t = H(t, S_t, V_t, Z_t)$, where $H(u, x, v, z)$ is a deterministic, Lipschitz-continuous function in v, z, uniformly in u. Besides $H(u, x, 0, 0)$ is continuous in x. This means that we can included H_t in the dynamics, if we assume a δ-hedging of the product (see [1,2,7,8]);

Using the flow notation, we assume that the market model is given by S satisfying:

$$S_s^{t,x} = x + \int_t^s r_u S_u^{t,x} du + \int_t^s \sigma S_u^{t,x} dW_u, \ \sigma > 0, \ t \le u \le T,$$

with default intensities following a CIR dynamics

$$\lambda_s^{i,t,w} = w + \int_t^s \gamma_i(\psi_i - \lambda_u^{i,t,w}) du + \int_t^s \eta_i \sqrt{\lambda_u^{i,t,w}} dB_u^i, \ i = 1, 2$$

with

$$W_t = \rho_1 B_t^1 + \rho_2 B_t^2 + \sqrt{1 - \rho_1^2 - \rho_2^2} B_t^3, \quad \rho_1^2 + \rho_2^2 \le 1, \ -1 \le \rho_i \le 1$$

where (B_t^1, B_t^2, B_t^3) is 3-dimensional standard Brownian motion, and $\gamma_i, \psi_i, \eta_i \ge 0, \ i = 1, 2$, that verify the *Feller condition*, $2\gamma_i\psi_i \ge \eta_i^2$, to ensure the processes' positivity.

Here, we choose the two default intensities independent of each other to simplify calculations, but this assumption may be easily removed by adding a further parameter to the correlation structure.

As a shown in [1] assuming a δ-hedging of this product, an appropriate change of probability, we can rewrite in flow notation Eq. (3) as

$$dV_s^{t,x,y,z} = -\left[(1-\alpha_t)\left[-f_t V_s^{t,x,y,z} - LGD_1\lambda_s^{1,t,y}V_s^{t,x,y,z,+} + LGD_2\lambda_s^{2,t,y}V_s^{t,x,y,z,-}\right]\right.$$

$$\left. - \alpha_t c_t V_s^{t,x,y,z} - (r_t - h_t)\frac{\partial V_s^{t,x,y,z}}{\partial S}S_s^{t,x}\right]dt + Z_s^{t,x,y,z}dW_t + d\mathcal{M}_t$$

$$V_T^{t,x} = \Phi(S_T^{t,x}).$$

(4)

Since the triple $(S^{t,x},\lambda^{1,t,y},\lambda^{2,t,z})$ is Markovian, $V_s^{t,x,y,z}$ is a deterministic function of the state variables, $u(s,S_s^{t,x},\lambda_s^{1,t,y},\lambda_s^{2,t,z})$, with $u(t,x,y,z)\in C^{1,2}([0,T]\times\mathbb{R}_+^3)$.

By applying Ito's formula and comparing the two expressions, it can be shown that u verifies the non-linear PDE

$$\begin{cases} \mathcal{L}(u)(t,x,y,z) + (1-\alpha)\left[-LGD_1 yu(t,x,y,z)^+ + LGD_2 zu(t,x,y,z)^-\right] = 0 \\ u(T,x,y,z) = \Phi(x), \end{cases}$$

(5)

where

$$\mathcal{L}(u)(t,x,y,z) = \partial_t u(t,x,y,z) + \gamma_1(\psi_1 - y)\partial_y u(t,x,y,z) + \gamma_2(\psi_2 - z)\partial_z u(t,x,y,z)$$

$$+ hx\partial_s u(t,x,y,z) + \frac{1}{2}\eta_1^2 y\partial_y^2 u(t,x,y,z) + \frac{1}{2}\eta_2^2 z\partial_z^2 u(t,x,y,z) + \frac{1}{2}\sigma^2 x^2\partial_x^2 u(t,x,y,z)$$

$$+ \frac{1}{2}\rho_1\sigma x\eta_1\sqrt{y}\partial_{xy}u(t,x,y,z) + \frac{1}{2}\rho_2\sigma x\eta_2\sqrt{z}\partial_{xz}u(t,x,y,z) - \alpha cu(t,x,y,z)$$

$$- (1-\alpha)fu(t,x,y,z).$$

When considering a triple of stochastic processes, Monte Carlo simulations to approximate Eq. (2) are bound to be extremely costly in terms of machine time, thus we suggest a discretization of (5) that seems to work efficiently in terms of computational times and accuracy.

4   The Method of Lines

The method of lines [11,12,15,16] is a numerical method to solve PDEs by approximating the spatial derivatives with finite differences, so generating a system of ODEs at each point of the discretization grid that can be solved by some method of time integration, such as the one-step Euler method.

The spatial domain $\mathbb{R}_+^3$ is unbounded, so we need to restrict it to an appropriate bounded rectangle $[a_x,b_x]\times[a_y,b_y]\times[a_z,b_z]\subset\mathbb{R}_+^3$. This truncation requires defining appropriate boundary conditions, which can be done exploiting the Black Scholes's pricing function $\phi(t,x;w,\sigma)$, with adjusted rates to include the default intensities

$$u(t,a_x,y,z) = 0, \qquad u(t,b_x,y,z) = \phi(t,b_x;r+\lambda,\sigma),$$
$$u(t,x,a_y,z) = \phi(t,x;r+\lambda,\sigma), \quad u(t,x,b_y,z) = \phi(t,x;r+\lambda,\sigma), \qquad (6)$$
$$u(t,x,y,a_z) = \phi(t,x;r+\lambda,\sigma), \quad u(t,x,y,b_z) = \phi(t,x;r+\lambda,\sigma),$$

We equispaced the three space intervals by taking, $x_i = a_x + i\Delta x$, $y_i = a_y + i\Delta y$, $z_i = a_z + i\Delta z$ with $\Delta x = \frac{(b_x - a_x)}{m}$, $\Delta y = \frac{(b_y - a_y)}{m}$, $\Delta z = \frac{(b_z - a_z)}{m}$ for $i = 0, \ldots, m$, and we apply the finite difference method to the space partial derivatives.

At each grid point x_k, y_i, z_j, the solution $u_{k,i,j}(t)$ verifies the following non-linear ODE

$$u_{k,i,j}(t)' = \mathcal{DL}(u_{k,i,j}) + (1 - \alpha)\big(LGD_1 y_i u_{k,i,j}(t)^+ - LGD_2 z_j u_{k,i,j}(t)^-\big) \quad (7)$$

for $k, i, j = 0, \ldots, m$, and $\mathcal{DL}(u_{k,i,j})$ is the discretized operator of $\mathcal{L}(u)$.

In matrix form

$$\bar{u}(t)' = \mathbf{A}(\bar{x}, \bar{y}, \bar{z})\bar{u}(t) + (1 - \alpha)\big(LGD_1 \bar{y}\bar{u}(t)^+ - LGD_2 \bar{z}\bar{u}(t)^-\big), \quad (8)$$

where $\mathbf{u}(t)', \mathbf{u}(t)$, and $\mathbf{A}(\bar{x}, \bar{y}, \bar{z})$ are a 3-dimensional tensor respectively, and $\bar{x}, \bar{y}, \bar{z}$ are vectors in $\mathbb{R}^{m+1}$ given by

$$\bar{x} = (a_x, x_1, \ldots, x_{m-1}, b_x), \quad \bar{y} = (a_y, y_1, \ldots, y_{m-1}, b_y), \quad \bar{z} = (a_z, z_1, \ldots, z_{m-1}, b_z)$$

and the final condition $u(T, \bar{x}, \bar{y}, \bar{z}) = \bar{\Phi}(x)$ holds, where $\bar{\Phi}(x) = \big(\Phi_0(x), \Phi_1(x), \ldots, \Phi_m(x)\big)$.

To solve the system (8), we use the Euler scheme with N ($0 = t_0 < t_1 < \cdots < t_{N-1} < t_N = T$) time sub-intervals of uniform length $\Delta t = t_{i+1} - t_i$ for $i = 0, \ldots, N - 1$, so we get

$$\bar{u}(t_i) = \bar{u}(t_{i+1}) - \Delta t\big(\mathbf{A}(\bar{x}, \bar{y}, \bar{z})\bar{u}(t_{i+1}) + (1 - \alpha)(LGD_1 \bar{y}\bar{u}(t_{i+1})^+ - LGD_2 \bar{z}\bar{u}(t_{i+1})^-)\big)$$
$$i = 0, \ldots, N - 1. \quad (9)$$

We denote the piecewise approximation of $u(t, x, y, z)$ by $u_{k,i,j}(t)$ for $x \in [x_k, x_{k+1})$, $y \in [y_i, y_{i+1})$, $z \in [z_j, z_{j+1})$ with $i, j, k = 0, \ldots, m - 1$.

For $t = 0$, we are interested in computing the value $u(0, x, y, z)$ for given x, y, z. To do so, we simply choose the closest points of the grid such that $x_k \approx x$, $y_i \approx y$, $z_j \approx z$ for some $k, i, j = 0, \ldots, m$ and we approximate the solution value by $u(0, x_k, y_i, z_j)$.

5   Numerical Results

In this section, we present some numerical results of our method. We study a simplified case when the intensities are deterministic, and we use as a benchmark the results obtained in Brigo et al.'s papers [7] by Monte Carlo simulations, with the same set of parameters. Since in [7] were not reported the machine time, we reproduced their simulations.

In this case, only one state variable, represented by underlying price, is present.

All the algorithms were implemented in MatLab(R2021a).

We consider a European call option with six months maturity, and strike price $K = 90$.

In Table 2 we report the results of our methods with the relative computational times.

Table 2. Prices of a European call with maturity 6 months and deterministic intensities.

Monte Carlo simulations			
N_t	Seconds	Price	by Brigo
10^3	616	16.4454	**16.4534**
Method of lines			
N_x	N_t	Seconds	Price
30	500	0.31	16.4453258
50	500	0.28	16.4272255
90	1000	0.57	16.4643242
150	5000	1.93	16.4555334
200	5000	1.52	16.4568071
300	10000	3.7	16.4574087
500	50000	18.48	16.4574889

As shown in the Table 2, Monte Carlo simulations give 16.4454 in about 10 minutes (fairly close to 16.4543 in [7]), while with 30 nodes, we get a result close to the benchmark with almost nihil computational time. If we want better accuracy with Monte Carlo simulations, we have to increase the number of sample paths, but it implies a high increase in computational time. Differently our method, one might increase the number of spatial and time nodes getting results in less than 20 s. We achieve better performance and comparable accuracy also with respect to [3], where the computational time is about 25 s. By increasing the number of spatial and temporal nodes, the third and fourth digits stabilize, showing the convergence of the method. The first two decimal digits coincide with those obtained by Brigo et al. [7], and we probably achieve better accuracy.

The Fig. 1 shows the surface of value for the European call option in the function of time and stock price.

Here, we show another case when one intensity is diffusive, whether the other is deterministic. We compared these results with the constant intensity case using the same number of nodes and time steps with different maturities.

The Table 3 shows that randomness of the intensity effect that we notice up to the first decimal digit, when maturity increases, confirming it might be significant to consider stochastic intensity models. Moreover, the computational time increased, but it is yet competitive with respect to Monte Carlo simulations. The Fig. 2 show the surfaces of value for the European call option to fixed time $t = 0$, intensity $y = y_0$ and stock price $S = S_0$ respectively.

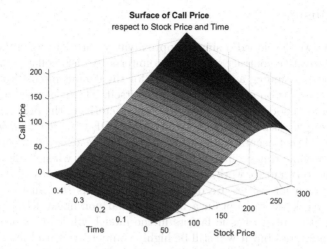

Fig. 1. Surface for a European call option with input arguments: $S_0 \in [50, 300]$, $K = 90$, $r = 0.005$ $\sigma = 0.4$, $\lambda_1 = 0.04$, $LGD_1 = 0.6$, $\lambda_2 = 0.02$, $LGD_2 = 0.6$, $c = 0.002$, $f = r$, $T = 0.5$.

Table 3. Price a European call with different maturities in the deterministic and stochastic case

Maturity	Deterministic case		One stochastic case	
	Seconds	Price	Seconds	Price
6 months	1.73	16.456	3.38	16.445
9 months	2.38	18.675	4.88	18.513
1 year	3.08	20.459	6.43	19.872

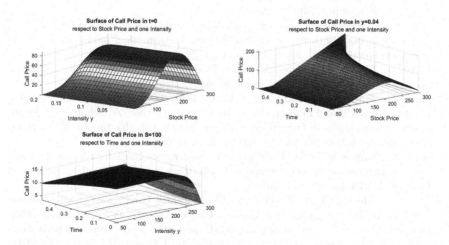

Fig. 2. Surface for a European call option to fixed time $t = t_0$, $y = y_0$ and $S = S_0$ respectively.

6 Conclusion

In this work, we developed a simple approximation procedure for the adjusted value of a derivative contract subject to counterparty risk, collateralization and founding costs, assuming a diffusion model for the default intensities and close-out values as a portion of the adjusted price itself. This generated a non-linear BSDE, with an associated non-linear PDE characterizing the price.

By the simple method of lines applied to this PDE with deterministic intensities, we showed that accurate approximations could be achieved in very manageable computational times, differently from what happens when employing Monte Carlo simulations. Future work will concern the numerical study of the complete model, i.e. when intensities are diffusive processes. As seen in the theoretical part of the work we will obtain a 3-dimensional non-linear PDE. We expect that the addition of stochastic factors in the model will lead to an increase in computational times but it will still be highly competitive with the Monte Carlo simulations machine times, which will be prohibitive. Moreover, we will study a sensitivity analysis and theoretical convergence in the complete case and finally will also regard the implementation of the solver in high-performance computing environments.

References

1. Antonelli, F., Ramponi, A., Scarlatti, S.: Approximate value adjustments for European claims. Eur. J. Oper. Res. **300**(3), 1149–1161 (2021)
2. Antonelli, F., Ramponi, A., Scarlatti, S.: CVA and vulnerable options pricing by correlation expansions. Ann. Oper. Res. **299**(1), 401–427 (2021)
3. Arregui, I., Salvador, B., Vázquez, C.: PDE models and numerical methods for total value adjustment in European and American options with counterparty risk. Appl. Math. Comput. **308**, 31–53 (2017)
4. Arregui, I., Salvador, B., Ševčovič, D., Vázquez, C.: Total value adjustment for European options with two stochastic factors. Mathematical model, analysis and numerical simulation. Comput. Math. Appl. **76**(4), 725–740 (2018)
5. Brigo, D., Liu, Q., Pallavicini, A., Sloth, D.: Nonlinear valuation under collateralization, credit risk, and funding costs. Springer, Heidelberg (2016)
6. Brigo, D., Francischello, M., Pallavicini, A.: Analysis of nonlinear valuation equations under credit and funding effects. In: Glau, K., Grbac, Z., Scherer, M., Zagst, R. (eds.) Innovations in Derivatives Markets. SPMS, vol. 165, pp. 37–52. Springer, Cham (2016). https://doi.org/10.1007/978-3-319-33446-2_2
7. Brigo, D., Francischello, M., Pallavicini, A.: Nonlinear valuation under credit, funding, and margins: existence, uniqueness, invariance, and disentanglement. Eur. J. Oper. Res. **274**(2), 788–805 (2019)
8. Brigo, D., Morini, M., Pallavicini, A.: Counterparty Credit Risk, Collateral and Funding: With Pricing Cases for All Asset Classes, vol. 478. Wiley, Hoboken (2013)
9. Burgard, C., Kjaer, M.: Partial differential equation representations of derivatives with bilateral counterparty risk and funding costs. J. Credit Risk **7**(3), 1–19 (2011)
10. Crépey, S., Bielecki, T.R., Brigo, D.: Counterparty Risk and Funding: A Tale of Two Puzzles. Chapman and Hall/CRC, London (2014)

11. D'Ambrosio, R., Moccaldi, M., Paternoster, B.: Adapted numerical methods for advection-reaction-diffusion problems generating periodic wavefronts. Comput. Math. Appl. **74**(5), 1029–1042 (2017)
12. D'Ambrosio, R., Di Giovacchino, S., Pera, D.: Parallel numerical solution of a 2D chemotaxis-stokes system on GPUs technology. In: Krzhizhanovskaya, V.V., et al. (eds.) ICCS 2020. LNCS, vol. 12137, pp. 59–72. Springer, Cham (2020). https://doi.org/10.1007/978-3-030-50371-0_5
13. Gnoatto, A., Reisinger, C., Picarelli, A.: Deep xVA Solver-A neural network based counterparty credit risk management framework. Available at SSRN 3594076 (2020)
14. Gregory, J.: Counterparty Credit Risk and Credit Value Adjustment: A Continuing Challenge for Global Financial Markets. Wiley, Hoboken (2012)
15. Isaacson, E., Keller, H.B.: Analysis of numerical methods. Courier Corporation (2012)
16. LeVeque, R.J.: Finite difference methods for ordinary and partial differential equations: steady-state and time-dependent problems. SIAM (2007)
17. Jeanblanc, M., Yor, M., Chesney, M.: Mathematical Methods for Financial Markets. Springer, London (2009)
18. Pardoux, E., Râşcanu, A.: Stochastic Differential Equations, Backward SDEs, Partial Differential Equations, vol. 69. Springer, Cham (2014). https://doi.org/10.1007/978-3-319-05714-9
19. Piterbarg, V.: Funding beyond Discounting: Impact of Stochastic Funding and Collateral Agreements and Derivatives Pricing. Risk (2010)

Hermite Parametric Bicubic Patch Defined by the Tensor Product

Vaclav Skala[✉][iD]

Faculty of Applied Sciences, Department of Computer Science and Engineering,
University of West Bohemia, 301 00 Pilsen, Czech Republic
skala@kiv.zcu.cz
http://www.VaclavSkala.eu

Abstract. Bicubic parametric plates are essential for many geometric applications, especially for CAD/CAM systems used in the automotive industry, mechanical and civil engineering applications. Usually the Hermite, Bézier, Coons or NURBS plates are used. There is always a problem to explain how the Hermit bicubic plate is constructed. This contribution describes a novel formal approach to Hermite bi-cubic plate construction using the tensor product.

Keywords: Hermite curve · Hermite bicubic patch · Interpolation · Tensor product · Parametric patches · Kronecker product

1 Introduction

This contribution describes a novel approach for deriving Hermite bicubic parametric patch. Simple and understandable formal derivation of the Hermite is crucial for the understanding it. Especially, within computer graphics and geometric modeling courses, mostly only the mathematical definition is presented. The standard derivation of the Hermite form is quite complex.

The presented approach based on tensor product with linear operators is simple, easy to understand especially convenient for computer graphics and geometric modeling introductory courses. The Bézier parametric patch $S(u, v)$, Bézier [3], is actually based on the tensor product of Bézier curves, i.e. $S(u, v) = C(\mathbf{u}) \otimes C(\mathbf{v})$. In general, cubic parametric curves and bicubic parametric patches are described in Cogen [4], Goldman [6], Prautzsch [11], Holliday [7] and Rockwood [12], etc.

It should be noted, that in the case of the bicubic parametric patches the "border curves" are cubic parametric curves. However, the diagonal and anti-diagonal curves, i.e. for $u = v$ and $u = 1 - v$, the curves are of degree 6. If restrictions to the curve degree 3 are introduced, additional requirements are obtained. Such restrictions were specified in Skala [14, 16] for the Hermite parametric patch and Kolcun [9], Skala [15] for the Bézier parametric patch. Geometric interpretation of the tensor-product diagonal of a Bézier volume was investigated by Holliday and Farin [7]. Triangular patches were desrcibed in Farin [5], Karim [8].

Research supported by the University of West Bohemia - Institutional research support.

2 Tensor Product

The tensor product [19] is not frequently used, however it is very useful. Generally, it is the non-commutative product on two vectors $\mathbf{v} = [v_1, v_2, \ldots, v_n]^T$ and $\mathbf{w} = [w_1, w_2, \ldots, w_m]^T$ defined as:

$$
\mathbf{v} \otimes \mathbf{w} =
\begin{bmatrix}
v_1 w_1 & v_1 w_2 & \cdots & v_1 w_m \\
v_2 w_1 & v_2 w_2 & \cdots & v_2 w_m \\
\vdots & \vdots & \ddots & \vdots \\
v_n w_1 & v_n w_2 & \cdots & v_n w_m
\end{bmatrix}
\tag{1}
$$

The Kronecker product [17], named after the German mathematician Leopold Kronecker (1823–1891), is a generalization of the outer product and a special case of the tensor product [19].

$$
\begin{aligned}
\mathbf{A} \otimes \mathbf{B} &=
\begin{bmatrix} a_{1,1} & a_{1,2} \\ a_{2,1} & a_{2,2} \end{bmatrix} \otimes
\begin{bmatrix} b_{1,1} & b_{1,2} \\ b_{2,1} & b_{2,2} \end{bmatrix} \\
&=
\begin{bmatrix}
a_{1,1} \begin{bmatrix} b_{1,1} & b_{1,2} \\ b_{2,1} & b_{2,2} \end{bmatrix} & a_{1,2} \begin{bmatrix} b_{1,1} & b_{1,2} \\ b_{2,1} & b_{2,2} \end{bmatrix} \\
a_{2,1} \begin{bmatrix} b_{1,1} & b_{1,2} \\ b_{2,1} & b_{2,2} \end{bmatrix} & a_{2,2} \begin{bmatrix} b_{1,1} & b_{1,2} \\ b_{2,1} & b_{2,2} \end{bmatrix}
\end{bmatrix} \\
&=
\begin{bmatrix}
a_{1,1}b_{1,1} & a_{1,1}b_{1,2} & a_{1,2}b_{1,1} & a_{1,2}b_{1,2} \\
a_{1,1}b_{2,1} & a_{1,1}b_{2,2} & a_{1,2}b_{2,1} & a_{1,2}b_{2,2} \\
a_{2,1}b_{1,1} & a_{2,1}b_{1,2} & a_{2,2}b_{1,1} & a_{2,2}b_{1,2} \\
a_{2,1}b_{2,1} & a_{2,1}b_{2,2} & a_{2,2}b_{2,1} & a_{2,2}b_{2,2}
\end{bmatrix}
\end{aligned}
\tag{2}
$$

If the tensor product is applied on differential operators, the following matrix is obtained:

$$
\begin{bmatrix} 1 \\ \frac{\partial}{\partial u} \end{bmatrix} \otimes
\begin{bmatrix} 1 \\ \frac{\partial}{\partial v} \end{bmatrix} =
\begin{bmatrix} 1 & \frac{\partial}{\partial v} \\ \frac{\partial}{\partial u} & \frac{\partial}{\partial u}\left(\frac{\partial}{\partial v}\right) \end{bmatrix} =
\begin{bmatrix} 1 & \frac{\partial}{\partial v} \\ \frac{\partial}{\partial u} & \frac{\partial^2}{\partial u \partial v} \end{bmatrix}
\tag{3}
$$

The tensor and Kronecker products are multilinear [18] and can be also applied on functions Mochizuki [10].

3 Hermite Cubic Curve

The Hermite parametric cubic curve segment uses two end-points x_1, x_2 and two tangential vectors x_3, x_4 of the cubic segment end-points, see Fig. 1.

The position of the point $x(u)$ is given by Eq. 4:

$$
x(u) = a_1 u^3 + a_2 u^2 + a_3 u + a_4
$$

$$
x(u) = \sum_{i=1}^{4} a_i u^{4-i}, \quad u \in <0, 1>
\tag{4}
$$

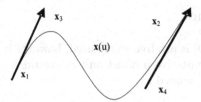

Fig. 1. Hermite cubic curve (tangential vectors shortened)

and the tangent vector $x'(u) = \frac{dx(u)}{du}$ is given by Eq. 5:

$$x^{(u)}(u) = 3a_1u^2 + 2a_2u + a_3$$

$$x^{(u)}(u) = \sum_{i=1}^{3}(4-i)\, a_iu^{3-i}, \quad u \in <0,1> \tag{5}$$

The Eq. 4 can be rewritten using the *dot product* as

$$x(u) = [a_1, a_2, a_3, a_4]^T\, [u^3, u^2, u, 1] = \mathbf{a}^T\mathbf{u} \tag{6}$$

Solving the Eq. 4 and Eq. 5 for the curve segment end-points, i.e. $u = 0$ and $u = 1$ the following system of linear equations is obtained:

$$
\begin{aligned}
x(0) &= a_4 \\
x(1) &= a_1 + a_2 + a_3 + a_4 \\
x^{(u)}(0) &= a_3 \\
x^{(u)}(1) &= 3a_1 + 2a_2 + a_3
\end{aligned}
\tag{7}
$$

where $x^{(u)} = \frac{\partial x}{\partial u}$.

It leads to a system of equations for the unknown coefficients $\mathbf{a} = [a_1, a_2, a_3, a_4]^T$ for the given end-points property

$\boldsymbol{\xi} = [x(0), x(1), x^{(u)}(0), x^{(u)}(1)]^T \stackrel{\text{def}}{=} [x_1, x_2, x_1^{(u)}, x_2^{(u)}]^T.$

$$
\begin{bmatrix} 0 & 0 & 0 & 1 \\ 1 & 1 & 1 & 1 \\ 0 & 0 & 1 & 0 \\ 3 & 2 & 1 & 0 \end{bmatrix}
\begin{bmatrix} a_1 \\ a_2 \\ a_3 \\ a_4 \end{bmatrix}
=
\begin{bmatrix} x_1 \\ x_2 \\ x_1^{(u)} \\ x_2^{(u)} \end{bmatrix}, \quad
\mathbf{Ba} = \boldsymbol{\xi}
\tag{8}
$$

Solving the linear system of equations $\mathbf{Ba} = \boldsymbol{\xi}$, Eq. 7, the coefficients of the Hermite form are obtained.

Then

$$
\begin{aligned}
x(u) &= a_1u^3 + a_2u^2 + a_3u + a_4 = \\
&\quad (\mathbf{B}^{-1}\boldsymbol{\xi})^T\mathbf{u} = \boldsymbol{\xi}^T\mathbf{B}^{-T}\mathbf{u}
\end{aligned}
\tag{9}
$$

where $\mathbf{u} = [u^3, u^2, u, 1]^T$, $\mathbf{B}^{-T}$ is transposed the inverse matrix. Now, the Hermite parametric curve is then described as:

$$x(u) = \boldsymbol{\xi}^T \mathbf{M}_H \mathbf{u}$$

$$= \boldsymbol{\xi}^T \begin{bmatrix} 2 & -3 & 0 & 1 \\ -2 & 3 & 0 & 0 \\ 1 & -2 & 1 & 0 \\ 1 & -1 & 0 & 0 \end{bmatrix} \mathbf{u} = \mathbf{u}^T \mathbf{M}_H^T \boldsymbol{\xi} \tag{10}$$

where $\mathbf{u} = [u^3, u^2, u, 1]^T$, $\mathbf{M}_H = \mathbf{B}^{-1}$ is the matrix of the Hermite form and $\boldsymbol{\xi} = [x(0), x(1), x^{(u)}(0), x^{(u)}(1)]^T \equiv [x_1, x_2, x_1^{(u)}, x_2^{(u)}]^T$ are the control values of the curve $x(u)$.

It should be noted that the Eq. 10 represents only the $x(u)$-coordinate and for the other coordinates, i.e. $y(u)$, $z(u)$, it is similar.

Generally for the E^3 case, for a curve $\mathbf{C}(\mathbf{u})$ we can write:

$$\mathbf{C}(u) = [\mathbf{P}_1, \mathbf{P}_2, \mathbf{P}_3, \mathbf{P}_4]^T \mathbf{M}_H [u^3, u^2, u, 1]$$
$$= [\mathbf{P}_1, \mathbf{P}_2, \mathbf{P}_3, \mathbf{P}_4]^T \mathbf{M}_H \mathbf{u} \tag{11}$$

where $\mathbf{P}_1 = [x_1, y_1, z_1]^T$, $\mathbf{P}_2 = [x_2, y_2, z_2]^T$ are vectors of the curve end-points, $\mathbf{P}_3 = [x_1^{(u)}, y_1^{(u)}, z_1^{(u)}]^T$, $\mathbf{P}_4 = [x_2^{(u)}, y_2^{(u)}, z_2^{(u)}]^T$ are vectors of the tangential vectors at the curve end-points. The Eq. 10 can be rewritten as:

$$\mathbf{C}(u) = [\mathbf{P}_1, \mathbf{P}_2, \mathbf{P}_3, \mathbf{P}_4]^T \mathbf{M}_H \begin{bmatrix} u^3 \\ u^2 \\ u \\ 1 \end{bmatrix}, \tag{12}$$

i.e.

$$\begin{bmatrix} x(u) \\ y(u) \\ z(u) \end{bmatrix} = \begin{bmatrix} x_1^{(u)} & x_2^{(u)} & x_3^{(u)} & x_4^{(u)} \\ y_1^{(u)} & y_2^{(u)} & y_3^{(u)} & y_4^{(u)} \\ z_1^{(u)} & z_2^{(u)} & z_3^{(u)} & z_4^{(u)} \end{bmatrix} \mathbf{M}_H \begin{bmatrix} u^3 \\ u^2 \\ u \\ 1 \end{bmatrix} \tag{13}$$

Note that the Eq. 10 is formally valid also for the Bézier, Catmul, Ferguson, etc. curves, however, the control vector $\boldsymbol{\xi}$ has different properties.

The Bézier curve of the degree n is defined as:

$$^{(B)}x(u) = \sum_{i=0}^{n} x_i \binom{n}{i} u^i (1-u)^{n-i} \tag{14}$$

and the tangential vectors are defined as:

$$x^{(u)}(0) = n(x_1 - x_0) \quad x^{(u)}(1) = n(x_n - x_{n-1}) \tag{15}$$

It can be seen direct connection between the Hermite and Bézier forms. Therefore the Hermite, Bézier, Ferguson, etc. curves are mutually convertible, see Anand [2].

It should be noted, that an invertible matrix $\mathbf{M}_{H \to B}$ (4×4) exists, which transforms the Hermite form to the Bézier form:

$$^{(B)}x(u) = \mathbf{M}_{H \to B} \,\, ^{(H)}x(u) \tag{16}$$

where $^{(B)}x(u)$, resp. $^{(H)}x(u)$ means the x-coordinate of the Hermite cubic curve, resp. Bézier cubic curve, see Anand [2]. Continuity conditions were also studied in Ali [1], Skala [13].

4   Hermite Patch

The Hermite bicubic patch is actually two dimensional case of the multi-variate interpolation. The bicubic parametric patch for the x-coordinate is defined as:

$$x(u, v) = (\sum_{i=1}^{4} a_i u^{4-i})(\sum_{j=1}^{4} b_j v^{4-j})$$

$$= \sum_{i=1}^{4} \sum_{j=1}^{4} a_i b_j \,\, u^{4-i} v^{4-j} \tag{17}$$

$$= \sum_{i=1}^{4} \sum_{j=1}^{4} u^{4-i} \,\, s_{i,j} \,\, v^{4-j}$$

It can be seen that the Eq. 17 can be rewritten as:

$$x(u, v) = \mathbf{u}^T \mathbf{S} \, \mathbf{v} \tag{18}$$

where: $\mathbf{u} = [u^3, u^2, u, 1]^T$, $\mathbf{v} = [v^3, v^2, v, 1]^T$ and the matrix $\mathbf{S}$ has the $s_{i,j}$ elements. Similarly for the y and z-coordinates.

Using the tensor product on functions a simple formula is obtained:

$$x(u, v) = x(u) \otimes x(v) \tag{19}$$

The Eq. 18 describes a parametric patch $x(u, v)$. Each point of the curve $x(u)$ in the Eq. 10 is parameterized by the second parameter v. As the

$$x(u, v) = \mathbf{u}^T \mathbf{M}_H^T \boldsymbol{\xi}(\mathbf{v}) \tag{20}$$

where: $\boldsymbol{\xi}(\mathbf{v}) = [x_1(v), x_2(v), x_1^{(v)}(u), x_2^{(v)}(u)]^T$ It should be noted that all elements of the vector $\boldsymbol{\xi}(\mathbf{v})$ are the Hermite curves again. It means, that

$$\begin{aligned}
x_1(v) &= [x_{11}, x_{12}, x_{11}^{(v)}, x_{12}^{(v)}]\mathbf{M}_H \mathbf{v} \\
x_2(v) &= [x_{21}, x_{22}, x_{21}^{(v)}, x_{22}^{(v)}]\mathbf{M}_H \mathbf{v} \\
x_1^{(v)}(u) &= [x_{11}^{(u)}, x_{12}^{(u)}, x_{11}^{(uv)}, x_{12}^{(uv)}]\mathbf{M}_H \mathbf{v} \\
x_2^{(v)}(u) &= [x_{21}^{(u)}, x_{22}^{(u)}, x_{21}^{(uv)}, x_{22}^{(uv)}]\mathbf{M}_H \mathbf{v}
\end{aligned} \tag{21}$$

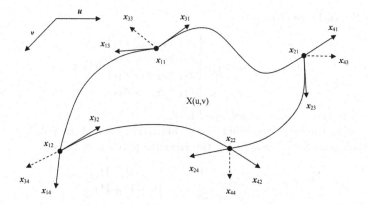

Fig. 2. Hermite bi-cubic patch (tangential and twist vectors scaled)

where $x^{(uv)} \stackrel{\text{def}}{=} \frac{\partial^2 x}{\partial u \partial v}$ and $\mathbf{v} = [v^3, v^2, v, 1]^T$.

Now, the Hermite patch $x(u,v)$ for the x-coordinate can be rewritten as:

$$x(u,v) = \mathbf{u}^T \mathbf{M}_H^T \begin{bmatrix} x_{11} & x_{12} & x_{11}^{(v)} & x_{12}^{(v)} \\ x_{21} & x_{22} & x_{21}^{(v)} & x_{22}^{(v)} \\ x_{11}^{(u)} & x_{12}^{(u)} & x_{11}^{(uv)} & x_{12}^{(uv)} \\ x_{21}^{(u)} & x_{22}^{(u)} & x_{21}^{(uv)} & x_{22}^{(uv)} \end{bmatrix} \mathbf{M}_H \mathbf{v} \tag{22}$$

or using more compact form:

$$x(u,v) = \mathbf{u}^T \mathbf{M}_H^T \mathbf{X} \mathbf{M}_H \mathbf{v} \tag{23}$$

where the matrix $\mathbf{X}$ is the matrix of the control values of the Hermite patch form.

It can be seen, that it is the bi-quadratic form. This formal notation is common for the other bicubic patches, e.g. for the Bézier, Ferguson, etc.

5   Hermite Bicubic Plate Using Tensor Product

The Hermite bicubic plate can be expressed by using tensor product as:

$$\mathbf{S}(u,v) = \mathbf{C}(u) \otimes \mathbf{C}(v) \tag{24}$$

Using the tensor product and more compact form with the block matrix notation:

$$x(u,v) = \mathbf{u}^T \mathbf{M}_H^T \begin{bmatrix} x_{11} & x_{12} & x_{11}^{(v)} & x_{12}^{(v)} \\ x_{21} & x_{22} & x_{21}^{(v)} & x_{22}^{(v)} \\ x_{11}^{(u)} & x_{12}^{(u)} & x_{11}^{(uv)} & x_{12}^{(uv)} \\ x_{21}^{(u)} & x_{22}^{(u)} & x_{21}^{(uv)} & x_{22}^{(uv)} \end{bmatrix} \mathbf{M}_H \mathbf{v} \tag{25}$$

The Eq. 25 can be rewritten to:

$$x(u,v) = \mathbf{u}^T \mathbf{M}_H^T \begin{bmatrix} x_{11} & x_{12} & x_{13} & x_{14} \\ x_{21} & x_{22} & x_{23} & x_{24} \\ x_{31} & x_{32} & x_{33} & x_{34} \\ x_{41} & x_{42} & x_{43} & x_{44} \end{bmatrix} \mathbf{M}_H \mathbf{v} \qquad (26)$$

where x_{ij} are the control values, see Fig. 2.

Now, using the tensor product and a submatrix 4×4 of the patch end-points a more "compact form" describing the Hermite patch is obtained as:

$$\mathbf{P}(u,v) = \mathbf{u}^T \mathbf{M}_H^T \begin{bmatrix} 1 & \frac{\partial}{\partial y} \\ \frac{\partial}{\partial u} & \frac{\partial^2}{\partial u \partial v} \end{bmatrix} \otimes \begin{bmatrix} \mathbf{P}_{11} & \mathbf{P}_{12} \\ \mathbf{P}_{21} & \mathbf{P}_{22} \end{bmatrix} \mathbf{M}_H \mathbf{v}$$

$$= \mathbf{u}^T \mathbf{M}_H^T \begin{bmatrix} \begin{bmatrix} \mathbf{P}_{11} & \mathbf{P}_{12} \\ \mathbf{P}_{21} & \mathbf{P}_{22} \end{bmatrix} & \frac{\partial}{\partial v} \begin{bmatrix} \mathbf{P}_{11} & \mathbf{P}_{12} \\ \mathbf{P}_{21} & \mathbf{P}_{22} \end{bmatrix} \\ \frac{\partial}{\partial u} \begin{bmatrix} \mathbf{P}_{11} & \mathbf{P}_{12} \\ \mathbf{P}_{21} & \mathbf{P}_{22} \end{bmatrix} & \frac{\partial^2}{\partial u \partial v} \begin{bmatrix} \mathbf{P}_{11} & \mathbf{P}_{12} \\ \mathbf{P}_{21} & \mathbf{P}_{22} \end{bmatrix} \end{bmatrix} \mathbf{M}_H \mathbf{v} \qquad (27)$$

If the differential tensor operator Eq. 3 is applied on the Hermit bicubic corners, the matrix form is obtained as follows:

$$\begin{bmatrix} 1 & \frac{\partial}{\partial y} \\ \frac{\partial}{\partial u} & \frac{\partial^2}{\partial u \partial v} \end{bmatrix} \otimes \begin{bmatrix} \mathbf{P}_{11} & \mathbf{P}_{12} \\ \mathbf{P}_{21} & \mathbf{P}_{22} \end{bmatrix}$$

$$= \begin{bmatrix} \begin{bmatrix} \mathbf{P}_{11} & \mathbf{P}_{12} \\ \mathbf{P}_{21} & \mathbf{P}_{22} \end{bmatrix} & \frac{\partial}{\partial v} \begin{bmatrix} \mathbf{P}_{11} & \mathbf{P}_{12} \\ \mathbf{P}_{21} & \mathbf{P}_{22} \end{bmatrix} \\ \frac{\partial}{\partial u} \begin{bmatrix} \mathbf{P}_{11} & \mathbf{P}_{12} \\ \mathbf{P}_{21} & \mathbf{P}_{22} \end{bmatrix} & \frac{\partial^2}{\partial u \partial v} \begin{bmatrix} \mathbf{P}_{11} & \mathbf{P}_{12} \\ \mathbf{P}_{21} & \mathbf{P}_{22} \end{bmatrix} \end{bmatrix} \qquad (28)$$

$$= \begin{bmatrix} \mathbf{P}_{11} & \mathbf{P}_{12} & \frac{\partial}{\partial u}\mathbf{P}_{11} & \frac{\partial}{\partial u}\mathbf{P}_{12} \\ \mathbf{P}_{21} & \mathbf{P}_{22} & \frac{\partial}{\partial y}\mathbf{P}_{21} & \frac{\partial}{\partial y}\mathbf{P}_{22} \\ \frac{\partial}{\partial v}\mathbf{P}_{11} & \frac{\partial}{\partial v}\mathbf{P}_{12} & \frac{\partial^2}{\partial u \partial v}\mathbf{P}_{11} & \frac{\partial^2}{\partial u \partial v}\mathbf{P}_{12} \\ \frac{\partial}{\partial v}\mathbf{P}_{21} & \frac{\partial}{\partial v}\mathbf{P}_{22} & \frac{\partial^2}{\partial u \partial v}\mathbf{P}_{21} & \frac{\partial^2}{\partial u \partial v}\mathbf{P}_{22} \end{bmatrix}$$

It can be seen that this matrix clearly shows the Hermite form properties.

It should be noted that the Hermite bicubic parametric patch can be converted to the Bézier bicubic patch similarly as in the case of cubic curves, see Anand [2].

6 Conclusion

This contribution presents a different approach for the Hermite cubic curve and Hermite bicubic patch definition using the tensor product, as the tensor product might be applied not only on vectors and matrices, but also on functions. Unfortunately, especially in computer graphics courses, vector or matrix formulation is presented only, without deeper derivation of the formulas.

The derivation of the Hermite form using the tensor matrix operations is more understandable, especially in the case of the Hermite bicubic patch.

Acknowledgement. The author would like to thank colleagues at the University of West Bohemia for hints provided, to students and colleagues at the University of West Bohemia, Plzen and VSB-Technical University, Ostrava for their recent suggestions, to anonymous reviewers for their critical comments and recommendations that improved this paper significantly.

References

1. Ali, F., Karim, S., Dass, S., Skala, V., Saaban, A., Hasan, M., Hashim, I.: New cubic timmer triangular patches with C^1 and G^1 continuity. J. Teknol. **81**(6), 1–11 (2019). https://doi.org/10.11113/jt.v81.13759
2. Anand, V.B.: Computer Graphics and Geometric Modeling for Engineers, 1st edn. John Wiley & Sons Inc., New York (1993)
3. Bézier, P.: The mathematical basis of the UNIURF CAD system. Butterworth-Heinemann (1986). https://doi.org/10.1016/C2013-0-01005-5
4. Cohen, E., Riesenfeld, R., Elber, G.: Geometric Modeling with Splines: An Introduction. A K Peters/CRC Press, Boca Raton (2019)
5. Farin, G.: Chapter 18 - bézier triangles. In: Farin, G. (ed.) Curves and Surfaces for Computer-Aided Geometric Design (3rd Edn.), pp. 321–351. Academic Press, Boston (1993). https://doi.org/10.1016/B978-0-12-249052-1.50023-4
6. Goldman, R.: An Integrated Introduction to Computer Graphics and Geometric Modeling, 1st edn. CRC Press Inc., Boca Raton (2009)
7. Holliday, D., Farin, G.: Geometric interpretation of the diagonal of a tensor-product Bézier volume. Comput. Aided Geom. Des. **16**(8), 837–840 (1999). https://doi.org/10.1016/S0167-8396(99)00004-7
8. Karim, S.A.A., Saaban, A., Skala, V., Ghaffar, A., Nisar, K.S., Baleanu, D.: Construction of new cubic Bézier-like triangular patches with application in scattered data interpolation. Adv. Differ. Equ. **2020**(1), 1–22 (2020). https://doi.org/10.1186/s13662-020-02598-w
9. Kolcun, A.: Biquadratic S-Patch in Bézier form. In: WSCG 2011 proceedings 2019, pp. 201–207 (2011). http://wscg.zcu.cz/DL/wscg_DL.htm
10. Mochizuki, N.: The tensor product of function algebras. Tohoku Math. J. **17**(2), 139–146 (1965). https://doi.org/10.2748/tmj/1178243579
11. Prautzsch, H., Boehm, W.: Geometric Concepts for Geometric Design. A K Peters/CRC Press, Boca Raton (1993). https://doi.org/10.1201/9781315275475
12. Rockwood, A., Chambers, P.: Interactive Curves and Surfaces: A Multimedia Tutorial on CAGD, 1st edn. Morgan Kaufmann Publishers Inc., San Francisco (1996)
13. Skala, V.: New geometric continuity solution of parametric surfaces. AIP Conf. Proc. **1558**, 2500–2503 (2013). https://doi.org/10.1063/1.4826048
14. Skala, V., Ondracka, V.: S-Patch: Modification of the Hermite parametric patch. In: ICGG 2010–14th International Conference on Geometry and Graphics, pp. 255–262 (2010)
15. Skala, V., Ondracka, V.: BS-patch: constrained Bézier parametric patch. WSEAS Trans. Math. **12**(5), 598–607 (2013)
16. Skala, V., Smolik, M., Ondracka, V.: HS-patch: a new Hermite smart bicubic patch modification. J. Int. J. Math. Comput. Simul. **8**, 292–299 (2014)
17. Wikipedia contributors: Kronecker product – Wikipedia, the free encyclopedia (2021). https://en.wikipedia.org/wiki/Kronecker_product. Accessed 7 Oct 2021
18. Wikipedia contributors: Multilinear polynomial – Wikipedia, the free encyclopedia (2021). https://en.wikipedia.org/wiki/Multilinear_polynomial
19. Wikipedia contributors: Tensor product – Wikipedia, the free encyclopedia (2021). https://en.wikipedia.org/wiki/Tensor_product. Accessed 7 Oct 2021

Comparative Compression Robustness
Evaluation of Digital Image Forensics

Oliver Remy, Sebastian Strumegger, Jutta Hämmerle-Uhl, and Andreas Uhl[(⊠)]

Visual Computing and Security Lab (VISEL), Department of Artificial Intelligence and Human Interfaces, University of Salzburg, Salzburg, Austria
uhl@cs.sbg.ac.at

Abstract. The robustness of two important digital image forensic tasks (i.e. SIFT-based copy-move forgery detection and PRNU-based camera sensor identification) against four different lossy compression techniques is investigated (while typically, only JPEG compression is considered) to identify the best suited technique for this application scenario. Overall, we find that the accuracy of forensic tasks is reduced for increasing compression strength as expected, however, the relative performance of the compression schemes is different for the two tasks. While JPEG is superior for realistic application settings (where accuracy is in an acceptable range) in SIFT-based copy-move forgery detection, JPEG XR and BPG provide the best option for PRNU-based camera sensor identification, whereas JPEG is clearly impacting this forensic application most severely.

1 Introduction

In the past, images were considered as most authentic source of information – with increasing popularity and the availability of low-cost image editing software such as Adobe photoshop, corel paint shop, GIMP and recent techniques to produce "deep fakes", the truthfulness of an image can no longer be taken for granted. Among other forgery types, copy move forgery and object removal forgery are the most prominent ones. In a *copy move forgery*, a part of the image itself is copied and pasted into another part of the same image to conceal an important object or information, or to conceal that an object has been removed from the image in an *object removal forgery*. In most cases of image forgery, it is extremely difficult to distinguish between an original image and the forged one. Therefore, it is required to develop methods/techniques to assess the authenticity of an image – Digital Image Forensics (DIF [1]) has served this purpose to a large extent. Whenever an image is forged, there are some traces which are left behind in the forged image. These traces are useful for the forensic researcher to detect a forgery.

A wide range of DIF forgery detection techniques have been established in the recent years [2–5]. Besides recent deep learning based schemes [6,7], techniques relying on Scale Invariance Feature Transform (SIFT) keypoints have been shown to be effective. In particular, SIFT keypoints (and other local texture descriptors) have been proposed to reveal copy move forgeries [3,8–10] and image cloning [11], as well as to detect copyrighted material using CBIR techniques [12].

Another important DIF task is camera device identification and device linking. Besides its use in forgery detection [13], the photo response non-uniformity

O. Gervasi et al. (Eds.): ICCSA 2022, LNCS 13376, pp. 236–246, 2022.
https://doi.org/10.1007/978-3-031-10450-3_19

(PRNU [14]) of an imaging sensor has emerged as an important forensic tool for the realisation of these tasks. Slight variations among individual pixels during the conversion of photons to electrons in digital image sensors are considered as the source of the PRNU; thus, it is an intrinsic property which forms an inherent part of all digital imaging sensors and their output, respectively. All digital image sensors cast this weak, noise-like pattern into each and every image they capture. The most prominent way how to compute the PRNU is due to Fridrich in [15], the method describes how to estimate the PRNU image from set of images taken by the same camera, the PRNU estimator is derived using a maximum likelihood estimator (MLE), the MLE is modeled from the simplified sensor output model [15].

Typically, DIF techniques rely on subtle changes or properties in an image. Therefore, lossy compression is a "natural enemy" of such techniques as it removes high-frequency detail and thus can be considered an anti-forensic technique itself (e.g. robustness of copy-move detection under high compression is reduced [16, 17], as it is the case for forensic image age approximation [18] and PRNU-based camera identification [19]). This is the reason why the detection of JPEG compression [20] is considered to be important for DIF, while corresponding anti-forensic techniques have already been developed to remove forensically significant indicators of compression from an image [21, 22]. Also, the detection of recompression/double compression [23] is often intepreted as an indicator for image manipulation as the originally JPEG-compressed images might have undergone a second JPEG compression stage after image manipulation has taken place. Taken these observations together, it is obvious that techniques have been developed to increase the compression robustness for forensic techniques [24–26].

When talking about lossy compression, papers seen so far deal almost exclusively with lossy JPEG. In this paper, we look at the question of DIF compression robustness from a different perspective: We consider four different lossy compression schemes, i.e. JPEG, JPEG2000 (J2K), JPEG XR, and BPG (a H.265 derivative), and compare their impact on the DIF compression robustness. The aim is to answer the question which compression technique is favorable in case least impact of DIF is desired, and to also learn which technique is best suited to conceal forensic traces (in order to raise alarm in case this compression format is observed). For the experimental investigation we consider SIFT-based copy-move detection and PRNU-based camera identification as our target DIF techniques.

Section 2 reviews the applied SIFT-based copy-move detection and PRNU-based camera identification techniques, respectively. In Sect. 3, we briefly characterize the employed lossy compression tools. Section 4 describes the experimental settings and presents corresponding results on compression robustness. Section 5 concludes the paper and provides an outlook to future work in this direction.

2 Digital Image Forensics

2.1 SIFT-Based Copy-Move Detection

To detect a copy-move forgery, SIFT keypoints are computed together with their descriptors and then for each keypoint the two nearest neighbours from all remaining keypoints are identified using a K-d tree based on Euclidean distance d_1 and d_2 (where

d_1 and d_2 are distances and d_1 corresponds to the closest neighbour) [27]. $T \in (0,1)$ defines the fraction of distances d_1 and d_2 used to assess the relation between the the nearest neighbours. [28] and [29] suggested that there is a match only if $\frac{d_1}{d_2} < T$ holds. In these papers $T = 0.6$ but we looked also into results for $T = 0.53$. To classify if an image is forged or not, agglomerative hierarchical clustering is applied to the spatial locations ((x, y) coordinates) of the keypoints. This method creates a hierarchy of clusters which can be represented by means of a tree structure. If there are two or more clusters with at least n matched keypoints, these regions are considered cloned.

2.2 PRNU-Based Camera Identification

The PRNU (i.e. sensor fingerprint) can be obtained as follows:

$$\hat{K} = \sum_{i=1}^{N} R_i I_i \bigg/ \sum_{i=1}^{N} I_i^2 \tag{1}$$

where the PRNU is denoted by $\hat{K}$ which is a noise-like signal carrying the PRNU. I_i is an image and R_i is the noise residual of an image which is obtained by (Eq. 2), note that i stands for the i th image out of N images which have been taken from a particular sensor (see Fig. 1a).

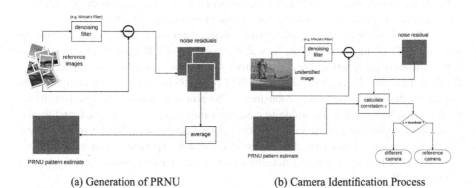

(a) Generation of PRNU   (b) Camera Identification Process

Fig. 1. Schematic workflow of PRNU-based camera identification.

The residual image R_i is calculated by subtracting the original image from a denoised version of the image obtained by applying e.g. a wavelet denoising filter to an original image:

$$R_i = I_i - F(I_i) \tag{2}$$

where F denotes the denoising method. Eventually, a Wiener Filter (WF) [30] is applied additionally.

To detect whether the Residual of an image I (R_I) is taken by the sensor with PRNU estimator $\hat{K}$, we use normalized cross-correlation (NCC), which is illustrated in Fig. 1b:

$$\rho_{[R_I, I\hat{K}]} = NCC(R_I, I\hat{K}) \tag{3}$$

NCC as well as Peak Correlation Energy (PCE) have been proposed [15] as similarity metrics.

3   Lossy Image Compression Techniques

We consider three different ISO/IEC (lossy) image compression standards for increasing compression rates (i.e. ratio between original file size and file size after compression) using the respective default configurations unless stated otherwise:

1. JPEG (JPG): The well-known (ISO/IEC IS 10918-1) DCT-based image compression method [31]. By adjusting the divisors in the quantization phase, different compression ratios can be achieved. We adjust the quality parameter iteratively to achieve a file size closest to the desired compression rate.
2. JPEG 2000 (J2K): The wavelet-based image compression standard (ISO/IEC IS 15444-1) can operate also at higher compression ratios [32]. J2K is also a part of the DICOM standard where it replaced lossless JPEG compression. Results typically do not generate block-based artifacts as the original DCT-based JPG standard. J2K facilitates explicit rate control, i.e. target bitrates are met with high accuracy.
3. JPEG-XR (JXR): This compression standard based on Microsoft's HD Photo is known to produce higher quality than JPEG, but provides faster compression than JPEG 2000 [33]. In the default configuration the Photo Overlay/Overlap Transformation is only applied to high pass coefficients prior to the Photo Core Transformation (ISO/IEC IS 29199-2). We adjust quantization levels iteratively to achieve a target bitrate closest to the desired one.

Additionally, we use the "Better Portable Graphics" (BPG) algorithm which is based on a subset of the H.265 (HEVC, ISO/IEC 23008-2) video compression standard [34]. We adjust quantisation levels iteratively to achieve a target bitrate closest to the desired one.

While comparisons of these algorithms' compression performance wrt. image quality metrics are difficult to identify (except for specific image types, e.g. medical images [35]), application oriented comparisons have been done before, e.g. in biometrics (iris [36] and ear recognition [37], respectively) and in document image compression [38,39], and promising results have been obtained for JXR and in particular for BPG.

4   Experiments

4.1   Experimental Settings

Concerning image compression, we use Imagemagick and NConvert for the three ISO standards and the BPG image library and utilities[1].

---

[1] https://bellard.org/bpg/.

Fig. 2. Compression example from the CoMoFoD public dataset.

Figure 2 displays the application of JPEG, JXR, and J2K to an example image of the CoMoFoD public dataset (see below) using compression ratio 60. The typical JPEG block artefacts and colour inconsistencies are clearly visible in the leftmost image. For the JXR case (middle image) we also notice some blocking artefacts while colouring is fine. The rightmost J2K case is a bit more blurry as compared to JXR while the colour display is equally well.

(a) True positive   (b) False positive

Fig. 3. Examples from the CoMoFoD public dataset.

For copy-move detection, forged images are taken from the CoMoFoD public dataset for assessing forensic techniques [40], which contain simple translated copies of objects/regions. The 200 images of the small image category (512×512) have been used, however, we removed 58 of them as these indicated inconsistent results due to identical object parts within distinct objects. OpenCV[2] was used to compute SIFT keypoints and descriptor distances, while hierarchical clustering was implemented in Python. We consider compression ratios of up to 100 in steps of 10 - for some images,

---

[2] http://opencv.org/.

it was not possible to achieve the higher rates using JPEG; in this case, the affected images have been discarded for all compression schemes to maintain comparability. Figure 3 shows two examples of identified SIFT keypoint matches where Fig. 3b shows an example where the result incorrectly suggests the presence of a copy-move attack.

For PRNU-based camera identification tests we used a subset of the Dresden Image Database [41] containing images of one Afga 505 x, Canon Ixus 55, Nikon D70, and Sony H50 each, plus images from two Canon Ixus 70. Experiments have been done using software from the Matlab version of the Camera Fingerprint Library[3]. We consider compression ratios of 1.25, 1.66, 2.5, 5, 10.0, and 20.0.

4.2 Experimental Results

In Figs. 4 and 5 we visualise the effect of increasing compression strength on the accuracy the copy-move detection process (two different parameter settings as given in the figure are used).

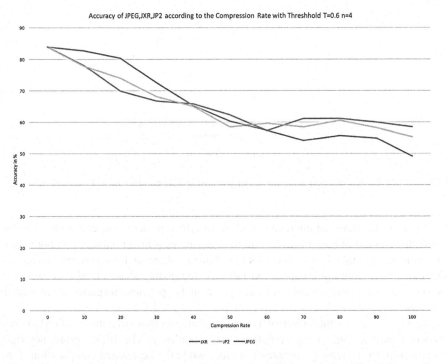

Fig. 4. Copy-move detection accuracy under increasing J2K compression ($T = 0.6, n = 4$).

For both settings, we observe clear trends: (i) For increasing compression strength, copy-move detection accuracy is decreasing. (ii) Up to compression ratio of 40, JPEG

---

[3] https://dde.binghamton.edu/download/camera_fingerprint/.

compression delivers accuracy superior to the other two compression schemes, for higher compression ratios above 70, JXR and J2K are clearly better. However, an accuracy of 60% for a binary decision is only slightly above guessing, so that this scenario is hardly realistic in practice.

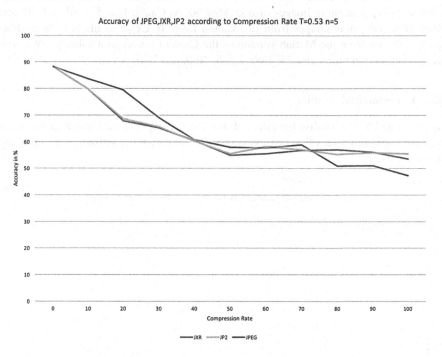

Fig. 5. Copy-move detection accuracy under increasing J2K compression ($T = 0.53$, $n = 5$).

Figure 6 illustrates an interesting additional effect of increasing compression ratio: While the amount of false positives and false negatives is rather balanced without compression being applied, we clearly notice that the share of false positive detections decreases for increasing compression ratio. A dominating share of false negatives is problematic for a forensic technique, as most actual copy-move forgeries are missed in this case.

In Fig. 7, we see the effect of increasing compression strength on PRNU-based camera identification, where we notice a clear tendency: The JPEG results detoriate significantly for increasing compression ratio, while the best suited compression techniques for this application case are JXR and BPG with J2K ranging in-between. Overall, this task suffers already significantly for moderate compression ratios as applied in our experiments.

(a) $T = 0.53$, $n = 5$

(b) $T = 0.6$, $n = 4$

Fig. 6. Distribution of false negatives vs. false positives under increasing compression.

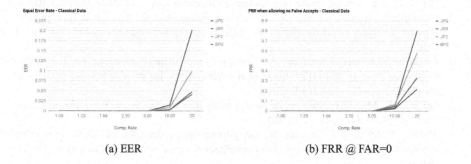

(a) EER

(b) FRR @ FAR=0

Fig. 7. Camera identification results under increasing compression.

5   Conclusion

We have investigated the robustness of two important digital image forensic tasks against JPEG, JPEG XR, JPEG 2000, and BPG lossy compression. SIFT-based copy-move forgery detection and PRNU-based camera sensor identification are considered. While it is expected that the accuracy of forensic tasks is reduced for increasing compression strength, the relative performance of the compression schemes turns out to be different for the two tasks. While JPEG is superior for realistic application settings (where accuracy is in an acceptable range) in SIFT-based copy-move forgery detection, JPEG XR and BPG provide the best option for PRNU-based camera sensor identification, whereas JPEG is clearly impacting this forensic application most severely. When considering the properties of the two investigated forensic applications, this result could have been expected: SIFT is a very robust algorithm, and not by chance SIFT keypoints are also used in content-based retrieval applications. Additionally, artefacts generated in the same way in copied areas may additionally assist in the respective detection. When the image quality gets too poor, the other algorithms take the lead, however, the overall accuracy is already relatively low. On the other hand, PRNU and noise residuals are noise-like signals and severely impacted by the overall much lower compression performance of JPEG. For this reason all three other compression schemes turn out to be superior for this forensic application case.

Future work will include the consideration of JPEG XL as well as deep learning-based lossy compression schemes to observe their respective performance in a forensic context.

Acknowledgments. The authors gratefully acknowlege the contribution of the further Media Data Formats Lab students Max Göttl, Christoph Schwengler, Dennis Strähhuber, Benedikt Streitwieser, and Tim Ungerhofer. This work has been partially supported by the Salzburg State Government project "Artificial Intelligence in Industrial Vision Salzburg".

References

1. Sencar, H.T., Memon, N.: Digital Image Forensics: There is More To a Picture than Meets the Eye. Springer Verlag, New York (2012). https://doi.org/10.1007/978-1-4614-0757-7
2. Ardizzone, E., Bruno, A., Mazzola, G.: Detecting multiple copies in tampered images. In: 2010 IEEE International Conference on Image Processing, pp. 2117–2120. IEEE (2010)
3. Christlein, V., Riess, C., Jordan, J., Riess, C., Angelopoulou, E.: An evaluation of popular copy-move forgery detection approaches. IEEE Trans. Inf. Forensics Secur. 7(6), 1841–1854 (2012)
4. Zandi, M., Mahmoudi-Aznaveh, A., Mansouri, A.: Adaptive matching for copy-move forgery detection. In: 2014 IEEE International Workshop on Information Forensics and Security (WIFS), pp. 119–124. IEEE (2014)
5. Mushtaq, S., Mir, A.H.: Image copy move forgery detection: a review. Int. J. Future Gener. Commun. Netw. 11(2), 11–22 (2018)
6. Abdalla, Y., Iqbal, M.T., Shehata, M.: Copy-move forgery detection and localization using a generative adversarial network and convolutional neural-network. Information 10, 286 (2019)

7. Wu, Y., Abd-Almageed, W., Natarajan, P.: BusterNet: detecting copy-move image forgery with source/target localization. In: Ferrari, V., Hebert, M., Sminchisescu, C., Weiss, Y. (eds.) ECCV 2018. LNCS, vol. 11210, pp. 170–186. Springer, Cham (2018). https://doi.org/10. 1007/978-3-030-01231-1_11

8. Huang, H.-Y., Ciou, A.-J.: Copy-move forgery detection for image forensics using the superpixel segmentation and the Helmert transformation. EURASIP J. Image Video Process. **2019**(1), 1–16 (2019). https://doi.org/10.1186/s13640-019-0469-9

9. Pavlović, A., Glišović, N., Gavrovska, A., Reljin, I.: Copy-move forgery detection based on multifractals. Multimed. Tools Appl. **78**(15), 20655–20678 (2019). https://doi.org/10.1007/ s11042-019-7277-1

10. Bilal, M., Habib, H.A., Mehmood, Z., Yousaf, R.M., Saba, T., Rehman, A.: A robust technique for copy-move forgery detection from small and extremely smooth tampered regions based on the DHE-SURF features and mDBSCAN clustering. Australian J. Forensic Sci. **53**, 1–24 (2020)

11. Saleem, M.: A key-point based robust algorithm for detecting cloning forgery. In: IEEE International Conference on Control System, Computing and Engineering (ICCSCE), vol. 4, pp. 2775–2779 (2014)

12. Do, T.T., Kijak, E., Furon, T., Amsaleg, L.: Deluding image recognition in SIFT-based CBIR systems. In: Proceedings of the 2nd ACM Workshop on Multimedia in Forensics, Security and Intelligence, pp. 7–12. ACM (2010)

13. Chierchia, G., Poggi, G., Sansone, C., Verdoliva, L.: PRNU-based forgery detection with regularity constraints and global optimization. In: 2013 IEEE 15th International Workshop on Multimedia Signal Processing (MMSP), pp.236–241 (2013)

14. Lukas, J., Fridrich, J., Goljan, M.: Digital camera identification from sensor pattern noise. IEEE Trans. Inf. Forensics Secur. **1**(2), 205–214 (2006)

15. Fridrich, J.: Digital image forensics. IEEE Signal Process. Mag. **26**(2), 26–37 (2009)

16. Huang, D.Y., Huang, C.N., Hu, W.C., Chou, C.H.: Robustness of copy-move forgery detection under high jpeg compression artifacts. Multimed. Tools Appl. **76**, 1509–1530 (2015)

17. Huang, D.Y., Huang, C.N., Hu, W.C., Chou, C.H.: Robustness of copy-move forgery detection under high jpeg compression artifacts. Multimedia Tools Appl. **76**(1), 1509–1530 (2017)

18. Joechl, R., Uhl, A.: Effects of image compression on image age approximation. In: 20th International Workshop on Digital-forensics and Watermarking (IWDW2021), Beijing, China (2021)

19. Goljan, M., Chen, M., Comesara, P., Fridrich, J.: Effect of compression on sensor-fingerprint based camera identification. Electron. Imaging. Media Watermark. Secur. Forensics **2016**, 1–10 (2016)

20. Kumawat, C., Pankajakshan, V.: A robust jpeg compression detector for image forensics. Signal Process. Image Commun. **89**, 116008 (2020)

21. Stamm, M.C., Liu, K.R.: Anti-forensics of digital image compression. IEEE Trans. Inf. Forensics Secur. **6**(3), 1050–1065 (2011)

22. Stamm, M.C., Tjoa, S.K., Lin, W.S., Liu, K.R.: Undetectable image tampering through jpeg compression anti-forensics. In: 2010 IEEE International Conference on Image Processing, pp. 2109–2112 (2010)

23. Lu, W., Zhang, Q., Luo, S., Zhou, Y., Huang, J., Shi, Y.Q.: Robust estimation of upscaling factor on double jpeg compressed images. IEEE Trans. Cybern. 1–13 (2021)

24. Diallo, B., Urruty, T., Bourdon, P., Fernandez-Maloigne, C.: Robust forgery detection for compressed images using CNN supervision. Forensic Sci. Int. Rep. **2**, 100112 (2020)

25. Diallo, B., Urruty, T., Bourdon, P., Fernandez-Maloigne, C.: Improving robustness of image tampering detection for compression. In: MMM 2019: MultiMedia Modeling, Thessaloniki, Greece, January 2019

26. Mandelli, S., Bonettini, N., Bestagini, P., Tubaro, S.: Training CNNs in presence of jpeg compression: Multimedia forensics vs computer vision. In: 2020 IEEE International Workshop on Information Forensics and Security (WIFS), pp. 1–6 (2020)
27. Amerini, I., Ballan, L., Caldelli, R., Del Bimbo, A., Serra, G.: A sift-based forensic method for copy-move attack detection and transformation recovery. IEEE Trans. Inf. Forensics Secur. 6(3), 1099–1110 (2011)
28. Mahdian, B., Saic, S.: Detection of copy-move forgery using a method based on blur moment invariants. Forensic Sci. Int. 171(2–3), 180–189 (2007)
29. Huang, H., Guo, W., Zhang, Y.: Detection of copy-move forgery in digital images using SIFT algorithm. In: Pacific-Asia Workshop on Computational Intelligence and Industrial Application, 2008. PACIIA 2008, vol. 2, pp. 272–276. IEEE (2008)
30. Mihcak, M.K., Kozintsev, I., Ramchandran, K.: Spatially adaptive statistical modeling of wavelet image coefficients and its application to denoising. In: Proceedings of 1999 IEEE International Conference on Acoustics, Speech, and Signal Processing, 1999, vol. 6, pp. 3253–3256. IEEE (1999)
31. Pennebaker, W., Mitchell, J.: JPEG - Still Image Compression Standard. Van Nostrand Reinhold, New York (1993)
32. Taubman, D., Marcellin, M.: JPEG2000 – Image Compression Fundamentals. Standards and Practice. Kluwer Academic Publishers, The Nethrlands (2002)
33. Dufaux, F., Sullivan, G.J., Ebrahimi, T.: The JPEG XR image coding standard. IEEE Signal Process. Mag. 26(6), 195–199 (2009)
34. Li, F., Krivenko, S., Lukin, V.: An approach to better portable graphics (BPG) compression with providing a desired quality. In: 2020 IEEE 2nd International Conference on Advanced Trends in Information Theory (ATIT), pp. 13–17 (2020)
35. Liu, F., Hernandez-Cabronero, M., Sanchez, V., Marcellin, M.W., Bilgin, A.: The current role of image compression standards in medical imaging. Information 8(4), 131 (2017)
36. Hofbauer, H., Rathgeb, C., Wagner, J., Uhl, A., Busch, C.: Investigation of better portable graphics compression for iris biometric recognition. In: Proceedings of the International Conference of the Biometrics Special Interest Group (BIOSIG 2015), Darmstadt, Germany, p. 8 (2015)
37. Rathgeb, C., Busch, C., Wagner, J., Pflug, A.: Effects of image compression on ear biometrics. IET Biom. 5(3), 252–261 (2016)
38. Darwiche, M., Pham, T.A., Delalandre, M.: Comparison of jpeg's competitors for document images. In: 2015 International Conference on Image Processing Theory, Tools and Applications (IPTA), pp. 487–493 (2015)
39. Wild, P., Štolc, S., Valentín, K., Daubner, F., Clabian, M.: Compression effects on security document images. In: 2016 European Intelligence and Security Informatics Conference (EISIC), pp. 76–79 (2016)
40. Ardizzone, E., Bruno, A., Mazzola, G.: Copy-move forgery detection by matching triangles of keypoints. IEEE Trans. Inf. Forensics Secur. 10(10), 2084–2094 (2015)
41. Gloe, T., Böhme, R.: The Dresden image database for benchmarking digital image forensics. In: SAC 2010: Proceedings of the 2010 ACM Symposium on Applied Computing, pp. 1584–1590ACM (2010)

ECG-Based Heartbeat Classification for Arrhythmia Detection Using Artificial Neural Networks

Eduardo Cepeda[1]([✉])[iD], Nadia N. Sánchez-Pozo[2][iD],
Diego H. Peluffo-Ordóñez[3][iD], Juan González-Vergara[2][iD],
and Diego Almeida-Galárraga[1][iD]

[1] School of Biological Sciences and Engineering, Universidad Yachay Tech,
Urcuquí 100119, Ecuador
eduardo.cepeda@sdas-group.com
[2] Smart Data Analysis Systems Group (SDAS Research Group), 47963 Ben Guerir,
Morocco
[3] Modeling, Simulation and Data Analysis (MSDA) Research Program,
Mohammed VI Polytechnic University, Lot 660, Hay Moulay Rachid,
43150 Ben Guerir, Morocco
http://www.sdas-group.com

Abstract. Cardiovascular disease (CVD) has quickly grown in prevalence over the previous decade, becoming the major cause of human morbidity on a global scale. Due to the massive number of ECG data, manual analysis is regarded as a time-consuming, costly and prone to human error task. In the other hand, computational systems based on biomedical signal processing and machine learning techniques might be suited for supporting arrhythmia diagnostic processes, while solving some of those issues. In general, such systems involve five stages: acquisition, preprocessing, segmentation, characterization, and classification. Yet numerous fundamental aspects remain unresolved, including sensitivity to signal fluctuation, accuracy, computing cost, generalizability, and interpretability. In this context, the present study offers a comparative analysis of ECG signal classification using two artificial neural networks created by different machine learning frameworks. The neural nets were built into a pipeline that aims to strike an appropriate balance among signal robustness, variability, and accuracy. The proposed approach reaches up to 99% of overall accuracy for each register while keeping the computational cost low.

Keywords: ANN · ECG · Multi layer perceptron · Neural network

1 Introduction

Cardiovascular disease (CVD) has quickly grown in prevalence over the previous decade, becoming the major cause of human morbidity on a global scale [1]. It is estimated to account for 30% of fatalities globally [4]. Cardiac arrhythmia is

O. Gervasi et al. (Eds.): ICCSA 2022, LNCS 13376, pp. 247–259, 2022.
https://doi.org/10.1007/978-3-031-10450-3_20

a particular CVD that refers to an irregular heartbeat. Although the majority of arrhythmias are harmless, some are dangerous or even life-threatening [2]. For example, atrial fibrillation may result in strokes and cardiac arrest [3], which is very hazardous and should be treated promptly. Additionally, the expense of cardiovascular disease-related therapies, including medicine, is quite expensive [5]. The electrocardiogram (ECG) is the most often used measuring technique for diagnosing CDV and is the primary tool for diagnosing CVD both in and out of hospitals. An ECG signal is made up of a sequence of periodic beats that depict the electrical activity of the heart throughout time [6].

Currently, the enormous amount of ECG data makes manual analysis by physicians a time-consuming, costly, and prone to human error activity [7]. Additionally, ECG signals are often constituted of several frequency components and even noise, which complicates the task of extracting discriminative features manually, so it is recommended to use an artificial intelligence-based technique.

Wavelet shape transforms (WT) or short-time Fourier transforms are employed for this propose; in general, WT produces more accurate time-frequency analysis findings than Fourier transform. As a result, computational system that include biomedical signal processing and machine learning techniques are well suited for this job supporting arrhythmia diagnosis processes [8]. In general, these systems provide aid with machine learning at five stages: acquisition, preprocessing, beat segmentation, characterization, and classification. There are a variety of methods for classifying ECG signal beats for these purposes.

Some studies have addressed the cardiac arrhythmia identification problem from the perspective of classical machine learning pipelines [9,10]. Various techniques, including artificial neural networks, support vector machines, multi-view based learning, and linear discriminates, are utilized for these goals [11]. Despite these approaches superior performance, some fundamental concerns like as sensitivity to signal fluctuation, accuracy, computing cost, generalizability, and interpretability remain unresolved. With the fats development of artificial neural networks in recent years, approaches based on machine learning have garnered more interest.

This article presents a comparative analysis of ECG signals processing approaches in this respect. To this end, an artificial neural network technique capable of identifying and categorizing cardiac arrhythmia-related beats is created and developed within a framework that finds an optimum balance between signal robustness, variability, and accuracy. To develop an automated approach for ECG signal categorization based on multi layer perceptron technique and artificial neural network (ANN). Where ANN is a machine learning technique that is capable of simulating the human visual system and has been effectively used to image classification and video recognition [12,13].

The ECG beat signal is transformed into the time-frequency domain using continuous wavelet transform (CWT) [13,14], and features are extracted from the 2D scalogram consisting of the previously decomposed time frequency components using ANN. To fully use all available information for ECG signal classification, we extract and combine RR interval features into our ANN. This is accomplished with the assistance of the MIT-BIH arrhythmia database [15]. The created technique is compared to current and suggested multi layer perceptron technique in the literature [16]. Comparative analysis of EEG signal processing approach enables the optimal trade-off between robustness, signal variability, and accuracy. In comparison to typical machine learning systems, the ANN technique are promising.

The following is the organization of the paper. Section 2 discusses the currently available approaches. Section 3 discusses the suggested approach for classifying ECG signals. Section 4 contains the results. Section 5 contains the discussion and conclusion of the results. This paper closes with Sect. 5.

2   Existing Methods

Alaa Sheta et al. [17] diagnosed obstructive sleep apnea from ECG signals using machine learning and deep learning classifiers, achieving an accuracy of up to 86.25%. Alaa Sheta et al. used the following popular classifiers: decisio tree (DT), linear discriminate analysis (LDA), k-nearest neighbors (KNN), logistic regression (LR), Naive Bayes (NB), support vector machine (SVM), ensemble decision tree (EDT), and boosted tress (BT).

2.1   Convolutional Neural Network (CNN)

Serkan K. et al. [18] provide an overview of the primary signal processing applications that use CNNs. The research reveals that using a methodical methodology, CNNs may attain a performance of up to 97.6% with minimum computing complexity. Xiaolong Z. et al. [19] utilizes a double beat ECG coupling matrix to propose a CNN based framework for heartbeat categorization. This two-dimensional encoded dual beat ECG coupling matrix effectively represents both the morphology and rhythm of the heartbeat. The suggested technique was validated against the MIT-BIH database and demonstrated more than 90% accuracy.

2.2   K Nearest Neighbour (KNN)

Vedavathi G et al. [20] Propose a classification method for cardiac arrhythmias based on the K-Nearest Neighbor (K-NN) classifier. This method involves phases such as data preprocessing, module extraction, and feature classification. This approach is applied to the MIT-BIH database of ECG signals, which are then categorized using the KNN method. The dataset achieves a classification accuracy of 98.4%, illustrating the accuracy of K-NN classifiers.

2.3   Deep Neural Network (DNN)

Raghu N et al. [21] classified arrhythmias based on ECG signals using Deep neural networks. They compared their results to those obtained using neural network (NN) and support vector machine (SVM) approaches, which produced much lower results than the DNN classifier. The suggested DNN classifier is used to execute 100 iterations on the MIT-BIH database, obtaining an accuracy of around 98.33%. The authors conclude that by properly characterizing the data, it is essential to increase the suggested method's accuracy.

2.4 Fog Computing Based (FCB)

Alessandro S. et al. [22] assessed the end-to-end method's capacity to recognize beats and categorize them into four categories: normal beats, supraventricular ectopic beats (VEBs), and ventricular ectopic beats. Beats generated from the fusion of normal and VEBs, as well as any beats that do not belong into the MIT-BIH arrythmia database's N, S, V, or F classifications. The resultant method obtains an accuracy of 89.1% in classifying arrhythmias. These findings are significant because the suggested technique minimizes power consumption by using hardware assisted execution of machine learning algorithms.

3 Methodology

3.1 Comparative Methodology

Artificial learning has become the most widely used artificial intelligence technique in recent years, making significant improvements in a variety of fields, including voice recognition, computer vision, and image processing [12,13]. Artificial intelligence approaches have shown their ability to significantly cut time and physical labor. Concentrating on artificial intelligence technologies, the literature has several uses for ECG data [17]. To facilitate cardiovascular health management, the majority of these approaches use artificial neural networks in ECG diagnosis [18–21].

To do this, a ECG signal monitoring method is carried out in a pipeline that aims to strike an appropriate balance between the signal's resilience and variability and accuracy. The proposed machine learning process, as shown in Fig. 1, identifies beats associated with cardiac arrhythmias through several preprocessing, segmentation, and characterization techniques. The resulting data is then fed to the neural nets, which are compared for better performance.

3.2 Database

The code for this work is written in Python and utilizes the MIT-BIH arrhythmia database as a reference dataset for evaluating the ANN and multilayer perceptron technique for developing comparative research. The MIT-BIH arrhythmia database is a freely accessible dataset that contains the data essential for detecting cardiac arrhythmias with 48 half-hourly two-channel ambulatory ECG recordings from 47 participants are included in the database, 23 records were chosen D analog ECG recordings [15].

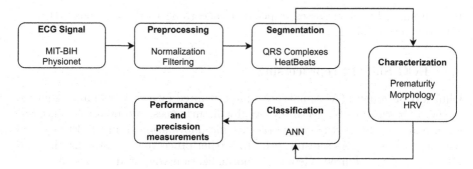

Fig. 1. Diagram depicting the steps for detecting cardiac arrhythmias. This identifies beats associated with cardiac arrhythmias through acquisition, preprocessing, segmentation, characterization, and classification techniques.

The remaining 25 records were collected from prior ambulatory ECG recordings and similarly exhibit rare but clinically severe arrhythmias. Each record has two leads and operates at a sampling rate of 360 samples per second with a resolution of 11 bits in the range of 10 mv ECG signals. The first lead is modified lead II (ML II), while the second lead is one of the following: lead VI, VII, V2, V4, or V5. Due to the prevalence of ML II in recordings, we will utilize it to classify ECGs in this study. Two or more cardiologists name each tape independently and classify into one of fifteen arrhythmia categories. As shown in Table 1 the annotations used are those from the original MIT-BIH database, which have

Table 1. Main categories of beats present in the MIT-BIH database. Where you can see the division of the superclasses N, SVEB, VEB, F and Q respectively.

Group	Annotation	Description
N	N	Normal beat
Any heartbeat not categorized as	L	Left bundle branch block beat
SVEB, VEB, F or Q	R	Right bundle branch block beat
	e	Atrial escape beat
	j	Nodal (junctional) escape beat
SVEB	A	Atrial premature beat
Supraventricular ectopic beat	a	Aberrated atrial premature beat
	S	Supraventricular premature beat
	J	Nodal (junctional) premature beat
VEB	V	Premature ventricular contraction
Ventricular ectopic beat	E	Ventricular escape beat
	!	Ventricular flutter wave
F - Fusion beat	F	Fusion of ventricular and normal beat
Q	Q	Unclassifiable beat
Unknown beat	/	Paced beat
	f	Fusion of paced and normal beat

been grouped by superclasses respectively according to the previous article by Eduardo Jose et al. [23].

3.3 ECG Signal Preprocessing

Clinically obtained ECG signals are often disrupted by a variety of noise sources, including baseline drift, electromyography disturbances, and power line interference, making it impossible to extract usable information from the ECG signal without processing. As a result, prior to further processing, a normalization and filtering step is required. Geometric normalization was used to normalize the signals in question [24], as expressed in Eq. (1). This normalization reduces the signal to noise ratio. The term $E\{s\}$ denotes the expectation operator, the arithmetic mean is considered in the instance is considered, correcting for the impact of a zero-mean transformation.

$$s \leftarrow \frac{s - E\{s\}}{\max |s|} \tag{1}$$

Due to the fact that excessive filtering would result in the loss of vital information, we eliminate just the noise: the baseline deviation, which has a significant effect on the categorization of ECG signals. The patient's respiration or movement causes base-line drift. In accordance with prior work [25], a simple 1s window with overlap filter is used to decrease signal disruptions and artifacts. The influence of noise on the ECG signal is seen in Fig. 2. In comparison to other filtering approaches, the simple 1s window with overlap filter effectively removes outliers without causing phase distortion [26].

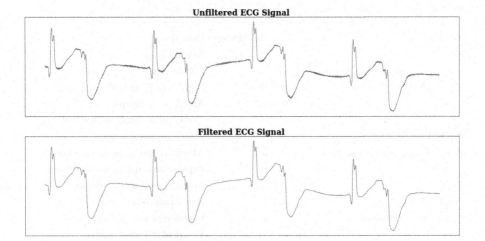

Fig. 2. ECG signal filtering impact

3.4   Hearbeat and QRS Segmentation

To correctly segment individual beats from the ECG signal, the QRS waves and beat reference points must be detected [27]. Numerous studies in the literature demonstrate that this procedure has a success rate of more than 99% [29]. The R peak is used as a reference point in this experiment, and the ECG signal is divided as shown in Eqs. (2) and (3).

$$b_i = y(p_i - 0.3RR_i : p_i - 0.6RR_i) \tag{2}$$

and

$$c_i = y(p_i - \alpha\ F_s : p_i + \beta\ F_s), \tag{3}$$

where p_i denotes the location of the i-th beat's R peak, p_i denotes the i-th beat's QRS complex, RR denotes the vector storing the distance between the R_i peaks, and Fs is the frequency of the vector v between places a and b ($b > a$). Because the times are derived from a dynamic variable, the duration of each extracted time is unique. The complexes were extracted using a 200 ms window width and centered on the R peak it means $\alpha = \beta = 0.1$ s. As seen in Fig. 3, these positions correspond to the most significant beat waves.

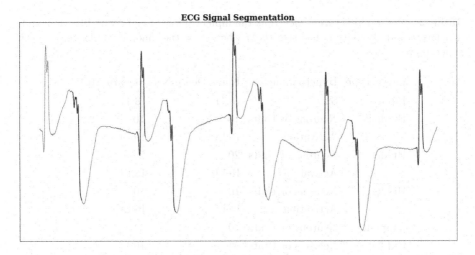

Fig. 3. ECG signal segmentation of QRS complexes.

Typically, arrhythmia alter not only the form of the pulse, but also the surrounding RR intervals (also knowns as peak R intervals). As a result, we include RR interval data into our ANN for ECG categorization. Three extensively utilized characteristics of RR intervals are extracted. The anterior RR interval is the time interval between the current and future beats. The RR ratio is the difference between the previous and subsequent RRs. The local RR is calculated as the average of the current beat's 10 prior RR intervals. To remove interpatient variance, the anterior RR, posterior RR, and local RR have been subtracted from the mean RR interval.

3.5   Classification of ECG Signals Using Neural Networks

To address the objective, the open source, low-code machine learning library PyCaret was used [28], from which two ANN were created to automatically extract possible relationships between various arrhythmias and regular heartbeats. The first ANN was built using [30], `MLPClassifier` function. All hyperparameters were set as default except for the following: `alpha` $= 1 \cdot 10^{-5}$, `hidden_layer_sizes` $= (10,20,10)$, `max iter` $= 500$. The second ANN was built using [31] sequential `Dense Layer`. All hyperparameters were set as default except for the following: `epochs` $= 500$, `batch_size` $= 100$, `loss` = categorical_crossentropy, `optimizer` = adam, `metrics` = accuracy. In both cases, given that Rectified learning unit (ReLU) activation function minimizes the model's computational complexity, increases its statistical efficiency and reaches nonlinear capabilities, it was chosen for most of the layers. In comparison to other optimizers, Adam often accelerates the network training process. Details of each model architectures are displayed in Table 2 and Fig. 4.

Table 2. ANN architectures, such that the input consist of eight variables, four hidden layers and the output has size $(k, 1)$ where $k =$ the amount of classes for each supergroup.

Layer Type	Hyperparameter	Keras Dense NN	Sklearn MLP
Input	Size	(8,1)	(8,1)
Hidden	Neurons or Units	10	10
	Activation	ReLU	ReLU
Hidden	Neurons or Units	20	20
	Activation	ReLU	ReLU
Hidden	Neurons or Units	10	10
	Activation	ReLU	ReLU
Dropout	Neurons or Units	10	-
Hidden	Neurons or Units	9	10
	Activation	Softmax	ReLU
Output	Size	$(k, 1)$	$(k, 1)$

4   Results

Our method offers an accuracy rate of up to 99% utilizing machine learning and a simple and easy to understand neural network (ANN) for the same application. Although existing approaches usually anticipate discriminative features,

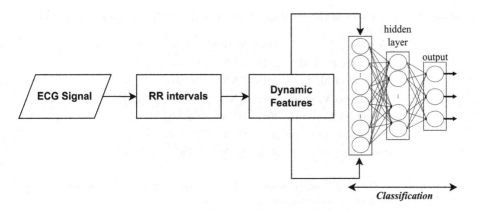

Fig. 4. Artificial neural network classification. Where is appreciated ECG signal, RR intervals, Dynamic Features and ANN Classification with their input, hidden and output layers respectively.

Table 3. ANN performance

Register	Precision	Recall	F1_score	Error	Accuracy
118	97.64	97.80	97.65	0.020	0.98
124	99.49	99.75	99.62	0.002	1.00
217	98.94	98.94	98.94	0.015	0.99
Overall	98.69	98.83	98.74	0.012	0.99

our method uses ANN and compares with the multilayer perceptron technique, which shows a much better appreciation of the results, moreover, the following Table 3 show the performance of the ANN structure, employing the 8 records of the analog recording F of the MIT-BIH Arrhythmia Database and performing the average of all the records used.

Also, the Table 4 compares the performance of the results with other authors who used different classifiers. The records of database recording D were chosen because they have a big variety of data that easily cluster into the superclasses (see Table 1), in addition to the records having a considerable and imbalanced variety compared to the other database recordings of the MIT-BIH Arrhythmia. With machine learning approaches, the ANN methodology is not sophisticated, is of low computing cost and achieves competitive accuracy with earlier studies where more complex and computationally expensive techniques are utilized (see Table 4). One of the key benefits achieved from our technique is related to the grouping by superclasses, which makes our neural network cheap computational cost, non-complex, competitive and achieves an accuracy of up to 99%.

Finally, the comparison of our methodology ANN-based keras dense with sklearn MLP classification method was undertaken, which yielded promising results, despite being a more complicated neural network than the suggested

Table 4. Performance of the results with other authors who used different classifiers.

Author	Year	Method	Accuracy	Reference
Kiranyaz S. et al.	2019	CNN	97.60%	[18]
Zahi X. et al.	2018	CNN	90.00%	[19]
Rangappa V. et al.	2018	KNN	98.40%	[20]
Meshram V. et al.	2017	DNN	98.33%	[21]
Scire A. et al.	2019	FCB	89.10%	[22]
Our method	2022	ANN	99%	

Table 5. Keras Dense NN and sklearn MLP comparison. Where the precision, Recall and F1-score of each class are found

Record	Class	Keras Dense NN			Sklearn MLP		
		Precision	Recall	F1-score	Precision	Recall	F1-score
118	N	0.98	0.99	0.99	0.98	1.00	0.99
	SVEB	0.77	0.61	0.68	0.86	0.64	0.73
	VEB	1.00	0.60	0.75	0.75	0.60	0.67
124	N	1.00	1.00	1.00	1.00	1.00	1.00
	SVEB	0.00	0.00	0.00	0.00	0.00	0.00
	VEB	1.00	1.00	1.00	1.00	1.00	1.00
217	N	0.99	1.00	0.99	0.97	0.99	0.98
	Q	0.99	1.00	1.00	1.00	1.00	1.00
	VEB	0.96	0.92	0.94	0.94	0.92	0.93

one. It can be observed from the Table 5 that, despite adopting a non-complex and cheap computing cost strategy, our method is competitive and produces outstanding results.

5   Discussion and Conclusion

This work classifies distinct forms of cardiac arrhythmias using ANN-based deep learning characteristics. The approach takes advantage of ANN's capability for feature representation, which is a nonlinear dimensionality reduction technique that is frequently utilized in machine learning. Obtaining the signal from the database, signal preprocessing, and signal segmentation are critical for this goal. Additionally, the effect of various strategies utilized for the same aim is examined. Our ANN-based technique can automatically extract discriminative features from data as a representation learning method. QRS segmentation of the signal is required for this purpose, with the peak R serving as a reference point. To validate this capacity, the accuracy score is employed, thereby comparing it with the multilayer perceptron machine learning approach and establishing that the suggested method is better.

To conclude, this study proposes the building of a machine learning technique capable of identifying cardiac arrhythmias. A comparison of the model described in this work to some of the approaches presently available in the literature reveals a good outcome. This model correctly diagnoses several kinds of cardiac arrhythmias using ACC classification, with an accuracy of up to 99%. Additionally, this strategy requires little computing resources. The manner in which this study was conducted enables comparison between multilayer perceptron classification techniques and the suggested approach, which produces promising results with an accuracy comparable to conventional methods.

As a future work, both new characterization (including wavelet transform), and classification approaches will be explored. Also, techniques for adding interpretability as well as lowering computational cost are to be incorporated in further releases of the software.

Acknowledgments. The authors would like to acknowledge the valuable support given by the SDAS Research Group (https://sdas-group.com/).

References

1. Radha, R., Shahzadi, S.K., Al-Sayah, M.H.: Fluorescent immunoassays for detection and quantification of cardiac troponin I: a short review. Molecules. **26**(16), 4812 (2021). https://doi.org/10.3390/molecules26164812
2. Wongthida, T., Lumkul, L., Patumanond, J., Wongtheptian, W., Piyayotai, D., Phinyo, P.: Development of a clinical risk score for prediction of life-threatening arrhythmia events in patients with ST elevated acute coronary syndrome after primary percutaneous coronary intervention. Int. J. Environ. Res. Public Health **19**(4), 1997 (2022). https://doi.org/10.3390/ijerph19041997
3. Kelley, R.E., Kelley, B.P.: Heart-brain relationship in stroke. Biomedicines. **9**(12), 1835 (2021). https://doi.org/10.3390/biomedicines9121835
4. Shaghiera, A.D., Widiyanti, P., Yusuf, H.: Synthesis and characterization of injectable hydrogels with varying collagen-chitosan-thymosin $\beta4$ composition for myocardial infarction therapy. J. Func. Biomater. **9**(2), 33 (2018). https://doi.org/10.3390/jfb9020033
5. Patel, P., et al.: Improved blood pressure control to reduce cardiovascular disease morbidity and mortality: the standardized hypertension treatment and prevention project. J. Clin. Hypertens. **18**(12), 1284–1294 (2016). https://doi.org/10.1111/jch.12861
6. Sannino, G., de Pietro, G.: A deep learning approach for ECG-based heartbeat classification for arrhythmia detection. Future Gener. Comput. Syst. **86**, 446–455 (2018). https://doi.org/10.1016/j.future.2018.03.057
7. Vizitiu, A., Nita, C.I., Toev, R.M., Suditu, T., Suciu, C., Itu, L.M.: framework for privacy-preserving wearable health data analysis: proof-of-concept study for atrial fibrillation detection. Appl. Sci. **11**(19), 9049 (2021). https://doi.org/10.3390/app11199049
8. Sraitih, M., Jabrane, Y., el Hassani, A.H.: An automated system for ECG arrhythmia detection using machine learning techniques. J. Clin. Med. **10**(22), 5450 (2021). https://doi.org/10.3390/jcm10225450

9. Vargas-muñoz, A.M., Chamorro-sangoquiza, D.C., Umaquinga-criollo, A.C.: Diseño de un prototipo de bajo coste computacional para detección de arritmias cardiacas, pp. 470–480 (2020)

10. Rodríguez-Sotelo, J.L., Peluffo-Ordoñez, D., Cuesta-Frau, D., Castellanos-Domínguez, G.: Unsupervised feature relevance analysis applied to improve ECG heartbeat clustering. Comput. Methods Programs Biomed. **108**(1), 250–261 (2012). https://doi.org/10.1016/J.CMPB.2012.04.007

11. Sansone, M., Fusco, R., Pepino, A., Sansone, C: Electrocardiogram pattern recognition and analysis based on artificial neural networks and support vector machines: a review (2013). http://www.sciencedirect.com/

12. Tripathy, S., Singh, R.: Convolutional neural network: an overview and application in image classification. In: Poonia, R.C., Singh, V., Singh Jat, D., Diván, M.J., Khan, M.S. (eds.) Proceedings of Third International Conference on Sustainable Computing. AISC, vol. 1404, pp. 145–153. Springer, Singapore (2022). https://doi.org/10.1007/978-981-16-4538-9_15

13. Wang, J., Yang, Y., Mao, J., Huang, Z., Huang, C, Xu, W.: CNN-RNN: a unified framework for multi-label image classification (2016)

14. Ghorbanian, P., Ghaffari, A., Jalali, A., Nataraj, C.: Heart arrhythmia detection using continuous wavelet transform and principal component analysis with neural network classifier. Comput. Cardiol. **2010**, 669–672 (2010)

15. Moody, G.B., Mark, R.G.: The impact of the MIT-BIH arrhythmia database. IEEE Eng. Med. Biol. Mag. **20**(3), 45–50 (2001). https://doi.org/10.1109/51.932724

16. Ramkumar, M, Ganesh Babu, C., Vinoth Kumar, K., Hepsiba, D., Manjunathan, A., Sarath Kumar, R.: ECG cardiac arrhythmias classification using DWT, ICA and MLP neural networks. J. Phys. Conf. Ser. **1831**(1), 012015 (2021). https://doi.org/10.1088/1742-6596/1831/1/012015

17. Sheta, A., et al.: Diagnosis of obstructive sleep apnea from ECG signals using machine learning and deep learning classifiers. Appl. Sci. **11**(14), 6622 (2021). https://doi.org/10.3390/app11146622

18. Kiranyaz, S., Ince, T., Abdeljaber, O., Avci, O., Gabbouj, M.: 1-D convolutional neural networks for signal processing applications. In: ICASSP, IEEE International Conference on Acoustics, Speech and Signal Processing - Proceedings, May 2019, vol. 2019, pp. 8360–8364 (2019). https://doi.org/10.1109/ICASSP.2019.8682194

19. Zhai, X., Tin, C.: Automated ECG classification using dual heartbeat coupling based on convolutional neural network. IEEE Access **6**, 27465–27472 (2018). https://doi.org/10.1109/ACCESS.2018.2833841

20. Rangappa, V.G., Prasad, S.V.A.V., Agarwal, A.: Classification of cardiac arrhythmia stages using hybrid features extraction with K-nearest neighbour classifier of ECG signals. Int. J. Intell. Eng. Syst. **11**(6), 21–32 (2018). https://doi.org/10.22266/IJIES2018.1231.03

21. Nanjundegowda, R., Meshram, V.A.: Arrhythmia detection based on hybrid features of T-wave in Electrocardiogram. Int. J. Intell. Eng. Syst. **11**(1), 153–162 (2018). https://doi.org/10.22266/ijies2018.0228.16

22. Scirè, A, Tropeano, F., Anagnostopoulos, A., Chatzigiannakis, I.: Fog-computing-based heartbeat detection and arrhythmia classification using machine learning. Algorithms. 12(2), 32 (2019). https://doi.org/10.3390/a12020032

23. Luz, E.J.S., Schwartz, W.R., Cámara-Chávez, G., Menotti, D.: ECG-based heartbeat classification for arrhythmia detection: a survey. Comput. Methods Progr. Biomed. **127**, 144–164 (2016). https://doi.org/10.1016/j.cmpb.2015.12.008

24. Patro, K.K., Kumar, P.R.: De-noising of ECG raw signal by cascaded window based digital filters configuration. In: 2015 IEEE Power, Communication and Information Technology Conference, PCITC 2015 - Proceedings, March 2016, pp. 120–124 (2016). https://doi.org/10.1109/PCITC.2015.7438145
25. Blanco-Velasco, M., Weng, B., Barner, K.E.: ECG signal denoising and baseline wander correction based on the empirical mode decomposition. Comput. Biol. Med. **38**(1), 1–13 (2008). https://doi.org/10.1016/j.compbiomed.2007.06.003
26. Pinto, J.R., Cardoso, J.S., Lourenço, A., Carreiras, C.: Towards a continuous biometric system based on ECG signals acquired on the steering wheel. Sensors **17**(10), 2228 (2017). https://doi.org/10.3390/s17102228
27. Lourenço, A., Silva, H., Leite, P., Lourenço, R., Fred, A.: Real time electrocardiogram segmentation for finger based ECG biometrics. In: BIOSIGNALS 2012 - Proceedings of the International Conference on Bio-Inspired Systems and Signal Processing, pp. 49–54 (2012). https://doi.org/10.5220/0003777300490054
28. Ali, M.: PyCaret: an open source, low-code machine learning library in Python, PyCaret version 1.0.0, April 2020. https://www.pycaret.org
29. Oweis, R., Oweis, R.J., Al-Tabbaa, B.O.: QRS detection and heart rate variability analysis: a survey. Biomed. Sci. Eng. **2**(1), 13–34 (2014). https://doi.org/10.12691/bse-2-1-3
30. Pedregosa, F., et al.: Scikit-learn: machine learning in Python. J. Mach. Learn. Res. **12**, 2825–2830 (2011)
31. Chollet, F.: Keras: the python deep learning library. Astrophys. Source Code Libr. ASCL-1806 (2018)

Modelling the Drivers of Urban Densification to Evaluate Built-up Areas Extension: A Data-Modelling Solution Towards Zero Net Land Take

Anasua Chakraborty[1]([✉]) [ID], Hichem Omrani[2] [ID], and Jacques Teller[1] [ID]

[1] University of Liege, Liege, Belgium
A.Chakraborty@uliege.be
[2] LISER, Luxembourg University, Esch-sur-Alzette, Luxembourg

Abstract. The impact of urbanization is determined by the amount of land taken and the intensity with which it is used, such as soil sealing and population density. Land take can be referred to the loss of agricultural, forest, and other semi-natural and natural land to urban and other artificial land development. It is closely linked to urban expansion. City centers play an important role to curb such land take issues in allocating the growing population through urban densification. In order to assess how built-up, environmental, and socio-economic factors impacts zero net land take, this paper aims at using Multinomial regression model (MLR) to evaluate the built-up densification. This model is built, calibrated, and validated for the area of Brussels Capital region and its peripheral Brabant's using cadastral data. Three 100×100 m built-up maps are created for 2000, 2010 and 2020 where the map for 1990–2000 were used for calibration and was further validated using 2000–2010 maps. The causative factors are calibrated using MLR and validated using ROC curve and goodness of fit. The results show that areas at closer periphery of the city center with high densities have high probability for allocating further growth as they provide a broad range of facilities and local services along with an established connectivity infrastructure. This can be observed as a pragmatic solution for the policy makers and urban planners to achieve the intended policy of "zero net land take".

Keywords: Urban densification · Multinomial logistic regression · Zero land take

1 Introduction

In the recent few years, there has been an exponential growth in the demand of developed land worldwide [1, 7]. The prime reason for this demand is due to the urban lifestyle that require more space per capita for residential use, and the increased competition between municipalities to attract new developments for economic gain [14]. From the standpoint of sustainability, these demands affect the preservation of growth potential for future generations, thus enhancing problems related to urbanization [8]. While urbanization

© The Author(s), under exclusive license to Springer Nature Switzerland AG 2022
O. Gervasi et al. (Eds.): ICCSA 2022, LNCS 13376, pp. 260–270, 2022.
https://doi.org/10.1007/978-3-031-10450-3_21

causes economic growth and increase in real estate pricing, the underlying problem of urbanization lies within housing shortages to accommodate a growing population [3]. This increase in housing density can influence land take and other related problem such as soil quality, land degradation and citizen's social experience [5].

Land take is defined as "the loss of agricultural, forest, and other semi-natural and natural land to urban and other man-made land development" [6]. The concept behind the EU "No net land take 2050" relates land take as the balance between taken and recultivated lands. The rate of rise in land take is substantially quicker than the rate of increase in population [10]. Land take is influenced by a variety of factors, including demography, socio-economic development, and environmental factors (Fig. 1).

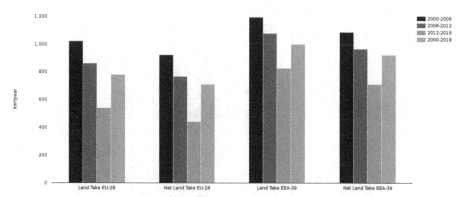

Fig. 1. Area of land take and net land take for all Corine Land Cover observation periods between 2000–2018 for the EU-28 and EEA-39 regions (Source: EEA, Europa)

In Europe, cities are becoming less dense, thus facing slower urban redevelopment and regeneration. In addition, land take can be related to urban sprawl either in the form of low density or dispersed development [13]. Land take also occurs outside of urban and peri-urban areas, thus developing high fragmentation [16]. A better understanding of underlying mechanisms of land take can be associated with urban densification [15] to aide in the EU28 "No net land take 2050" program.

The objective of this paper is to evaluate the drivers of urban densification can be viewed as a strategy for increasing the efficiency of utilizing natural resources while also bringing out a more efficient use of the city core. A multinomial logistic regression (MNL) was employed to explore the relationship between land take and densification.

2   Materials and Methods

2.1   Study Area

The selected study area (Fig. 2) comprises of Capital region of Brussels, Vlaams Brabant and Walloon Brabant. This area has been selected for its high geographical and political importance. It covers an area of 3376 km^2 which is 11% of total area of Belgium. To present an idea of the study area, Brussels Capital region is a highly clustered area with population of 2,109,631 which has grown almost by 0.78% within a span of five years. On the other hand, the area of Walloon Brabant comprises of a small cluster of urban cores with mostly peri urban landscapes. According to EEA report on Urban sprawls, Belgium is one of the two greatest hubs of urban sprawl with a weighted urban proliferation index greater than 6 (Urban permeation unit) UPU/m^2 [6]. This is because of the mixed landscape of dense urban core towards the north especially in Flanders and highly fragmented rural area in the south in Wallonia. Thus, urban sprawl limits the scope for more sustainable land use as it follows a ribbon and scattered pattern both in Flanders and Wallonia. In this context, densification policies are important to limit the increasing land take off and strategi the urban sprawl in an effective and sustainable way [5].

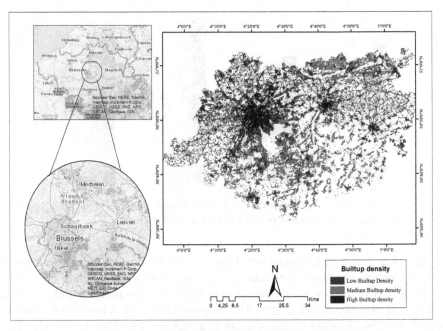

Fig. 2. Study area

2.2 Framework of Multinomial Logistic Regression (MLR) Model

A MLR model have been employed to analyze the impact of the controlling factors that impact the urban expansion and densification of our study area. While working with MLR model the two most important aspects considered were 1. The dependent variable (Y) 2. The independent variables (X). Initially the dependent variables were considered as categorial having a natural ordering between them (low-high). However, the chi square test statistic is <0.001 which establish that the supposition of natural ordering of the dependent variable remain unsatisfied. Therefore, a MLR model has been implied considering that the dependent variable as multi-nominal. The general formula of MLR model is

$$Log(k_n) = \alpha_{k_1} + \beta_{k_{11}}X_1 + \beta_{k_{12}}X_2 + \ldots + \beta_{k_{1v}}X_v$$

where $log(k_n)$ is the natural logarithm of class k_n, X is a set of explanatory variables (X_1, X_2.....X_v), α_{kn} is the intercept term for class k_n, and β is the slopes for classes.

2.3 Dependent Variable

The Cadastral Data (CAD) by Belgian Land registry has been used as the dependent variable for the model. Cadastral data provides information of parcels and plots and is widely used for fiscal purposes. CAD data is mainly a vector data consisting of spatial information about plots and parcels of a geographical area. Each building has its own set of attributes, the most crucial of which is the "construction year" for our purposes. Three raster maps, also called built-up maps in this context were created using the construction year for 2000, 2010 and 2020. These maps were rasterized into 2 * 2 m cell for obtaining a fine resolution raster image. Due to high computational time of 2 * 2 m cell, the images were further aggregated at 100 * 100 m raster. This cell size has been chosen as it is the best combination of aggregation and sensitivity analysis of Moran's I [11] are commonly used for Landuse modelling at regional level [12].

Each class contains the density values of 2 * 2 m cell. A threshold of 25 m^2 in aggregated raster was determined to consider a cell as built-up. Each aggregated cell value < 25 m^2 were considered as non-built up because this threshold corresponds to an average residential building in Belgium [17].The aggregated raster was classified based on density values into four classes (Table 1) using geometric interval classification method which is useful for highly skewed data which are do not follow a normal distribution [2].

Table 1. Built-up density classes range in number of 2 × 2 cells (% of 100 × 100 cell area)

Class	Minimum	Maximum
Class-0 (non builtup)	0	24 (1)
Class-1 (low builtup density)	25	117 (5)
Class-2 (medium builtup density)	118	541 (22)
Class-3 (high builtup density)	542	2500 (100)

A built-up transition matrix has been represented for the four density classes over the two modelled period. Table 2 suggests that transition from low to medium density areas are mostly predominant across both the year, which shows that there is a tendency of significant urban sprawl present in majority of new development. This can lead to proliferation in land take resulting in urban fragmentation. On the other hand, transition from low to medium is peripheral in nature, which is why the transition from class 0 to class 1, 2 and 3 is considered as expansion while transition from class 1–2 and class 2–3 is considered as densification.

Table 2. Class-to-class changes (% of total changes)

2000–2010	Class-0	Class-1	Class-2	Class-3
Class-0	401504 (99.25%)	–	–	–
Class-1	1478(0.37%)	27418 (91.36%)	–	–
Class-2	1149(0.28%)	2424 (8.08%)	63257 (94.95%)	–
Class-3	416(0.10%)	170 (0.57%)	3363 (5.05%)	30261
2010–2020	Class-0	Class-1	Class-2	Class-3
Class-0	399288 (99.45%)	–	–	–
Class-1	1030 (0.26%)	27197 (94.12%)	–	–
Class-2	860 (0.21%)	1551 (5.37%)	64095 (95.91%)	–
Class-3	326 (0.08%)	148 (0.51%)	2735 (4.09%)	34210

2.4 Drivers Controlling Built up Extension: Independent Variable

Primarily thirty-six (36) literatures have been considered out of many for selecting the drivers that impact the urban built up extension largely on combination of major factors: a) Relevant literatures with most common factors controlling changes under European context, b) Combination of various drivers with high impact on built up development under different territorial scenarios. However, to avoid multicollinearity a VIF (Variance Inflation factor) test has been conducted (Fig. 3) as otherwise the model exhibit bias result making it statistically irrelevant.

Hereto a total of eighteen (18) drivers has been selected under four categories of (i) accessibility factors, (ii) geophysical factors, (iii) environmental, and (iv) socio-economic factors. Accessibility was measured by Euclidian distance from Highways,

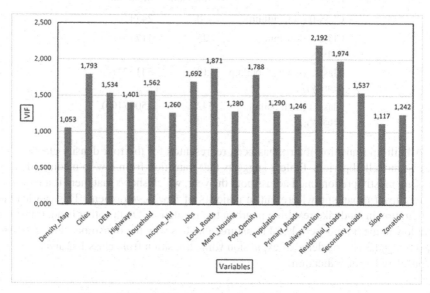

Fig. 3. Variance Inflation factors for all the driving factors

Primary roads, secondary roads, residential and local roads which were obtained from open street maps. Euclidian distance from cities considers the two major urban cores of Brussels and Leuven along with few minor cities. Another important driver that has been considered was distance to railway stations. The locations of the railways station were obtained from Open Street maps.

Digital Elevation Model (DEM) was provided by Belgian National Institute and was used to calculate the slope in percentages. Euclidean distances were also calculated for parks, natural reserves which will facilitate us to understand the role of environment in impacting Built up land take extensions. Statistical data was obtained from Statbel in delimited text format and mapped to raster images with a resolution of 100×100 m. These included number of jobs, Income household, Mean number of housings, total number of populations (Table 3).

Table 3. List of selected driving factors

Factor	Name	Type	Unit	Source
X_1	Elevation (DEM)	Continuous	Meter	Belgian National Geographic institute
X_2	Slope	Continuous	Percent Rise	Own calculation based on DEM
X_3	Dist. to highways	Continuous	Meter	OpenStreet maps
X_4	Dist. to primary roads	Continuous	Meter	OpenStreet maps
X_5	Dist. to secondary roads	Continuous	Meter	OpenStreet maps
X_6	Dist. to residential roads	Continuous	Meter	OpenStreet maps
X_7	Dist. to local roads	Continuous	Meter	OpenStreet maps
X_8	Dist. to cities	Continuous	Meter	OpenStreet maps
X_9	Dist. to parks	Continuous	Meter	OpenStreet maps
X_{10}	Dist. to reserves	Continuous	Meter	OpenStreet maps
X_{11}	Dist. to station	Continuous	Meter	OpenStreet maps
X_{12}	Household	Continuous	Number	Statbel
X_{13}	Income household	Continuous	Number	Statbel
X_{14}	Jobs	Continuous	Number	Statbel
X_{15}	Mean housing	Continuous	Number	Statbel
X_{16}	Population density	Continuous	Number	Statbel
X_{17}	Population	Continuous	Number	Statbel
X_{18}	Zoning	Categorical	Binary	SPW (Walloon Brabant), Geopunt (Flemish Brabant), perspective Brussels (Brussels Capital Region

2.5 Validation of MNL Model

Receiver operating characteristic (ROC) curve was used to validate the model performance. It compares the probability values produced from MNLto a reference values of urban cells in each class. Plotting the True Positive Rate (TPR) against the False Positive Rate (FPR) yielded the ROC curve (FPR). The ROC values are 0.5 (totally random) and 1 (perfect fit).

3 Result and Discussion

The impact of different drivers on expansion and densification process have been presented through Table 4 and 5, respectively. The odds ratio (OR) which equals exponential B has been derived from the model to show the relative measurement of contribution of each driver. An OR >1 shows a positive impact of development with an increasing probability, whereas OR <1 designates towards a negative impact.

Land development is more difficult due to elevation and slope. There is a negative relationship between slope and elevation for low and medium density expansion. As in densification process, the slopes OR value <1 signifies that built up areas in rugged terrains are more dispersed than in flatter areas. In both periods, Distance to natural amenities, parks and reserves shows a positive impact on densification as well as expansion. This is in line with the findings of [18] suggesting that natural amenities can encourage highly dispersed settlements, thus affecting global net land take through spatial segregation.

Transportation infrastructure can be seen as a form of land take as it not only takes up space but also support housing and commercial activities. All significant drivers related to road class has an OR <1 thus suggesting that probability of urban development is higher for locations such as highways, roads, stations, and urban centers. Distance to highways and secondary roads negatively contributes to all densification process. Other distance related factor, i.e., distance to residential roads contributed positively to the densification of medium to high density areas in 2010–2020, thus deeming towards higher land take.

Expansion highly corelated with zoning status., which is in line with [11]. In both the periods there is a gradual upward trend from low to medium and medium to high density areas. Land use planning are one of the most common instruments to explain land take. This suggests that zonation policies can directly affect land take, for ex strong zonation policies can result in fragmentation of non-urban area. Planning regulations favor excessive land take by means of low-density zoning which can be seen through Table 4. It suggests that during the period of 2000–2010, the expansion of low density was 23 times likely to be in the zones designated for urban use. Conversely, the effect of zoning status in densification from medium to high densities are non-significant. This can help in limiting the impervious surface of land take and thus decreasing fragmentation.

Table 4. The coefficients (β) of the MNL model for urban expansion (reference: class-0). Sample size 31000

	2000–2010			2010–2020		
	Coefficients β (odds ratio)			Coefficients β (odds ratio)		
	Class 1	Class 2	Class 3	Class 1	Class 2	Class 3
DEM	−0.086* (0.918)	−0.257* (0.774)	−0.207* (0.813)	−0.153* (0.858)	−0.284* (0.753)	−0.380* (0.684)
Slope	−0.020 (1.020)	−0.013* (0.987)	−0.110* (0.896)	−0.005 (0.995)	−0.060* (0.941)	−0.148* (0.862)
Dist. to highways	0.032 (1.032)	−0.041 (0.960)	−0.287* (0.751)	0.027 (1.028)	−0.010 (0.990)	−0.081 (0.992)
Dist. to primary roads	−0.010 (0.990)	−0.048* (0.953)	−0.091 (0.913)	−0.002 (0.998)	−0.021 (0.979)	0.015 (1.015)
Dist. to secondary roads	0.064* (1.066)	−0.023 (0.978)	−0.153* (0.858)	0.050* (1.051)	0.020 (1.021)	−0.277* (0.758)
Dist. to residential roads	−0.038 (0.963)	0.002 (1.002)	0.043 (1.043)	−0.069* (0.933)	−0.149* (0.862)	0.067 (1.070)
Dist. to local roads	−0.028 (0.973)	−0.018 (0.982)	−0.070 (0.932)	0.019 (1.019)	0.057* (1.058)	0.057 (1.058)
Dist. to cities	0.102* (1.107)	0.093* (1.098)	−0.021 (0.979)	0.054* (1.055)	0.066* (1.068)	0.089 (1.093)
Dist. to parks	0.000 (1.000)	−0.010 (0.990)	0.017 (1.017)	0.004 (1.004)	−0.050* (0.951)	−0.057 (0.945)
Dist. to reserves	−0.069* (1.072)	0.141* (1.152)	0.163* (1.177)	0.108* (1.114)	−0.212* (1.236)	−0.272* (1.313)
Dist. to stations	0.029 (1.029)	−0.013 (0.988)	−0.553* (0.575)	0.048* (1.049)	0.087* (1.091)	−0.313* (0.731)
Household	0.125* (1.133)	0.057* (1.058)	−0.408* (0.665)	−0.041* (0.960)	0.013* (1.013)	0.115* (1.121)
Income household	0.130* (1.139)	−0.036 (0.964)	−0.434* (0.648)	0.114* (1.121)	−0.117* (0.889)	−0.313* (0.731)
Jobs	−0.081* (0.922)	0.006 (1.006)	0.080 (1.083)	−0.041* (0.960)	0.013* (1.013)	0.115* (1.121)
Mean housing	−0.038 (0.963)	−2.042* (0.130)	−0.013 (0.987)	−0.821* (0.440)	−1,719* (0.179)	−7.201* (0.001)
Population density	−0.139 (0.871)	0.001 (1.001)	0.093* (1.098)	−0.098* (0.907)	−0.004 (0.996)	−0.026* (0.974)
Population	0.05 (1.005)	−0.123 (0.974)	−0.056 (0.945)	−0.009 (0.991)	−0.020 (0.980)	0.031 (1.032)
Zoning	3.174 (23.903)	2.639 (13.999)	3.518 (33.717)	2.344 (10.423)	2.644 (14.069)	3.174 (23.903)
ROC	**0.668**	**0.676**	**0.794**	**0.665**	**0.684**	**0.745**

* Indicate significance at P ≤ 0.05 level

The ROC for medium to high densification process produced the best performing descriptive for the both the periods. Estimation of the potential urban expansion produced many false positives, which were estimated at ROC values 0.66–0.79. This implies that the driving factors used in this study were statistically significant for urban densification process.

Table 5. The coefficients (β) of the MNL model for urban densification

	2000–2010		2010–2020	
	Coefficients β (odds ratio)		Coefficients β (odds ratio)	
	Reference: class 1 Sample Size: 22300	Reference: class 2 Sample size: 18000	Reference: class 1 Sample Size: 22300	Reference: class 2 Sample size: 18000
	Class 2	Class 3	Class 2	Class 3
DEM	−0.203* (0.816)	−0.068 (1.070)	−0.133 * (0.875)	−0.075 (0.928)
Slope	−0.086* (0.917)	0.003 (1.003)	−0.046* (0.955)	−0.065 (0.937)
Dist. to highways	−0.016 (0.537)	−0.107 (0.898)	−0.059 * (0.943)	0.015 (1.015)
Dist. to primary roads	−0.031 (0.970)	−0.002 (0.998)	0.002 (1.002)	−0.012 (0.989)
Dist. to secondary roads	−0.109 * (0.897)	−0.040 (0.960)	−0.013 (0.987)	−0.408* (0.665)
Dist. to residential roads	0.074 (1.077)	0.081 (1.085)	−0.048 (0.953)	0.327* (1.387)
Dist. to local roads	−0.041 (0.960)	−0.120 (0.887)	0.008 (1.008)	−0.001 (0.999)
Dist. to cities	−0.012 (0.988)	−0.035 (0.641)	−0.003 (1.003)	−0.065 (0.937)
Dist. to parks	−0.055 (0.947)	−0.106 (0.900)	−0.082* (0.922)	0.075 (1.078)
Dist. to reserves	−0.129 * (1.138)	−0.050 (0.952)	0.124 * (1.132)	0.053 (1.054)
Dist. to stations	−0.018 (0.982)	−0.596 * (0.551)	0.003 (1.00	−0.198 (0.821) *
Household	−0.070* (0.932)	−0.279 * (0.757)	−0.043** (0.958)	−0.169 (0.845)
Income household	−0.172* (0.842)	0.225 * (1.252)	−0.233 * (0.792)	−0.333* (1,395)

(*continued*)

Table 5. (*continued*)

	2000–2010		2010–2020	
	Coefficients β (odds ratio)		Coefficients β (odds ratio)	
	Reference: class 1 Sample Size: 22300	Reference: class 2 Sample size: 18000	Reference: class 1 Sample Size: 22300	Reference: class 2 Sample size: 18000
	Class 2	Class 3	Class 2	Class 3
Jobs	0.075* (1.078)	0.096 (1.101)	0.049* (1.050)	0.179* (1.196)
Mean housing	−2.999* (0.050)	−0.333 (0.717)	−0.899 * (0.407)	0.161 (1.174)
Population density	0.110* (1.116)	0.096 (1.101)	0.064* (1.066)	−0.056 (0.946)
Population	−0.029 (0.952) *	−0.175 (0.840)	−0.004 (1.004)	0.001 (1.000)
Zoning	0.083 (1.087)	−0.018 (0.982)	−0.038 (1.039)	−0.064 (0.938)
ROC	**0.804**	**0.728**	0.828	**0.685**

* Indicate significance at P ≤ 0.05 level

4 Conclusion

Jaeger and Schwick in 2014 suggested limiting urban sprawl through social action by introducing targets and regulate design of the use of landscape as a common property resource as a step to move towards No land take mission by 2050 [9]. In our study, Brussels Capital region, cities of Flemish and Walloon Brabant has been the area of interest presenting a cross border scenario with multiple governance. Dense urban core like Brussels and Leuven shows significant infill development over the years, while Wallonia is mainly dominated by urban sprawl. Most of the research considers sprawl as matter of concern. On the upside, densification can be seen as a workaround to these problems at multi-class level. Belgium has a land take of 104 km^2 [6] from 2012–2018 which is comparatively lesser than its neighboring countries like France and Germany, but it is counterintuitive while taking recultivation into account which is only 18%. Our study identified that drivers like zoning, distance to roads, natural amenities and geophysical features play a significant role in expansion process. Thus, it can be recommended from the study that robust regional policies and effective planning method will complement a national policy, providing a progressive shift towards no land take strategy.

Acknowledgment. This research was funded by the INTER program, co-funded by the Fond National de la Recherche, Luxembourg (FNR) and the Fund for Scientific Research-FNRS, Belgium (F.R.S—FNRS), grant number 19-14016367—'Sustainable Residential Densification' project (SusDens, 2020–2023).

References

1. Preidl, S., Lange, M., Doktor, D.: Introducing APiC for regionalised land cover mapping on the national scale using Sentinel-2A imagery. Remote Sens. Environ. **240**, 111673 (2020)
2. Arlinghaus, S.L., Kerski, J.J.: Spatial Mathematics: Theory and Practice Through Mapping. CRC Press, Boca Raton (2013)
3. Artmann, M., Inostroza, L., Fan, P.: Urban sprawl, compact urban development and green cities. How much do we know, how much do we agree? Ecol. Ind. **96**, 3–9 (2019)
4. Colsaet, A., Laurans, Y., Levrel, H.: What drives land take and urban land expansion? A systematic review. Land Use Policy **79**, 339–349 (2018)
5. de Smet, F., Teller, J.: Characterising the morphology of suburban settlements: a method based on a semi-automatic classification of building clusters. Landsc. Res. **41**, 113–130 (2016)
6. European Environment Agency: Land take in Europe. Indicator Assessment (2019). https://www.eea.europa.eu/data-and-maps/indicators/land-take-3/assessment. Accessed 8 Apr 2022
7. Gennaio, M.-P., Hersperger, A.M., Bürgi, M.: Containing urban sprawl – evaluating effectiveness of urban growth boundaries set by the Swiss Land Use Plan. Land Use Policy **26**, 224–232 (2009)
8. Hanzl, M.: Urban sprawl in Europe: landscapes, land-use change and policy. Plan. Pract. Res. **25**, 273–274 (2010)
9. Jaeger, J.A.G., Schwick, C.: Improving the measurement of urban sprawl: weighted urban proliferation (WUP) and its application to Switzerland. Ecol. Ind. **38**, 294–308 (2014)
10. Montgomery, D.C., Runger, G.C.: Applied Statistics and Probability for Engineers (1994)
11. Mustafa, A.M., Van Rompaey, A., Cools, M., Saadi, I., Teller, J.: Addressing the determinants of built-up expansion and densification processes at the regional scale. Urban Stud. **55**, 3279–3298 (2018)
12. Poelmans, L., Rompaey, A.V.: Complexity and performance of urban expansion models. Comput. Environ. Urban Syst. **34**, 17–27 (2010)
13. Schatz, E., Bovet, J., Lieder, S., Schroeter-Schlaack, C., Strunz, S., Marquard, E.: Land take in environmental assessments: recent advances and persisting challenges in selected EU countries. Land Use Policy **111**, 105730 (2021)
14. Science for Environment Policy: No net land take by 2050? Future Brief 14. Produced for the European Commission DG Environment by the Science Communication Unit, UWE, Bristol (2016). http://ec.europa.eu/science-environment-policy
15. Shukla, A., Jain, K., Ramsankaran, R., Rajasekaran, E.: Understanding the macro-micro dynamics of urban densification: a case study of different sized Indian cities. Land Use Policy **107**, 105469 (2021)
16. Stavi, I., Lal, R.: Achieving zero net land degradation: challenges and opportunities. J. Arid Environ. **112**, 44–51 (2015)
17. Tannier, C., Thomas, I.: Defining and characterizing urban boundaries: a fractal analysis of theoretical cities and Belgian cities. Comput. Environ. Urban Syst. **41**, 234–248 (2013)
18. Wu, W.: Migrant housing in urban China: choices and constraints. Urban Aff. Rev. **38**(1), 90–119 (2002)

Differences and Incongruences in Land Take Monitoring Techniques

Barbara Lopatriello[1], Lucia Saganeiti[2]([⊠]) [iD], and Beniamino Murgante[1] [iD]

[1] Laboratory of Urban and Regional Systems Engineering (LISUT), School of Engineering, University of Basilicata, Viale dell'ateneo Lucano 10, 85100 Potenza, Italy
beniamino.murgante@unibas.it
[2] Department of Civil, Building-Architecture and Environmental Engineering, University of L'Aquila, Via G. Gronchi, 18, 67100 L'Aquila, Italy
lucia.saganeiti@univaq.it

Abstract. The new European standards and directives on land take raise critical issues concerning the techniques for measuring and monitoring the phenomenon in order to achieve the targets fixed. The directive "No Net Land Take by 2050", makes it necessary to homogenize both the terminology used to define land take or consumption and the standardization of a computational methodology for its quantification. In order to achieve the goals, set by the EU regarding land take and soil sealing, it is necessary for EU member states to produce comparable data. It is essential to use the same data sources with standardized coding and to share the same meaning of the concept of land take. Therefore, with the aim of highlighting the criticalities and inconsistencies arising from the use of different techniques and datasets for monitoring land take, we will analyze, first, different definitions of land take derived from institutional sources including the European Environment Agency (EEA); then to each definition we will associate the corresponding land cover classes derived from the Copernicus Corine Land Cover (CLC) project. For the quantitative analysis we will use continuous and discontinuous datasets (raster and vectors) whose results will be compared with the data of the annual report on land take of the Superior Institute for environmental protection and research of Italy (ISPRA 2020).

Keywords: Land take · Corine land cover · Land consumption

1 Introduction

The great loss of soil and ecosystem services is one of the biggest challenges that Europe is already facing for several decades [1]. The extreme importance of the soil issue stems from its being considered a non-renewable resource (at least in the short term) and whose transformations are, therefore, irreversible [2]. The "uncontrolled" consumption of soil, resulting from processes of anthropization and soil sealing, produces economic, social, and environmental damages, reducing or destroying the capacity of soil to perform its basic ecosystem functions, with consequent impacts on biodiversity [3–6]. For these reasons, the sustainable management of soils, their preservation and the protection of

© The Author(s), under exclusive license to Springer Nature Switzerland AG 2022
O. Gervasi et al. (Eds.): ICCSA 2022, LNCS 13376, pp. 271–277, 2022.
https://doi.org/10.1007/978-3-031-10450-3_22

biodiversity are issues that in recent years are assuming particular importance in the field of territorial planning, land governance and in all those disciplinary contexts that show a particular sensibility towards issues related to environmental, social and economic sustainability [7]. Moreover, the recent territorial transformations due to the extreme effects of climate change have made the topic of considerable public interest [8]. To approach these challenges, the European Community has set several targets to be achieved (by now in the short term) including zero net land take by 2050 (EU Environment Action Programme to 2020 (7th EAP) [9–12]. The definition and implementation of such policies, rules and actions aimed at reducing land take appears to be as urgent and priority. In this regard, the recent recovery and resilience tool approved by the European Union (in order to cope with the crisis generated by the pandemic spread of COVID - 19), Next Generation EU and subsequent recovery plans at the national level such as the National Recovery and Resilience Plan (PNRR) [13], are also concerned with the environment, sustainability and the fight against climate change.

In Italy, land take has never been addressed in a systematic way. In 2021 there are countless drafts and proposals of laws with the common objective of limiting soil sealing, but which have never passed to the next level, that of transformation into law. In fact, in recent years the legislative proposals have succeeded each other without ever completing the discussion and approval process, postponed, sometimes depreciated in their basic principles, and completely covered by the amendments [14, 15]. Land take is defined by the Superior Institute for environmental protection and research (ISPRA) as the growth of artificial land cover at the expense of agricultural, natural and semi-natural areas. This definition corresponds to a change in land cover classes from non-artificial (natural or semi-natural) to artificial land cover (consumed land). The main and most impactful component of land take is soil sealing as it poses an increased risk of flooding and water scarcity, contributes to global warming, threatens biodiversity and is particularly worrying when fertile agricultural land is covered [16].

Among the main phenomena related to land take, are to be mentioned certainly, those related to settlement dispersion such as urban sprawl (more popular and known phenomena) [17, 18] and urban sprinkling (phenomena prevalent in internal areas of the Mediterranean context) [19–22]. These are urban transformation patterns characterized by low or very low population and settlement density indices that result in unsustainable land use. These phenomena, in fact, lead to, increased infrastructuring with consequent exploitation of agricultural or natural areas and increased management costs of technological and transport networks [4, 5]. These urban transformation patterns are not sustainable both from an environmental and economic point of view because they tend to consume a limited resource, converting those soils intended for other uses or with a different vocation (agricultural or natural) into artificial soils. In addition to the direct negative effects related to the amount of land take, the indirect effects are related to the total dependence of mobility on private cars, resulting in increased pollution, overall economic and social inefficiency, dependence on fossil fuels and mining [23, 24]. These phenomena have been fueled by the weakness, or (in some cases) total absence, of measures and policies to limit the phenomenon of land take, increasingly favoring the occupation of vacant land distant from urban centers rather than reconstruction or redevelopment within established urban areas [25, 26].

From this synthetic framework, it emerges the need to address the issue of land take in a systematic way, proposing a computational methodology that allows to quantify the phenomenon and compare it at national level first, and then at European level. In this article it is proposed an analysis of the datasets currently available for the quantification of the phenomenon of land take with interpretations of some definitions related to it and from official sources including the Environmental European Agency (EEA) glossary [27]. The purpose is to highlight the differences and incongruences arising from the use of different techniques and datasets for monitoring land take. For the quantitative analysis we will use continuous and discontinuous datasets (raster and vectors) whose results will be compared with the data of the ISPRA 2020 report.

2   Land Take in Italy, Definitions, and Monitoring System

At the national level, land monitoring activities in terms of land use, coverage and consumption are ensured by the National System for Environmental Protection (SNPA). The methodology adopted for analysis, using since 2015, in a unitary and homogeneous way on a national scale, the Sentinel satellite images produced by the European Copernicus Program. In 2015, the first national map of land take at very high resolution was produced. From the ISPRA report on land take 2018 [28], the land take is divided into two categories: permanent and reversible with an additional third level classification (for reversible) that has been detailed and refined over the years based also on the latest texts of the legislative proposal under discussion in the Senate Committees. In this paper we take as a reference for a final comparison of the results the ISPRA 2020 report from which emerges an estimate of land take, between 2018 and 2019, equal to 57.50 km^2 and an amount equal to 5.60 km^2 of restored areas (from other uses to natural use), i.e., that amount of areas identified as reversible consumed soil. Soil consumption monitoring methodologies are further complicated by the absence of an unambiguous definition of land take at European level. The presence of various definitions, sometimes very dissimilar from each other, makes it difficult to measure the phenomenon, whose non-univocity at European level makes the results incomparable. In this regard, three definitions of land take from EEA reports and glossaries were analyzed in this paper. Based on the definitions, Corine Land Cover (CLC) land cover classes with level III and IV detail were associated [29, 30]. The CLC level III at year 2018 and the dataset in vector and raster format with 100 m resolution were used to calculate the areas. The CLC level IV detail is only available for some thematic insights and, in this case was useful to highlight differences in definitions that, with a total national coverage would lead to a substantial difference in the calculation of land consumption. The aim of the work is to highlight incongruences in the results obtained by considering different definitions of land take.

3   Land Take Surfaces Based on Different Definitions

Table 1 shows the three definitions identified with their respective references and in the last columns the CLC classes identified for each of them. The first definition: (1) consumption of land cover, whose source is the EEA glossary [27], has been divided into two parts to highlight the different components. The first part of the definition contains point a while the second contains points b and c together. Points b and c of the definition are different, since point b considers extensive agriculture, while point c considers intensive agriculture. This distinction is possible only with the IV level of CLC with which class 2.1.1.1 refers to intensive crops while class 2.1.1.2 to extensive crops and for this reason in the calculation of the occupied area the two points are used jointly. The second definition: (2) Land take (Glossary EEA [27]), unlike the first definition, which refers to land consumption, considers the "taking" of land or, more appropriately, the occupation of land by infrastructure and related facilities. This definition is specific to infrastructure and should therefore be referred to with a different terminology that includes the infrastructure itself. The third definition: (3) land take (European Union [16]) describes land consumption as an increase in settlement areas over time. Therefore,

Table 1. Selected definitions of land take/consumption and assignment of land cover classes based on CLC III and IV levels.

Num.	Definition	CLC III level	CLC IV level
1	***Consumption of land cover* means:** (a) The expansion of built-up area which can be directly measured;	1.1.1 1.1.2 1.1.3 1.2.1	1.1.1.1 1.1.2.1 1.1.2.2 1.1.2.3 1.1.3.1 1.1.3.2 1.2.1.1 1.2.1.2 1.2.1.3 1.2.1.4
	(b) the absolute extent of land that is subject to exploitation by agriculture, forestry or other economic activities; (c) the overintensive exploitation of land that is used for agriculture and forestry EEA glossary [27]	1.3.1 1.3.2 2.1.1 2.1.2 2.4.4	2.1.1.1 2.1.1.2
2	***Land Take*: the area of land that is taken by** infrastructure itself and other facilities that necessarily go along with the infrastructure, such as filling stations on roads and railway stations EEA glossary [27]	1.2.2 1.2.3 1.2.4	1.2.2.1 1.2.2.2 1.2.2.3
3	***Land take* also referred to as land consumption,** describes an increase of settlement areas over time. This process includes the development of scattered settlements in rural areas, the expansion of urban areas around an urban nucleus (including urban sprawl), and the conversion of land within an urban area (densification). Depending on local circumstances, a greater or smaller part of the land take will result in actual soil sealing [16]	1.1.1 1.1.2 1.4.1 1.4.2	1.1.2.1 1.1.2.2 1.1.2.3

this classification includes rural settlements, urban areas and everything related to them (green areas, area for sports and recreation). It is interesting to note that, in the same definition, the terms land take and land consumption are used almost interchangeably.

Based on each definition of land take, the calculation of the corresponding surfaces was performed with both vector and raster data. Due to the different level of structuring of the two databases, there are some differences whose results are shown in the table below.

Table 2. Surface determination based on selected definitions

Definition Num.	Vector Surface [ha]	Raster Surface [ha]	Δ [ha]
1(a)	15.205	14.954	1,68
1(b)	82.689	82.451	0,29
2	560	517	8,32
3	12.570	12.321	2,02

Table 2 shows the surfaces calculated (on a raster and vector basis) according to the chosen definitions of land take and their associated CLC classes. Considering that the vector surfaces have resulted, for each definition, greater than the raster ones, the Δ represents the percentage difference of the raster compared to the vector. It means that, for example, taking definition 1(a) the raster data produces an underestimation of land consumption equal to 1.65% of the vector data. It should be noted that the area of land consumption related to the definition 1(c) was not analyzed because its specificity required the IV detail level of the CLC, not available for the totality of the study area considered.

The highest differences (Δ) emerge in definition 2 concerning the land covered by infrastructure. This occurs because in the raster data only the linear elements with such an extension as to cover at least 50% of a cell are detected and, consequently, all linear elements of minor entity (secondary roads of small size in terms of width of roadway) are excluded.

4   Discussions and Conclusions

In the ISPRA 2020 Report, consumed soil is defined as the total amount of soil with artificial cover and all classes of permanent and reversible soil consumption are indicated in the relative classification. Moreover, the new classification system no longer considers interventions related to the conduct of agricultural activity in which the natural conditions of the soil are ensured. The database is very detailed and refers to data available within the Copernicus Program, in particular to the Sentinel-2 mission which provides multispectral data with a resolution of 10 m. Thanks to this large availability of data, from last year the quantification of land consumption made by ISPRA has been increasingly refined, being able to detail the results obtained by specifying coverage classes and types of land consumption (reversible, irreversible and permanent).

In order to highlight the main differences in the dataset, a comparison was made first on a national basis, then on a provincial basis (for brevity we do not report all the results on a provincial level), considering the set of two of the definitions listed above, in which only surface completely impermeable are considered (definition 1(a) and definition 2). This results in a difference of 35%, a banal result if we refer to the different resolution of the two databases.

Positive and negative differences emerge from the comparison. The negative differences are attributable to the configuration of urbanized areas, which in most cases are compact and of big dimensions. The positive differences are instead attributable to dispersed spatial configurations and small dimensions of urban settlements. In fact, the spatial resolution of the CLC dataset, contrary to those used by ISPRA, does not allow the identification of small size urban areas. On the contrary, on compact and large spatial configurations of urban settlements, CLC overestimates the land consumption compared to ISPRA.

From the calculation of land take in accordance with the different definitions identified in this research it emerges that the type of data used (vector or raster) involves differences in the average result of 3%. In addition, each definition of land consumption involves a different and not negligible result.

The comparison with the land consumption of the ISPRA 2020 report is not significant since the level of detail of the databases used are not comparable at all. This shows how, even though at the national level the research on soil consumption is continuing with good results, identifying accurate definitions and allowing to divide the phenomenon into different sub processes, at the higher level of governance, the European one, this result becomes not comparable. The most used databases at European level for monitoring land consumption are CLC or ATLAS (with a higher level of detail) but without any unambiguous definition of the phenomenon. Urban ATLAS dataset is very detailed but does not have uniform coverage. Data is only available for cities that are provincial capitals.

References

1. Couch, C., Leontidou, L., Petschel-Held, G.: Urban sprawl in Europe: landscapes, land-use change & policy. Plan. Pract. Res. **25**(2), 273–274 (2007)
2. EEA: Land and soil in Europe (2019). https://doi.org/10.2800/779710
3. Pilogallo, A., Saganeiti, L., Scorza, F., Murgante, B.: Assessing the impact of land use changes on ecosystem services value. In: Gervasi, O., et al. (eds.) ICCSA 2020. LNCS, vol. 12253, pp. 606–616. Springer, Cham (2020). https://doi.org/10.1007/978-3-030-58814-4_47
4. Freilich, R.H., Peshoff, B.G.: The social costs of sprawl. Urban Lawyer **29**, 183–198 (1997). https://doi.org/10.2307/27895056
5. Manganelli, B., Murgante, B., Saganeiti, L.: The social cost of urban sprinkling. Sustainability **12**, 2236 (2020). https://doi.org/10.3390/su12062236
6. Beniamino, M., et al.: A methodological proposal to evaluate the health hazard scenario from COVID-19 in Italy. Environ. Res. **209**, 112873 (2022). https://doi.org/10.1016/J.ENVRES.2022.112873
7. Bencardino, M.: Land take and urban sprawl: drivers e contrasting policies (2015). https://doi.org/10.13128/BSGI.V8I2.339

8. Anderegg, W.R.L., Goldsmith, G.R.: Public interest in climate change over the past decade and the effects of the 'climategate' media event. Environ. Res. Lett. **9**, 054005 (2014). https://doi.org/10.1088/1748-9326/9/5/054005

9. Brown, L.A.: The city in 2050: a kaleidoscopic perspective. Appl. Geogr. **49**, 4–11 (2014). https://doi.org/10.1016/j.apgeog.2013.09.003

10. Cobbinah, P.B., Aboagye, H.N.: A Ghanaian twist to urban sprawl. Land Use Policy **61**, 231–241 (2017). https://doi.org/10.1016/j.landusepol.2016.10.047

11. United Nations, Department of Economic and Social Affairs, Population Division: World Urbanization Prospects The 2018 Revision (2018)

12. European Union: FUTURE BRIEF: No net land take by 2050? (2016). https://doi.org/10.2779/537195

13. Piano Nazionale di ripresa e resilienza #NextGenerationITALIA (2021)

14. Munafò, M.: Consumo di suolo, dinamiche territoriali e servizi ecosistemici. Edizione 2020. Report SNPA, no. 15, 224 (2020). 978-88-448-0964-5

15. Munafò, M. (a cura di): Consumo di suolo, dinamiche territoriali e servizi ecosistemici. Edizione 2019. Report SNPA, 08/19 (2019). 978-88-448-0964-5

16. European Commission: Guidelines on best practice to limit, mitigate or compensate soil sealing (2012). https://doi.org/10.2779/75498

17. Brueckner, J.K.: Urban sprawl: diagnosis and remedies. Int. Reg. Sci. Rev. **23**, 160–171 (2000). https://doi.org/10.1177/016001700761012710

18. Nechyba, T.J., Walsh, R.P.: Urban sprawl. J. Econ. Perspect. **18**, 177–200 (2004). https://doi.org/10.1257/0895330042632681

19. Romano, B., Zullo, F., Fiorini, L., Ciabò, S., Marucci, A.: Sprinkling: an approach to describe urbanization dynamics in Italy. Sustainability **9**, 97 (2017). https://doi.org/10.3390/su9010097

20. Saganeiti, L., Favale, A., Pilogallo, A., Scorza, F., Murgante, B.: Assessing urban fragmentation at regional scale using sprinkling indexes. Sustainability **10**, 3274 (2018). https://doi.org/10.3390/su10093274

21. Saganeiti, L., Mustafa, A., Teller, J., Murgante, B.: Modeling urban sprinkling with cellular automata. Sustain. Cities Soc. **65**, 102586 (2020). https://doi.org/10.1016/j.scs.2020.102586

22. Romano, B., Fiorini, L., Zullo, F., Marucci, A.: Urban growth control DSS techniques for de-sprinkling process in Italy. Sustainability **9**, 1852 (2017). https://doi.org/10.3390/su9101852

23. Gonzalez, G.A.: Urban sprawl, global warming and the limits of ecological modernisation. Environ. Politics **14**, 344–362 (2007). https://doi.org/10.1080/09644010500087558

24. Johnson, M.P.: Environmental impacts of urban sprawl: a survey of the literature and proposed research agenda. Environ. Plan. A Econ. Sp. **33**, 717–735 (2001). https://doi.org/10.1068/a3327

25. Scorza, F., Saganeiti, L., Pilogallo, A., Murgante, B.: Ghost planning: the inefficiency of energy sector policies in a low population density region. Arch. di Stud. Urbani e Reg. 34–55 (2020). https://doi.org/10.3280/ASUR2020-127-S1003

26. Romano, B., Zullo, F., Marucci, A., Fiorini, L.: Vintage urban planning in Italy: land management with the tools of the mid-twentieth century. Sustainability **10**, 4125 (2018). https://doi.org/10.3390/SU10114125

27. European Environment Agency: EEA Glossary—European Environment Agency. https://www.eea.europa.eu/help/glossary/eea-glossary. Accessed 23 Nov 2020

28. Munafò, M. (a cura di): Consumo di suolo, dinamiche territoriali e servizi ecosistemici. Edizione 2018. ISPRA (2018)

29. Feranec, J., Soukup, T., Hazeu, G., Jaffrain, G.: Detailed CLC data: member states with CLC level 4/level 5 and (semi-) automated solutions. In: European Landscape Dynamics. CORINE L. Cover Data, pp. 307–334 (2016). https://doi.org/10.1201/9781315372860-41

30. Kosztra, B., Büttner, G., Hazeu, G., Arnold, S.: Updated CLC illustrated nomenclature guidelines. Service Contract No 3436/R0-Copernicus/EEA.57441 (2019)

Gender Dis-equality and Urban Settlement Dispersion: Which Relationship?

Lucia Saganeiti[✉] [iD] and Lorena Fiorini [iD]

Department of Civil, Building-Architecture and Environmental Engineering,
University of L'Aquila, Via G. Gronchi, 18, 67100 L'Aquila, Italy
{lucia.saganeiti,lorena.fiorini}@univaq.it

Abstract. In the last 50 years, the phenomenon of urban land occupation in Europe has become increasingly relevant, leading to the development of low-density and highly dispersed settlements. The shapes and extensions of urban settlements have moved away from the more traditional and recognized dynamics of urban expansion, acquiring different forms and very low values of settlement density. These are models of unsustainable development because they tend to consume a limited resource, converting those soils intended for other uses or with a different natural vocation into artificial soils. In addition to the direct negative effects related to the amount of land consumed, the indirect effects are related to the total dependence on private cars for daily commuting, resulting in increased pollution, overall economic and social inefficiency, dependence on fossil fuels and minerals and services deficiency.

The shape of the urban settlement inevitably influences the quality of life of men and women, and if we consider that, in Italy, there are still important differences in terms of gender equality, we propose the first developments of a research project in which we want to investigate whether and how the dispersion of urban settlement affects and influences the quality of life of women.

Keywords: Urban dispersion · Gender gap · Urban sprinkling

1 Introduction

The issues of low-density cities characterized by phenomena of urban sprawl or urban sprinkling, have been highlighted in different studies and mainly concern the uncontrolled consumption of land [1, 2], the inefficient use of energy sources [3], and the higher economic and social costs that they involve [4–6]. These phenomena of dispersed expansion, in fact, compared to the phenomena of compact expansion, require a greater amount of infrastructure with consequent exploitation of agricultural or natural areas and increased costs of management of technological networks and transport [4].

As evidenced by Romano et al. (2017) [7], urban sprinkling generates effects significantly more critical than urban sprawl because of its irreversible character (except in the medium to long term). This uncontrolled land consumption leads to a landscape fragmentation that affects the reduction of the resilience of habitats, populations and more

O. Gervasi et al. (Eds.): ICCSA 2022, LNCS 13376, pp. 278–284, 2022.
https://doi.org/10.1007/978-3-031-10450-3_23

generally the ecosystem services loss [8–11]. In addition to these direct negative effects, the indirect effects are related to the total dependence of mobility on private cars, resulting in increased pollution, overall economic-social inefficiency, and dependence on fossil and mineral sources [12, 13]. In fact, the sprawl and sprinkling models are characterized by very different parameters, i.e. 10–20 build/hectares and 20–50 inhabitants/hectares for international sprawl and 0.1 built/hectares and 0.2–0.5 inhabitants/hectares for urban sprinkling [14]. The compact settlement is characterized by very high value of population and building densities.

The irreversibility of the land consumption phenomenon and the poor effectiveness of urban and territorial policies aimed at limiting its progression are elements of considerable importance [15, 16] and the high-density city characterized by a more compact spatial configuration (monocentric development) remains today the most sustainable form of development [17]. It follows that: a dispersed settlement is extremely dissipative compared to a compact one. If urban planning and political choices affect spatial transformations, these in turn affect the quality of life of men and women, then the question of this research is: is it possible to assess how spatial transformations and settlement patterns affect the quality of life of women?

The women's quality of life can not depend only on economic indicators such as the flattening of salaries of men and women or the presence of female figures in positions of value work but also from the provision of services, access to career and employment opportunities, contractual and tax benefits, gender violence, performance in sports and other.

Statistically, women take longer to travel by transport than men, who on average use faster means of transport such as private cars rather than public transport [18]. Women's trips are also characterized to be short but more numerous (multi-stop) since, compared to men whose trips are mostly for work reasons, they tend to perform diversified activities [19, 20]. According to Italian Statistical Institute (ISTAT) the employment rate of women (between 25 and 49 years of age) with pre-school children is 53.3% in Italy and only 35.2% in the regions of Southern Italy, which, except for a few cases, are characterized by strong settlement dispersion. In addition, family aspects have a differential influence on the lives of women and men, affecting accessibility to basic services and, consequently, on the quality of life.

Assuming this, the basic hypothesis is that a dispersed and low-density settlement context generates negative effects on the quality of life of women resulting from the dilatation of travel time to access basic services and the reduced availability of services (nurseries, sports facilities, hospitals, collective spaces and so on) with all the resulting consequences. In this contribute we will show the first results obtained in a research project aimed at investigating the existence of a relationship between urban settlement dispersion and women's quality of life.

The activities of the project include the application of geostatistical analysis to identify the relationship between the phenomena described above in the Italian territory. To start we will employ in these article: (i) the data already analyzed (of urban settlement dispersion), in the contribution presented in the annual report on land consumption ISPRA 2021 [21] (by the same authors); (ii) the data of the quality of life of women developed by the "Il Sole 24Ore" on the basis of statistical ISTAT data.

2 Research Goals and Innovativeness

Overcoming the Gender Gap is one of the Agenda 2030 goals (Goal 5 - Gender Equality) as well as a central position in post-pandemic recovery and relaunch policies [22].

In these relaunch policies, issues concerning the leveling of salaries to shorten the gaps due to gender differences are addressed more than anything else. In contrast, this research aims to demonstrate how the shape of an urban settlement affects women's quality of life. In this analysis, a fundamental role is played by land management policies that could act on factors related to gender differences, with well-designed and appropriate land transformations to ensure a high quality of life for both women and men. The innovative character of this research lies precisely in the intention to investigate the relationships existing between spatial planning and human behavior, a factor that both are reflected in the quality of life. In fact, the territorial strategies that are apparently unrelated to certain phenomena, on the contrary, deeply affect the choices and daily behavior of human beings, improving or worsening all those parameters intrinsically linked to the quality of life.

In order to highlight how a dispersed urban context contributes to increasing gender inequality, the methodology proposed in the research project is based on quantitative indices that, independently of subjective perceptions, scientifically identify the phenomenon that we want to examine. Through the available data (both open source and proprietary) composite indicators will be tested and, through spatial autocorrelation analysis, will be related to the values of settlement dispersion. As for women's quality of life, indicators derived from official data sources at national and international level such as ISTAT [23], The World Bank [24], Eurostat will be considered [25].

The work plan of the research is articulated in the following points: (i) recognition of data and indicators useful to express the relationship between gender dis-equality and urban settlement dispersion; (ii) experimentation of composite indicators and spatial autocorrelation analysis that allow to represent the phenomenon exposed above; (iii) proposal of addresses of land management and urban transformations, which allow to cancel/reduce gender dis-equality in dispersed urban settlements.

We are at the initial point of the development of research and therefore in this article we will present the first results obtained that already show a certain relationship between the two phenomena.

3 Women Quality of Life and Urban Settlement Dispersion

At the methodological level, it is proposed to analyze the relationship between urban settlement dispersion and women quality of life through indices of spatial correlation. Specifically, we will use: the LISA index (Local Indicator for Spatial Association) [26, 27] for the local scale, and in the next stages of the research, we will use the Moran I index for analysis on a global scale, as well as other indices of spatial autocorrelation such as Geary [28, 29]. These indices, given a set of variables, allow us to analyze the shape of spatial patterns and their relationships in the space.

LISA index (Ii) is expressed with the following formula (1):

$$I_i = Z_i \sum\nolimits_{j=1}^{N} w_{ij} Z_j \qquad (1)$$

where: Zi represents the ratio of the difference between the i-th element x and the mean of all elements divided by the standard deviation, Wij is the standardized weight matrix representing the degree of similarity of places i and j.

In this initial phase of the research, the LISA index has been experimented in order to preliminarily identify the relationships between the phenomena to be analyzed. The first results reported in Fig. 1 show the existence of a dependence between the index of women quality of life (Fig. 1(b)) and the index of urban settlement dispersion (Fig. 1(a)).

The index of women quality of life derives from the data elaborated by "Il Sole 24 Ore", the quality of life of women grows as the index increases. The index is composed of 12 indicators, including: life expectancy at birth; women's employment rate; youth employment; gender employment gap; job non-participation rate; gender pay gap; number of women-owned businesses; women administrators in businesses; women administrators in municipalities; gender violence; performance in sports; Olympic performance.

The index of urban settlement dispersion has been evaluated with the Moran I index and has a range of values between 0 and 1 where higher values correspond to urban compact settlement and lower values to urban dispersed settlement.

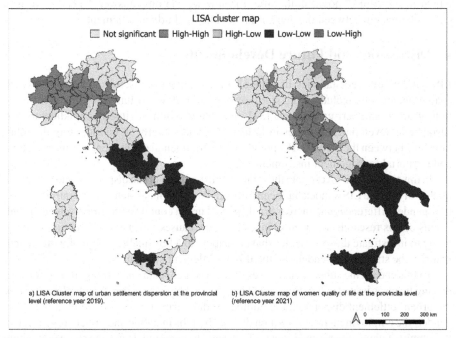

Fig. 1. LISA cluster map: relationship between women quality of life and urban settlement dispersion.

Cluster values indicate respectively:

LOW-LOW: this cluster identifies provinces with low values of the index of women quality of life adjacent to provinces characterized by low values of the same index. The same is valid for urban settlement dispersion, for which a low Moran index corresponds to high urban settlement dispersion;

HIGH-HIGH: this cluster identifies provinces with high values of the index of women quality of life adjacent to provinces characterized by high values of the same index. This applies also to the settlement dispersion, for which a high Moran index corresponds to low urban settlement dispersion, i.e. a compact form of urban settlement;

HIGH-LOW and LOW-HIGH: these clusters identify provinces with high/low values of the index of women quality of life and urban settlement dispersion adjacent to provinces with low/high values of the indices and vice versa.

The results of this first analysis show the presence, in southern Italy, of a cluster of LOW-LOW values while in north-central Italy there is a cluster of HIGH-HIGH values with respect to both variables.

Therefore, to the question "Gender dis-equality and urban settlement dispersion: which relationship?" posed in the title, for now we can only answer: "YES, there is a clear relationship between the gender dis-equality and urban settlement dispersion".

4   Discussions and Future Developments

LISA index and geo-statistics in general, turned out to be useful to describe several spatial phenomena including the study of migration flows in Italy [30], the identification of urban and peri-urban areas [31], the identification of clusters of indicators for sustainable development policies in France [32] and recently, in investigating the relationships between the COVID-19 spread and environmental components, climate factors and territorial management instrument [33].

In this research, to investigate the relationship between urban dispersion and women's quality of life, the LISA index has been utilized. It is evident, as stated in the introduction, how gender differences can increase in dispersed urban contexts. Starting from the initial results of this research, we want to investigate the causes/effects of this relationship by going to investigate those variables that contribute to a low quality of life of women and that may be strongly dependent on the urban settlement structure.

To this end, in the subsequent phases of the research, data concerning: the number of driving licenses issued at the provincial level divided by gender in order to relate them to the urban settlement dispersion; the number of daily trips for work or study divided by gender; the employment rate of women divided by jobs in public and private institutions; the supply of day-care centers, requests for access to maternity leave, the share of women time dedicated to unpaid work, domestic work and care, will be analyzed.

This research aims to investigate how spatial planning and strategic choices can affect women's quality of life, considering that in dispersed urban contexts travel time to reach basic services is longer and that these services are in turn not uniformly distributed throughout the territory. The organization and the structure of the urban settlement could have a significant impact on gender issues, increasing dis-equality.

An urban planning aimed at the development of a sustainable city as much as possible (non-dissipative system) in terms of optimization of routes, efficiency of services, improvement of the 'training/work offer and effective and efficient organization of urban spaces can only positively affect the women's quality of life by contributing to the levelling of the gender gap that can not depend only on economic indicators such as the flattening of salaries of men and women or the presence of female figures in positions of value work.

Funding. This research is funded by the University Research Project for Basic and Initial Research 2022 (University of L'Aquila): "Gender dis-equality e dispersione insediativa" (Gender dis-equality and urban dispersion).

References

1. Romano, B., Zullo, F., Fiorini, L., Marucci, A., Ciabò, S.: Land transformation of Italy due to half a century of urbanization. Land Use Policy **67**, 387–400 (2017). https://doi.org/10.1016/j.landusepol.2017.06.006
2. Saganeiti, L., Favale, A., Pilogallo, A., Scorza, F., Murgante, B.: Assessing urban fragmentation at regional scale using sprinkling indexes. Sustainability **10**, 3274 (2018). https://doi.org/10.3390/su10093274
3. Saganeiti, L., Pilogallo, A., Faruolo, G., Scorza, F., Murgante, B.: Territorial fragmentation and renewable energy source plants: which relationship? Sustainability **12**, 1828 (2020). https://doi.org/10.3390/su12051828
4. Freilich, R.H., Peshoff, B.G.: The social costs of sprawl. The Urban Lawyer **29**, 183–198 (1997). https://doi.org/10.2307/27895056
5. Carruthers, J.I., Ulfarsson, G.F.: Urban sprawl and the cost of public services. Environ. Plan. B Plan. Des. **30**, 503–522 (2003). https://doi.org/10.1068/b12847
6. Manganelli, B., Murgante, B., Saganeiti, L.: The social cost of urban sprinkling. Sustainability **12**, 2236 (2020). https://doi.org/10.3390/su12062236
7. Romano, B., Fiorini, L., Zullo, F., Marucci, A.: Urban growth control DSS techniques for de-sprinkling process in Italy. Sustainability **9**, 1852 (2017). https://doi.org/10.3390/su9101852
8. Bender, D.J., Contreras, T.A., Fahrig, L.: Habitat loss and population decline: a meta-analysis of the patch size effect. Ecology **79**, 517–533 (1998). https://doi.org/10.1890/0012-9658(1998)079[0517:HLAPDA]2.0.CO;2
9. Pilogallo, A., Saganeiti, L., Scorza, F., Murgante, B.: Ecosystem services approach to evaluate renewable energy plants effects. In: Misra, S., et al. (eds.) ICCSA 2019. LNCS, vol. 11624, pp. 281–290. Springer, Cham (2019). https://doi.org/10.1007/978-3-030-24311-1_20
10. Pilogallo, A., Saganeiti, L., Scorza, F., Murgante, B.: Ecosystem services' based impact assessment for low carbon transition processes. TeMA J. Land Use Mobil. Environ. **12**, 127–138 (2019). https://doi.org/10.6092/1970-9870/6117
11. Pilogallo, A., Saganeiti, L., Scorza, F., Murgante, B.: Assessing the impact of land use changes on ecosystem services value. In: Gervasi, O., et al. (eds.) ICCSA 2020. LNCS, vol. 12253, pp. 606–616. Springer, Cham (2020). https://doi.org/10.1007/978-3-030-58814-4_47
12. Gonzalez, G.A.: Urban sprawl, global warming and the limits of ecological modernisation. Environ. Politics **14**, 344–362 (2007). https://doi.org/10.1080/09644410500087558
13. Johnson, M.P.: Environmental impacts of urban sprawl: a survey of the literature and proposed research agenda. Environ. Plan. A Econ. Sp. **33**, 717–735 (2001). https://doi.org/10.1068/a3327

14. Romano, B., Zullo, F., Fiorini, L., Ciabò, S., Marucci, A.: Sprinkling: an approach to describe urbanization dynamics in Italy. Sustainability **9**, 97 (2017). https://doi.org/10.3390/su9010097

15. Scorza, F., Saganeiti, L., Pilogallo, A., Murgante, B.: Ghost planning: the inefficiency of energy sector policies in a low population density region. Arch. di Stud. Urbani e Reg. 34–55 (2020). https://doi.org/10.3280/ASUR2020-127-S1003

16. Romano, B., Zullo, F., Marucci, A., Fiorini, L.: Vintage urban planning in italy: land management with the tools of the mid-twentieth century. Sustainability **10**, 4125 (2018). https://doi.org/10.3390/su10114125

17. Jenks, M., Burton, E., Williams, K.: The Compact City: A Sustainable Urban Form. Routledge, Milton Park (2003). https://doi.org/10.4324/9780203362372

18. Olivieri, C., Fageda, X.: Urban mobility with a focus on gender: the case of a middle-income Latin American city. J. Transp. Geogr. **91**, 102996 (2021). https://doi.org/10.1016/j.jtrangeo.2021.102996

19. Crane, R.: Is there a quiet revolution in women's travel? Revisiting the gender gap in commuting. J. Am. Plan. Assoc. **73**, 298–316 (2007). https://doi.org/10.1080/01944360708977979

20. Wachter, I., Holz-Rau, C.: Gender differences in work-related high mobility differentiated by partnership and parenthood status. Transportation 1–28 (2021). https://doi.org/10.1007/s11116-021-10226-z

21. Munafò, M. (a cura di): Consumo di suolo, dinamiche territoriali e servizi ecosistemici Edizione 2021 Report SNPA 22/21 (2021)

22. Piano Nazionale di ripresa e resilienza #NextGenerationITALIA (2021)

23. Istat.it. https://www.istat.it/. Accessed 06 Apr 2022

24. The world bank. https://datacatalog.worldbank.org/home. Accessed 06 Apr 2022

25. Home – Eurostat. https://ec.europa.eu/eurostat/web/main/home. Accessed 26 Mar 2020

26. Anselin, L.: Spatial Econometrics: Methods and Models. Springer, Dordrecht (1988). https://doi.org/10.1007/978-94-015-7799-1

27. Anselin, L.: Local indicators of spatial association—LISA. Geogr. Anal. **27**, 93–115 (1995). https://doi.org/10.1111/J.1538-4632.1995.TB00338.X

28. Moran, P.A.P.: The Interpretation of Statistical Maps (1948)

29. Getis, A., Ord, J.K.: The analysis of spatial association by use of distance statistics. Geogr. Anal. **24**, 189–206 (1992). https://doi.org/10.1111/j.1538-4632.1992.tb00261.x

30. Murgante, B., Borruso, G.: Analyzing migration phenomena with spatial autocorrelation techniques. In: Murgante, B., et al. (eds.) ICCSA 2012. LNCS, vol. 7334, pp. 670–685. Springer, Heidelberg (2012). https://doi.org/10.1007/978-3-642-31075-1_50

31. Las Casas, G.B., Murgante, B., Nolè, G., Pontrandolfi, P., Sansone, A.: L'uso della geostatistica per la delimitazione degli ambiti periurbani della Provincia di Potenza. Presented at the (2005)

32. Bonnet, J., Coll-Martínez, E., Renou-Maissant, P.: Evaluating sustainable development by composite index: evidence from French departments. Sustainability **13**, 761 (2021). https://doi.org/10.3390/SU13020761

33. Murgante, B., Borruso, G., Balletto, G., Castiglia, P., Dettori, M.: Why Italy first? Health, geographical and planning aspects of the COVID-19 outbreak. Sustainability **12**, 5064 (2020). https://doi.org/10.3390/su12125064

Temporal Changes of Green Roofs Retention Capacity

Roberta D'Ambrosio[✉], Antonia Longobardi, and Mirka Mobilia

Dipartimento di Ingegneria Civile, Università degli Studi di Salerno, Via Giovanni Paolo II, 132, 84084 Fisciano, SA, Italy
robdambrosio@unisa.it

Abstract. Green roofs experience an evolution over the years of physical and chemical properties of the substrate layer that may lead to substantial changes in their hydrological behavior. This study, benefiting from a 5-years monitoring period, aims at assessing changes in the retention capacity of two experimental green roofs (GR1 and GR2), located in Southern Italy and different in drainage layer, by comparing pairs of similar rainfall-runoff events which occurred respectively in 2018 and early 2019, one year after installation, and in 2022. To this end, once identified the retention capacity of each, differences among similar events occurred four years apart were assessed and compared for the two green roof configurations to detect: possible changes in their hydrological performance, the configuration most affected by aging and the evolution of their differences over time. The results obtained so far suggest a general decay of the green roofs retention capacity with some differences according to the drainage characteristics. GR1, with a drainage layer made by 5-cm depth expanded clay, reported a 79% reduction of retention capacity while GR2, with a drainage layer made by MODI' plastic panel filled with expanded clay, experienced a reduction of about 53%. Differences between the two green roof configurations also increase due to aging effects because the substrate, initially crucial in the retention dynamics, seems affected by a progressive performance loss. Conversely, the drainage layer, that appears to play a secondary role in the early operational period, becomes determinant in the medium observation period.

Keywords: Green roofs · Retention capacity · Aging

1 Introduction

During the last decades, the combined effects of urbanization and climate change led to the need for sustainable drainage strategies, capable of supporting the traditional technologies in the management of flooding phenomena at the catchment scale [1].

Among the different solutions, there are certainly green roofs, vegetated roofs able to mitigate volumes and flow rates through the implementation of two fundamental processes: retention and detention [2, 3].

The retention capacity of green roofs depends on numerous factors such as climatic conditions, design choices, technological characteristics and aging [4, 5]. In particular,

© The Author(s), under exclusive license to Springer Nature Switzerland AG 2022
O. Gervasi et al. (Eds.): ICCSA 2022, LNCS 13376, pp. 285–291, 2022.
https://doi.org/10.1007/978-3-031-10450-3_24

the evolution of the physical and chemical properties of the substrate can significantly influence the hydrological performance of these infrastructures [6, 7]. However, due to the need for long monitoring periods of experimental sites, few are the studies that focused on assessing aging effects on the green roofs hydrological response and their results are often conflicting [8, 9].

Therefore, starting from a monitoring activity of about five years (2017–2022), this study aims at assessing the retention capacity of two experimental green roofs [10] by comparing rainfall-runoff events, similar for precipitation depth and initial soil moisture conditions, which occurred respectively in 2018 and early 2019, one year after installation, and in 2022.

2 Materials and Methodology

2.1 The Experimental Site

Two extensive green roofs test beds were installed at the Maritime and Environmental Hydraulic Laboratory of the University of Salerno in January 2017. Each one of them has an area of 2.5 m^2 and a total thickness of 15 cm. They are made up of a vegetation layer, a substrate layer and drainage layer with a filter mat of non-woven fabric interposed between the latter two. The vegetation layer consists in succulent plant called Mesembryanthemum, typical of Mediterranean areas. The 10-cm depth substrate layer consists of a soil mix made of peat, zeolites, coconut fibres and bio stimulant algae as fertilizer. The two green roofs differ for the 5-cm depth drainage layer. In fact, for one of them (GR1) it is made up by expanded clay while for the other (GR2) it is made up of a commercial plastic trays (MODI') with truncated cone shape concavity filled with expanded clay. Laboratory experiments aimed at the characterization of the retention capacity of these drainage layers pointed out that GR2 system is than featured by a moderate larger retention capacity (about 18%) if compared to GR1. The experimental site is continuously monitored by a weather station that includes tipping bucket rain gauge, hygrometer, pyranometer, anemometer and four FDR probes (Reflectometry in the Frequency Domain) located at opposite ends of the green roofs to measure the soil moisture content. Since these values could be affected by the presence of roots in the substrate layer, they are appropriately calibrated with relationships function of the root growth stage. The runoff generated by green roofs is measured at 5-min time steps (Fig. 1).

2.2 Methodology

The analyses required the identification of six rainfall-runoff events recorded in the year 2022 (EV_{2022}_h1; EV_{2022}_h2; EV_{2022}_h3; EV_{2022}_h4; EV_{2022}_h5; EV_{2022}_h6) to be compared with six events selected from the database of the years 2018–2019, similar in terms of rainfall depth and initial soil moisture content, SMC (EV_{2018}_h1; EV_{2018}_h2; EV_{2018}_h3; EV_{2018}_h4; EV_{2018}_h5; EV_{2019}_h6).

Fig. 1. Experimental site evolution: a. green roofs in 2018; b. substrate in 2018; c. green roofs in 2021; d. substrate in 2021.

Moreover, for each event identified the cumulative runoff was measured and the retention capacity (RC), representative of the hydrological performance of the green roofs, was calculated as follows:

$$RC(\%) = \left(1 - \frac{R}{P}\right) \cdot 100 \tag{1}$$

where:

R = runoff depth (mm)
P = precipitation depth (mm)

The similarity criterion made it possible to identify six pairs of events for both the green roofs (EV$_{2022\_h1}$-EV$_{2018\_h1}$; EV$_{2022\_h2}$-EV$_{2018\_h2}$; EV$_{2022\_h3}$-EV$_{2018\_h3}$; EV$_{2022\_h4}$-EV$_{2018\_h4}$; EV$_{2022\_h5}$-EV$_{2018\_h5}$; EV$_{2022\_h6}$-EV$_{2019\_h6}$).

Tables 1 and 2 show respectively the characteristics of the rainfall-runoff events selected from the databases relating to the years 2022 and 2018–2019. It is possible to notice that, under the same precipitation event, GR1 and GR2, which differs for the drainage layer, exhibit a different behavior in terms of runoff and therefore of retention capacity.

Table 1. Characteristics of rainfall-runoff events registered in 2022.

2022 Events	P (mm)	SMC GR1 (%)	SMC GR2 (%)	RC GR1 (%)	RC GR2 (%)
EV$_{2022}$_h1	0.60	33.15	28.39	87	89
EV$_{2022}$_h2	1.27	34.18	31.43	80	65
EV$_{2022}$_h3	5.33	30.84	29.16	82	79
EV$_{2022}$_h4	8.00	32.93	27.78	58	66
EV$_{2022}$_h5	15.49	31.88	31.31	15	25
EV$_{2022}$_h6	35.56	30.89	28.62	23	26

Table 2. Characteristics of rainfall-runoff events registered in 2018–2019.

2018 Events	P (mm)	SMC GR1 (%)	SMC GR2 (%)	RC GR1 (%)	RC GR2 (%)
EV$_{2018}$_h1	0.51	27.18	28.58	100	100
EV$_{2018}$_h2	1.78	29.17	31.24	87	82
EV$_{2018}$_h3	5.84	20.76	21.19	85	81
EV$_{2018}$_h4	7.11	25.06	27.01	84	80
EV$_{2018}$_h5	13.46	28.92	31.20	49	51
EV$_{2019}$_h6	32.00	11.59	15.05	63	66

It can be observed that the selected precipitations are characterized by rainfall depths ranging from 0.60 mm to 35.56 mm. These are events of mild or moderate intensity, for which the effectiveness of sustainable drainage systems should achieve important results. This study foresaw three main levels of analysis: the assessment of the differences between the retention capacities (RC) of GR1 and GR2 obtained under similar rainfall events occurred during the whole period of observation; the identification of the configuration most affected by the aging effects; the study of the evolution of the hydrological differences between GR1 and GR2. The following relationship was used to assess the differences between the retention capacities of GR1 and GR2 between 2018 and 2022 (DR$_{aging}$):

$$DRxaging(\%) = \left(\frac{RCx2022 - RCx2018}{RCx2022} \right) \cdot 100 \qquad (2)$$

where:

RCx2022 = retention capacity of infrastructure "x" (GR1 or GR2) in 2022 (%).
RCx2018 = retention capacity of infrastructure "x" (GR1 or GR2) in 2018 (%).

In order to assess, instead, the differences between GR1 and GR2 depending on the year of observation and thus on the aging stage ($DR_{drainage}$), their relative difference was computed as follows:

$$DRydrainage(\%) = \left(\frac{RCyGR2 - RCyGR1}{RCyGR2} \right) \cdot 100 \tag{3}$$

where:

RCyGR2 = retention capacity of GR2 in the "y" year (2018 or 2022) (%).
RCyGR1 = retention capacity of GR1 in the "y" year (2018 or 2022) (%).

3 Results

The results are reported in Table 3 and in Fig. 2. As regards the evaluation of the effects of the aging phenomenon on the retention capacity (DR_{aging}), a substantial decrease of the hydrological performance can be observed for both green roof configurations (GR1 and GR2).

Furthermore, GR1 seems to be more affected by the phenomenon of aging. The latter, in fact, registered an average reduction in retention capacity of approximately 79% while GR2, which differs only for the drainage layer made by MODI' plastic panels, of about 53%.

Table 3. Comparison of retention capacity under the aging and drainage effects.

	RAIN (mm)		RC GR1 (%)		RC GR2 (%)		DR_aging (%)		DR_drainge (%)	
	2018	2022	2018	2022	2018	2022	GR1	GR2	2018	2022
EV_h1	0.51	0.60	100	87	100	89	−15	−12	0	3
EV_h2	1.78	1.27	87	80	82	65	−9	−26	−6	−23
EV_h3	5.84	5.33	85	82	81	79	−3	−3	−5	−4
EV_h4	7.11	8.00	84	58	80	66	−43	−22	−5	11
EV_h5	13.46	15.49	49	15	51	25	−230	−105	3	40
EV_h6	32.00	35.56	63	23	66	26	−174	−154	5	12
						Mean	**−79**	**−53**	**−1**	**6**

According to the characteristics of the events selected in 2018, during the early operational period, the differences between GR1 and GR2 are almost undetectable with GR1 performances on average moderately higher than GR2 [5]. This is confirmed by the 2018 $DR_{drainage}$ values shown in Table 3 that, even if for a modest number of events, indicates that in 2018 the RC differences between the two roofs were on average equal to 1%. Provided GR1 and GR2 only differ for the drainage layer properties, this seems to be reasonably attributable to the fact that the drainage layer does not play a fundamental role in the retention process, at least in the first operational period. However, in 2022, five years after the experimental site set up, the hydrological performance appears very different. The differences between the two roofs increased up to about 23% in the case of "EV_h2" and 40% in the case of "EV_h5" with an average value of the differences equal to 6% in favor of GR2.

Overall, the results would lead to think that the evolution of the chemical and physical characteristics of the substrate brings to a double effect. The first and most noticeable one is the reduction of the retention capacity of the green roofs, more specifically related to a progressive performance loss of the substrate layer. Whereas, the second is the relevance of the drainage layer in the medium observation period, not appreciable during the early stages of the infrastructure where the retention effect of the substrate is undoubtedly predominant.

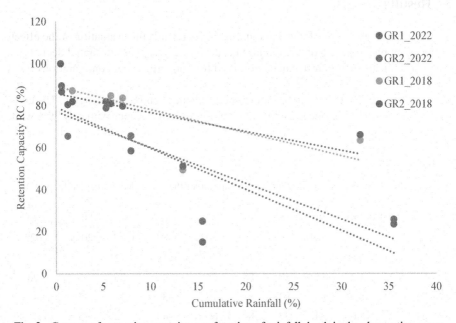

Fig. 2. Green roofs retention capacity as a function of rainfall depth in the observation years.

4   Conclusions

This research work aimed at assessing the evolution of the hydrological performance of two experimental green roofs, different for the drainage layers properties, through a 5-years monitoring period of the meteorological characteristics and the runoff at a small temporal resolution.

The results obtained so far suggest a physiological decay of the retention capacity of green roofs, certainly attributable to a change in the chemical-physical characteristics of the substrate. The characteristics of the drainage layer seem to influence the response of these infrastructures to the effects of aging. In fact, GR1 registers on average 79% reductions in retention capacity over time while GR2 53%.

The differences between GR1 and GR2 also increase due to aging effects because over time the substrate, the main actor in the management of retention dynamics in the early stages of the infrastructure's life, is affected by a progressive reduction of its potentiality that makes the role of the drainage layer increasingly decisive over time.

The drainage layer of GR2 still confirmed to have the highest performance. A more extensive study, aimed at analyzing the evolution of green roofs based on a larger number of rainfall-runoff events, is certainly necessary for confirmation of the quantitative assessments set out so far.

References

1. Fletcher, T.D., et al.: SUDS, LID, BMPs, WSUD and more – the evolution and application of terminology surrounding urban drainage. Urban Water J. **12**, 525–542 (2015)
2. Mentens, J., Raes, D., Hermy, M.: Green roofs as a tool for solving the rainwater runoff problem in the urbanized 21st century. Landsc. Urban Plan. **77**, 217–226 (2006)
3. Akter, M., He, J., Chu, A., Huang, J., van Duin, B.: A review of green roof applications for managing urban stormwater in different climatic zones. Sustainability **10**(8), 2864 (2018)
4. Mobilia, M., D'Ambrosio, R., Claverie, R., Longobardi, A.: Substrate soil moisture impact on green roof performance for an experimental site in Tomblaine, France. In: Gervasi, O., et al. (eds.) Computational Science and Its Applications – ICCSA 2021. LNCS, vol. 12950, pp. 563–570. Springer, Cham (2021). https://doi.org/10.1007/978-3-030-86960-1_39
5. D'Ambrosio, R., Mobilia, M., Khamidullin, I.F., Longobardi, A., Elizaryev, A.N.: How substrate and drainage layer materials affect the hydrological performance of Green roofs: CHEMFLO-2000 numerical investigation. In: Gervasi, O., et al. (eds.) Computational Science and Its Applications – ICCSA. LNCS, vol. 12956, pp. 254–263. Springer, Cham (2021). https://doi.org/10.1007/978-3-030-87010-2_17
6. De-Ville, S., Menon, M., Stovin, V.: Temporal variations in the potential hydrological performance of extensive green roof systems. J. Hydrol. **558**, 564–578 (2018)
7. Piana, M., Carlisle, S.: Green roofs over time: a spatially explicit method for studying green roof vegetative dynamics and performance. Cities Environ. **7**(2), 1 (2014)
8. Bouzouidja, R., Séré, G., Claverie, R., Ouvrard, S., Nuttens, L., Lacroix, D.: Green roof aging: quantifying the impact of substrate evolution on hydraulic performances at the lab-scale. J. Hydrol. **564**, 416–423 (2018)
9. Yang, Y., Davidson, C.I.: Green roof aging effect on physical properties and hydrologic performance. J. Sustain. Water Built Environ. **7**(3), 0401007(2021)
10. Longobardi, A., D'Ambrosio, R., Mobilia, M.: Predicting stormwater retention capacity of green roofs: an experimental study of the roles of climate, substrate soil moisture, and drainage layer properties. Sustainability **11**(24), 6956 (2019)

Machine Learning Based Approach to Assess Territorial Marginality

Simone Corrado[(✉)] [iD] and Francesco Scorza [iD]

Laboratory of Urban and Regional System Engineering (LISUT), School of Engineering,
University of Basilicata, Potenza, Italy
`simone.corrado@studenti.unibas.it`

Abstract. The territorial cohesion is one of the primary objectives for the European Union and it affects economic recovery pushing the role of Public Administration in promoting territorial development actions. The National Strategy for Inner Areas (SNAI) is a public policy promoting endogenous development processes in marginal territories with low settlement density. Specific contexts where rules and standards defined for the organization of large metropolitan aggregates lose their effectiveness whose identification represents a critical stage for policy efficacy and the actual map of SNAI target areas appears to be the results of a weak and simplified analytical approach. These considerations are the origin of the research question that underlies this work: identify the typical characteristics of Basilicata's marginal areas through machine learning techniques and, subsequently, reclassify the national territory using the trained model. However, outlining the boundary of this territories is only a preliminary task. The following step is the identification of the dynamics within the different territorial sub-systems that make up the inner peripheries. This paper presents the results of the local model-agnostic method for interpreting the obtained results. It emerges, thought cooperative game theory by Shapley values, the need to refine analytical methods that are sensitive to the measurement of the different context conditions. Future perspectives of the research regard the extensive deepening of the application on the basis of wider datasets able to make explicit spatial components of the distribution of the observed phenomena.

Keywords: Territorial cohesion · Inner periphery · Interpretable machine learning

1 Introduction

The territorial cohesion is one of the primary objectives for the European Union [1, 2]. Rural areas host almost a third of the EU population, and in the Italian national context about a quarter of the entire population lives in marginal areas: the inner peripheries [3, 4]. The Italian territory is organized in a multiplicity of minor centers connected to main metropolitan poles [5]. This spatial arrangement brings out the extraordinary variety of inner areas at all levels i.e., geographic, economic, social, cultural, eco-systemic. The identification of the differences between local systems of marginal areas is the first step

© The Author(s), under exclusive license to Springer Nature Switzerland AG 2022
O. Gervasi et al. (Eds.): ICCSA 2022, LNCS 13376, pp. 292–302, 2022.
https://doi.org/10.1007/978-3-031-10450-3_25

in recognizing the intrinsic complexity of these territories. Hence arise the needs for integrated spatial planning based on sustainable development, a substantial and particularly critical exercise in the management of so-called weak demand territories, i.e., with low settlement density, where rules and standards defined for the organization of large metropolitan aggregates lose their effectiveness [6]. In fact, Italian inner areas have been facing process of marginalization since the 1950s. Intense phenomena of de-antrophization have led to a substantial decrease in population and progressive demographic aging, the reduction of the active population with a consequent reduction in employment and under-use of local territorial resources [7]. Therefore, inner peripheries are considered a national issue, because of their development potential, as well as their community costs due to their social condition and the unequal access to basic services compared to the more developed centers [8].

The national strategy for inner areas seeks to reverse these trends, through a gradual, integrated and monitored approach and by evaluating land governance and development strategies [9]. Such innovative policy aims to improve the quality of life of residents, contributing to national economic recovery and the achievement of the European Union's territorial cohesion objectives [10]. In organizing such complex policy framework, the primary issue is the identification of the boundaries of the target areas. SNAI reduces this issue to an operative simplification based on a limited set of indices at national level.

In this paper a broader analytical procedure is proposed for the identification of inner areas according to a robust spatial appraisal including multivariate datasets. We base such analysis on the application of machine learning techniques to a database including socio-economic indicators and variables descriptive of the morphological characteristics linked to spatial measures of accessibility. This approach tends to improve the selection of target areas for the policies promoted by the SNAI by bringing out different functional specializations on the basis of which endogenous development policies can be better structured. In particular, the analytical approach takes into account, for the definition of the reference labels, the characteristics of the marginal territories identified in the Basilicata Region. The working hypothesis it's to consider Basilicata as a benchmark role for the model. The results obtained propose a new map of the inner areas that is scarcely comparable with that of the SNAI. It opens up critical considerations on the potential impact of the development support policy and confirms the need to refine analytical methods that are sensitive to the measurement of the different context conditions. The conclusions highlight how the mapping of territorial marginality obtained through the proposed analytical approach is, in fact, conditioned by specific structural variables such as "resident population", characteristics linked to "ageing", and the "low productive specialization" of municipalities. They confirm the need to deepen the application on the basis of more extensive datasets able to make explicit spatial components of the distribution of the observed phenomena.

2 Materials and Method

The previous section already introduced the growing importance of data in the progress of spatial development strategies for the future [11, 12]. To better explain what big-Data is, it is necessary to specify what is meant as data. The DIKW method is introduces as a hierarchical framework to get insight and find pattern into data [13]. Data are closely related to places, are potentially reproducible, are part of larger information structures, and can be processed and stored in digital formats [14]. Raw-data itself are neutral to the human mind, they become information when they are extracted, processed and used for certain purposes. The framework of information often consisting of multiple data from the same and different types of domains becomes knowledge when they are interpreted through tools, applications, methods, cross-references, indicators etc. [15]. Knowledge, finally, gains the value of awareness -in the case of Open Data it can certainly be defined as collective, in the broadest sense of common benefit- when it is able to perform well the complexity of the real world [16]. The issues in big-data management are well known and concern volume, velocity and variety without ignoring two additional dimensions: variability and authenticity of the information [17].

The SNAI database was chosen as basic dataset for this research. This is an informative infrastructure of accessible and interoperable data certified by the national agency of territorial cohesion in which the minimum statistical unit is the municipality. It contains variables and indicators for individual municipality related to the scopes of the SNAI Strategy. The thematic areas analyzed are: social, demographic, economic situation and consistency of essential services. The data are extremely heterogeneous both by topic and year of release. Some variables are collected from 1971 to 2011 on a 10-year basis for statistical trend setting others cover only the year 2011. The following Table 1 gives a summary of the characteristics of SNAI database.

Table 1. Summary of SNAI database

Context	Indicator	Variable	Total
Demography	9	13	22
Economy	10	19	29
Morphology	6	6	12
Health	3	5	8
School	3	51	54
Transport	1	5	6
Digital divide	2	-	2
Total	34	99	133

Supervised Machine Learning (ML) techniques emerge to be the most capable at handling such informational heterogeneity. As known, ML is a set of methods that computers use to make and improve predictions or behaviors based on data. Specifically, supervised learning allows finding patterns between data and labels that can be expressed mathematically as functions [18]. The model will then learn from train data by identifying relationships in feature space - refers to the n-dimensions where variables are distributed - over the homogeneous reference group given by the labels. Then the ML model will be used to make predictions about the new data not assessed during training phase. For this property, the ML model will be used to make predictions about the unseen municipality data. Python programming language was preferred because it integrates many ML and data visualization libraries. In particular, the Numpy and Pandas libraries were used as data analysis and manipulation tools, scikit-learn for data engineering and ML models, and the seaborn library for visualize, explore and understand the data [19–21].

To achieve the aim of the research, it is necessary to deconstruct the analysis problem into distinct moments. Firstly, more than one million data from the 8092 Italian municipalities were analyzed to seek for possible statistical mismatches and to assess their frequency distribution. The in-depth analysis identified the transformation most akin to the distribution of the data and the best techniques to impute the missing values. Commonly, ML algorithms don't perform well if feature have very different scales, -in SNAI database data varies widely, some indicators are percentages, while other demographic variables ranging from 1e3 to 1e6 and so on-, thus a feature scaling is needed [22]. In fact, most of the features have a lognormal distribution with metropolitan cities set as outliers for many variables. After this validation check, data engineering process was performed. In particular, data have been transformed for stabilizing variance and minimizing skewness with a quintile transform feature-wise to make distribution more Gaussian-like (see Fig. 1).

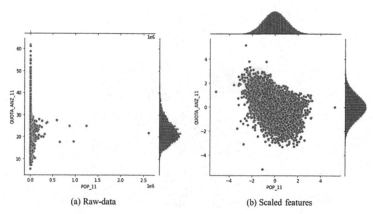

(a) Raw-data   (b) Scaled features

Fig. 1. Comparison between raw (a) and transformed (b) data distribution of residential population and demographic aging index.

Labels of the Basilicata municipalities are assumed from a previous work that investigated the hierarchy of policentricity ranks according to Christaller's Central place theory and PCA statistics performed on in deep analysis of a peculiar set of variables describing the services supply and the rarity index for services categories as a way to detect territorial marginality [23, 24].On the basis of the frequency of each service category, an aggregate assessment of the rank of each Basilicata municipality was drawn up in 4 classes (R1- main urban center, R2, R3, R4 – inner periphery). This is not a simple ranking of the cities, but a hierarchical dependence, in the sense that those of higher rank also encompass in their sphere of superior services areas gravitating for common services on cities of lower rank. Thus, in this work all municipalities classified as the lowest rank are considered inner peripheries.

The ML classification algorithm used is the "decision-tree" (see Fig. 2). It allows a significant interpretation of the territorial marginality since it is more closely mirror human decision-making. In facts, tree-based models split the data multiple times in order to obtain subsets which minimize the Gini index or the entropy of the system. The algorithm hence tends to search within the dataset for those predictors that best split the sample into pure subsets, that is, data that all fall into the same class. The model therefore predicts that each new observation belongs to the class most commonly found in training observations in the rank to which it belongs. The algorithm continues to split the data recursively until the Gini index drop to zero. This process produces a tree that resulting in a perfectly fit on training set, but is likely to over-fit the data, leading to a poor generalization [22]. A better strategy is to grow a smaller tree with fewer data splits in order to have lower variance and a better interpretation at the cost of purity leaf split. Thus, a tree pruning is set on the fourth leaf. However, after an initial attempt with a single decision-tree model, a tree bagging was carried out through the use of random forest algorithm to overcome the over-fitting issues and substantially improve the predictive performance.

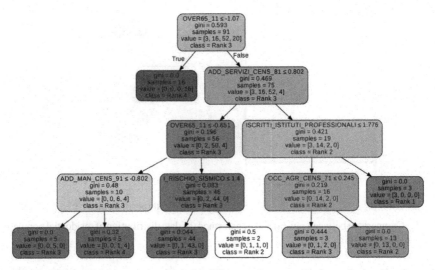

Fig. 2. Single decision-tree in which the different colors specify the rank classification.

3   ML Interpretability and Results

Trained ML models are designed to make the most accurate predictions from data. The accuracy of the model allows to evaluate its effectiveness and avoid the over-fitting issue. There are several metrics to assess multi-label classification score. The simplest one is accuracy score. This function computes general model accuracy com-paring the set of labels predicted for a sample against the same subset true label. The output model has a score on the train subset of 0.94 instead on the test subset equal to 0.87. Also, a confusion matrix can be displayed. This metric makes it possible to investigate in more depth on which group the model fails (see Fig. 3).

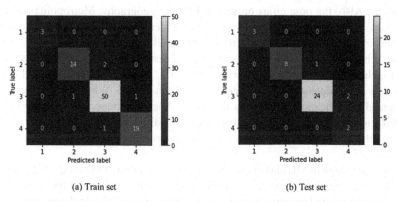

(a) Train set   (b) Test set

Fig. 3. Confusion matrix on train (a) and test (b) split database.

The overall accuracy of the classification model is considered adequate, and the confusions matrix analysis allows to estimate negligible losses over rank 4. Once the model was trained and tested, the classification of municipal ranks was transferred to the Italian municipalities (See Fig. 4).

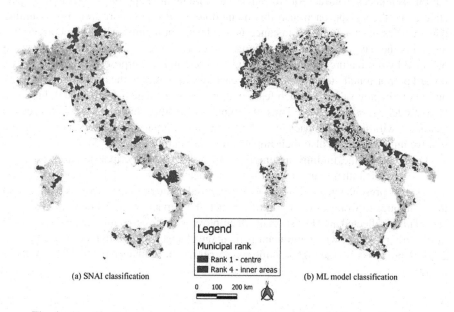

(a) SNAI classification   (b) ML model classification

Fig. 4. Classification comparison between SNAI (a) and trained ML algorithm (b).

The classification of the inner areas obtained with the trained ML model is scarcely comparable with the SNAI. The resulting classification is much more fragmented. This is mainly due to the hypothesis to consider as labels for inner areas those municipalities that in the Basilicata hierarchy was the weakest and rarest ones. In other words, those territory presenting the highest development demand on the basis of the regional conditions. Also, the pole cities present a different geography. Metropolitan areas are identifiable in the results and their scope is even wider. This depends also on the training set where Potenza and Matera (effectively two small town) are classified in the highest rank as urban poles. Moreover, the greatest differences are found in the west Alpine region included in the inner peripheries by the ML model while in the SNAI classification it was not considered an inner area for such extend. What also emerges is the fragmented classification throughout the whole Apennine bone. This also depends on the characteristics of the training subset used for ML. Eventually additional appraisal of morphological features and more accurate accessibility analysis may improve such result.

A relevant stage in ML classification is the interpretation of the model [25]. It means going into the specific informative contribution of each variable and understanding its relevance within it and overcome the concern of black-box model. In detail, interpretable ML refers to methods and models that make the behavior and predictions of machine learning systems more understandable to humans [26–28]. As previously mention, decision tree models are very interpretable because they are similar to human thinking and decision-making. In fact, a single decision tree can be displayed to understand how it's work and why it used some feature rather than others to split the subsets. Instead, the Random-forest algorithm improve prediction accuracy at the expense of interpretability but this is a necessary trade-off for having a more flexible approach. Through cooperative game theory approach also this methodology becomes more intuitive assuming that each feature value of the instance is a "player" in a game where the correct prediction is the payout [29]. In fact, Shapley value is a system for distributing a reward obtained by the feature among its coalition subset, and its purpose is to distribute that reward proportionally to the contribution each player makes to the coalition. The distribution of Shapley values for each feature allows to investigate the ML model through a local model-agnostic method. Thus, the impacts of features on the model's choices are estimated with the SHAP package. The following summary plot represent the feature relative importance and also their impact on model output (See Fig. 5).

Depicting to the finding, assumptions regarding inner peripheries are validated. Socio-economic rather than morphological characteristics defined the inner peripheries. These areas present a general situation of structural demographic weakness with a trend that continues to worsen due to inertia. In fact, the impact on model choices is significant. This is reflected also in a shortage of employees in the economic sectors, especially in the tertiary sector, with significant percentage changes in employment from 1971 to 2001. A proxy is also the high seismic risk territories that enhance the isolation of these areas.

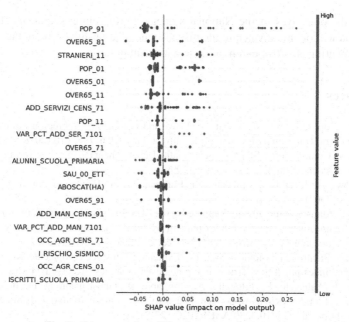

Fig. 5. Summary plot of Shapley values for inner areas

4 Conclusions

ML and model interpretation have proved to be two effective tools supporting the territorial research for the identification of inner areas. Among results, detecting features relevance in the model represents a first driver to better orient the strategic actions: i.e., if ageing population represents a key component in inner areas classifications, the policy should prioritize actions oriented to support the needs for those inhabitants and to adopt measure to reduce the relative weight of this population components in favor of the others ones. This analytic approach is meaningful also in validating existing assumptions about inner peripheries, grasp and anticipate changes that might set-in and design place-based development policies, put in practice effective territorial monitoring tools.

Measuring the effects of the SNAI strategy on demographics therefore becomes a key-factor in assessing the impact of local development policies and projects [30]. However, a study has already shown that the SNAI database requires revision both in the accuracy of some municipal scale indicators and in the consistency of some features [31]. In fact, the database is unbalanced towards demographic feature rather than economic and especially geo-morphological variables. Such unbalanced classes could affect the deciphering of patterns within the data [32]. Reference studies to be considered in order to extend the informative bases regards: accessibility and mobility management [33, 34] in urban and territorial scale, impact of regional development policies funded by EU [35, 36], territorial fragmentation and anthropic pressure on relevant ecosystem values [37–40], energy transition and climate proof municipalities [41–44]. Future research perspectives are: revisiting the database by identifying additional Open Government dataset that have been activated since 2011, and integrating trends and indices deemed useful to the objectives of the National strategy. Furthermore, spatial inequality and segregation will be investigated to identify also the relationship between the inner area for implementing effective community management policies.

References

1. Dax, T., Copus, A.: Towards vibrant, inclusive and sustainable rural regions: orientations for a future rural cohesion policy. Eur. Struct. Invest. Funds J. **6**, 198–210 (2018)
2. European Commission: ESDP European Spatial Development Perspective: Towards Balanced and Sustainable of the European Union (1999)
3. Matthews, A.: Rural Development in the European Union: Issues and Objectives, pp. 1–14. Citeseer (2007)
4. Eurostat: Statistics on regional typologies in the EU - Statistics Explained. https://ec.europa.eu/eurostat/statistics-explained/index.php?title=Statistics_on_rural_areas_in_the_EU#Source_data_for_figures_and_maps_.28MS_Excel.29. Accessed 24 May 2022
5. Eurostat: Territorial typologies - Statistics Explained. https://ec.europa.eu/eurostat/statistics-explained/index.php?title=Territorial_typologies#Typologies. Accessed 24 May 2022
6. Scorza, F., Saganeiti, L., Pilogallo, A., Murgante, B.: Ghost planning: the inefficiency of energy sector policies in a low population density region. Arch. di Stud. Urbani e Reg. 34–55 (2020). https://doi.org/10.3280/ASUR2020-127-S1003
7. Dax, T., Fischer, M.: An alternative policy approach to rural development in regions facing population decline. Eur. Plan. Stud. **26**, 297–315 (2018). https://doi.org/10.1080/09654313.2017.1361596
8. Balzan, M.V., Caruana, J., Zammit, A.: Assessing the capacity and flow of ecosystem services in multifunctional landscapes: evidence of a rural-urban gradient in a Mediterranean small island state. Land Use Policy **75**, 711–725 (2018). https://doi.org/10.1016/j.landusepol.2017.08.025
9. Carrosio, G.: A place-based perspective for welfare recalibration in the Italian inner peripheries: the case of the Italian strategy for inner areas. Sociol. E Polit. Soc. 50–64 (2016). https://doi.org/10.3280/sp2016-003004
10. Knickel, K., et al.: Between aspirations and reality: making farming, food systems and rural areas more resilient, sustainable and equitable. J. Rural Stud. **59**, 197–210 (2018). https://doi.org/10.1016/j.jrurstud.2017.04.012
11. Athey, S.: Beyond prediction: using big data for policy problems. Science. **355**, 483–485 (2017). https://doi.org/10.1126/SCIENCE.AAL4321
12. Höchtl, J., Parycek, P., Schöllhammer, R.: Big data in the policy cycle: policy decision making in the digital era. J. Organ. Comput. Electron. Commer. **26**, 147–169 (2016). https://doi.org/10.1080/10919392.2015.1125187
13. Rowley, J.: The wisdom hierarchy: representations of the DIKW hierarchy. J. Inf. Sci. **33**, 163–180 (2007). https://doi.org/10.1177/0165551506070706
14. Murgante, B., Borruso, G., Lapucci, A.: Geocomputation and Urban Planning. Springer, Heidelberg (2009). https://doi.org/10.1007/978-3-540-89930-3_1
15. Zins, C.: Conceptual approaches for defining data, information, and knowledge. J. Am. Soc. Inf. Sci. Technol. **58**, 479–493 (2007). https://doi.org/10.1002/asi.20508
16. Las Casas, G., Murgante, B., Scorza, F.: Regional local development strategies benefiting from open data and open tools and an outlook on the renewable energy sources contribution. In: Papa, R., Fistola, R. (eds.) Smart Energy in the Smart City. GET, pp. 275–290. Springer, Cham (2016). https://doi.org/10.1007/978-3-319-31157-9_14

17. Laney, D.: others: 3D data management: controlling data volume, velocity and variety. META Gr. Res. note. **6**, 1 (2001)
18. Mitchell, T.M.: Machine Learning. McGraw-Hill, New York (1997)
19. McKinney, W.: Data structures for statistical computing in Python. In: Proceedings of the 9th Python in Science Conference, pp. 56–61 (2010). https://doi.org/10.25080/majora-92b f1922-00a
20. Harris, C.R., et al.: Array programming with NumPy. Nature **585**, 357–362 (2020). https://doi.org/10.1038/s41586-020-2649-2
21. Waskom, M.: seaborn: statistical data visualization. J. Open Source Softw. **6**, 3021 (2021). https://doi.org/10.21105/joss.03021
22. Hastie, T., Tibshirani, R., James, G., Witten, D.: An Introduction to Statistical Learning (2nd ed.). Springer Texts, vol. 102, 618. Springer, New York (2021). https://doi.org/10.1007/978-1-0716-1418-1
23. Getis, A., Getis, J.: Christaller's central place theory. J. Geog. **65**, 220–226 (1966)
24. Curatella, L., Scorza, F.: Una Valutazione della struttura policentrica dell'insediamento nella Regione Basilicata. LaborEst. **20**, 37–42 (2020)
25. Doshi-Velez, F., Kim, B.: Towards A Rigorous Science of Interpretable Machine Learning (2017). https://doi.org/10.48550/arxiv.1702.08608
26. Molnar, C.: Interpretable Machine Learning. A Guide for Making Black Box Models Explainable (2019)
27. Miller, T.: Explanation in artificial intelligence: insights from the social sciences. Artif. Intell. **267**, 1–38 (2019). https://doi.org/10.1016/j.artint.2018.07.007
28. Murdoch, W.J., Singh, C., Kumbier, K., Abbasi-Asl, R., Yu, B.: Definitions, methods, and applications in interpretable machine learning. Proc. Natl. Acad. Sci. U.S.A. **116**, 22071–22080 (2019). https://doi.org/10.1073/PNAS.1900654116/SUPPL_FILE/PNAS.190 0654116.SAPP.PDF
29. Shapley, L.S.: A Value for N-Person Games. RAND Corporation, Santa Monica, CA (1952). https://doi.org/10.7249/P0295
30. Las Casas, G., Scorza, F., Murgante, B.: Conflicts and sustainable planning: peculiar instances coming from Val d'agri structural inter-municipal plan. In: Papa, R., Fistola, R., Gargiulo, C. (eds.) Smart Planning: Sustainability and Mobility in the Age of Change. GET, pp. 163–177. Springer, Cham (2018). https://doi.org/10.1007/978-3-319-77682-8_10
31. Rossitti, M., Dell'ovo, M., Oppio, A., Torrieri, F.: The italian national strategy for inner areas (SNAI): a critical analysis of the indicator grid. Sustainability. **13**, 6927 (2021). https://doi.org/10.3390/su13126927
32. Géron, A.: Book Review: Hands-on Machine Learning with Scikit-Learn, Keras, and Tensorflow, 2nd edn. O'Reilly Media, Sebastopol (2019)
33. Scorza, F., Fortunato, G.: Cyclable cities: building feasible scenario through urban space morphology assessment. J. Urban Plan. Dev. **147**, 05021039 (2021). https://doi.org/10.1061/(asce)up.1943-5444.0000713
34. Scorza, F., Fortunato, G., Carbone, R., Murgante, B., Pontrandolfi, P.: Increasing urban walkability through citizens' participation processes. Sustain. **13**, 5835 (2021). https://doi.org/10.3390/su13115835
35. Scorza, F.: Improving EU cohesion policy: the spatial distribution analysis of regional development investments funded by EU structural funds 2007/2013 in Italy. In: Murgante, B., et al. (eds.) Computational Science and Its Applications – ICCSA 2013. LNCS, vol. 7973, pp. 582–593. Springer, Heidelberg (2013). https://doi.org/10.1007/978-3-642-39646-5_42
36. Scorza, F., Casas, G.L.: Territorial specialization in attracting local development funds: an assessment procedure based on open data and open tools. In: Murgante, B., et al. (eds.) Computational Science and Its Applications – ICCSA 2014. LNCS, vol. 8580, pp. 750–757. Springer, Cham (2014). https://doi.org/10.1007/978-3-319-09129-7_54

37. Curatella, L., Scorza, F.: Polycentrism and insularity metrics for in-land areas. In: Gervasi, O., et al. (eds.) Computational Science and Its Applications – ICCSA 2020. LNCS, vol. 12255, pp. 253–261. Springer, Cham (2020). https://doi.org/10.1007/978-3-030-58820-5_20

38. Scorza, F., Fortunato, G.: Active mobility oriented urban development: a morpho-syntactic scenario for mid-sized town. Eur. Plan. Stud. (2022).https://doi.org/10.1080/09654313.2022.2077094

39. Pilogallo, A., Saganeiti, L., Scorza, F., Las Casas, G.: Tourism attractiveness: main components for a spacial appraisal of major destinations according with ecosystem services approach. In: Gervasi, O., et al. (eds.) Computational Science and Its Applications – ICCSA 2018. LNCS, vol. 10964, pp. 712–724. Springer, Cham (2018). https://doi.org/10.1007/978-3-319-95174-4_54

40. Scorza, F., Pilogallo, A., Saganeiti, L., Murgante, B.: Natura 2000 areas and sites of national interest (SNI): measuring (un)integration between naturalness preservation and environmental remediation policies. Sustainability. 12, 2928 (2020). https://doi.org/10.3390/su12072928

41. Corrado, S., Giannini, B., Santopietro, L., Oliveto, G., Scorza, F.: Water management and municipal climate adaptation plans: a preliminary assessment for flood risks management at urban scale. In: Gervasi, O., et al. (eds.) Computational Science and Its Applications – ICCSA 2020. LNCS, vol. 12255, pp. 184–192. Springer, Cham (2020). https://doi.org/10.1007/978-3-030-58820-5_14

42. Scorza, F., Santopietro, L.: A systemic perspective for the sustainable energy and climate action plan (SECAP). Eur. Plan. Stud. 1–21 (2021). https://doi.org/10.1080/09654313.2021.1954603

43. Santopietro, L., Scorza, F.: The Italian experience of the covenant of mayors: a territorial evaluation. Sustainability. 13, 1289 (2021). https://doi.org/10.3390/su13031289

44. Santopietro, L., Scorza, F., Murgante, B.: Multiple components in GHG stock of transport sector: technical improvements for SECAP baseline emissions inventory assessment. TeMA J. L. Use Mobil. Environ. 15, 5–24 (2022). https://doi.org/10.6092/1970-9870/8391

Computational Model for Fluid and Elastic Solid Interaction Based on Symmetric Hyperbolic Thermodynamically Compatible Systems Theory

Evgeniy Romenski[1]([⊠])[iD] and Galina Reshetova[2][iD]

[1] Sobolev Institute of Mathematics SB RAS, Novosibirsk 630090, Russia
evrom@math.nsc.ru
[2] Institute of Computational Mathematics and Mathematical Geophysics SB RAS, Novosibirsk 630090, Russia
kgv@nmsf.sscc.ru

Abstract. A computational model of interaction of a compressible fluid and deformable elastic solid is presented. The model is derived from the general solid-fluid two-phase mixture model and its derivation is based on the Symmetric Hyperbolic Thermodynamically Compatible (SHTC) systems theory. The governing equations form a symmetric hyperbolic system of partial differential equations of the first order, the solutions of which satisfy the thermodynamic law of conservation of energy. These properties allow the direct application of advanced high accuracy computational methods to solve model equations and ensure the reliability of numerically obtained solutions. Some preliminary results of numerical simulation are presented, showing the applicability of the model for studying complex problems of the solid-fluid interaction.

Keywords: Fluid solid interaction · Symmetric Hyperbolic Thermodynamically Compatible system · Runge-Kutta WENO method · Diffuse interface

1 Introduction

The solid-fluid interaction is a complex multiphysics problem of interest for various industrial applications, see, for example, [1]. One of the main challenges in modeling this type of problems is the numerical treatment of the interface between a fluid and a deformable moving solid. The difficulty here consists in

The development of the model is supported by the state contract of the Sobolev Institute of Mathematics (project no. FWNF-2022-0008), implementation of numerical methods and simulations are supported by the Russian Science Foundation (project no. 19-77-20004).

O. Gervasi et al. (Eds.): ICCSA 2022, LNCS 13376, pp. 303–313, 2022.
https://doi.org/10.1007/978-3-031-10450-3_26

the formulation of a moving curvilinear interface boundary condition and its numerical implementation. In recent decades, a diffuse interface approach has emerged that has an advantage of being able to use a rectangular mesh in the 2D case and a parallelepiped mesh in the 3D case. An application of various high-order numerical methods combined with a diffuse interface approach to multi-material problems can be found in a recently published review paper [2]. The main idea of this approach is to formulate a general multiphase model, rather than to combine separate models for each material through the boundary interaction. In this case, the interface is taken into account as a jump in the volume fraction of the phases, and the interaction of the phases is automatically described by the conservation laws of the general multiphase model. Such an approach is highly convenient for numerical implementation and high-performance numerical simulations.

The objective of the present paper is to develop a computational model for fluid interaction with a deformable solid combining a high accuracy Runge-Kutta WENO numerical method and diffuse interface approach. The mathematical model is based on a general theory of Symmetric Hyperbolic Thermodynamically Compatible (SHTC) equations [3–6], which has been successfully applied to modeling processes in complex media and development of the unified model of continuum [7–9]. We consider a compressible solid-fluid mixture theory [10] formulated within the class of SHTC equations. In this formulation, fluid and solid constituents are characterized by their own set of state variables, material constants, and a thermodynamic equation of state. The closure relations of the model depend on the volume and mass fraction of the phases according to some mixture rules. Thus, for the case of a vanishing phase volume fraction, one can obtain the governing equations for a pure fluid or pure elastic solid phases. This property is highly attractive, because it allows one to simulate in domains of a complex structure by the single PDE system with the use of diffuse interfaces. This approach has already been used in [11] to simulate the propagation of small amplitude waves, and in this paper we apply it to nonlinear processes.

The rest of the paper is organized as follows. Section 2 formulates the governing equations of the model and discusses their properties. Section 3 briefly describes high accuracy Runge-Kutta WENO numerical method, and Sect. 4 presents some preliminary results of solving a numerical test problem.

2   Model Formulation and Governing Equations

The mathematical model presented in the paper for simulations the interaction of an elastic solid and a compressible fluid can be formulated using a solid-fluid two-phase two-pressure two-velocity model from [10]. The derivation is based on the one velocity and one pressure approximation of the above model and a special choice of the volume fraction balance equation. Denote the fluid and solid phase parameters by indexes 1 and 2, respectively. Assume that the solid-fluid mixture is characterised by the volume fractions of the fluid α_1 and the solid $\alpha_2 = 1 - \alpha_1$. The other state variables characterizing the medium are: v^i -

velocity of the medium (common for both phases), ρ_1, ρ_2 - phase mass densities of the fluid and solid, respectively, $A_{ij}(i, j = 1, 2, 3)$ - the distortion field for the entire mixture.

The resulting system of equations consists of the total momentum conservation law, phase densities conservation laws for the fluid and solid phases and evolution equation for the distortion, which can be obtained from the PDE system presented in [10] assuming that the phase velocities of the mixture are equal to v^i and the phase pressure is equal to the common value $p_1(\rho_1) = p_2(\rho_2) = p$. We should also add an additional balance equation for the volume fraction, which in our case differs from that presented in [10]. The equation for the volume fraction in physically consistent two-phase models contains a transport term and a source term which is responsible for the phase pressures relaxation. In our case, we neglect the mentioned source term and consider only a term describing transport with the velocity of the medium. This means that the transition zone between the phases is not correctly simulated from the point of view of physics, and the volume fraction simply plays the role of a color function. Nevertheless, such an approach for modeling a two-phase flow with interfaces was proposed in [12] and was successfully applied to diffuse interphase simulations in many multimaterial problems.

Thus, the complete system of the governing PDEs reads as

$$\frac{\partial \rho v^i}{\partial t} + \frac{\partial(\rho v^i v^k + p\delta_{ik} - \sigma_{ik})}{\partial x_k} = 0,$$

$$\frac{\partial \alpha_1 \rho_1}{\partial t} + \frac{\partial \alpha_1 \rho_1 v^k}{\partial x_k} = 0,$$

$$\frac{\partial \alpha_2 \rho_2}{\partial t} + \frac{\partial \alpha_2 \rho_2 v^k}{\partial x_k} = 0, \tag{1}$$

$$\frac{\partial A_{ik}}{\partial t} + \frac{\partial A_{im} v^m}{\partial x_k} + v^j \left(\frac{\partial A_{ik}}{\partial x_j} - \frac{\partial A_{ij}}{\partial x_k} \right) = 0,$$

$$\frac{\partial \rho \alpha_1}{\partial t} + \frac{\partial \rho \alpha_1 v^k}{\partial x_k} = 0.$$

Here $\rho = \alpha_1 \rho_1 + \alpha_2 \rho_2$ is the mixture total density, ρ_1, ρ_2 are the phase densities, $p = p_1(\rho_1) = p_2(\rho_2)$ is the pressure of the mixture, coinciding with the pressures of both phases, A_{ik} is the distortion, $\sigma_{ik}(A_{mn}, \alpha_1)$ is the shear stress, whose definition is given below.

Note that the energy conservation law holds for system (1)

$$\frac{\partial \rho(E + v^i v^i / 2)}{\partial t} + \frac{\partial(\rho v^k(E + v^i v^i / 2) + v^k p - v^i \sigma_{ik})}{\partial x_k} = 0, \tag{2}$$

that means that the model is thermodynamically compatible. Here $E(\alpha_1, \rho_1, \rho_2, A_{ij})$ is the specific internal energy of the mixture.

System (1) has an additional important property. An additional stationary conservation law (constraint) holds

$$\frac{\partial A_{ik}}{\partial x_j} - \frac{\partial A_{ij}}{\partial x_k} = 0 \tag{3}$$

for all the time moments if it holds in the initial data at $t = 0$.

We emphasize that system (1) can be used to simulate a "pure" compressible fluid flow if $\alpha_2 = \epsilon, \alpha_1 = 1 - \epsilon$, where ϵ is a very small number. And vice versa, it can be used to simulate the finite deformations of a "pure" elastic medium if $\alpha_1 = \epsilon, \alpha_2 = 1 - \epsilon$, with a very small ϵ. This can be done by a special choice of closing relations and material constants. Note that it is possible to take into account the non-elastic deformation of a solid medium by introducing a source term into the right-hand side of the equation for distortion A_{ik}, as is described, for example, in [7].

System (1) belongs to the class of the SHTC systems, i.e. it is thermodynamically compatible and can be converted to a symmetric hyperbolic form. These properties ensure the reliability of the numerically obtained solutions.

Closing relations for system (1) are the dependence of phase pressures on the density of the corresponding phases and the dependence of shear stress on distortion. These relations can be obtained from the internal energy thermodynamic potential E, which provides the closure of the general two-phase fluid-solid mixture model (see the details in [10]).

In this paper, we use the stiffened gas equation of state for each phase that means that the energy for each phase takes the following form

$$e(\rho) = \frac{C^2}{\gamma(\gamma - 1)} \left(\frac{\rho}{\rho_0} \right)^{(\gamma-1)} + \frac{\rho_0 C^2 - \gamma p_0}{\gamma \rho}, \tag{4}$$

where C is the bulk sound velocity, γ is the adiabatic constant, ρ_0 is the reference density and p_0 is the common reference pressure for two phases. Based on the thermodynamic definition of the pressure $p = \rho^2 \partial e / \partial \rho$, the pressure for each phase is computed as

$$p_i(\rho_i) = \frac{\rho_{i0} C_i^2}{\gamma_i} \left(\left(\frac{\rho_i}{\rho_{i0}} \right)^{\gamma_i} - 1 \right) + p_0, \quad i = 1, 2, \tag{5}$$

where material constants for each phase are different. The shear stress is defined as (see [10])

$$\sigma_{ik}(A_{mn}) = -\frac{\rho c_2 C_s^2}{2} \left(g_{i\alpha} g_{\alpha k} - \frac{1}{3} g_{\alpha\beta} g_{\beta\alpha} \delta_{ik} \right), \tag{6}$$

where $g_{ij} = G_{ij}(detG)^{-1/3}$ is the normalized Finger tensor $G_{ij} = A_{\alpha i} A_{\alpha j}$, C_s^2 is the squared shear velocity of sound in the solid, $c_2 = \alpha_2 \rho_2 / \rho$ is the mass fraction of the solid phase. It can be seen from (6) that in the pure fluid ($c_2 = 0$) the shear stress vanishes, whereas in the pure solid ($c_2 = 1$) it corresponds to the Hooke law for the elastic medium.

3   Numerical Method

The governing equations of the model formulated in the previous section form a first order hyperbolic system, and therefore the modern high accuracy methods developed for solving such equations can be applied to numerical simulations. We consider two-dimensional processes and reduced two-dimensional equations in the coordinates $x_1 = x, x_2 = y$ in the presence of possible source terms (for example, gravity) can be written down as

$$\frac{\partial \mathbf{U}}{\partial t} + \frac{\partial \mathbf{F}(\mathbf{U})}{\partial x} + \frac{\partial \mathbf{G}(\mathbf{U})}{\partial y} + B_1(\mathbf{U})\frac{\partial \mathbf{U}}{\partial x} + B_2(\mathbf{U})\frac{\partial \mathbf{U}}{\partial y} = \mathbf{S}(\mathbf{U}). \qquad (7)$$

Here $\mathbf{U}$ is the vector of conservative variables

$$\mathbf{U} = (\rho v_1, \rho v_2, \alpha_1 \rho_1, \alpha_2 \rho_2, A_{11}, A_{21}, A_{12}, A_{22}, \alpha_1)^T. \qquad (8)$$

Note that in the two-dimensional case $A_{13} = A_{31} = 0, A_{33} = 1$.

The non-conservative terms in (7) with the matrices $B_1(\mathbf{U}), B_2(\mathbf{U})$ correspond to the $curl A$ term in the fourth equation of system (1). In this paper, we assume that the numerical approximation gives us the value of $curl A$ close to zero due to compatibility condition (3) and therefore we neglect the non-conservative terms in (7). Of course, this assumption is made only to test the performance of the model and should be discarded in the future when developing more accurate methods.

We also introduce the vector of primitive variables

$$\mathbf{V} = (v_1, v_2, \rho_1, \rho_2, A_{11}, A_{21}, A_{12}, A_{22}, \alpha_1)^T. \qquad (9)$$

The fluxes $\mathbf{F}(\mathbf{U})$ and $\mathbf{G}(\mathbf{U})$ in the x and y directions are computed as

$$\mathbf{F}(\mathbf{U}) = (\rho v_1^2 - \Sigma_{11}, \rho v_1 v_2 - \Sigma_{21}, \alpha_1 \rho_1 v_1, \alpha_2 \rho_2 v_1, A_{1j} v_j, A_{2j} v_j, 0, 0, \alpha_1 v_1)^T, \quad (10)$$

$$\mathbf{G}(\mathbf{U}) = (\rho v_1 v_2 - \Sigma_{12}, \rho v_2^2 - \Sigma_{22}, \alpha_1 \rho_1 v_2, \alpha_2 \rho_2 v_2, 0, 0, A_{1j} v_j, A_{2j} v_j, \alpha_1 v_2)^T, \quad (11)$$

where $\Sigma_{ij} = \sigma_{ij} - p\delta_{ij}, i, j = 1, 2$.

Finally, if the gravity is taken into account, the vector of source terms is computed as

$$\mathbf{S}(\mathbf{U}) = (0, -\rho g, 0, 0, 0, 0, 0, 0, 0)^T, \qquad (12)$$

where $g = 9.8 \, \text{m/s}^2$ is the acceleration of gravity.

To solve system (7), we apply the standard Runge-Kutta WENO method [14], which is successfully used in modeling various problems of fluid dynamics and solid mechanics. The chosen order of accuracy of the method is the fifth order in space and time. Since we apply the diffuse interface method, the spatial approximation uses a square grid, which is highly convenient for the numerical implementation.

The numerical experiments described below were performed in the square domain $(x, y) \in [0, L] \times [0, L]$ with the cells $I_{ij} = [x_{i-1/2}, x_{i+1/2}] \times [y_{j-1/2}, y_{j+1/2}]$, where $x_{i\pm 1/2} = x_i \pm h/2$, $y_{j\pm 1/2} = y_j \pm h/2$, $h = L/N$, N is the number of intervals along the axes X and Y. The spatial finite difference approximation of system (7) for the mesh cell I_{ij} reads as

$$\frac{d\mathbf{U}_{ij}}{dt} + \frac{\mathbf{F}_{i+1/2,j} - \mathbf{F}_{i-1/2,j}}{h} + \frac{\mathbf{G}_{i,j+1/2} - \mathbf{G}_{i,j-1/2}}{h} = \mathbf{S}_{ij}, \qquad (13)$$

where $\mathbf{U}_{ij}$ is the value of the vector of conservative variables corresponding to the mesh cell I_{ij}, the fluxes $\mathbf{F}_{i\pm 1/2,j}$, $\mathbf{G}_{i,j\pm 1/2}$ are computed at the cell boundaries, and $\mathbf{S}_{ij}$ is the value of the source terms in this cell.

Thus, if the values of the fluxes at the cell boundaries are known, we obtain an ordinary differential equation for $\mathbf{U}_{ij}$ which can be written in the following form:

$$\frac{d\mathbf{U}_{ij}}{dt} = \mathcal{L}(\mathbf{U}), \qquad (14)$$

where $\mathcal{L}(\mathbf{U}) = -(\mathbf{F}_{i+1/2,j} - \mathbf{F}_{i-1/2,j})/h - (\mathbf{G}_{i,j+1/2} - \mathbf{G}_{i,j-1/2})/h + \mathbf{S}_{ij}$. This means that if the cell boundary fluxes are known, we have the ordinary differential equation for $\mathbf{U}_{ij}$ which can be numerically solved by the high order Runge-Kutta method. In the present paper, we use the SSPRK (Strong Stability Preserving Runge-Kutta) method [15], whose formulae for ODE system (14) at the time moment t_n read as

$$\mathbf{U}^{(0)} = \mathbf{U}_{ij}^n,$$

$$\mathbf{U}^{(k)} = \mathbf{U}^{(k-1)} + \frac{\Delta t}{2}\mathcal{L}(\mathbf{U}^{k-1}), \quad k = 1, ..., K-1 \qquad (15)$$

$$\mathbf{U}^{(K)} = \sum_{m=0}^{K-2} \alpha_{K,m}\mathbf{U}^{(m)} + \alpha_{K,K-1}\left(\mathbf{U}^{(K-1)} + \frac{\Delta t}{2}\mathcal{L}(\mathbf{U}^{K-1})\right),$$

$$\mathbf{U}^{(n+1)} = \mathbf{U}^{(K)},$$

We take the fifth order SSPRK method with $K = 6$ and coefficients $\alpha_{K,0} = 1/9$, $\alpha_{K,1} = 2/5$, $\alpha_{K,2} = 0$, $\alpha_{K,3} = 4/9$, $\alpha_{K,4} = 0$, $\alpha_{K,5} = 2/45$.

The time step Δt must be chosen in accordance with the Courant-Friedrichs-Lewy stability condition $\Delta t = C_{CFL} \times \min(h/V_{ij})$ with $0 < C_{CFL} < 1$, where V_{ij} is the velocity of fastest wave in the mesh cell I_{ij}.

For the evaluation of fluxes on the cell boundaries we use the fifth order WENO reconstruction for primitive variables in conjunction with the Lax-Friedrichs method [13]. We do not give here the formulas for the WENO reconstruction, which can be found in [14]. This gives us the values of all variables on the left and on the right of the cell boundary for each spatial direction. After the reconstruction, we can compute the fluxes as follows. If the reconstructed values of the variables U_L to the left and U_R to the right of the boundary located at the point $x_{i+1/2,j}$ between cells in the x-direction are known, the flux on this boundary is computed as

$$\mathbf{F}_{i+1/2,j} = \frac{1}{2}(\mathbf{F}(\mathbf{U}_L) + \mathbf{F}(\mathbf{U}_R)) - \frac{1}{2}\frac{h}{\Delta t}(\mathbf{U}_R - \mathbf{U}_L). \qquad (16)$$

Similarly, the flux in the y-direction for the intercell boundary located at $y_{i,j+1/2}$ is computed as

$$\mathbf{G}_{i,j+1/2} = \frac{1}{2}(\mathbf{G}(\mathbf{U}_L) + \mathbf{G}(\mathbf{U}_R)) - \frac{1}{2}\frac{h}{\Delta t}(\mathbf{U}_R - \mathbf{U}_L), \qquad (17)$$

where U_L, U_R are reconstructed values from the left and the right sides of the boundary.

Finally, it should be noted that the numerical approximation of the equation for the volume fraction should be done separately in order to avoid spurious oscillations caused by a jump in the volume fraction in the initial data. We take the following approximation:

$$\frac{d(\alpha_1)_{i,j}}{dt} = \qquad (18)$$

$$-\frac{1}{2h}\left((v_1)^n_{i,j}\left((\alpha_1)^L_{i+1/2,j} + (\alpha_1)^R_{i+1/2,j}\right) - \frac{h}{\Delta t}\left((\alpha_1)^R_{i+1/2,j} - (\alpha_1)^L_{i+1/2,j}\right)\right)$$

$$+\frac{1}{2h}\left((v_1)^n_{i,j}\left((\alpha_1)^L_{i-1/2,j} + (\alpha_1)^R_{i-1/2,j}\right) - \frac{h}{\Delta t}\left((\alpha_1)^R_{i-1/2,j} - (\alpha_1)^L_{i-1/2,j}\right)\right)$$

$$-\frac{1}{2h}\left((v_2)^n_{i,j}\left((\alpha_1)^L_{i,j+1/2} + (\alpha_1)^R_{i,j+1/2}\right) - \frac{h}{\Delta t}\left((\alpha_1)^R_{i,j+1/2} - (\alpha_1)^L_{i,j+1/2}\right)\right)$$

$$+\frac{1}{2h}\left((v_2)^n_{i,j}\left((\alpha_1)^L_{i,j-1/2} + (\alpha_1)^R_{i,j-1/2}\right) - \frac{h}{\Delta t}\left((\alpha_1)^R_{i,j-1/2} - (\alpha_1)^L_{i,j-1/2}\right)\right)$$

This approximation can be derived from fulfilling the requirement of maintaining the homogeneity of the phase density fields in a medium with a discontinuity only in the volume concentration (see, for example [16]). When deriving, specific formulas (16), (17) for the Lax-Friedrichs flux must be used.

4 Numerical Simulations

The numerical approach is tested on a two-dimensional model of a "pure" elastic ball falling in a "pure" compressible fluid under the gravity action. For the simulation, we use system (1) and fifth order in space and time Runge-Kutta WENO numerical techniques discussed in the previous sections. Note that to include the gravity force in the model, it is necessary to put the source term $-\rho g$ into the equation for v_2, where g is the gravitational acceleration. In the simulations, we took an artificial acceleration value $g = 900.8 \times 10^3$ to speed up the falling process.

To describe this test model in terms of the solid-fluid mixture, we put a small value of fluid with the volume fraction $\alpha_1 = \epsilon = 10^{-6}$ ($\alpha_2 = 1 - \epsilon$) in the solid phase and vice versa put the same value of the solid phase $\alpha_2 = \epsilon = 10^{-6}$ ($\alpha_1 = 1 - \epsilon$) in the fluid phase. The material parameters of the fluid phase (Fluid) and the solid phase (Solid) are given in Table 1. The adiabatic constant in formula (5) is equal to $\gamma = 2$.

The computational domain is 4-m square with uniform 400×400 mesh, and the initial ball with radius 0.3 m located at $x = 2$ m and $y = 0.7$ m. The simulation is performed with a Courant number of 0.8.

Figure 1 shows the results of numerical simulations at the initial time (the upper snapshot) and after each 1000 time steps. Figure represents the distribution of the fluid volume fraction α_1. We can observe the numerical diffusion of the sharp interface between the ball and the fluid, but the diffusion is not crucial and the overall shape is preserved (Fig. 2). It is possible to reduce this numerical diffusion by employing the Tangent of Hyperbola INterface Capturing (THINC) method [17, 18] which we plan to incorporate in our numerical techniques.

Table 1. Physical parameters used for simulation.

State	Property	Parameters	Value	Unit
Fluid (water):	Fluid density	$\rho_f = \rho_{10}$	1040	kg/m^3
	Sound velocity	c_f	1500	m/s
	Bulk modulus	$K_f = K_1 = \rho_f c_f^2$	2.34	GPa
Solid (granite):	Solid density	$\rho_s = \rho_{20}$	2500	kg/m^3
	P-wave velocity	v_p	6155	m/s
	Bulk velocity	c_s	4332	m/s
	Shear velocity	c_{sh}	3787	m/s
	Bulk modulus	$K_s = K_2 = \rho_s c_s^2$	46.91	GPa
	Shear modulus	$\mu_s = \mu_2 = \rho_s c_{sh}^2$	35.85	GPa

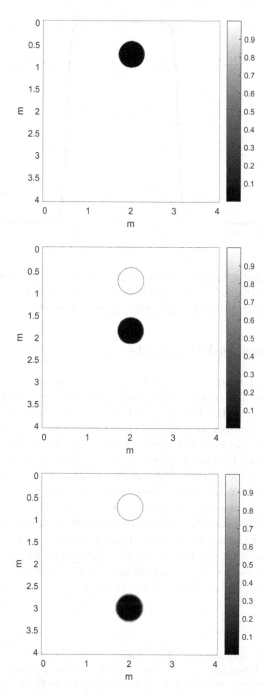

Fig. 1. The snapshots of the fluid volume fraction α_1 at the initial time (upper figure), after 1000 time steps (middle figure) and after 2000 time steps (lower figure).

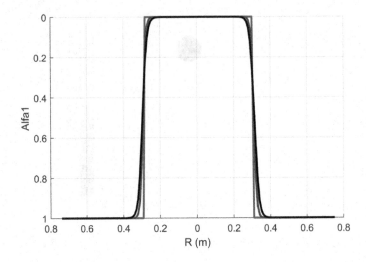

Fig. 2. Comparison of diffusion of the fluid volume fraction α_1 near the sharp interface between the ball of radius R and the fluid. Red - at the initial time, Blue - after 1000 time steps and Black - after 2000 time steps. (Color figure online)

5   Conclusions and Prospects

We have presented a new computational model applicable for the simulation of the interaction of a compressible fluid and an elastic deformable solid. Its derivation is based on the theory of SHTC systems. The governing equations of the model are well-posed (they can be transformed to a symmetric hyperbolic system, and existence and uniqueness of the solution is provided at least locally in time) and thermodynamically correct (the first and second laws of thermodynamics are satisfied). The interfaces between the fluid and the solid are represented by a jump in the phase volume fraction in the single system of PDEs, which allows one to use a diffuse interface model and rectangular (2D) or parallelepiped (3D) meshes. A numerical example is presented that illustrates the applicability of the model for simulation the problem of the solid-fluid interaction. Further research will involve the development of more accurate methods for the diffuse interface, such as THINK [17, 18], as well as the application of the method to solve various problems of the interaction of a fluid and a solid.

References

1. Peksen, M.: Multiphysics modelling of interactions in systems. In: Peksen, M. (ed.) Multiphysics Modelling, pp. 139–159. Academic Press, Cambridge (2018)
2. Maltsev, V., Skote, M., Tsoutsanis, P.: High-order methods for diffuse-interface models in compressible multi-medium flows: a review. Phys. Fluids **34**, 021301 (2022)
3. Godunov, S.K., Romenskii, E.I.: Elements of Continuum Mechanics and Conservation Laws. Kluwer Academic/Plenum Publishers, New York (2003)

4. Godunov, S.K., Mikhaĭlova, T.Y., Romenskii, E.I.: Systems of thermodynamically coordinated laws of conservation invariant under rotations. Siberian Math. J. **37**, 690–705 (1996)
5. Romenski, E.: Hyperbolic systems of thermodynamically compatible conservation laws in continuum mechanics. Math. Comput. Model. **28**, 115–130 (1998)
6. Peshkov, I., Pavelka, M., Romenski, E., Grmela, M.: Continuum mechanics and thermodynamics in the Hamilton and the Godunov-type formulations. Continuum Mech. Thermodyn. **30**(6), 1343–1378 (2018). https://doi.org/10.1007/s00161-018-0621-2
7. Dumbser, M., Peshkov, I., Romenski, E., Zanotti, O.: High order ADER schemes for a unified first order hyperbolic formulation of continuum mechanics: viscous heat-conducting fluids and elastic solids. J. Comput. Phys. **314**, 824–862 (2016)
8. Dumbser, M., Peshkov, I., Romenski, E., Zanotti, O.: High order ADER schemes for a unified first order hyperbolic formulation of Newtonian continuum mechanics coupled with electro-dynamics. J. Comput. Phys. **348**, 298–342 (2017)
9. Peshkov, I., Dumbser, M., Boscheri, W., Romenski, E., Chiocchetti, S., Ioriatti, M.: Simulation of non-Newtonian viscoplastic flows with a unified first order hyperbolic model and a structure-preserving semi-implicit scheme. Comput. Fluids **224**, 104963 (2021)
10. Romenski, E., Reshetova, G., Peshkov, I., Dumbser, M.: Modeling wavefields in saturated elastic porous media based on thermodynamically compatible system theory for two-phase solid-fluid mixtures. Comput. Fluids **206**, 104587 (2020)
11. Reshetova, G., Romenski, E.: Diffuse interface approach to modeling wavefields in a saturated porous medium. Appl. Math. Comput. **398**, 125978 (2021)
12. Allaire, G., Clerc, S., Kokh, S.: A five-equation model for the simulation of interfaces between compressible fluids. J. Comput. Phys. **181**, 577–616 (2002)
13. Toro, E.F.: Riemann Solvers and Numerical Methods for Fluid Dynamics. A Practical Introduction, 3rd edn. Springer, Heidelberg (2009). https://doi.org/10.1007/b79761
14. Jiang, G.-S., Shu, C.-W.: Efficient implementation of weighted ENO schemes. J. Comput. Phys. **126**, 202–228 (1996)
15. Gottlieb, S.: On high order strong stability preserving Runge-Kutta and multi step time discretizations. J. Sci. Comput. **25**, 105–128 (2005)
16. Saurel, R., Abgrall, R.: A simple method for compressible multifluid flows. SIAM J. Sci. Comput. **21**, 1115–1145 (1999)
17. Deng, X., Inaba, S., Xie, B., Shyue, K.-M., Xiao, F.: High fidelity discontinuity-resolving reconstruction for compressible multiphase flows with moving interfaces. J. Comput. Phys. **371**, 945–966 (2018)
18. Xiao, F., Honma, Y., Kono, T.: A simple algebraic interface capturing scheme using hyperbolic tangent function. Int. J. Numer. Meth. Fluids **48**(9), 1023–1040 (2005)

Electronic, Chemical, Thermodynamics Properties Screening of $[M(SDPH)(VDPH)(X)a(Y)b)]^n$ (M = Cr, Mn, Fe, Co, Ni; X = NH_3; Y: H_2O; a = 0 or 1; b = 1 or 2; n = 0 or 1) Metal Complexes with an Extended Tight Binding Quantum Chemical Method

Winda Eka Pratiwi[✉], Irma Mulyani, and Atthar Luqman Ivansyah

Departement of Chemistry, Faculty of Mathematics and Naturals Science, Bandung Institute of Technology, Bandung, Indonesia
windaekapratiwi17@gmail.com, irma@chem.itb.ac.id,
atthar@csx.itb.ac.id

Abstract. The capability of the Schiff's base complex from the *hydrazine* group, which has *azomethine* (-NHN=CH-) as the main group, has been studied for its potential in the medical field, such as anticancer, antioxidant, and antibacterial. The synthesis method and its reaction condition for coordinating the first-row transition complex compound with base Schiff's ligands SDPH (Salicylaldehyde-2,4-Dinitrophenylhydrazine) and VDPH (Vanillin-Dinitrophenylhydrazine) were still challenging to be applied as not all reaction conditions can succeed in the synthesis experiment. To determine the potential of first-row transition metal ions coordinating with SDPH and VDPH ligands, this research studies computationally the Extended Tight Binding Quantum Chemical method, called GFN2-xTB. Variations of the octahedral complex molecular formula used in computational calculations are $[M(L)_2X_aY_b]$ and $[M(L)_2X_aY_b]^+$ with M = (Cr, Mn, Fe, Co, Ni); L = SDPH and VDPH; X = NH_3 (a = 0 or 1); and Y = H_2O (b = 1 or 2). In addition, these complex compounds, which have metal ions with electron configuration d^4-d^7, were studied for their stability under high and low spin conditions. The data indicate the presence of stable complexes with more negative ΔG values were generally found in: (i) complexes with VDPH ligands, (ii) complexes containing the NH_3 ligand, (iii) complexes with metal ions M^{+3}, (iv) complexes having low spin magnetic properties. These results were also supported by the characteristics of global reactive descriptors, including a global electrophilicity index, electronegativity, chemical potential, chemical hardness, and chemical softness. It also included studies related to the HOMO-LUMO electronic energy to determine the reactivity and stability of the studied complex compounds.

Keywords: SDPH and VDPH complexes · First-row transition metals · GFN2-xTB

O. Gervasi et al. (Eds.): ICCSA 2022, LNCS 13376, pp. 314–332, 2022.
https://doi.org/10.1007/978-3-031-10450-3_27

1 Introduction

The coordination functionality of the central atom and the ligand is still one of the interesting issues that are currently being developed. One of the ligands that have various applications in the field of chemistry is Schiff's base ligand. The coordination of a Schiff's base ligand with a transition metal has received much more attention because it has many medical, pharmacology, and biological studies applications [1]. In addition, this research is supported by several studies reporting that Schiff's base has broad biological activities, especially as an antibacterial, antifungal antiviral and anti-inflammatory agent [2, 3] which are closely related to the characteristics of the ligand properties and the functionality of a complex [4]. Therefore, it is important to understand the character of the ligand and the central atom to be able to make coordination of complex compounds that are useful for life, especially in the biomedical field. Schiff base group hydrazone is a compound produced from the reaction of aldehydes with hydrazine. These hydrazone compounds can act as multidentate ligands with transition metals and show development in biological applications. [5, 6] Hydrazone in a Schiff's base compound with the main group of azomethine is (C=N), which is a substantial part for biological application [7–9]. This was stated in a study saying that Schiff's base complex with transition metals Fe(III), Cu(II), Zn(II) has been synthesized and produced complexes that are useful in the field of antimicrobials [10]. A group of Schiff's base derived from salicylaldehyde can provide a medium for producing valuable compounds with desirable certain biological and industrial attributes [11–13]. One of the Schiff base groups derived from salicylaldehyde is SDPH or (*Salicylaldehyde-2,4-dinitrophenyl hydrazine*) which has successfully demonstrated in the presence of antioxidants activity when coordinated with Co(II) to form complex compounds [Co(II)(SDPH)] [14].

Modification of the hydrazone-derived ligand group with the main compounds salicylaldehyde vanillin, and hydrazine is a modification of the complex formula of the Schiff base, especially the SDPH and VDPH ligands which have not been widely synthesized yet. Consequently, this study was conducted to analyze the stability of a complex when formed and its characteristics, including reactivity and chemical stability.

Through the use of computational calculation methods, it is easier to identify possible non-covalent interactions of a compound that will be synthesized since this non-covalent interaction can increase the potential for biological activity for bioactive compounds [15]. One of the computational study is the semi-empirical quantum chemical, especially GFNn-xTB method. The GFNn-XTB method is a method that is popularly being developed. It has also a good performance in terms of of organic chemistry and several organometallic [16]. This is one of the reasons for using the GFN2-xTB method in this research. As it is known that this method is not yet commonly used, it will be a special appeal to develop it. In addition, it can help the calculation of complex compounds and transition metals which have hundreds or thousands of atoms. Besides, this is supported by a higher speed on GFNn-xTB than the DFT method. Therefore, this study focuses on the identification and screening of the Schiff's base complexes, especially the complex compound SDPH (*Salicylaldehyde-2,4-Dinitrophenylhydrazine*) and VDPH (*Vanillin-Dinitrophenylhydrazine*) with any transition metals first row using the GFN2-xTB method.

2 Computational Study

The methodology used in this study is the GFN2-xTB method, where extended tight binding is the scope of the atomistic-based semi-empirical method or SQM method which is usually used for atomistic modelling, biochemical and organometallic applications [17]. XTB comes from the expansion of density functional disturbances or DFT from electron density in a fluctuating to several massages alike as a broader or extended functional density binding model known as "xTB" [18]. The GFNn-xTB energy expressions are represented as a robust electronic structure scheme for the calculation of harmonic frequencies used in a calculated free energy, especially GFN2-xTB which is highly advised on a vibrational big scale frequency [19]. Another advantage of choosing GFN2-xTB method is more efficient, reasonable cost accuracy ratio, and high resistance [20]. Recently, the GFN2-xTB method has been developed to optimize the complex structure, such as optimization of the structure of La(III) complex compounds [21]. Complex compounds consisting of tens or even hundreds of atoms in a computational chemistry study require special methods because they are often limited to chemical compounds that have a simple number of atoms. This GFN2-xTB has been a thorough development and evaluation of a semi-empirical quantum chemical method. The common method used in the semi-empirical quantum chemical is the DFT which is usually used for complex compounds. The advantage of using the DFT method is that it has a fairly good level of accuracy, but it has the disadvantage of a fairly long calculation process so over time, quantum chemical methods were found that provide the right calculation process, one of which is GFN2-xTB. The GFN2-xtb method was developed because it has good geometry optimization results and is full of simple compounds to complex compounds [22]. Furthermore, GFN2-xtb methods can test benchmark sets regarding reaction energies on organometallic reactions. The GFNn-xTB method has calculation results which are shown by the success of the simulation of mass spectrum electron ionization, conformer-rotamer in organic chemistry, and optimization of lanthanoid complexes [22]. GFNn-xTB is also used in calculating the pKa of a reaction [23].

The results of the optimization of the structure of organometallic complex compounds studied produced an excellent structure and the GFNn-xTB method is considered to have excellent performance in optimizing the structure of complex compounds. xTB [16]. The advantages of GFNn-xTB compared to DFT are efficiency and speed in the performance of calculations carried out especially in complex compounds [17]. This is evidenced by optimization of the geometric structure with all SQM methods in all finite elements $Z = 86$ including lanthanoids. This of course can also open up opportunities for finding conformational searches for systems with transition metals bonded to other compounds for optimizing their use in the chemical field. Optimizing the accuracy of the geometric structure produced by the GFNn-xTB method can be used as an alternative to the theory of the DFT method. The DFT method fails to describe a system that occurs in transition metals such as breaking chemical bonds and characterizing the correlation of static theory. This is due to the difficulty in describing the interactions of the degenerated states [24]. This tight bind extended method is designed not only for the calculation of the structure but also the energy of non-covalent interactions in a system with large molecules and atomic numbers such as complex compounds. The advantages of good computational efficiency compared to its predecessor methods make the GFNn-xTB method considered appropriate for exploring the conformational space of molecular systems [25].

The study carried out is the optimization of molecular orbital geometry where there are a dozens of complex structure variations as well as major ligands, which include SDPH (*Salicylldehyde-2,4-Dinitrophenylhydrazine*) and VDPH (*Vanillindinitrophenylhydrazine*) ligands and L = SDPH and VDPH X = NH_3 and Y = H_2O, which reviewed based on electronic, chemical, and thermodynamic properties pada temperature standard 298K and the pressure constant which mean 1 atm. For the preparation of optimization of molecular structures of complex compound, we used Avogadro software to input geometry of the complexes. All calculations were executed with ORCA 4.2.0 software. The calculation of electronic properties is through the highest occupied molecular orbital- the lowest unoccupied molecular orbital (HOMO-LUMO) energy analysis. While the thermodynamic properties are based on changes in the resulting Gibbs free energy, while global reactivity descriptors are calculated for the stability and reactivity of complex compounds, including Softness (S), Electronegativity (χ), Electrophilicity index (ω), global electrophilicity, frontier molecular orbitals (FMO), Chemical Potential (μ) and Hardness (η).

3   Results and Discussion

3.1   Stabilization of Complex Compounds with Variation of First-Row Transition Metal Ions

The transition metal is an essential parameter in a complex compound playing a pivotal role in addition to ligands. In this study, the nature of each transition metal, especially the central first-row metals: [M: Cr, Mn, Fe, Co, Ni], was studied to determine the effect of variations in metal ion charge or oxidation number on the overall stability of the SDPH and VDPH complex compounds.

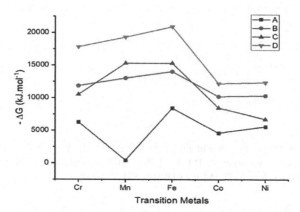

Fig. 1. ΔG energy any complexes with molecular formula: $[M(II)(L)_2(Y)]^n$ with (n = 0 or 1) and Y = H_2O. The complexes consist of, (A) $[M(II)(SDPH)_2(H_2O)_2]$; (B) $[M(II)(VDPH)_2(H_2O)_2]$; (C) $[M(III)(SDPH)_2(H_2O)_2]^+$; (D) $[M(III)(VDPH)_2(H_2O)_2]^+$

According to Fig. 1 in a complex compound, the total change in Gibbs free energy produced by each complex with variations in the charge of metal ions 2+ and 3+, and also from variations in the molecular formula of different complex compounds can produce the most negative total Gibbs free energy is D [M(III)(VDPH)$_2$(H$_2$O)$_2$]$^+$ complex. This indicates that complex compounds with a charge of 3+ and with variations in VDPH ligands have the highest negative energy. The value is -20909 kJ.mol^{-1}, followed by complex compounds C [M(III)(SDPH)$_2$(H$_2$O)$_2$]$^+$ and complex B:[M(II)(VDPH)$_2$(H$_2$O)$_2$], while the lowest negative value is A [M(II)(SDPH)$_2$(H$_2$O)$_2$]. As a result, the change in Gibbs free energy from the most negative value is D (-20909 kJ.mol^{-1}) > C ($-15306,2$ kJ.mol^{-1}) > B ($-14029,7$ kJ.mol^{-1}) > A (-8443 kJ.mol^{-1}). The negative value of the change in Gibbs free energy occurring in the several complex compounds indicates that these are more thermodynamically stable than complex compounds with other types of metal ions. According to Fig. 1, complex compound with the molecular formula [M(III)(SDPH)$_2$(H$_2$O)$_2$]$^+$ has a more negative value since the central metal ion with a 3+ charge is more acidic than the metal ion with a 2+ charge. The more acidic the metal center, the easier the complex formation and the more stable complex compounds.

3.2   Effect of NH$_3$ Ligand on the Stability of Complex Compounds

This study carried out calculations on various types of complex compounds with different molecular formulas. The aim is to analyze the presence of NH$_3$ ligand effect on complex compounds for in terms of its stability.

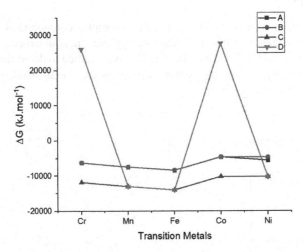

Fig. 2. ΔG energy any complexes with molecular formula [M(II)(L)$_2$X(Y)] with X = NH$_3$ and Y = H$_2$O. The complexes consist of (A) [M(II)(SDPH)$_2$(H$_2$O)$_2$]; (B) [M(II)(SDPH)$_2$(NH$_3$)(H$_2$O)]; (C) [M(II)(VDPH)$_2$(H$_2$O)$_2$]; (D) [M(II)(VDPH)$_2$(NH$_3$)(H$_2$O)]

Figure 2 depicts a plot energy of total Gibbs free energy change for each complex compound. D [M(II)(VDPH)$_2$(NH$_3$)(H$_2$O)] compound has the most negative energy at -14029.7 kJ.mol^{-1}.This value is slightly different compared to C [M(II)(VDPH)$_2$

$(H_2O)_2]$ compound value at -13025.4 kJ.mol^{-1}. According to this plot energy, the change of Gibbs free energy on the various complex compounds results not only a change of negative energy, but also a change of positive energy. This is proven by the number of total change in Gibbs free energy produced by complex compounds $[Cr(II)(VDPH)_2(NH_3)(H_2O)]$ and $[Co(II)(VDPH)_2(NH_3)(H_2O)]$ from molecular formula $[M(II)(VDPH)_2(NH_3)(H_2O)]$ at 25986 kJ.mol^{-1} and 27641 kJ.mol^{-1} respectively. Hence, not all complex compounds produce a negative total energy change. This negative energy value indicates that the complex is stable and occurs spontaneously. This is different from the results of several other complexes which are positive indicating a less stable complex. The complexes containing the NH3 ligan results more stable complexes compared to complexes without the NH3 ligan. This is because the NH3 ligand is a ligand that has a better field strength than water although both are sigma donor ligands. Consequently, it has an implication for the formation of complexes that are easier and more stable. This occurs due to the character of the NH3 ligand, apart from being a good base by being able to donate electrons to metal ions and being a suitable sigma donor ligand. Furthermore, the density of the electron environment around the complex becomes stable and makes the change in the Gibbs free energy bigger.

3.3 Effect of Electron Distribution on the Stability of Complex Compounds

The bar chart in Fig. 3 explains the effect of distributed electron of any complexes which results a total Gibbs free energy change. In this chart, the electron configurations d4-d7 of complexes with metal ions are Cr^{2+}, Mn^{2+}, Fe^{2+}, Co^{2+}, Ni^{2+}, Cr^{3+}, Mn^{3+}, Fe^{3+}, Co^{3+}, Ni^{3+}.

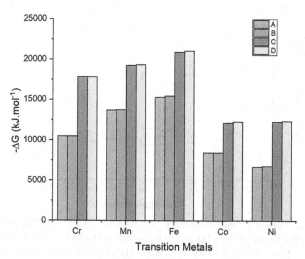

Fig. 3. ΔG energy any complexes with molecular formula $[M(II)(L)_2(Y)]$ with L = SDPH or VDPH, Y = H_2O. The complexes consist of (A) $[M(II)(SDPH)_2(H_2O)_2]$ HS; (B) $[M(II)(SDPH)_2(H_2O)_2]$ LS; (C) $[M(II)(VDPH)_2(H_2O)_2]$ HS; (D) $[M(II)(VDPH)_2(H_2O)_2]$ LS (with HS = High Spin) and LS = Low Spin)

Based on the results of the calculations, the results of the electron distribution of each complex were different. In this case, one representative of the calculation of complex compounds was taken with the molecular formula [M(II)(L)$_2$(Y)$_2$] where L = SDPH or VDPH, and Y = H$_2$O) with spin variations, called high spin and low spin. The complex with a low spin state turned out to have the most negative Gibbs free energy change value. Although thermodynamically, the values for the high and low spin states were not much different for each complex. The value of the most negative Gibbs free energy change in the complex with the molecular formula [M(II)(VDPH)$_2$(H$_2$O)$_2$] LS was −21087 kJ.mol^{-1}, whereas the smallest negative Gibbs free energy change value was the complex [M(II)(SDPH)$_2$(H$_2$O)$_2$] HS at −6703 kJ.mol^{-1}. This indicates that the most stable complexes are found for complex compounds with variations in central metal and electron distribution, called complex compounds with the molecular formula [M(II)(L)$_2$(Y)$_2$] with low spin.

3.4   Global Reactivity Descriptors

In the computational theory of quantum mechanics, where the global reactivity descriptor characteristic can explain the reactivity of a compound, in this study, the Schiff's base complex compound has been studied and can determine the chemical reactivity of a molecule, chemical stability, and polarization tendencies of the molecule [26]. In addition, this study related to the global quantum descriptor can also analyze a molecule selection [27].

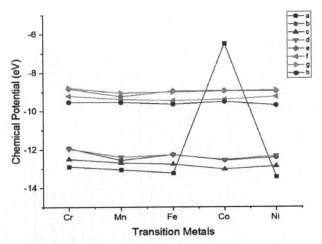

Fig. 4. Chemical Potential any complexes that consist of (a) [M(III)(SDPH)$_2$(H$_2$O)$_2$]$^+$; (b) [M(III)(VDPH)$_2$(H$_2$O)$_2$]$^+$ (c) [M(III)(SDPH)$_2$(NH$_3$)(H$_2$O)]$^+$; (d) [M(III)(VDPH)$_2$(NH$_3$)(H$_2$O)]$^+$; (e) [M(II)(VDPH)$_2$(H$_2$O)$_2$]; (f) [M(II)(SDPH)$_2$(NH$_3$)(H$_2$O)]; (g) [M(II)(VDPH)$_2$(NH$_3$)(H$_2$O)]; (h) [M(II)(SDPH)$_2$(H$_2$O)$_2$]

1) Chemical Potential (μ)

The chemical potential can describe the tendency of electrons to escape from equilibrium as the electronegativity of the molecule [27]. If the value of the chemical potential of the complex is greater than the others, the energy of the complex is more sensitive to the change of the electron's number [28]. The molecule's chemical potential indicates a tendency to donate or accept electrons. The lowest chemical potential shown in the complex compound is -6.477 eV for complex [M(II)(VDPH)2(H2O)2]. The lowest value indicates that the complex compound can stabilize a system with its electronic energy. In contrast, the highest value is -13.4208 eV in complex [M(III)(SDPH)$_2$(H$_2$O)$_2$]$^+$. This highest value of chemical potential indicates a lack of a complex compound with this structure in stabilizing the system (Fig. 4).

2) The Chemical Hardness (η) and Softness (S)

The Chemical hardness characteristics can describe a complex's hard or soft characteristics, while the hardness value can also be correlated with the obtained softness value like the concept of hard soft acid base. A large HOMO-LUMO gap can be found in a hard molecule. This molecule will be more stable if they have a large gap of HOMO-LUMO and also need much energy excitation to reach the manifold of excited states [28] (Fig. 5).

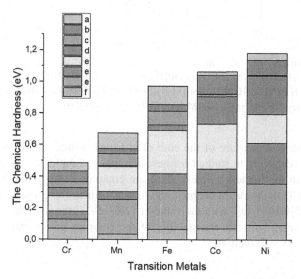

Fig. 5. The Hardness of complexes with any molecular formula, The complexes consist of: (a) [M(II)(VDPH)$_2$(NH$_3$)(H$_2$O)]; (b) [M(II)(SDPH)$_2$(NH$_3$)(H$_2$O)]; (c) [M(II)(VDPH)$_2$(H$_2$O)$_2$]; (d) [M(II)(SDPH)$_2$(H$_2$O)$_2$]; (e) [M(III)(VDPH)$_2$(NH$_3$)(H$_2$O]$^+$; (f) [M(III)(SDPH)$_2$(NH$_3$)(H$_2$O)]$^+$; (g) [M(III)(VDPH)$_2$(H$_2$O)$_2$]$^+$; (h) [M(III)(SDPH)$_2$(H$_2$O)$_2$]$^+$

The chemical hardness of each complex shown that the complex with the smallest hardness value is at [M(II)(VDPH)$_2$(H$_2$O)$_2$] with a value of 0.0049 eV and the highest value of the hardness is to complex [M(III)(VDPH)$_2$NH$_3$H$_2$O]$^+$ with a value of

0.2836 eV. This hardness is also a measure of the molecule resistance which can be used to change its electronic structure. It can be shown that complex compounds with high hardness values have a tendency to stabilize the system [29]. Meanwhile, a low hardness value indicates that complex compounds tend to be less stable in stabilizing a system. Complex compounds that have high chemical hardness indicate a measure of the resistance system for changing its electronic structure. It is also in line with the principles of HSAB (Soft Hard Acids and Bases) [29] (Fig. 6).

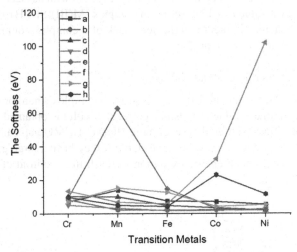

Fig. 6. The softness of any molecular complexes, the complexes consist of: (a) $[M(III)(SDPH)_2(H_2O)_2]^+$; (b) $[M(III)(VDPH)_2(H_2O)_2]^+$; (c) $[M(III)(SDPH)_2(NH_3)(H_2O)]^+$; (d) $[M(III)(VDPH)_2(NH_3)(H_2O)]^+$; (e) $[M(II)(SDPH)_2(H_2O)_2]^+$; (f) $[M(II)(SDPH)_2(H_2O)_2]$; (g) $[M(II)(SDPH)_2(NH_3)(H_2O)]$; (h) $[M(II)(VDPH)_2(NH_3)(H_2O)]$;

The softness is a measure of the ease of change transfer related to a high polarizability [30]. According to studied softness of various complex compounds, complex compounds with the highest softness value are complex compounds $[M(II)(VDPH)_2(H_2O)_2]$ with 102.0408 eV. In contrast, the lowest softness of complex compounds is $[M(III)(VDPH)_2NH_3H_2O]^+$ with the value of 1.763 eV. If the complex compound has the most significant softness, the stability of the complex compounds will decrease, while its reactivity will increase.

3) Electronegativity (χ)

The electronegativity value of various complex compounds, shown that the complex compounds which have a greater electronegativity than others are complex compounds with the molecular formula $[M(III)(SDPH)_2(H_2O)_2]^+$ with the central metal being Ni with the value of 13.4208 eV. While the lowest electronegativity value was obtained from $[M(III)(SDPH)_2(H_2O)_2]^+$ complex compounds with the same molecular formula but with different types of central metal, namely complex compounds with Co metal with a value of 6.477 eV (Fig. 7).

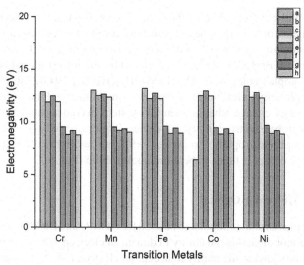

Fig. 7. Electronegativity of any molecular complexes. The complexes consist of: (a) $[M(III)(SDPH)_2(H_2O)2]^+$; (b) $[M(III)(VDPH)_2(H_2O)2]^+$; (c) $[M(III)(SDPH)_2 (NH_3)(H_2O)]^+$; (d) $[M(II)(VDPH)_2(NH_3)(H_2O)]^+$; (e) $[M(II)(SDPH)_2(H_2O)2]$; (f) $[M(II)(VDPH)_2(H_2O)_2]$; (g) $[M(II)(SDPH)_2(NH_3)(H_2O)]$; (h) $[M(II)(VDPH)_2(NH_3)(H_2O)]$

4) Global Electrophilicity (ω)

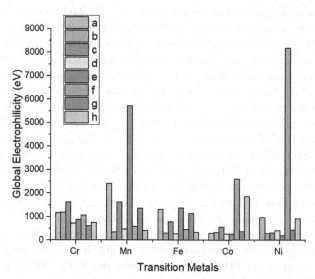

Fig. 8. Global Electrophilicity of any molecular complexes, the complexes consist of: (a) $[M(III)(SDPH)_2(H_2O)_2]^+$; (b) $[M(III)(VDPH)_2(H_2O)_2]^+$; (c) $[M(III)(SDPH)_2 (NH_3)(H_2O)]^+$; (d) $[M(II)(VDPH)_2(NH_3)(H_2O)]^+$; (e) $[M(II)(SDPH)_2(H_2O)_2]$; (f) $[M(II)(VDPH)_2(H_2O)_2]$; (g) $[M(II)(SDPH)_2(NH_3)(H_2O)]$; (h) $[M(II)(VDPH)_2(NH_3)(H_2O)]$

Global Electrophilicity (ω) can show the species capability to accept electrons [31, 32]. The characteristics of various types of complex compounds indicated by the highest global electrophilicity value was found in complex compounds with the molecular formula [M(II)(VDPH)$_2$(H$_2$O)$_2$] 8179.38772 eV, while the lowest global electrophilicity value was in complex compounds [M(II)(SDPH)$_2$(H$_2$O)$_2$] 194.42736 eV. This shows that the electrophilicity index, when viewed in terms of thermodynamic properties, can measure the energy change when a chemical system becomes saturated while adding electrons. This global electrophilicity value that a large value indicates that the complex tends to have high electrophilic properties, while a low global electrophilicity value indicates that the complex tends to be more nucleophilic (Fig. 8).

3.5 Frontier Molecular Orbital

Frontier Molecular Orbital is popular to be used for HOMO and LUMO [33]. The HOMO is an electron donor depicting the ability to donate an electron, whereas the LUMO is an electron acceptor showing the ability to accept an electron [34, 35]. Frontier Molecular Orbitals analysis is one parameter that is quite important to be able to estimate and explain chemical reactivity, hardness, and softness of the compound such as complex compound. As is known, HOMO (π donor) [36] acts as a place to receive the highest electrons, while LUMO(π acceptor) [36] acts as an electron acceptor which acts to attract electrons, and the lowest energy orbital that can accept electrons [37]. FMO provides insight into the contribution of atoms to reactivity. HOMO-LUMO describes the basic fundamentals for examining chemical reactivity, compound stability, and compound stability.

The ability to accept electrons is attributed to the LUMO orbitals which are electronically vacant or unfilled orbitals. HOMO-LUMO energy difference. The highest HOMO-LUMO gap value indicates that the complex has high stability, but negligible or low reactivity of the compound. This is because a molecule with a small HOMO-LUMO gap (ΔE) explains that the molecule is more polarized and is generally related to high chemical reactivity. Furthermore, a low kinetic stability and HOMO-LUMO energy can show whether is it easy or not for a compound to accept electrons (Fig. 9).

The complex with the highest HOMO-LUMO gap value are complex with the molecular formula [M(III)(VDPH)(NH$_3$)(H$_2$O)]$^+$ 0.5672 eV, while complex compounds with the lowest HOMO-LUMO gap values are complex compounds with the molecular formula [M(II)(SDPH)$_2$(H$_2$O)$_2$] 0.0159 eV. Complex that has highest HOMO-LUMO gap or ΔE indicated that more stable and less reactive and hard compound. Besides, the complex with the lowest HOMO-LUMO gap or ΔE are complex indicated less stable and more reactive and consist of soft compound (Table 1).

The highest H-L gap is NH$_3$ ligand which indicates that the NH$_3$ metal tends to have high stability and low chemical reactivity compared to other ligands [38]. While the lowest H-L gap is the VDPH ligand describing that the VDPH molecule without binding to other compounds has a high chemical reactivity and low stability. The order of the H-L gap from the highest is in the ligand NH$_3$ > H$_2$O > SDPH > VDPH.

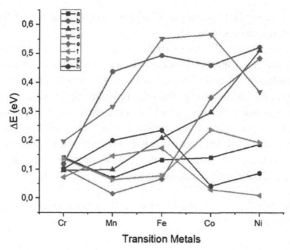

Fig. 9. ΔE (eV) energy of any molecular complex consist of: (a) $[M(III)(SDPH)_2(H_2O)_2]^+$; (b) $[M(III)(VDPH)_2(H_2O)_2]^+$; (c) $[M(III)(SDPH)_2\ (NH_3)(H_2O)]^+$; (d) $[M(II)(VDPH)_2(NH_3)(H_2O)]^+$; (e) $[M(II)(SDPH)_2(H_2O)_2]$; (f) $[M(II)(VDPH)_2(H_2O)_2]$; (g) $[M(II)(SDPH)_2(NH_3)(H_2O)]$; (h) $[M(II)(VDPH)_2(NH_3)(H_2O)]$

Table 1. HOMO-LUMO energy of Ligands

Ligand	Energy of HOMO (eV)	Energy of LUMO (eV)	Energy of H-L Gap (eV)
SDPH	−9.8412	−9.0725	0.7687
VDPH	−9.4101	−9.2350	0.1751
NH_3	−10.6157	1.6655	14.1541
H_2O	−12.1657	1.9884	12.2812

4   Conclusions

The electronic, chemical, and thermodynamic properties of the SDPH and VDPH complexes with various types first -row transition metals have been thoroughly investigated and screened by extended tight binding or GFN2-xTB. Stabilization of the complexes with various molecular formula was examined systematically. The result reveals that SDPH and VDPH complexes with first-row transition metals tend to have stable and spontaneous conditions complex compounds. However, there are several complexes that also produce an unstable state proven by the total value of the positive Gibbs free energy change. The outcome depicts those complex compounds consisting of VDPH ligands tend to have a more negative total value of Gibbs free energy changes than complex compounds with SDPH ligands. The charge of 3+ complex compounds also tends to have more stable complex compounds. Furthermore, the influence of electron distribution at low spins results in a more negative Gibbs free energy change and makes the complex compound in a stable state. In this study, the NH_3 as a ligand gave the impact to stabilize the complexes. It means NH3 has a good influence on the stability of the complex and makes the complexes more stable.

The acquired results are also supported by analysis of global reactivity descriptors consisting of a global electrophilicity index (ω), electronegativity (χ), chemical potential (μ), chemical hardness (η), and chemical softness (S) and frontier molecular orbitals. The results of any component of the global reactivity descriptors can support the previous results of thermodynamic (ΔG energy) which mean the complex compounds have high stability with low reactivity and the complex compounds with low stability with high reactivity are obtained which later are expected to be supporting data in the development of investigations on the conditions of synthesis of a complex compound with the main ligands SDPH and VDPH with experimentally.

Acknowledgment. We would like to thank Indonesian Endowment Funds for Education (LPDP) for all supports given to this research.

Appendixes

ΔG energy of any SDPH and VDPH Complexes

Complex	ΔG (kJ.mol^{-1})	Complex	ΔG (kJ.mol^{-1})
Co(II)(SDPH)$_2$(H$_2$O)$_2$ HS	−4610	Fe(II)(VDPH)$_2$(NH$_3$)(H$_2$O) LS	−14109.8
Co(II)(SDPH)$_2$(H$_2$O)$_2$ LS	−4699	Fe(III)(SDPH)$_2$(H$_2$O)$_2$ HS	−15306.2
Co(II)(VDPH)$_2$(H$_2$O)$_2$ HS	−10204	Fe(III)(SDPH)$_2$(H$_2$O)$_2$ LS	−15486.9
Co(II)(VDPH)$_2$(H2O)$_2$ LS	−10280	Fe(III)(VDPH)$_2$(H$_2$O)$_2$ HS	−20909
Co(II)(SDPH)$_2$(NH$_3$)(H$_2$O) HS	−6411	Fe(III)(VDPH)$_2$(H$_2$O)$_2$ LS	−21087
Co(II)(SDPH)$_2$(NH$_3$)(H$_2$O) LS	−6423	Fe(III)(SDPH)$_2$(NH$_3$)(H$_2$O) HS	−40205.6
Co(II)(VDPH)$_2$(NH$_3$)(H$_2$O) HS	27641	Fe(III)(SDPH)$_2$(NH$_3$)(H$_2$O) LS	−40366
Co(II)(VDPH)$_2$(NH$_3$)(H$_2$O) LS	27552	Fe(III)(VDPH)$_2$(NH$_3$)(H$_2$O) HS	−20903.8
Co(III)(SDPH)$_2$(H$_2$O)$_2$ HS	−8479	Fe(III)(VDPH)$_2$(NH$_3$)(H$_2$O) LS	−21078.8
Co(III)(SDPH)$_2$(H$_2$O)$_2$ LS	−8479	Mn(II)(SDPH)$_2$(H$_2$O)$_2$ HS	−7444.62
Co(III)(VDPH)$_2$(H$_2$O)$_2$ HS	−12187	Mn(II)(SDPH)$_2$(H$_2$O)$_2$ LS	−7554.65
Co(III)(VDPH)$_2$(H$_2$O)$_2$ LS	−12325	Mn(II)(VDPH)$_2$(H$_2$O)$_2$ HS	−13025.4
Co(III)(SDPH)$_2$(NH$_3$)(H$_2$O) HS	−8292	Mn(II)(VDPH)$_2$(H$_2$O)$_2$ LS	−13128.6
Co(III)(SDPH)$_2$(NH$_3$)(H$_2$O) LS	−8486	Mn(II)(SDPH)$_2$(NH$_3$)(H$_2$O) HS	−7446.41
Co(III)(VDPH)$_2$(NH$_3$)(H$_2$O) HS	25682	Mn(II)(SDPH)$_2$(NH$_3$)(H$_2$O) LS	−7561.83
Co(III)(VDPH)$_2$(NH$_3$)(H$_2$O) LS	27552	Mn(II)(VDPH)$_2$(NH$_3$)(H$_2$O) HS	−13028.8
Cr(II)(SDPH)$_2$(H$_2$O)$_2$ HS	−6295.86	Mn(II)(VDPH)$_2$(NH$_3$)(H$_2$O) LS	−13144.2
Cr(II)(SDPH)$_2$(H$_2$O)$_2$ LS	−6402.44	Mn(III)(SDPH)$_2$(H$_2$O)$_2$ HS	−13720.5

(*continued*)

(*continued*)

Complex	ΔG (kJ.mol^{-1})	Complex	ΔG (kJ.mol^{-1})
Cr(II)(VDPH)$_2$(H$_2$O)$_2$ HS	−11847.1	Mn(III)(SDPH)$_2$(H$_2$O)$_2$ LS	−13770.7
Cr(II)(VDPH)$_2$(H$_2$O)$_2$ LS	−11944	Mn(III)(VDPH)$_2$(H$_2$O)$_2$ HS	−19303.3
Cr(II)(SDPH)$_2$(NH$_3$)(H$_2$O) HS	−6265.45	Mn(III)(VDPH)$_2$(H$_2$O)$_2$ LS	−19363
Cr(II)(SDPH)$_2$(NH$_3$)(H$_2$O) LS	−6358.84	Mn(III)(SDPH)$_2$(NH$_3$)(H$_2$O) HS	−13713.1
Cr(II)(VDPH)$_2$(NH$_3$)(H$_2$O) HS	25986.1	Mn(III)(SDPH)$_2$(NH$_3$)(H$_2$O) LS	−13781.3
Cr(II)(VDPH)$_2$(NH$_3$)(H$_2$O) LS	25892.7	Mn(III)(VDPH)$_2$(NH$_3$)(H$_2$O) HS	−367978
Cr(III)(SDPH)$_2$(H$_2$O)$_2$ HS	−10507	Mn(III)(VDPH)$_2$(NH$_3$)(H$_2$O) LS	−368047
Cr(III)(SDPH)$_2$(H$_2$O)$_2$ LS	−10507	Ni(II)(SDPH)$_2$(H$_2$O)$_2$ HS	−5573
Cr(III)(VDPH)$_2$(H$_2$O)$_2$ HS	−15765.8	Ni(II)(SDPH)$_2$(H$_2$O)$_2$ LS	−5573
Cr(III)(VDPH)$_2$(H$_2$O)$_2$ LS	−16104	Ni(II)(VDPH)$_2$(H$_2$O)$_2$ HS	−10304
Cr(III)(SDPH)$_2$(NH$_3$)(H$_2$O) HS	−10515.5	Ni(II)(VDPH)$_2$(H$_2$O)$_2$ LS	−10304
Cr(III)(SDPH)$_2$(NH$_3$)(H$_2$O) LS	−10515.5	Ni(II)(SDPH)$_2$(NH$_3$)(H$_2$O) HS	−4719
Cr(III)(VDPH)$_2$(NH$_3$)(H$_2$O) HS	21567.5	Ni(II)(SDPH)$_2$(NH$_3$)(H$_2$O) LS	−4719
Cr(III)(VDPH)2(NH$_3$)(H$_2$O) LS	21567.5	Ni(II)(VDPH)$_2$(NH$_3$)(H$_2$O) HS	−10302
Fe(II)(SDPH)$_2$(H$_2$O)$_2$ HS	−8442.99	Ni(II)(VDPH)$_2$(NH$_3$)(H$_2$O) LS	−10302
Fe(II)(SDPH)$_2$(H$_2$O)$_2$ LS	−8540.33	Ni(III)(SDPH)$_2$(H$_2$O)$_2$ HS	−6703
Fe(II)(VDPH)$_2$(H$_2$O)$_2$ HS	−14029.7	Ni(III)(SDPH)$_2$(H$_2$O)$_2$ LS	−6800
Fe(II)(VDPH)$_2$(H$_2$O)$_2$ LS	−14119.9	Ni(III)(VDPH)$_2$(H$_2$O)$_2$ HS	−12319
Fe(II)(SDPH)$_2$(NH$_3$)(H$_2$O) HS	−8427.06	Ni(III)(VDPH)$_2$(H$_2$O)$_2$ LS	−12409
Fe(II)(SDPH)$_2$(NH$_3$)(H$_2$O) LS	−8529.86	Ni(III)(SDPH)$_2$(NH$_3$)(H$_2$O) HS	−6709
Fe(II)(VDPH)$_2$(NH$_3$)(H$_2$O) HS	−14015	Ni(III)(SDPH)$_2$(NH$_3$)(H$_2$O) LS	−6801
		Ni(III)(VDPH)$_2$(NH$_3$)(H$_2$O) HS	−12292
		Ni(III)(VDPH)$_2$(NH$_3$)(H$_2$O) LS	−12376

The Global Reactive Descriptors

Complex	Chemical Potential (eV)	Chemical Hardness (eV)	The Softness (eV)	The Electronegativity (eV)	Global Electrophilicity (eV)	ΔE (eV)
Co(II)(SDPH)$_2$(H$_2$O)$_2$ HS	−9.238	0.043	11.682	9.238	996.88	9.195
Co(II)(SDPH)$_2$(H$_2$O)$_2$ LS	−9.503	0.174	2.873	9.503	259.45	9.329
Cr(II)(SDPH)$_2$(H$_2$O)$_2$ LS	−9.531	0.052	9.615	9.531	873.44	9.479
Cr(II)(SDPH)$_2$(H$_2$O)$_2$ HS	−9.331	0.032	15.699	9.331	1.366.94	9.300
Fe(II)(SDPH)$_2$(H$_2$O)$_2$ LS	−9.635	0.034	14.815	9.635	1.375.26	9.601
Fe(II)(SDPH)$_2$(H$_2$O)$_2$ HS	−9.181	0.055	9.017	9.181	760.07	9.126
Ni(II)(SDPH)$_2$(H$_2$O)$_2$ HS	−9.696	0.242	2.068	9.696	194.43	9.454
Ni(II)(SDPH)$_2$(H$_2$O)$_2$ LS	−9.696	0.242	2.068	9.696	194.43	9.454
Mn(II)(SDPH)$_2$(H$_2$O)$_2$ LS	−9.537	0.008	62.893	9.537	5.720.94	9.530
Mn(II)(SDPH)$_2$(H$_2$O)$_2$ HS	−9.216	0.035	14.368	9.216	1.220.33	9.181

(*continued*)

(*continued*)

Complex	Chemical Potential (eV)	Chemical Hardness (eV)	The Softness (eV)	The Electronegativity (eV)	Global Electrophilicity (eV)	ΔE (eV)
Cr(II)(VDPH)$_2$(H$_2$O)$_2$ LS	−8.829	0.037	13.643	8.829	1.063.44	8.792
Cr(II)(VDPH)$_2$(H$_2$O)$_2$ HS	−8.715	0.090	5.556	8.715	421.99	8.625
Mn(II)(VDPH)$_2$(H$_2$O)$_2$ HS	−8.862	0.026	19.120	8.862	1501.64	8.836
Mn(II)(VDPH)$_2$(H$_2$O)$_2$ LS	−9.231	0.073	6.817	9.231	580.84	9.158
Fe(II)(VDPH)$_2$(H$_2$O)$_2$ LS	−8.944	0.087	5.770	8.944	461.55	8.857
Fe(II)(VDPH)$_2$(H$_2$O)$_2$ HS	−8.609	0.068	7.310	8.609	541.76	8.541
Co(II)(VDPH)$_2$(H$_2$O)$_2$ LS	−8.931	0.015	32.680	8.931	2606.68	8.916
Co(II)(VDPH)$_2$(H$_2$O)$_2$ HS	−8.688	0.060	8.382	8.688	632.71	8.628
Ni(II)(VDPH)$_2$(H$_2$O)$_2$ HS	−8.953	0.005	102.041	8.953	8179.39	8.948
Ni(II)(VDPH)$_2$(H$_2$O)$_2$ LS	−8.953	0.005	102.041	8.953	8179.39	8.948
Cr(III)(SDPH)$_2$(H$_2$O)$_2$ HS	−12.889	0.071	7.062	12.889	1173.26	12.819
Cr(III)(SDPH)$_2$(H$_2$O)$_2$ LS	−12.889	0.071	7.062	12.889	1173.26	12.819
Mn(III)(SDPH)$_2$(H$_2$O)$_2$ LS	−13.051	0.035	14.144	13.051	2409.19	13.016
Mn(III)(SDPH)$_2$(H$_2$O)$_2$ HS	−12.709	0.326	1.532	12.709	247.40	12.383
Fe(III)(SDPH)$_2$(H$_2$O)$_2$ LS	−13.233	0.067	7.508	13.233	1314.60	13.166
Fe(III)(SDPH)$_2$(H$_2$O)$_2$ HS	−12.252	0.046	10.811	12.252	1622.95	12.206
Co(III)(SDPH)$_2$(H$_2$O)$_2$ LS	−6.477	0.071	7.072	6.477	296.69	6.406
Co(III)(SDPH)$_2$(H$_2$O)$_2$ HS	−6.276	0.069	7.210	6.276	283.99	6.207
Ni(III)(SDPH)$_2$(H$_2$O)$_2$ LS	−13.421	0.093	5.365	13.421	966.30	13.328
Ni(III)(SDPH)$_2$(H$_2$O)$_2$ HS	−12.671	0.521	0.959	12.671	154.00	12.150
Cr(III)(VDPH)$_2$(H$_2$O)$_2$ LS	−11.927	0.060	8.396	11.927	1194.35	11.867
Cr(III)(VDPH)$_2$(H$_2$O)$_2$ HS	−11.927	0.060	8.396	11.927	1194.35	11.867
Mn(III)(VDPH)$_2$(H$_2$O)$_2$ LS	−12.550	0.219	2.285	12.550	359.95	12.332
Mn(III)(VDPH)$_2$(H$_2$O)$_2$ HS	−12.158	0.166	3.008	12.158	444.67	11.991
Fe(III)(VDPH)$_2$(H$_2$O)$_2$ LS	−12.260	0.247	2.024	12.260	304.22	12.013
Fe(III)(VDPH)$_2$(H$_2$O)$_2$ HS	−11.308	0.083	6.013	11.308	768.91	11.225
Co(III)(VDPH)$_2$(H$_2$O)$_2$ LS	−12.559	0.230	2.174	12.559	342.88	12.329
Co(III)(VDPH)$_2$(H$_2$O)$_2$ HS	−11.397	0.075	6.631	11.397	861.38	11.322
Ni(III)(VDPH)$_2$(H$_2$O)$_2$ LS	−12.406	0.261	1.913	12.406	294.40	12.145
Ni(III)(VDPH)$_2$(H$_2$O)$_2$ HS	−11.843	0.027	18.727	11.843	2626.66	11.817
Co(II)(SDPH)$_2$(NH$_3$)(H$_2$O) HS	−9.022	0.092	5.408	9.022	440.24	8.930
Co(II)(SDPH)$_2$(NH$_3$)(H$_2$O) LS	−9.383	0.118	4.225	9.383	371.99	9.265
Cr(II)(SDPH)$_2$(NH$_3$)(H$_2$O) LS	−9.208	0.069	7.252	9.208	614.91	9.140
Cr(II)(SDPH)$_2$(NH$_3$)(H$_2$O) HS	−9.065	0.107	4.658	9.065	382.75	8.958
Fe(II)(SDPH)$_2$(NH$_3$)(H$_2$O) LS	−9.451	0.039	12.739	9.451	1137.74	9.411
Fe(II)(SDPH)$_2$(NH$_3$)(H$_2$O) HS	−8.944	0.086	5.794	8.944	463.44	8.857
Ni(II)(SDPH)$_2$(NH$_3$)(H$_2$O) HS	−9.235	0.096	5.208	9.235	444.20	9.139
Ni(II)(SDPH)$_2$(NH$_3$)(H$_2$O) LS	−9.235	0.096	5.208	9.235	444.20	9.139
Mn(II)(SDPH)$_2$(NH$_3$)(H$_2$O) LS	−9.379	0.032	15.456	9.379	1359.64	9.347
Mn(II)(SDPH)$_2$(NH$_3$)(H$_2$O) HS	−8.978	0.082	6.075	8.978	489.73	8.896
Cr(II)(VDPH)$_2$(NH$_3$)(H$_2$O) LS	−8.788	0.051	9.804	8.788	757.22	8.737
Cr(II)(VDPH)$_2$(NH$_3$)(H$_2$O) HS	−8.788	0.051	9.804	8.788	757.22	8.737

(*continued*)

(continued)

Complex	Chemical Potential (eV)	Chemical Hardness (eV)	The Softness (eV)	The Electronegativity (eV)	Global Electrophilicity (eV)	ΔE (eV)
Mn(II)(VDPH)$_2$(NH$_3$)(H$_2$O) HS	−8.819	0.078	6.443	8.819	501.17	8.742
Mn(II)(VDPH)$_2$(NH$_3$)(H$_2$O) LS	−9.045	0.100	5.000	9.045	409.07	8.945
Fe(II)(VDPH)$_2$(NH$_3$)(H$_2$O) LS	−8.993	0.118	4.255	8.993	344.16	8.876
Fe(II)(VDPH)$_2$(NH$_3$)(H$_2$O) HS	−8.636	0.087	5.754	8.636	429.10	8.549
Co(II)(VDPH)$_2$(NH$_3$)(H$_2$O) LS	−8.942	0.022	23.148	8.942	1850.70	8.920
Co(II)(VDPH)$_2$(NH$_3$)(H$_2$O) HS	−8.673	0.101	4.941	8.673	371.64	8.572
Ni(II)(VDPH)$_2$(NH$_3$)(H$_2$O) HS	−8.909	0.043	11.574	8.909	918.64	8.866
Ni(II)(VDPH)$_2$(NH$_3$)(H$_2$O) LS	−8.909	0.043	11.574	8.909	918.64	8.866
Cr(III)(SDPH)$_2$(NH$_3$)(H$_2$O) HS	−12.492	0.048	10.352	12.492	1615.53	12.444
Cr(III)(SDPH)$_2$(NH$_3$)(H$_2$O) LS	−12.492	0.048	10.352	12.492	1615.53	12.444
Mn(III)(SDPH)$_2$(NH$_3$)(H$_2$O) LS	−12.686	0.050	10.040	12.686	1615.73	12.636
Mn(III)(SDPH)$_2$(NH$_3$)(H$_2$O) HS	−12.419	0.159	3.139	12.419	484.09	12.260
Fe(III)(SDPH)$_2$(NH$_3$)(H$_2$O) LS	−12.759	0.104	4.787	12.759	779.23	12.654
Fe(III)(SDPH)$_2$(NH$_3$)(H$_2$O) HS	−11.781	0.095	5.271	11.781	731.67	11.686
Co(III)(SDPH)$_2$(NH$_3$)(H$_2$O) LS	−13.027	0.149	3.355	13.027	569.27	12.878
Co(III)(SDPH)$_2$(NH$_3$)(H$_2$O) HS	−11.898	0.124	4.026	11.898	569.87	11.774
Ni(III)(SDPH)$_2$(NH$_3$)(H$_2$O) LS	−12.854	0.256	1.952	12.854	322.59	12.598
Ni(III)(SDPH)$_2$(NH$_3$)(H$_2$O) HS	−12.220	0.133	3.748	12.220	559.74	12.087
Cr(III)(VDPH)$_2$(NH$_3$)(H$_2$O) LS	−11.960	0.098	5.079	11.960	726.52	11.862
Cr(III)(VDPH)$_2$(NH$_3$)(H$_2$O) HS	−11.960	0.098	5.079	11.960	726.52	11.862
Mn(III)(VDPH)$_2$(NH$_3$)(H$_2$O) LS	−12.387	0.159	3.154	12.387	483.85	12.228
Mn(III)(VDPH)$_2$(NH$_3$)(H$_2$O) HS	−12.154	0.069	7.236	12.154	1068.92	12.085
Fe(III)(VDPH)$_2$(NH$_3$)(H$_2$O) LS	−12.274	0.276	1.809	12.274	272.53	11.998
Fe(III)(VDPH)$_2$(NH$_3$)(H$_2$O) HS	−11.337	0.127	3.953	11.337	507.98	11.210
Co(III)(VDPH)$_2$(NH$_3$)(H$_2$O) LS	−12.530	0.284	1.763	12.530	276.79	12.246
Co(III)(VDPH)$_2$(NH$_3$)(H$_2$O) HS	−11.438	0.165	3.024	11.438	395.58	11.272
Ni(III)(VDPH)$_2$(NH$_3$)(H$_2$O) LS	−12.332	0.184	2.720	12.332	413.60	12.148
Ni(III)(VDPH)$_2$(NH$_3$)(H$_2$O) HS	−11.814	0.021	23.529	11.814	3283.93	11.793

References

1. Uddin, M.N., Ahmed, S.S., Alam, S.M.R.: REVIEW: biomedical applications of Schiff base metal complexes. J. Coord. Chem. **73**(23), 3109–3149 (2020). https://doi.org/10.1080/009 58972.2020.1854745

2. Przybylski, P., Huczynski, A., Pyta, K., Brzezinski, B., Bartl, F.: Biological properties of Schiff bases and Azo derivatives of phenols. Curr. Org. Chem. **13**(2), 124–148 (2009). https://doi.org/10.2174/138527209787193774

3. Qin, W., Long, S., Panunzio, M., Biondi, S.: Schiff bases: a short survey on an evergreen chemistry tool. Molecules **18**(10), 12264–12289 (2013). https://doi.org/10.3390/molecules 181012264

4. Kumhar, D., Patel, R.N., Patel, S.K., Patel, A.K., Patel, N., Butcher, R.J.: Structural diversity of copper(II) complexes with three dimensional network: crystal structure, Hirshfeld surface

analysis, DFT calculations and catalytic activity. Polyhedron **214**, 115633 (2022). https://doi.org/10.1016/j.poly.2021.115633

5. Iha, M.E.V.S., Pehkonen, S.O., Hoffmann, M.R.: Stability, stoichiometry, and structure of Fe(II) and Fe(III) complexes with Di-2-pyridyl ketone benzoylhydrazone: environmental applications. Environ. Sci. Technol. **28**(12), 2080–2086 (1994). https://doi.org/10.1021/es00061a016

6. Ávila Terra, L.H.S., Da Cunha Areias, M.C., Gaubeur, I., Suárez-Iha, M.E.V.: Solvent extraction-spectrophotometric determination of nickel(II) in natural waters using di-2-pyridyl ketone benzoylhydrazone. Spectrosc. Lett. **32**(2), 257–271 (1999). https://doi.org/10.1080/00387019909349981

7. Naureen, B., Miana, G.A., Shahid, K., Asghar, M., Tanveer, S., Sarwar, A.: Iron (III) and zinc (II) monodentate Schiff base metal complexes: synthesis, characterisation and biological activities. J. Mol. Struct. **1231**, 129946 (2021). https://doi.org/10.1016/j.molstruc.2021.129946

8. Cinarli, A., Gürbüz, D., Tavman, A., Birteksöz, A.S.: Synthesis, spectral characterizations and antimicrobial activity of some Schiff bases of 4-chloro-2-aminophenol. Bull. Chem. Soc. Ethiop. **25**(3), 407–417 (2011). https://doi.org/10.4314/bcse.v25i3.68593

9. Al Zoubi, W., Al-Hamdani, A.A.S., Ahmed, S.D., Ko, Y.G.: Synthesis, characterization, and biological activity of Schiff bases metal complexes. J. Phys. Org. Chem. **31**(2), 1–7 (2018). https://doi.org/10.1002/poc.3752

10. Al-Hazmi, G.A.A., Abou-Melha, K.S., El-Metwaly, N.M., Althagafi, I., Shaaban, F., Zaky, R.: Green synthesis approach for Fe (III), Cu (II), Zn (II) and Ni (II)-Schiff base complexes, spectral, conformational, MOE-docking and biological studies. Appl. Organomet. Chem. **34**(3), 1–15 (2020). https://doi.org/10.1002/aoc.5403

11. Sriram, D., Yogeeswari, P., Myneedu, N.S., Saraswat, V.: Abacavir prodrugs: Microwave-assisted synthesis and their evaluation of anti-HIV activities. Bioorganic Med. Chem. Lett. **16**(8), 2127–2129 (2006). https://doi.org/10.1016/j.bmcl.2006.01.050

12. Wang, P.H., Lien, E.J., Keck, J.G., Lai, M.M.C.: Design, synthesis, testing, and quantitative structure-activity relationship analysis of substituted salicylaldehyde Schiff bases of 1-amino-3-hydroxyguanidine tosylate as new antiviral agents against coronavirus. J. Med. Chem. **33**(2), 608–614 (1990). https://doi.org/10.1021/jm00164a023

13. Rauf, A., et al.: Synthesis, spectroscopic characterization, DFT optimization and biological activities of Schiff bases and their metal (II) complexes. J. Mol. Struct. **1145**, 132–140 (2017). https://doi.org/10.1016/j.molstruc.2017.05.098

14. Azizah, Y.N., Mulyani, I., Wahyuningrum, D., Bima, D.N.: Synthesis, characterization and antioxidant activity of Kobalt (II)-Hydrazone complex. EduChemia (Jurnal Kim. dan Pendidikan) **5**(2), 119 (2020). https://doi.org/10.30870/educhemia.v5i2.7987

15. Beyramabadi, S.A., Saadat-Far, M., Faraji-Shovey, A., Javan-Khoshkholgh, M., Morsali, A.: Synthesis, experimental and computational characterizations of a new quinoline derived Schiff base and its Mn(II), Ni(II) and Cu(II) complexes. J. Mol. Struct. **1208**, 127898 (2020). https://doi.org/10.1016/j.molstruc.2020.127898

16. Bursch, M., Neugebauer, H., Grimme, S.: Structure optimisation of large transition-metal complexes with extended tight-binding methods. Angew. Chemie - Int. Ed. **58**(32), 11078–11087 (2019). https://doi.org/10.1002/anie.201904021

17. Dohm, S., Bursch, M., Hansen, A., Grimme, S.: Semiautomated transition state localization for organometallic complexes with semiempirical quantum chemical methods. J. Chem. Theory Comput. **16**(3), 2002–2012 (2020). https://doi.org/10.1021/acs.jctc.9b01266

18. Komissarov, L., Verstraelen, T.: Improving the silicon interactions of GFN-xTB. J. Chem. Inf. Model. **61**(12), 5931–5937 (2021). https://doi.org/10.1021/acs.jcim.1c01170

19. Bannwarth, C., et al.: Extended tight-binding quantum chemistry methods. Wiley Interdiscip. Rev. Comput. Mol. Sci. **11**(2), 1–49 (2021). https://doi.org/10.1002/wcms.1493

20. Ásgeirsson, V., Bauer, C.A., Grimme, S.: Quantum chemical calculation of electron ionization mass spectra for general organic and inorganic molecules. Chem. Sci. **8**(7), 4879–4895 (2017). https://doi.org/10.1039/c7sc00601b

21. Gao, S., et al.: A new mixed-ligand lanthanum(III) complex with salicylic acid and 1,10-phenanthroline: synthesis, characterization, antibacterial activity, and underlying mechanism. J. Mol. Struct. **1225**, 129096 (2021). https://doi.org/10.1016/j.molstruc.2020.129096

22. Bursch, M., Hansen, A., Grimme, S.: Fast and reasonable geometry optimization of lanthanoid complexes with an extended tight binding quantum chemical method. Inorg. Chem. **56**(20), 12485–12491 (2017). https://doi.org/10.1021/acs.inorgchem.7b01950

23. Pracht, P., Wilcken, R., Udvarhelyi, A., Rodde, S., Grimme, S.: High accuracy quantum-chemistry-based calculation and blind prediction of macroscopic pKa values in the context of the SAMPL6 challenge. J. Comput. Aided. Mol. Des. **32**(10), 1139–1149 (2018). https://doi.org/10.1007/s10822-018-0145-7

24. Cohen, A.J., Mori-Sánchez, P., Yang, W.: Insights into current limitations of density functional theory. Science **321**(5890), 792–794 (2008). https://doi.org/10.1126/science.1158722

25. Bannwarth, C., Ehlert, S., Grimme, S.: GFN2-xTB - an accurate and broadly parametrized self-consistent tight-binding quantum chemical method with multipole electrostatics and density-dependent dispersion contributions. J. Chem. Theory Comput. **15**(3), 1652–1671 (2019). https://doi.org/10.1021/acs.jctc.8b01176

26. Choudhary, V.K., Bhatt, A.K., Dash, D., Sharma, N.: DFT calculations on molecular structures, HOMO–LUMO study, reactivity descriptors and spectral analyses of newly synthesized diorganotin(IV) 2-chloridophenylacetohydroxamate complexes. J. Comput. Chem. **40**(27), 2354–2363 (2019). https://doi.org/10.1002/jcc.26012

27. Khan, S.A., Rizwan, K., Shahid, S., Noamaan, M.A., Rasheed, T., Amjad, H.: Synthesis, DFT, computational exploration of chemical reactivity, molecular docking studies of novel formazan metal complexes and their biological applications. Appl. Organomet. Chem. **34**(3), 1–24 (2020). https://doi.org/10.1002/aoc.5444

28. Pratiwi, R., Ibrahim, S., Tjahjono, D.H.: Reactivity and stability of metalloporphyrin complex formation: DFT and experimental study. Molecules **25**(18), 1–8 (2020). https://doi.org/10.3390/molecules25184221

29. Trofymchuk, O.S., Ortega, D.E., Gutiérrez-Oliva, S., Rojas, R.S., Toro-Labbé, A.: The performance of methallyl nickel complexes and boron adducts in the catalytic activation of ethylene: a conceptual DFT perspective. J. Mol. Model. **21**(9), 1 (2015). https://doi.org/10.1007/s00894-015-2770-6

30. Joshi, R., Pandey, N., Tilak, R., Yadav, S.K., Mishra, H., Pokharia, S.: New triorganotin(IV) complexes of quinolone antibacterial drug sparfloxacin: synthesis, structural characterization, DFT studies and biological activity. Appl. Organomet. Chem. **32**(5), 1–15 (2018). https://doi.org/10.1002/aoc.4324

31. Feng, X.T., Yu, J.G., Lei, M., Fang, W.H., Liu, S.: Toward understanding metal-binding specificity of porphyrin: a conceptual density functional theory study. J. Phys. Chem. B **113**(40), 13381–13389 (2009). https://doi.org/10.1021/jp905885y

32. Chattaraj, P.K., Giri, S.: Electrophilicity index within a conceptual DFT framework. Annu. Reports Prog. Chem. Sect. C **105**, 13–39 (2009). https://doi.org/10.1039/b802832j

33. Nora, M., et al.: Interactions in inclusion complex of β-cyclodextrin/l-Metheonine: DFT computational studies. J. Incl. Phenom. Macrocycl. Chem. **96**(1–2), 43–54 (2019). https://doi.org/10.1007/s10847-019-00948-0

34. Gümüş, H.P., Tamer, Ö., Avci, D., Atalay, Y.: Quantum chemical calculations on the geometrical, conformational, spectroscopic and nonlinear optical parameters of 5-(2-Chloroethyl)-2,4- dichloro-6-methylpyrimidine. Spectrochim. Acta Part A Mol. Biomol. Spectrosc. **129**, 219–226 (2014). https://doi.org/10.1016/j.saa.2014.03.031

35. Gümüş, H.P., Tamer, Ö., Avci, D., Atalay, Y.: Effects of donor-acceptor groups on the structural and electronic properties of 4-(methoxymethyl)-6-methyl-5-nitro-2-oxo-1,2-dihydropyridine-3-carbonitrile. Spectrochim. Acta Part A Mol. Biomol. Spectrosc. **132**, 183–190 (2014). https://doi.org/10.1016/j.saa.2014.04.128
36. El-Gammal, O.A., Rakha, T.H., Metwally, H.M., Abu El-Reash, G.M.: Synthesis, characterization, DFT and biological studies of isatinpicolinohydrazone and its Zn(II), Cd(II) and Hg(II) complexes. Spectrochim. Acta Part A Mol. Biomol. Spectrosc. **127**, 144–156 (2014). https://doi.org/10.1016/j.saa.2014.02.008
37. Nejati, K., Bakhtiari, A., Bikas, R., Rahimpour, J.: Molecular and electronic structure, spectroscopic and electrochemical properties of Copper(II)complexes: experimental and DFT studies. J. Mol. Struct. **1192**, 217–229 (2019). https://doi.org/10.1016/j.molstruc.2019.04.135
38. Mariappan, G., Sundaraganesan, N.: Spectral and structural studies of the anti-cancer drug Flutamide by density functional theoretical method. Spectrochim. Acta Part A Mol. Biomol. Spectrosc. **117**, 604–613 (2014). https://doi.org/10.1016/j.saa.2013.09.043

Approaching a Common Conscious Dataspace from a Data Provider Perspective – Requirements and Perspectives

Markus Jobst[1]([✉]) [iD] and Tatjana Fischer[2] [iD]

[1] Federal Office of Metrology and Surveying, Vienna, Austria
markus@jobstmedia.at
[2] Department of Landscape, Spatial and Infrastructure Sciences, University of Natural Resources and Life Sciences, Vienna, Austria

Abstract. Many use cases give the impression that fundamental spatial data themes could help to bridge the gap of data silos and even approach a common conscious dataspace. Starting from the fundamental data themes of UNGGIM, we evaluate the minimal consensus for spatial data quality and create evidence for a missing common spatial data space by pragmatic examples from a data provider viewpoint. By the hand of given examples, the main challenges to start a common conscious dataspace in terms of the geospatial perspective can be highlighted, which leads to the need for a foundational semantic structure and sustainable persistent information structures. One possible approach to establish the baseline for a common persistent information space are geographical grid systems.

Keywords: Conscious dataspace · Spatial knowledge infrastructure · Map · Grid system · Graph structures

1 Introduction

The more data become available and follow FAIR principles (findable, accessible, interoperable, reusable), the easier gaps or discrepancies can be observed for the different data silos. Different qualities due to various use cases, different velocities and contradicting semantics make it hard to work within a common homogeneous dataspace that establishes a single market for economy and supports data sovereignty.

The combination of geographical grids with fundamental data themes and their foundational geospatial ontology encapsulates semantics by grids [1]. The spatial information space becomes more comparable. Therefore, this grid graph approach creates the ability to persistently compare against spatial phenomena, stays independent from detailed spatial feature changes and their spatial movements throughout time and may offer a spatial storage container. In general, these characteristics are needed for the conscious data space, where consciousness describes some kind of long-term information memory to observe and verify phenomena across different data spaces.

This contribution discusses the situation, gaps and requirements for a common conscious dataspace. We will highlight the need for a foundational semantic structure and

© The Author(s), under exclusive license to Springer Nature Switzerland AG 2022
O. Gervasi et al. (Eds.): ICCSA 2022, LNCS 13376, pp. 333–343, 2022.
https://doi.org/10.1007/978-3-031-10450-3_28

evaluate their implementation by using geographical grids systems [18] as baseline for a common information space. The resulting geographical grid graph approach can highlight characteristics that are needed in a conscious data space, but is also accompanied with restrictions. We will discuss the perspectives and restrictions of the proposed geographic grid graph approach and come to a first assessment for its usability.

2 Fundamental Spatial Data Sources in Action for a Common Conscious Dataspace

A common dataspace is fed with different data sources, which in their complexity are computed according to an occurring use case. The different velocities and contradicting semantics within the common dataspace need to be considered. At least the characteristic of each data source need to be understood in order to reduce incompatibilities. This kind of transparency of the data source supports data sovereighty and brings competences of the data production and its provider into the common data space [15]. This organisational inclusive step becomes an important part of a common conscious dataspace, where a long-term memory within the dataspace is established. This means that specific data (if they are important enough) stay available in the long term for various use cases [3].

Considering the spatial dimension in a common dataspace opens additional possibilities in terms of data linking. This enhanced cross-linking of data and their semantics are a core component of a spatial-driven conscious dataspace, which mainly builds upon spatial knowledge infrastructures and smart environments. An applicable spatial component within the common dataspace requires persistent IDs, a documentation of its lifetime and precise as well as comprehensive semantic anchoring [11]. At least these requirements should be valid for fundamental data themes, a set of spatial core information that initially structures space.

Pragmatic approaches for domain-specific dataspaces highlight the evidence for the importance of spatial information in a common conscious dataspace. A minimum consensus for spatial data quality and structures for the different data providers is needed on one hand. Flexibility and openess for new dynamic information input and semantic structures, like it is produced by self-managing algorithms [16] or citizen science, is needed on the other hand.

2.1 Spatial Knowledge Networks

The spatial knowledge infrastructure (SKI) unites evaluated pieces of information in a network [21]. This is the result of data collection and enrichment processes, feedback of information success and its fitting into the specified knowledge space [17]. The SKI is more than a connected collection and mutual orchestration of microservices that are offered by different providers. It includes intelligent processes of spatial information analysis, transformations and formation of semantic links [12].

A "cartographic added value" within the spatial knowledge infrastructure as part of a conscious dataspace fulfills two tasks. First: the rules of cartography allow for a better perception of retrieved information. Second: cartography embedded as foundational ontology allows to identify topographical relations.

2.2 Smart Environment

Smart environments can be described as small worlds with mutual interacting components, like smart devices, that continuously record, analyse and process to make specialists tasks and even human life more comfortable [23]. Applications fields reach from hazardous work, physical labors to a very general view of automated agents.

The core concept focuses on dynamically created mashups and a high degree of flexibility, instead of statically determined process driven approaches with service-mashups [19]. The most promising approach uses Web patterns with fault-tolerant relations, low-level protocol semantics, information ontologies and a standard Web architecture style [4]. This concept supports the integration of big data and IoT technologies for a variety of application fields.

2.3 Fundamental Spatial Data Themes

A sustainable development of environment and society requires continuous measurements, monitoring and governance according to the results. A common dataspace that includes all relevant information in a flexible but consistent way over time supports evidence-informed policy and decision making [10]. Spatial data and cartography are highly relevant in this information environment because it puts information into spatial context, mutually connects information pieces and brings in scale dependent semantics.

A set of fundamental data themes have been defined by the United Nations Expert Group of Global Geoinformation Management. Theses data themes cover the global geodetic reference frame, orthoimagery, elevation and depth, buildings and constructions, geographical names as identification of places, geology, land cover and its proposed land use, land parcels and land ownership, transport networks and their connectivity, physical infrastructure including public facilities and functional areas of public life that is used for different kind of administration [25].

2.4 The Role of Citizen Science in a Common Dataspace

In a common dataspace as comprehensive information source, information quality (IQ) of its components is of focal interest. The integration of different sources identifies quality concerns and discrepancies [24]. It is therefore a key task to mutually enhance quality within the data. For example, the correlation of administrative units, addresses and geographical names will immediately highlight a non-harmonized naming of the features and call for a common definition and guidance for the naming.

Citizen science with its open, frequently and in general anonymous participation adds further possibilities to the IQ enhancement. In many cases this citizen information can be classified as collective intelligence. In fact, citizen science brings in a user perspective - what is important to a participating user? - and refers to a large application scale. If considered carefully, it is a trigger for quality improvement within a common dataspace.

2.5 Functional Space and Its Impact on a Common Conscious Dataspace

The following pragmatic view on a use case in the field of spatial research and regional planning highlights the requirements for reliant data sources, transparent information quality and the recursive processing in a common conscious dataspace [14].

It is important to understand that functional regions are spatial structures that consist of communities with different characteristics that are in (exchange) relationships with each other [26]. This (exchange) relationship, in turn, must be "significant", i.e. relevant in quantitative terms. To this end, the relationship must be made measurable. In a first step, the characteristics must be defined (e.g. schools, hospitals in central places) and the relationship between the municipalities must be conceptualized (e.g. use of the facility by local residents as well as by and inhabitants of other (neighboring) municipalities). It is then necessary to identify and decide for secondary data that are suitable for calculating a defined indicator (e.g. catchment area of a nursing home). This approach also makes it possible to spatially delimit the functional region on the basis of the a priori defined threshold values for the required minimum strength of the relationship between the municipalities [6].

By taking into account other previously defined relevant boundary conditions such as the reasonable accessibility of the infrastructure and the spatial information required and available for this (e.g. the topology), the calculation model can be refined and more differentiated conclusions can be drawn on infrastructural oversupply and undersupply as well as on (intra-regional) supply rates..

The complex regional problem analysis of the functional space incorporates a diversity of data sources that are not harmonized, but deliver important impact on the analysis model. The recursive approach of regional planning corresponds to a machine learning procedure as long as discrete conclusions are the result of the analysis. Therefore, discretisation of indicators can be seen as core requirement for a common conscious dataspace from a functional space perspective.

3   Initial Challenges to Start a Common Conscious Dataspace

Initial challenges for a common conscious dataspace exist. These challenges mainly concern new roles in a common dataspace [13]. These roles are integrative parts in autonomous data silos, but need to be available and to interact in a common dataspace. Central roles are for example identity management or content brokering [8]. A conscious dataspace requests a full automation of these roles in order to fulfill the requirements of long-term availability.

Any knowledge persistence on the basis of a common dataspace assumes ongoing continuous processes for the fundamental (spatial) data sources, which is supported by a flexible but defined stewardship model and the governance of critical rules. From a geospatial perspective, consciousness within a common dataspace depends on trustworthy spatial data sources that appropriately describe space in an actual way, are historically available, offer an acceptable information quality and bind into a common consensual semantic structure [7].

3.1   A Shared Understanding of the Term "Common Dataspace"

A common dataspace is not only a collection of microservices or data sources. It is a network of reliable and self-determined exchange of information among known or unknown partners. The level of trusting available information in the dataspace can be defined by the stewardship of participating parties and their core competencies, which at least refer to "data sovereignty" [27].

3.2 The Conscious Framework from a Geospatial Perspective

A conscious framework within a common dataspace requests a historicized understanding of space. The description of space and its understanding is permanently changing. Due to legal frameworks or organizational collaboration the imagery and meaning of information evolves, which again influences a persistent semantic structuring of space [9]. The geospatial perspective helps to understand spatial related situations, where e.g. topography impacts a sustainable delivery of professional care for the elderly. In this context, it can be assumed that spatial-related challenges such as overcoming geographical distances in alpine areas are likely to fuel the reflection on whether to decide for a job in mobile care or nursing... The creation of a foundational semantic structure of space is a first step to persist the understanding of a geospatial imagery.

3.3 The Need for a Foundational Ontology

A universal topographic semantic structure across different scales, cartographic simplifications and spatial structures creates a foundational topographic ontology that helps to connect existing structures of meaning by its spatial characteristic [20]. It verifies another role of modern maps: a universal semantic structure of topographic content.

The need for a foundational topographic ontology can be anticipated, whenever semantic interoperability and efficient knowledge transmission on the basis of modern SDI lacks [21].

The foundational topographic ontology enhances a cross-domain networking of information structures. It therefore prevents spatial information spoofing and thus 'fake facts'. This can be achieved by cross-correlation of information, clear responsibilities of definitions and its universal semantic thesaurus of geographies.

Given by the aspects of initial challenges, a common conscious dataspace envisages a collaborative information landscape with enabled trust, mutual understanding, comprehensive knowledge, informed decisions, full automation of spatial data integration and adaptive analytics for knowledge expansion.

4   Geographic Grids Establishing the Baseline for a Common Information Space

In the recent years the integration of thematic and spatial information, especially concerning the UN sustainable development goals indicators, led to the realization that common geographies and geocoding are of high importance. Within the GSGF (Global Statistical Geospatial Framework) evidence has been built to move to gridded data delivery.

Gridded data are in use for the statistical domain for decades [1]. These statistical grid systems have regional restrictions. There are national and regional definitions. Some use cases call for global coverages. Therefore, a discrete global grid system (DGGS) has been developed under the auspices of the Open Geospatial Consortium (OGC). The main aim of a grid system is to provide a geospatial reference frame and establish persistent location for spatial values measured. As consequence the grid enables comparison in time and space. Values are bound to a location on one hand, the size of the grid cell and its value is comparable throughout the defined grid on the other hand. The grid is a multiscale definition which establishes a discrete hierarchical tessellation of progressively finer resolution cells. The numbering of cells follows a unique and multiple scale spanning index that facilitates rapid computation.

A common conscious dataspace could benefit from the comparable and timelessness characteristic of a grid system. Its geospatial reference and multiscale index hierarchy establish a baseline for a common conscious dataspace, at least for specific analysis and cross-domain-linking.

5   A Geographical Grid Graph Approach (GGGA)

Many use cases in spatial-related planning require a persistent framework of information structuring on one hand, but also call for flexibility for data structures on the other hand. From the viewpoint of the authors, a geographical grid graph approach (GGGA) could fulfill both requirements. In pragmatic use cases of regional planning this approach has been established and delivered first comparable results.

The GGGA is an established geographical grid and combines the functionalities and characteristics of space within a graph database. The geographical grid discretizes space into comparable tiles. The graph database introduces flexibility for data structures. In addition, the graph points to original geometries in a spatial index for deep learning procedures.

5.1   Encapsulating Semantics by Grids

The meaning of a spatial situation is defined by an ontology based spatial structure [28], something like a foundational topographic ontology combined with thematic classifications. Thematic classifications depend on the given use case and help to identify "important" information [29]. A graph describes this spatial semantic, whereas geographical features represent natural objects as geometries [30]. These geometries may change during time and often can hardly be compared. For example, a forest area will change its shape, but still stays the same semantic object. As described in the previous section, the relation of the spatial semantic to a grid establishes a baseline for a continuous comparison.

Two relations have to be established for a GGGA:

(1)   the information of geographical features has to be related to one or more specified grids. This is done by georeferencing, a dataintegration method by space: in which grid cell is the geographical feature located? The persistent identifier (PID) of the geographical feature then becomes part of the grid cell as "consist of" relation. In addition, the PID of the grid cell could become part of the geographical feature as "refers to" relation.

(2) the grid has to be connected to the spatial semantic. This connection to spatial semantic is done with the help of all the information of geographical features within the grid cell.

The spatial semantic could evolve with research questions and a proposed analysis. Changes also occur with new insights. Then relations between the grid and a new semantic have to be modified or extended.

5.2 Observations in a Regional Planning Use Case

In our use case of regional planning and the analysis of functional space, we identified several datasources, created a thematic semantic for the functional space, considered the foundational topographic ontology and established a semantic grid by a standardized regional statistical raster grid.

The open dataspace for the analysis of functional space is increasing, but inhomogeneous. Authoritative sources and volunteered geographic information mix up, which delivers a good variety. Reliance of the different sources differs:

Authoritative data seem to be complete depending to the meaning of data. For example, one source will embed all childcare facilities run by public authorities, others will list all childcare facilities including private ones, but exclude church-affiliated and other confessional institutions. Given a varying georeference (location) and a missing feature identifier accross all data sources, one may easily step into the trap of "counting too much".

Volunteered geographic information includes a diverse but consistent semantic. Functional description like childcare facilities, hospitals, police stations or museums exist. But the information only exists if it was interesting for the volunteer. Therefore, a lot of information is missing. Often authoritative feature identifiers, if they exist, are not considered. The volunteered geographic sources within the common dataspace for a functional analysis could extend authoritative collections and but could not be reliably considered for the categorisation of municipalities in our use case.

The thematic semantic for the functional space has been designed according to different scientific publications. This means that the thematic semantic structure is flexible and may change according to new insights.

The chosen "standardized regional statistical raster grid" has been designed in a way that it is compatible with the European statistical grid system based on the coordinate reference system (CRS) epsg: 3035 with 100 m grid cells. 100 m seems to be a rough resolution for geographical features, but it is a microscale for statistical themes, which may call for statistical disclosure control [22].

This setting of the grid allows for the integration of a lot more statistical data, such as demographic characteristics, health status and labor market structure.

6 Requirements, Perspectives and Restrictions of the Proposed Geographic Grid Graph Approach (GGGA)

Our ongoing work on approaching a common conscious dataspace with the proposed geographic grid graph approach from a data provider perspective exposes some requirements, perspectives and restrictions. In general, graph structures and their ontologies, combined with discrete and comparable spatial cells, could establish a sustainable structure for a common conscious dataspace. The main characteristics of this GGGA approach are the persistence of spatial discretisation with the grid and the flexibility of information structures with the graph.

The spatial discretisation with the grid supports a massive integration with time- and information layers, which then will lead to a so-called datacube [2]. The datacube as multidimensional data container has specific performance characteristics and owns specific operations to extract data. The connection to spatial data on the web is supported by a RDF data cube vocabulary (ref: RDF data cube vocabulary).

In this section we highlight the most important requirements and restrictions according to our observations.

6.1 Requirements

The main observed requirements for a common conscious dataspace are quality governance and a common understanding.

Quality Governance. Information sources within a common conscious dataspace consist of differing qualities that may not match or even create wrong results. A quality categorization for information chunks or geographic features has to be embedded in addition to the time stamp and persistent identifier in order to characterize this piece of information and differentiate its importance within a given use case. The quality categorization could be issue to modification if integration procedures can improve precision, reliability, coverage, completeness or conformance [5].

Foundational Ontology. The common understanding for spatial structures in a common conscious dataspace is driven by ontologies, a categorization and linking of information taxonomy [31]. In general, these ontologies are driven by applications fields and use cases and may differ in a single common dataspace. Therefore, the common understanding has to be supported by a foundational ontology for spatial components, which connect spatial information to a common knowledge base.

6.2 Restrictions

The grid within GGGA is accompanied by some restrictions. The discretisation of space enables timelessness comparison, but it depends on its specification. Grids with different specifications (e.g. starting point, grid cell size), geographical projections or cell geometries (e.g. square, hexagon) cannot be compared, because the information content of the cell will differ. This means that the specification of the grid as vehicle for stability is an apriori task that considers the scale, density, regional- and global needs of any approaching use case in future.

In our presented example the use case is restricted to a regional bounding box. In order to consume official European data sources, the regional grid has been specified according to the official statistical grid of Europe. An extension to the discrete global grid system is not possible, because the shape and projection of both grids does not match and therefore the information value cannot be compared.

A conceivable approach to overcome the incompatibility of different grid specifications could make use of the original spatial source data and rebuild the information grid. The most critical point here is, that any location modification within the data source will lead to an information change in the grid. These location modifications often come along with quality improvements.

7   Concluding Remarks

As we understand it, a common conscious dataspace is an extended concept of a common dataspace that establishes long-term memory with spatial relevance. From the perspective of a data provider and the application field of regional planning a common conscious dataspace is of "extreme" high value.

This paper tells about our work in progress and the observed difficulties to approach a common conscious dataspace that could be used for cross-sectoral spatial-related planning. In this paper we focused on spatial requirements and perspectives. We did not go into details on the new roles, like broker or identity manager in common dataspaces. We highlighted our approach to introduce stability in space and time with a geographical grid graph approach and resulted in its main requirements and restrictions.

Further actions of our work concern the embedding of statistical evaluations and derivation of effective geo-visualisations on the basis of the geographical grid graph.

References

1. Sato, A.-H., Nishimura, S., Namiki, T., Makita, N., Tsubaki, H.: World grid square data reference framework and its potential applications. In: 2018 IEEE 42nd Annual Computer Software and Applications Conference (COMPSAC), pp. 398–409 (2018), https://doi.org/10.1109/COMPSAC.2018.00062
2. Baumann, P., Team, R.: The EarthServer global datacube federation. In: IEEE, pp.3192–3194 (2020). https://ieeexplore.ieee.org/abstract/document/9324386
3. Bensmann, F., et al.: An infrastructure for spatial linking of survey data. Data Sci. J. **19**(19). https://datascience.codata.org/articles/https://doi.org/10.5334/dsj-2020-027/
4. Berners-Lee, T.: Linked data design issues. [online] W3C (2021). https://www.w3.org/DesignIssues/LinkedData. Accessed 25 Mar 2021
5. Döllner, J.: Geospatial artificial intelligence: potentials of machine learning for 3D point clouds and geospatial digital twins. PFG. J. Photogram. Remote Sens. Geoinform. Sci. **88,** 15–24 (2020). https://link.springer.com/article/10.1007%2Fs41064-020-00102-3
6. Dunford, M.: Area definition and classification and regional development finance: the European Union and China. In: Pike, A., Rodriguez-Pose, A., Tomaney, J. (eds.) Routledge Handbook of Local and Regional Development. Routledge, pp. 527–548 (2010). https://doi.org/10.4324/9780203842393.CH44

7. European Commission, J.: Guidelines for the RDF encoding of spatial data (2017). Github.io. http://inspire-eu-rdf.github.io/inspire-rdf-guidelines/. Accessed 8 Apr 2021
8. European Commission: Policy: Destination earth (DestinE). [online] European Commission (2020). https://ec.europa.eu/digital-single-market/en/destination-earth-destine
9. Gould, N., Mackaness, W.: From taxonomies to ontologies: formalizing generalization knowledge for on-demand mapping. Cartogr. Geogr. Inf. Sci. **43**(2016), 208–222 (2016). https://www.tandfonline.com/doi/abs/https://doi.org/10.1080/15230406.2015.1072737
10. Hadley, C.: The global fundamental geospatial data themdes journey. United Nations Committee of Experts on Global Geospatial Information Management (2018). https://ggim.un.org/documents/Fundamental%20Data%20Publication.pdf
11. Haldorson, M., Moström, J.: Developing a statistical geospatial framework for the European statistical system. In: Service-Oriented Mapping. Springer, pp.185–206. https://link.springer.com/chapter/https://doi.org/10.1007/978-3-319-72434-8_9
12. Hyvönen, E.: Linked open data infrastructure for digital humanities in Finland. In: Proceedings of Digital Humanities in Nordic Countries (DHN 2020) (2020). https://helda.helsinki.fi/bitstream/handle/10138/320220/hyvonen_lodi4dh_dhn_2020.pdf?sequence=1
13. International Data Spaces Association: IDSA rule book. Internationaldataspaces.org (2019). https://internationaldataspaces.org/download/19008/
14. ISO - International Organization for Standardization: ISO 37120:2014, Sustainable development of communities — Indicators for city services and quality of life ISO (2017). https://www.iso.org/standard/62436.html
15. ISO - International Organization for Standardization: ISO/IEC JTC 1/SC 41, Internet of things and digital twin. ISO (2020b). https://www.iso.org/committee/6483279.html
16. ISO - International Organization for Standardization: ISO/IEC JTC 1/SC 42Artificial intelligence. ISO (2020c). https://www.iso.org/committee/6794475.html
17. Janowicz, K., Scheider, S., Pehle, T., Hart, G.: Geospatial semantics and linked spatiotemporal data–past, present, and future. Semantic Web **3**, 321–332 (2012). https://content.iospress.com/articles/semantic-web/sw077. Accessed 8 Apr 2021
18. Sahr, K., White, D., Jon Kimerling, A.: Geodesic discrete global grid systems. Cartogr. Geogr. Inf. Sci. **30**(2), 121–134 (2003). https://doi.org/10.1559/152304003100011090
19. Mohammadi, H., Rajabifard, A., Williamson, I.P.: Development of an interoperable tool to facilitate spatial data integration in the context of SDI. Int. J. Geogr. Inf. Sci. **24**, 487–505 (2010). https://www.tandfonline.com/doi/abs/https://doi.org/10.1080/13658810902881903. Accessed 8 Apr 2021
20. Partridge, C., Mitchell, A., Cook, A., Sullivan, J., West, M.: A survey of top-level ontologies-to inform the ontological choices for a foundation data model. Cambridge University Research Outputs (2020). https://www.repository.cam.ac.uk/handle/1810/313452. Accessed 8 Apr 2021
21. Rieke, M., et al.: Geospatial IoT—the need for event-driven architectures in contemporary spatial data infrastructures. ISPRS Int. J. Geo-Inf. **7**, 385 (2018). https://www.mdpi.com/2220-9964/7/10/385. Accessed 8 Apr 2021
22. Ritchie, F.: Disclosure detection in research environments in practice. Paper presented at UNECE/Eurostat Work Session on Statistical Data Confidentiality (2007). https://doi.org/10.2901/Eurostat.C2007.004
23. Mayer, S., Verborgh, R., Kovatsch, M., Mattern, F.: Smart configuration of smart environments. IEEE Trans. Autom. Sci. Eng. **13**(3), 1247–1255 (2016). https://doi.org/10.1109/TASE.2016.2533321
24. Schade, S., Granell, C., Diaz, L.: Augmenting SDI with linked data. In: Citeseer. (2010). http://citeseerx.ist.psu.edu/viewdoc/download?doi=10.1.1.414.9301&rep=rep1&type=pdf

25. Scott, G.P.: A national strategic geospatial information framework to support the implementation of the sustainable development goals (SDGs) (2020). https://minerva-access.unimelb.edu.au/handle/11343/243052
26. Statistics Austria (Ed.): Urban-Rural Typology of Statistics Austria. Information on Methodology in German Language. https://www.statistik.at/web_en/classifications/regional_breakdown/urban_rural/index.html. Accessed 8 May 2022
27. Taneski, N., Petrovski, A., Bogatinov, D.: Geography in geospatial intelligence-C4IRS and cyber security. Security and crisis management–theory and practice, Regional Association for Security and Crisis Management S4 GLOSEC Global , pp. 65–73 (2019)
28. vd Brink, L., et al.: Best practices for publishing, retrieving, and using spatial data on the web. Semantic Web **10**, 95–114 (2019). https://content.iospress.com/articles/semantic-web/sw305. Accessed 8 Apr 2021
29. W3C: Spatial data on the web working group. W3.org (2015). https://www.w3.org/2015/spatial/wiki/Main_Page. Accessed 8 Apr 2021
30. W3C: DCAP AP. W3.org (2020). https://www.w3.org/ns/dcat. Accessed 8 Apr 2021
31. Wang, T.D., Parsia, B., Hendler, J.: A survey of the web ontology landscape. In: Cruz, et al. (eds.) The Semantic Web - ISWC 2006 ISWC 2006 5th International Semantic Web Conference, ISWC 2006, Athens, GA, USA, 5–9 November 2006, LNCS 4273, pp. 682–694. Springer, Heidelberg (2006). https://doi.org/10.1007/11926078_49

Evaluation of Spatial Variables Related to the Provision of Essential Services in the Basilicata Region

Valentina Santarsiero[1,2](✉) (iD), Gabriele Nolè[2], Francesco Scorza[1], and Beniamino Murgante[1]

[1] IMAA-CNR C.da Santa Loja, Zona Industriale, Tito Scalo, Italy
{valentina.santarsiero,gabriele.nole}@imaa.cnr.it
[2] School of Engineering, University of Basilicata, Viale dell'Ateneo Lucano 10, 85100 Potenza, Italy
{valentina.santarsiero,francesco.scorza,
beniamino.murgante}@unibas.it

Abstract. Basilicata is composed by many small municipalities that offer poor accessibility to essential services. The key theme of this work is the evaluation of the endowment of these services, analyzing, in a GIS environment, their accessibility in terms of temporal distance. This work explores the specific issues and challenges for accessibility to internal areas and reflects on the future development prospects of the 131 Lucanian municipalities. The analysis was conducted on the basis of two types of information layers in relation to the totality of the municipalities: demographic structure of the population and provision of essential services, divided into 3 macro classes: education, health and mobility. Evaluations were thus extracted which provided a comparative-objective analysis of the presence of essential services. The result is a picture that shows serious difficulties linked to the socio-cultural and territorial fabric, the railway and motorway networks are profoundly lacking, showing a clear gap between the municipalities in terms of provision of services.

Keywords: Inland areas · GIS · Remote sensing · Basilicata region · Accessibility

1 Introduction

Urban areas have been identified, both internationally and nationally, as a crucial ladder for the development and advancement of civilization.

Much of the Lucanian territory is characterized by a spatial organization based on smaller centers which, in many cases, are able to guarantee limited accessibility to essential services. The characteristics of these smaller centers consist in a significant distance from the main centers offering essential services (education, health and mobility). These inland areas represent a very varied territory, the result of the dynamics of the various territorial processes and of the phenomena of anthropization that have occurred. The identification of internal areas is a polycentric interpretation of the regional territory, characterized by different levels of spatial periphery.

From a spatial point of view, the level of periphery of the territories with respect to the network of urban centers, home to a vast plurality of services, profoundly influences the quality of life of citizens and the level of social inclusion. In these, the presence of essential services can act as an attractor capable of generating discrete catchment areas.

The center of the supply of essentials is identified in that municipality capable of supplying at least the whole supply, an essential hospital and a railway station.

In a similar context, giving an adequate definition to a territorial model represents a challenge, since spatial data and information must be able to understand the mechanisms that determine, on a local scale, and supply demand for services [1–4]. It consists of an interpretative approach to the dynamics of settlement, territorial, infrastructural endowments and organizational models that condition, for example, territorial accessibility and that lead citizens to self-determine residence and systematic travel according to criteria for optimizing the methods of use of space and territory.

It is in this perspective that the concept of accessibility is grafted. The concept of accessibility is widely used even if there are many definitions that can be attributed to it and that give it a changeable and indefinite outline.

We can understand it as a right and intrinsic condition of living in cities and in the territory [5–7].

Too often, however, this concept is taken into consideration only in the territory of the planning and design phases, thus not responding to the real needs of those who live the term. This is the result of an objective and not subjective approach, the planning of the territory does not focus on the single individual and his needs-possibilities, but following an equitable live ability.

We have gone from a strictly connected link to the productive and economic sector and then, after the war, to take root in that of services of social interest such as education, health and ambitious recreation. Among the variables that most affect the way of understanding accessibility is the territorial context to which reference is made. The latter can in fact aggravate or bring out, in a marked way, forms of social inequality in terms of equal opportunities or, even more, isolate and marginalize some urban contexts. Recent studies have highlighted the possibility between social exclusion and use of the city by showing combinations of use of the latter monotonous and mono-place [8, 9]. This is the case of the Basilicata Region characterized by a serious delay in development and a secular infrastructural deficit [9, 10] especially for rural and mountain areas. The National Strategy for Internal Areas (SNAI) promotes an approach based on the provision of structural conditions for territorial (including accessibility) and local development [10, 11].

Basilicata presents this criticality in the management of the territories, being one of the regions with the lowest settlement density.

This thesis work explores the specific themes and challenges for accessibility in inland areas and reflects on future development prospects. It wants to promote the development of a spatial analysis methodology aimed at analyzing essential services in terms of accessibility and capable of providing a detailed picture of the territory in terms of local development. The work aims to study the spatial relations existing between the 131 municipalities of the Region and to promote the themes of territorial and spatial planning in order to outline a strategic development framework. It is important to define the urban poles in which the essential services are concentrated to connect them neighboring cases by developing, improving and improving in some cases, trying to eliminate programmatic interiors, trying to eliminate internal imbalances.

2 Material and Method

The Basilicata Region is mainly mountainous and hilly, with a single wider plain in the Metaponto area (Ionian coast) and four valleys that rise from the great rivers from south to north of the region. Urban centers are mainly located in the higher areas of the region for historically defensive reasons, generally surrounded by large uninhabited areas and scattered houses or small civil or industrial aggregates. Thirty percent of the territory is affected by areas subject to environmental constraints; these data further highlight the need for prudence and more sustainable use of natural soil.

Most of the small Italian urban centers, despite having development potential linked to cultural tourism, suffer from serious economic and above all social hardships, mainly due to depopulation processes. Basilicata is one of the Italian regions with a high rate of depopulation as a result of migratory processes [12] and adverse territorial conditions; according to Istat sources [12], the resident population in the region increased from about 600,000 in 2000 to about 547,000 inhabitants in 2022. Most urban centers have a population that on average does not exceed 5,000 inhabitants, exceptions are the two capital cities and some industrial centers with a strong tourist and agricultural vocation. The SNAI (National Strategy of Internal Areas) [13] divides the Lucanian territory into four internal zones: Alto Bradano; Platano marble; Mercure - Sinni, Sarmento Valley and Matera Montain.

This classification is based on accessibility indicators in terms of minutes of travel, and is intended to show the remoteness of these areas from essential services.

2.1 Methodology

In this work, two main types of information layers were considered to analyze the framework of the territorial accessibility of the 131 Lucanian municipalities: the demographic structure of the resident population and the provision of essential services, which then made it possible to carry out an accessibility analysis. The classification of the demographic structure refers to Istat data, while the essential services are obtained from a detailed survey and mapping of the offer of public services, which together determine the different types of territorial endowments.

The first methodological approach was to reconstruct the stock of essential services (education, health and mobility) with the use of open data [14, 15] in a GIS environment. The provision of services is a fundamental parameter against which to evaluate the quality of life in a specific area. It can also be understood as an assessment of deficits, or the absence of minimum requirements for the supply of essential services with reference to the urban functions exercised by each territorial unit.

In order to frame a first summary view of the main socio-economic variables of the territory, read with respect to the trends that emerge from the Istat census data, the demographic trend was analyzed. A significant elaboration to describe the severity of the aging process of the population is the construction of indicators that frame the resident population in percentage terms, divided into three classes: Youth population (aged between 14 and 35 years), Adult population (over 55 years) and Elderly population (over 80 years). This information base describes the socio-demographic structure to which we refer for the proposal of territorial organizational models aimed at balancing the demand for services. The variables related to the presence of the latter, organized on two levels of very detailed classification, describe the supply side of these and therefore the territorial endowment.

3   Results

All the municipalities of the Region were evaluated taking into consideration variables linked to information relating to the structure of the population and the provision of essential services. These were divided into three macro classes: education, health and mobility.

The spatial analysis on education initially focused on a survey of the regional school supply through the use of public datasets [14] and subsequently an analysis of the spatial distribution of secondary schools was carried out (Fig. 1).

It can be seen from the map in Fig. 1, a fairly varied trend in inland areas with maximum distances of 44 min for some urban centers located on the border with Calabria and for some inland areas.

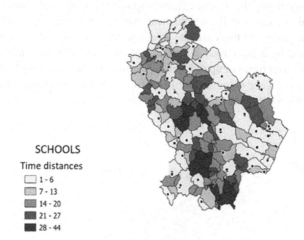

Fig. 1. Time distance, expressed in minutes, of each municipality to the nearest upper secondary school.

The analysis of essential services concerning the health aspect focused on spatial analyzes that related the availability of these services and their spatial and temporal distribution on the analyzed territory. An initial analysis concerned the recognition of all public health facilities, emergency rooms present in the Region through the use of open datasets [15] and subsequently maps of the distribution of hospital facilities were drawn up (Fig. 2) and the Emergency room (Fig. 3).

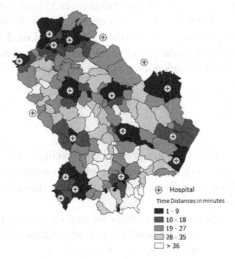

Fig. 2. Time distance, expressed in minutes, of each municipality to the nearest Hospital.

A highly fragmented and varied picture emerges in the three areas analyzed. From the analyzes concerning the distance from hospitals it emerges, in some cases, that the closest hospital is located in the neighboring regions of Campania and Puglia. Travel times vary widely. Also in this case, the most internal and isolated areas of the territory are characterized by a poor road infrastructure network; they are therefore the most penalized, with travel times of up to 55 min. A similar picture emerges from the analysis carried out for Emergency Room. In this case as well, the penalized urban centers are those falling within the innermost band of the Region (Fig. 3).

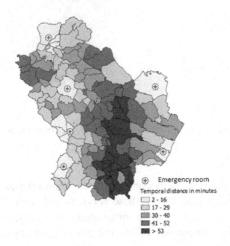

Fig. 3. Time distance, expressed in minutes, of each municipality to the nearest Emergency Room.

The following tables (Figs. 4 and 5) represent the temporal distances from the main mobility services such as airports and Highway Tollbooths. Figure refers to the temporal accessibility in minutes of the urban centers of Basilicata from the two nearest airports of Bari and Naples, located in Campania and Apulia Region. It can be seen that the nearest airport is at a distance of no less than 59 min, while the one furthest away shows temporal distances greater than 150 min.

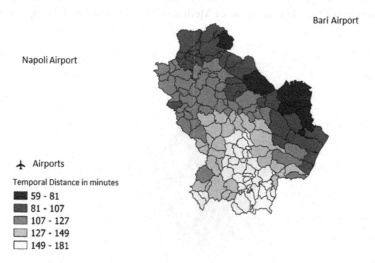

Fig. 4. Time distance, expressed in minutes, of each municipality to the nearest Airports.

The Basilicata Region does not have highways. The nearest freeway exits are those of Mercato San Severino, Candela, Barriera Taranto Nord and Bari. Figure 5 shows the temporal distance of the urban centers from the above-mentioned freeway tollbooths; it can be seen that the minimum distance is slightly more than 20 min and the maximum is more than 99 min.

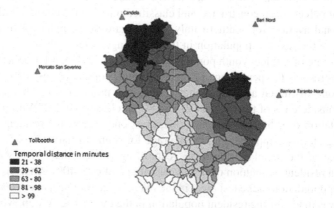

Fig. 5. Time distance, expressed in minutes, of each municipality to the nearest Highway Tollbooths.

The Basilicata region has a resident population of about 545000 inhabitants, a figure that is declining in view of the negative trend accompanied by an aging population and a decrease in the number of young people [20]. The demographic analysis (Fig. 6) shows us a region characterized by a strong centralization in a few urban centers, with consequent depopulation of inland areas and intensification of regional disparities [11]. We identify urban aggregates with high rates of resident population, where over the years there is a weak increase in population. These areas coincide with the two provincial capitals and the hinterland of the industrial pole of Melfi and the tourist poles of Metapontino.

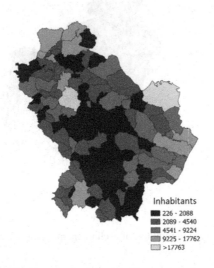

Inhabitants
■ 226 - 2088
■ 2089 - 4540
■ 4541 - 9224
▨ 9225 - 17762
☐ >17763

Fig. 6. Distribution of resident population as of 2021.

The results of calculating the indicators by age group for the year 2021 are very significant (Fig. 7). The indicators measure, as a percentage of age, the population in the three age groups considered (young (14–34 years), over 55 and over 80) out of the total resident population. These values were compared to the national average values. The indicators have been constructed and classified into 5 value classes, with reference to the national average for southern Italy. With regard to the indicator relative to the percentage of the resident population in the 14–34 age bracket, the class with value 5 represents a rate of resident youth population greater than 27% until decreasing to value 1, which represents the percentage of resident youth population less than 18%. What emerges from this initial analysis is that the resident population for this age group in the areas considered is of the order of 21%–18% of classes 3 and 2. With regard to the adult population over 55, the indicator measures, once again, the resident population in percentage terms compared with the average for southern Italy. Class 5 is attributed a percentage of the population over 55 years of age of less than 30%, while class 1 represents a resident population over 55 years of age of over 40%. Analysis shows that the resident population in the test area, in the over 55 age group, is over 40%. A similar argument was made for the resident population in the over 80 age group, where in class 5 a resident population of less than 3% is represented while in class 1 a value of the resident elderly population greater than 10% is represented. In this case it emerges that the percentage of the resident population in this age group in the area is between 7% and 10%.

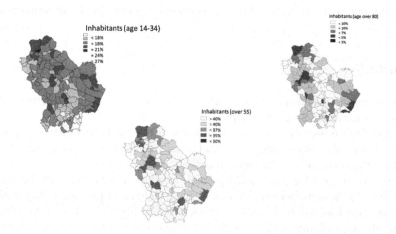

Fig. 7. Distribution of resident population by age group.

4 Discussion

This study proposed the use of a basic analytical methodology capable of evaluating the potential for local development of an area and highlighting its critical points. Numerical evaluations and maps have been extracted to allow an objective and quantifiable comparative analysis of the endowment of essential services.

The picture that emerges shows serious difficulties deriving from socio-cultural issues, but also territorial ones.

Analyzing the network of infrastructures and services that can be used in the regional territory, what is an indispensable and fundamental component for full and active participation in social life [8], significant shortcomings are revealed that specifically concern the rail and freeway networks. The regional rail network runs on a discontinuous line of 365 km that divides the region into two sectors. The entire territory, moreover, is devoid of freeway network and its tollbooths, the only points of entry to a fast road are present in the municipalities of Lagonegro and Lauria crossed by the Salerno-Reggio Calabria.

The low settlement density of Lucanian urban centers, confirmed by demographic analysis, and the characteristics of fragility and geological and geomorphological instability, are associated with considerable distances from essential services and also from the consequent opportunities for social development.

The population as a whole is aging and aging more rapidly in areas where there is more emigration of young people, aggravating the economic difficulties and social discomfort, in a spiral that seems unstoppable.

From the preliminary study carried out in this thesis emerges a region characterized by deep structural gaps between the 131 municipalities, those located inland, equipped with essential services, are in a favorable position compared to other centers located in inland areas difficult to connect and lacking basic services.

This preliminary research provides a methodology for the application of spatial analysis to map the endowment of basic services in inland areas and the existing gap in accessibility, and can be a useful tool in future development planning for these marginal areas.

5   Conclusion

This work represents the main elements of a first experimentation, at the municipal level, of the methodology in the previous chapters.

The objective has been to create a spatial framework that can be used in future spatial elaborations, with the aim of integrating traditional methodologies and geostatistical approaches in the definition of the regional socio-economic framework.

The work carried out has thus made it possible to bring out the existing gap between municipalities in the same region in terms of accessibility and provision of essential services, showing how this is one of the parameters that affects regional development. Improving the accessibility of these territories means bringing, for example, essential services back to the most isolated areas, strengthening the mobility offer and acting on the local territorial capital.

Although an improvement in infrastructure endowment is not a very feasible prospect, forms of territorial cooperation oriented towards the efficient organization of the supply of the main public services should be undertaken on the basis of a strongly contextualized model of territorial organization [16, 17]. This work, on a preliminary basis, offers a synthetic representation useful for comparing localization choices of local policies with the current levels of supply of basic services on a regional scale.

References

1. Danese, M., Nolè, G., Murgante, B.: Visual impact assessment in urban planning. Stud. Comput. Intell. **176**, 133–146 (2009). https://doi.org/10.1007/978-3-540-89930-3_8
2. Fortunato, G., Scorza, F., Murgante, B.: Hybrid oriented sustainable urban development: a pattern of low-carbon access to schools in the City of Potenza. In: Gervasi, O., et al. (eds.) ICCSA 2020. LNCS, vol. 12255, pp. 193–205. Springer, Cham (2020). https://doi.org/10.1007/978-3-030-58820-5_15
3. Murgante, B., Borruso, G., Lapucci, A.: Geocomputation and urban planning. Stud. Comput. Intell. **176**, 1–17 (2009). https://doi.org/10.1007/978-3-540-89930-3_1
4. Pontrandolfi, P., Dastoli, P.S.: Comparing impact evaluation evidence of EU and local development policies with new urban agenda themes: The Agri Valley Case in Basilicata (Italy). Sustainability **13**, 9376 (2021). https://doi.org/10.3390/SU13169376
5. Bacci, E., Cotella, G., Vitale Brovarone, E.: La sfida dell'accessibilità nelle aree interne: riflessioni a partire dalla Valle Arroscia. Territorio. 77–85 (2021). https://doi.org/10.3280/TR2021-096007
6. Calvaresi, C.: A national strategy for internal areas: Rights of citizenship and local development. Territorio. 78–79 (2015). https://doi.org/10.3280/TR2015-074013

7. Scorza, F., Saganeiti, L., Pilogallo, A., Murgante, B.: Ghost Planning: The Inefficiency of Energy Sector Policies in Low Population Density Region, pp. 34–55 (2020). https://doi.org/10.3280/ASUR2020-127-S1003

8. Borlini, B., Memo, F.: Ripensare l'accessibilità urbana. (2009)

9. Bonaiuto, M., Fornara, F., Bonnes, M.: Indexes of perceived residential environment quality and neighbourhood attachment in urban environments: a confirmation study on the city of Rome. Landsc. Urban Plan. **65**, 41–52 (2003). https://doi.org/10.1016/S0169-2046(02)002 36-0

10. Dastoli, P.S., Scorza, F., Murgante, B.: Impact evaluation: an experiment on development policies in Agri Valley (Basilicata, Italy) compared with new urban agenda themes. In: Gervasi, O., et al. (eds.) ICCSA 2021. LNCS, vol. 12957, pp. 621–633. Springer, Cham (2021). https://doi.org/10.1007/978-3-030-87013-3_48

11. Curatella, L., Scorza, F.: Polycentrism and insularity metrics for In-land areas. In: Gervasi, O., et al. (eds.) ICCSA 2020. LNCS, vol. 12255, pp. 253–261. Springer, Cham (2020). https://doi.org/10.1007/978-3-030-58820-5_20

12. Popolazione residente al 1° gennaio : Basilicata. http://dati.istat.it/Index.aspx?QueryId=18564. Accessed 23 Nov 2021

13. Ministro per il Sud e la Coesione territoriale - Strategia Nazionale Aree Interne. https://www.ministroperilsud.gov.it/it/approfondimenti/aree-interne/strategia-nazionale-aree-int erne/. Accessed 2 Mar 2021

14. Portale Unico dei Dati della Scuola|MIUR: https://dati.istruzione.it/opendata/. Accessed 2 Mar 2022

15. Open Data - Dati - Posti letto per struttura ospedaliera. https://www.dati.salute.gov.it/dati/det taglioDataset.jsp?menu=dati&idPag=18. Accessed 2 Mar 2022

16. Saganeiti, L., Favale, A., Pilogallo, A., Scorza, F., Murgante, B.: Assessing urban fragmentation at regional scale using sprinkling indexes. Sustainability **10**, 3274 (2018). https://doi.org/10.3390/su10093274

17. Nolè, G., Murgante, B., Calamita, G., Lanorte, A., Lasaponara, R.: Evaluation of urban sprawl from space using open source technologies. Ecol. Inform. **26**, 151–161 (2015). https://doi.org/10.1016/J.ECOINF.2014.05.005

Abandoned Agricultural Areas: From Quantification to Qualification by Integration of GIS and Remote Sensing

Giuseppe Cillis[1], Valentina Santarsiero[1,2(✉)], Gabriele Nolè[1], Antonio Lanorte[1], and Beniamino Murgante[2]

[1] IMAA-CNR C.da Santa Loja, Zona Industriale, Tito Scalo, Italy
{giuseppe.cillis,valentina.santarsiero,gabriele.nole,
antonio.lanorte}@imaa.cnr.it
[2] School of Engineering, University of Basilicata, Viale dell'Ateneo Lucano 10, 85100 Potenza, Italy
{valentina.santarsiero,beniamino.murgante}@unibas.it

Abstract. The agricultural areas abandonment has become one of phenomena that is most influencing the land transformation. This has been evident for some decades already, especially in inland mountainous and hilly areas of the Mediterranean where some types of agricultural activities have been abandoned as less profitable. The effects of this abandonment are not yet very clear but above all vary greatly in relation to morphological, geological and microclimatic characteristics of territory. The drivers of abandonment are also linked to these territorial characteristics with the addition of socio-economic factors. Therefore, studying this process from a spatial and geographical point of view is crucial. To do this, the integration of GIS and remote sensing in an open source environment represents a key approach as it allows to address the issues in a multi-temporal and multi-disciplinary way in an accurate way. In this paper, a case study of Southern Italy (Alto Bradano area - Basilicata region) has been chosen to quantify and qualify abandoned agricultural areas. First, a methodology for quantification of abandoned agricultural areas has been implemented through the time series analysis of spectral indices obtained starting from freely available satellite imagery, then a qualitative analysis has been carried out by relating abandoned agricultural areas to some spatial variables. In this way, we want to better define the drivers of change and contextualize them with respect to the local geography in order to have an overall view of the phenomenon of agricultural abandonment.

Keywords: Land changes · Agricultural abandonment · GIS · Remote sensing · FoSS · Basilicata region

1 Introduction

In the last decades, the territory of the most disadvantaged rural areas from a morphological and socio-economic point of view is undergoing significant transformations in

© The Author(s), under exclusive license to Springer Nature Switzerland AG 2022
O. Gervasi et al. (Eds.): ICCSA 2022, LNCS 13376, pp. 354–363, 2022.
https://doi.org/10.1007/978-3-031-10450-3_30

its landscape and environmental pattern [1]. This is mainly due to the abandonment of traditional agricultural activities (pastoralism and small-scale agriculture). It is a very common phenomenon in the inland areas of many Mediterranean regions [2]. However, in recent years, also due to climatic transformations, this process of abandonment is affecting also areas with high agricultural profitability [3].

Land transformation due to agricultural abandonment is very complex to evaluate and analyse because there are many biophysical, political and socio-economic variables that determine the development and intensity. Indeed, the drivers of abandonment of agricultural activities differs according to both the territorial and geographical context [4]. Even the impacts are complex to assess because they can be positive or negative in relation to the territorial context [5, 6]. Therefore, it is necessary to deepen both the causes of abandonment and the effects on the basis of methodologies that are as multidisciplinary as possible [7]. In view of the transformations taking place in the environmental, agricultural and social policies of the European community, these abandoned areas are also at the attention of the European Green Deal [8].

The first step for a more in-depth study of this phenomenon is linked to the quantification and qualification of agricultural areas that are abandoned. This mapping, however, must not be based on single years, but should be based on the trend of agricultural land over time, also because from a planning point of view the Common Agricultural Policy considers cultivated fields abandoned only after a certain number of years [9]. For this reason, the quantification of abandoned agricultural areas must be based on the use of time series realized by exploiting the different types of geodata available. One of the classical approaches is based on the use of historical cartography, aerial photos and orthophotos processed manually or semi-automatically in a GIS environment [10]. The use of historical cartography and aerial photos, although with some problems related to the accuracy of the estimate, is one of the fundamental methodologies for the assessment of agricultural abandonment as they allow to go back in time even more than a century [11]. However, one of the most used approaches is the one based on satellite images from different missions. This is because they allow to standardize the analysis for continuous and well-defined periods in order to create time series comparable over time [12].

Moreover, more and more often, in the literature it is possible to find case studies where integration between different remote sensing data is used. Among the commonly used satellite images there are Moderate Resolution Imaging Spectroradiometer (MODIS), Visible Infrared Imaging Radiometer Suite (VIIRS), or SPOT VEGETATION which, given their spatial resolution, allow a quantification mainly at geographical scale [13]. However, among the most used for investigations at small spatial scale are the images provided by the Landsat and Sentinel-2 missions. Indeed, there are many works that use different classification algorithms to evaluate land use and land cover transformations useful to estimate land abandonment rates [14]. In this type of classification algorithms in most cases are based on the use of vegetation indices that are able to perceive the photosynthetic changes or water content of the vegetation and thus assess its health and phonological status [15].

Increasingly common is the use of these techniques and methodologies in open source GIS environment since, in addition to the ease of use of the most common classification techniques, they also allow for more complex spatial analysis based on other types of geodata [16]. This is fundamental in multidisciplinary researches such as those related to the qualification of abandoned agricultural areas. Indeed, qualifying patterns of abandonment is one of the preliminary analyses that follows quantification as it allows to make initial assessments of the drivers and impacts of agricultural abandonment [17].

This work is part of this context, as integrated techniques between free and open source software (FoSS) GIS and remote sensing are applied in a rural landscape typical of Southern Italy and with significant problems of land take and land degradation [16] (Basilicata Region - Alto Bradano area) to quantify and qualify the abandonment of agricultural areas in a period ranging from 1990 to 2020. In particular, the mapping of abandoned agricultural areas was based on the use of time series of NDVI (Normalized Difference Vegetation Index) extrapolated from images of Landsat missions. These were then correlated with some variables (altitude, slope and exposure) in order to qualify the abandoned areas from a biophysical point of view and thus make an initial assessment of the process of abandonment. These two steps are preliminary but fundamental for all phases of land-use planning as they are at the base of the compression of the abandonment problem.

2   Material and Methods

2.1   Study Area

The study covered an area of approximately 155.000 hectares within the Basilicata Region (Southern Italy) (Fig. 1), including 17 municipalities and in part corresponds to the landscape area delimited by the high and medium Bradano rivers. The study area does not include some municipalities in their totality because those used in a previous study based on a single Sentinel-2 tile were used as boundaries [18]. This scenario corresponds to an agricultural landscape in which the vast cereal cultivations mixed with arboreal pastures and forages extend on the hills up to the Bradano river, interspersed, in the steepest slopes, with oak woods and wooded spots. Close to the inhabited centres, the agrarian mosaic changes and thickens in olive groves, orchards, vineyards and specialized crops. The cultivations, often interspersed by the presence of natural elements; hedges, trees and small bushes or minor roads, are fragmented into smaller plots until they reach the slopes of the settlements.

The population is concentrated almost exclusively in the population centres and there is little or no settlement in the surrounding area. The demographic dynamics of the context record, as in all the smaller municipalities of the region, a trend and a negative migration balance and, consequently, a consequent and worrying index of aging. The degree of "dispersion" of settlements and the poor infrastructure of the area represent the main constraints to the development potential of the area.

This social problem and the morphological conditions represent the main themes for the planning strategies that are being implemented to reduce the abandonment and degradation of the territory.

2.2   Abandoned Agricultural Areas Quantification

The quantification of abandoned agricultural areas was based on the reconstruction of the NDVI time series from 1990 to 2020 already implemented in a previous study [18].

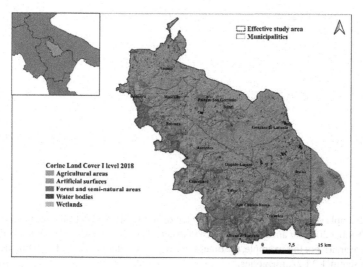

Fig. 1. Localization of the study area within Southern Italy and the Basilicata Region with a detail on land cover according to the 2018 Corine Land Cover I level.

The NDVI index is the most widely used remote sensing indicator to assess the health of vegetation (natural or cultivated) based on leaf reflectance. Indeed, it is the most accurate in estimating plant biomass because it is related to photosynthetic activity. It is based (Eq. 1) on the difference in leaf reflectance at different wavelengths. The value varies from −1 to +1 a lot but in general the higher it is, the better the vegetation is in a health state.

$$NDVI = \frac{NIR - RED}{NIR + RED} \tag{1}$$

Given the characteristics of this index, it is possible to use NDVI to evaluate over a one-year time frame how the vegetation status varies [20]. This is very useful to discriminate even one type of vegetation from another on the basis of a phenological curve and in particular to differentiate cereal crops from natural grasslands [19]. Effectively, the two land covers differ because cereal crops have an annual cycle that shows maximum NDVI values in spring (between March and April) and a minimum in autumn. In the same period, if we compare with natural meadows (where there is no more agricultural activity) we can see that in the autumn period the NDVI value is much higher and in the first part of spring the opposite. This is summarized in the example in Fig. 2 and can be explained by the differences in the phenological cycle between cereal crops and wild herbaceous species.

After the NDVI 1990–2020 time series was created, the difference between fall and spring for each year was calculated through change detections analyses. Finally, with subsequent spatial analyses as presented in a previous work [18], abandoned agricultural areas were identified. At the end of this phase, informed layers related to the abandoned agricultural areas between 1990 and 2020 were made. The satellite images used refer

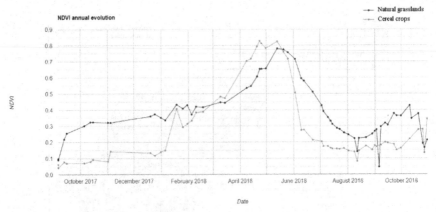

Fig. 2. Example of a phenology curve calculated on a historical NDVI time series from October 2017 to October 2018 for an agricultural area with cereal crops and a natural grassland (abandoned agricultural area). For this example, the time series was calculatedin Google Earth Engine platform based on Sentinel-2 L2A imageries.

to the Landsat 4/5 TM and Landsat 8 OLI mission. All operations were performed with the open source software QGIS.

2.3 Abandoned Agricultural Areas Qualification

Following the quantification, a preliminary assessment of the abandoned areas was made based on three indicators commonly used in studies involving land transformation [21]. Therefore, the information layer elaborated in the first part of the study, was related to altitude (meters above sea level), slope (in degrees) and aspect (in degrees). This procedure was carried out through a zonal spatial analysis with the altitude, slope and exposure raster processed from the digital terrain model provided by the geoportal of the Basilicata region [22]. The modules within QGIS allow to export the information in tabular format in order to better interpret them (Fig. 3). In fact, these data were exported in Comma Separated Value (.csv) format and processed within RStudio for the realization of box plots for the statistical interpretation of the data which is useful to start a process of more precise understanding of the process of abandoned agricultural areas.

3 Results and Discussions

The realization of the NDVI time series from 1990–2020 and the subsequent evaluation of the differences (ΔNDVI) allowed to map the areas that in this period of time have undergone a process of agricultural abandonment as they present several consecutive years with absence of cereal crops (Fig. 4).

The total number of abandoned hectares is about 4033, distributed mainly in patches of the same size as the single pixel (0.09 ha), demonstrating that the analyses must be integrated with subsequent spatial analyses to better determine abandonment. Through a random validation through a visual interpretation with orthophotos (1988 and 2020)

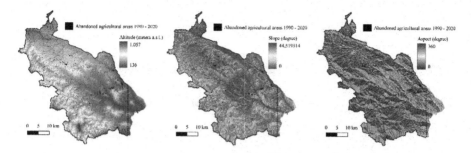

Fig. 3. Elevation, slope, and aspect maps for the study area.

the general accuracy of the identified areas has been verified (Fig. 5). The procedure, which will be improved in the next steps of the work, shows that time series and change detection represent the reference for this type of investigation and that NDVI is certainly sensitive but must be integrated with other spectral indices.

A problem is due to the temporal resolution of the Landsat missions which has a return time on the same area of 16 days and this leads to gaps in the time series when the cloud cover is high. In the future, the use of Sentinel-2, even if it allows to realize time series from 2015, will be fundamental because the return time is reduced up to 5 days in some cases.

Regarding the qualitative analysis of the abandoned agricultural areas identified with respect to some morphological variables (altitude, slope and aspect), the result has been statistically evaluated by making three different box plots (Fig. 6).

This preliminary analysis shows that the areas in which abandonment is most concentrated are at an average altitude of about 400 m above sea level and at a slope of about 7°. In both cases there is a concentration of values around a narrow range. Instead for what concerns the aspect, the values are more concentrated around a very wide range that goes from about 70° to 250 (from East to West) but that however represent the portions of the territory more sunny. This demonstrates that the phenomenon of agricultural abandonment should be analyzed and studied even at the local level because the complexity and the variables that determine it are diversified even within the same geographical area.

This was also confirmed by basic statistics calculated directly on the information layer in QGIS (Table 1).

The ease with which QGIS manages statistical databases makes it possible to quickly calculate all types of descriptive statistics accurately within the same work environment.

In the following steps of the study, further biophysical variables will be included and, above all, they will be related to planning and infrastructural variables such as the distance from roads and inhabited centres. This qualitative analysis, although preliminary, gives us an indication of a very important aspect, namely that in this study area the abandonment (from a topographical point of view) was not concentrated at the highest altitudes and steepest slopes, which are those considered at greater risk [23, 24]. Obviously the analysis is much simplified but the fact that it can be replicated in series within QGIS for all the layers and the possibility of replicating the scripts of RStudio directly within the same

Fig. 4. Mapping abandoned farmland between 1990 and 2020.

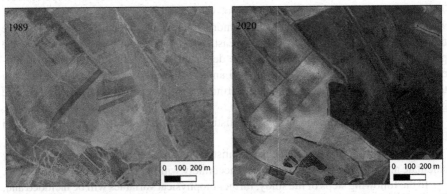

Fig. 5. Example of abandoned agricultural area where the difference between abandoned agricultural area and agricultural area with cereal crops is clear.

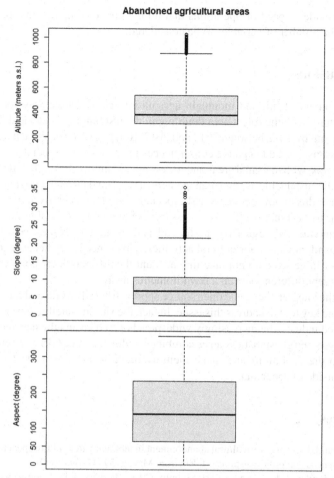

Fig. 6. Relative box plots of relationships between abandoned agricultural area and morphological variables (elevation, slope and aspect). Outliers (circles), median value (line inside the box), first quartile (bottom of the box), third quartile (top of the box) and variability beyond the quartiles (whiskers) are indicated.

Table 1. Average, minimum, maximum and standard deviation of morphological variables

Morphological variabiles	Avarage	Minimum	Maximum	Standard deviation
Altitude (meters)	434.99	160.06	1030.5	165.33
Slope (degree)	7.33	0	35.67	4.91
Aspect (degree)	153.90	0	358.53	98.55

software, provide a speed of operations that do not create computational problems by increasing the number of variables to be considered.

4 Conclusions

The abandonment of hill and mountain agriculture has paved the way for a massive return of nature, with the forest area doubling in the last hundred years and the number of trees growing by 4.7% between 2012 and 2017. But this, while positive it may seem in ecological terms, has had negative consequences in some cases especially in economic and social terms, with marginal areas and its few inhabitants increasingly left to their own devices. So the sustainable use and management of rural land through integrated planning could mitigate this ongoing process and especially avoid the negative impacts. In order for planning to be functional, it is necessary to implement replicable and updatable techniques and methodologies to quantify and analyze with the highest possible level of detail the abandonment of agricultural activities. This is necessary because the analysis at regional or large scale do not take into account the different local contexts that may present different differences even a few kilometres away.

Surely, the integrated free and open source approach based on GIS and remote sensing represents the key tool to address this issue. In fact, the various satellite missions in orbit, the developed indices, the increasingly widespread open data and the new techniques of spatial analysis and geostatistics can be combined within the same GIS work environment to speed up the operations and make them available to those who deal with spatial planning outside of academia.

References

1. MacDonald, D., et al.: Agricultural abandonment in mountain areas of Europe: environmental consequences and policy response. J. Environ. Manag. **59**, 47–69 (2000)
2. Van der Zanden, E.H., Verburg, P.H., Schulp, C.J.E., Verkerk, P.J.: Trade-offs of European agricultural abandonment. Land Use Policy **62**, 290–301 (2017)
3. Hatna, E., Bakker, M.M.: Abandonment and expansion of arable land in Europe. Ecosystems **14**, 720–731 (2011). https://doi.org/10.1007/s10021-011-9441-y
4. Rey Benayas, J.M.: Abandonment of agricultural land: an overview of drivers and consequences. CAB Rev. Perspect. Agric. Vet. Sci. Nutr. Nat. Resour. **2** (2007)
5. Cramer, V.A., Hobbs, R.J., Standish, R.J.: What's new about old fields? Land abandonment and ecosystem assembly. Trends Ecol. Evol. **23**, 104–112 (2008)
6. Stoate, C., et al.: Ecological impacts of early 21st century agricultural change in Europe—a review. J. Environ. Manag. **91**, 22–46 (2009)
7. Fayet, C.M.J., Reilly, K.H., Van Ham, C., Verburg, P.H.: What is the future of abandoned agricultural lands? A systematic review of alternative trajectories in Europe. Land Use Policy **112**, 105833 (2022)
8. Fayet, C.M.J., Reilly, K.H., Van Ham, C., Verburg, P.H.: The potential of European abandoned agricultural lands to contribute to the Green Deal objectives: policy perspectives. Environ. Sci. Policy **133**, 44–53 (2022)
9. Renwick, A., et al.: Policy reform and agricultural land abandonment in the EU. Land Use Policy **30**, 446–457 (2013)

10. Praticò, S., Solano, F., Di Fazio, S., Modica, G.: A multitemporal fragmentation-based approach for a dynamics analysis of agricultural terraced systems: the case study of Costa Viola Landscape (Southern Italy). Land **11**(4), 482 (2022)
11. Cillis, G., Statuto, D., Picuno, P.: Historical GIS as a tool for monitoring, preserving and planning forest landscape: a case study in a Mediterranean Region. Land **10**, 851 (2021)
12. Estel, S., Kuemmerle, T., Alcantara, C., Levers, C., Prishchepov, A., Hostert, P.: Mapping farmland abandonment and recultivation across Europe using MODIS NDVI time series. Remote Sens. Environ. **163**, 312–325 (2015)
13. Du, Z., Yang, J., Ou, C., Zhang, T.: Agricultural land abandonment and retirement mapping in the Northern China crop-pasture band using temporal consistency check and trajectory-based change detection approach. IEEE Trans. Geosci. Remote Sens. **60**, 1–12 (2022)
14. Yin, H., et al.: Monitoring cropland abandonment with Landsat time series. Remote Sens. Environ. **246**, 111873 (2020)
15. Conte, A.L., et al.: Oak decline in the Mediterranean basin: a study case from the southern Apennines (Italy). Plant Sociol. **56**, 69–80 (2019)
16. Santarsiero, V., Nolè, G., Lanorte, A., Tucci, B., Cillis, G.; Murgante, B.: Remote sensing and spatial analysis for land-take assessment in Basilicata Region (Southern Italy). Remote Sens. **14**, 1692 (2022). https://doi.org/10.3390/rs1407169
17. Castillo, C.P., Jacobs-Crisioni, C., Diogo, V., Lavalle, C.: Modelling agricultural land abandonment in a fine spatial resolution multi-level land-use model: an application for the EU. Environ. Modell. Softw. **136**, 104946 (2020)
18. Santarsiero, V., et al.: A remote sensing methodology to assess the abandoned arable land using NDVI index in Basilicata region. In: Gervasi, O., et al. (eds.) Proceedings of the Computational Science and Its Applications—ICCSA 2021, Cagliari, Italy, 13–16 September 2021, vol. 12954, pp. 685–703. Springer: Cham (2021). https://doi.org/10.1007/978-3-030-86979-3_49
19. Filizzola, C., et al.: On the use of temporal vegetation indices in support of eligibility controls for EU aids in agriculture. Int. J. Remote Sens. **39**(14), 4572–4598 (2018). https://doi.org/10.1080/01431161.2017.1395973
20. Sarti, M., Vaccari, F.P., Calfapietra, C., Brugnoli, E., Scartazza, A.: A statistical approach to detect land cover changes in Mediterranean ecosystems using multi-temporal Landsat data: the case study of Pianosa Island, Italy. Forests **11**, 334 (2020)
21. Terres, J.M., et al.: Farmland abandonment in Europe: identification of drivers and indicators, and development of a composite indicator of risk. Land Use Policy **49**, 20–34, (2015)
22. RSDI – Basilicata Region Geoportal. https://rsdi.regione.basilicata.it/. Accessed 4 Feb 2022
23. Lasanta, T., Arnáez, J., Pascual, N., Ruiz-Flaño, P., Errea, M.P., Lana-Renault, N.: Space–time process and drivers of land abandonment in Europe. Catena **149**, 810–823 (2017)
24. Padial-Iglesias, M., et al.: Driving forces of forest expansion dynamics across the Iberian Peninsula (1987–2017): a spatio-temporal transect. Forests **13**, 475 (2022)

Land Use Change Evaluation in an Open-Source GIS Environment: A Case Study of the Basilicata Region (Southern Italy)

Valentina Santarsiero[1,2](✉) [iD], Antonio Lanorte[1] [iD], Gabriele Nolè[1] [iD],
Giuseppe Cillis[1] [iD], and Beniamino Murgante[2] [iD]

[1] IMAA-CNR C.da Santa Loja, Zona Industriale, Tito Scalo, Italy
{valen-tina.santarsiero,antonio.lanorte,gabriele.nole,
giuseppe.cillis}@imaa.cnr.it
[2] School of Engineering, University of Basilicata, Viale dell'Ateneo Lucano 10, 85100 Potenza,
Italy
{valentina.santarsiero,beniamino.murgante}@unibas.it

Abstract. Soil is an essential, non-renewable natural resource that provides vital goods and services for ecosystems, human life, and the production of crops and fuels. The phenomena of land consumption and land use change have a considerable impact on ecosystems. In addition, the poor and confusing regulatory framework contributes to the spread of processes related to soil sealing, such as the wild installation of wind farms, resulting in an increasing fragmentation of the territory with related phenomena of soil degradation.

The research work has proposed an innovative methodological approach on issues related to land consumption and land use change, based on a robust territorial and landscape study. The whole research has been focused on the use and integration between geographic information systems and remote sensing techniques for the study of the territory. The increasing availability of cartographic data and the evolution of satellite data is the basis of a system that provides a continuous phase of analysis of the phenomenon. The work defines the picture of the phenomenon in Basilicata, investigating various aspects of land consumption, going into specific detail of some sample areas. The objective was the application of remote sensing techniques and change detection analysis for the qualitative and quantitative estimation of land take related to degradation phenomena. The methodologies and data developed in this work, could be the basis for the creation of a regional database on soil consumption, which could be made up of a robust infrastructure of spatial data and could provide a service and a system of data collection and collect data and reports from citizens, companies, institutions, research organizations, would support public bodies in the definition of policies, strategies and actions aimed at the containment of the phenomenon and would implement, in addition, measures of limitation, prevention, monitoring and mitigation of the same.

Keywords: Land use change · Remote sensing · GIS

O. Gervasi et al. (Eds.): ICCSA 2022, LNCS 13376, pp. 364–372, 2022.
https://doi.org/10.1007/978-3-031-10450-3_31

1 Introduction

Land take and land degradation represent the most dramatic consequences of the loss of the natural characteristics and functions of soils, due to an increase in artificial land cover, linked to settlement and infrastructural dynamics [1, 2]. The increase in land take is a very important indicator of land management policies, both for the assessment of settlement processes, and for the protection and enhancement policies of the agricultural, rural and natural areas of the territory [3–6]. Land degradation is the main cause of soil degradation in Europe, triggering an increase in environmental risks, urban fragmentation and all related problems [7]. This has led to the definition of standards with the aim of regulating and stemming the phenomenon [8, 9]. Over time, land take has been linked to different phenomena, such as urban/industrial expansion, the construction of infrastructures, the productive exploitation of specific natural and mineral resources etc. [10, 11]. These degradation processes involve different types of environmental risks such as hydrogeological instability, soil erosion, salinization, loss of organic matter [7, 12–15].

The innovative approach of this research was based on the construction of methodologies that allowed a detailed and accurate historical analysis on the issues of land consumption, land use change and land degradation based on a robust spatial study [16, 17].

The whole work has been based on the use and integration between geographic information systems and remote sensing techniques for the study of the territory.

In particular, the study of areas subject to land consumption and land degradation, was conducted with the use of innovative tools, models and techniques, using mainly satellite data. In fact, the methodological framework put in place is robust to monitoring the dynamics of land consumption and land use change over time. The research conducted defines the framework of Land Use Change (LCC) in Basilicata, investigating the various aspects, analyzing in detail some specific areas. The work has been articulated, therefore, analyzing and articulating the different aspects of LCC in different workpages (Land take, LCC, Land Degradation related to soil erosion), described in the following sections.

2 Material and Method

2.1 Definition of Land Take Monitoring System

The first part of the research was aimed at creating a land use classification model that would allow for expeditious monitoring of impermealized areas. The work was divided into two phases, the first involved the use of an experimental model for the classification and historical analysis of land take based primarily on Landsat satellite data (analysis of historical land consumption trends) [16–20].

Particular emphasis has been placed on the identification and classification of land use changes due to the installation of renewable energy sources to quantify the consumption of land take in the period 2010, 2014, 2018 [18].

In fact, subsequently, with the use of Sentinel 2 data, which has a higher spatial resolution than the Landsat data, it was possible to further improve the methodology created by increasing the degree of detail in the classification process. The use of Sentinel

2 data has allowed to study and estimate the land take due to the installation of renewable energy sources. Both methodologies developed saw the use of Support Vector Machine (SVM) algorithms for classification [18, 21, 22].

2.2 Analysis of Land Use and Land Cover Change

The objective of this analysis was the creation of a database of land use maps based on historical analysis of past trends, analyzed by land cover change detection through the use of satellite data. Specifically, the work was divided into two parts [21–23]. In the first, a regional scale approach was used in which land cover maps were created.

Maps of land cover, land cover changes were made 1990/2018 and mapping of some dynamics related to specific cover classes (grasslands) using MODIS satellite data. In the second part, a local scale approach was used based on innovative methodologies of satellite image classification. The local scale approach has allowed to determine with greater detail the dynamics that occur on the territory, to improve the methodology and to develop more prudent land-use planning strategies. Specifically, in this phase a case study (Regional Park of Gallipoli Cognato Piccole Dolomiti Lucane) and a supervised classification methodology for the land cover of the Basilicata Region.

One of the objectives of this part of the work was to improve knowledge and techniques related to the creation of land cover databases and analysis of the dynamics of transformation in such a way as to be used at different levels. The work carried out in the first part has allowed to highlight a trend of abandonment of agricultural areas and subsequent agricultural areas and subsequent renaturalization that is not very clear and detailed (especially in the case of the Land Monitoring Service) and(especially in the case of the Land Monitoring Service) and that instead has emerged with greater clarity in the second part thanks to a local scale approach and a very accurate preliminary methodology of identification of the accurate preliminary methodology for identifying land cover changes.

2.3 Assessment and Monitoring of Soil Erosion Risk and Land Degradation

This part of the work aimed at applying remote sensing techniques and change detection analysis for the qualitative and quantitative estimation of land consumption related to land degradation phenomena and spatial dynamics related to land use changes.

The analyses applied in this work page have allowed to evaluate, first of all, the existing link between the erosion phenomena and degradation in agricultural areas. Erosion in fact occurs more in areas that have areas that have undergone a change of land use and/or abandonment, while in stable agricultural areas the stable agricultural areas the phenomenon has less impact. The analysis techniques developed have made it possible to highlight the areas in degradation with respect to changes in the rate of erosion, developing maps of vulnerability to land degradation of areas that are currently arable land and post-crop vegetation. The relationships between spatial dynamics related to land use change and erosion were investigated. In addition, it was possible to estimate any existing connections between the age of agricultural abandonment of arable land and current erosion rates [15, 16, 24].

2.4 Methodology

The research was based on the integration between remote sensing techniques and Geographic Information Systems (GIS), using different datasets of open spatial data, this offers the possibility to study and monitor the evolution of the territory at a wide temporal and spatial scale, allowing to adopt the same techniques and models of analysis in different territorial contexts. Satellite data provide detailed information and insight into landscape characteristics and changes in urban and rural areas. Land cover changes are among the main fields of application of remote sensing [24–26]. The reference satellite data used are the Sentinel 2 products of the Copernicus Mission, data from the Landsat constellation and Modis satellite data.

The use of satellite data and GIS tools can provide useful data for estimating land use land degradation, erosion risk, and for mapping and monitoring degraded areas.

These methods are mainly based on the use of indices obtained from the combination of different spectral bands, which emphasize and detect any change in the state of vegetation. In the present work, the integration of the soil erosion model (RUSLE model) with GIS and remote sensing were found to be effective tools to map and quantify areas and rates of soil erosion for the development of better conservation plans and land monitoring. In addition, the use of spatially explicit geostatistical surveys allowed for a more accurate quantitative analysis of the various results obtained.

In order to provide a more fluent understanding of the methodologies, techniques, and analyses performed, the following are listed:

1. Supervised classification, through the use of the SVM algorithm, with the integration of ancillary data (orthophotos, ground truth data), of the historical trend (1994–2014) to create land cover maps subsequently used as input for estimating land take. In order to produce a synthetic map of land take, the Sentinel-2 images were classified using a supervised classification. Using Map Algebra, the 10-m rasterized information layers, or subsets thereof, were inserted on the previous classification map, replacing the corresponding pixels. A first map of land take was obtained divided the area characterized by urbanization from the area with the presence of the renewable energy sources. Eolic class have been reclassified discriminate the relevant street from the turbine pad and subdivided into other subclasses referred to the power wind turbines, in order to quantify the land take related to each one;
2. Estimation of land transformations in terms of land cover and land use through a comparison of differences in quantitative surface area Surface area associated with each land cover category. A quantitative spatial diachronic analysis of Land Use Land Cover (LULC) data has been carried out in order to identify and evaluate in detail the trends of changes within each class.
3. Calculation of the Revised Universal Soil Loss Equation (RUSLE) for estimating monthly erosion and overall annual erosion (October 2019 - September 2020);
4. General statistical investigation between land cover classes and monthly and annual RUSLE values;
5. Clustering of RUSLE, through Getis & Ord. autocorrelation algorithm, in order to highlight areas that, month after month, show a continuous erosion phenomenon;
6. Survey of Normalized Difference Vegetation Index (NDVI) time series for the period 1990–2020 in order to create a database on the transition dynamics of land cover;

7. Susceptibility to land degradation of areas classified as arable land and areas with post-crop vegetation on the basis of deviations from the average values of RUSLE and mapping of Areas of vegetation degradation, related to arable land, through statistical correlation with the vegetation factor C.

3 Results and Discussion

3.1 Definition of Land Take Monitoring System

In this study, a new method of classification of Landsat and Sentinel satellite data was proposed to perform a multi-temporal analysis to identify changes in LCC and subsequently quantify the change in impermeabilized areas. Moreover, within the defined model, the use of the Geotopographic Database (GTDB) spatial information layers was fundamental for the detailed definition of land take. The application of the proposed method allowed us to quickly extract detailed maps of land take with an overall accuracy greater than 90%, reducing the cost and the processing time [21].

Analyzed the land take due to urban expansion and renewable energy is evident how in the first case the trend is constantly growing, while in the latter trend shows a strongly increment starting from 2014 caused by the development of small and large Eolic stations.

3.2 Analysis of Land Use and Land Cover Change

Change detection has allowed us to highlight the areas in which changes in agricultural land use have occurred agricultural land use changes occurred. In most cases there has been a reduction of agricultural areas (e.g. sometimes fields close to others have been abandoned) and in other cases a new land use has been established. Statistical data indicate a value of class 4 (agricultural) equal to about 421000 ha in 1985 which have decreased to about 365000 ha in 2011, recording a loss of about 55000 ha. The transformations that have taken place show differences depending on the local contexts. In some cases, agricultural land has given way to shrub land, in others to wooded land, etc. In general, statistics on the entire region give a prevalence of new land use (which in 1985 was agricultural) of areas with shrubs (about 70%).

The analysis at a smaller scale, even if it requires more time and more knowledge of the territory, certainly guarantee a better accuracy and specificity of the data. So doing so, it is possible to use these techniques (generally used only for scientific purposes) also to support decision-making and planning activities of the various bodies.

Moreover, given the increasing number of open techniques and tools, it is possible to automate or make more accessible the however, make more accessible methodologies of land classification. In fact, using an analysis at the regional scale but with more specific techniques and with a knowledge of the territory allows to have a higher level of accuracy than that present in datasets than that present in the Corinne Land Cover (CLC) datasets. In fact, with the methodology applied it is recorded that, in a comparable but not identical period of reference, there has been a reduction in the agricultural areas and not an increase as reported in the CLC datasets.

In addition, the ability to access ancillary data of different types to implement supervised classifications is critical to improving and detailing the classes of land cover. Certainly, the main challenge in this field of research is to understand the methods for extracting useful information from the data, as well as properly interpreting signals of the time series, so that we can understand both slow variations, caused by gradual changes in the ecosystem, as well as faster variations due to external disturbances or other events.

3.3 Assessment and Monitoring of Soil Erosion Risk and Land Degradation

The results of this work page have allowed to realize preliminary maps of susceptibility to land degradation related to the spatial dynamics of land use changes. The mapping of the results allows, in general, to identify areas or large clusters that must be focused on both for further study and from a planning point of view as they are precisely those planning point of view as they are precisely those areas that may be subject to land degradation. The normalized values allow the subdivision into equal classes which in this preliminary investigation have been classified only by following an algebraic logic and without taking into account further aspects. The analyses applied in this work have allowed to evaluate the relationships existing between agricultural land use changes and land degradation phenomena, as erosion phenomena are more evident in areas that have undergone land degradation. erosive phenomena are more evident in areas which have undergone land use change and/or abandonment, while in stable agricultural areas the phenomenon has less impact. With the methodologies applied in this study, it was possible to create different datasets, both tabular and in the form of maps, for an assessment of the process of land degradation related to the dynamics of land use and land cover. The transition phase of these areas towards low-density urbanization has a marginal impact on the marginal compared to the phenomena of abandonment and/or agricultural transition (moving from one type of cultivation to arable farming to another type of cultivation) on the phenomenon of degradation. Starting with the application of the RUSLE model, soil erosion for the period October 2019/September 2020 was preliminarily estimated, based on which basic statistics were performed to evaluate the contribution of the various factors and investigations with respect to each land cover class. This allowed for the evaluation of land cover classes that had high erosion values over the period. In addition, for a general assessment, a preliminary and detailed survey was carried out on the state of arable land and areas defined as post-crop, which represent two classes of cover whose dynamics most influence the processes of land degradation in the region. Subsequently, models have been developed to specifically understand the relationship between land cover, erosion and land degradation. In addition, at this stage of the work, we began to analyze the cause-effect relationship between degradation and erosion. This allowed us to highlight the areas in degradation simply with respect to changes in erosion rates, producing maps of vulnerability to land degradation of areas that are currently arable land and post-crop vegetation.

Taking advantage of the link between lack of soil productivity and degradation, vulnerable areas were identified by correlating vegetation cover and erosion.

The two approaches, allow to systematically monitor the areas that present erosion problems and that are vulnerable to degradation. The outputs are represented by indications in the form of maps of the areas to be monitored and by data (in different formats) useful to support public decision-makers in the various activities of agro-forestry planning.

4 Conclusion

Land take and land use change have a considerable impact on the territory and on the ecosystems. The importance of biodiversity is recognized globally for its key role in maintaining key role in maintaining ecosystem services. Appropriate LCC data play a key role in several areas of land use planning. The problem of land transformation is one of those research fields that needs up-to-date LCC geodata that allow for standardized and repeated surveying over time.

The work currently carried out defines the framework of LCC in Basilicata, investigating various aspects of land consumption, going into specific details of some sample areas.

In this work we tried to propose new approaches for data management and processing applicable to the entire regional territory, in order to better understand the LCC and all its facets and monitor its evolution over time. For this reason, the completion of the analysis of historical trends of the phenomena analyzed is essential.

The complexity, the relevance of the topics discussed with and the usefulness of the contents produced so far, underline the need for a continuation of this research.

References

1. Marquard, E., et al.: Land consumption and land take: enhancing conceptual clarity for evaluating spatial governance in the EU context. Sustainability **12**, 8269 (2020). https://doi.org/10.3390/SU12198269
2. Schatz, E.M., Bovet, J., Lieder, S., Schroeter-Schlaack, C., Strunz, S., Marquard, E.: Land take in environmental assessments: recent advances and persisting challenges in selected EU countries. Land Use Policy (2021). https://doi.org/10.1016/j.landusepol.2021.105730
3. Seto, K., Güneralp, B., Hutyra, L.R.: Global forecasts of urban expansion to 2030 and direct impacts on biodiversity and carbon pools. Natl. Acad Sci. (2012). https://doi.org/10.1073/pnas.1211658109
4. Keesstra, S.D., et al.: The significance of soils and soil science towards realization of the United Nations Sustainable Development Goals. Soil **2**, 111–128 (2016). https://doi.org/10.5194/soil-2-111-2016
5. Las Casas, G., Scorza, F., Murgante, B.: New urban agenda and open challenges for urban and regional planning. In: Calabrò, F., Della Spina, L., Bevilacqua, C. (eds.) ISHT 2018. SIST, vol. 100, pp. 282–288. Springer, Cham (2019). https://doi.org/10.1007/978-3-319-92099-3_33
6. Nolè, G., Murgante, B., Calamita, G., Lanorte, A., Lasaponara, R.: Evaluation of urban sprawl from space using open source technologies. Ecol. Inform. **26**, 151–161 (2015). https://doi.org/10.1016/J.ECOINF.2014.05.005
7. Pacheco, F.A.L., Sanches Fernandes, L.F., Valle Junior, R.F., Valera, C.A., Pissarra, T.C.T.: Land degradation: multiple environmental consequences and routes to neutrality. Curr. Opin. Environ. Sci. Heal. **5**, 79–86 (2018). https://doi.org/10.1016/J.COESH.2018.07.002

8. COM/2016/0767 final - 2016/0382 (COD)$ - Publications Office of the EU. https://op.eur opa.eu/it/publication-detail/-/publication/151772eb-b7e9-11e6-9e3c-01aa75ed71a1/langua ge-en. Accessed 23 Nov 2021

9. Abuelaish, B., Olmedo, M.T.C.: Scenario of land use and land cover change in the Gaza Strip using remote sensing and GIS models. Arab. J. Geosci. **9**(4), 1–14 (2016). https://doi.org/10. 1007/s12517-015-2292-7

10. Puertas, O.L., Henríquez, C., Meza, F.J.: Assessing spatial dynamics of urban growth using an integrated land use model. Application in Santiago Metropolitan Area, 2010–2045. Land Use Policy **38**, 415–425 (2014). https://doi.org/10.1016/j.landusepol.2013.11.024

11. Saganeiti, L., Favale, A., Pilogallo, A., Scorza, F., Murgante, B.: Assessing urban fragmen- tation at regional scale using sprinkling indexes. Sustainability **10**, 3274 (2018). https://doi. org/10.3390/su10093274

12. Morabito, M., Crisci, A., Guerri, G., Messeri, A., Congedo, L., Munafò, M.: Surface urban heat islands in Italian metropolitan cities: tree cover and impervious surface influences. Sci. Total Environ. **751**, 142334 (2021). https://doi.org/10.1016/j.scitotenv.2020.142334

13. Le Houérou, H.N.: Climate change, drought and desertification. J. Arid Environ. **34**, 133–185 (1996). https://doi.org/10.1006/JARE.1996.0099

14. Pilogallo, A., Saganeiti, L., Scorza, F., Murgante, B.: Soil ecosystem services and sediment production: the Basilicata region case study. In: Gervasi, O., et al. (eds.) ICCSA 2020. LNCS, vol. 12253, pp. 421–435. Springer, Cham (2020). https://doi.org/10.1007/978-3-030-58814- 4_30

15. Cillis, G., et al.: Soil erosion and land degradation in rural environment: a preliminary GIS and remote-sensed approach. In: Gervasi, O., et al. (eds.) ICCSA 2021. LNCS, vol. 12954, pp. 682–694. Springer, Cham (2021). https://doi.org/10.1007/978-3-030-86979-3_48

16. Santarsiero, V., et al.: A remote sensing methodology to assess the abandoned arable land using NDVI index in Basilicata region. In: Gervasi, O., et al. (eds.) ICCSA 2021. LNCS, vol. 12954, pp. 695–703. Springer, Cham (2021). https://doi.org/10.1007/978-3-030-86979-3_49

17. Santarsiero, V., Nolè, G., Lanorte, A., Tucci, B., Baldantoni, P., Murgante, B.: Evolution of soil consumption in the municipality of Melfi (southern Italy) in relation to renewable energy. In: Misra, S., et al. (eds.) ICCSA 2019. LNCS, vol. 11621, pp. 675–682. Springer, Cham (2019). https://doi.org/10.1007/978-3-030-24302-9_48

18. Di Palma, F., Amato, F., Nolè, G., Martellozzo, F., Murgante, B.: A SMAP supervised clas- sification of landsat images for urban sprawl evaluation. ISPRS Int. J. Geo-Inform. **5**, 109 (2016). https://doi.org/10.3390/IJGI5070109

19. Murgante, B., Borruso, G., Lapucci, A.: Sustainable development: concepts and methods for its application in urban and environmental planning. Stud. Comput. Intell. **348**, 1–15 (2011). https://doi.org/10.1007/978-3-642-19733-8_1

20. Baldantoni, P., Nolè, G., Lanorte, A., Tucci, B., Santarsiero, V., Murgante, B.: Trend definition of soil consumption in the period 1994–2014 - municipalities of Potenza, Matera and Melfi. In: Misra, S., et al. (eds.) ICCSA 2019. LNCS, vol. 11621, pp. 683–691. Springer, Cham (2019). https://doi.org/10.1007/978-3-030-24302-9_49

21. Santarsiero, V., Nolè, G., Lanorte, A., Tucci, B., Cillis, G., Murgante, B.: Remote Sensing and Spatial Analysis for Land-Take Assessment in Basilicata Region (Southern Italy) (2022). https://doi.org/10.3390/rs14071692

22. Statuto, D., Cillis, G., Picuno, P.: Using historical maps within a GIS to analyze two centuries of rural landscape changes in southern Italy. Land **6**, 65 (2017). https://doi.org/10.3390/LAN D6030065

23. Cillis, G., Tucci, B., Santarsiero, V., Nolè, G., Lanorte, A., Ballesta, J.: Understanding Land Changes for Sustainable Environmental Management: The Case of Basilicata Region (Southern Italy) (2021). https://doi.org/10.3390/pollutants1040018

24. Tucci, B., et al.: Assessment and monitoring of soil erosion risk and land degradation in arable land combining remote sensing methodologies and RUSLE factors. In: Gervasi, O., et al. (eds.) ICCSA 2021. LNCS, vol. 12954, pp. 704–716. Springer, Cham (2021). https://doi.org/10.1007/978-3-030-86979-3_50
25. Adam, E., Mutanga, O., Odindi, J., Abdel-Rahman, E.M.: Land-use/cover classification in a heterogeneous coastal landscape using RapidEye imagery: evaluating the performance of random forest and support vector machines classifiers. Int. J. Remote Sens. **35**(10), 3440–3458 (2014). https://doi.org/10.1080/01431161.2014.903435
26. Aung, H.P.P., Aung, S.T.: Analysis of land cover change detection using satellite images in Patheingyi Township. In: Zin, T., Lin, J.W. (eds.) Big Data Analysis and Deep Learning Applications, vol. 744. Springer, Singapore (2019). https://doi.org/10.1007/978-981-13-0869-7_41

A Preliminary Study on Electrocardiogram Response During Pain Induction

Ana Bento[1]($\boxtimes$), Susana Brás[2,3], and Raquel Sebastião[2,3]

[1] Department of Physics (DFis), University of Aveiro, 3810-193 Aveiro, Portugal
analuisa98@ua.pt
[2] Institute of Electronics and Informatics Engineering of Aveiro (IEETA),
University of Aveiro, 3810-193 Aveiro, Portugal
susana.bras@ua.pt, raquel.sebastiao@ua.pt
[3] Department of Electronics, Telecommunications and Informatics (DETI),
University of Aveiro, 3810-193 Aveiro, Portugal

Abstract. Pain is a complex phenomenon that arises from the interaction of multiple neuroanatomic and neurochemical systems with several cognitive and affective processes. Nowadays, the assessment of pain intensity still relies on the use of self-reports. However, recent research has shown a connection between the perception of pain and exacerbated stress response on the Autonomic Nervous System (ANS). The ANS, which is divided into the Parasympathetic Nervous System (PNS) and the Sympathetic Nervous System (SNS), functions as the subconscious regulator of the body. As a result, there has been increasing analysis of the autonomic reactivity with the objective to assess pain. The goal of this study was to explore and understand different responses in the electrocardiogram (ECG) signal when in the experience of pain. For this study, ECG was simultaneously recorded while a pain-inducing protocol (Cold Pressor Task - CPT) was implemented. Several features were extracted from the ECG to analyse differences related to pain induction tasks. The results obtained showed a statistically significant increase in the heart rate during the painful periods in comparison with non-painful periods. Additionally, heart rate variability features demonstrated a decrease in the PNS influence. These results are a step further in understanding the ECG response during the experience of pain, supporting the awareness and insights over physiological interactions within the pain experience.

Keywords: ANS · CPT · ECG · Pain induction · Feature extraction · Pain assessment

O. Gervasi et al. (Eds.): ICCSA 2022, LNCS 13376, pp. 373–383, 2022.
https://doi.org/10.1007/978-3-031-10450-3_32

1   Introduction

Pain is a complex biopsychosocial phenomenon caused by damage or potential damage in the tissues and serves a vital protective function. The International Association for the Study of Pain revised the definition of pain as "an unpleasant sensory and emotional experience associated with, or resembling that associated with, actual or potential tissue damage" [1]. Pain is a common symptom in almost every clinical practice. This is particularly true in neurological and musculoskeletal problems [5].

The presence of pain and, moreover, its intensity, influences a physician's clinical judgement, the selection of treatments and therapeutics, the potential surgical indications, and the subsequent prognosis. An accurate assessment is a critical factor, affecting decision making in patient management, treatment, and outcomes. As of today, pain assessment still relies primarily on self-report, both in clinical and experimental settings. Self-reports are generally easy to obtain, require practically little to no equipment, allow for comprehensive information collection, and exhibit typically good reliability [5]. Nonetheless, circumstances exist where this is not possible or where it is unreliable [2]. In these situations, surrogate markers utilise changes in behavioural or psychological parameters. However, their use may be inaccurate, hampered by observational bias, or influenced by disease processes or pharmacological interventions [6]. Thus, objective approaches to measuring pain experience would provide an important complement to self-reports [2]. Although the study of how physiological indicators correlate to pain is still at an early stage, it has become a promising research area. Consequently, the main goal of this study aims to explore and describe ANS reactions related to pain and identify relevant features from physiological signals associated with it.

This work is organized as follows. The next Sect., 2, presents related works on exploring physiological reactions, namely through ECG, in the experience of pain. Section 3 presents the data collection and methodology for data analysis, while Sect. 4 presents the obtained results. Finally, the results are discussed in Sect. 5 prior to presenting the conclusions of our study in Sect. 6.

2   Related Works

Pain is thought to exacerbate the autonomic response to stress, a rationale supported by evidence showing a neuroanatomical overlap between nociceptive and autonomic pathways [2]. For example, studies have shown that the application of pain stimuli induces significant heart rate acceleration. Therefore, there has been a growing interest in the use of autonomic reactivity as an objective marker of pain [3–5].

Loggia et al. [5] studied the alterations in the Heart Rate (HR), skin conductance, and pain ratings in response to heat stimulus of different intensities, which range from warm to pain-inducing. The data was analysed from two different perspectives: the correlation between the autonomic response and pain intensity in subjects separately (subject analysis) and the correlation between the average pain intensity and the autonomic responses to the same temperature in all individuals (group analysis). The results demonstrated that an increase in pain intensity generated an increase in both HR and skin conductance. The subject analysis revealed a higher correlation with skin conductance, leading to a belief that this metric is more sensitive to changes in perception. However, the magnitude increases of the skin conductance did not significantly correlate with the magnitude of pain intensity, suggesting that this measure alone does not predict the absolute level of pain reported by the subject. The opposite was true for HR, as it did not reliably predict verbal responses to pain on a subject basis but did on the group level. These differences suggest that, although HR is affected by pain perception, it is a very noisy measure.

The Cold Pressor Task (CPT) is a pain-inducing method that requires individuals to immerse one hand (or forearm) in cold water for as long as they can tolerate or during a fixed period of time. The main advantages of this method rely on its portability, minimal training to use, and few risks. The primary disadvantage of the CPT is the significant methodological divergences in its implementation and in the measurement of pain outcomes, crippling the comparison of results from different studies [3, 4, 8, 9]. There is increasing information linking the feeling of pain with the ANS. Therefore, several studies have investigated and recorded the alterations of the ANS with the use of the CPT.

One such case was the work of Hampf [3], who planned to quantify the changes in skin impedance, HR, and facial skin temperature when healthy volunteers were subjected to acute pain through a CPT (with water at 0 °C). A total of nineteen participants were included in the study. The results showed an increase in all the parameters calculated during the CPT, in comparison to those calculated during the baseline. However, only the skin conductance increase was statistically significant.

Kregel. et al. [4] analysed the relation between efferent sympathetic nervous system activity to skeletal muscle (MNSA) and pain sensation during localised skin cooling. Ten subjects took part in the study, immersing their hand in different temperature water baths for three minutes each. The levels of temperature in the bath range from warm non-pain inducing to mid-level (14 °C) to cold (7 °C and 0 °C - pain-inducing). The participants went in order from the warmest to coldest temperature, with a ten-minute interval between the recovery three-minute period of the last water tank and the three-minute baseline of the next. While the study was being performed, the MNSA, BP (blood pressure), HR, and breathing were continuously recorded. The observations of this study demonstrated that there was no evident influence on MNSA when the participants were subjected to non-painful skin cooling. During the hand immersion in ice water, there was a progressive rise in MSNA as skin temperature started to decrease. Regarding HR, there was a significant rise during the initial phase of the 0 °C, which was expected. Even so, the HR consistently increased in less painful water temperatures, although on a smaller scale. As for the BP, it showed no changes [4].

3 Materials and Methods

This section describes the protocol for data collection and presents the methods applied for analysing the ECG response during the induction of pain through cold pain stimuli implemented as a CPT. The different methods used to analyse the data were implemented in Matlab R2021a (MATLAB R2021a & Simulink R2021a) [7]. As the proposed work focuses on the ECG response in the experience of pain, it will be only presented the protocol for ECG data collection.

3.1 Data Collection

Aiming to study the physiological changes that pain provokes, 45 participants were subjected to a pain-inducing protocol (CPT), while the ECG signal was being collected. This study was approved by the Ethics and Deontological Council of the University of Aveiro (number 09-CED/2019).

All the participants were recruited from the local community, they were healthy, did not suffer from any disease that causes chronic pain, did not present any mental illness or neurological disorder, and, lastly, could comprehend and answer to self-report measures. As explained before, we studied a total of 45 participants, 27 male and 17 female, with ages between 21 and 59, with an average age and standard deviation of 33 and 11 years old, respectively.

To perform the CPT, two specially designed tanks were used. These were produced to be able to sustain the water at the desired temperature. The physiological data were collected with the Biosignalsplux® Explorer tool kit, with a sampling frequency of 1000 Hz. The ECG was collected with a triode configuration: two electrodes were placed on the right and left side of the participant's ribcage, and a reference electrode was placed above the pelvic bone. Additionally, to mark the different epochs, a handheld switch directly connected to the hub was used.

After obtaining the participant's informed consent, and before starting the procedure, the participants had to respond to the instrument for data collection regarding their age, gender, and health status, thus ensuring that they complied with the inclusion criteria. That same data collection sheet was later used to fill out their pain level. The participants were asked which hand was their non-dominant and seated accordingly. All the participants were facing a wall during the study, to ensure as few distractions as possible. The protocol started with a five-minute baseline recording, where the participant had to be seated, at a comfortable position, with their arm close to their body, trying to avoid movements. After, they were asked to immerse their hand and forearm inside the warm water tank for two minutes, to ensure that all the participants started the CPT with similar skin temperatures (37 °C). Before the end of this task, the level of pain, with a numerical rating scale (NRS), was assessed. Afterwards, for the induction of pain, the participants immersed the arm into the cold-water tank and the CPT started. If the participant was unable to withstand the CPT for the whole two minutes, they could withdraw their hand from the cold tank. In this case, the participant was advised to notify their wish to remove the arm from the tank and, before doing so, to report their current pain level and the level of the maximum pain experienced during the CPT. If the participant was able to withstand the entire CPT, the current and maximum pain levels were reported at the two-minute mark. Right after removing the arm, they again reported their pain level and the BP was measured. The participant transferred the arm to the warm water tank for two minutes of immersion. Next, the hand and forearm were dried, and, while seated in a comfortable position, a five-minute rest period, similar to the initial baseline, commenced. At the three-minute point during this rest period (around five minutes after the end of the CPT), they were asked to give their current pain level and to report the maximum level of pain they felt in retrospect.

3.2   Data Analysis

After data acquisition, the raw ECG was filtered considering the frequencies between 0.5 Hz and 40 Hz. After, the ECG data was normalized according to the baseline epoch, which corresponds to the first five minutes of this study. The feature extraction was done using the Neurokit2[1] in Python. After the data was processed, it was divided into epochs according to the pressing of the triggers. The five epochs created are the five-minute baseline recording (Baseline), the first two-minute recordings of the hand and arm in the warm water tank (WarmWater1), the CPT recording, the two minute recordings of the warm water tank for the second time (WarmWater2) and, finally, the last five minute rest (Rest). Afterwards, all features were subjected to statistical analysis, in which the significance level (α) was set at 0.05, to investigate differences in the extracted features in the several epochs. As all of the features failed to be normally distributed, the differences between the five different epochs were evaluated with the non-parametric Friedmann. When a significant difference was found between the five epochs, the Wilcoxon signed-rank test, with Bonferroni correction, was performed to evaluate which epochs were significantly different from each other. The statistical analysis was done using scikit posthocs [11]. This python package provides posthoc tests for pairwise multiple comparisons. Scikit posthocs package is dependable on the statsmodels module, in which the multiple test is responsible for adjusting the p values to minimize type I and type II errors [12]. The results were then plotted on a heatmap to facilitate their interpretation.

4   Results

Six of the 45 original volunteers had to be taken out of the study. As such, a total of 39 individuals were used in this study.

Regarding ECG features, the HR was computed and the maximum and minimum values of each ECG cycle were calculated, R peaks and S peaks, respectively. Afterwards, for each epoch, the averages of those were computed.

---

[1] https://neurokit2.readthedocs.io/en/latest/.

Table 1. Description of the extracted ECG features.

Feature	Description
Mean HR	Number of beats per minute (mean)
R peaks	Maximum value of the ECG cycles (upward deflections)
S peaks	Minimum value of the ECG cycles (downward deflections)
RMSSD	Root mean square of successive differences between normal heartbeats. It is a reflection of the beat-to-beat difference in the HR and is used to estimate the alteration of the HRV caused by the vagus nerve
pNN50	Percentage of successive RR intervals that are greater than 50 ms. Firmly correlated with the PNS activity
SampEn	Measures the regularity and complexity of a given signal. Smaller values indicate a regular and predictable signal

With respect to the HRV features, and due to the different lengths of the epochs and the short term of the CPT epoch, only the following features were considered: RMSSD, pNN50 (time-domain features), and SampEn (non-linear feature). The description of the used features is presented in Table 1.

Figure 1, represents the results for the normalised mean HR. It is clear that the most prominent boxplot is the CPT, being the epoch with the higher HR values, showing a response to the stress caused by the pain. Observing the matrix statistical results, there is a statistically significant difference between the mean HR during the CPT and from the remaining epochs.

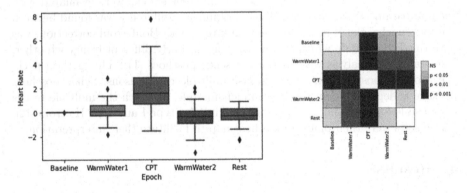

Fig. 1. Boxplot of mean HR values for each epoch (left) and respective p-values between different epochs, with Bonferroni correction (right).

Figure 2 regards the maximum value of the ECG cycles, which correspond to the R-peaks, showing a median value increase for the normalised R-peak amplitude from the Baseline to the WarmWater1, with little variation of the dispersion. This increase is about 7.7% from the Baseline (4.04 mV) to the WarmWater1 (4.35 mV). However, this is followed by a decrease of 2.55% during the CPT (4.24 mV). The median, rises, once again, reaching its peak with an increase of about 6% during the WarmWater2. The amplitude returns to near its original value (4.11 mV) during the Rest period. Although slight, there seems to be a reaction when the participants placed their hand on the water. However, there is no significant difference between the non-pain inducing and pain-inducing water temperatures on the maximum amplitude of the ECG cycles. The statistical analysis corroborates this, as it did not show any inter-epochs significant differences, with exception of the WarmWater2 for the Baseline and the Rest, the epochs with the highest and lowest amplitude values, respectively. These results suggest that the maximum ECG amplitude is not a suitable feature to examine the presence of pain in an individual when subjected to the CPT.

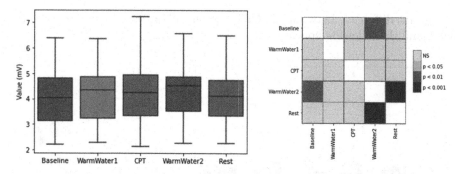

Fig. 2. Boxplot for the mean maximum ECG cycle values (left) and respective matrix of calculated p-values between different epochs, with Bonferroni correction, for the (right).

Another ECG-feature studied was the minimum value of the ECG cycles, which corresponds to the S-peak. Figure 3 shows a decrease of the median value from the Baseline to the WarmWater1, followed by a decrease from this epoch to the CPT. After the pain-inducing procedure, the minimum amplitude of the ECG cycles gradually increased. The statistical analysis for this feature shows that the CPT had significant differences from all the other epochs, being statistically more significant with the Baseline and Rest periods. There were no significant differences between the Baseline and Rest. Finally, regarding the WarmWater1 and WarmWater2, there was, also, no significant difference between them. Nevertheless, both had statistically significant differences from the other groups.

Figure 4 shows the RMSSD results. Looking at the graph, the epoch with the lowest values is the CPT. As for the other epochs, the RMSSD values are higher. However, the Baseline and, especially, the WarmWater1 appear, in general, to have slightly lower levels when compared to the Rest and WarmWater2 epochs. Finally, analysing the p-values obtained by the Wilcoxon test, there is only a

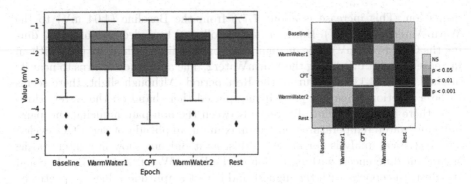

Fig. 3. Boxplot for the mean minimum ECG cycles (left) and respective matrix of calculated p-values between different epochs, with Bonferroni correction, for the (right).

significant difference between the CPT and the WarmWater1 and between the CPT and the following epochs.

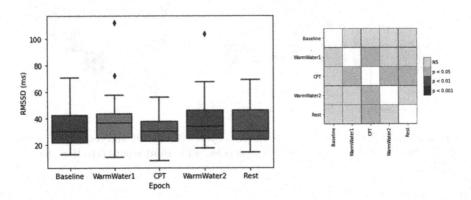

Fig. 4. Boxplot of RMSSD values for each epoch (left) and respective p-values between different epochs, with Bonferroni correction (right).

Figure 5 displays the pNN50 results. In accordance with the findings of the RMSSD, the epoch with the lowest pNN50 values was the CPT. In this epoch, the participant with the highest pNN50 had less than 40% of their heartbeats longer than 50 ms. Overall, the median values in each epoch seem to be similar. Even so, the epoch with the lowest median was the CPT (7.7%), with a 0.9% difference when compared to the Baseline and 2.4% compared with the WarmWater1 and Rest, while the WarmWater2 was the epoch with the highest median pNN50 (11.4%). There seems to be a consistent positive skewness on the boxplots, which means that the values of the upper quartile are more dispersed. This may be due to natural differences between the participants. Along with the protocol, there is a general increase of values from the Baseline to the WarmWater1, followed by a decrease during the CPT and a subsequent rise during the WarmWater2 and

Rest epochs, indicating a recovery after the CPT. Unlike the previous features, there was no significant statistical difference shown between the epochs.

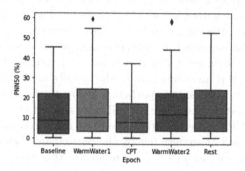

Fig. 5. Boxplot of pNN50 values for each epoch.

Finally, the regularity and complexity of each epoch are presented in Fig. 6, through the SampEn values. The epoch with the lowest value was the CPT. Another interesting observation is the results in the WarmWater2, which had generally higher values and a noticeable increase in the median value, which implies less predictability. Looking at the Baseline and WarmWater1, both have equal median values (1.45). However, the values showed greater dispersion on the latter, which denotes greater behavioural differences in participants when compared to the former epoch. Lastly, the Rest epoch had a similar mean value to the two initial epochs and smaller dispersion, suggesting that, overall, the participants were able to recover after the CPT. The statistical analysis (Fig. 6-right) only indicates a statistically significant difference between the CPT and the remaining epochs, with the exception of the Rest.

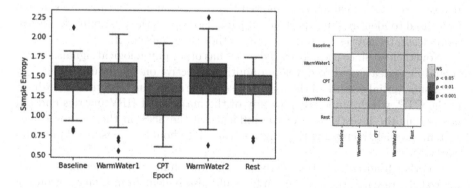

Fig. 6. Boxplot of SampEn values for each epoch (left) and respective p-values between different epochs, with Bonferroni correction (right).

5   Discussion

For the study of induced pain, the features extracted from the ECG seemed to respond in accordance with what was hypothesized. The results on the meanHR, were similar to what was described in previous literature [2,3,5,10], and is most likely a result of the increased sympathetic outflow on the body. The Wilcoxon results also showed significant differences between epochs. As for the RMSSD, a HRV metric which is an estimation of the vagally mediated changes, demonstrated a decrease in the parasympathetic outflow to the cardiovascular system during the pain inducing task. The RMSSD also showed lower values for the two epochs before the CPT, when compared to those that preceded it. This may be a result of a higher level of anxiety felt by the participants before being subjected to pain. The statistical analysis also corroborates this conjecture, as there were no significant differences observed between the Baseline and CPT. The SampEn, which measures the regularity of the signal, demonstrated that the pain induced by the CPT caused a reaction in the participants that lead to a more consistent heartbeat pattern in their cardiac system. As described above, the WarmWater2 had higher values. This implies less predictability and may be attributed to the recovery time that the body needed to return to the initial state by decreasing its HR. Lastly, the mean amplitude of S-peaks showed a progressive decrease in values until the CPT, followed by a progressive increase in the latter epochs. The statistical analysis for this feature also endorsed that there was a response in the S-waves of the ECG to the pain. In general, the results for the ECG features show that the cardiac system seems to react to the cold-painful stimulus.

6   Conclusions

Overall, the results of this induced pain study are quite similar to what was discovered in previous related works. With the exception of the pNN50 and the R-peaks, the statistical analysis showed that the remaining features are suitable to be used to identify the experience of pain. This opens the possibility for derive more accurate metrics to evaluate pain rather than self-reports.

Nonetheless, since the collected dataset has other physiological signals, efforts should be endeavoured to develop a multi-perspective on the induced pain.

A substantial setback of the used dataset is the short length of time recordings of the CTP, which hindered the study of the majority of HRV metrics and did not permit the investigation of the influence of the SNS on the cardiovascular system. As such, increasing the length of the CPT should be considered in future works.

Another hindrance to this study was the low number of participants, which limited the research scope. The study would also benefit from a larger group of individuals, allowing additional gender or aged based studies to find group-based differences.

Acknowledgments. This work was funded by national funds through FCT - Fundação para a Ciência e a Tecnologia, I.P., under the Scientific Employment Stimulus - Individual Call - CEECIND/03986/2018, and is also supported by the FCT through national funds, within IEETA/UA R&D unit (UIDB/00127/2020). This work is also funded by national funds, European Regional Development Fund, FSE through COMPETE2020, through FCT, in the scope of the framework contract foreseen in the numbers 4, 5, and 6 of the article 23, of the Decree-Law 57/2016, of August 29, changed by Law 57/2017, of July 19.

References

1. Raja, S..N., et al.: The revised international association for the study of pain definition of pain: concepts, challenges, and compromises. Pain **161**(9), 1976–1982 (2020)
2. Cowen, R., Stasiowska, M.K., Laycock, H., Bantel, C.: Pain diagnosis and management would benefit from the development of objective markers of nociception and pain. Current research. Anaesthesia **70**(7), 828–847 (2015)
3. Hampf, G.: Influence of cold pain in the hand on skin impedance, heart rate and skin temperature. Physiol. Behav. **47**(1), 217–218 (1990)
4. Kregel, K.C., Seals, D.R., Callister, R.: Sympathetic nervous system activity during skin cooling in humans: relationship to stimulus intensity and pain sensation. J. Physiol. **454**(1), 359–371 (1992)
5. Loggia, M.L.: Multi-parameter autonomic-based pain assessment: more is more? Pain **153**(9), 217–218 (2012)
6. Lukas, A., et al.: Pain and dementia: a diagnostic challenge. Zeitschrift fur Gerontologie und Geriatrie **45**(1), 45–49 (2012)
7. MATLAB version 9.10.0.1684407 (R2021a). The Mathworks Inc., Massachusetts (2021)
8. McCaul, K.D., Monson, N., Maki, R.H.: Does distraction reduce pain-produced distress among college students? Health Psychol. **11**(4), 210–217 (1992)
9. Myers, C.D., Robinson, M.E., Riley, J.L., Sheffield, D.: Sex, gender, and blood pressure: contributions to experimental pain report. Psychosom. Med. **63**(4), 545–550 (2001)
10. Streff, A., Kuehl, L.K., Michaux, G., Anton, F.: Differential physiological effects during tonic painful hand immersion tests using hot and ice water. Eur. J. Pain **14**(3), 266–272 (2010)
11. Terpilowski, M.: scikit-posthocs: pairwise multiple comparison tests in Python. J. Open Source Softw. **36**(4), 1169 (2019)
12. Seabold, S., Perktold, J.: Statsmodels: econometric and statistical modeling with python. In: 9th Python in Science Conference (2010)

First Experiences on Parallelizing Peer Methods for Numerical Solution of a Vegetation Model

Dajana Conte[1], Pasquale De Luca[2]([⊠]), Ardelio Galletti[3],
Giulio Giunta[3], Livia Marcellino[3], Giovanni Pagano[1],
and Beatrice Paternoster[1]

[1] Department of Mathematics, University of Salerno,
Via Giovanni Paolo II, 132, 84084 Fisciano, SA, Italy
{dajconte,gpagano,beapat}@unisa.it
[2] International PhD Programme/UNESCO Chair "Environment,
Resources and Sustainable Development", Department of Science and Technology,
Parthenope University of Naples, Centro Direzionale, Isola C4, 80143 Naples, Italy
pasquale.deluca@uniparthenope.it
[3] Department of Science and Technology, Parthenope University of Naples,
Centro Direzionale, Isola C4, 80143 Naples, Italy
{ardelio.galletti,giulio.giunta,livia.marcellino}@uniparthenope.it
https://www.dipmat.unisa.it

Abstract. The purpose of this paper is to provide a parallel acceleration of peer methods for the numerical solution of systems of Ordinary Differential Equations (ODEs) arising from the space discretization of Partial Differential Equations (PDEs) modeling the growth of vegetation in semi-arid climatic zones. The parallel algorithm is implemented by using the CUDA environment for Graphics Processing Units (GPUs) architectures. Numerical experiments, showing the performance gain of the proposed strategy, are provided.

Keywords: Self-organization in ecology · Vegetation · PDEs · Peer methods · Parallel strategies · GPGPU

1 Introduction

This paper focuses on efficient numerical solution of PDEs arising in vegetation problems, by means of parallel numerical methods employing GPUs. We consider the following system of PDEs [12]:

The authors are members of the GNCS group. This work is supported by GNCS-INDAM project and by the Italian Ministry of University and Research (MUR), through the PRIN 2020 project (No. 2020JLWP23) "Integrated Mathematical Approaches to Socio-Epidemiological Dynamics" (CUP: E15F21005420006) and the PRIN 2017 project (No. 2017JYCLSF) "Structure preserving approximation of evolutionary problems".

O. Gervasi et al. (Eds.): ICCSA 2022, LNCS 13376, pp. 384–394, 2022.
https://doi.org/10.1007/978-3-031-10450-3_33

$$\begin{cases} \dfrac{\partial u_1}{\partial t} = \dfrac{\partial^2 u_1}{\partial x^2} + w u_1 (u_1 + H u_2) - B_1 u_1 - S u_1 u_2, \\[2mm] \dfrac{\partial u_2}{\partial t} = D \dfrac{\partial^2 u_2}{\partial x^2} + F w u_2 (u_1 + H u_2) - B_2 u_2, \qquad (x,t) \in [x_0, X] \times [t_0, T], \\[2mm] \dfrac{\partial w}{\partial t} = d \dfrac{\partial^2 w}{\partial x^2} + A - w - w(u_1 + u_2)(u_1 + H u_2), \end{cases}$$

$$(1)$$

with initial conditions:

$$\begin{cases} u_1(x,t_0) = U_{1,0}(x), \\ u_2(x,t_0) = U_{2,0}(x), \qquad x \in [x_0, X]. \\ w(x,t_0) = W_0(x), \end{cases} \qquad (2)$$

The PDEs system (1) represents a model of vegetation in semi-arid climatic zones, and constitutes an example of the principle of self-organization in ecology. It was introduced to study how two herbaceous species compete for the same limiting resource (the water) managing to resist. To better understand how the model works, you can imagine that the function u_1 describes the density of grass present on the soil x at the instant t, that the function u_2 represents the same for trees, and that w is the quantity of water available. In [12], the authors analytically study the existence of states in which both species coexist, proving that coexistence is not a stable solution of the system. That is, coexistence occurs as metastable state, i.e. as a state appearing as stable solution of the system for very long times. However, for infinite times one of the two plants dies.

An approach that is usually followed (and that we will use in this paper) to numerically solve a PDEs system is given by the Method Of Lines (MOL), which consists in spatially discretizing the problem, then deriving a large system of ODEs (whose size is proportional to the number of grid points used in each spatial direction). To efficiently solve this ODEs system, it would be preferable to use a cheap method (i.e. a method involving the least possible number of function evaluations, matrix inversions, and so on), equipped with excellent stability properties. The latter request derives from the fact that ODEs coming from PDEs related to real applications are endowed with severe stiffness.

The requirements of cheapness and excellent stability are difficult to be fulfilled at the same time. In fact, the most widely used numerical methods for solving stiff ODEs are implicit Runge-Kutta [1,2], linearly implicit Runge-Kutta (see e.g. [4,8,27]), Rosenbrock [30], or IMEX (see an overview on all these methods, e.g., also in [26]). All these methods are implicit, which means that it is necessary to solve at each integration step, and for each stage, systems of linear or non-linear equations. That is, it is necessary to numerically compute inversions of matrices having dimension proportional to the size of the problem. The implicit methods are therefore expensive, but they are the only ones that enjoy excellent stability properties. On the other hand, using explicit methods does not involve the solution of systems of equations, but requires the use of very small time steps for the numerical solution to not explode, as explicit methods have bounded stability regions. Therefore, their use for the numerical solution of stiff ODEs becomes problematic.

In this paper, we overcome the mentioned difficulties by solving the model (1) making use of a class of explicit methods, known as peer methods, together with a parallel strategy. Peer methods [9–11,14–18,28,29,32] are two-step numerical schemes belonging to the class of general linear methods [3]. They are newer than the Runge-Kuttas, and have two properties whereby their use can be very convenient. Indeed, in these methods, all stages are calculated with the same accuracy as the advancing solution, and this ensures that peer methods do not suffer from order reduction when integrating stiff problems, unlike what happens for Runge-Kutta methods [31]. Furthermore, since in peer methods the next stages just depend on the previous ones, we have been able to provide a new formulation, for the case study (1), which has been implemented in a parallel environment.

Thanks to this approach, a computational gain can be achieved also when a large amount of data have to be processed. We highlight that some initial attempts to parallelize peer methods have been addressed (see [13]), where software, for multicore system is presented. Here, we refine the parallel strategy in order to exploit the GPUs (Graphics Processing Units) architectures powerful by employing the CUDA environment [19]. We remark that nowadays the choice of the GPUs becomes almost mandatory thanks to the possibility they offer to solve large size problems, by means of suitable parallel algorithms, in a reduced execution time [5–7,20–23].

The rest of the paper is organized as follows. Section 2 recalls peer methods and shows the chosen numerical scheme. In Sect. 3, the sequential and parallel algorithms and the related GPU-CUDA implementation are presented. The experiments are discussed in Sect. 4 to confirm the efficiency of the proposed implementation in terms of performance. Finally, conclusions in Sect. 5 close the paper.

2   Numerical Scheme

In this section, numerical difference schemes and peer methods, with their use for discretizing in space and time Eq. (1), are presented. In the first step a spatial semi-discretization, via the MOL method, is described, while second step shows general details about peer methods and how they can be adapted to be used in problem (1).

2.1   Spatial Semi-discretization

First step is based on the MOL technique. Hence, we spatially semi-discretize (1), by dividing the spatial interval $[x_0, X]$ into $M - 1$ sub-intervals, using central finite differences to approximate the involved second derivatives, as follows:

$$\frac{\partial^2 u}{\partial x^2} = \frac{u(x - \Delta x, t) - 2u(x, t) + u(x + \Delta x, t)}{\Delta x^2}, \quad u = u_1, u_2, w, \quad \Delta x = \frac{X - x_0}{M - 1}.$$

Therefore, the following ODEs system of size $3M$ is obtained:

$$\begin{cases} \dfrac{\partial U_1}{\partial t} = \dfrac{1}{\Delta x^2} L_{Diff} U_1 + F_1, \\[2mm] \dfrac{\partial U_2}{\partial t} = \dfrac{D}{\Delta x^2} L_{Diff} U_2 + F_2, \\[2mm] \dfrac{\partial W}{\partial t} = \dfrac{d}{\Delta x^2} L_{Diff} W + F_3. \end{cases} \tag{3}$$

For simplicity of notation, we have omitted the time dependence of all the involved functions. We have used the following notation:

$$x_m = x_0 + m\Delta x; \quad m = 0, \ldots, M-1; \quad x_{M-1} = X, \tag{4}$$

and:

$$u_1^m = u_1(x_m, t), \qquad u_2^m = u_2(x_m, t), \qquad w^m = w(x_m, t),$$

$$U_1 = \left(u_1^m(t)\right)_{m=0}^{M-1}, \quad U_2 = \left(u_2^m(t)\right)_{m=0}^{M-1}, \quad W = \left(w^m(t)\right)_{m=0}^{M-1},$$

$$\frac{\partial U_1}{\partial t} = \left(\frac{\partial u_1^m}{\partial t}\right)_{m=0}^{M-1}, \quad \frac{\partial U_2}{\partial t} = \left(\frac{\partial u_2^m}{\partial t}\right)_{m=0}^{M-1}, \quad \frac{\partial W}{\partial t} = \left(\frac{\partial w^m}{\partial t}\right)_{m=0}^{M-1},$$

$$F_1 = \left(w^m u_1^m (u_1^m + H u_2^m) - B_1 u_1^m - S u_1^m u_2^m\right)_{m=0}^{M-1},$$

$$F_2 = \left(F w^m u_2^m (u_1^m + H u_2^m) - B_2 u_2^m\right)_{m=0}^{M-1},$$

$$F_3 = \left(A - w^m - w^m (u_1^m + u_2^m)(u_1^m + H u_2^m)\right)_{m=0}^{M-1}.$$

If u_1, u_2, w are assumed to be zero outside their domain, it turns out that matrix L_{Diff} is tridiagonal and it is given by:

$$L_{Diff} = \begin{pmatrix} -2 & 1 & & & \\ 1 & -2 & 1 & & \\ & & \ddots & \ddots & \\ & & 1 & -2 & 1 \\ & & & 1 & -2 \end{pmatrix} \in \mathbb{R}^{M,M}. \tag{5}$$

While, by using periodic boundary conditions, the matrix L_{Diff} must actually be slightly modified, setting $L_{Diff}(M, 1) = L_{Diff}(1, M) = 1$. Finally, by further compacting the semi-discrete ODEs system (3), we get:

$$y'(t) = L \cdot y(t) + NL\big(y(t)\big), \tag{6}$$

where

$$y(t) = [U_1, U_2, W]^T \in \mathbb{R}^{3M} \qquad \text{and} \qquad NL\big(y(t)\big) = [F_1, F_2, F_3]^T \in \mathbb{R}^{3M}, \tag{7}$$

while matrix L takes the form:

$$L = \frac{1}{\Delta x^2} \begin{pmatrix} L_{Diff} & 0 & 0 \\ 0 & D L_{Diff} & 0 \\ 0 & 0 & d L_{Diff} \end{pmatrix} \in \mathbb{R}^{3M,3M}. \tag{8}$$

Next step aims to discretize the ODEs system (6) by means of peer methods.

2.2   Time Discretization by Peer Methods

Peer methods are a class of two-step numerical schemes that solve first order ODEs systems, in the general form $y'(t) = f(t, y(t))$ $(t \in [t_0, T])$ with initial condition $y_0 = y(t_0) \in \mathbb{R}^d$. Let consider the time discretization:

$$t_n = t_0 + nh; \quad n = 0, \ldots, N; \quad t_N = T, \tag{9}$$

of the integration interval $[t_0, T]$ related to (1), and therefore to (6). Explicit s-stage two-step peer methods, with fixed step-size h, are of the following form:

$$Y_{n,i} = \sum_{j=1}^{s} b_{ij} Y_{n-1,j} + h \sum_{j=1}^{s} a_{ij} f(t_{n-1,j}, Y_{n-1,j}), \qquad n = 0, \ldots, N-1,$$
$$Y_{n,i} \approx y(t_{n,i}), \quad t_{n,i} = t_n + h c_i, \qquad i = 1, \ldots, s. \tag{10}$$

where c_i are nodes in $[0, 1]$ and $c_s = 1$. Then, the advancing solution $Y_{n,s}$ is the computed approximation of $y(t_n + h)$, i.e. the last stage computes the numerical solution at the grid points. Coefficients in matrices $A = (a_{ij})_{i,j=1}^{s}$ and $B = (b_{ij})_{i,j=1}^{s}$ characterize the peer method used. In particular, to choose the methods free coefficients, we need to recall some theoretical results: firstly, peer methods are said to be optimally zero-stable by setting:

$$(b_{ij})_{i,j=1}^{s-1} = 0, \qquad \text{and} \qquad b_{is} = 1, \forall i = 1, \ldots, s.$$

This choice is linked to the stability of peer methods near the origin [32]. Furthermore, the A matrix coefficients are assigned by imposing the consistency order of peer methods [32], i.e. by annihilating the necessary number of residuals, defined as

$$h\Delta_i := y(t_{n,i}) - \sum_{j=1}^{s} b_{ij} y(t_{n-1,j}) - h \sum_{j=1}^{s} a_{ij} y'(t_{n-1,j}), \quad i = 1, \ldots, s.$$

where y spans over suitable polynomial bases.
Note that the i-th residual measures the error between the i-th stage and its exact value.

Hence, assuming s-stages peer methods of order $p = s$, the coefficients $(a_{ij})_{i,j=1}^{s}$ have to satisfy [32]

$$A = (CV_0 D^{-1})V_1^{-1} - B(C - I_s)V_1 D^{-1}V_1^{-1},$$

where $V_0 = (c_i^{j-1})_{i,j=1}^{s}$, $V_1 = ((c_i - 1)^{j-1})_{i,j=1}^{s}$, $C = diag(c_i)$, $D = diag(1, \ldots, s)$, and I_s is the Identity matrix of dimension s. In particular, in our scheme, we choose to use both values $s = 2$ and $s = 3$ for stages. In these settings, we get:

$$A = \begin{pmatrix} 0 & 0 \\ -1/2 & 3/2 \end{pmatrix}, \qquad B = \begin{pmatrix} 0 & 1 \\ 0 & 1 \end{pmatrix}, \qquad (c_1, c_2) = (0, 1), \tag{11}$$

for $s = 2$, and:

$$A = \begin{pmatrix} 0 & 0 & 0 \\ 5/24 & -2/3 & 23/24 \\ 7/6 & -10/3 & 19/6 \end{pmatrix}, \quad B = \begin{pmatrix} 0\ 0\ 1 \\ 0\ 0\ 1 \\ 0\ 0\ 1 \end{pmatrix}, \quad (c_1, c_2, c_3) = (0, 1/2, 1), \quad (12)$$

for $s = 3$. Notice that therefore that all the stages $Y^{[n]} = (Y_{n,i})_{i=1}^s$ in the interval $[t_n, t_n + h]$ are functions of all the stages in the interval $[t_n - h, t_n]$ only, which are totally known at the current time step. Then, by denoting by $\mathcal{F}$ the function evaluations of the stages at each discrete point $t_{n,i}$, i.e.,

$$\mathcal{F}(Y^{[n]}) = \big(f(t_{n,i}, Y_{n,i})\big)_{i=1}^s$$

peer methods (10) can take the more compact vector representation:

$$Y^{[n]} = (B \otimes I_d)Y^{[n-1]} + h(A \otimes I_d)\mathcal{F}(Y^{[n-1]}), \tag{13}$$

being d the solution dimension and I_d is the identity matrix of order d. Finally, we can derive the whole numerical procedure by setting in formulation (13) $d = 3M$ and:

$$\mathcal{F}(Y^{[n-1]}) = \big(LY_{n-1,i} + NL(Y_{n-1,i})\big)_{i=1}^s, \tag{14}$$

where L and NL are as in (7) and (8), and by applying the scheme to the vegetation problem in the ODE form (6).

3   Sequential and Parallel Implementation

Previous discussions allow us to introduce an algorithm which recalls main numerical steps described above.

Algorithm 1 shows the main operations needed to find numerical solution of problem (1) based on discretization discussed in Sect. 2. This algorithm has been implemented, in a first version, through a sequential C code whose details are below described.

In particular, the algorithm initializes the necessary parameters for time and space discretization (lines 1–4). Then, to perform the spatial semi-discretization, in lines 5–6 the procedure builds the tridiagonal matrix L_{Diff}, as in Eq. (5), and the tridiagonal block matrix L, as in (8). Now, to apply the peer method, it is mandatory to prime it, that is for time step $n = 0$ we need precompute the values of $Y_{0,i}$ at all stages (lines 7–8). To this aim, in the algorithm we used the explicit one-step four order Runge-Kutta that guarantees the peer method maintains the same order of accuracy when computing next values $Y_{n,i}$. Finally, lines 9–12 illustrate the main core of the procedure, i.e. the *loop-for* on time steps ($n = 1, \ldots, N$).

We remark that, when small step sizes are chosen large space-time discretized grids occur, generating a remarkably increase of the procedure time complexity, which in turn implies possibly huge execution times of the whole procedure. To address this issue, here, we propose an accelerated implementation that parallelizes the sequential Algorithm 1, by exploiting the powerful parallel nature of GPUs. The idea comes from taking advantages of large number of threads equipped by a GPU and decomposing the problem among them.

Algorithm 1. Sequential pseudo-algorithm for problem (1)

Input : $s, x_0, X, N, t_0, T, M, y_0, NL_0, a, B1, B2, H, F, S, d, D,$ Output : Y

   % Initialization:

1: **set** $\Delta x = (X - x_0)/(M-1)$

2: **set** x_m $(m = 0, \ldots, M-1)$ as in (4)

3: **set** $h = (T - t_0)/N$

4: **set** t_n $(n = 0, \ldots, N)$ as in (9)

   % Spatial semi-discretization:

5: **build** L_{Diff} as in (5)

6: **build** L as in (8)

   % Peer method

      % initialization: time step $n = 0$

7:     **set** $t_{0,i} = t_0 + h \cdot c_i,$ $(i = 1, \ldots, s)$

8:     **compute** $Y_{0,i}$ **for** $i = 1, \ldots, s$

      % loop on time steps

9:     **for** $n = 1, \ldots, N$ **do**

10:       **set** $t_{n,i} = t_n + h \cdot c_i,$ $(i = 1, \ldots, s)$

11:       **compute** $Y_{n,i}$ as in (10), **for** $i = 1, \ldots, s.$

12:     **end for**

3.1 Parallel Approach

Due to the high computational time required by the procedure on finding solution of Eq. (10), we chose to parallelize the majority of the overall work. The parallel pseudo-code Algorithm 2 highlights the main features to be addressed to implement the numerical procedure in a GPU environment.

In this work, we have implemented Algorithm 2 in a GPU parallel software by means of suitably built parallel functions. Details and main operations are listed in following steps:

    Line 1: The discrete space-time grids are defined by using the *loop-unrolling* strategy, in order to optimize the computation and memory accesses.

    Lines 2,8: These instructions are related to the data transfer from host-to-device and vice-versa. The procedures are carried out only during the starting and final phases of the GPU-parallel code, in order to improve the software performance.

    Line 3: Here, the spatial semi-discretization operation is considered. A specific CUDA kernel has been designed for building, firstly the L_{Diff} matrix, and then the L matrix in a parallel way. We use the structural properties of matrix L, in order to perform a fair work-load balancing among domain problem and threads number. In other words, we set as threads number $T = 3$, then each thread computes own part of L matrix (each thread is related to

---

Algorithm 2. GPU pseudo-algorithm for problem (1)

Input: $s, x_0, X, N, t_0, T, M, y_0, NL_0, a, B1, B2, H, F, S, d, D.$ Output: Y

% initialization, as at lines 1–4 of Algorithm 1

1: generate x_m, t_n $(m = 0, \ldots, M - 1, \quad n = 0, \ldots, N)$

% GPU computation starting

2: transfer Input data Host-To-Device

% Spatial semi-discretization

3: dynamic parallel building of L_{Diff} and L, as in (5), (8)

% Parallel peer method

   % initialization: time step $n = 0$

4:    dynamic parallel computing of $Y_{0,\tau}$ for $\tau = 1, \ldots, s$

   % loop on time steps

5:    for $n = 1, \ldots, N$ do

6:        parallel computing of $Y_{n,i}$ for $i = 1, \ldots, s.$

7:    end for

8: transfer Output data Device-To-Host

   % end GPU computation

---

one of variables u_1, u_2,w) by performing operations concurrently. This parallel step is implemented by using the *dynamic parallelism* which characterizes the CUDA environment and allows us to design a nested parallelization strategy [24].

Line 4: In this step, a kind of nested parallelism is adopted. More specifically, each threads τ $(\tau = 1, \ldots, s)$ computes concurrently $Y_{0,\tau}$ by means the Runge-Kutta four order method, which in turn has been implemented parallelized, by distributing basic linear algebra operating among further threads.

Lines 5-7: At each time step $n = 1, \ldots, N$, similarly in previous step, a nested kind of parallelism is used for solving the basic linear algebraic operations. Also in this step, we need to implement three specific CUDA kernels in order to perform evaluation of linear and nonlinear terms in (14), and generic loop iteration required in (13). Moreover, the gathering process of the local results is done by guaranteeing a coalescent memory access. This final step is implemented by ensuring any memory contention and a fair work-load balancing among threads.

4   Experimental Tests

In this section, we propose tests and experiments to prove the reliability and the main features of our implementation. In the whole section, we assume to consider the problem (1) with parameters (see [12]) $A = 1.5$, $B_1 = 0.45$, $B_2 = 0.3611$, $F = 0.802$, $H = 0.802$, $S = 0.0002$, $d = 500$, $D = 0.802$, and space and time intervals $[-50, 50]$ and $[0, 50]$, respectively. According to what has been done in [12], we also set randomly the solution initial values in the interval $[1.4, 2.1]$ for u_1 and u_2, and in the interval $[0.14, 0.21]$ for w. Furthermore, the experiments are carried out in the following high-performance computer with technical specifications:

- 1 Intel(R) Xeon(R) Gold 5218 CPU @ 2.30 GHz, 16 cores, 2 threads per core, 192 GB of RAM, 4 channels 51 Gb/s memory bandwidth
- 1 NVIDIA V100-SXM2, 5120 CUDA cores, 1370 MHz clock speed for core, 16 GB DDR5, 900.1 Gb/s as bandwidth.

Table 1. CPU vs. GPU execution times. `block` × `threads`: 128 × 3125

	Execution times (s)	
N	CPU	GPU
2.0×10^5	2 055.23	63.21
4.0×10^5	6 410.54	191.46
8.1×10^5	10 293.11	318.14
1.6×10^6	36 322.95	701.84
3.2×10^6	∼	1 293.19
1.3×10^7	∼	1 820.95

Table 1 shows an execution time comparison between sequential and parallel implementation for solving problem (1). The test is conducted by varying N, and fixing $M = 64$. A standard GPU-CUDA computation provides to preliminarly set the grid threads through the `block` × `threads` and here, after testing the algorithm with different configurations, we used `block` × `threads` = 128 × 3125 that gave best performance. First column of the Table refers to sequential implementation of Algorithm 1 which runs on a single core machine. Last column exhibits the execution times of GPU implementation of Algorithm 2. We observe a significant gain with respect to the serial version. The time of the sequential version grows considerably as N increases. However a noticeable speed-up is observed in the GPU-accelerated version. In detail, due to high resource hardware limits of CPU, the tests are stopped to 1.6×10^6. Thanks to different memory layer equipped by the GPU, and the specific parallel approach employed, we pushed the boundaries from CPU. This means that a fair analysis in accuracy and efficiency terms can be done.

5 Conclusions

In this work we presented a parallel strategy, and a related implementation in a GPU environment, for computing approximate solution of a vegetation model.

The underlying numerical procedure combines a spatial semi-discretization and the use of Peer methods for the numerical solution of systems of Ordinary Differential Equations. Numerical results and test are provided and show the gain in terms of performance of the proposed algorithm.

Acknowledgements. The authors are members of the GNCS group. This work is supported by GNCS-INDAM project and by the Italian Ministry of University and Research (MUR), through the PRIN 2020 project (No. 2020JLWP23) "Integrated Mathematical Approaches to Socio-Epidemiological Dynamics" (CUP: E15F21005420006) and the PRIN 2017 project (No. 2017JYCLSF) "Structure preserving approximation of evolutionary problems".

References

1. Butcher, J.C.: Implicit Runge-Kutta processes. Math. Comp. **18**, 50–64 (1964)
2. Butcher, J.C.: Numerical Methods for Ordinary Differential Equations, 2nd edn. Wiley, Chichester (2008)
3. Butcher, J.C.: General linear methods. Acta Numer. **15**, 157–256 (2006)
4. Calvo, M.P., Gerisch, A.: Linearly implicit Runge-Kutta methods and approximate matrix factorization. Appl. Math. **53**(2–4), 183–200 (2005)
5. Conte, D., D'Ambrosio, R., Paternoster, B.: GPU-acceleration of waveform relaxation methods for large differential systems. Numer. Algorithms **71**(2), 293–310 (2015). https://doi.org/10.1007/s11075-015-9993-6
6. Conte, D., Paternoster, B.: Parallel methods for weakly singular Volterra integral equations on GPUs. Appl. Numer. Math. **114**, 30–37 (2016)
7. Cuomo, S., De Michele, P., Galletti, A., Marcellino, L.: A GPU-parallel algorithm for ECG signal denoising based on the NLM method. In: 2016 30th International Conference on Advanced Information Networking and Applications Workshops (WAINA), pp. 35–39, March 2016
8. Conte, D., D'Ambrosio, R., Pagano, G., Paternoster, B.: Jacobian-dependent vs. Jacobian-free discretizations for nonlinear differential problems. Comput. Appl. Math. **39**(3), 1–12 (2020). https://doi.org/10.1007/s40314-020-01200-z
9. Conte, D., Mohammadi, F., Moradi, L., Paternoster, B.: Exponentially fitted two-step peer methods for oscillatory problems. Comput. Appl. Math. **39**(3), 1–19 (2020). https://doi.org/10.1007/s40314-020-01202-x
10. Conte, D., Pagano, G., Paternoster, B.: Jacobian-dependent two-stage peer method for ordinary differential equations. In: Gervasi, O., et al. (eds.) ICCSA 2021, Part I. LNCS, vol. 12949, pp. 309–324. Springer, Cham (2021). https://doi.org/10.1007/978-3-030-86653-2_23
11. Conte, D., Pagano, G., Paternoster, B.: Two-step peer methods with equation-dependent coefficients. Comput. Appl. Math. **41**(4), 140 (2022)
12. Eigentler, L., Sherratt, J.A.: Metastability as a coexistence mechanism in a model for dryland vegetation patterns. Bull. Math. Biol. **81**, 2290–2322 (2019). https://doi.org/10.1007/s11538-019-00606-z
13. Schmitt, B.A., Weiner, R.: Parallel start for explicit parallel two-step peer methods. Numer. Algorithms **53**(2), 363–381 (2010). https://doi.org/10.1007/s11075-009-9267-2
14. Schmitt, B.A., Weiner, R., Jebens, S.: Parameter optimization for explicit parallel peer two-step methods. Appl. Numer. Math. **59**(3–4), 769–782 (2009)

15. Schmitt, B.A., Weiner, R., Podhaisky, H.: Multi-implicit peer two-step W-methods for parallel time integration. BIT Numer. Math. **45**(1), 197–217 (2005). https:// doi.org/10.1007/s10543-005-2635-y

16. Schmitt, B.A., Weiner, R., Erdmann, K.: Implicit parallel peer methods for stiff initial value problems. Appl. Numer. Math. **53**(2–4), 457–470 (2005)

17. Weiner, R., Schmitt, B.A., Podhaisky, H.: Parallel "Peer" two-step W-methods and their application to MOL-systems. Appl. Numer. Math., **48**(3–4), 425–439 (2004)

18. Schmitt, B.A., Weiner, R.: Parallel two-step W-methods with peer variables. SIAM J. Numer. Anal. **42**(1), 265–282 (2004)

19. https://developer.nvidia.com/cuda-zone

20. De Luca, P., Galletti, A., Marcellino, L.: A Gaussian recursive filter parallel implementation with overlapping. In: 2019 15th International Conference on Signal-Image Technology and Internet-Based systems (SITIS), pp. 641–648 (2019)

21. De Luca, P., Galletti, A., Giunta, G., Marcellino, L.: Accelerated Gaussian convolution in a data assimilation scenario. In: Krzhizhanovskaya, V.V., et al. (eds.) ICCS 2020, Part VI. LNCS, vol. 12142, pp. 199–211. Springer, Cham (2020). https:// doi.org/10.1007/978-3-030-50433-5_16

22. De Luca, P., Galletti, A., Ghehsareh, H.R., Marcellino, L., Raei, M.: A GPU-CUDA framework for solving a two-dimensional inverse anomalous diffusion problem. In: Foster, I., Joubert, G.R., Kučera, L., Nagel, W.E., Peters, F. (eds.) Parallel Computing: Technology Trends, Advances in Parallel Computing, vol. 36, pp. 311–320 (2020)

23. De Luca, P., Galletti, A., Giunta, G., Marcellino, L.: Recursive filter based GPU algorithms in a data assimilation scenario. J. Comput. Sci. **53**, 101339 (2021)

24. Jones, S.: Introduction to dynamic parallelism. In: GPU Technology Conference Presentation, vol. 338 (2012)

25. Hairer, E., Norsett, S.P., Wanner, G.: Solving Ordinary Differential Equations I: Nonstiff Problems, 2nd edn. Springer, Berlin (1993). https://doi.org/10.1007/978-3-540-78862-1

26. Hundsdorfer, W., Verwer, J.: Numerical Solution of Time-Dependent Advection-Diffusion-Reaction Equations. Springer Series in Computational Mathematics, Berlin (2003). https://doi.org/10.1007/978-3-662-09017-6

27. Ixaru, L.G.: Runge-Kutta methods with equation dependent coefficients. Comput. Phys. Commun. **183**(1), 63–69 (2012)

28. Jebens, S., Weiner, R., Podhaisky, H., Schmitt, B.: Explicit multi-step peer methods for special second-order differential equations. Appl. Math. Comput. **202**(2), 803–813 (2008)

29. Klinge, M., Weiner, R., Podhaisky, H.: Optimally zero stable explicit peer methods with variable nodes. BIT Numer. Math. **58**(2), 331–345 (2017). https://doi.org/10.1007/s10543-017-0691-8

30. Rosenbrock, H.H.: Some general implicit processes for the numerical solution of differential equations. Comput. J. **5**(4), 329–330 (1963)

31. Sanz-Serna, J.M., Verwer, J.G., Hundsdorfer, W.H.: Convergence and order reduction of Runge-Kutta schemes applied to evolutionary problems in partial differential equations. Numer. Math. **50**, 405–418 (1986). https://doi.org/10.1007/BF01396661

32. Weiner, R., Biermann, K., Schmitt, B., Podhaisky, H.: Explicit two-step peer methods. Comput. Math. Appl. **55**(4), 609–619 (2008)

A Preliminary Case Study: Predicting Postoperative Pain Through Electrocardiogram

Raquel Sebastião[(✉)] [iD]

Institute of Electronics and Informatics Engineering of Aveiro (IEETA),
Department of Electronics, Telecommunications and Informatics (DETI),
University of Aveiro, 3810-193 Aveiro, Portugal
`raquel.sebastiao@ua.pt`

Abstract. Currently pain is mainly evaluated by resorting to self-reporting instruments, turning the objective evaluation of pain barely impossible. Besides the inherent subjectivity due to these reports, the perception of pain is influenced by several factors. Moreover, cognitive impairments and difficulties in expressing pose a burden difficulty in pain evaluation. Beyond less efficient pain management, the consequences of an incorrect pain assessment may result in over or under dosage of analgesics, with potentially harmful consequences due to the undesirable side-effects of wrong doses. Therefore, a quantitative and accurate assessment of pain is critical for the adaptation of healthcare strategies, providing a step further in personalized medicine. Thus, the analysis of Autonomic Nervous System (ANS) reactions, which can be assessed continuously with minimally invasive equipment, offers an excellent opportunity to monitor physiological indicators when in the experience of pain. The goal of the proposed work is to classify the presence of pain in postoperative records. The results show accuracy and precision of around 85%, and recall and F_1-score of 92%, indicating that the experience of postoperative pain can be classified by relying on physiological data.

Keywords: Postoperative pain · ECG · Signal processing · Prediction problems · Machine learning · Decision support

1 Introduction

Pain involves dysregulations in the Autonomic Nervous System (ANS), a primary behavioral regulation system [20]. As the experience of pain induces reactions in the ANS, and, as it functions without conscious control [4], the study of such reactions is a feasible way to assess pain.

The ANS controls various organ systems inside the body, namely muscles, glands, and organs within the body. While maintaining the equilibrium of the body's systems according to both internal and external stimuli, many physiological signals reflect the activity of the ANS. The activation of the ANS can suppress or, in pathological states, aid pain.

O. Gervasi et al. (Eds.): ICCSA 2022, LNCS 13376, pp. 395–403, 2022.
https://doi.org/10.1007/978-3-031-10450-3_34

Due to the lack of quantified pain measures, currently, pain is mainly evaluated by resorting to self-reporting instruments. Besides the inherent subjectivity due to these types of reports, the perception of pain is influenced by several factors. Moreover, cognitive impairments and difficulties in expressing pose a burden hazard in pain evaluation.

An incorrect assessment of pain may lead to undertreatment or overtreatment of pain [5,16], difficult the overall recovery [9,18], and lead to adverse psychological and cognitive effects [7,15]. Moreover, in postoperative pain, the correct management of pain is a critical task of utmost relevance to ensure patient comfort. Thus, researchers have been using statistical inference to describe and characterize the experience of pain and proposed machine learning models to identify pain and/or classify pain levels.

Considering that it is of utmost importance to proper assess pain, there are recent studies showing that common symptoms associated with pain seem to induce a broad heightened sympathetic branch activation of the Autonomic Nervous System (ANS), including increased electrodermal and respiratory activities, cardiac acceleration and heightened muscle contraction [3,6,8,11–13,19,20].

In [11], the authors agree that the severity of postoperative pain significantly influences SC (skin conductance). From a sample of 25 patients subjected to surgery (11 general surgical patients, 9 orthopedic, and 5 plastics cases), they demonstrated a correlation between NFSC (number of fluctuations within the mean SC per second) and self-assessed pain measured using a NRS (numeric rating scale), concluding that changes in levels of patient-rated postoperative pain on a NRS are reflected by corresponding changes of NFSC as a parameter of SC.

A total of 180 children within 3 different age groups (with valid pain assessments in 165 patients), undergoing elective surgery, had participated in the study [6]. The authors proposed using changes in the NFSC as a biomarker to assess acute postoperative pain, being able to predict moderate to severe postoperative pain from NFSC.

Based on the relationship between lowered heart rate variability (HRV) and poor health, the authors of [3] proposed HRV as a biomarker. Participants included 104 healthy control children and 48 children with chronic pain, aged from 8 to 17 years, and laboratory sessions involved four pain induction tasks (evoked pressure, cold pressor, focal pressure, and a conditioned pain modulation task).

1.1 Motivation, Goals, and Structure

The above studies sustained the importance of an accurate assessment of acute pain as an essential component of postoperative care, improving pain control, avoiding undesirable side-effects from under/overdosage, and promoting health-care.

During the postoperative period, the pain that the patient is being subjected to, and the pain reported, varies a lot according to the overthrow of the anesthesia and the effects of analgesics administered. Thus, these changes may be rendered by physiological signals, such as the ECG.

The purpose of the present study is to go beyond the characterization of postoperative pain, proposing the classification of postoperative pain through features computed from Heart Rate (HR), which render the influence of pain in ECG.

Regarding the evaluation of postoperative pain, assessed in the recovery room, the goal of this work is to address the classification of pain experience through HR-based features. To the best of our knowledge, this is the first attempt to classify postoperative pain experience through physiological data.

The remainder of this work is organized as follows: Sect. 2 describes the setup, the equipment, and the methodology of data collection and physiological monitoring, as well as the methods used for data analysis. In Sect. 3 the results are presented and discussed. Final remarks and future research lines are presented in Sect. 4.

2   Dataset Description and Methodology

This section describes the setup and data collection, as well as the ECG processing techniques for feature extraction, and provides a description of the data used for postoperative pain prediction. The machine learning methodology applied to classify pain in postoperative scenarios is also explained. Data analysis was performed in MATLAB [14] and Python, using the NeuroKit2[1], which provides biosignal processing routines.

2.1   Setup and Data Collection

The study was conducted in accordance with the Declaration of Helsinki, and under the approval of the Ethics Committee for Health of Centro Hospitalar Tondela-Viseu (CHTV), with document number 894, 30/11/2018, and the Ethics and Deontology Council of the University of Aveiro, with document number 36/2018, 03/04/2019.

This study required the participation of adults patients who underwent elective neck and thorax surgeries at CHTV, recruited on a volunteer base after written informed consent. The exclusion criteria applied included the presence of major systems diseases, congenital syndromes, pacemakers, and psychological/psychiatric/mental disorders. The data used in this study was collected in the recovery room, after surgery, during the standard clinical practices of analgesia, fulfilling all the clinical aspects, and without compromising the patient's well-being.

During data monitoring, through the Vital Jacket® [1], with a sampling rate 500 Hz, and using two electrodes placed on the right and left side of the participant's ribcage and a reference electrode placed above the pelvic bone, the patients' health and well-being was always the first concern.

All the procedures were explained to the voluntary participants, as well as being informed that there were no risks involved in participating and that they could decline from participating in the study at any time.

---

[1] https://neurokit2.readthedocs.io/en/latest/.

Besides the ECG signals, this dataset contains information on patient age, gender, type of surgical intervention, and type of anesthesia protocol. The procedures performed during the postoperative recovery of patients were also registered, including self-reports of pain, pain relief therapeutics, and other medical interventions, such as patient repositioning. These procedures are associated with time triggers that mark the event occurrence in the ECG signal. The evaluation of pain was based on self-report instruments (Numerical Rating Scale - NRS [21]) and several assessments, as necessary accordingly to the clinical team, were obtained until discharge.

Of the twenty patients in the dataset, one patient was withdrawn from the study because of the lack of pain assessment annotations during the ECG recording, resulting in a total of nineteen patients (60 ± 21 years old), ten females.

2.2 Feature Extraction

The ECG signals are affected by noise, such as skin-electrode interference (low-frequency noise, which is amplified by motion, movements, and respiratory variation), powerline (with a frequency 50 Hz), and electronic devices (high-frequency noise) namely from the clinical apparatus that concern this specific clinical scenario [2,10]. To attenuate the effects of noise and improve the quality of the signal, the raw ECG was low-pass filtered at a cut-off frequency 40 Hz, as the useful band of frequencies for these research purposes, without clinical relevance, varies between 0.5 Hz and 40 Hz. Afterward, the baseline wander was removed with a moving average filter, and Heart Rate was computed using the distance between R peaks locations.

The HR-features used for postoperative pain prediction had been proposed by [17] for early classification of mortality prediction based on ECG information, with F1-score around 93%. Thus, based on the reasoning provided for that problem, the proposed work attains to predict postoperative pain using the same features. Considering that postoperative pain can be assessed within the time-period before ('pain') and after ('no pain') analgesia administration, ECG-epochs of 1 min before and 1 min after the administration of analgesia for pain relief were used. For the ECG data after the administration of pain, it was considered different time epochs with a duration of 1 min, however with different initial times regarding the administration of analgesia. Namely, one, two, and three minutes after the administration of pain relief drugs. This strategy, besides assessing pain, will also allow reasoning on the time-effect of analgesia. Thus, using sliding windows of 10 s, HR-features were computed for these different epochs and, thereafter, were normalized before the classification task. To describe useful insights about the distribution of HR, after the signal processing methodology, 12 quantitative features were computed:

- Maximum: maximum value of HR;
- Minimum: minimum value of HR;
- Mean: mean value of HR;
- Median: median value of HR;

- Mode: mode of HR;
- Standard deviation: standard deviation of HR;
- Variance: HR's variance;
- Range: HR's range;
- Kurtosis: thickness of the tails of HR's distribution;
- Skewness: symmetry of HR's distribution;
- Energy: HR's averaged power;
- Periodogram Power: the periodogram power spectral density (PSD) estimate of HR;

2.3 Data Analysis Methodology

For performance comparison, using a 5-fold cross-validation strategy, 6 classifiers were used: decision tree, linear discriminant, random forest, boosted trees, Gaussian support vector machine (SVM), and k-nearest neighborhood (kNN), with the default hyperparameters.

The performance of classification models was assessed through several metrics, such as *accuracy, precision, recall,* and F_1-*score. Accuracy* gives the ratio between the corrected classified examples and the total examples to be classified. *Precision* measures the ratio between the correct predictions and all the predictions of a given class (usually, denoted as positive), while *Recall* is the ratio of correct predictions and all the examples that actually belong to that class. In the case both metrics get high values, then the different classes are properly handled by the classifier.

Precision and *recall* are closely related to the concepts of type I and type II errors: a classifier with high recall has a low type II error rate, which means that it misses few detections. While a classifier with high precision has a low type I error rate, which means that is resilient to false alarms. Combining both, the F_1-*score* is defined as the harmonic mean of these two evaluation metrics.

3 Results and Discussion

As detailed above, the workflow process for data analysis consisted of several steps, from the collection of data to the evaluation of the results, including the preprocessing of ECG data, the selection of 'pain' and 'no pain' epochs according to the reports and analgesia, the extraction of features and distribution's analysis, and the computation of machine learning models for pain prediction. This workflow is illustrated in Fig. 1.

The HR-features computed for the different pain epochs will be fed into different machine learning algorithms with the purpose of pain prediction and comparing the performance of the used models in the classification task. Also, different epochs of 'no pain' will be considered to infer the influence of time-effect of analgesia on the pain experience. Figure 2 shows the distribution of the 12 computed HR-features (for the 'no pain' features computed from 1-min interval of ECG recorded 1-min after analgesia administration). It can be observed that

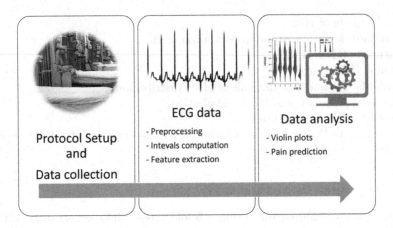

Fig. 1. Workflow for postoperative pain prediction.

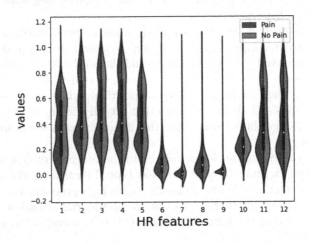

Fig. 2. Violin plots showing the HR-features distribution.

these features reveal distinct distributions among 'no pain' and 'pain' records, which supports the use of these features for pain prediction purposes.

Thereafter, the HR-features were used to compute classification models for pain prediction, and performance comparison was performed with different evaluation metrics. From Fig. 3 it can be observed that, with the exception of DT, the *accuracy* of the used classifiers are similar, reaching around 85%.

Figure 3 also shows that the 6 models get high and similar values of *precision* (around 85%). Regarding *recall*, except for the DT, the used models achieved almost 99%. For F_1-*score*, the performances of the 5 models (excluding DT) are quite the same, with values of almost 92%. For the four metrics used, the high values obtained sustain the feasibility of using these HR-features for postoper-

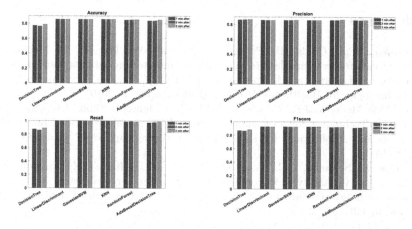

Fig. 3. Evaluation metrics of the 6 classification models.

ative pain prediction. Although the performance was slightly better than the remaining comparable models, the LDA achieved the best overall results.

4 Conclusions and Further Research

The obtained results indicate that the experience of postoperative pain can be predicted by relying on physiological data. Moreover, advancing classification models based on features computed from the ECG signal, which is continously recorded through minimally invasive equipment, can help pave the way for future research in self-regulation strategies for pain management, i.e., biofeedback, promoting health, and well-being.

Through this preliminary study it is shown that the obtained results should be further explored and explained. This is critical for the adaptation of healthcare strategies, providing a step further in personalized medicine. Thus, future research should be concerned with the explanations of the contributions of these features to the experience of postoperative pain. Moreover, efforts should also be devoted to the exploration of the meaningful features for this purpose and the contributions of other physiological signals, attempting a multimodal classification approach. This designed future research, aiming at a more accurate pain assessment, can support therapeutic approaches, namely through a better dosage of analgesics, either by different pharmacological interventions or by cognitive-behavioral therapies.

Acknowlegments. This work was funded by national funds through FCT - Fundação para a Ciência e a Tecnologia, I.P., under the Scientific Employment Stimulus - Individual Call - CEECIND/03986/2018, and is also supported by the FCT through national funds, within IEETA/UA R&D unit (UIDB/00127/2020).

Particular thanks are due to the clinical team for allowing and supporting the researchers of this work during the procedure of data collection. The author also acknowledges all volunteers that participated in this study.

References

1. Cunha, J.P.S., Cunha, B., Pereira, A.S., Xavier, W., Ferreira, N., Meireles, L.: Vital-jacket®: a wearable wireless vital signs monitor for patients' mobility in cardiology and sports. In: 4th International ICST Conference on Pervasive Computing Technologies for Healthcare (PervasiveHealth), pp. 1–2 (2010)
2. do Vale Madeiro, J.P., Cortez, P.C., da Silva Monteiro Filho, J.M., Rodrigues, P.R.F.: Techniques for noise suppression for ECG signal processing. In: Developments and Applications for ECG Signal Processing, pp. 53–87. Academic Press (2019)
3. Evans, S., Seidman, L.C., Tsao, J.C., Lung, K.C., Zeltzer, L.K., Naliboff, B.D.: Heart rate variability as a biomarker for autonomic nervous system response differences between children with chronic pain and healthy control children. J. Pain Res. **6**, 449–457 (2013)
4. Gabella, G.: Autonomic Nervous System. Wiley, Hoboken (2012)
5. Gan, T.J.: Poorly controlled postoperative pain: prevalence, consequences, and prevention. J. Pain Res. **10**, 2287–2298 (2017)
6. Hullett, B., et al.: Monitoring electrical skin conductance: a tool for the assessment of postoperative pain in children? Anesthesiology **111**(3), 513–517 (2009)
7. Joshi, G.P., Ogunnaike, B.O.: Consequences of inadequate postoperative pain relief and chronic persistent postoperative paint. Anesthesiol. Clin. North Am. **23**(1), 21–36 (2005)
8. Joshi, M.: Evaluation of pain. Indian J. Anaesth. **50**(5), 335–339 (2006)
9. Kang, S., Brennan, T.J.: Mechanisms of postoperative pain. Anesth. Pain Med. **11**, 236–248 (2016)
10. Berkaya, S.K., Uysal, A.K., Gunal, E.S., Ergin, S., Gunal, S., Gulmezoglu, M.B.: A survey on ECG analysis. Biomed. Signal Process. Control **43**, 216–235 (2018)
11. Ledowski, T., Bromilow, J., Paech, M.J., Storm, H., Hacking, R., Schug, S.A.: Monitoring of skin conductance to assess postoperative pain intensity. Br. J. Anaesth. **97**, 862–865 (2006)
12. Ledowski, T., Bromilow, J., Paech, M.J., Storm, H., Schug, S.A.: The assessment of postoperative pain by monitoring skin conductance: results of a prospective study. Anaesthesia **62**, 989–993 (2007)
13. Ledowski, T., Preuss, J., Schug, S.A.: The effects of neostigmine and glycopyrrolate on skin conductance as a measure of pain. Eur. Soc. Anaesthesiol **26**, 777–781 (2009)
14. MATLAB version 9.10.0.1684407 (R2021a). The Mathworks, Inc., Natick, Massachusetts (2021)
15. Middleton, C.: Understanding the physiological effects of unrelieved pain. Nurs. Times **99**(37), 28 (2003)
16. Pogatzki-Zahn, E., Segelcke, D., Schug, S.: Postoperative pain-from mechanisms to treatment. PAIN Rep. **2**, 1 (2017)
17. Sadeghi, R., Banerjee, T., Romine, W.: Early hospital mortality prediction using vital signals. Smart Health **9–10**, 265–274 (2018). CHASE 2018 Special Issue
18. Segelcke, D., Pradier, B., Pogatzki-Zahn, E.: Advances in assessment of pain behaviors and mechanisms of post-operative pain models. Curr. Opin. Physio. **11**, 07 (2019)
19. Storm, H.: Changes in skin conductance as a tool to monitor nociceptive stimulation and pain. Curr. Opin. Anesthesiol. **21**, 796–804 (2008)

20. Storm, H.: The capability of skin conductance to monitor pain compared to other physiological pain assessment tools in children and neonates. Pediatr. Ther. **3**, 168 (2013)
21. Williamson, A., Hoggart, B.: Pain: a review of three commonly used pain rating scales. J. Clin. Nurs. **14**(7), 798–804 (2005)

Using an Economically Justified Trend for the Stationarity of Time Series in ARMA Models

Victor Dostov[1,2] , Pavel Pimenov[1,2(✉)] , Pavel Shoust[1,2] , and Rita Fedorova[3]

[1] Federal State Budgetary Educational Institution of Higher Education "Saint-Petersburg State University", 7-9 Universitetskaya Emb., St. Petersburg 199034, Russia
dostov@npaed.ru, pavpimenov@gmail.com
[2] Russian Electronic Money and Remittance Association, 5/2 Orlikov per, Moscow 107078, Russia
[3] Federal State Budgetary Educational Institution of Higher Education "Saint-Petersburg State Agrarian University", 2 Peterburgskoe Shosse, St. Petersburg 196601, Russia

Abstract. The ARMA models are used in econometric studies to predict the behavior of a time series. In case of non-stationarity of the initial data ARIMA models get time series to stationarity by differentiation. The problem is applying differentiation provide the loss of essential information. The paper is trying to prove that ARMA model based on the differences between non-stationarity initial data and trend line can provide the same with classic ARIMA approach level of prediction force. For this purpose, the comparison of the quality indicators of the model constructed according to the ARIMA model based on the initial data and the ARMA model based on trend line was carried out. The cryptocurrency market has been chosen as the sphere of research. It was found that the two approaches give approximately the same prediction error and variations from the initial data.

Keywords: ARIMA · Bass's theory of diffusion of innovations · Stationarity · Cryptocurrencies · Differentiation

1 Introduction

Time series analysis is an important sphere in statistic and econometric. In the professional community, there are many models and methods for predicting and analyzing the behavior of time series. ARMA family models (autoregressive moving average model) are one of the most mathematically and statistically coherent models.

The ARMA method assumes that any stationary time series satisfy the criteria:

- theoretical mathematical expectation and variance of the series are independent of time,
- the covariance between its values at moments t and $t + n$ depends only on s, not on time.

O. Gervasi et al. (Eds.): ICCSA 2022, LNCS 13376, pp. 404–415, 2022.
https://doi.org/10.1007/978-3-031-10450-3_35

For ARMA models the stationarity of time series is critical for obtaining a reliable level of forecasting. In case of non-stationary time series, the ARIMA (autoregressive integrated moving average) model is used [7]. ARIMA uses differentiation of initial data to bring non-stationary time series. The main disadvantage of this method is that the level of differentiation carried out by simple brute force method. Besides differentiation can provide a loss of significant information.

In this paper we want to analyze an alternative approach to the problem of stationarity when using ARMA family models. We suppose the usage the difference between initial time series and economy-based trend line as a training data for ARMA model can provide the same with classic ARIMA approach level of prediction force and explanation of initial data.

To prove this assumption, we tested the efficiency of the classical ARIMA and our approach at the number of active crypto wallets of Bitcoin and Ethereum data in different time periods. The Python programming language with extended statistical packages is used for analysis.

2 Methodology

2.1 ARMA and ARIMA Models Construction Methods

To compare the effectiveness of the proposed method with the classical ARIMA, we use the following algorithm:

1. Building trend lines.
2. Calculation of the trend line deviation from initial time series.
3. Checking the obtained deviation for stationarity by the Dickey-Fuller method [12].
4. Calculation of the parameters of the classical ARIMA model based on the initial data using the pmdarima.autoarima package for the python programming language (ARIMA optimization method is the Powell Method).
5. Calculation of ARMA parameters, based on trend line deviation, using the pmdarima.auto_arima package with a given $d = 0$.
6. Calculation of ARIMA parameters using the pmdarima.auto_arima package (in this case, parameter d will not be used).
7. Calculation of the Root Mean Square Error (RMSE), the mean absolute error (MAE), as well as mean absolute percentage error (MAPE) for ARIMA and ARMA models.
8. Calculation of the predictive force indicators of models.

For all calculated quality parameters, we use the sklearn and pandas' libraries for the python programming language.

2.2 Trend Identification Approach

In case of initial data, we conduct a series of comparative tests on the number of active wallets of cryptocurrencies Bitcoin (hereinafter BTC) and Ethereum (hereinafter ETH) for two large-scale periods – from 2013 to 2019 (the period of the first speculative peak in 2018), and from 2013 to 2021 (the period including two speculative peaks – the peak of 2018 and the peak of the beginning of 2021, caused by the speculative interventions of Elon Musk) [1]. Time series of cryptocurrency price dynamics are a popular object for research. Machine learning methods [9], correlated stochastic differential equations [2] and ARMA family models [8] are usually used for their analysis. Nevertheless, the focus of such papers is to predict the dynamics of cryptocurrencies prices. In our previous research [3–6], we focused on considering cryptocurrencies as payment system. It's not the price that interests us, but the audience. Therefore, in this paper we propose to test classical ARIMA approach and our approach on the number of cryptocurrencies' active wallets.

Each time series was considered by us in two states. In the first case, training will be performed on the initial data (2517 days for the first period and 4517 for the second period). This allows to simulate the situation of data analysis with a high proportion of random noise. It also can show the difference of ARMA prediction force depending on the training period. In the second case, we transform the data into weekly japanese candlesticks (reducing the sample size by 7 times). Thus, we get smoothed data, which are free from random noise, but preserving the main directions of the trend development:

- BTC_1 - Dynamics of active BTC wallets for 2517 days of observations (daily data);
- BTC_1_light - Dynamics of active BTC wallets for 2517 days of observations (weekly data);
- BTC_2 - Dynamics of active BTC wallets for 4517 days of observations (daily data);
- BTC_2_light - Dynamics of active BTC wallets for 4517 days of observations (weekly data);
- ETH_1 - Dynamics of active ETH wallets for 2517 days of observations (daily data);
- ETH_1_light - Dynamics of active ETH wallets for 2517 days of observations (weekly data);
- ETH_2 - Dynamics of active ETH wallets for 4517 days of observations (daily data);
- ETH_2_light - Dynamics of active ETH wallets for 4517 days of observations (weekly data).

In our previous work [3], we demonstrated that the growth dynamics of Bitcoin and Ethereum users is well described by the Bass equation, originally developed by us to predict the dynamics of the development of payment systems.

In our previous works [4–6], we were able to establish that the development of payment systems can be described using a modified equation of Bass [10]. The advantage of this approach is that the indicators used in the model have a pronounced economic meaning. We modified classical Bass equation for the purpose of payment systems behavior forecast. The following parameters are used:

- current number of users x_0;
- the maximum number of users, for example, the entire audience of a given country, N. Therefore, the number of potential users not currently participating in the system is $N - x_0$;
- audience capture rate, which reflects the probability that a given user will start using the service: $r > 0$ (the reverse time of the decision) within a given period;

- audience fatigue coefficient, which reflects the probability that the customer will stop using the service: $b > 0$ (inverse decision-making time) during a given period.

The modified equation for predicting payment systems behavior forecast has the following form [3]:

$$\frac{dx}{dt} = a(N - x)x - bx \tag{1}$$

We also proposed a generalized equation for predicting payment systems behavior forecast [3]:

$$x = \frac{x_0 N e^{rKt}}{x_0\left(e^{rKt}-1\right) + N} \tag{2}$$

3 Construction and Quality Analysis of ARMA and ARIMA Models

3.1 Construction and Analysis of Trend Lines for Time Series

First, we built trend lines for the initial time series. The trend lines are shown in Table 2. On the next step we calculated deviation of the trend line from initial data. The obtained time series are presented in Table 3. Received time series was tested by The Dickey-Fuller criterion [12]. This is a popular method in machine learning for checking the stationarity of a time series. The main idea of the test is searching for single roots. If a single root exists, the series is non-stationary, if there is no such root, it is stationary.

The coefficients for the Bass equation and the presence or absence of stationarity according to the Dickey-Fuller test are presented in Table 1.

Table 1. Bass equation coefficients

	K	r	x_0	Is stationarity achieved by the Dickey-Fuller criterion
BTC_1	705 027	0,00240	29 540	Yes
BTC_1_light	551 209	0,00260	29 540	Yes
BTC_2	729 526	0,00236	29 540	Yes
BTC_2_light	651 667	0,00238	29 540	Yes
ETH_1	396 582	0,00823	959	Yes
ETH_1_light	381 595	0,00812	959	Yes
ETH_2	445 028	0,00804	959	No
ETH_2_light	478 891	0,00773	959	No

Table 2. Investigated time series and trend lines based on the Bass equation

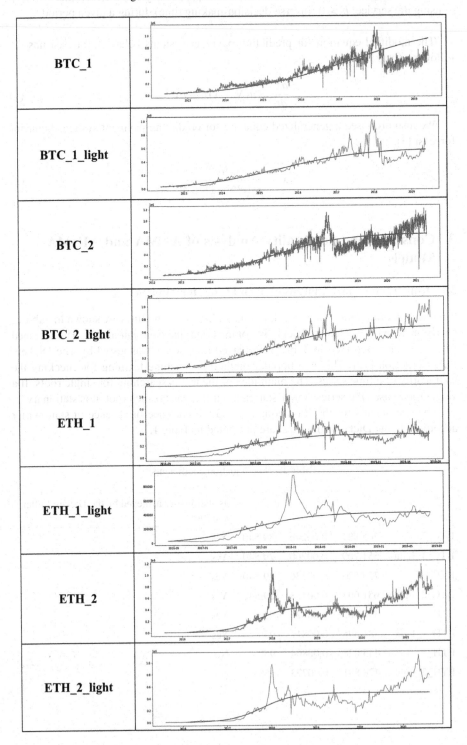

Table 3. Graphs of the difference between real time series data and trend lines based on the Bass equation

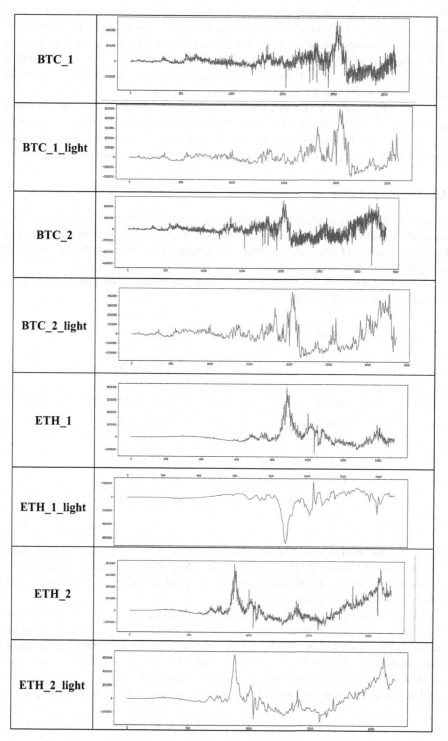

The stationarity of the time series based on deviation of the trend line from initial data is achieved in almost all cases. The exception is a series based on the dynamics of ETH fluctuations in the period from 2012 to 2021. This is because ETH is close to investment instrument, unlike BTC, which keep characteristics of the payment system. In addition, the price movement of many cryptocurrencies, as well as the level of investor confidence in the market, depend on fluctuations in BTC prices. Thus, in 2018, following the fall in the price of BTC, faith in ETH and other cryptocurrencies has been seriously decreased. This behavior is atypical for payment systems.

This example shows the meaning of trend line equation choice. In our case, increasing the number of ETH active wallets since 2018 has a high market effect and can't be explained by modified Bass equation. Nevertheless, the dynamics of another time series is generally described by the Bass equation, which allows us to continue our research.

3.2 Building Models

Based on the initial data and the trend lines constructed using the modified Bass equation, we calculated the ARIMA and ARMA models. The calculation is based on pmarima.autoarima Python library with a fixed value of $d = 0$ for ARMA models, and computed d for ARIMA.

Table 3 shows the best combinations of parameters obtained by pmarina.autoarima for ARMA and ARIMA models.

Table 4. ARMA and ARMA models parameters

	ARIMA models parameters	ARMA models parameters
BTC_1	*p: 0 d: 1 q: 2*	*p: 5 d: 0 q: 4*
BTC_1_light	*p: 0 d: 1 q: 1*	*p: 1 d: 0 q: 1*
BTC_2	*p: 5 d: 1 q: 3*	*p: 5 d: 0 q: 4*
BTC_2_light	*p: 0 d: 1 q: 1*	*p: 1 d: 0 q: 1*
ETH_1	*p: 2 d: 1 q: 4*	*p: 5 d: 0 q: 5*
ETH_1_light	*p: 2 d: 1 q: 3*	*p: 2 d: 0 q: 1*

ARMA and ARIMA models' parameters have a significant spread. Basically, large spread is fixed for data with a high random noise. In case of the weekly candle data, the q indicator is quite close. The largest deviations are observed in the parameter p – the behavior of the autoregressive model.

The difference in parameters may indicate a different quality of the model's description of real data. To check this, we trained ARMA and ARIMA modes used model parameters from Table 4 by ARIMA.predict_in_sample. Obtained data was compared with initial data by RMSE, MAE, and MAPE indicators. These indicators are often used in studies of the cryptocurrency market predictions methods [2, 11].

The results of comparing ARMA and ARMA models are presented in Table 5.

Table 5. Quality analysis of ARMA and ARIMA models

	Criteria	ARIMA models parameters	ARMA models parameters
BTC_1	RMSE	29 924,54	31 794,92
	MAE	19 047,39	20 224,71
	MAPE	0,06	0,06
BTC_1_light	RMSE	23 947,90	25 406,85
	MAE	14 591,15	15 552,61
	MAPE	0,05	0,05
BTC_2	RMSE	44 985,68	44 752,18
	MAE	28 461,57	28 192,13
	MAPE	0,07	0,07
BTC_2_light	RMSE	24 715,78	26 104,84
	MAE	15 645,47	17 224,74
	MAPE	0,04	0,04
ETH_1	RMSE	11 938,82	12 889,05
	MAE	6 192,17	6 616,09
	MAPE	0,05	0,04
ETH_1_light	RMSE	8 353,00	17 101,50
	MAE	4 851,60	9 444,31
	MAPE	0,13	0,10

The analysis shows that the ARIMA and ARMA models have approximately the same percentage of error in comparison with initial data. For weekly candles, ARIMA models describe initial data generally better than ARMA (in the corridor from 0.1 to 1% accuracy). In case of unprepared initial data with high random noise, ARMA models give a slightly more accurate distribution (in a similar corridor). It means that, in general, the quality of ARMA models based on trend deviation from the initial time series is comparable to ARIMA models based on initial data.

3.3 Prediction Force

In scientific research, ARIMA-type models are mainly used to obtain short-term forecasts [8, 11]. The reason is ARMA and ARMA models in the long-term predictions is trying to balance itself into some stationary.

To test the predictive force of the models, we train them on a part of the initial time series using the pindorama.arima package for Python and the ARIMA.predict_in_sample method. According to another scientific research, the ARIMA family models lose their predictive power at the 4th prediction period [11]. Therefore, to obtain the dynamics of the loss of predictive force by models, we consider 3 cases relative to the last observation period (T):

- Prediction for the next period (for first day for models trained on the full variation series and 1 week for "light" models).
- Prediction for the period $T + 2$ (for second day for models trained on the full variation series and 2 weeks for "light" models).
- Prediction for the period $T + 3$ (for third day for models trained on the full variation series and 3 weeks for "light" models).

For each case, let's make a prediction for 5 periods. For each period, we train the model on initial data (or on the difference between real data and the Bass equation) using pmdarima.auto_arima and build a forecast for $T + 1(T + 2, T + 3)$ using ARIMA.predict_in_sample. The obtained value is compared with the real number of wallets in this period (this period did not participate in the training of the model). If the number of BTC wallets increased in the period $T + 1$, and the predicted value also shows an increase, we think that there is a correct prediction. If the value predicted by the model shows a decrease, when real number of wallets growth a conclusion is made about an incorrect prediction. Then the real value of the time series is added to the trained data and the process repeats.

The results of model predictions are presented in Tables 6 and 7.

It is easy to see that increase in the prediction distance provides a decrease in the number of correct predictions (for example, for ARMA models in the period $T + 1$ there are 23 times of correct prediction, but in the period $T + 3$ there are only 14 correct predictions). This data coincides with the ARIMA models behaviour which was identified by other researchers on analyzing cryptocurrencies [8, 11].

We also can see that the prediction force for models based on short time series (BTC_1, BTC_1_light, ETH_1, ETH_1_light) is stronger that for models based on full data set (BTC_2, BTC_2_light, ETH_2, ETH_2_light). This behaviour can be explained by the fact that cryptocurrencies have a high speculative effect. The dynamics of interest in cryptocurrencies strongly depends on the price of coins and can vary greatly in different time periods. ARMA predictions based on a complete time series try to describe the behavior of the number of wallets during a period of strong volatility in the markets. At the same time, short time series predict the dynamics in a calm market. This is an important conclusion that should be considered when determining the amount of data to train the ARMA model.

Table 6. The number of model predictions coinciding with the actual data of the time series

		$T + 1$ prediction	$T + 2$ prediction	$T + 3$ prediction
		Prediction force:	Prediction force:	Prediction force:
BTC_1	ARIMA	4	3	3
	ARMA	3	3	3
BTC_1_light	ARIMA	3	2	2
	ARMA	3	2	1
BTC_2	ARIMA	3	2	0
	ARMA	2	1	1
BTC_2_light	ARIMA	3	3	2
	ARMA	3	3	2
ETH_1	ARIMA	2	2	2
	ARMA	2	2	2
ETH_1_light	ARIMA	3	2	1
	ARMA	3	2	2
ETH_2	ARIMA	4	3	3
	ARMA	4	3	3
ETH_2_light	ARIMA	1	1	1
	ARMA	0	0	0
Total correct predictions	ARIMA	**23**	**18**	**14**
	ARMA	**20**	**16**	**14**

In general, the classical ARIMA model and the ARMA model based on the Bass equation both demonstrate similar predictive force. For the $T + 1$ period models guess the correct direction of the time series in 3 or 4 cases out of 5. The weakest prediction is on the ETH_2_light time series.

It is also necessary to mention the dynamics of the decline in forecasting efficiency. If in the $T + 1$ period ARIMA models were better than ARMA models based on the Bass equation (23 correct forecasts versus 20). In the $T + 3$ period the predictive power of all models has become comparable. At the same time, ARMA (except for ETH_2_light) was generally more accurate.

Table 7. Absolute error of model predictions

		$T + 1$ prediction	$T + 2$ prediction	$T + 3$ prediction
		prediction_mistake:	prediction_mistake:	prediction_mistake:
BTC_1	ARIMA	5.31%	5.92%	4.93%
	ARMA	5.60%	4.71%	4.42%
BTC_1_light	ARIMA	17.35%	17.80%	15.46%
	ARMA	16.68%	16.46%	13.98%
BTC_2	ARIMA	3.43%	4.53%	4.99%
	ARMA	4.48%	4.81%	4.60%
BTC_2_light	ARIMA	7.51%	12.63%	7.45%
	ARMA	7.43%	11.99%	6.63%
ETH_1	ARIMA	4.56%	7.49%	6.69%
	ARMA	4.49%	6.70%	6.86%
ETH_1_light	ARIMA	5.88%	4.26%	6.45%
	ARMA	4.85%	3.96%	4.61%
ETH_2	ARIMA	3.09%	4.06%	4.52%
	ARMA	2.65%	3.10%	3.20%
ETH_2_light	ARIMA	3.22%	4.77%	6.42%
	ARMA	4.37%	7.15%	11.53%

4   Conclusions

The paper showed that the usage of the difference between the initial data and the economically justified trend as a stationary time series for making of ARMA model allows to obtain a level of accuracy like classical ARIMA. It allows us to describe the behavior of the time series without differentiation. Moreover, the study shows in case of high data noise, the usage of a trend live is preferable, because the differentiation of the initial time series leads to more significant errors.

Nevertheless, the study showed that the quality of proposed method depends on the quality of the explanation of real data by an economically justified trend. The example with ETH demonstrates how weak explanation force of the trend can provide the loss of ARMA prediction potential. Nevertheless, we believe that this problem can be overcome by adjusting the model. Ultimately, this method opens additional opportunities for empirical prediction and analysis of time series.

References

1. Bitcoin Active Addresses historical chart Homepage. https://bitinfocharts.com/comparison/bitcoin-activeaddresses.html. Accessed 13 Mar 2022

2. Dipple, S., Choudhary, A., Flamino, J., Szymanski, B.K., Korniss, G.: Using correlated stochastic differential equations to forecast cryptocurrency rates and social media activities. Appl. Netw. Sci. **5**(1), 1–30 (2020). https://doi.org/10.1007/s41109-020-00259-1
3. Dostov, V., Pimenov, P., Shoust, P., Titov, V.: The impact of short-term hype on predicting the long-term behavior of cryptocurrencies. In: 38th International Business Information Management Conference (38th IBIMA) (2021)
4. Dostov, V., Shoust, P., Krivoruchko, S.: A using mathematical models for analysis and prediction of payment systems behaviour. In: Proceedings of Fifth International Congress on Information and Communication Technology – ICICT 2020 Volume 2 (2020)
5. Dostov, V., Shoust, P., Popova, E.: Using mathematical models to describe the dynamics of the spread of traditional and cryptocurrency payment systems. In: Misra, S., et al. (eds.) ICCSA 2019. LNCS, vol. 11620, pp. 457–471. Springer, Cham (2019). https://doi.org/10.1007/978-3-030-24296-1_36
6. Dostov, V., Shust, P.: A generalization of bass equation for description of diffusion of cryptocurrencies and other payment methods and some metrics for cooperation on market. In: Gervasi, O., et al. (eds.) ICCSA 2020. LNCS, vol. 12251, pp. 3–13. Springer, Cham (2020). https://doi.org/10.1007/978-3-030-58808-3_1
7. Hyndman, R.J., Athanasopoulos, G.: Forecasting: Principles and Practice. In: OTexts, 360 p (2018)
8. Safiullin, M.R., Abdukaeva, A.A., El'shin, L.A.: Methodological approaches to forecasting dynamics of cryptocurrencies exchange rate using stochastic analysis tools (on the example of bitcoin). Finance Theory Pract. **22**(4), 38–51 (2018). https://doi.org/10.26794/2587-5671-2018-22-4-38-51
9. Saurabh, K.: Forecasting cryptocurrency prices using ARIMA and neural network: a comparative study. J. Prediction Markets **13**, 33–34 (2020). https://doi.org/10.5750/jpm.v13i2.1780
10. The Bass Model Homepage. http://bassbasement.org/BassModel/Default.aspx. Accessed 15 Mar 2021
11. Wirawan, I.M., Widiyaningtyas, T., Hasan, M.M.: Short term prediction on bitcoin price using ARIMA METHOD. In: International Seminar on Application for Technology of Information and Communication (iSemantic), Semarang, Indonesia, pp. 260–265 (2019). https://doi.org/10.1109/ISEMANTIC.2019.8884257
12. Yugesh, V.: Complete guide to dickey-fuller test in time-series analysis. Analytics India Magazine (2022)

Time Series Based Frequency Analysis of Violence and Criminalization Related Dynamic Mental Health Media News

Ahu Dereli Dursun[✉][iD]

Institute of Social Sciences, Communication Studies, Istanbul Bilgi University,
Istanbul, Turkey
ahu.dereli.dursun@bilgiedu.net, ahudereli@yahoo.com

Abstract. Violence, displaying a dynamic and multivariate nature with different biological, psychodynamic, social and individual factors, is reflected in media texts related to mental health and mental illness which embody numerous variables that are not simple to address and assess. The problematic issues around mental health are not only concerned with the medical aspect of mental problems, including the definition, diagnosis and treatment thereof, but also with respect to negative attitudes of people towards those with psychological problems, which may bring about cases of stigmatization. Media can play a significant role in criminalization of the mentally ill and be instrumental in shaping and changing attitudes towards mental illness. Accordingly, the current study aims to assess the trends in national discourse through media texts by looking into the volume and content of a sample of 496 news stories about mental illness, with a particular focus on bipolar disorder, from 2014 to 2019. Three national daily newspapers constitute the sample addressed in the study where frequency analysis has been performed on the media text dataset in accordance with the changes over the years. The frequency analyses based on time series conducted in the study demonstrate that violence and criminalization have been found to be the most frequently addressed topic among the ones mentioned across the study period. Based on the results derived from the analyses, it is seen that focus of the news media on violence is not proportional to actual rates of violence among the mentally ill. Thus, the research suggests that such a continued emphasis on violence and criminalization may intensify social stigmatization and hinder attempts to seek professional help. All these mental health-related considerations and raising public awareness point to ultimate strategies in public health domain regarding the socially constructed model which significantly affects the benefits of and barriers to action in health-promoting attitudes and behaviors.

Keywords: Dynamic mental health media news · Time series · Frequency analysis · Criminalization · Violence · Public health · Public awareness · Bipolar disorder · Affective disorder

1   Introduction

Time-series analysis, having a substantial place in social sciences, preliminarily aims at understanding how patterns change over time allowing researchers to investigate trends and shifts at multiple time points [1]. Frequency distribution, which is a summary of data showing the number of times a particular observation occurs (namely frequency), is employed to organize extensive amounts of data. A frequency distribution is constructed by arranging the data into categories that represent value ranges of the variables at stake [2]. Accordingly, structuring and modeling the quintessentially dynamical changes in the size and volume of content as well as trends of changes makes up integral parts pertaining to various stages of research from data description to data analysis.

Social constructionism, as a theory addressed in sociology, social ontology and communication theory, puts forth that reality can never be stable or self-evident, so reality is not an objective truth but rather a product of activities of humans whose experience is mediated culturally, historically and linguistically [3]. For this reason, a critical standpoint is required to be adopted regarding the taken-for-granted ways of understanding the world and people, which encourages human beings to be critical of the idea that our observations of the world straightforwardly produce its nature [4]. Discourse, being time and culture specific, is subject to change over time, which frequently produces social transformations [5]. Regarding the connection between mental illness and social constructionism as a theoretical position, it can be said that social constructionism has contributed significantly to health and illness in various ways, contending that medical knowledge and practices are socially constructed. It is further argued that psychiatry has no privileged understanding of mental disorder and social as well as cultural contexts need to be emphasized [6]. Even though the biomedical approach which focuses on diagnosis and medication is prevalent in clinical psychiatry, not all psychiatrists adhere to its logic [7]. Hence, alternative perspectives like social constructionism have become common in the context of public and mental health.

In this context, there are quite a huge number of challenges when one considers the dynamics of mental health that interacts between multiple factors and actors as well as the requirement of media production to consider not only discourse manufactured in newsrooms but also other factors like journalistic practices, specific networks, structural contexts with ideological assumptions embedded and technologies [8]. To complicate things further, unlike other health issues, mental illness is at times linked to violence in media portrayals. Mental conditions such as schizophrenia, for instance, often come to media attention in crime settings or court proceedings, which many believe can gratuitously stigmatize not only individuals with that diagnosis but with any mental illness, and may also bring about public safety being placed undue attention in mental health policy [9]. As surveyed by [10], individuals with mental illness became implicitly and explicitly associated with criminality through the process of stigmatization that associated unpredictability, violence and danger with mental illness. In reality, Gunn and Taylor found out in their study [11] that out of 5189 homicide cases, 61% of the murders were committed by mentally ill people [12]. In addition, emphasis on interpersonal violence in news coverage of mental illness is found to be concerning since most people with mental illness are never violent and around 4% of interpersonal violence in the US is said to be attributable to mental illness [13]. These studies reveal that being mentally ill does not necessarily come to mean that this situation will necessarily lead to criminality or violence. Another point is that with negative stories prevailing around mental problems, it can be stated that the stories rarely cover cases of success, recovery or accomplishment. The study by [14] verifies this particular point by finding out that the most frequently mentioned topic was violence (55%), while only 14% provided a description of successful treatment or recovery from mental illness.

The article [15] deals with news coverage in science journalism and employs a novel input-output analysis for the investigation of over eight million scientific study results published between 2014 and 2018 have been selected by global journalism to a relevant degree. The input-output analysis searches the patterns in the coverage of all scientific results published with regard to related distributions. The study by [16] is concerned with temporal mental health dynamics and social media where the authors describe a set of experiments to build the related system utilizing a methodology of data mining and deploying the system during the COVID-19 pandemic toward strategic decision-making. Another study [17], concerned with mental illness and social media, highlights the recent attempts that examine the potential to leverage social media postings towards the understanding of mental illness among individuals and populations. The study points out the significance of developing tools to identify the onset of depressive disorders toward being more proactive about mental health. Advancements in technologies have enabled computational methods to investigate different types and facets of media. Consequently, respective studies have become rampant like the one by [18] in which the authors perform a comparative computer-based text analysis of three news organizations regarding the COVID-19 issues using MAXQDA software. The study reveals the way the media outlets frame their news using word frequency, multiple words' combination and semantic relationships on 105 news. Another study [19] employs multifractal methods to detect and analyze self-repeating patterns for ensuring regularity and self-similarity in the digital-based complex media dataset and attaining accurate categorization of words in texts by one of the Natural Language Processing (NLP) methods, namely Bidirectional Encoder Representations from Transformers (BERT). The analysis results of the datasets compared by BERT demonstrate that the most optimal result could be achieved by multifractal Bayesian method. Regarding global news items and construction of risk in media, the study [20] provides a quantitative analysis and content analysis to elucidate parameters of risk society-related concepts focusing on economic uncertainty and risk.

In tandem with the tendency to represent mental illnesses in a way which links violence and dangerousness with the mental problem, descriptive studies of the US news media content of the last two decades of the previous millennium show that news stories about mental illness put emphasis on interpersonal violence with dangerousness seeming to be the most common theme in coverage involving accounts of violent criminal activity committed by people with mental illness [21,22]. The findings in the aforementioned studies are also consistent with those concerning other countries like the UK [23], Spain [24] and Canada [25]. In the light of the previous literature, this study, with a different perspective and setting, examines the content of the recent news coverage related to mental illness and assesses the trends of violence and criminalization over time in Turkish context through a computational application approach.

2   Material and Methods

2.1   Mental Health Media News Dataset

The newspaper items related to *mental health (with key words including mental health, mental distress, mental disorders, bipolar disorder, depression, depressive, manic and affective disorder)* printed between 2014 and 2019 in the top three highest-circulation daily papers in Turkey as of 2022 (Hürriyet, Sabah and Sözcü) as accessible via electronic newspaper database make up the mental health media news dataset addressed in the study. Out of a total number of 725 news items, 496 items (Hürriyet (n = 218), Sabah (n = 168) and Sözcü (n = 110), respectively) are handled with a focus on violence and criminalization as the related features. The original larger size dataset is a part of the dissertation thesis entitled "News Media Portrayal of Mental Health and Psychological Problems: An Analysis of Daily Newspapers in Turkey". The circulation rates of Hürriyet, Sabah and Sözcü as of March 2022 are 185.655, 179.341 and 153.773, respectively [26]. Table 1 provides the number of news stories covered in the three newspapers mentioned above.

Table 1. The number of news stories by newspapers.

Newspaper	The total number of news items (N)
Hürriyet	218
Sabah	168
Sözcü	110

2.2   Methods

Time series analysis is a particular means employed to analyze a sequence of data points collected over an interval of time. Rather than recoding the data points randomly or intermittently, time series analysis enables the recording of the data points at consistent intervals across a set period of time, which means that this analysis does not only constitute data collection act over time. In addition to this advantage, time series analysis can also show how variables change over time, and time is the crucial variable since it shows how the data adjust over the course of the data points and the final results. Another noteworthy benefit is related to its provision of an additional source of information and a set order of dependencies between the data [27].

Time Series Based Frequency Analysis based on Dynamic Mental Health Media News

Frequency of an event is the number of times the event has occurred in a study or experiment. The description of the characteristics of a set of data belongs to the area of descriptive statistics, and frequency analysis is one part of this area. Frequency distributions are generally employed to describe both nominal and interval data along with ordinal data. Since they are condense and capable of summarizing large amounts of data in applicable formats, they have a facilitating role in graphic presentation of data [28].

Frequencies are often represented in histograms graphically with values of events being plotted to produce a frequency distribution. In mathematical terms, a histogram is an m function that counts the number of observations that fall into discrete categories. n refers to the total number observations (sample) and k refers to the total number of boxes; so m histogram fulfills the following conditions for the calculation as per Eq. (1):

$$n = \sum_{i=1}^{k} m_i \qquad (1)$$

3 Experimental Results and Discussion

The subsequent stages were followed in the study dataset (media text dataset) made up of repetitive numbers in order to construct the histogram. First, the data were sequenced; then the frequencies were found out. Afterwards, the width of the data group was measured through its frequency and finally, histogram was drawn graphically based on the tables. All the analyses and depictions were performed by Matlab [29] (Table 2).

Table 2. Time series based frequency distribution of violence content in news items.

(a) number of violence content		(b) year the violence content seems the highest	
Newspaper	Year	Year	Violence content (Yes/No)
Hürriyet	71	2014	16
Sabah	45	2015	43
Sözcü	22	2016	55
		2017	38
		2018	36
		2019	42

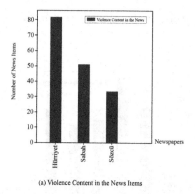

(a) Violence Content in the News Items

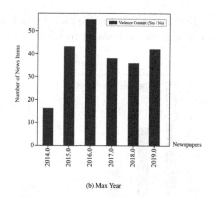

(b) Max Year

Fig. 1. Histogram for the time series based frequency analysis of violence content in the news items per newspaper (a) number of news (b) the year the content seems the highest.

Figure 1 Depicts the frequency analysis of violence content in the news items based on time series in a histogram form.

The results of the frequency analyses derived from histogram distributions reveal that the highest number of criminalization content is covered by Hürriyet and the lowest number by Sözcü (Fig. 1(a), Table 3(a)). The year when the maximum content of criminalization was covered is 2016 and the minimum is 2014 (Fig. 1(b), Table 3(b)).

Table 3 provides the frequency distribution of criminalization content in news items based on time series.

Table 3. Time series based frequency distribution of violence content in news items (a) number of content (b) year the violence content seems the highest.

(a) number of violence content		(b) year the violence content seems the highest	
Newspaper	Year	Year	Violence content (Yes/No)
Hürriyet	71	2014	16
Sabah	45	2015	43
Sözcü	22	2016	54
		2017	37
		2018	35
		2019	43

The results of the frequency analyses derived from histogram distributions reveal that the highest number of criminalization content is covered by Hürriyet and the lowest number by Sözcü (Fig. 1(a), Table 3(a)). The year when the maximum content of criminalization was covered is 2016 and the minimum is 2014 (Fig. 1(b), Table 3(b)).

Figure 2 presents the frequency analysis of criminalization content in the news items based on time series in histogram.

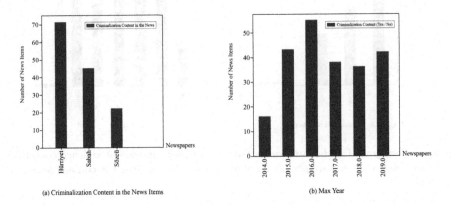

(a) Criminalization Content in the News Items   (b) Max Year

Fig. 2. Time series based frequency distribution of criminalization content in news items (a) number of content (b) year the criminalization content seems the highest.

The results of the frequency analyses derived from histogram distributions reveal that the highest number of criminalization content is covered by Hürriyet and the lowest number by Sözcü (Fig. 2(a), Table 3(a)). The year when the maximum content of criminalization was covered is 2016 and the minimum is 2014 (Fig. 2(b), Table 3(b)).

4   Conclusions and Future Directions

Time-series analysis holds a significant place in social sciences with an overarching aim of understanding the way patterns change over time, which enables researchers to investigate trends and shifts at multiple time points. Frequency distribution, on the other hand, is used to organize rampant amounts of data and constructed to show the number of times a particular observation occurs to show the value ranges of variables in question. Mental illness associated with violence and criminalization in media coverage is a problematic issue since media coverage has its effects on public beliefs and attitudes toward public health. The present study has assessed the trends in national discourse through media texts by examining the volume and content of a sample of 496 news stories about mental illness from 2014 to 2019. Subsequently, frequency analysis has been performed on the media text dataset in accordance with the changes over the years. The frequency analyses based on time series conducted in the study demonstrate that violence (interpersonal and/or self-directed) and criminalization have been found to be the most frequently addressed topic among the ones mentioned across the study period. The results derived from the analyses reveal that focus of the news media on violence is not proportional to the real rates of violence among individuals with mental illnesses. The research suggests that such a persistent emphasis on violence and criminalization may intensify social stigmatization, hinder attempts to seek professional help and deterioration in the life quality of individuals suffering from mental health as well as their families and/or acquaintances. The findings of the current study can be used as future directions to guide journalistic practices, training and reporting in terms of news items content. In addition, promoting public awareness can be another future direction to cover the importance of providing accurate accounts of mental illness. All the discussed mental health-related considerations point toward a way regarding the ultimate strategies in public health domain through the socially constructed model that has significant effects on the benefits of and barriers to action in health-promoting attitudes and behaviors.

Limitations of the Study. The further analyses conducted have not been presented in this study due to page restrictions.

References

1. Box-Steffensmeier, J.M., Freeman, J.R., Hitt, M.P., Pevehouse, J.C.: Time Series Analysis for the Social Sciences. Cambridge University Press, Cambridge (2014)
2. Fleming, M.C., Nellis, J.G.: Describing data tables, charts, and graphs. In: Principles of Applied Statistics, 2nd edn., pp. 13–50. Thomson Learning, New York (2000)
3. O'Reilly, M., Lester, J.N.: Introduction the social construction of normality and pathology. In: The Palgrave Handbook of Adult Mental Health, pp. 1–19. Palgrave Macmillan, London (2016)
4. Burr, V.: Social Constructionism, 2nd edn. Routledge, London (2003)
5. Burr1, V., Dick P.: Social constructionism. In: Gough B. (eds.) The Palgrave Handbook of Critical Social Psychology. Palgrave Macmillan, London (2017). https://doi.org/10.1057/978-1-137-51018-1_4
6. Bracken, P., Thomas, P.: Postpsychiatry: a new direction for mental health. Bmj **322**(7288), 724–727 (2001)
7. Rogers, A., Pilgrim, D.: A Sociology of Mental Health and Illness. McGraw-Hill Education, London (2014)
8. Henderson, L., Hilton, S.: The media and public health: where next for critical analysis? Crit. Pub. Health **28**(4), 373–376 (2018)
9. Holland, K.: Making mental health news: Australian journalists' views on news values, sources and reporting challenges. J. Stud. **19**(12), 1767–1785 (2018)
10. Wilcox, S.: Media and the Criminalization of Mental Illness: The Impact of Stigma Reduction Videos (2016)
11. Taylor, P.J., Gunn, J.: Homicides by people with mental illness: myth and reality. Br. J. Psychiatry **174**(1), 9–14 (1999)
12. Murphy, N.A.: The Influence of Media Representations on Mental Health Practitioners. University of Salford, Salford (2015)
13. Swanson, J.W., McGinty, E.E., Fazel, S., Mays, V.M.: Mental illness and reduction of gun violence and suicide: bringing epidemiologic research to policy. Ann. Epidemiol. **25**(5), 366–376 (2015)

14. McGinty, E.E., Kennedy-Hendricks, A., Choksy, S., Barry, C.L.: Trends in news media coverage of mental illness in the United States: 1995–2014. Health Aff. **35**(6), 1121–1129 (2016)

15. Lehmkuhl, M., Promies, N.: Frequency distribution of journalistic attention for scientific studies and scientific sources: an input-output analysis. PLoS One **15**(11), e0241376 (2020)

16. Tabak, T., Purver, M.: Temporal Mental Health Dynamics on Social Media. arXiv preprint arXiv:2008.13121 (2020)

17. De Choudhury, M.: Role of social media in tackling challenges in mental health. In Proceedings of the 2nd International Workshop on Socially-Aware Multimedia, pp. 49–52 (2013)

18. Hossain, A., Wahab, J.A., Khan, M.S.R.: A computer-based text analysis of Al Jazeera, BBC, and CNN news shares on Facebook: framing analysis on Covid-19 issues. SAGE Open **12**(1), 21582440211068496 (2022)

19. Karaca, Y., et al. Multifractal complexity analysis-based dynamic media text categorization models by natural language processing with BERT (Chapter 6). In: Multi-Chaos, Fractal and Multi-Fractional Artificial Intelligence of Different Complex Systems. Elsevier, Amsterdam (2021)

20. Dursun, A.D.: Reconsidering the risk society: its parameters and repercussions evaluated by a statistical model with aspects of different social sciences. In: Gervasi, O., et al. (eds.) ICCSA 2020, Part II. LNCS, vol. 12250, pp. 394–409. Springer, Cham (2020). https://doi.org/10.1007/978-3-030-58802-1_29

21. Wahl, O.E., Wood, A., Richards, R.: Newspaper coverage of mental illness: is it changing? Psychiatr. Rehabil. Skills **6**(1), 9–31 (2002)

22. Wahl, O.F.: Mass media images of mental illness: a review of the literature. J. Commun. Psychol. **20**(4), 343–352 (1992)

23. Philo, G., Secker, J., Platt, S., Henderson, L., McLaughlin, G., Burnside, J.: The impact of the mass media on public images of mental illness: media content and audience belief. Health Educ. J. **53**(3), 271–281 (1994)

24. Aragones, E., López-Muntaner, J., Ceruelo, S., Basora, J.: Reinforcing stigmatization: coverage of mental illness in Spanish newspapers. J. Health Commun. **19**(11), 1248–1258 (2014)

25. Day, D.M., Page, S.: Portrayal of mental illness in Canadian newspapers. Can. J. Psychiatry **31**(9), 813–817 (1986)

26. https://www.medyajans.com/gazete-tirajlari.html

27. Kaplan, D.: The Sage Handbook of Quantitative Methodology for the Social Sciences. Sage Publication, Thousand Oak (2004)

28. Winkler, O.W.: Interpreting Economic and Social Data: A Foundation of Descriptive Statistics. Springer, Heidelberg (2009). https://doi.org/10.1007/978-3-540-68721-4

29. The Mathworks, MATLAB r 2021b. 2021. The MathWorks, Inc., Natick, MA (2021)

Author Index

Printed in the United States
by Baker & Taylor Publisher Services